Willa J. Dean

MORNING & EVENING

NEW INTERNATIONAL VERSION

MORNING & EVENING

A devotional classic for daily encouragement

CHARLES SPURGEON

HENDRICKSON PUBLISHERS

MORNING AND EVENING
Complete and Unabridged
Updated edition based on the New International Version

© 1995 Hendrickson Publishers Marketing, LLC
P. O. Box 3473
Peabody, Massachusetts 01961-3473

ISBN 978-1-56563-819-8

Printed in the United States of America

Eleventh Printing — January 2014

Publisher's Preface to the New Updated Edition

HE need for new translations and updated and modernized editions will always be with us as long as writings of a past time continue to have value for new generations. This is one of the chief reasons that new Bible translations appear: language is never static, but fluid, alive, and changeable. What makes sense in one time may not make sense in another; usage of a particular word may disappear, or a word's meaning may change entirely, as in the case of "suffer," whose primary meaning of the seventeenth century, "permit," has all but vanished today. Whether it's Homer's *Iliad*, Shakespeare's *Romeo and Juliet*, or John Bunyan's *Pilgrim's Progress*, the need to make the original accessible to a contemporary audience will always exist. Charles Haddon Spurgeon's beloved and time-honored *Morning and Evening* merits such an updating and modernizing of language in order to make it accessible to a new generation.

This new edition has been carefully revised; every effort has been made to retain Spurgeon's knack of turning a phrase and his extraordinary command of the English language. All changes have been guided by a desire to preserve the integrity of Spurgeon's own voice, a voice which necessarily echoes with a certain historical particularity. Spurgeon (1834–92) served as preacher and pastor at London's six-thousand seat Metropolitan Tabernacle for thirty years. He wrote *Morning and Evening* for Christians who were in late nineteenth-century England struggling with, among other things, the separation of church and state, the enhancement of public education, urban poverty, imperialistic foreign policy in Africa and the Far East, and the ethics of war. Spurgeon was a Christian dedicated to living and speaking his faith in every aspect of his life. He thus addresses several such timely concerns in his writings—issues which, in fact, many contemporary Christians face as well. It is in the timeless power of God's Holy Word, however, and in Spurgeon's passionate application of that Word to the human condition, that past meets present and the Christian today receives a fresh word from the living God.

Updates in language and usage have been made to facilitate understanding for the modern reader. Nothing has been omitted, no meaning changed. At the same time, archaic words and unfamiliar phrases have been replaced with fresh and contemporary language. Spurgeon's occasional recitation in King James English is also modified. All occurrences of words such as *thee, thine, thou, wert, ye,* and *speaketh* have been appropriately substituted. British spellings, like *honour, favour,* and *offence,* are also adapted to modern American forms. Replacing the text of the King James Version of the Bible with the New International Version enlivens the Scripture passages for today's reader and complements the overall desire to introduce *Morning and Evening* to a contemporary audience. By using one of today's most popular translations of the Bible, and by contemporizing *Morning and Evening* for modern readers, we think that we are fully in keeping with Spurgeon's own drive to preach the gospel to his generation and to make its riches known more fully.

*"He wakens me morning by morning, wakens
my ear to listen like one being taught."*
— *Isaiah 50:4*

*"My soul will be satisfied as with the richest of foods;
with singing lips my mouth will praise you.
On my bed I remember you; I think of you
through the watches of the night."*
— *Psalm 63:5, 6*

*"That year they ate of the produce
of Canaan." — Joshua 5:12*

 SRAEL'S weary wanderings were all over;
they had reached their promised rest. No
more moving tents, fiery serpents, fierce
Amalekites, and howling wildernesses. They
came to the land which flowed with milk
and honey and ate the old corn of the land.
Perhaps this year, dear Christian reader, this may be your
case or mine. The prospect is exciting. If we exercise our
faith, it will yield pure joy. To be with Jesus in the rest
which is waiting for the people of God is a cheerful hope
indeed; to expect this glory sooner than later is double
bliss. Unbelief shudders at the Jordan which still rolls
between us and the heavenly land, but let's rest assured
that we have already experienced more harm than death at
its worst can cause us. Let's banish every fearful thought,
and rejoice with exceedingly great joy in the prospect that
this year we shall begin to be "forever with the Lord."

A part of the host will stay on earth this year to serve
their Lord. If this should be our lot, there is no reason why
the New Year's text shouldn't still be true. "We who have
believed enter that rest." The Holy Spirit is the promise
guaranteeing our inheritance; He gives us "glory begun
below." In heaven they are secure, and we are preserved in
Christ Jesus also; there they triumph over their enemies,
and we have victories, too. Celestial spirits enjoy communion with their Lord, and so do we; they rest in His love,
and we have perfect peace in Him; they sing His praise,
and it is our privilege to bless Him, too. During this year
we will gather a heavenly harvest on earthly ground, where
faith and hope turn a desert into the garden of the Lord.
Humanity ate angels' food long ago, and why can't we
now? O for grace to feed on Jesus, and so to eat of the
produce of the land of Canaan this year!

"We rejoice and delight in you." — *Song of Songs 1:4*

 E rejoice and delight in You. We will not open the gates of the year to the dolorous notes of the lyre but to the sweet strains of the harp of joy and the high-sounding cymbals of gladness. "Come, let us sing for joy to the LORD; let us shout aloud to the Rock of our salvation." We, the called, faithful, and chosen, will drive away our griefs and set up our banners of confidence in the name of God. Let others lament over their troubles; we who have the sweetening tree to cast into Marah's bitter pool will joyfully magnify the Lord. Eternal Spirit, our effectual Comforter, we who are the temples in which You dwell will never cease from adoring and blessing the name of Jesus. *We* WILL, we are resolved about it, Jesus must have the crown of our heart's delight; we will not dishonor our Bridegroom by mourning in His presence. We are ordained to be the minstrels of the skies. Let's rehearse our everlasting anthem before we sing it in the halls of the New Jerusalem. *We will* REJOICE AND DELIGHT: two words with one sense, double bliss, blessedness upon blessedness. Need there be any limit to our rejoicing in the Lord even now? Don't people of grace find their Lord to be camphor and spikenard, calamus and cinnamon even now, and what better fragrance do they have in heaven itself? *We will rejoice and delight* IN YOU. That last word is the meat in the dish, the kernel of the nut, the soul of the text. What heavens are laid up in Jesus! What rivers of infinite bliss have their source and, yes, every drop of their fullness in Him! Since, O sweet Lord Jesus, You are the present portion of Your people. Favor us this year with such a sense of your preciousness that, from its first to its last day, we may rejoice and delight in You. Let January open with joy in the Lord, and December close with gladness in Jesus.

"Devote yourselves to prayer." — *Colossians 4:2*

 T is interesting to notice how many pages of Sacred Writ are taken up with the subject of prayer, either by providing examples, enforcing precepts, or pronouncing promises. We can scarcely begin reading the Bible before encountering a phrase such as "At that time men began to call on the name of the LORD;" and, just as we are about to complete our reading, the "Amen" of an earnest supplication meets our ear. There are numerous examples of this. Here we find a wrestling Jacob — there a Daniel who prayed three times a day — and a David who, with all his heart, called upon his God. On the mountain we see Elias; in the dungeon Paul and Silas. We have multitudes of commands and myriads of promises. What do these examples teach us? Specifically, the sacred importance and necessity of prayer! We may be certain that whatever stands out prominently in God's Word is intended to be observable in our lives. If He has said a great deal about prayer, it is because He knows we have great need of it. Our necessities are so deep that, until we are in heaven, we mustn't stop praying. Don't you lack anything? Then, I am afraid you do not know the extent of your poverty. Don't you have some mercy to ask of God? Then, may the Lord's mercy show you your misery! A prayerless soul is a Christless soul. Prayer is the lisping of the believing infant, the shout of the fighting believer, the requiem of the dying saint falling asleep in Jesus. It is the breath, the watchword, the comfort, the strength, the honor of a Christian. If you are a child of God, you will seek your Father's face and live in your Father's love. Pray that this year you may be holy, humble, zealous, and patient; have closer communion with Christ, and enter more often into the banqueting house of His love. Pray that you may be an example and a blessing to others, and that you may live more to the glory of your Master. The motto for this year must be: "Devote yourselves to prayer."

"Let the nations renew their strength."
— Isaiah 41:1

LL things on earth need to be renewed. No created thing continues by itself. "You renew the face of the earth," the Psalmist uttered. Even the trees, which don't wear themselves out with anxious concern, nor shorten their lives with work, must drink the rain of heaven and draw on the hidden treasures of the soil. The cedars of Lebanon, which God has planted, only live because each new day they are full of fresh sap drawn from the earth. Likewise, our lives cannot be sustained without renewal from God. We know the only way to prevent the body from wasting away is to eat meals frequently. It is just as necessary, in order to restore the soul, to feed on the Book of God, listen to the preached Word, and partake of the Lord's table. How diminished our graces become when the means of grace are neglected! What poor starvelings some saints are who live without the diligent use of the Word of God and secret prayer! If our piety can live without God it is not divinely created by God but a fantasy; for if God had begotten it, our piety would wait upon Him as the flowers wait upon the dew. Without constant restoration we are not ready for the perpetual assaults of hell, or the stern afflictions of heaven, or even for the strifes within. When the whirlwind shall be loosed, woe to the tree that has not drawn into itself fresh sap, and grasped the rock with many intertwined roots. When tempests arise, woe to the sailors who have not strengthened their mast, nor cast their anchor, nor sought the haven. If we allow the good to grow weaker, the evil will surely gather strength and struggle desperately for mastery over us; and, because of this situation, a painful desolation and a lamentable disgrace may perhaps follow. Let's move closer to the footstool of divine mercy with our humble appeals; only then shall the promise that "those who hope in the LORD will renew their strength" be fulfilled for us.

*"I will make you to be a covenant
for the people." — Isaiah 49:8*

 ESUS Christ is Himself the sum and substance of the covenant and, as one of its gifts, He is the property of every believer. Can you estimate what you have received in Christ? "In Christ all the fullness of the Deity lives in bodily form." Consider that word "Deity" and its infinity, and then meditate upon "perfect human being" and all his beauty; for all that Christ, as God and man, ever had, or can have, is yours — out of pure, free kindness, transferred to you to be your inheritance forever. Our blessed Jesus, as God, is omniscient, omnipresent, omnipotent. Doesn't it console you to know that all these great and glorious attributes are entirely yours? Does He have power? That power is yours to support and strengthen you, to overcome your enemies, and to preserve you even to the end. Does He have love? Well, there isn't a drop of love in His heart which isn't yours; you may dive into the immense ocean of His love, and you may say about all of it, "It is mine." Does He have justice? It may seem a stern attribute, but even that is yours for, by His justice, He will see to it that all which is promised to you in the covenant of grace shall be most certainly secured to you. And all that He has as *perfect human being* is yours. As a perfect human being the Father was delighted with Him. He stood accepted by the Most High. O believer, God's acceptance of Christ is your acceptance. Don't you realize that the love which the Father set on a perfect Christ, He *now* sets on you? For all that Christ did is yours. That perfect righteousness which Jesus worked out when, through His stainless life, He kept the law and made it honorable, is yours, and is assigned to you. Christ is in the covenant.

> "My God, I am thine — what a comfort divine!
> What a blessing to know that the Savior is mine!
> In the heavenly Lamb thrice happy I am,
> And my heart it doth dance at the sound of His name."

"A voice of one calling in the desert,
Prepare the way for the Lord, make straight
paths for him." — *Luke 3:4*

HE voice crying in the wilderness demanded *a way for the Lord, a way prepared, and a way prepared in the desert.* I need to pay attention to the Master's proclamation, and open for Him a pathway to my heart, which is caught up with indulgent behaviors through the desert of my nature. The four instructions in the text require my serious attention.

Every valley must be exalted. Low and groveling thoughts of God must be given up; doubting and despairing must be removed; and self-seeking and physical desires must be forsaken. Across these deep valleys a glorious causeway of grace must be raised.

Every mountain and hill shall be laid low. Proud self-sufficiency and boastful self-righteousness must be leveled to make a highway for the King of kings. Divine fellowship is never bestowed on haughty, high-minded sinners. The Lord respects the lowly and visits the contrite in heart, but the lofty are an abomination to Him. My soul, beg the Holy Spirit to set you right in this respect.

The crooked shall be made straight. The wavering heart must have a straight path of decision for God and holiness marked out for it. Double-minded people are strangers to the God of truth. My soul, take heed to be honest and true in all things, as in the sight of the heart-searching God.

The rough places shall be made smooth. Obstacles of sin must be removed, and thorns and briers of rebellion must be uprooted. Such an eminent visitor must not find muddy paths and stony places when He comes to honor His favored ones with His company. O that this evening the Lord may find in my heart a highway prepared by His grace, that His progression to the farthest limits of my soul will be triumphal from the beginning of this year to its end.

"Grow in grace and knowledge of our Lord
and Savior Jesus Christ." — 2 Peter 3:18

ROW in grace" — not in one grace only, but in *all* grace. Grow in that root of grace, *faith*. Believe the promises more firmly than you have done. Let faith increase in fullness, constancy, simplicity. Grow also in *love*. Ask that your love may become extended, more intense, more practical, influencing every thought, word, and deed. Grow likewise in *humility*. Seek to lie very low and know more of your own nothingness. As you grow *downward* in humility, seek also to grow *upward* — having nearer approaches to God in prayer and more intimate fellowship with Jesus. May God the Holy Spirit enable you to *"grow in grace and knowledge of our Lord and Savior Jesus Christ."* Those who don't grow in the knowledge of Jesus refuse to be blessed. To know Him is "life eternal," and to advance in the knowledge of Him is to increase in happiness. Those who don't long to know more of Christ know nothing of Him yet. Whoever has sipped this wine will thirst for more for, although Christ does satisfy, yet it is such a satisfaction that the appetite is not cloyed but whetted. If you know the love of Jesus — as the deer pants for streams of water, so will you pant after the deeper depths of His love. If you don't desire to know Him better, then you don't love Him, for love always cries, "Nearer, nearer." Absence from Christ is hell; but the presence of Jesus is heaven. Don't be content to not increase your familiarity with Jesus. Seek to know more of Him in His divine nature, in His human relationship, in His finished work, in His death, in His resurrection, in His present glorious intercession, and in His future royal advent. Live close by the Cross and search the mystery of His wounds. An increase of love for Jesus and a more perfect apprehension of His love for us is one of the best tests of growth in grace.

"Although Joseph recognized his brothers, they did not recognize him." — Genesis 42:8

THIS morning our desires were directed toward increasing our familiarity with the Lord Jesus. It may be appropriate tonight to consider a kindred topic, namely, *our heavenly Joseph's knowledge of us.* This was most blessedly perfect long before we had the slightest knowledge of Him. "Your eyes saw my unformed body. All the days ordained for me were written in Your book before one of them came to be." Before we had a being in the world we had a being in His heart. When we were enemies to Him, He knew us, our misery, our madness, and our wickedness. When we wept bitterly in despairing repentance, and viewed Him only as a judge and a ruler, He viewed us lovingly as His kin, and His heart yearned towards us. He never mistook His chosen, but always looked on them as objects of His infinite affection. "The Lord knows those who are His," is as true of the prodigals who are feeding swine as of the children who sit at the table.

But, alas! *we did not know our royal Brother,* and out of this ignorance grew a host of sins. We withheld our hearts from Him and did not allow Him access to our love. We mistrusted Him and gave no credit to His words. We rebelled against Him and paid Him no loving homage. The Sun of Righteousness shone forth, and we couldn't see Him. Heaven came down to earth, and earth perceived it not. Let God be praised, those days are over for us; yet even now we know so little of Jesus compared with what He knows of us. We have just begun to study Him, but He knows us completely. It is a blessed circumstance that this ignorance is not on His side, for then it would be a hopeless case for us. He will not say to us, "I never knew you," but He will confess our names in the day of His appearing and, meanwhile, will make Himself known to us in ways He does not show the world.

*"God saw that the light was good, and he separated
the light from the darkness." — Genesis 1:4*

IGHT might well be good since it sprang from that fiat of goodness, "Let there be light." We who enjoy it should be more grateful for it than we are, and see more of God in it and by it. *Physical* light is said by Solomon to be sweet, but *gospel* light is infinitely more precious because it reveals eternal things and ministers to our immortal natures. When the Holy Spirit gives us *spiritual* light, and opens our eyes to behold the glory of God in the face of Jesus Christ, we behold sin in its true colors, and ourselves in our real position; we see the Most Holy God as He reveals Himself, the plan of mercy as He propounds it, and the world to come as the Word describes it. Spiritual light has many beams and prismatic colors, but whether they be knowledge, joy, holiness, or life, all are divinely good. If the light received is good in this way, what must the *essential* light be, and how glorious must be the place where He reveals Himself! O Lord, since light is so good, give us more of it, and more of Yourself, the true light.

No sooner is there a good thing in the world, than *a division is necessary*. Light and darkness have no communion; God has divided them, let's not confuse them. Sons of light must not have fellowship with deeds, doctrines, or deceits of darkness. The children of the day must be sober, honest, and bold in their Lord's work, leaving the works of darkness to those who shall dwell in it forever. Our churches should by discipline divide the light from the darkness, and we should by our distinct separation from the world do the same. In judgment, in action, in hearing, in teaching, in association, we must discern between the precious and the vile, and maintain the great distinction which the Lord made upon the world's first day. O Lord Jesus, be our light throughout the whole of this day, for Your light is the light of all people.

"God saw the light." — Genesis 1:4

 HIS morning we noticed the goodness of the light, and the Lord's dividing it from the darkness. We now note the special eye which the Lord had for the light. "God saw the light" — He looked at it with complacency, gazed upon it with pleasure, saw that it "was good." If the Lord has given you light, dear reader, He looks on that light with peculiar interest; for not only is it dear to Him as His own handiwork, but because it is like Himself, for "He is light." It is pleasant for the believer to know that, in this manner, God's eye is tenderly observant of that work of grace which He has begun. He never loses sight of the treasure which He has placed in our earthen vessels. Sometimes we cannot see the light, but God always sees the light, and that is much better than our seeing it. Better for the judge to see my innocence than for me to think I see it. It is very comfortable for me to know that I am one of God's people — but whether *I* know it or not, if the Lord knows it, I am still safe. This is the foundation, "The Lord knows them that are His." You may be sighing and groaning because of inbred sin, and mourning over your darkness, yet the Lord sees "light" in your heart, for He has put it there, and all the cloudiness and gloom of your soul cannot conceal your light from His gracious eye. You may have sunk low in despondency, and even despair; but if your soul has any longing towards Christ, and if you are seeking to rest in His finished work, God sees the "light." He not only *sees* it, but He also *preserves* it in you. "I, the Lord, do keep it." This is a precious thought to those who, after anxious watching and guarding of themselves, feel their own powerlessness to do so. The light which is being preserved by His grace in this manner, He will one day develop into the splendor of noonday, and the fullness of glory. The light within is the dawn of the eternal day.

*"Cast all your anxiety on him because
he cares for you."* — *1 Peter 5:7*

T is a happy way of soothing sorrow when we can feel — "HE cares for *me*." Christian! don't dishonor religion by always wearing a brow of care. Come, cast your burden upon your Lord. You are staggering beneath a weight which your Father would not feel. What seems to you a crushing burden would be to Him but as the small dust of the balance. Nothing is so sweet as to

"Lie passive in God's hands,
And know no will but His."

O child of suffering, be patient. God has not passed you over in His providence. He who feeds sparrows will also furnish *you* with what you need. Don't sit down in despair, but hope on, hope ever. Take up the arms of faith against a sea of trouble and your opposition shall yet end your distresses. *There is* One who cares for you. His eye is fixed on you, His heart beats with pity for your woe, and His omnipotent hand shall yet bring you the needed help. The darkest cloud shall scatter itself in showers of mercy. The blackest gloom shall give place to the morning. If you are one of His family, He will bind up your wounds and heal your broken heart. Don't doubt His grace because of your tribulation, but believe that He loves you as much in seasons of trouble as in times of happiness. What a serene and quiet life you would lead if you could leave providing to the God of providence! With a little oil in the cruse and a handful of meal in the barrel, Elijah outlived the famine, and you will do the same. If God cares for you, why do you need to care too? Can you trust Him just for your soul, and not for your body? He has never refused to bear your burdens, He has never fainted under their weight. Come, then, soul, stop fretting! Leave all your concerns in the hand of a gracious God.

*"Now [in] the evening . . . the hand of the LORD
was upon me."* —Ezekiel 33:22

N the way of *judgment* this may be the case,
and, if so, I must consider the reason for
such a visitation, and bear the rod and Him
that has appointed it. I'm not the only one
who is chastened in the night season; let me
submit to the affliction cheerfully, and carefully seek to profit by it. But the hand of the Lord may also
be felt in another manner: *strengthening* the soul and lifting
the spirit upward towards eternal things. O that I may feel
the Lord dealing with me in this sense! A feeling of the
divine presence and indwelling bears the soul towards
heaven as upon the wings of eagles. At such times we are
full to the brim with spiritual joy and forget the cares and
sorrows of earth. The invisible is near, and the visible loses
its power over us. Servant-body waits at the foot of the hill,
and the master-spirit worships upon the summit in the
presence of the Lord. O that a sacred time of divine
communion may be bestowed on me this evening! The
Lord knows how much I need it. My graces languish, my
corruptions rage, my faith is weak, my devotion is cold; all
these are reasons why His healing hand should be laid
upon me. His hand can cool the heat of my burning brow
and stay the tumult of my palpitating heart. That glorious
right hand which molded the world can create my mind
anew; the unwearied hand which bears the earth's huge
pillars up can sustain my spirit; the loving hand which
encloses all the saints can cherish me; and the mighty
hand which breaks the enemy into pieces can subdue my
sins. Why shouldn't I feel that hand touching me this
evening? Come, my soul, address your God with the potent
plea, that Jesus' hands were pierced for your redemption,
and you shall surely feel that same hand upon you which
once touched Daniel and set him upon his knees that he
might see visions of God.

"For to me, to live is Christ." — *Philippians 1:21*

ELIEVERS did not always live to Christ. They began to do so when God the Holy Spirit convinced them of sin, and when, by grace, they were brought to see the dying Savior making a propitiation for their guilt. From the moment of the new and celestial birth a person begins to live to Christ. To believers, Jesus is the one pearl of great price for whom we are willing to part with all that we have. He has so completely won our hearts that they beat alone for Him. We live to His glory and would die in defense of His gospel. He is the pattern of our life and the model after which we would sculpt our character. Paul's words mean more than most people think they do. They imply that the *aim and end of his life was Christ* — no, his life itself was Jesus. In the words of an ancient saint, he ate, drank and slept eternal life. Jesus was his very breath, the soul of his soul, the heart of his heart, the life of his life. As a professing Christian, can you say that you live up to this idea? Can you honestly say that for you to live is Christ? Your business — are you doing it *for Christ?* Is it not done for self-aggrandizement and for family advantage? Do you ask, "Is that an inferior reason?" For *Christians* it is. They profess to live for Christ; how can they live for another object without committing a spiritual adultery? There are many who carry out this principle in some measure, but which of you dares to say, as the apostle did, that you have lived wholly for Christ? Yet, this alone is the true life of a Christian — its source, its sustenance, its fashion, its end, all gathered up in one word — *Christ Jesus.* Lord, accept me. I here present myself, praying to live only in You and to You. Let me be as the bull which stands between the plow and the altar, to work or to be sacrificed; and let my motto be: "Ready for either."

"My sister, my bride." — *Song of Songs 4:12*

 BSERVE the sweet titles with which the heavenly Solomon with intense affection addresses His bride the church. *"My sister,* one near to me by ties of nature, partaker of the same sympathies. *My bride,* nearest and dearest, united to me by the tenderest bands of love; my sweet companion, part of my own self. *My sister,* by my Incarnation, which makes me bone of your bone and flesh of your flesh; *my bride,* by heavenly betrothal, in which I have espoused you to myself in righteousness. *My sister,* whom I knew of old, and over whom I watched from her earliest infancy; *my bride,* taken from among the daughters, embraced by arms of love, and pledged to me forever. See how true it is that our royal Kinsman is not ashamed of us, for He dwells with obvious delight upon this twofold relationship. We have the word "my" twice in our version; as if Christ dwelt with rapture on His possession of His church; "delighting in humanity," because those people were His own chosen ones. He, the Shepherd, sought the sheep, because they were *His* sheep; He has gone about "to seek and to save what was lost" because that which was lost was *His* long before it was lost to itself or lost to Him. The church is the exclusive portion of her Lord; none else may claim a partnership, or pretend to share her love. Jesus, your church delights to have it so! Let every believing soul drink solace from these wells. Soul! Christ is near to you in ties of relationship; Christ is dear to you in bonds of marriage union, and you are dear to Him; behold He grasps both of your hands with both His own, saying, *"My* sister, *my* bride." Mark the two sacred holdfasts by which your Lord gets such a double hold of you that He neither can nor will ever let you go. O beloved, don't be slow to return the hallowed flame of His love.

"The guilt involved in the sacred gifts." — *Exodus 28:38*

HAT a veil is lifted up by these words and what a disclosure is made! It will be humbling and profitable for us to pause awhile and see this sad sight. The iniquities of our public worship, its hypocrisy, formality, lukewarmness, irreverence, wandering of heart and forgetfulness of God, what a full measure we have there! Our work for the Lord, its emulation, selfishness, carelessness, slackness, unbelief, what a mass of defilement is there! Our private devotions, their laxity, coldness, neglect, sleepiness, and vanity, what a mountain of dead earth is there! If we looked more carefully we should find this iniquity to be far greater than appears at first sight. Dr. Payson, writing to his brother, says, "My parish, as well as my heart, very much resembles the garden of the sluggard and, what is worse, I find that very many of my desires for the melioration of both proceed either from pride or vanity or indolence. I look at the weeds which overspread my garden, and breathe out an earnest wish that they were eradicated. But why? What prompts the wish? It may be that I may walk out and say to myself, 'In what fine order is my garden kept!' This is *pride*. Or, it may be that my neighbors may look over the wall and say, 'How finely your garden flourishes!' This is *vanity*. Or I may wish for the destruction of the weeds just because I am tired of pulling them up. This is *indolence*." It is so, then, that our desire for holiness could be tainted by evil motives. Under the greenest sods worms hide themselves; it doesn't take long to discover them. How comforting the thought is that, when the High Priest bore the iniquity of the holy things, he wore upon his brow the words, "HOLY TO THE LORD." Likewise, while Jesus bears our sin, He presents before His Father's face not our unholiness, but His own holiness. O for grace to view our great High Priest by the eye of faith!

"Your love is more delightful than wine."
— *Song of Songs 1:2*

 OTHING gives us believers as much joy as fellowship with Christ. We have the same enjoyment as others have in the common mercies of life; we can enjoy both God's gifts and God's works. However, in all of these, separately and added together, we don't find as much substantial pleasure as in the matchless person of our Lord Jesus. He has wine which no vineyard on earth ever yielded; He has bread which all the cornfields of Egypt could never bring forth. Where can such sweetness be found as we have tasted in communion with our Beloved? In our esteem, the joys of earth are little better than husks for swine compared with Jesus, the heavenly manna. We would rather have one mouthful of Christ's love, and a sip of His fellowship, than a whole world full of carnal delights. What is the chaff to the wheat? What is the sparkling paste to the true diamond? What is a dream to the glorious reality? What is time's mirth, in its best trim, compared to our Lord Jesus in His most despised estate? If you know anything of the inner life, you will confess that our highest, purest, and most enduring joys must be the fruit of the tree of life which is in the midst of the Paradise of God. No spring yields such sweet water as that well of God which was dug with the soldier's spear. All earthly bliss is of the earth and earthy, but the comforts of Christ's presence are like Himself, heavenly. We can review our communion with Jesus, and find no regrets of emptiness therein; there are no dregs in this wine, no dead flies in this ointment. The joy of the Lord is solid and enduring. Vanity has not looked upon it, but discretion and prudence testify that it abides the test of years, and is in time and in eternity worthy to be called "the only true delight." For nourishment, consolation, exhilaration, and refreshment, no wine can rival the love of Jesus. Let's drink to the full this evening.

"I will be their God." — *Jeremiah 31:33*

CHRISTIAN! here is everything you can possibly need. To make you happy you want something that shall *satisfy* you; and isn't this enough? If you can pour this promise into your cup, won't you say, with David, "My cup overflows; I have more than heart can wish"? When this is fulfilled, *"I am your God,"* aren't you possessor of all things? Desire is as insatiable as death, but He who fills all in all can fill it. Who can measure the capacity of our wishes? But the immeasurable wealth of God can more than overflow it. I ask you, aren't you complete when God is yours? Do you want anything but God? Isn't His all-sufficiency enough to satisfy you if all else should fail? But you want more than quiet satisfaction; you desire *rapturous delight.* Come, soul, here is music fit for heaven in this your portion, for God is the Maker of Heaven. Not all the music blown from sweet instruments, or drawn from living strings, can yield such melody as this sweet promise, "I will be their God." Here is a deep sea of bliss, a shoreless ocean of delight; come, bathe your spirit in it; swim an age, and you shall find no shore; dive throughout eternity, and you shall find no bottom. "I will be their God." If this does not make your eyes sparkle and your heart beat high with bliss, then your soul is definitely not in a healthy state. But you want more than present delights — you crave something concerning which you may exercise *hope;* and what more can you hope for than the fulfillment of this great promise, "I will be their God"? This is the masterpiece of all the promises; its enjoyment makes a heaven below, and will make a heaven above. Dwell in the light of your Lord, and let your soul always be captivated by His love. Get out the marrow and fatness which this portion yields you. Live up to your privileges, and rejoice with unspeakable joy.

"Worship the LORD *with gladness."* — *Psalm 100:2*

ELIGHT in divine service is a token of acceptance. Those who worship God with a sad countenance, because they do what is unpleasant to them, aren't worshipping Him at all; they bring the form of homage, but the life is absent. Our God requires no slaves to grace His throne. He is the Lord of the empire of love and would have His servants dressed in the livery of joy. The angels of God worship Him with songs, not with groans; a murmur or a sigh would be a mutiny in their ranks. That obedience which isn't voluntary is disobedience, for the Lord looks at the heart, and if He sees that we worship Him from force, and not because we love Him, He will reject our offering. Worship coupled with cheerfulness is heart worship, and therefore true. Take away joyful willingness from the Christian, and you have removed *the test of his sincerity.* If a man is driven to battle, he is not patriotic; but he who marches into the fight with flashing eye and beaming face, singing, "It is sweet to die for one's country," proves himself to be sincere in his patriotism. Cheerfulness is *the support of our strength;* in the joy of the Lord are we strong. It acts as *the remover of difficulties.* It is to our worship what oil is to the wheels of a railway carriage. Without oil the axle heats up and accidents occur; and if there isn't any holy cheerfulness to oil our wheels, our spirits will be clogged with weariness. Those who are cheerful worshipping God, prove that obedience is their element; they can sing,

> "Make me to walk in Thy commands,
> 'Tis a delightful road."

Reader, let's put this question — do *you* worship the Lord *with gladness?* Let's show to the people of the world, who think our religion to be slavery, that it is to us a delight and a joy! Let our gladness proclaim that we worship a good Master.

"There is in store for me the crown of righteousness."
— *2 Timothy 4:8*

OUBTING one! you have often said, "I fear I shall never enter heaven." Don't be afraid! all the people of God shall enter there. I love the quaint saying of a dying man, who exclaimed, "I have no fear of going home; I have sent all before me; God's finger is on the latch of my door, and I am ready for Him to enter." "But," said one, "aren't you afraid you might lose your inheritance?" "No," said he, "no; there is one crown in heaven which the angel Gabriel could not wear, it will fit no head but mine. There is one throne in heaven which Paul the apostle could not fill; it was made for me, and I shall have it." O Christian, what a joyous thought! your portion is secure; "there remains a rest." "But can it be forfeited?" No, it is inherited. If I am a child of God, I will not lose it. It is mine as securely as if I were there. Come with me, believer, and let's sit upon the top of Nebo, and view the sizable land, even Canaan. Do you see that little river of death glistening in the sunlight, and do you see across from it the pinnacles of the eternal city? Do you see the pleasant country, and all its joyous inhabitants? Know, then, that if you could fly across you would see written upon one of its many mansions, "This remains for such a one; it is preserved for you and you alone, and you will be caught up to dwell forever with God." Poor doubting one, see the fair inheritance; it is *yours.* If you believe in the Lord Jesus, if you have repented of sin, if you have been renewed in heart, you are one of the Lord's people, and there is a place reserved for you, a crown laid up for you, a harp specially provided for you. No one else shall have your portion, it is reserved in heaven for you, and you shall have it before long, for there shall be no vacant thrones in glory when all the chosen are gathered in.

"In my flesh I will see God." — Job 19:26

ARK the subject of Job's devout anticipation — "I shall see God." He doesn't say, "I shall see the saints" — though undoubtedly that will be untold bliss — but, "I shall see *God*." It isn't — "I shall see the pearly gates, I shall behold the walls of jasper, I shall gaze upon the crowns of gold," but "I shall see God." This is the sum and substance of heaven, this is the joyful hope of all believers. It is their delight to see Him now in the ordinances by faith. They love to behold Him in communion and in prayer; but there in heaven they shall have an open and unclouded vision, and thus seeing "Him as He is," shall be made completely like Him. *Likeness to God* — what more can we wish for? And *a sight of God* — what better desire can we have? Some read the passage, "Yet, I shall see God in my flesh," and find here an allusion to Christ, as the "Word made flesh," and that glorious beholding of Him which shall be the splendor of the latter days. Whether this is so or not, what is certain is that Christ shall be the object of our eternal vision; nor shall we ever want any joy beyond that of seeing Him. Don't think that this will be a narrow sphere for the mind to dwell in. It is but one source of delight, but that source is infinite. All His attributes shall be subjects for contemplation, and as He is infinite under each aspect, there is no fear of exhaustion. His works, His gifts, His love to us, and His glory in all His purposes, and in all His actions, these shall make a theme which will be ever new. The patriarch looked forward to this sight of God as a *personal* enjoyment. "I myself will see him with my own eyes — I, and not another." Take a real look at heaven's bliss; think of what it will be *to you*. "*Your* eyes will see the King in His beauty." All earthly brightness fades and darkens as we gaze upon it, but here is a brightness which can never dim, a glory which can never fade — "*I will see God.*"

"They have no root." — Luke 8:13

Y soul, examine yourself this morning by the light of this text. You have received the word with joy. Your feelings have been stirred and a lively impression has been made. However, remember, that to receive the word in the ear is one thing, and to receive Jesus into your very soul is quite another. Superficial feeling is often joined to inward hardness of heart, and a lively impression of the word isn't always a lasting one. In the parable, the seed in one case fell upon ground having a rocky bottom, covered over with a thin layer of earth. When the seed began to take root, its downward growth was hindered by the hard stone. Therefore it spent its strength in pushing its green shoot aloft as high as it could, but having no inward moisture derived from root nourishment, it withered away. Is this my case? Have I been making a fair show in the flesh without having a corresponding inner life? Good growth takes place upwards and downwards at the same time. Am I rooted in sincere fidelity and love to Jesus? If my heart remains unsoftened and unfertilized by grace, the good seed may germinate for a season, but it must ultimately wither, for it cannot flourish on a rocky, unbroken, unsanctified heart. Let me dread a godliness as rapid in growth and as wanting in endurance as Jonah's vine; let me count the cost of being a follower of Jesus. Above all, let me feel the energy of His Holy Spirit, and then I shall possess an abiding and enduring seed in my soul. If my mind remains as stubbornly impenitent as it was by nature, the sun of trial will scorch, my hard heart will help to cast the heat the more terribly upon the poorly-covered seed, my religion will soon die, and my despair will be terrible; therefore, O heavenly Sower, plow me first, and then cast the truth into me, and let me yield a bounteous harvest for You.

"I have prayed for you." — *Luke 22:32*

OW encouraging the thought of the Redeemer's unceasing intercession is for us. When we pray, He pleads for us; and then we are *not* praying, He is advocating our cause, and by His supplications shielding us from unseen dangers. Notice the word of comfort addressed to Peter — "Simon, Simon, Satan has asked to sift you as wheat; but" — what? "But go and pray for yourself." That would be good advice, but it isn't written that way. Neither does He say, "But I will keep you watchful, and so you shall be preserved." That would be a great blessing. No, it is, *"But I have prayed for you,* Simon, that your faith may not fail." Little do we know of what we owe to our Savior's prayers. When we reach the hilltops of heaven, and look back upon all the ways in which the Lord our God has led us, how we shall praise Him who, before the eternal throne, undid the mischief which Satan was doing upon earth. How we shall thank Him because He never held His peace, but day and night pointed to the wounds upon His hands, and carried our names upon His breastplate! Even before Satan had begun to tempt, Jesus had forestalled him and entered a plea in heaven. Mercy outruns malice. Notice, He doesn't say, "Satan has sifted you, and therefore I will pray," but "Satan has *asked* to sift you." He checks Satan even in his very desire, and nips it in the bud. He doesn't say, "But I have desired to pray for you." No, but "I *have* prayed for you: I have done it already; I have gone to court and entered a counterplea even before an accusation is made." O Jesus, what a comfort it is that You have pleaded our cause against our unseen enemies; countermined their mines, and unmasked their ambushes. Here is a matter for joy, gratitude, hope, and confidence.

"You are of Christ." — 1 Corinthians 3:23

OU *are* of Christ." You are His by donation, for the Father gave you to the Son; His by His bloody purchase, for He counted down the price for your redemption; His by dedication, for you have consecrated yourself to Him; His by relation, for you are named by his name, and made one of His brethren and co-heirs. Work practically to show the world that you are the servant, the friend, the bride of Jesus. When tempted to sin, reply, "I cannot do this great wickedness, for I am of Christ." Immortal principles forbid the friend of Christ to sin. When wealth is before you to be won by sin, say that you are of Christ, and don't touch it. Are you exposed to difficulties and dangers? Stand fast in the evil day, remembering that you are of Christ. Are you placed where others are sitting down idly, doing nothing? Rise to the work with all your powers; and when the sweat stands upon your brow, and you are tempted to loiter, cry, "No, I cannot stop, for I am of Christ. If I were not purchased by blood, I might be like Issachar, crouching between two burdens; but I am of Christ, and cannot loiter." When the siren song of pleasure would tempt you from the path of right, reply, "your music cannot charm me; I am of Christ." When the cause of God invites you, give yourself to it; when the poor require you, give your goods and yourself away, for you are of Christ. Never belie your profession. Always be one of those whose manners are Christian, whose speech is like the Nazarene, whose conduct and conversation are so redolent of heaven, that all who see you may know that you are the Savior's, recognizing in you His features of love and His countenance of holiness. "I am a Roman!" was proof of integrity in ages past; far more, then, let it be your proof of holiness, "I am of Christ!"

"There is more to be said in God's behalf."
— *Job 36:2*

E ought not to court publicity for our virtue, or notoriety for our zeal; but, at the same time, it is a sin to be always seeking to hide that which God has bestowed upon us for the good of others. A Christian isn't to be a village in a valley, but "a city on a hill;" nor a lamp under a bowl, but a lamp on its stand, giving light to all. Withdrawal may be lovely in its season, and to hide one's self is doubtless modest, but the hiding of *Christ* in us can never be justified, and the keeping back of truth which is precious to ourselves is a sin against others and an offense against God. If you are of a nervous temperament and of retiring disposition, take care that you don't indulge this trembling propensity too often, lest you should be useless to the church. In the name of Him who was not ashamed of you, seek to do some little violence to your feelings, and tell to others what Christ has told to you. If you cannot speak with trumpet tongue, use the still small voice. If the pulpit must not be your platform, if the press may not carry on its wings your words, yet say with Peter and John, "Silver or gold I do not have, but what I have I give you." Talk to the Samaritan woman at the well of Sychar if you cannot preach a sermon on the mountain. Utter the praises of Jesus in the house if not in the temple, in the field if not upon the exchange, among your own family if not among the great family of humankind. From the hidden springs within let sweetly flowing rivulets of testimony flow forth, giving drink to every passer-by. Don't hide your talent. Trade with it, and you shall bring in good interest to your Lord and Master. To speak for God will be refreshing to us, encouraging to saints, useful to sinners, and honoring to the Savior. Mute children are an affliction to their parents. Lord, unloosen all Your children's tongues.

*"Now Jehoshaphat built a fleet of trading ships
to go to Ophir for gold, but they never set sail —
they were wrecked at Ezion Geber." — 1 Kings 22:48*

 OLOMON'S ships had returned in safety, but Jehoshaphat's vessels never reached the land of gold. Providence prospers one, and frustrates the desires of another, in the same business and at the same spot, yet the Great Ruler is as good and wise at one time as another. May we have grace today, in the remembrance of this text, to bless the Lord for ships broken at Ezion Geber, as well as for vessels freighted with temporal blessings; let's not envy the more successful, nor murmur at our losses as though we were singularly and specially tried. Like Jehoshaphat, we may be precious in the Lord's sight, although our schemes end in disappointment.

The secret cause of Jehoshaphat's loss is well worth noticing, for it is the root of very much of the suffering of the Lord's people; it was his alliance with a sinful family, his fellowship with sinners. In 2 Chron. 20:37, we are told that the Lord sent a prophet to declare, "Because you have made an alliance with Ahaziah, the LORD will destroy what you have made." This was a fatherly chastisement, which appears to have been blessed to him; for in the verse which succeeds our morning's text we find him refusing to allow his servants to sail in the same vessels with those of the wicked king. Would to God that Jehoshaphat's experience might be a warning to the rest of the Lord's people to avoid being unequally yoked together with unbelievers! A life of misery is usually the lot of those who are united in marriage, or in any other way of their own choosing, with the people of the world. O for such love for Jesus that, like Him, we may be holy, harmless, undefiled, and separate from sinners; for if it isn't so for us, we may expect to hear it often said, "The LORD will destroy what you have made."

"Elisha . . . made the iron [axhead] float."
— *2 Kings 6:6*

HE axhead seemed hopelessly lost and, since it was borrowed, the honor of the prophetic band was likely to be jeopardized and, thereby, the name of their God compromised. Contrary to all expectation, the iron was made to rise from the depth of the stream and to swim; for things impossible with man are possible with God. I knew a man in Christ who was called to undertake a work far exceeding his strength. It appeared so difficult that the mere idea of undertaking it was absurd. Yet he was called to that work and his faith rose with the occasion. God honored his faith, unforeseen aid was sent, and the axhead floated. Another of the Lord's family was in grievous financial straits, he was able to meet all claims, and much more if he could have realized a certain portion of his estate, but he was overtaken with a sudden pressure; he sought for friends in vain, but faith led him to the unfailing Helper, and lo, the trouble was averted, his footsteps were enlarged, and the axhead floated. A third had a sorrowful case of depravity to deal with. He had taught, reproved, warned, invited, and interceded, but all in vain. Old Adam was too strong for young Melancthon, the stubborn spirit would not relent. Then came an agony of prayer, and before long a blessed answer was sent from heaven. The hard heart was broken, the axhead floated.

Beloved reader, what is your desperate situation? What heavy matter do you have in hand this evening? Bring it here. The God of the prophets lives, and lives to help His saints. He will not allow you to lack any good thing. Believe in the Lord of hosts! Approach Him pleading the name of Jesus, and the axhead shall float; you, too, shall see the finger of God working marvels for His people. According to your faith will it be done to you, and yet again the axhead shall float.

"Mighty to save." — Isaiah 63:1

Y the words "to save" we understand the whole of the great work of salvation, from the first holy desire onward to complete sanctification. The words are *multum in parro;* indeed, here is all mercy in one word. Christ isn't only "mighty to save" those who repent, but He is able to make us repent. He will carry those to heaven who believe; but He is, moreover, mighty to give us new hearts and to work faith in them. He is mighty to make the person who hates holiness love it, and to constrain the despiser of His name to bend the knee before Him; and that's not all, for the divine power is equally seen in the work afterwards. The life of a believer is a series of miracles wrought by "the Mighty God." The bush burns, but isn't consumed. He is mighty to keep His people holy after He has made them so, and to preserve them in His fear and love until He consummates their spiritual existence in heaven. Christ's might doesn't lie in making a believer and then leaving him to shift for himself; but He who begins the good work carries it on; He who imparts the first germ of life in the dead soul, prolongs the divine existence, and strengthens it until it bursts asunder every bond of sin, and the soul leaps from earth, perfected in glory. Believer, here is encouragement. Are you praying for some loved one? Oh, don't give up praying, for Christ is "mighty to save." You are powerless to reclaim the rebel, but your Lord is Almighty. Lay hold on that mighty arm, and rouse it to put forth its strength. Does your own situation trouble you? Don't be afraid, for His strength is sufficient for you. Whether to begin with others, or to carry on the work in you, Jesus is "mighty to save;" the best proof of which lies in the fact that He has saved *you*. What a thousand mercies that you have not found Him mighty to destroy!

"Beginning to sink, [he] cried out, Lord, save me!"
— *Matthew 14:30*

INKING *times are praying times* with the Lord's servants. Peter neglected prayer at starting upon his venturous journey, but, when he began to sink, his danger made him a suppliant, and his cry, though late, was not too late. In our hours of bodily pain and mental anguish, we find ourselves as naturally driven to prayer as the wreck is driven upon the shore by the waves. The fox hurries to its hole for protection; the bird flies to the wood for shelter; and even so the tried believer hastens to the mercy seat for safety. Heaven's great harbor of refuge is All-prayer; thousands of weather-beaten vessels have found a haven there, and the moment a storm comes on, it is wise for us to make for it with full sail.

Short prayers are long enough. There were only three words in the petition which Peter gasped out, but they were sufficient for his purpose. Not length but strength is desirable. A sense of need is a mighty teacher of brevity. If our prayers had less of the tail feathers of pride and more wing they would be all the better. Verbiage is to devotion as chaff to the wheat. Precious things lie in small compass, and all that is real prayer in many long addresses could be uttered in a petition as short as Peter's.

Our extremities are the Lord's opportunities. As soon as a keen sense of danger forces an anxious cry from us, the ear of Jesus hears, and with Him ear and heart go together, and the hand doesn't linger very long. At the last moment we appeal to our Master, but His swift hand makes up for our delays by instant and effectual action. Are we nearly engulfed by the boisterous waters of affliction? Then let's lift up our souls to our Savior, and we may rest assured that He will not allow us to perish. When we can do nothing Jesus can do all things; let's enlist His powerful aid upon our side, and all will be well.

"Do as you promised." — *2 Samuel 7:25*

OD'S promises were never meant to be thrown aside as waste paper. He intended that they should be used. God's gold isn't miser's money but is minted for trading. Nothing pleases our Lord better than to see His promises put in circulation. He loves to see His children bring them up to Him, and say, "Lord, do as You promised." We glorify God when we plead His promises. Do you think that God will be any the poorer for giving you the riches He has promised? Do you dream that He will be any the less holy for giving holiness to you? Do you imagine He will be any the less pure for washing you from your sins? He has said, "Come now, let us reason together," says the LORD. "Though your sins are like scarlet, they shall be as white as snow; though they are red as crimson, they shall be like wool." Faith embraces the promise of pardon. It doesn't delay, saying, "This is a precious promise, I wonder if it is true?" but goes straight to the throne with it, and pleads, "Lord, here is the promise. 'Do as You promised.' " Our Lord replies, "Be it to you even as you will." When a Christian grasps a promise but doesn't take it to God, then God is dishonored; but when one hastens to the throne of grace, and cries, "Lord, I have nothing to recommend me but this, 'You have said it;' " then the desire shall be granted. Our heavenly Banker delights to cash His own notes. Never let the promise rust. Draw the word of promise out of its scabbard, and use it with holy violence. Don't think that God will be troubled by your importunately reminding Him of His promises. He loves to hear the loud outcries of needy souls. It is His delight to give favors. He is more ready to hear than you are to ask. The sun isn't weary of shining, nor the fountain of flowing. It is God's nature to keep His promises. Therefore, go at once to the throne with "Do as You promised."

"But I am a man of prayer." — Psalm 109:4

YING tongues were busy against the reputation of David, but he did not defend himself. He moved the case into a higher court and pleaded before the great King Himself. Prayer is the safest method of replying to words of hatred. The Psalmist did not pray in a cold-hearted manner. He *gave himself* to the exercise — threw his whole soul and heart into it — straining every sinew and muscle, as Jacob did when wrestling with the angel. Thus, and thus only, shall any of us speed at the throne of grace. As a shadow has no power because there is no substance in it, even so that supplication in which one's true self isn't thoroughly present in agonizing earnestness and vehement desire, is utterly ineffectual, for it lacks that which would give it force. "Fervent prayer," says an old divine, "like a cannon planted at the gates of heaven, makes them fly open." The common fault with most of us is our readiness to yield to distractions. Our thoughts go roving hither and thither, and we make little progress towards our desired end. Like quicksilver our minds will not hold together, but roll off this way and that. How great an evil this is! It injures us, and what is worse, it insults our God. What should we think of a petitioner, if, while having an audience with a prince, he should be playing with a feather or catching a fly?

Continuance and perseverance are intended in the expression of our text. David didn't cry once, and then relapse into silence; his holy clamor was continued until it brought down the blessing. Prayer must not be our chance work, but our daily business, our habit and vocation. As artists give themselves to their models, and poets to their classical pursuits, so must we addict ourselves to prayer. We must be immersed in prayer as in our element, and so pray without ceasing. Lord, teach us so to pray that we may be more and more prevalent in supplication.

"I myself will help you, declares the LORD." — Isaiah 41:14

HIS morning let's hear the Lord Jesus speak to each one of us: "I myself will *help* you." "It is a small thing for Me, your God, to *help* you. Consider what I have done already. What! not help you? Why, I bought you with My blood. What! not help you? I have died for you; and if I have done the greater, won't I do the less? *Help* you! It is the least thing I will ever do for you; I *have* done more, and *will* do more. Before the world began I chose you. I made the covenant for you. I laid aside My glory and became a man for you; I gave up My life for you; and if I did all this, I will surely help you now. In helping you, I am giving you what I have bought for you already. If you needed a thousand times as much help, I would give it to you; you require little compared with what I am ready to give. It is much for you to need, but it is nothing for me to give. 'Help you?' Don't be afraid! If there were an ant at the door of your granary asking for help, it would not ruin you to give him a handful of your wheat; and you are nothing but a tiny insect at the door of My all-sufficiency. 'I myself will help you.' "

O my soul, isn't this enough? Do you need more strength than the omnipotence of the United Trinity? Do you want more wisdom than exists in the Father, more love than displays itself in the Son, or more power than is manifest in the influences of the Spirit? Bring your empty pitcher here! Surely this well will fill it. Hurry, gather up your wants, and bring them here — your emptiness, your woes, your needs. Behold, this river of God is full for your supply; what can you desire besides? Go forth, my soul, in this your might. The Eternal God is your helper!

> "Fear not, I am with thee, oh, be not dismay'd!
> I, I am your God, and will still give thee aid."

"The Anointed One will be cut off." — Daniel 9:26

LESSED be His name, there was no cause of death in Him. Neither original nor actual sin had defiled Him, and therefore death had no claim upon Him. No man could have taken His life from Him justly, for He had done no man wrong, and no man could even have slain Him by force unless He had been pleased to yield Himself to die. But lo, one sins and another suffers. Justice was offended by us, but found its satisfaction in Him. Rivers of tears, mountains of offerings, seas of the blood of bulls, and hills of frankincense, could not have availed for the removal of sin; but Jesus was cut off for us, and the cause of wrath was cut off at once, for sin was put away forever. This is the wisdom whereby substitution, the sure and speedy way of atonement, was devised! This is the condescension which brought the Messiah, the Prince, to wear a crown of thorns and die upon the cross! This is the love which led the Redeemer to lay down His life for His enemies!

It isn't enough, however, to admire the spectacle of the innocent bleeding for the guilty, we must make sure of our interest in that context. The special object of the Messiah's death was the salvation of His church. Do we have a part and a place among those for whom He gave His life a ransom? Did the Lord Jesus stand as our representative? Are we healed by His stripes? It will be a terrible thing indeed if we should come short of a portion in His sacrifice; it would be better for us if we had never been born. As solemn as the question is, it is a joyful circumstance that it is one which may be answered clearly and without mistake. To all who believe on Him the Lord Jesus is a present Savior, and upon them all the blood of reconciliation has been sprinkled. Let all who trust in the merit of the Messiah's death be joyful at every remembrance of Him, and let their holy gratitude lead them to the fullest consecration to His cause.

"Then I looked, and there before me was the Lamb, standing on Mount Zion." — *Revelation 14:1*

 HE apostle John was privileged to look within the gates of heaven, and in describing what he saw, he begins by saying, "I looked, and there before me was the Lamb!" This teaches us that the chief object of contemplation in the heavenly state is "the Lamb of God, who takes away the sin of the world." Nothing else attracted the apostle's attention so much as the person of that Divine Being who has redeemed us by His blood. He is the theme of the songs of all glorified spirits and holy angels. Christian, here is joy for you. You have looked and you have seen the Lamb. Through your tears your eyes have seen the Lamb of God taking away your sins. Rejoice, then. In a little while, when your eyes shall have been wiped from tears, you will see the same Lamb *exalted on His throne.* It is the joy of your heart to hold daily fellowship with Jesus; you shall have the same joy to a higher degree in heaven; you shall enjoy the constant vision of His presence; you shall dwell with Him forever. "I looked, and there before me was the Lamb!" Why, that Lamb is heaven itself; for as good Rutherford says, "Heaven and Christ are the same thing;" to be with Christ is to be in heaven, and to be in heaven is to be with Christ. That prisoner of the Lord very sweetly writes in one of his glowing letters — "O my Lord Jesus Christ, if I could be in heaven without You, it would be a hell; and if I could be in hell, and have You still, it would be a heaven to me, for You are all the heaven I want." Isn't it true, Christian? Doesn't your soul say so?

"Not all the harps above
Can make a heavenly place,
If God His residence remove,
Or but conceal His face."

All you need to make you blessed, supremely blessed, is "to be with Christ."

*"One evening David got up from his bed and
walked around on the roof of the palace."*
— 2 Samuel 11:2

T that hour David saw Bathsheba. We are
never out of the reach of temptation. Both at
home and abroad we are liable to meet with
allurements to evil. The morning opens with
peril, and the shades of evening find us still
in jeopardy. They are well kept whom God
keeps, but woe to those who go forth into the world, or even
dare to walk around their own house unarmed. Those who
think themselves secure are more exposed to danger than
any others. The armor bearer of Sin is Self-confidence.

David should have been engaged in fighting the Lord's
battles, but he lingered at Jerusalem, instead, and gave
himself up to luxurious repose, for he arose from his bed at
evening. Idleness and luxury are the devil's jackals, and
find him abundant prey. In stagnant waters poisonous
creatures swarm, and neglected soil soon yields a dense
tangle of weeds and briars. Oh for the constraining love of
Jesus to keep us active and useful! When I see the King of
Israel sluggishly leaving his couch at the close of the day,
and falling at once into temptation, let me take warning,
and set holy watchfulness to guard the door.

Is it possible that the king had mounted his housetop
for retirement and devotion? If so, what a caution is given
us to count no place, however secret, a sanctuary from sin!
While our hearts are so like a tinder box, and sparks so
plentiful, we must be diligent in all places to prevent a
blaze. Satan can climb housetops and enter closets, and
even if we could shut out that foul fiend, our own corruptions are enough to work our ruin unless grace intervenes.
Reader, beware of evening temptations. Don't be secure.
The sun is down but sin is up. We need a watchman for the
night as well as a guardian for the day. O blessed Spirit,
keep us from all evil this night. Amen.

*"There remains, then, a Sabbath-rest for
the people of God." — Hebrews 4:9*

 OW different the state of believers in heaven
will be from what it is here! Here they are
born to toil and suffer weariness, but in
the land of the immortal, fatigue is never
known. Anxious to serve their Master, they
find their strength unequal to their zeal:
their constant cry is, "Help me to serve You, O my God." If
they are thoroughly active, they will have much work; not
too much for their will, but more than enough for their
power, so that they will cry out, "We are not tired *of* the
work, but we are weary *in it.*" Ah! Christian, the hot day of
weariness doesn't last forever. The sun is nearing the
horizon; it shall rise again with a brighter day than you
have ever seen upon a land where they serve God day and
night, and yet rest from their labors. *Here,* rest is only
partial. *There,* it is *perfect. Here,* Christians are always
unsettled; they feel that they have not yet attained. *There,*
all are at rest; they have attained the summit of the
mountain; they have ascended to the bosom of their God.
They cannot go higher. Ah, toil-worn laborer, only think
when you shall rest forever! Can you conceive of it? It is a
rest *eternal;* a rest that "remains." Here, my best joys bear
"mortal" on their brow; my fair flowers fade; my dainty
cups are drained to dregs; my sweetest birds fall before
Death's arrows; my most pleasant days are shadowed into
nights; and the flood tides of my bliss subside into ebbs of
sorrow; but *there,* everything is immortal; the harp abides
unrusted, the crown unwithered, the eye undimmed, the
voice unfaltering, the heart unwavering, and the immortal
being is wholly absorbed in infinite delight. Happy day!
happy! when mortality shall be swallowed up by life, and
the Eternal Sabbath shall begin.

> *"He explained to them what was said in all the*
> *Scriptures concerning himself." — Luke 24:27*

HE two disciples on the road to Emmaus had a most profitable journey. Their companion and teacher was *the best of tutors;* the interpreter, one of a thousand, in whom are hid all the treasures of wisdom and knowledge. The Lord Jesus condescended to become a preacher of the gospel, and He was not ashamed to exercise His calling before an audience of two persons; neither does He now refuse to become the teacher of even one. Let's court the company of such an excellent Instructor, for until He is made wisdom to us, we shall never be wise to salvation.

This unrivaled tutor used as His textbook *the best of books.* Although able to reveal fresh truth, He preferred to expound the old. He knew by His omniscience what was the most instructive way of teaching, and by turning at once to Moses and the prophets, He showed us that the surest road to wisdom isn't speculation, reasoning, or reading human books, but meditation upon the Word of God. The quickest way to be spiritually rich in heavenly knowledge is to dig in this mine of diamonds, to gather pearls from this heavenly sea. When Jesus Himself sought to enrich others, He worked in the quarry of Holy Scripture.

The favored pair were led to consider *the best of subjects,* for Jesus spoke of Jesus, and expounded the things concerning Himself. Here the diamond cut the diamond, and what could be more admirable? The Master of the House unlocked His own doors, conducted the guests to His table, and placed His own dainties upon it. He who hid the treasure in the field Himself guided the searchers to it. Our Lord would naturally discourse upon the sweetest of topics, and He could find none sweeter than His own person and work: with an eye to these we should always search the Word. O for grace to study the Bible with Jesus as both our teacher and our lesson!

"I looked for him but did not find him."
— *Song of Songs 3:1*

ELL me where you lost the company of Christ, and I will tell you the most likely place to find Him. Have you lost Christ in the closet by restraining prayer? Then it is there you must seek and find Him. Did you lose Christ by sin? You will find Christ in no other way but by the giving up of the sin, and seeking by the Holy Spirit to mortify the member in which the lust dwells. Did you lose Christ by neglecting the Scriptures? You must find Christ in the Scriptures. It is a true proverb, "Look for a thing where you dropped it, it is there." So look for Christ where you lost Him, for He has not gone away. But it is hard work to go back for Christ. Bunyan tells us that Pilgrim found the piece of the road back to the Arbor of Ease, where he lost his roll, the hardest he had ever traveled. Twenty miles onward is easier than to go one mile back for the lost evidence.

Take care, then, when you find your Master, to cling closely to Him. But how is it you have lost Him? One would have thought you would never have parted with such a precious friend, whose presence is so sweet, whose words are so comforting, and whose company is so dear to you! How is it that you did not watch Him every moment for fear of losing sight of Him? Yet, since you have let Him go, what a mercy that you are seeking Him, even though you mournfully groan, "O that I knew where I might find Him!" Go on seeking, for it is dangerous to be without your Lord. Without Christ you are like a sheep without its shepherd; like a tree without water at its roots; like a withered leaf in the tempest — not bound to the tree of life. Seek Him with your whole heart, and He will be found by you: only give yourself thoroughly up to the search, and truly, you shall discover Him to your joy and gladness.

*"He opened their minds so they could understand
the Scriptures." — Luke 24:45*

 E whom we observed last evening as opening
Scripture, we now perceive opening the understanding. In the first work He has many
fellow laborers, but in the second He stands
alone. Many can bring the Scriptures to
mind, but the Lord alone can prepare the
mind to receive the Scriptures. Our Lord Jesus differs from
all other teachers. They reach the ear, but He instructs the
heart. They deal with the outward letter, but He imparts an
inward taste for the truth, by which we perceive its savor and
spirit. The most unlearned of individuals become ripe scholars in the school of grace when the Lord Jesus by His Holy
Spirit unfolds the mysteries of the kingdom to them, and
grants the divine anointing by which they are enabled to
behold the invisible. Happy are we if we have had our
understandings cleared and strengthened by the Master!
How many persons of profound learning are ignorant of
eternal things! They know the killing letter of revelation,
but its living spirit they cannot discern; they have a veil
upon their hearts which the eyes of carnal reason cannot
penetrate. Such was our case a little time ago. We who now
see were once utterly blind; truth was to us as beauty in the
dark, a thing unnoticed and neglected. Had it not been for
the love of Jesus we should have remained to this moment in
utter ignorance, for without His gracious opening of our
understanding, we could no more have attained to spiritual
knowledge than an infant can climb the Pyramids, or an
ostrich fly up to the stars. Jesus' College is the only one in
which God's truth can be really learned; other schools may
teach us what is to be believed, but Christ's alone can show
us how to believe it. Let's sit at the feet of Jesus, and in
earnest prayer summon His blessed aid that our dull wits
may grow brighter and our feeble understandings may receive heavenly things.

"Abel kept flocks." — *Genesis 4:2*

 S a shepherd Abel *sanctified his work to the glory of God, and offered a sacrifice of blood upon his altar, and the Lord looked with favor on Abel and his offering.* This early type of our Lord is exceedingly clear and distinct. Like the first streak of light which tinges the east at sunrise, it doesn't reveal everything, but it clearly manifests the great fact that the sun is coming. As we see Abel, a shepherd and yet a priest, offering a sacrifice of sweet smell to God, we discern our Lord, who brings before His Father a sacrifice which Jehovah ever looks on with favor. Abel was hated by his brother — hated without a cause; and even so was the Savior: the natural and carnal man hated the accepted man in whom the Spirit of grace was found, and did not rest until his blood had been shed. Abel fell, and sprinkled his altar and sacrifice with his own blood, and therein sets forth the Lord Jesus slain by the enmity of man while serving as a priest before the Lord. "The good Shepherd lays down His life for the sheep." Let's weep over Him as we view Him slain by the hatred of mankind, staining the horns of His altar with His own blood. *Abel's blood speaks.* "The Lord said to Cain, 'Your brother's blood cries out to Me from the ground.' " The blood of Jesus has a mighty tongue, and the import of its prevailing cry isn't vengeance but mercy. It is precious beyond all preciousness to stand at the altar of our good Shepherd! to see Him bleeding there as the slaughtered priest, and then to hear His blood speaking peace to all His flock, peace in our conscience, peace between Jew and Gentile, peace between man and his offended Maker, peace all down the ages of eternity for blood-washed humanity. Abel is the first shepherd in order of time, but our hearts will always place Jesus first in order of excellence. Great Keeper of the sheep, we the people of Your pasture bless You with our whole hearts when we see You slain for us.

*"Turn my eyes away from worthless things; preserve
my life according to your word."* — *Psalm 119:37*

HERE are various kinds of vanity. The cap
and bells of the fool, the mirth of the world,
the dance, the lyre, and the cup of the disso-
lute, these are recognized by all as vanities;
by their conspicuous behavior, they display
their proper name and title. Far more treacherous are those equally vain things, the cares of this world
and the deceitfulness of riches. A person may follow vanity
as truly in the counting house as in the theater. The days of
a life spent acquiring wealth pass in a vain show. Unless we
follow Christ, and make our God the great object of life, we
only differ in appearance from the most frivolous. Clearly,
we are in great need of the first prayer of our text.

"Lord, preserve my life." The Psalmist confesses that he
is dull, heavy, lumpy, all but dead. Perhaps, dear reader,
you feel the same. We are so sluggish that the best motives
cannot revive us, apart from the Lord Himself. What! will
not hell revive me? Shall I think of sinners perishing, and
yet not be awakened? Will not heaven revive me? Can I
think of the reward that awaits the righteous, and yet be
cold? Will not death revive me? Can I think of dying and
standing before my God, and yet be lazy in my Master's
service? Will not Christ's love constrain me? Can I think
of His dear wounds, can I sit at the foot of His cross, and
not be stirred with fervency and zeal? It seems so! No mere
consideration can awaken us to zeal. God Himself must do
it, hence the cry, "*Lord,* preserve my life." The Psalmist
breathes out his whole soul in vehement pleadings: his
body and his soul unite in prayer. "Turn my eyes away,"
says the body: "*Lord,* preserve my life," cries the soul. This
is a suitable prayer for each day. O Lord, hear it in my
particular situation this night.

"All Israel will be saved." — *Romans 11:26*

HEN Moses sang at the Red Sea, it was his joy to know that *all* Israel was safe. Not a drop of spray fell from that solid wall until the last of God's Israel had safely set foot on the other side of the flood. That done, immediately the floods dissolved into their proper place again, but not until then. Part of that song was, "In Your unfailing love You will lead the people You have redeemed." In the last time, when the elect shall sing the song of Moses, the servant of God, and of the Lamb, it shall be the boast of Jesus, "Of all whom You have given me, I have lost none." In heaven there shall not be a vacant throne.

> "For all the chosen race
> Shall meet around the throne,
> Shall bless the conduct of His grace,
> And make His glories known."

As many as God has chosen, as many as Christ has redeemed, as many as the Spirit has called, as many as believe in Jesus, shall safely cross the dividing sea. We are not all safely landed yet:

> "Part of the host has crossed the flood,
> And part is crossing now."

The vanguard of the army has already reached the shore. We are marching through the depths. We are this day following closely after our Leader into the heart of the sea. Let's be of good cheer: the rearguard shall soon be where the vanguard already is; the last of the chosen ones shall soon have crossed the sea, and then shall be heard the song of triumph, when all are secure. But oh! if one were absent — oh! if one of His chosen family should be cast away — it would make an everlasting discord in the song of the redeemed, and cut the strings of the harps of paradise, so that music could never be extorted from them.

*"Because he was very thirsty, he cried out to the
LORD, You have given your servant this great
victory. Must I now die of thirst?"* — *Judges 15:18*

AMSON was thirsty and ready to die. The
difficulty was totally different from any
which the hero had met before. Merely to get
thirst assuaged is not as great a matter as to
be delivered from a thousand Philistines!
However, when the thirst was upon him,
Samson felt that small present difficulty weighed more
heavily upon him than the great past difficulty out of
which he had so specially been delivered. It is very usual
for God's people, when they have enjoyed a great deliverance, to find a small trouble too much for them. Samson
slays a thousand Philistines, and piles them up in heaps,
and then faints for a little water! Jacob wrestles with God
at Peniel, and overcomes Omnipotence itself, and then
goes "limping because of his hip!" Strange that there *must*
be a shrinking of the sinew whenever we win the day. As if
the Lord *must* teach us our littleness, our nothingness, in
order to keep us within bounds. Samson boasted extremely
loudly when he said, "I have killed a thousand men." His
boastful throat soon grew hoarse with thirst, and he committed himself to prayer. God has many ways of humbling
His people. Dear child of God, if after great mercy you are
laid very low, your case isn't an unusual one. When David
had mounted the throne of Israel, he said, "Today, though
I am the anointed king, I am weak." You must expect to
feel weakest when you are enjoying your greatest triumph.

If God has carried out great deliverances for you in the
past, your present difficulty is only like Samson's thirst,
and the Lord will not let you faint, nor allow the daughter
of the uncircumcised to triumph over you. The road of
sorrow is the road to heaven, but there are wells of refreshing water all along the route. So, tested brother or sister,
cheer your heart with Samson's words, and rest assured
that God will deliver you before long.

*"Son of Man, how is the wood of a vine better
than that of a branch on any of the trees in the forest?"*
— *Ezekiel 15:2*

THESE words are for the humbling of God's people; they are called God's vine, but what are they by nature more than others? They, by God's goodness, have become fruitful, having been planted in good soil; the Lord has trained them upon the walls of the sanctuary, and they bear fruit to His glory; but what are they without their God? What are they without the continual influence of the Spirit, begetting fruitfulness in them? O believer, learn to reject pride, seeing that you have no ground for it. Whatever you are, you have nothing to make you proud. The more you have, the more you are in debt to God; and you should not be proud of that which renders you a debtor. Consider your origin; look back to what you were. Consider what you will have been but for divine grace. Look upon yourself as you are now. Doesn't your conscience reproach you? Don't your thousand wanderings stand before you, and tell you that you are unworthy to be called His son or daughter? And if He has made you anything, aren't you taught thereby that it is grace which has made you to differ? Great believer, you would have been a great sinner if God had not made you to differ. O you who are valiant for truth, you would have been as valiant for error if grace had not laid hold upon you. Therefore, don't be proud, though you have a large estate — a wide domain of grace, once did not have a single thing to call your own except your sin and misery. Oh! strange infatuation, that you, who have borrowed everything, should think of exalting yourself; a poor dependent pensioner upon the bounty of your Savior, one who has a life which dies without fresh streams of life from Jesus, and yet proud! Shame on you, O silly heart!

"Does Job fear God for nothing?" — *Job 1:9*

HIS was Satan's wicked question concerning that upright man of old, but there are many today about whom this question can be justifiably asked, for they love God after a fashion because He prospers them; but if things went badly for them, they would give up all their boasted faith in God. If they can clearly see that, since the time of their supposed conversion, everything has gone prosperously well for them, then they will love God in their poor carnal way; but if they endure adversity, they rebel against the Lord. Their love is the love of the table, not of the host; a love to the cupboard, not to the master of the house. As for true Christians, they expect to have their reward in the next life, and to endure hardship in this. The promise of the old covenant was prosperity, but the promise of the new covenant is adversity. Remember Christ's words — "He cuts off every branch in me that bears no fruit, while every branch that does bear fruit" — What? *"He prunes so that it will be even more fruitful."* If you bear fruit, you will have to endure affliction. "Alas!" you say, "that is a terrible prospect." But this affliction works out such precious results, that the Christian who is the subject of it must learn to rejoice in tribulations, because as his tribulations abound, so his consolations abound by Christ Jesus. Rest assured, if you are a child of God, you will be no stranger to the rod. Sooner or later every bar of gold must pass through the fire. Fear not, but rather rejoice that such fruitful times are in store for you, for in them you will be weaned from earth and will qualify to share in the inheritance of the saints in the kingdom of light; you will be delivered from clinging to the present, and made to long for those eternal things which are so soon to be revealed to you. When you feel that, as regards the present, you serve God in vain, you will then rejoice in the infinite reward of the future.

"I have exalted a young man from among the people."
— Psalm 89:19

HY was Christ chosen out of the people? Speak, my heart, for thoughts from the heart are best. Wasn't it that He might be able to be *our brother*, in the blessed tie of kindred blood? Oh, what a relationship there is between Christ and the believer! The believer can say, "I have a Brother in heaven; I may be poor, but I have a Brother who is rich, and is a King, and will He let me be needy while He is on His throne? Oh, no! He loves me; He is my Brother." Believer, wear this blessed thought, like a necklace of diamonds, around the neck of your memory; put it, as a golden ring, on the finger of recollection, and use it as the King's own seal, stamping the petitions of your faith with confidence of success. He is a brother born for adversity, treat Him as such.

Christ was also chosen out of the people that He might know our wants and sympathize with us. He was "Tempted in every way, just as we are — yet was without sin." In all our sorrows we have His sympathy. Temptation, pain, disappointment, weakness, weariness, poverty — He knows them all, for He has felt all. Remember this, Christian, and let it comfort you. However difficult and painful your road, it is marked by the footsteps of your Savior; and even when you reach the dark valley of the shadow of death, and the deep waters of the swelling Jordan, you will find His footprints there. No matter where we go, He has been our forerunner; each burden we have to carry, has once been laid on the shoulders of Immanuel.

"His way was much rougher and darker than mine;
Did Christ, my Lord, suffer, and shall I repine?"

Take courage! Royal feet have left a blood-red track upon the road, and consecrated the thorny path forever.

"We will praise your love more than wine."
— *Song of Songs 1:4*

 ESUS will not let His people forget His love. If all the love they have enjoyed were to be forgotten, He would visit them with fresh love. "Do you forget My cross?" says He, "I will cause you to remember it; for at My table I will manifest Myself anew to you. Do you forget what I did for you in the council chamber of eternity? I will remind you of it, for you shall need a advisor, and shall find Me ready at your call." Mothers don't let their children forget them. If the boy goes to Australia, and doesn't write home, his mother writes — "Has John forgotten his mother?" Then an affectionate letter comes back in reply, which proves that the gentle reminder was not in vain. So is it with Jesus, He says to us, "Remember Me," and our response is, "We will praise Your love." We *will* praise Your love and its matchless history. It is as ancient as the glory which You had with the Father before the world was. We praise, O Jesus, Your eternal love when You became our Surety, and espoused us as Your betrothed. We praise the love which suggested the sacrifice of Yourself, the love which, until the fullness of time, mused over that sacrifice, and we long for the hour of which in the scroll it was written of You, "Here I am, I have come." We praise Your love, O Jesus as it was revealed to us in Your holy life, from the manger of Bethlehem to the garden of Gethsemane. We trace You from the cradle to the grave — for every word and deed of Yours was love — and we rejoice in Your love, which death did not exhaust; Your love which shone resplendent in your resurrection. We praise that burning fire of love which will never let You hold your peace until Your chosen ones are all safely housed, until Zion is glorified, and Jerusalem settled on her everlasting foundations of light and love in heaven.

"Surely he will save you from the fowler's snare."
— Psalm 91:3

 OD delivers His people from the snare of the fowler in two senses. *From,* and *out of.* First, He delivers them *from* the snare — doesn't let them enter it; and secondly, if they should be caught therein, He delivers them *out of* it. The first promise is the most precious to some; the second is the best to others.

"He shall deliver you *from* the snare." How? Trouble is often the means whereby God delivers us. God knows that our backsliding will soon end in our destruction, and He in mercy sends the rod. We say, "Lord, why is this?" not knowing that our trouble has been the means of delivering us from far greater evil. Many have been thus saved from ruin by their sorrows and their crosses; these have frightened the birds from the net. At other times, God keeps His people *from* the snare of the fowler by giving them great spiritual strength, so that when they are tempted to do evil they say, "How can I do this great wickedness, and sin against God?" But what a blessed thing it is that if, in an evil hour, we come into the net, at this time God will bring us *out* of it! O backsliders, be downcast, but don't despair. Although you have been wanderers, hear what your Redeemer says — "Return, O backsliding children; I will have mercy upon you." But you say you cannot return, for you are a captive. Then listen to the promise — "Surely he will save you from the fowler's snare." You shall yet be brought out of all evil into which you have fallen, and though you shall never cease to repent of your ways, yet He that has loved you will not cast you away; He will receive you, and give you joy and gladness, that the bones which He has broken may rejoice. No bird of paradise shall die in the fowler's net.

*"Martha was distracted by all the preparations that
had to be made." — Luke 10:40*

ER fault was not that she *served:* the de-
meanor of a servant is always becoming to
every Christian. "I serve," should be the
motto of all the members of the royal family
of heaven. Nor was it her fault that she had
to make "all the preparations." We cannot do
too much. Let's do all that we possibly can; let head, and
heart, and hands, be engaged in the Master's service. It was
not her fault that she was busy preparing a feast for the
Master. Happy Martha, to have an opportunity of enter-
taining so blessed a guest; and happy, too, to have the spirit
to throw her whole soul so heartily into the engagement.
Her fault was that she grew "distracted by all the preparations," so that she forgot *Him,* and only remembered the
service. She allowed service to override communion, and
so presented one duty stained with the blood of another.
We ought to be Martha and Mary in one: we should
perform all the necessary preparations, and engage in the
communion at the same time. For this we need great grace.
It is easier to serve than to commune. Joshua never grew
weary in fighting with the Amalekites; but Moses, on the
top of the mountain in prayer, needed two helpers to
sustain his hands. The more spiritual the exercise, the
sooner we tire in it. The choicest fruits are the hardest to
rear: the most heavenly graces are the most difficult to
cultivate. Beloved, while we don't neglect external things,
which are good enough in themselves, we ought also to see
to it that we enjoy living, personal fellowship with Jesus.
See to it that sitting at the Savior's feet isn't neglected,
even though it is under the specious pretext of doing Him
service. The first thing for our soul's health, the first thing
for His glory, and the first thing for our own usefulness, is
to keep ourselves in perpetual communion with the Lord
Jesus, and to see that the vital spirituality of our religion is
maintained over and above everything else in the world.

*"I will tell of the kindnesses of the LORD, the deeds
for which he is to be praised, according to all
the LORD has done for us."* — *Isaiah 63:7*

OU can't do this? Are there mercies which you *haven't experienced*? Even though you are gloomy now, how can you forget that blessed hour when Jesus met you, and said, "Come to me"? Can't you remember that rapturous moment when He snapped your fetters, dashed your chains to the earth, and said, "I came to break your bonds and set you free"? Or if you've forgotten the love you felt at your wedding, surely there must be some precious milestone along the road of life not quite grown over with moss on which you can read a happy memorial of His mercy towards you? What, didn't you ever have a sickness like the one you are suffering now, and did He not restore you? Were you never poor before, and didn't He supply your needs? Weren't you ever in tight situations before, and didn't He deliver you? Arise, go to the river of your experience, and pull up a few bulrushes, and braid them into an ark, wherein your childlike faith may float safely on the stream. Don't forget what your God has done for you; turn over the pages of your mind, and remember the days gone by. Can't you remember the hill Mizar? Didn't the Lord ever meet with you at Hermon? Haven't you ever climbed the Delectable Mountains? Haven't you ever been helped in time of need? On the contrary! I know you have. Go back, then, a little way to the choice mercies of yesterday, and though all may be dark *now*, light up the lamps of the past, they shall glitter through the darkness, and you shall trust in the Lord until the day breaks and the shadows flee away. "Remember, O LORD, your great mercy and love, for they are from long ago."

"Do we, then, nullify the law by this faith? Not at all! Rather, we uphold the law." — Romans 3:31

HEN the believer is adopted into the Lord's family, his relationship to old Adam and the law ceases at once; but then he is under a new rule, and a new covenant. Believer, you are God's child; it is your first duty to obey your heavenly Father. This has nothing to do with a servile spirit. You are not a slave, but a child; and now, inasmuch as you are a beloved child, you are bound to obey your Father's faintest wish, the smallest hint of His will. Does He request you to fulfill a sacred ordinance? It is not a safe thing for you to neglect it, for you will be disobeying your Father. Does He command you to seek the image of Jesus? Is it not your joy to do so? Does Jesus tell you, "Be perfect, therefore, as your heavenly Father is perfect"? Then you will work to be perfect in holiness, not because the law requires this, but because your Savior commands it. Does He invite His saints to love one another? Do it! Not because the law says, "Love your neighbor," but because Jesus says, "If you love me, you will obey what I command;" and this is the commandment that He has given to you, "that you love one another." Are you told to distribute to the poor? Do it! not because charity is a burden which you dare not shirk, but because Jesus teaches, "Give to the one who asks you." Does the Word say, "Love God with all your heart"? Look at the commandment and reply, "Ah! commandment, Christ has fulfilled you already — I have no need, therefore, to fulfill you for my salvation, but I rejoice to yield obedience to you because God is my Father now and He has a claim upon me, which I would not dispute." May the Holy Spirit make your heart obedient to the constraining power of Christ's love, that your prayer may be, "Direct me in the path of Your commands, for there I find delight." Grace is the mother and nurse of holiness, and not the apologist of sin.

"Your heavenly Father." — Matthew 6:26

 OD'S people are doubly His children, they are His offspring by creation, and they are His children by adoption in Christ. Hence they are privileged to call Him, "Our Father in heaven." Father! Oh, what a precious word that is. Here is *authority:* "If I am a father, where is the honor due me?" If you are sons and daughters, where is your obedience? Here is *affection* mingled with authority; an authority which doesn't provoke rebellion; an obedience demanded which is most cheerfully rendered — which wouldn't be withheld even if it could be. The obedience which God's children yield to Him must be *loving* obedience. Don't go about serving God as slaves to their taskmaster's toil, but run in the way of His commands because it is your *Father's* way. Yield your bodies as instruments of righteousness, because righteousness is your Father's will, and *His* will should be the will of His child. *Father!* — Here is a kingly attribute so sweetly veiled in love, that the King's crown is forgotten in the King's face, and His scepter becomes, not a rod of iron, but a silver scepter of mercy — the scepter indeed seems to be forgotten in the tender hand of Him who wields it. Father! — Here is honor and love. How great is a Father's love to his children! That which friendship cannot do, and mere benevolence will not attempt, a father's heart and hand must do for his children. They are his offspring, he must bless them; they are his children, he must show himself strong in their defense. If an earthly father watches over his children with unceasing love and care, how much more does our heavenly Father? Abba, Father! Those who can say this have uttered better music than cherubim or seraphim can reach. There is heaven in the depth of that word — Father! There is all I can ask; all my necessities can demand; all my wishes can desire. I have all in all to all eternity when I can say, "Father."

"All who heard it were amazed." — *Luke 2:18*

 E must not cease to wonder at the great marvels of our God. It would be very difficult to draw a line between holy wonder and *real worship;* for when the soul is overwhelmed with the majesty of God's glory, though it may not express itself in song, or even utter its voice with bowed head in humble prayer, yet it silently adores. Our incarnate God is to be worshipped as "the Wonderful." That God should consider His fallen creatures, human beings, and instead of sweeping them away with the broom of destruction, should Himself undertake to be the Redeemer of humanity, and to pay the ransom price, is, indeed marvelous! But to each believer redemption is most marvelous as he views it in relation to himself. It is a miracle of grace indeed, that Jesus should forsake the thrones and royalties above, to suffer ignominiously below *for you.* Let your soul lose itself in wonder, for wonder is in this way a very practical emotion. Holy wonder will lead you to *grateful worship* and *heartfelt thanksgiving.* It will cause within you *godly watchfulness;* you will be afraid to sin against such a love as this. Feeling the presence of the mighty God in the gift of His dear Son, you will put off your shoes from off your feet, because the place whereon you stand is holy ground. You will be moved at the same time to *glorious hope.* If Jesus has done such marvelous things on your behalf, you will feel that heaven itself isn't too great for your expectation. Who can be astonished at anything, when he has once been astonished at the manger and the cross? What is left that is wonderful after one has seen the Savior? Dear reader, it may be that from the quietness and seclusion of your life, you are scarcely able to imitate the shepherds of Bethlehem, who told what they had seen and heard, but you can, at least, fill up the circle of the worshippers before the throne, by wondering at what God has done.

"From the fullness of his grace we have all received."
— *John 1:16*

 HESE words tell us that there is a fullness in Christ. There is a fullness of essential Deity, for "in Christ all the fullness of the Deity lives in bodily form." There is a fullness of perfect humanity, for in Him, bodily, that Godhead was revealed. There is a fullness of atoning efficacy in His blood, for "the blood of Jesus, His Son, purifies us from all sin." There is a fullness of justifying righteousness in His life, for "therefore, there is now no condemnation for those who are in Christ Jesus." There is a fullness of divine prevalence in His plea, for "He is able to save completely those who come to God through Him, because He always lives to intercede for them." There is a fullness of victory in His death, for through death He destroyed him that had the power of death, that is the devil. There is a fullness of efficacy in His resurrection from the dead, for by it "He has given us new birth into a living hope." There is a fullness of triumph in his ascension, for "when He ascended on high, He led captives in His train and gave gifts to men." There is a fullness of blessings of every sort and shape; a fullness of grace to pardon, of grace to regenerate, of grace to sanctify, of grace to preserve, and of grace to perfect. There is a fullness at all times; a fullness of comfort in affliction; a fullness of guidance in prosperity. A fullness of every divine attribute, of wisdom, of power, of love; a fullness which is impossible to survey, much less explore. "For God was pleased to have all His fullness dwell in Him," Oh, what a fullness this must be if *all* receive it! Fullness, indeed, there must be when the stream is always flowing, and yet the well springs up as free, as rich, as full as ever. Come, believer, and get all your needs supplied; ask largely, and you shall receive largely, for this "fullness" is inexhaustible, and is stored where all the needy may reach it, even in Jesus, Immanuel — God with us.

"But Mary treasured up all these things and pondered them in her heart." — Luke 2:19

 N the part of this blessed woman, three powers of her being were being exercised: her *memory* — she treasured all these things; her *affections* — she kept them in her heart; her *intellect* — she pondered them; so that memory, affection, and understanding together were applied to the things which she had heard. Beloved, remember what you have heard of your Lord Jesus, and what He has done for you; make your heart the golden pot of manna to preserve the memorial of the heavenly bread upon which you have fed in days gone by. Let your memory treasure up everything about Christ which you have either felt, or known, or believed, and then let your fond affections hold *Him* close forevermore. Love the person of your Lord! Bring forth the alabaster box of your heart, even though it is broken, and let all the precious ointment of your affection pour onto His pierced feet. Let your intellect be exercised concerning the Lord Jesus. Meditate upon what you read: don't be superficial; dive into the depths. Don't be like the swallow which touches the brook with her wing, but like the fish which penetrates the lowest wave. Stay with your Lord: don't let Him be just a passer-by who only stays the night, but urge Him strongly, saying, "Stay with us, for it is nearly evening; the day is almost over." Hold Him, and don't let Him go. The word "ponder," means to weigh. Prepare the balances of judgment. Oh, but where are the scales that can weigh the Lord Christ? "He weighs the islands as though they were fine dust:" — who shall take *Him* up? "He weighed the mountains on the scales" — on what scales shall we weigh *Him*? So be it. If your understanding cannot comprehend, let your affections apprehend; and if your spirit cannot compass the Lord Jesus in the grasp of understanding, let it embrace Him in the arms of affection.

"Perfect in Christ." — *Colossians 1:28*

ON'T you feel in your own soul that perfection isn't in you? Doesn't every day teach you that? Every tear which trickles from your eye weeps "imperfection;" every sigh which bursts from your heart, cries "imperfection;" every harsh word which proceeds from your lip, mutters "imperfection." You have too frequently had a view of your own heart to dream for a moment of any perfection *in yourself.* But in the midst of this sad consciousness of imperfection, here is comfort for you — you are "perfect *in Christ Jesus.*" In God's sight, you are "complete in Him;" *even now* you are given "grace . . . in the One he loves." But there is a second perfection, yet to be realized, which is sure to all the seed. Isn't it wonderful to look forward to the time when every stain of sin shall be removed from all believers, and we shall be presented faultless before the throne, without spot, or wrinkle, or any such thing? The church of Christ then will be so pure that not even the eye of Omniscience will see a spot or blemish in her; so holy and so glorious, that Hart did not go beyond the truth when he said —

> "With my Savior's garments on,
> Holy as the Holy One."

Then we shall know, taste, and feel the happiness of this vast but short sentence, "Perfect in Christ." Not until then shall we fully comprehend the heights and depths of the salvation of Jesus. Doesn't your heart leap for joy at the thought of it? Sinful as you are, you shall be sinless one day; filthy as you are, you shall be clean. Oh, what is a marvelous salvation this is! Christ takes a worm and transforms it into an angel; Christ takes a dirty and deformed thing and makes it clean and matchless in His glory, peerless in His beauty, and fit to be the companion of seraphs. O my soul, stand and admire this blessed truth of perfection in Christ.

*"The shepherds returned, glorifying and praising
God for all the things they had heard and seen,
which were just as they had been told." — Luke 2:20*

 HAT was the subject of their praise? They *praised God for what they had heard* — for the good tidings of great joy that a Savior was born to them. Let's mimic them; let's also raise a song of thanksgiving that we have heard of Jesus and His salvation. They also *praised God for what they had seen.* There is the sweetest music — what we have experienced, what we have felt within, what we have made our own — our "verses for the King." It isn't enough to *hear* about Jesus: mere hearing may tune the harp, but the fingers of living faith must create the music. If you have seen Jesus with the God-giving sight of faith, don't allow any cobwebs to linger among the harpstrings, but loud to the praise of sovereign grace, awake your psaltery and harp. One point for which they praised God was *the agreement between what they had heard and what they had seen.* Observe the last part of the sentence — "just as they had been told." Haven't you found the gospel to be in yourselves just what the Bible said it would be? Jesus said He would give you rest — haven't you enjoyed the sweetest peace in Him? He said you should have joy, and comfort, and life through believing in Him — haven't you received all these? Aren't His ways ways of pleasantness, and His paths paths of peace? Surely you can say with the queen of Sheba, "Not even half was told me." I have found Christ sweeter than His servants ever said He was. I looked upon His likeness as they painted it, but it was a mere paint smear compared with Himself; for the King in His beauty outshines all imaginable loveliness. Surely what we have *"seen"* keeps pace with, no, far exceeds what we have *"heard."* Let's, then, glorify and praise God for a Savior so precious, and so satisfying.

"What is unseen." — 2 Corinthians 4:18

 N our Christian pilgrimage it is well, for the most part, to be looking forward. Forward lies the crown, and onward is the goal. Whether it be for hope, for joy, for consolation, or for the inspiring of our love, the future must, after all, be the grand object of the eye of faith. Looking into the future we see sin cast out, the body of sin and death destroyed, the soul made perfect, and fit to be a participant in the inheritance of the saints in light. Looking further yet, the believers' enlightened eyes can see death's river passed, the gloomy stream forded, and the hills of light attained on which stands the celestial city; we sees ourselves enter within the pearly gates, hailed as more than conqueror, crowned by the hand of Christ, embraced in the arms of Jesus, glorified with Him, and made to sit together with Him on His throne, even as He has overcome and has sat down with the Father on His throne. The thought of this future may well relieve the darkness of the past and the gloom of the present. The joys of heaven will surely compensate for the sorrows of earth. Hush, my fears! this world is but a narrow span, and you shall soon have passed it. Hush, hush, my doubts! death is but a narrow stream, and you shall soon have forded it. Time, how short — eternity, how long! Death, how brief — immortality, how endless! It seems to me that even now I am eating of Eshcol's clusters, and sipping from the well which is within the gate. The road is so very short! I shall soon be there.

> "When the world my heart is rending
> With its heaviest storm of care,
> My glad thoughts to heaven ascending,
> Find a refuge from despair.
> Faith's bright vision shall sustain me
> Till life's pilgrimage is past;
> Fears may vex and troubles pain me,
> I shall reach my home at last."

"The dove returned to him in the evening."
— *Genesis 8:11*

 LESSED be the Lord for another day of mercy, even though I am now weary with its toils. To the preserver of humankind I lift up my song of gratitude. The dove found no rest out of the ark, and therefore returned to it; similarly, my soul has learned more fully than ever today that there is no satisfaction to be found in earthly things — God alone can give rest to my spirit. As to my business, my possessions, my family, my attainments, these are all well enough in their way, but they cannot fulfill the desires of my immortal nature. "Be at rest once more, my soul, for the Lord has been good to you." It was at the still hour, when the gates of the day were closing, that with weary wing the dove came back to her master: O Lord, enable me this evening thus to return to Jesus. She could not endure to spend a night hovering over the restless waste, nor can I bear to be even for another hour away from Jesus, the consolation of my heart, the home of my spirit. She did not merely alight upon the roof of the ark, she "returned to him;" even so would my longing spirit look into the secret of the Lord, pierce to the interior of truth, enter into that which is within the veil, and reach to my Beloved in very deed. I must come to Jesus: my longing spirit cannot stop short of the nearest and dearest communication with Him. Blessed Lord Jesus, be with me, reveal Yourself, and abide with me all night, so that when I awake I may be still with You. I notice that the dove brought in her mouth an olive branch which she had plucked off, the memorial of the past day, and a prophecy of the future. Have I no pleasing record to bring home? No pledge and earnest of loving-kindness yet to come? Yes, my Lord, I present You my grateful acknowledgments for tender mercies which have been new every morning and fresh every evening; and now, I pray You, put forth Your hand and take Your dove into Your bosom.

"As soon as you hear the sound of marching in the tops of the balsam trees, move quickly." — *2 Samuel 5:24*

HE members of Christ's church should be very prayerful, always seeking the unction of the Holy One to rest upon their hearts, that the kingdom of Christ may come, and that His "will be done on earth as it is in heaven;" but there are times when God seems especially to favor Zion, such seasons ought to be to them like "the sound of marching in the tops of the balsam trees." We ought then to be doubly prayerful, doubly earnest, wrestling more at the throne than we have been accustomed to doing. Action should then be prompt and vigorous. The tide is flowing — now let's pull bravely for the shore. O for Pentecostal outpourings and Pentecostal labors. Christian, in *yourself* there are times when you "hear the sound of marching in the tops of the balsam trees." You have a peculiar power in prayer; the Spirit of God gives you joy and gladness; the Scripture is open to you; the promises are applied; you walk in the light of God's countenance; you have peculiar freedom and liberty in devotion, and more closeness of communion with Christ than what you were used to. Now, at such joyous periods when you hear the "sound of marching in the tops of the balsam trees," is the time to move quickly, wake yourself up; now is the time to get rid of any evil habit, while God the Spirit helps your infirmities. Spread your sail; but remember what you sometimes sing —

"I can only spread the sail;
Thou! Thou! must breathe the auspicious gale."

Only be sure you have the sail up. Don't miss the gale because you lacked the preparation for it. Seek God's help so that you may be more earnest in duty when you are made stronger in faith; so that you may be more constant in prayer when you have more liberty at the throne; so that you may be more holy in your conversation while you live more closely with Christ.

"In him we were also chosen." — *Ephesians 1:11*

HEN Jesus gave Himself for us, He gave us all the rights and privileges which went with Himself; so that now, although as eternal God, He has essential rights to which no creature may venture to pretend, yet as Jesus, the Mediator, the federal Head of the covenant of grace, He has no heritage apart from us. All the glorious consequences of His obedience to death are the joint riches of all who are in Him, and on whose behalf He accomplished the divine will. See, He enters into glory, but not for Himself alone, for it is written, "Jesus, who went before us, has entered on *our* behalf." Heb. 6:20. Does He stand in the presence of God? — Christ "appear[s] *for us* in God's presence." Heb. 9:24. Consider this, believer. You have no right to heaven in yourself: your right lies in Christ. If you are pardoned, it is through *His* blood; if you are justified, it is through *His* righteousness; if you are sanctified, it is because *He* is your sanctification; if you shall be kept from falling, it will be because you are preserved in Christ Jesus; and if you are perfected at the last, it will be because you are complete in *Him.* Thus Jesus is magnified — for all is in Him and by Him; thus the inheritance is made certain to us — for it is obtained in Him; each blessing is sweeter because of this, and even heaven itself is brighter because it is Jesus our Beloved "in whom" we have obtained all. Where is the person who shall estimate our divine portion? Weigh the riches of Christ in scales, and His treasure in balances, and then think to count the treasures which belong to the saints. Reach the bottom of Christ's sea of joy, and then hope to understand the bliss which God has prepared for them that love Him. Overleap the boundaries of Christ's possessions, and then dream of a limit to the fair inheritance of the elect. "All things are yours, for you are Christ's and Christ is God's."

"The LORD Our Righteousness." — *Jeremiah 23:6*

T will always give a Christian the greatest calm, quiet, ease, and peace, to think of the perfect righteousness of Christ. How often are the saints of God dejected and sad! I don't think they ought to be. I don't think they would be if they could always see their perfection in Christ. There are some who are always talking about corruption, and the depravity of the heart, and the innate evil of the soul. This is quite true, but why not go a little further, and remember that we are "perfect in Christ Jesus." It is no wonder that those who are dwelling upon their own corruption should wear such depressed looks; but surely if we call to mind that "Christ has become for us righteousness," we shall be of good cheer. What though distresses afflict me, though Satan assault me, though there may be many things to be experienced before I get to heaven, those are done for me in the covenant of divine grace; there is nothing wanting in my Lord, Christ has done it all. On the cross He said, "It is finished!" and if it is finished, then am I complete in Him, and can rejoice with joy unspeakable and full of glory, "Not having a righteousness of my own that comes from the law, but that which is through faith in Christ — the righteousness that comes from God and is by faith." You will not find a holier people this side of heaven than those who receive into their hearts the doctrine of Christ's righteousness. When the believer says, "I live in Christ alone; I rest on Him solely for salvation; and I believe that, however unworthy, I am still saved in Jesus;" then, motivated by gratitude, this thought occurs — "Why shouldn't I live to Christ? Why shouldn't I love Him and serve Him, seeing that I am saved by His merits?" "Christ's love compels us," "that those who live should no longer live for themselves but for Him who died for them." If saved by imputed righteousness, we shall greatly value imparted righteousness.

*"Then Ahimaaz ran by way of the plain and outran
the Cushite." — 2 Samuel 18:23*

RUNNING isn't everything; there is something to be said for the path we select: a swift foot over hill and down dale will not keep pace with a slower traveler upon level ground. How is it with my spiritual journey, am I laboring up the hill of my own works and down into the ravines of my own humiliations and resolutions, or do I run by the plain way of "Believe and live"? How blessed it is to wait upon the Lord by faith! The soul runs without weariness, and walks without fainting, in the way of believing. Christ Jesus is the way of life, and He is a plain way, a pleasant way, a way suitable for the tottering feet and feeble knees of trembling sinners: am I found in this way, or am I hunting after another track such as the call to the priesthood or metaphysics may promise me? I read about the path of holiness, that the traveler, though a fool, shall not make a mistake by taking it: have I been delivered from proud reason and been brought as a little child to rest in Jesus' love and blood? If so, by God's grace I shall outrun the strongest runner who chooses any other path. This truth I may remember to my profit in my daily cares and needs. It will be my wisest course to go at once to my God, and not to wander in a roundabout manner to this friend and that. He knows my wants and can relieve them, to whom should I repair but to Himself by the direct appeal of prayer, and the plain argument of the promise. "The best runner follows the most direct course." I will not deliberate with the runners, but go directly to their coach.

In reading this passage, it strikes me that, if we compete with each other in common matters and one outruns the other, in all seriousness I ought to run that I may obtain. Lord, help me to brace my mind and press on toward the goal to win the prize for which God has called me heavenward in Christ Jesus.

"May they sing of the ways of the LORD." — *Psalm 138:5*

HE time when Christians begin to sing the ways of the Lord is when they first lose their burden at the foot of the Cross. Not even the songs of the angels seem as sweet as the first song of rapture which gushes from the in-most soul of the forgiven child of God. You know how John Bunyan describes it. He says when poor Pilgrim lost his burden at the Cross, he gave three great leaps, and went on his way singing —

> "Blessed Cross! blessed Sepulchre! blessed rather be
> The Man that there was put to shame for me!"

Believer, do you recall the day when *your* fetters fell off? Do you remember when Jesus met you, and said, "I have swept away your offenses like a cloud, your sins like the morning mist. Return to Me, for I have redeemed you." Oh! what a sweet season is that when Jesus takes away the pain of sin. When the Lord first pardoned my sin, I was so joyous that I could scarcely refrain from dancing. On the road home from the house where I had been set free, I wanted to shout in the street the story of my deliverance. My soul was so happy that I wanted to tell every snowflake that was falling from heaven of the wondrous love of Jesus who had blotted out the sins of my most rebellious nature. But it is not only at the beginning of the Christian life that believers have a reason to sing; as long as they live they discover reasons to sing about the ways of the Lord, and their experiences of His constant loving-kindness lead them to say, "I will extol the LORD at all times; His praise will always be on my lips." See to it, brothers and sisters, that you praise the Lord *this day.*

> "Long as we tread this desert land,
> New mercies shall new songs demand."

"Your love for me was wonderful." — *2 Samuel 1:26*

 OME, dear readers, let's speak for ourselves of the wonderful love, not of Jonathan, but of Jesus. We will not relate what we have been told, but the things which we have tasted and handled — of the love of Christ. Your love to me, O Jesus, was wonderful when I was a stranger wandering far from You, fulfilling the desires of the flesh and of the mind. Your love restrained me from committing the sin which is to death, and you withheld me from self-destruction. Your love held back the ax when Justice said, "Cut it down! Why should it use up the soil?" Your love drew me into the wilderness, stripped me there, and made me feel the guilt of my sin, and the burden of my iniquity. Your love spoke this comfort to me when I was very dismayed — "Come to Me, and I will give you rest." Oh, how matchless your love is when, in a moment, You washed my sins away, and made my polluted soul, which was crimson with the blood of my nativity and filthy with the grime of my transgressions, pure as the driven snow and the finest wool. How You commended Your love when You whispered in my ear, "I am yours and you are Mine." In kindly tones You said, "The Father Himself loves you." In sweet moments You declared to me "the love of the Spirit." My soul shall never forget those chambers of fellowship where You have unveiled Yourself to me. Didn't Moses have his cleft in the rock, where he saw the train, the back parts of his God? We, too, have had our clefts in the rock, where we have seen the full splendors of the Godhead in the person of Christ. Didn't David remember the tracks of the wild goat, the land of Jordan and the Hermonites? We, too, can call to mind moments equal to these in holiness and happiness. Precious Lord Jesus, give us a fresh amount of Your wondrous love with which to begin the month. Amen.

"Without the shedding of blood there is no forgiveness."
— Hebrews 9:22

HIS is the voice of unalterable truth. In none of the Jewish ceremonies were sins, even the usual ones, removed without the shedding of blood. By no means can sin be pardoned without atonement. It is clear, then, that there is no hope for me outside of Christ; for there is no other blood-shedding which is worth a thought as an atonement for sin. Am I, then, believing in Him? Is the blood of His atonement truly applied to my soul? All of us are on the same level concerning our need for Him. Even if we were to behave in a moral, generous, amiable, or patriotic way, the rule would not be altered to make an exception for us. Sin will yield to nothing less potent than the blood of Him whom God has set forth as a propitiation. What a blessing that there is the one way of pardon! Why should we seek another?

Persons who understand religion as a mere formality cannot understand how we can rejoice that all our sins are forgiven us for Christ's sake. Their works, and prayers, and ceremonies give them very poor comfort; and well may they be uneasy, for they are neglecting the one great salvation, and endeavoring to get remission without blood. My soul, sit down, and behold the justice of God as bound to punish sin; see all that punishment executed upon your Lord Jesus, and fall down in humble joy, and kiss the dear feet of Him whose blood has made atonement for you. It is in vain when conscience is aroused to fly to feelings and evidences for comfort: this is a habit which we learned in the Egypt of our legal bondage. The only restorative for a guilty conscience is a look at Jesus suffering on the cross. "The blood is the life thereof," says the Levitical law, and let's rest assured that it is the life of faith and joy and every other holy grace.

> "Oh! how sweet to view the flowing
> Of my Savior's precious blood;
> With divine assurance knowing
> He has made my peace with God."

"These records are from ancient times."
— *1 Chronicles 4:22*

 ET not as ancient as those precious things which are the delight of our souls. Let's for a moment recount them, pouring over them the way misers count their gold. *The sovereign choice* of the Father, by which He elected us to eternal life, even before the earth was, is a matter of vast antiquity, since no date can be conceived for it in the human mind. We were chosen from before the foundations of the world. *Everlasting love* went with the choice, for it was not a bare act of divine will by which we were set apart, but the divine affections were involved. The Father loved us in and from the beginning. Here is a theme for daily contemplation. *The eternal purpose* to redeem us from our foreseen ruin, to purify and sanctify us, and at last to glorify us, was of infinite antiquity, and runs side by side with immutable love and absolute sovereignty. *The covenant* is always described as being everlasting, and Jesus, the second party in it, had His goings forth of old; He struck hands in sacred sponsorship long before the first of the stars began to shine, and it was in Him that the elect were ordained to eternal life. Thus, in the divine purpose, a most blessed covenant union was established between the Son of God and His elect people, which will remain as the foundation of their safety when time shall be no more. Isn't it worth our while to be versed in these ancient things? Isn't it a shame that they are neglected so much and even rejected by the majority of professors? If they knew more about their own sin, wouldn't they be more ready to adore distinguishing grace? Let's both admire and adore tonight, as we sing —

"A monument of grace,
A sinner saved by blood;
The streams of love I trace
Up to the Fountain, God;
And in His sacred bosom see
Eternal thoughts of Love to me."

"Therefore, brothers, we have an obligation."
— *Romans 8:12*

 S God's creatures, we are all debtors to Him: to obey Him with all our body, and soul, and strength. Having broken His commandments, as we all have, we are debtors to His justice, and we owe Him a vast amount which we are not able to pay. But of the *Christian* it can be said that he does not owe God's *justice* anything, for Christ has paid the debt His people owed; for this reason the believer owes the more to *love*. I am a debtor to God's grace and forgiving mercy; but I am no debtor to His justice, for He will never accuse me of a debt already paid. Christ said, "It is finished!" and by that He meant, that whatever His people owed was wiped away forever from the book of remembrance. Christ, to the utmost, has satisfied divine justice; the account is settled; the handwriting is nailed to the cross; the prescription is given, and we are debtors to God's justice no longer. But then, because we are not debtors to our Lord in that sense, we become ten times more debtors to God than we should have been otherwise. Christian, pause and ponder for a moment. What a debtor you are to divine *sovereignty!* How much you owe to His disinterested love, for He gave His own Son that He might die for you. Consider how much you owe to His forgiving *grace*, that after ten thousand affronts He loves you as infinitely as ever. Consider what you owe to His *power;* how He has raised you from your death in sin; how He has preserved your spiritual life; how He has kept you from falling; and how, though a thousand enemies have surrounded your path, you have been able to hold on to your way. Consider what you owe to His *immutability*. Though you have changed a thousand times, He has not changed once. You are as deep in debt as you can be to every attribute of God. To God you owe yourself, and all you have — yield yourself as a living sacrifice; this is your spiritual act of worship.

"Tell me . . . where you graze your flock and where you rest your sheep at midday." — *Song of Songs 1:7*

HESE words express the desire of the believer for Christ, and his longing for *present* communion with Him. Where do You feed your flock? In *Your house?* I will go, if I may find You there. In private *prayer?* Then I will pray without ceasing. In the *Word?* Then I will read it diligently. In Your *ordinances?* Then I will walk in them with all my heart. Tell me where You feed, for wherever You stand as the Shepherd, there will I lie down as a sheep; for no one but You can supply my need. I cannot be satisfied to be apart from You. My soul hungers and thirsts for the refreshment of Your presence. "Where do You rest your flock at midday?" for whether at dawn or at midday, my only rest must be where You and Your beloved flock are. My soul's rest must be a grace-given rest, and can only be found in You. Where is the shadow of that rock? Why should I not repose beneath it? "Why should I be like a veiled woman beside the flocks of your friends?" You have friends — why shouldn't I be one of them? Satan tells me I am unworthy; but I always was unworthy, and yet You have long loved me; and therefore my unworthiness cannot be an impediment to my having fellowship with You now. It is true I am weak in faith, and prone to fall, but my very feebleness is the reason why I should always be where You feed Your flock, that I may be strengthened and preserved in safety beside the still waters. Why should I turn aside? There is no reason why I should, but there are a thousand reasons why I should not, for Jesus beckons me to come. If He withdrew Himself a little, it is only to make me prize His presence more. Now that I am grieved and distressed at being away from Him, He will lead me yet again to that sheltered nook where the lambs of His fold are sheltered from the burning sun.

"As the LORD loves." — Hosea 3:1

ELIEVER, *look back* over all your experience, and think of the way in which the Lord your God has led you in the wilderness, and how He has fed and clothed you every day — how He has endured your bad manners — how He has put up with all your complaining, and all your longings after the pots of meat of Egypt — how He has opened the rock to supply you, and fed you with manna that came down from heaven. Think of how His grace has been sufficient for you in all your troubles — how His blood has been a pardon to you in all your sins — how His rod and His staff have comforted you. When you have looked back upon the love of the Lord in this manner, then let faith survey His love *in the future,* for remember that Christ's covenant and blood have something more in them than the *past.* He who has loved you and pardoned you, shall never cease to love and pardon. He is Alpha, and He shall be Omega also: He is first, and He shall be *last.* Therefore, remember, when you shall pass through the valley of the shadow of death, you needn't fear any evil, for He is with you. When you shall stand in the cold floods of the Jordan, you need not fear, for death cannot separate you from His love; and when you shall come into the mysteries of eternity you need not tremble, "For I am convinced that neither death nor life, neither angels nor demons, neither the present nor the future, nor any powers, neither height nor depth, nor anything else in all creation, will be able to separate us from the love of God that is in Christ Jesus our Lord." Now, soul, isn't your love refreshed? Doesn't this make you love Jesus? Doesn't a flight through limitless plains of the ether of love inflame your heart and compel you to delight yourself in the Lord your God? Surely as we meditate on "the love of the Lord," our hearts burn within us, and we long to love Him more.

"Protection from the avenger of blood." — Joshua 20:3

 T is said that in the land of Canaan, cities of refuge were so arranged, that a person could reach any one of them within half a day at most. Even so the word of our salvation is near to us; Jesus is a present Savior, and the way to Him is short; it is but a simple renunciation of our own merit, and a laying hold of Jesus, to be our all in all. With regard to the roads to the city of refuge, we are told that they were strictly preserved, every river was bridged, and every obstruction removed, so that the man who fled might find an easy passage to the city. Once a year the elders went along the roads and saw to their condition, so that nothing might impede the flight of any one, and cause him, through delay, to be overtaken and slain. How graciously the promises of the gospel remove stumbling blocks from the way! Wherever there were byways and turnings, there were handmade signs posted with the inscription — "To the city of refuge!" This is a picture of the road to Christ Jesus. It is no roundabout road of the law; it is no obeying this, that, and the other; it is a straight road: "Believe, and live." It is a road so hard, that no self-righteous man can ever tread it, but so easy, that every sinner, who knows himself to be a sinner, may by it find his way to heaven. No sooner did the person accused of murder reach the outlying areas of the city than he was safe; it was not necessary for him to pass far within the walls; the suburbs themselves were sufficient protection. Learn from now on that, if all you do is touch the hem of Christ's garment, you shall be made whole; if all you do is grasp Him with "faith as small as a mustard seed," you are safe.

> "A little genuine grace ensures
> The death of all our sins."

Only don't waste time or loiter by the way, for the avenger of blood is swift of foot; and it may be he is at your heels at this still hour of the evening.

"The Father has sent his Son to be the Savior of the world." — 1 John 4:14

 T is a sweet thought that Jesus Christ did not come forth without His Father's permission, authority, consent, and assistance. He was sent of the Father, that He might be the Savior of humankind. We are too apt to forget that, while there are distinctions as to the *persons* in the Trinity, there are no distinctions of *honor*. We, too, frequently ascribe the honor of our salvation, or at least the depths of its benevolence, more to Jesus Christ than we do the Father. This is a very great mistake. What if Jesus came? Didn't His Father send Him? If He spoke wondrously, didn't His Father pour grace into His lips, that He might be an able minister of the new covenant? Those who know the Father, and the Son, and the Holy Spirit as they should know them, never set one before another in their love; they see them at Bethlehem, at Gethsemane, and on Calvary, all equally engaged in the work of salvation. O Christian, have you put your confidence in the Man Christ Jesus? Have you placed your reliance solely on Him? And are you united with Him? Then believe that you are united to the God of heaven. Since to the Man Christ Jesus you are a sibling, and hold closest fellowship, you are linked thereby with God the Eternal, and "the Ancient of days" is your Father and your friend. Did you ever consider the depth of love in the heart of Jehovah, when God the Father equipped His Son for the great enterprise of mercy? If not, let this be today's meditation. The *Father* sent Him! Contemplate that. Think how Jesus works what the *Father* wills. In the wounds of the dying Savior see the love of the great I AM. Let every thought of Jesus be also connected with the Eternal, ever-blessed God, for "it was the LORD's will to crush Him and cause Him to suffer."

"At that time Jesus [answered and] said."
— *Matthew 11:25*

HIS is a singular way in which to begin a verse — "At that time Jesus said." If you will look at the context you will perceive that no one had asked Him a question, nor was He in conversation with any human being. Yet it is written, "Jesus [answered and] said, 'I praise You, Father.' " When you answer, you answer a person to whom you have been speaking. Who, then, had spoken to Christ? His Father. Yet there is no record of it; and this should teach us that Jesus had constant fellowship with His Father, and that God spoke into His heart so often, so continually, that it was not a circumstance singular enough to be recorded. It was the habit and life of Jesus to talk with God. Even as Jesus was, in this world, so are we; let's therefore learn the lesson which this simple statement concerning Him teaches us. May *we* likewise have silent fellowship with the Father, so that often we may answer Him, and though the world does not concern itself with who we are speaking to, may we be responding to that secret voice unheard by any other ear, which our own ear, opened by the Spirit of God, recognizes with joy. God has spoken to us, let's speak to God — either to set our seal that God is true and faithful to His promise, or to confess the sin of which the Spirit of God has convinced us, or to acknowledge the mercy which God's providence has given, or to express assent to the great truths which God the Holy Spirit has opened to our understanding. What a privilege intimate communion is with the Father of our spirits! It is a secret hidden from the world, a joy with which even the nearest friend does not interfere. If we would hear the whispers of God's love, our ear must be purged and fitted to listen to His voice. This very evening may our hearts be in such a state that, when God speaks to us, we, like Jesus, may be prepared at once to *answer* Him.

"Always keep on praying." — *Ephesians 6:18*

HAT multitudes of prayers we have put up from the first moment when we learned to pray. Our first prayer was a prayer for ourselves; we asked that God would have mercy upon us, and blot out our sin. He heard us. But when He had blotted out our sins like a cloud, then we had more prayers for ourselves. We have had to pray for sanctifying grace, for constraining and restraining grace; we have been led to crave for a fresh assurance of faith, for the comfortable application of the promise, for deliverance in the hour of temptation, for help in the time of duty, and for aid in the day of trial. We have been compelled to go to God for our souls, as constant beggars asking for everything. Bear witness, children of God, you have never been able to get anything for your souls elsewhere. All the bread your soul has eaten has come down from heaven, and all the water of which it has drunk has flowed from the living rock — Christ Jesus the Lord. Your soul has never grown rich in itself; it has always been dependent upon the daily bounty of God; and hence your prayers have ascended to heaven for a range of spiritual mercies all but infinite. Your wants were innumerable, and therefore the supplies have been infinitely great, and your prayers have been as varied as the mercies have been countless. Then don't you have cause to say, "I love the Lord, because He has heard the voice of my supplication"? For as your prayers have been many, so also have been God's answers to them. He has heard you in the day of trouble, has strengthened you, and helped you, even when you dishonored Him by trembling and doubting at the mercy seat. Remember this, and let it fill your heart with gratitude to God, who has thus graciously heard your poor weak prayers. "Praise the LORD, O my soul, and forget not all His benefits."

"Pray for each other." — *James* 5:16

A S an encouragement to cheerfully offer intercessory prayer, remember that *such prayer is the sweetest God ever hears,* for the prayer of Christ is of this character. In all the incense which our Great High Priest now puts into the golden censer, there is not a single grain for Himself. His intercession must be the most acceptable of all supplications — and the more similar our prayer is to Christ's, the sweeter it will be; thus while petitions for ourselves will be accepted, our pleadings for others through the precious merits of Jesus will be the sweetest oblation that we can offer to God, the very fat of our sacrifice, having in them more of the fruits of the Spirit, more love, more faith, more familial kindness. Remember, again, that *intercessory prayer is exceedingly prevalent.* It has worked wonders! The Word of God teems with its marvelous deeds. Believer, you have a mighty engine in your hand, use it well, use it constantly, use it with faith, and you shall surely be a benefactor to others. When you have the King's ear, speak to Him for the suffering members of His body. When you are favored to draw very near to His throne, and the King says to you, "Ask, and I will give you what you will," let your petitions be, not for yourself alone, but for the many who need His aid. If you have grace at all, and are not an intercessor, that grace must be small as a grain of mustard seed. You have just enough grace to float your soul clear from the quicksand, but you have no deep floods of grace, or else you would carry in your joyous vessel a weighty cargo of the wants of others, and you will bring back from your Lord, for them, rich blessings which, but for you, they might not have obtained: —

> "Oh, let my hands forget their skill,
> My tongue be silent, cold, and still,
> This bounding heart forget to beat,
> If I forget the mercy seat!"

"Get up, go away!" — *Micah 2:10*

HE hour is approaching when the message will come to us, as it comes to all — "Arise, and go forth from the home in which you have dwelled, from the city in which you have done your business, from your family, from your friends. Arise, and take your last journey." And what do we know of the journey? And what do we know of the country to which we are bound? We have read a little about it, and it has been revealed to us somewhat by the Spirit; but how little we know of the realms of the future! We know that there is a dark and stormy river called "Death." God requires us to cross it, promising to be with us. And, after death, what comes next? What world of wonder will open upon our astonished sight? What scene of glory will be unfolded to our view? No traveler has ever returned to tell. But we know enough of the heavenly land to make us welcome our summons there with joy and gladness. The journey of death may be dark, but we may go forth on it fearlessly, knowing that God is with us as we walk through the gloomy valley, and therefore we need fear no evil. We shall be departing from all we have known and loved here, but we shall be going to our Father's house — to our Father's home, where Jesus is — to that royal "city with foundations, whose architect and builder is God." This shall be our *last* removal, to dwell forever with Him whom we love, in the midst of His people, in the presence of God. Christian, meditate often on heaven; it will help you to carry on, and to forget the labor of the journey. This vale of tears is but the pathway to the better country: this world of woe is but the stepping-stone to a world of bliss.

> "Prepare us, Lord, by grace divine,
> For Thy bright courts on high;
> Then bid our spirits rise, and join
> The chorus of the sky."

> *"Then they heard a loud voice from heaven saying*
> *to them, Come up here." — Revelation 11:12*

ITHOUT considering these words in their prophetical connection, let's regard them as the invitation of our great Forerunner to His sanctified people. In due time there shall be heard "a loud voice from heaven" to every believer, saying, "Come up here." To the saints, this should be *the subject of joyful anticipation.* Instead of dreading the time when we shall leave this world to go to the Father, we should be longing for the hour of our emancipation. Our song should be —

> "My heart is with Him on His throne,
> And ill can brook delay;
> Each moment listening for the voice,
> 'Rise up and come away.' "

We are not called *down* to the grave, but *up* to the skies. Our heaven-born spirits should long for their native air. Yet the celestial summons should be *the object of patient waiting.* Our God knows best when to bid us "Come up here." We must not wish to antedate the period of our departure. I know that strong love will make us cry,

> "O Lord of Hosts, the waves divide,
> And land us all in heaven;"

but patience must have her perfect work. God ordains with accurate wisdom the most fitting time for the redeemed to stay below. Surely, if there could be regrets in heaven, the saints might mourn that they didn't live here longer to do more good. Oh, for more sheaves for my Lord's granary! more jewels for His crown! But how, unless there is more work? True, there is the other side of it, that, living so briefly, our sins are the fewer; but oh! when we are fully serving God, and He is giving us precious seed to scatter, and reap a hundredfold, we would even say that it is fitting for us to stay where we are. Whether our Master shall say "go," or "stay," let's be equally well pleased as long as He indulges us with His presence.

"You are to give him the name Jesus." — *Matthew 1:21*

WHEN a person is dear, everything connected with him becomes dear for his sake. Thus, so precious is the person of the Lord Jesus in the estimation of all true believers, that everything about Him they consider to be inestimable beyond all price. "All Your robes are fragrant with myrrh and aloes and cassia," said David, as if the very vestments of the Savior were so sweetened by His person that he couldn't help but love them. Certain it is, that there is not a spot where that hallowed foot has trampled — there is not a word which those blessed lips have uttered — nor a thought which His loving Word has revealed — which is not to us precious beyond all price. And this is true of the *names* of Christ — they are all sweet in the believer's ear. Whether He is called the Husband of the church, her Bridegroom, her Friend; whether He is styled the Lamb slain from the foundation of the world — the King, the Prophet, or the Priest — every title of our Master — Shiloh, Emmanuel, Wonderful, the Mighty Advisor — every name is like the honeycomb dropping with honey, and luscious are the drops that distill from it. But if there is one name sweeter than another in the believer's ear, it is the name of *Jesus*. Jesus! it is the name which moves the harps of heaven to melody. Jesus! the life of all our joys. If there is one name more charming, more precious than another, it is this name. It is woven into the very warp and woof of our psalmody. Many of our hymns begin with it, and scarcely any, if they are any good at all, end without it. It is the sum total of all delights. It is the music with which the bells of heaven ring; a song in a word; an ocean for comprehension, although a drop for brevity; a matchless oratorio in two syllables; a gathering up of the hallelujahs of eternity in five letters.

> "Jesus, I love Thy charming name,
> 'Tis music to mine ear."

"He will save his people from their sins."
— *Matthew 1:21*

ANY persons, if they are asked what they understand by salvation, will reply, "Being saved from hell and taken to heaven." This is one result of salvation, but it is not one tithe of what is contained in that boon. It is true our Lord Jesus Christ does redeem all His people from the wrath to come; He saves them from the fearful condemnation which their sins had brought upon them; but His triumph is far more complete than this. He saves His people "from their sins." Oh! sweet deliverance from our worst foes. Where Christ works a saving work, He casts Satan from his throne, and will not let him be master any longer. None of us is truly a Christian if sin reigns in our mortal body. Sin will be *in* us — it will never be utterly expelled until the spirit enters glory; but it will never have *dominion*. There will be a striving for dominion — a lusting against the new law and the new spirit which God has implanted — but sin will never get the upper hand so as to be absolute monarch of our nature. Christ will be Master of the heart, and sin must be mortified. The Lion of the tribe of Judah shall prevail, and the dragon shall be cast out. Christian! is sin subdued in you? If your *life* is unholy your *heart* is unchanged, and if your heart is unchanged you are an unsaved person. If the Savior has not sanctified you, renewed you, given you a hatred of sin and a love of holiness, He has done nothing in you of a saving character. The grace which does not make a man better than others is a worthless counterfeit. Christ saves His people, not *in* their sins, but *from* them. "Without holiness no one shall see the Lord." "Everyone who confesses the name of the Lord must turn away from wickedness." If not saved from sin, how shall we hope to be counted among His people. Lord, save me now from all evil, and enable me to honor my Savior.

"David inquired of the LORD." — *2 Samuel 5:23*

HEN David made this inquiry he had just fought the Philistines, and gained a remarkable victory. The Philistines came up in great hosts, but, by the help of God, David had easily put them to flight. Note, however, that when they came a second time, David didn't go up to fight them without inquiring of the Lord. Once he had been victorious, and he could have said, as many others have in other situations, "I shall be victorious again; I may rest quite sure that if I have conquered once I shall triumph yet again. So then why should I wait to seek at the Lord's hands?" Not David. He had gained one battle by the strength of the Lord; he would not venture upon another until he had insured the same. He inquired, "Shall I go up against them?" He waited until God's sign was given. Learn from David not to take a step without God. Christian, if you want know the path of duty, take God for your compass; if you want to steer your ship through the dark billows, put the tiller into the hand of the Almighty. Many rocks could be avoided if we would let our Father take the helm; many a shoal or quicksand we might well avoid, if we would leave to His sovereign will to choose and to command. The Puritan said, "As sure as sure can be, whenever Christians carve for themselves, they'll cut their own fingers;" this is a great truth. Said another old divine, "Those who go before the cloud of God's providence go on a fool's errand;" and so they do. We must note God's providence leading us; and if providence delays, wait until providence comes. Those who go before providence will be very glad to run back again. "I will instruct you and teach you in the way you should go," is God's promise to His people. Let's, then, take all our perplexities to Him, and say, "Lord, what will You have me to do?" Don't leave your room this morning without inquiring of the Lord.

"Lead us not into temptation." — *Luke 11:4*

HAT we are taught to seek or shun in prayer, we should equally pursue or avoid in action. We should, therefore, very earnestly avoid temptation, seeking to walk so guardedly in the path of obedience, that we may never tempt the devil to tempt us. We are not to enter the thicket in search of the lion. We may pay dearly for such presumption. This lion may cross our path or leap upon us from the thicket, but we have nothing to do with hunting him. Those who confront him, even though they save the day, will find their struggle a stern one. Let the Christian pray that to be spared the encounter. Our Savior, who had personally experienced what temptation meant, thus earnestly admonishes His disciples — "Pray that you will not fall into temptation."

But do what we will, we shall be tempted; hence the prayer "deliver us from evil." God had one Son without sin; but He has no son without temptation. Humankind is born to trouble as the sparks fly upwards, and the Christian is born to temptation just as certainly. We must always be on our watch against Satan, because, like a thief, he gives no intimation of his approach. Believers who have experienced Satan's ways know that there are certain times when he will most probably make an attack, just as at certain seasons bleak winds may be expected; thus the Christian is put on a double guard by fear of danger, and the danger is averted by preparing to meet it. Prevention is better than cure: it is better to be so well armed that the devil will not attack you, than to endure the perils of the fight, even though you come off as a conqueror. Pray this evening, first, that you may not be tempted, and next, that if temptation is permitted, you may be delivered from the evil one.

"I know what it is to have plenty." — *Philippians 4:12*

 HERE are many who know "how to be in need" who have not learned "how to have plenty." When they are set upon the top of a pinnacle their heads grow dizzy, and they are ready to fall. The Christian disgraces his profession far more often in prosperity than in adversity. It is a dangerous thing to be prosperous. The crucible of adversity is a less severe trial to the Christian than the refining experience of prosperity. Oh, what leanness of soul and neglect of spiritual things have been brought on through the very mercies and bounties of God! Yet this is not a matter of necessity, for the apostle tells us that he knew how to have plenty. When he had much he knew how to use it. Abundant grace enabled him to bear abundant prosperity. When he had a full sail he was loaded with much ballast, and so floated safely. It needs more than human skill to carry the brimming cup of mortal joy with a steady hand, yet Paul had learned that skill, for he declares, "I have learned the secret of being content in any and every situation, whether well fed or hungry." It is a divine lesson to know how to be full, for the Israelites were full once, but while the flesh was yet in their mouth, the wrath of God came upon them. Many have asked for mercies that they might satisfy their own hearts' lust. Fullness of bread has often made fullness of blood, and that has brought on wantonness of spirit. When we have much of God's providential mercies, it often happens that we have but little of God's grace, and little gratitude for the bounties we have received. We are full and we forget God: satisfied with earth, we are content to do without heaven. Rest assured it is harder to know how to have plenty than it is to know how to be in need — so desperate is the tendency of human nature to pride and forgetfulness of God. Take care that you ask in your prayers that God would teach you "what it is to have plenty."

"Let not the gifts Thy love bestows
Estrange our hearts from Thee."

"I have swept away your offenses like a cloud, your sins like the morning mist. Return to me, for I have redeemed you." — *Isaiah 44:22*

TTENTIVELY observe THE INSTRUCTIVE SIMILITUDE: our sins are like a *cloud*. As clouds are of many shapes and colors, so are our transgressions. As clouds obscure the light of the sun, and darken the landscape beneath, so do our sins hide the light of Jehovah's face from us and cause us to sit in the shadow of death. They are earth-born things, and rise from the miry places of our nature; and when collected so that their measure is full, they threaten us with storm and tempest. Alas! that, unlike clouds, our sins yield us no genial showers, but rather threaten to deluge us with a fiery flood of destruction. O black clouds of sin, how can there be fair weather in our souls while you remain?

Let our joyful eye dwell upon THE NOTABLE ACT of divine mercy — "swept away." God Himself appears upon the scene, and in divine benignity, instead of manifesting His anger, reveals His grace: He at once and forever effectually removes the mischief, not by blowing away the cloud, but by erasing it from existence once for all. Against the justified man no sin remains, the great transaction of the cross has eternally removed His transgressions from him. On Calvary's summit the great deed, by which the sin of all the chosen was forever put away, was completely and effectually performed.

Putting this into practice, let's obey THE GRACIOUS COMMAND, "return to Me." Why should pardoned sinners live at a distance from their God? If we have been forgiven all our sins, let no legal fear withhold us from the boldest access to our Lord. Let backslidings be lamented, but let's not carry on interminably about them. In the power of the Holy Spirit, let's strive to return to the closest possible proximity of communion with the Lord. O Lord, this night restore us!

*"And they took note that these men had been
with Jesus."* — Acts 4:13

Christian should bear a striking resemblance
to Jesus Christ. You have read lives of Christ,
beautifully and eloquently written, but the
best life of Christ is His living biography,
written out in the words and actions of His
people. If we were what we profess to be, and
what we should be, we would be pictures of Christ; yes, such
striking likenesses of Him, that the world wouldn't have to
hold all of us up all together by the hour and say, "Well,
there seems to be somewhat of a resemblance;" instead, they
would, when they first notice us, exclaim, "They have been
with Jesus; they have been taught by Him; they are like
Him; they have caught the very idea of the holy Man of
Nazareth, and they work it out in their lives and everyday
actions." A Christian should be like Christ in *boldness.* Never
blush to own your religion; your profession will never
disgrace you: take care you never disgrace *that.* Be like Jesus,
very valiant for your God. Imitate Him in your *loving* spirit;
think kindly, speak kindly, and do kindly, that men may say
of you, "He has been with Jesus." Imitate Jesus in His *holiness.*
Was He zealous for His Master? You be so, too, always going
about doing good. Let's not waste time: it is too precious.
Was He self-denying, never looking to His own interest? Be
the same. Was He devout? Be fervent in your prayers. Had
He deference to His Father's will? So submit yourselves to
Him. Was He patient? So learn to endure. And best of all, as
the highest representation of Jesus, try to forgive your
enemies, as He did; and let those sublime words of your
Master, "Father, forgive them, for they do not know what
they are doing," always ring in your ears. Forgive, as you
hope to be forgiven. Heap coals of fire on the head of your
foe by your kindness to him. Good for evil, remember, is
godlike. Be godlike, then; and in all ways and by all means,
so live that all may say of you, "You have been with Jesus."

"You have forsaken your first love." — *Revelation 2:4*

VER to be remembered is that best and brightest of hours, when we first saw the Lord, lost our burden, received the roll of promise, rejoiced in full salvation, and went on our way in peace. It was springtime in our soul; the winter was past; the mutterings of Sinai's thunders were hushed; the flashings of its lightnings were no more perceived; God was beheld as reconciled; the law threatened no vengeance, justice demanded no punishment. Then the flowers appeared in our heart; hope, love, peace, and patience sprung from the sod; the hyacinth of repentance, the snowdrop of pure holiness, the crocus of golden faith, the daffodil of early love, all decked the garden of the soul. The time for the singing of birds had come, and we rejoiced with thanksgiving; we magnified the holy name of our forgiving God, and our resolve was, "Lord, I am Yours, wholly Yours; all I am, and all I have, I would devote to You. You have bought me with Your blood — let me spend myself and be spent in Your service. In life and in death let me be consecrated to You." *How have we kept this resolve?* Our espousal love burned with a holy flame of devotion to Jesus — is it the same *now?* Might not Jesus justifiably say to us, "I hold this against you: You have forsaken your first love"? Alas! we have done so little for our Master's glory. Our winter has lasted all too long. We are as cold as ice when we should feel a summer's glow and bloom with sacred flowers. We give to God pennies when He deserves larger currency, no, He deserves our heart's blood to be coined in the service of His church and of His truth. But shall we continue in this manner? O Lord, after You have so richly blessed us, shall we be ungrateful and become indifferent to Your good cause and work? O alert us so that we may return to our first love, and do our first works! Send us a genial spring, O Sun of Righteousness.

*"For just as the sufferings of Christ flow
over into our lives, so also through Christ our
comfort overflows." — 2 Corinthians 1:5*

ERE is a blessed proportion. The Ruler of Providence bears a pair of scales — on one side He puts His people's trials, and on the other He puts their consolations. When the scale of trial is nearly empty, you will always find the scale of consolation in nearly the same condition; and when the scale of trials is full, you will find the scale of consolation just as heavy. When the black clouds gather most, the light is the more brightly revealed to us. When the night lowers and the tempest is coming on, the Heavenly Captain is always closest to His crew. It is a blessed thing, that when we are most cast down, then it is that we are most lifted up by the consolations of the Spirit. One reason is, because *trials make more room for consolation.* Great hearts can only be made by great troubles. The spade of trouble digs the reservoir of comfort deeper, and makes more room for consolation. God comes into our heart — He finds it full — He begins to break our comforts and to make it empty; then there is more room for grace. The more humble we are, the more comfort we will always get, because we will be more fitted to receive it. Another reason why we are often most happy in our troubles is this — *then we have the closest dealings with God.* When the barn is full, we can live without God: when the purse is bursting with gold, we try to do without so much prayer. But once our *gourds* are taken away, we want our *God;* once our household idols are purified, then we are compelled to honor Jehovah. "Out of the depths I cry to You, O LORD." There is no cry so good as that which comes from the bottom of the mountains; no prayer half so hearty as that which comes up from the depths of the soul, through deep trials and afflictions. Hence they bring us to God, and we are happier; for nearness to God is happiness. Come, troubled believer, don't brood over your heavy troubles, for they are the heralds of weighty mercies.

"He will give you another Counselor to be with you forever." — John 14:16

HE Great Father revealed Himself to believers of old before the coming of His Son, and was known to Abraham, Isaac, and Jacob as the God Almighty. Then Jesus came, and the ever-blessed Son in His own proper person, was the delight of His people's eyes. At the time of the Redeemer's ascension, the Holy Spirit became the head of the present dispensation, and His power was gloriously manifested in and after Pentecost. He remains at this hour the present Immanuel — God with us, dwelling in and with His people, life-giving, guiding, and ruling in their midst. Is His presence recognized as it ought to be? We cannot control His working; He is most sovereign in all His operations; but are we sufficiently anxious to obtain His help, or sufficiently watchful lest we provoke Him to withdraw His aid? Without Him we can do nothing, but by His almighty energy the most extraordinary results can be produced: everything depends upon His manifesting or concealing His power. Do we always look up to Him both for our inner life and our outward service with the respectful dependence which is fitting? Don't we too often run before His call and act independently of His aid? Let's humble ourselves this evening for past neglects, and now entreat the heavenly dew to rest upon us, the sacred oil to anoint us, the celestial flame to burn within us. The Holy Spirit is no temporary gift, He abides with the saints. We only have to seek Him properly, and He will be found of us. He is jealous, but He is compassionate; if He leaves in anger, He returns in mercy. Condescending and tender, He does not weary of us, but awaits to be gracious still.

> Sin has been hammering my heart
> Unto a hardness, void of love,
> Let suppling grace to cross his art
> Drop from above.

"How great is the love the Father has lavished
on us, that we should be called children of God! And
that is what we are! The reason the world does not know
us is that it did not know him. Dear friends, now we
are children of God." — 1 John 3:1, 2

OW great is the love the Father has lavished on *us*." Consider who we were, and what *we* feel ourselves to be even now when corruption is powerful in us, and you will wonder at our adoption. Yet *we* are called *"the children of God."* What a high relationship is that of a child, and what privileges it brings! What care and tenderness the child expects from the father, and what love the father feels towards the child! But all *that,* and more than *that,* we now have through Christ. As for the temporary drawback of suffering with the elder sibling, this we accept as an honor: "The reason the world does not know us is that it did not know Him." We are content to be unknown with Him in His humiliation, for we are to be exalted with Him. *"Dear friends, now we are children of God."* That is easy to read, but it is not so easy to feel. How does your heart feel this morning? Are you in the lowest depths of sorrow? Does corruption rise within your spirit, and grace seem like a poor spark trampled under foot? Does your faith almost fail you? Don't be afraid, it is neither your graces nor feelings on which you are to live: you must live simply by faith in Christ. With all these things against us, *now* — in the very depths of our sorrow, wherever we may be — *now,* as much in the valley as on the mountain, "Dear friends, *now* we are the children of God." "Ah, but," you say, "see how I am clothed! my graces are not bright; my righteousness doesn't shine with apparent glory." But read the next: *"What we will be has not yet been made known. But we know that when He appears, we shall be like Him."* The Holy Spirit shall purify our minds, and divine power shall refine our bodies, then shall *we see Him as He is.*

"Therefore, there is now no condemnation."
— *Romans 8:1*

OME, my soul, think of this. Believing in Jesus, you are actually and effectually cleared from guilt; you are led out of your prison. You are no longer in fetters as a bondservant; you are delivered *now* from the bondage of the law; you are freed from sin, and can walk at large as a free person, your Savior's blood has procured your full discharge. You have a right now to approach your Father's throne. No flames of vengeance are there to scare you now; no fiery sword; justice cannot strike the innocent. Your disabilities are taken away: you were once unable to see your Father's face: you can see it now. You could not speak with Him: but now you have access with boldness. Once there was a fear of hell upon you; but you have no fear of it now, for how can there be punishment for the guiltless? He who believes is not condemned, and cannot be punished. And above all, the privileges you might have enjoyed, if you had never sinned, are yours now that you are justified. All the blessings which you would have had if you had kept the law, and more, are yours because Christ has kept it for you. All of the love and the acceptance which perfect obedience could have obtained of God belongs to you, because Christ was perfectly obedient on your behalf, and has imputed all His merits to your account, that you might be exceedingly rich through Him, who for your sake became exceedingly poor. Oh! how great the debt of love and gratitude you owe to your Savior!

> "A debtor to mercy alone,
> Of covenant mercy I sing;
> Nor fear with your righteousness on,
> My person and offerings to bring:
> The terrors of law and of God,
> With me can have nothing to do;
> My Savior's obedience and blood
> Hide all my transgressions from view."

"Day by day the king gave Jehoiachin a regular allowance as long as he lived." — 2 Kings 25:30

EHOIACHIN wasn't sent away from the king's palace with provisions that would last him for months; rather, his allowance was given to him on a daily basis. In this he very much depicts the happy position of all the Lord's people. A daily portion is *all that a person really wants.* We don't need tomorrow's supplies; that day has not yet dawned, and its wants are as yet unborn. The thirst which we may allow in the month of June doesn't need to be quenched in February, for we don't feel it yet; if we have enough for each day as the days arrive we shall never know want. Sufficient for the day is *all that we can enjoy.* We cannot eat or drink or wear more than the day's supply of food and clothing; the surplus gives us the care of storing it, and the anxiety of watching against a thief. One staff aids a traveler, but a bundle of staves is a heavy burden. Enough is not only as good as a feast, but is all that the complete glutton can truly enjoy. This is *all that we should expect;* a craving for more than this is ungrateful. When our Father doesn't give us more, we should be content with His daily allowance. Jehoiachin's situation is ours; we have a *sure* portion, a portion *given to us by the king,* a *gracious* portion, and a *perpetual* portion. Here, surely, is grounds for thankfulness.

Dear Christian reader, in matters of grace *you need a daily supply.* You have no store of strength. Day by day you must seek help from above. It is a very sweet assurance that *a daily portion is provided for you.* In the word, through the ministry, by meditation, in prayer, and waiting upon God you shall receive renewed strength. In Jesus all necessary things are laid up for you. So, then, *enjoy your continual allowance.* Never go hungry while the daily bread of grace is on the table of mercy.

"She had been instantly healed." — *Luke 8:47*

NE of the most touching and teaching of the Savior's miracles is before us tonight. The woman was very ignorant. She imagined that virtue came out of Christ by a law of necessity, without His knowledge or direct will. Moreover, she was a stranger to the generosity of Jesus' character, or she wouldn't have gone behind to steal the cure which He was so ready to give. Misery should always place itself right in the face of mercy. Had she known the love of Jesus' heart, she would have said, "I have but to put myself where He can see me — His omniscience will teach Him my situation, and His love at once will work my cure." We admire her faith, but we marvel at her ignorance. After she had obtained the cure, she rejoiced with trembling: she was glad that the divine virtue had worked a marvel in her; but she feared lest Christ should retract the blessing, and negate the grant of His grace: little did she comprehend the fullness of His love! We have not so clear a view of Him as we could wish; we don't know the heights and depths of His love; but we know of a surety that He is too good to withdraw from a trembling soul the gift which it has been able to obtain. But here is the marvel of it: little as her knowledge was, her faith, because it was real faith, saved her, and saved her at once. There was no tedious delay — faith's miracle was instantaneous. If we have faith as a grain of mustard seed, salvation is our present and eternal possession. If in the list of the Lord's children we are written as the feeblest of the family, yet, being heirs through faith, no power, human or devilish, can eject us from salvation. If we don't dare lean our heads upon His bosom with John, yet if we can venture into the throng behind Him, and touch the hem of His garment, we are made whole. Courage, timid one! Your faith has saved you; go in peace. "Since we *have been* justified through faith, *we have* peace with God."

"To him be glory both now and forever!" — *2 Peter 3:18*

EAVEN will be full of the ceaseless praises of Jesus. Eternity! your unnumbered years shall speed their everlasting course, but forever and forever, "to Him be glory." Isn't He a "Priest forever after the order of Melchisedek"? "To Him be glory." Isn't He king forever? — King of kings and Lord of lords, the everlasting Father? "To Him be glory *forever.*" Never shall His praises cease. That which was bought with blood deserves to last while immortality endures. The glory of the cross must never be eclipsed; the luster of the grave and of the resurrection must never be dimmed. O Jesus! you shall be praised forever. As long as immortal spirits live — as long as the Father's throne endures — forever, forever, to You shall be glory. Believer, you are anticipating the time when you shall join the saints above in ascribing all glory to Jesus; but are you glorifying Him *now?* The apostle's words are, "To Him be glory both now and forever." Won't you make it your prayer today? "Lord, help me to glorify You; I am poor, help me to glorify You by contentment; I am sick, help me to give You honor by patience; I have talents, help me to extol You by spending them for You; I have time, Lord, help me to redeem it, that I may serve You; I have a heart to feel, Lord, let that heart feel no love but Yours and glow with no flame but affection for You; I have a head to think, Lord, help me to think *of* You and *for* You; You have put me in this world for something, Lord, show me what that is, and help me to work out my life purpose: I cannot do much, but as the widow put in her two small coins, which were all her living, so, Lord, I cast my time and eternity, too, into Your treasury; I am all Yours; take me, and enable me to glorify You *now,* in all that I say, in all that I do, and with all that I have."

"All . . . makes you glad." — *Psalm 45:8*

ND who are thus privileged to make the Savior glad? His church — His people. But is it possible? He makes *us* glad, but how can *we make Him glad?* By our love. Ah! we think it so cold, so faint; and so, indeed, we must sorrowfully confess it to be, but it is very sweet to Christ. Hear His own eulogy of that love in the golden Canticle: "How delightful is your love, my sister, my bride! How much more pleasing is your love than wine." See, loving heart, how He delights in you. When you lean your head on His bosom, you not only receive, but you give Him joy; when you gaze with love upon His all-glorious face, you not only obtain comfort, but impart delight. Our *praise,* also gives Him joy — not the song of the lips alone, but the melody of the heart's deep gratitude. Our *gifts,* too, are very pleasant to Him; He loves to see us lay our time, our talents, our substance upon the altar, not for the value of what we give, but for the sake of the motive from which the gift springs. To Him the lowly offerings of His saints are more acceptable than the thousands made of gold and silver. *Holiness* is like frankincense and myrrh to Him. Forgive your enemy, and you make Christ glad; distribute of your substance to the poor, and He rejoices; be the means of saving souls, and you give Him to see of the travail of His soul; proclaim His gospel, and you are a sweet savor to Him; go among the ignorant and lift up the cross, and you have given Him honor. It is in your power even now to break the alabaster box, and pour the precious oil of joy upon His head, as did the woman of old, whose memorial is to this day set forth wherever the gospel is preached. Will you be backward then? Won't you perfume your beloved Lord with the myrrh and aloes, and cassis of your heart's praise? Yes, ivory palaces, you shall hear the songs of the saints!

"I have learned to be content whatever the circumstances." — *Philippians 4:11*

HESE words show us that contentment is not a natural propensity of man. "Bad weeds grow in haste." Covetousness, discontent, and murmuring are as natural to man as thorns are to the soil. We needn't sow thistles and brambles; they come up naturally enough, because they are indigenous to earth: and so, we needn't teach men to complain; they complain fast enough without any education. But the precious things of the earth must be cultivated. If we would have wheat, we must plow and sow; if we want flowers, there must be the garden, and all the gardener's care. Now, contentment is one of the flowers of heaven, and, if we would have it, it must be cultivated. It will not grow in us by nature; it is the new nature alone that can produce it, and even then we must be especially careful and watchful that we maintain and cultivate the grace which God has sown in us. Paul says, "I have *learned* to be content;" as much as to say, he didn't know how at one time. It cost him some pains to attain to the mystery of that great truth. No doubt he sometimes thought he had learned, and then broke down. And when at last he had attained to it, and could say, "I have learned to be content whatever the circumstances," he was an old, gray-haired man, upon the borders of the grave — a poor prisoner shut up in Nero's dungeon at Rome. We might well be willing to endure Paul's infirmities, and share the cold dungeon with him, if we, too, might by any means attain to his good measure. Don't indulge the notion that you can be contented with *learning,* or learn without discipline. It is not a power that may be exercised naturally, but a science to be acquired gradually. We know this from experience. Brother and sister, hush that complaint, as natural as it is, and continue as a diligent scholar in the College of Content.

"Your good Spirit." — *Nehemiah 9:20*

 OMMON, too common, is the sin of forgetting the Holy Spirit. This is folly and in gratitude. He is good, supremely good, and deserves accordingly at our hands. As God, He is good essentially. He shares in the threefold ascription of Holy, holy, holy, which ascends to the Triune Jehovah. Unmixed purity and truth, and grace is He. He is *good benevolently,* tenderly bearing with our waywardness, striving with our rebellious wills; giving us life from our death in sin, and then training us for the skies as a loving nurse fosters her child. How generous, forgiving, and tender is this patient Spirit of God. He is *good operatively.* All His works are good in the most eminent degree: He suggests good thoughts, prompts good actions, reveals good truths, applies good promises, assists in good attainments, and leads to good results. There is no spiritual good in all the world of which He is not the author and sustainer, and heaven itself will owe the perfect character of its redeemed inhabitants to His work. He is *good officially;* whether as Comforter, Instructor, Guide, Sanctifier, Quickener, or Intercessor. He fulfills His office well, and each work is fraught with the highest good to the church of God. They who yield to His influences become good, they who obey His impulses do good, they who live under His power receive good. Let's then act towards so good a person according to the dictates of gratitude. Let's revere His person, and adore Him as God over all, blessed forever; let's own His power, and our need of Him by waiting upon Him in all our holy enterprises; let's seek His aid hourly, and never grieve Him; and let's speak to His praise whenever occasion occurs. The church will never prosper until it believes in the Holy Spirit more reverently. He is so good and kind, that it is sad, indeed, that He should be grieved by slights and negligences.

"Isaac ... lived near Beer Lahai Roi." — *Genesis 25:11*

AGAR had once found deliverance there and Ishmael had drunk from the water so graciously revealed by the God who lives and sees humankind; but this was a merely casual visit, such as worldlings pay to the Lord in times of need, when it serves their turn. They cry to Him in trouble, but forsake Him in prosperity. Isaac *lived* there, and made the well of the living and all-seeing God his constant source of supply. The usual tenor of a man's life, the *living* of his soul, is the true test of his state. Perhaps the providential visitation experienced by Hagar struck Isaac's mind, and led him to revere the place; its mystical name endeared it to him; his frequent musings by its brim at evening made him familiar with the well; his meeting Rebecca there had made his spirit feel at home near the spot; but best of all, the fact that he enjoyed fellowship there with the living God had made him select that hallowed ground for his dwelling. Let's learn to live in the presence of the living God; let's pray to the Holy Spirit that this day, and every other day, we may feel, "You, God, see me." May the Lord Jehovah be as a well to us, delightful, comforting, unfailing, springing up to eternal life. The bottle of the creature cracks and dries up, but the well of the Creator never fails; happy is he who lives at the well, and so has abundant and constant supplies near at hand. The Lord has been a sure helper to others: His name is Shaddai, God All-sufficient; our hearts have often had most delightful communication with Him; through Him our soul has found her glorious Husband, the Lord Jesus; and in Him this day we live, and move, and have our being; let's, then, live in closest fellowship with Him. Glorious Lord, constrain us that we may never leave You, but live by the well of the living God.

"Even though I the Lord was there."
— *Ezekiel 35:10*

DOM'S princes saw the whole country left
desolate, and counted upon its easy conquest;
but there was one great difficulty in their way
— quite unknown to them — *"The Lord was
there;"* and in His presence lay the special
security of the chosen land. Whatever may
be the machinations and devices of the enemies of God's
people, there is still the same effectual barrier to thwart their
design. *The saints* are God's heritage, and He is in the midst
of them, and will protect His own. What comfort this
assurance yields us in our troubles and spiritual conflicts!
We are constantly opposed, and yet perpetually preserved!
How often Satan shoots his arrows against our *faith*, but our
faith defies the power of hell's fiery darts; they are not only
turned aside, but they are quenched upon its shield, for "the
Lord was there." *Our good works* are the subjects of Satan's
attacks. A saint never yet had a virtue or a grace which was
not the target for hellish bullets: whether it was hope bright
and sparkling, or love warm and fervent, or patience all-en-
during, or zeal flaming like coals of fire, the old enemy of
everything that is good has tried to destroy it. The only
reason why anything virtuous or lovely survives in us is this,
"the Lord was there."

If the Lord is with us through life, we needn't fear for our
dying confidence; for *when we come to die,* we shall find that
"the Lord was *there;"* where the billows are most tempestuous, and the water is most chilly, we shall feel the bottom,
and know that it is good: our feet shall stand upon the Rock
of Ages when time is passing away. Beloved, from the first of a
Christian's life to the last, the only reason why we don't perish
is because *"the Lord was there."* When the God of everlasting love shall change and leave His elect to perish, then may
the church of God be destroyed; but not until then, because
it is written, JEHOVAH SHAMMAH, *"The Lord is there."*

"Tell me what charges you have against me." — Job 10:2

 ERHAPS, O tested soul, the Lord is doing this to develop your graces. There are some of your graces which would never be *discovered* if it were not for your trials. Don't you know that your faith never looks so grand in summer weather as it does in winter? Love is too often like a firefly, showing only a little light except if it is in the midst of surrounding darkness. Hope itself is like a star — not to be seen in the sunshine of prosperity, and only to be discovered in the night of adversity. Afflictions are often the black foils in which God does set the jewels of His children's graces, to make them shine the better. It was only a little while ago that on your knees you were saying, "Lord, I fear I have no faith: let me know that I have faith." Wasn't this really, though perhaps unconsciously, your praying for trials? — for how can you know that you have faith until your faith is exercised? Depend upon it, God often sends us trials that our graces may be discovered, and that we may be certified of their existence. Besides, it is not merely discovery, *real growth* in grace is the result of sanctified trials. God often takes away our comforts and our privileges in order to make us better Christians. He trains His soldiers, not in tents of ease and luxury, but by turning them out and exposing them to forced marches and hard service. He makes them ford through streams, and swim through rivers, and climb mountains, and walk many a long mile with heavy knapsacks of sorrow on their backs. Well, Christian, may not this account for the troubles through which you are passing? Isn't the Lord bringing out your graces, and making them grow? Isn't this the reason why He is contending with you?

> "Trials make the promise sweet;
> Trials give new life to prayer;
> Trials bring me to His feet,
> Lay me low, and keep me there."

"Father, I have sinned." — *Luke 15:18*

T is quite certain that those whom Christ has washed in His precious blood need not make a confession of sin, as culprits or criminals, before God the Judge, for Christ has forever taken away all their sins in a legal sense, so that they no longer stand where they can be condemned, but are once for all accepted in the Beloved; but having become children, and offending as children, oughtn't they go before their heavenly Father daily and confess their sin, and acknowledge their iniquity in that character? Nature teaches that it is the duty of erring children to make a confession to their earthly father, and the grace of God in the heart teaches us that we, as Christians, owe the same duty to our heavenly Father. We daily offend, and ought not to rest without daily pardon. For, supposing that my trespasses against my Father are not at once taken to Him to be washed away by the purifying power of the Lord Jesus, what will be the consequence? If I were not to have sought forgiveness and been washed from these offenses against my Father, I would feel distance from Him; I would doubt His love to me; I would tremble at Him; I would be afraid to pray to Him: I would grow like the prodigal, who, although still a child, was yet far off from his father. But if, with a child's sorrow at offending so gracious and loving a Parent, I go to Him and tell Him all, and do not rest until I realize that I am forgiven, then I shall feel a holy love to my Father, and shall go through my Christian career, not only as saved, but as one enjoying present peace in God through Jesus Christ my Lord. There is a wide distinction between confessing sin *as a culprit,* and confessing sin *as a child.* The Father's bosom is the place for penitent confessions. We have been cleansed once for all, but our feet still need to be washed from the defilement of our daily walk as children of God.

"This is what the Sovereign LORD says:
Once again I will yield to the plea of the house
of Israel and do this for them." — Ezekiel 36:37

 RAYER is the forerunner of mercy. Turn to sacred history, and you will find that scarcely ever did a great mercy come to this world unheralded by supplication. You have found this true in your own personal experience. God has given you many an unsolicited favor, but still great prayer has always been the prelude of great mercy with you. When you first found peace through the blood of the cross, you had been praying often, and earnestly interceding with God that He would remove your doubts, and deliver you from your distresses. Your assurance was the result of prayer. When at any time you have had high and rapturous joys, you have been obliged to look upon them as answers to your prayers. When you have had great deliverances out of sore troubles, and mighty helps in great dangers, you have been able to say, "I sought the LORD, and He answered me; He delivered me from all my fears." Prayer is always the preface to blessing. It goes before the blessing *as the blessing's shadow.* When the sunlight of God's mercies rises upon our necessities, it casts the shadow of prayer far down upon the plain. Or, to use another illustration, when God piles up a hill of mercies, He Himself shines behind them, and He casts on our spirits the shadow of prayer, so that we may be assured that, if we are often in prayer, our pleadings are the shadows of mercy. Prayer is thus connected with the blessing *to show us the value of it.* If we had the blessings without asking for them, we should think them common things; but prayer makes our mercies more precious than diamonds. The things we ask for are precious, but we don't realize their preciousness until we have sought for them earnestly.

"Prayer makes the darken'd cloud withdraw;
Prayer climbs the ladder Jacob saw;
Gives exercise to faith and love;
Brings every blessing from above."

*"The first thing Andrew did was to find
his brother Simon." — John 1:41*

THIS case is an excellent example of all situations where spiritual life is vigorous. *As soon as one has found Christ, one begins to find others.* I won't believe that you have tasted of the honey of the gospel if you can eat it all yourself. True grace puts an end to all spiritual monopoly. Andrew *first* found his own brother Simon, and then others. *Relationship has a very strong demand upon our first individual efforts.* Andrew, you did well to begin with Simon. I would be surprised if there were some Christians giving away the good news at other people's houses when they would do well to present the good news to their own — if there were some people engaged in useful works abroad who are neglecting their special sphere of usefulness at home. You may or you may not be called to evangelize the people in any particular locality, but certainly you are called to see after your own servants, your own kin and acquaintance. Let your religion begin at home. Many tradesmen export their best commodities — Christians shouldn't. They should have all their conversation everywhere of the best quality; but let them take care to put forth the sweetest fruit of spiritual life and testimony in his own family. When Andrew went to find his brother, little did he imagine how eminent Simon would become. *Simon Peter was worth ten Andrews* as far as we can gather from sacred history, and yet Andrew was instrumental in bringing him to Jesus. You may be very deficient in talent yourself, and yet you may be the means of drawing to Christ one who shall become eminent in grace and service. Ah! dear friend, you know very little about the possibilities that are in you. You may only speak a word to a child, and in that child there may be slumbering a noble heart which shall stir the Christian church in years to come. Andrew has only two talents, but he finds Peter. Go and do likewise.

"God, who comforts the downcast." — *2 Corinthians 7:6*

ND who comforts like Him? Go to some poor, melancholy, distressed child of God; tell him sweet promises, and whisper in his ear choice words of comfort; he is like the deaf adder, he doesn't hear the voice of the charmer, no matter how wisely he charms. He is drinking gall and wormwood, and comfort him as you may, it will be only a note or two of mournful resignation that you will get from him; you will not elicit psalms of praise, or hallelujahs, or joyful sonnets. But let *God* come to His child, let Him lift up his countenance, and the mourner's eyes glisten with hope. Don't you hear him sing —

> "'Tis paradise, if thou art here;
> If thou depart, 'tis hell"?

You couldn't have cheered him: but the Lord has done it; "He is the God of all comfort." There is no balm in Gilead, but there is balm in God. There is no physician among the creatures, but the Creator is Jehovah Rophi. It is marvelous how one sweet word of God will make whole songs for Christians. One word of God is like a piece of gold, where the Christian beats the piece of gold into gold leaf, and can hammer that promise out for whole weeks. So, then, poor Christian, you needn't sit down in despair. Go to the Comforter, and ask Him to give you consolation. You are a poor dry well. You have heard it said, that when a pump is dry, you must pour water down it first of all, and then you will get water, and so, Christian, when you are dry, go to God, ask Him to shed abroad His joy in your heart, and then your joy shall be full. Don't go to earthly acquaintances, for you will find them Job's comforters after all; but go first and foremost to your "God, who comforts the downcast," and you will soon say, "When anxiety was great within me, Your consolation brought joy to my soul."

"Then Jesus was led by the Spirit into the desert to be tempted by the devil." — Matthew 4:1

Holy character doesn't avert temptation — Jesus was tempted. When Satan tempts us, his sparks fall upon tinder; but in Christ's case, it was like striking sparks on water; yet the enemy continued his evil work. Now, if the devil goes on striking when there is no result, how much more will he do it when he knows what inflammable stuff our hearts are made of! Though you become greatly sanctified by the Holy Spirit, expect that the great dog of hell will bark at you still. In the haunts of men we expect to be tempted, but even seclusion will not guard us from the same trial. Jesus Christ was led away from human society into the wilderness, and was tempted of the devil. Solitude has its charms and its benefits, and may be useful in checking the lust of the eye and the pride of life; but the devil will follow us into the most lovely retreats. Don't suppose that it is only the worldly-minded who have dreadful thoughts and blasphemous temptations, for even spiritually-minded persons endure the same; and in the holiest position we may allow the darkest temptation. The utmost consecration of spirit will not insure you against Satanic temptation. Christ was consecrated through and through. It was His meat and drink to do the will of Him that sent Him: and yet He was tempted! Your hearts may glow with a seraphic flame of love to Jesus, and yet the devil will try to bring you down to Laodicean lukewarmness. If you will tell me when God permits Christians to lay aside their armor, I will tell you when Satan has given up temptation. Like the old knights in times of battle, we must sleep with helmet and breastplate buckled on, for the arch-deceiver will seize our first unguarded hour to make us his prey. The Lord keep us watchful in all seasons, and give us a final escape from the jaw of the lion and the paw of the bear.

"God has said." — *Hebrews 13:5*

F we can only grasp these words by faith, we have an all-conquering weapon in our hand. What doubt will not be slain by this two-edged sword? What fear is there which shall not fall smitten with a deadly wound inflicted by an arrow from the bow of God's covenant? Will not the distresses of life and the pangs of death; will not the corruptions within, and the snares without; will not the trials from above, and the temptations from beneath, all seem but light afflictions when we can hide ourselves beneath the bulwark of "God has said"? Yes; whether for delight in our quietude or for strength in our conflict, "God has said" must be our daily resort. And this may teach us the extreme value of *searching* the Scriptures. There may be a promise in the Word which would exactly fit your case, but you may not know of it, and therefore you miss its comfort. You are like prisoners in a dungeon where there could be one key on the key ring which would unlock your door and free you. However, if you won't look for it, you may remain a prisoner yet, though liberty is so close at hand. There may be a potent medicine in the great pharmacopoeia of Scripture, and you may yet continue sick unless you will examine and search the Scriptures to discover what "God has said." Besides reading the Bible, shouldn't you be filling your memories abundantly with the promises of God? You can recollect the sayings of great people; you treasure up the verses of renowned poets; oughtn't you to be profound in your knowledge of the words of God so that you may be able to quote them readily when you want to solve a difficulty, or overthrow a doubt? Since "God has said" is the source of all wisdom and the fountain of all comfort, let it dwell in you richly, as "A spring of water welling up to eternal life." So shall you grow healthy, strong, and happy in the divine life.

"Do you understand what you are reading?"
— *Acts 8:30*

E would be better able to teach others, and less liable to be carried about by every wind of doctrine, if we sought to have a more intelligent understanding of the Word of God. Since the Holy Spirit, the Author of the Scriptures, is He who alone who can enlighten us correctly to understand them, we should constantly ask His teaching, and His guidance into all truth. When the prophet Daniel would interpret Nebuchadnezzar's dream, what did he do? He set himself to earnest prayer that God would open up the vision. The apostle John, in his vision at Patmos, saw a book sealed with seven seals which none was found worthy enough to open, much less look upon. The book was afterwards opened by the Lion of the tribe of Judah, who had prevailed to open it; but it is written first — "I wept and wept." The tears of John, which were his liquid prayers, were, as far as he was concerned, the sacred keys by which the folded book was opened. Therefore, if, for your own and others' profit, you desire to be filled "with the knowledge of [God's] will through all spiritual wisdom and understanding," remember that prayer is your best means of study: like Daniel, you shall understand the dream, and the interpretation thereof, when you have sought God; and like John you shall see the seven seals of precious truth unloosed, after you have wept and wept. Stones are not broken, except by an earnest use of the hammer; and the stonecutter must go down on his knees. Use the hammer of diligence, and exercise the knee of prayer, and there is not a stony doctrine in revelation which is useful for you to understand which will not fly into shivers under the exercise of prayer and faith. You may force your way through anything with the leverage of prayer. Thoughts and reasonings are like the steel wedges which take a hold upon truth; but prayer is the lever, the crowbar which forces open the iron chest of sacred mystery, that we may get at the treasure hidden within.

*"His bow remained steady, his strong arms
stayed limber, because of the hand of the
Mighty One of Jacob."* — Genesis 49:24

 HAT strength which God gives to His Josephs is *real* strength; it is not a boasted valor, a fiction, a thing of which people talk, but which ends in smoke; it is true — *divine strength.* Why does Joseph stand against temptation? Because God gives him aid. We can do nothing without the power of God. All true strength comes from "the mighty God of Jacob." Notice in what a *blessedly familiar way* God gives this strength to Joseph — "His strong arms stayed limber because of the hand of the Mighty One of Jacob." Thus God is represented as putting His hands on Joseph's hands, placing His arms on Joseph's arms. Just like a father teaches his children, so the Lord teaches them that fear Him. He puts His arms upon them. Marvelous condescension! God Almighty, Eternal, Omnipotent, stoops from His throne and lays His hand upon the child's hand, stretching His arm upon the arm of Joseph, that he may be made strong! This strength was also covenant strength, for it is ascribed to "the *Mighty One of Jacob.*" Now, wherever you read of the God of Jacob in the Bible, you should remember the covenant with Jacob. Christians love to think of God's covenant. All the power, all the grace, all the blessings, all the mercies, all the comforts, all the things we have, flow to us from the principal source, through the covenant. If there were no covenant, then we would fail indeed; for all grace proceeds from it, as light and heat from the sun. No angels ascend or descend, save upon that ladder which Jacob saw, at the top of which stood a covenant God. Christian, it may be that the archers have bitterly attacked you, and shot at you, and wounded you, but still your bow abides in strength; be sure, then, to ascribe all the glory to Jacob's Mighty One.

"The LORD is slow to anger and great in power."
— *Nahum 1:3*

EHOVAH *"is slow to anger."* When mercy comes into the world she drives winged steeds; the axles of her chariot wheels are red hot with speed; but when wrath goes forth, it toils on with tardy footsteps, for God takes no pleasure in the sinner's death. God's rod of mercy is always in His outstretched hands; His sword of justice is in its scabbard, held down by that pierced hand of love which bled for the sins of humanity. "The Lord is slow to anger," because He is GREAT IN POWER. He is truly great in power who has power over himself. When God's power restrains Himself, then it is power indeed: the power that binds omnipotence is omnipotence surpassed. A man who has a strong mind can bear to be insulted for a long time, and only resents the wrong when a sense of right demands his action. The weak mind is irritated at the slightest thing: the strong mind bears it like a rock which doesn't move, even though a thousand breakers dash upon it, and cast their pitiful malice in spray upon its summit. God marks His enemies, and yet He doesn't rouse Himself, but holds His anger in. If He were less divine than He is, He would have sent forth the whole of His thunders long before this, and emptied the magazines of heaven; long before this He would have blasted the earth with the wondrous fires of its lower regions, and humankind would have been utterly destroyed; but the greatness of His power brings us mercy. Dear reader, what is your state this evening? Can you by humble faith look to Jesus, and say, "My substitute, You are my rock, my trust"? Then, beloved, don't be afraid of God's power; for by faith you have fled to Christ for refuge, the power of God needn't terrify you any more than the shield and sword of the warrior terrifies those whom he loves. Rather, rejoice that He who is "great in power" is your Father and Friend.

"Never will I leave you." — *Hebrews 13:5*

 O promise is for private interpretation. Whatever God has said to any one saint, He has
said to all. When He opens a well for one, it
is that all may drink. When He opens a
granary door to give out food, there may be
some one starving person who provides the
occasion for its being opened, but all hungry saints may
come and feed, too. Whether He gave the word to Abraham
or to Moses doesn't matter, O believer; He has given it to
you as one of the covenanted seed. There is not a high
blessing too lofty for you, nor a wide mercy too extensive
for you. Now, lift up your eyes to the north and to the
south, to the east and to the west, for all this is yours.
Climb to Pisgah's top, and view the utmost limit of the
divine promise, for the land is all your own. There is not a
brook of living water of which you may not drink. If the
land flows with milk and honey, eat the honey and drink
the milk, for both are yours. Be bold to believe, for He has
said, "Never will I leave *you;* never will I forsake *you.*" In
this promise, God gives to His people everything. "Never
will *I* leave you." Then no attribute of God can cease to be
engaged for us. Is He mighty? He will show Himself strong
on the behalf of them that trust Him. Is He love? Then
with loving-kindness He will have mercy upon us. Whatever attributes may compose the character of Deity, every
one of them to its fullest extent shall be engaged on our
side. To say it all in one space, there is nothing you can
want, there is nothing you can ask for, there is nothing you
can need in time or in eternity, there is nothing living,
nothing dying, there is nothing in this world, nothing in
the next world, there is nothing now, nothing at the
resurrection morning, nothing in heaven which is not
contained in this text — "Never will I leave you, never will
I forsake you."

"Carry [your] cross and follow me." — Luke 14:27

OU don't have the makings for your own cross, although unbelief is a master carpenter at making crosses; neither are you allowed to choose your own cross, although self-will would preferably be lord and master; rather, your cross is prepared and appointed for you by divine love, and you are to accept it cheerfully; you are to *carry* the cross as your chosen badge and burden, and not to stand judging it too severely. This night Jesus bids you to submit your shoulder to His easy yoke. Don't kick at it in petulance, or trample on it in vain conceit, or fall under it in despair, or run away from it in fear, but take it up like a true follower of Jesus. Jesus was a cross bearer; He leads the way in the path of sorrow. Surely you could not desire a better guide! And if He carried a cross, what nobler burden would you desire? The *Via Crucis* is the way of safety; don't be afraid to tread its thorny paths.

Beloved, the cross is not made of feathers, or lined with velvet, it is heavy and galling to disobedient shoulders; but it is not an iron cross, though your fears have painted it with iron colors, it is a wooden cross, and a man can carry it, for the Man of sorrows tried the load. Carry your cross, and by the power of the Spirit of God you will soon be so in love with it, that like Moses, you would not exchange the reproach of Christ for all the treasures of Egypt. Remember that Jesus carried it, and it will smell sweetly; remember that it will soon be followed by the crown, and the thought of the coming weight of glory will greatly lighten the present heaviness of trouble. The Lord help you to bow your spirit in submission to the divine will before you fall asleep this night, that waking with tomorrow's sun, you may go forth to the day's cross with the holy and submissive spirit which becomes a follower of the Crucified.

"I will send down showers in season; there will be showers of blessing." — Ezekiel 34:26

ERE is *sovereign mercy* — "I will send down showers in season." Is it not sovereign, *divine* mercy? — for who can say, "I will send down showers," except God? There is only one voice which can speak to the clouds, and cause them to bring the rain. Who sends down the rain upon the earth? Who scatters the showers upon the green herb? Don't I, the Lord? So grace is the gift of God, and is not to be created by man. It is also *needed* grace. What would the ground do without showers? You may break up the clods of dirt, you may sow your seeds, but what can you do without the rain? As absolutely needful is the divine blessing. You work in vain until God the generous shower gives and sends salvation down. Then, it is *generous grace*. "I will send down showers." It doesn't say, "I will send down drops," but "showers." So it is with grace. If God gives a blessing, He usually gives it in such a measure that there is not room enough to receive it. Generous grace! Ah! we want generous grace to keep us humble, to make us prayerful, to make us holy; generous grace to make us zealous, to preserve us through this life, and at last to land us in heaven. We cannot do without saturating showers of grace. Again, it is *seasonable grace*. "I will send down showers *in season.*" What is your season this morning? Is it the season of drought? Then that is the season for showers. Is it a season of great heaviness and dark clouds? Then that is the season for showers. "Your strength will equal your days." And here is a *varied* blessing. "There will be *showers* of blessing." The word is in the plural. God will send all kinds of blessings. All God's blessings go together, like links in a golden chain. If He gives converting grace, He will also give comforting grace. He will send "showers of blessing." Look up today, O parched plant, and open your leaves and flowers for a heavenly watering.

*"LORD Almighty, how long will you withhold mercy
from Jerusalem? . . . So the LORD spoke
kind and comforting words to the angel who
talked with me." — Zechariah 1:12, 13*

HAT a sweet answer to an anxious inquiry!
This night let's rejoice in it. O Zion, there
are good things in store for you; your time of
travail shall soon be over; your children
shall be brought forth; your captivity shall
end. Bear the rod patiently for a season, and
under the darkness still trust in God, for His love burns
towards you. God loves the church with a love too deep for
human imagination: He loves her with all His infinite
heart. Therefore let her members be of good courage; she
cannot be far from prosperity to whom God speaks "kind
and comforting words." What these comforting words are
the prophet goes on to tell us: "I am very jealous for
Jerusalem and Zion." The Lord loves His church so much
that He cannot bear that she should go astray to others;
and when she has done so, He cannot endure that she
should suffer too much or too heavily. He will not have his
enemies afflict her: He is displeased with them because
they increase her misery. When God seems most to leave
His church, His heart is warm towards her. History shows
that whenever God uses a rod to chasten His servants, He
always breaks it afterwards, as if He loathed the rod which
gave his children pain. "As a father has compassion on his
children, so the Lord has compassion on those who fear
Him." God has not forgotten us because He smites — His
blows are no evidences of want of love. If this is true of His
church *collectively,* it is of necessity true also of *each individual member.* You may fear that the Lord has passed you by,
but it is not so: He who counts the stars, and calls them by
their names, is in no danger of forgetting His own children. He knows your situation as thoroughly as if you were
the only creature He ever made, or the only saint He ever
loved. Approach Him and be at peace.

"The coming wrath." — *Matthew 3:7*

T is refreshing to walk in the country after a heavy rainstorm has passed over; to smell the freshness of the herbs after the rain has passed away, and to note the drops while they glisten like purest diamonds in the sunlight. That is the position of a Christian. We are going through a land where the storm has spent itself upon His Savior's head, and if there are a few drops of sorrow falling, they drop from clouds of mercy, and Jesus cheers us by the assurance that they are not for our destruction. But how terrible it is to witness the approach of a tempest: to note the forewarnings of the storm; to notice the birds of heaven as they droop their wings; to see the cattle as they lay their heads low in terror; to discern the face of the sky as it grows dark, and look at a sun which is not shining, and the heavens which are angry and frowning! How terrible to await the dread advance of a hurricane — such as occurs, sometimes, in the tropics — to wait in terrible apprehension until the wind shall rush forth in fury, tearing up trees from their roots, forcing rocks from their pedestals, and hurling down all the dwelling places of man! And yet, sinner, this is your present position. No hot drops have as yet fallen, but a shower of fire is coming. No terrible winds howl around you, but God's tempest is gathering its dread artillery. As yet the floodwaters are dammed up by mercy, but the floodgates shall soon be opened: the thunderbolts of God are still in His storehouse, but lo! the tempest hastens, and how awful shall that moment be when God, robed in vengeance, shall march forth in fury! Where, where, where, O sinner, will you hide your head, or to what place will you flee? O that the hand of mercy may now lead you to Christ! He is freely set before you in the gospel: His riven side is the rock of shelter. You know you need Him; believe in Him, throw yourself upon Him, and then the fury shall be passed over forever.

> *"But Jonah ran away from the LORD and headed*
> *for Tarshish. He went down to Joppa." — Jonah 1:3*

NSTEAD of going to Nineveh to preach the Word, as God commanded him, Jonah disliked the work, and went down to Joppa to escape from it. There are occasions when God's servants shrink from duty. But what is the consequence? What did Jonah lose by his conduct? *He lost the presence and comfortable enjoyment of God's love.* When we serve our Lord Jesus as believers should do, our God is with us; and though we have the whole world against us, if we have God with us, what does it matter? But the moment we start back, and seek our own inventions, we are at sea without a captain. Then we very well may bitterly lament and groan out, "O my God, where have You gone? How could I have been so foolish as to ignore Your service, and thus lose all the radiance of Your face? This is too high a price. Let me return to my allegiance, so that I may rejoice in Your presence." In the next place, Jonah *lost all peace of mind.* Sin soon destroys a believer's comfort. It is the poisonous upas tree, whose leaves yield deadly drops which destroy the life of joy and peace. Jonah *lost everything upon which he might have drawn for comfort in any other situation.* He couldn't plead the promise of divine protection, for he was not in God's ways; he couldn't say, "Lord, I meet with these difficulties in fulfilling my duty; therefore, help me through them." He was reaping his own deeds; he was filled with his own ways. Christian, don't play the Jonah, unless you wish to have all the waves and the billows rolling over your head. You will find in the long run that it is far harder to shun the work and will of God than to yield yourself at once to it. *Jonah lost his time,* for he had to go to Nineveh after all. It is hard to contend with God; let's yield ourselves at once.

"Salvation is of the Lord." — *Jonah 2:9*

 ALVATION is the work of God. It is He alone who rouses the soul "dead in transgressions and sins," and it is He also who maintains the soul in its spiritual life. He is both "Alpha and Omega." "Salvation is of the Lord." If I am prayerful, God makes me prayerful; if I have graces, they are God's gifts to me; if I hold on in a consistent life, it is because He upholds me with His hand. I do nothing whatever towards my own preservation, except what God Himself first does in me. Whatever I have, all my goodness is of the Lord alone. When I sin, that is my own doing; but when I act rightly, that is of God, wholly and completely. If I have repulsed a spiritual enemy, the Lord's strength nerved my arm. Do I live a consecrated life before others? It is not I, but Christ who lives in me. Am I sanctified? I didn't purify myself: God's Holy Spirit sanctifies me. Am I weaned from the world? I am weaned by *God's* chastisements sanctified to my good. Do I grow in knowledge? The great Instructor teaches me. All my jewels were fashioned by heavenly art. I find in God all that I want; but I find in myself nothing but sin and misery. "He alone is my rock and my salvation." Do I feed on the Word? That Word wouldn't be food for me unless the Lord made it food for my soul, and helped me to feed upon it. Do I live on the manna which comes down from heaven? What is that manna but Jesus Christ Himself incarnate, whose body and whose blood I eat and drink? Am I continually receiving fresh increase of strength? Where does my might come from? My help comes from heaven's hills: without Jesus I can do nothing. As a branch cannot bring forth fruit except it abide in the vine, no more can I, except I abide in Him. What Jonah learned in the great deep, let me learn this morning in my closet: "Salvation is of the Lord."

"If the disease has covered his whole body, he shall pronounce that person clean." — Leviticus 13:13

 TRANGE as this regulation seems, yet there was a reason for it, for the advancement of the disease proved that the constitution was sound. This evening it may be well for us to see the typical teaching of so singular a rule. We, too, are lepers, and may read the law of the leper as applicable to ourselves. When we see ourselves as completely lost and ruined, covered all over with the defilement of sin, and in no part free from pollution; when we disclaim all righteousness of our own, and plead guilty before the Lord, then we are clean through the blood of Jesus, and the grace of God. Hidden, unfelt, unconfessed iniquity is the true leprosy; but when sin is seen and felt, it has received its deathblow, and the Lord looks with eyes of mercy upon the soul afflicted with it. Nothing is more deadly than self-righteousness, or more hopeful than contrition. We must confess that we are "nothing else but sin," for no confession short of this will be the whole truth; and if the Holy Spirit is at work with us, convincing us of sin, we will have no difficulty in making such an acknowledgment — it will spring spontaneously from our lips. What comfort the text affords to truly awakened sinners: the very circumstance which so grievously discouraged them is here turned into a sign and symptom of a hopeful state! Stripping comes before clothing; digging out a foundation is the first step in building — and a thorough sense of sin is one of the earliest works of grace in the heart. O you poor leprous sinner, utterly destitute of a sound spot, take heart from the text, and come as you are to Jesus —

"For let our debts be what they may, however great or small,
As soon as we have nought to pay, our Lord forgives us all.
'Tis perfect poverty alone that sets the soul at large:
While we can call one mite our own, we have no full discharge."

"You make the Most High your dwelling — even the LORD, who is my refuge." — Psalm 91:9

HE Israelites *were continually exposed to change* in the wilderness. Whenever the pillar stood still, the tents were pitched; but the next day, before the morning sun had risen, the trumpet sounded, the ark was in motion, and the fiery, cloudy pillar was leading the way through the narrow gorges of the mountain, up the hillside, or along the arid waste of the wilderness. They had scarcely time to rest a little before they heard the sound of "Away! this is not your rest; you must still journey onward towards Canaan!" They never stayed very long in one place. Even wells and palm trees could not detain them. Yet they had an abiding home in their God, His cloudy pillar was their tree roof, and its flame by night their household fire. They must go onward from place to place, continually changing, never having time to settle, and to say, "Now we are secure; in this place we shall dwell." "Yet," says Moses, "though we are always changing, Lord, You have been our dwelling place throughout all generations." Christians knows no change with regard to God. We may be rich today and poor tomorrow; we may be sickly today and well tomorrow; we may be happy today, tomorrow we may be distressed — but there is no change with regard to our relationship to God. If He loved me yesterday, He loves me today. My unmoving mansion of rest is my blessed Lord. Let prospects be blighted; let hopes be blasted; let joy be withered; let mildews destroy everything; I have lost nothing of what I have in God. "Be my rock of refuge, to which I can always go." I am a pilgrim in the world, but at home in my God. In the earth I wander, but in God I dwell in a quiet habitation.

"Whose origins are from of old, from ancient times."
— *Micah 5:2*

HE Lord Jesus had originated for His people *as their representative before the throne, long before they appeared upon the stage of time.* It was "from everlasting" that He signed the compact with His Father, that He would pay blood for blood, suffering for suffering, agony for agony, and death for death, on the behalf of His people; it was "from everlasting" that He gave Himself up without a murmuring word. That from the crown of His head to the sole of His foot He might sweat great drops of blood, that He might be spit upon, pierced, mocked, rent asunder, and crushed beneath the pains of death. His origins as our Surety were from everlasting. Pause, my soul, and wonder! You have origins in the person of Jesus "from everlasting." Not only did Christ love us when we were born into the world, but His delights were with us before any human beings existed. He thought of them often; from everlasting to everlasting He had set His affection upon them. What! my soul, if He has been so long about your salvation, will He not finish it? Has He from everlasting gone about saving me, and will He lose me now? What! has He carried me in His hand, as His precious jewel, and will He now let me slip from between His fingers? Did He choose me before the mountains were brought forth, or the channels of the deep were dug, and will He reject me now? Impossible! I am sure He wouldn't have loved me for this long if He hadn't been a changeless Lover. If He was going to grow weary of me, He would have been tired of me long before now. If He hadn't loved me with a love as deep as hell, and as strong as death, He would have turned away from me long ago. Oh, joy above all joys, to know that I am His everlasting and inalienable inheritance, given to Him by His Father even before the earth existed! Everlasting love shall be the pillow for my head this night.

"My hope comes from Him." — *Psalm 62:5*

 T is the believer's privilege to use this language. If one is looking for anything whatsoever from the world, it is a poor "hope" indeed. But if we look to God for the supply of our wants, whether in temporal or spiritual blessings, our "hope" will not be in vain. We may constantly draw from the bank of faith, and get our needs supplied out of the riches of God's loving-kindness. This I know, I would rather have God for my banker than all the Rothschilds. My Lord never fails to honor His promises; and when we bring them to His throne, He never sends them back unanswered. Therefore I will wait at His door only, for He always opens it with the hand of munificent grace. At this hour I will try Him anew. But we have "hopes" beyond this life. We shall die soon; and then our "hope comes from Him." Don't we hope that, when we lie upon our sickbed, He will send angels to carry us to His bosom? We believe that when the pulse is faint, and the heart heaves heavily, some angelic messenger shall stand and look with loving eyes upon us, and whisper, "Kindred spirit, come away!" As we approach the heavenly gate, we expect to hear the welcome invitation, "Come, you who are blessed by my Father, take your inheritance, the kingdom prepared for you since the creation of the world." We are expecting harps of gold and crowns of glory; we are hoping soon to be among the multitude of shining ones before the throne; we are looking forward and longing for the time when we shall be like our glorious Lord — for "We shall see Him as He is." Then, if these be your "hopes," O my soul, live for God; live with the desire and resolve to glorify Him from whom comes all your supplies, and of whose grace in your election, redemption, and calling it is that you have any "hope" of coming glory.

"For the jar of flour was not used up and the jug of oil did not run dry, in keeping with the word of the LORD spoken by Elijah." — *1 Kings 17:16*

 EE the faithfulness of divine love. You observe that this woman had *daily necessities.* She had herself and her son to feed in a time of famine; and now, in addition, the prophet Elijah was to be fed, too. But though the need was threefold, yet the supply of flour was not wasted, for she had *a constant supply.* Each day she drew from the jar, yet each day it remained the same. You, dear reader, have daily necessities, and because they come so frequently, you are apt to fear that the jar of flour will one day be empty, and the jug of oil will fail you. Rest assured that, according to the Word of God, this shall not be the case. Each day, though it bring its trouble, shall bring its help; and though you should live to outnumber the years of Methuselah, and though your needs should be as many as the sands of the seashore, yet shall God's grace and mercy last through all your necessities, and you shall never know a real lack. For three long years, in this widow's days, the heavens never saw a cloud, and the stars never wept a holy tear of dew upon the wicked earth: famine, and desolation, and death made the land a howling wilderness, but this woman never was hungry, but always joyful in abundance. So shall it be with you. You shall see the sinner's hope perish, for he trusts his native strength; you shall see the proud Pharisee's confidence totter, for he builds his hope upon the sand; you shall see even your own schemes blasted and withered, but you yourself shall find that your place of defense shall be the munition of rocks: "Your bread shall be given you, and your water shall be sure." It is better to have God as your guardian than the Bank of England for your possession. You might spend the wealth of the Indies, but the infinite riches of God you can never exhaust.

"I have drawn you with loving-kindness." — Jeremiah 31:3

HE thunders of the law and the terrors of judgment are all used to bring us to Christ; but the final victory is effected by loving-kindness. The prodigal set out to his father's house from a sense of need. However, his father saw him a great way off and ran to meet him, so that the last steps he took towards his father's house were with the kiss still warm upon his cheek and the welcome still musical in his ears.

> "Law and terrors do but harden
> All the while they work alone;
> But a sense of blood-bought pardon
> Will dissolve a heart of stone."

The Master came one night to the door, and knocked with the iron hand of the law; the door shook and trembled upon its hinges; but the man piled every piece of furniture which he could find against the door, for he said, "I will not admit the man." The Master turned away, but before long He came back, and with His own soft hand, using most that part where the nail had penetrated, He knocked again — oh, so softly and tenderly. This time the door didn't shake, but, strange to say, it opened, and there upon his knees the once unwilling host was found rejoicing to receive his guest. "Come in, come in; You have so knocked that my heart laments for You. I could not think of Your pierced hand leaving its blood mark on my door, and of Your going away homeless, 'Your head drenched with dew, and Your hair with the dampness of the night.' I yield, I yield, Your love has won my heart." This is true for every situation: loving-kindness wins the day. What Moses with the tablets of stone could never do, Christ does with His pierced hand. Such is the doctrine of effectual calling. Do I understand it experimentally? Can I say, "He drew me, and I followed on, glad to confess the voice divine?" If so, may He continue to draw me, until at last I shall sit down at the marriage supper of the Lamb.

"We have . . . the Spirit who is from God,
that we may understand what God has
freely given us." — 1 Corinthians 2:12

EAR reader, have you received the Spirit who is from God, wrought by the Holy Spirit in your soul? The necessity of the work of the Holy Spirit in the heart may be clearly seen from this fact, that *all which has been done by God the Father, and by God the Son, must be ineffectual to us, unless the Spirit shall reveal these things to our souls.* What effect does the doctrine of election have upon any person until the Spirit of God enters into that person? Election is a dead letter in my consciousness until the Spirit of God calls me out of darkness into marvelous light. *Then* through my calling, I see my election, and knowing myself to be called of God, I know myself to have been chosen in the eternal purpose. A covenant was made with the Lord Jesus Christ, by His Father; but of what use is that covenant to us until the Holy Spirit brings us His blessings and opens our hearts to receive them? There hang the blessings on the nail — Christ Jesus; but being short of stature, we cannot reach them; the Spirit of God takes them down and hands them to us, and thus they actually become ours. Covenant blessings in themselves are like the manna in the skies, far out of mortal reach, but the Spirit of God opens the windows of heaven and scatters the living bread around the camp of the spiritual Israel. Christ's finished work is like wine stored in the winepress; through unbelief we can neither draw nor drink. The Holy Spirit dips our vessel into this precious wine, and then we drink; but without the Spirit we are as truly dead in sin as though the Father never had elected, and as though the Son had never bought us with His blood. The Holy Spirit is absolutely necessary to our well-being. Let's walk lovingly towards Him and tremble at the thought of grieving Him.

"Awake, north wind, and come, south wind!
Blow on my garden, that its fragrance may
spread abroad." — Song of Songs 4:16

NYTHING is better than the dead calm of indifference. Our souls may wisely desire the north wind of trouble if that alone can be sanctified to the drawing out of the perfume of our graces. As long as it cannot be said, "The Lord was not in the wind," we will not shrink from the most wintry blast that ever blew upon plants of grace. Didn't the spouse in this verse humbly submit herself to the reproofs of her Beloved, only appealing to Him to discharge His grace in some form, and making no specific request as to the manner in which it should come? Didn't she, like ourselves, become so utterly weary of deadness and unholy calm that she longed for any trial which would prepare her for action? Yet she desires the warm south wind of comfort, too, the smiles of divine love, the joy of the Redeemer's presence; these are often vigorously effective in arousing our sluggish life. She desires either one, or the other, or both, so that she may but be able to delight her Beloved with the spices of her garden. She cannot endure to be unprofitable, nor can we. How encouraging is the thought that Jesus can find comfort in our poor feeble graces. Can it be? It seems far too good to be true. We may well court trial, or even death itself, if they bring joy to Immanuel's heart. O that our heart were crushed to atoms if only by such bruising our sweet Lord Jesus could be glorified. Unexercised graces are as sweet perfumes slumbering in the cups of the flowers: the wisdom of the great Farmer overrules diverse and opposite causes to produce the one desired result, and makes both affliction and consolation draw out the grateful fragrances of faith, love, patience, hope, resignation, joy, and the other fair flowers of the garden. May we know, by sweet experience, what this means.

"This stone is precious." — *1 Peter 2:7*

 S all the rivers run into the sea, so all pleasures center in our Beloved. The glances from His eyes outshine the sun: the beauties of His face are fairer than the choicest flowers: no fragrance is like the breath of His mouth. Gems from the mine and pearls from the sea are worthless when measured against His value. Peter tells us that Jesus is precious, but he didn't and couldn't tell us *how* precious; nor could any of us compute the value of God's unspeakable gift. Words can't describe the preciousness of the Lord Jesus to His people, nor fully tell how essential He is to their satisfaction and happiness. Believer, haven't you found a painful famine in the midst of plenty if your Lord has been absent? The sun was shining, but Christ had hidden Himself, and all the world was dark to you; or it was night, and since the bright and morning star was gone, no other star could yield you so much as a ray of light. What a howling wilderness this world is without our Lord! If once He hides Himself from us, the flowers of our garden wither; our pleasant fruits decay; the birds stop singing, and a tempest overturns our hopes. All earth's candles cannot make daylight if the Sun of Righteousness is eclipsed. He is the soul of our soul, the light of our light, the life of our life. Dear reader, what in the world will you do without Him when you wake up and look forward to the day's battle? What will you do at night, when you come home jaded and weary without this door of fellowship between you and Christ? Blessed be His name. He will not allow us to attempt our destiny without Him, for Jesus never forsakes His own. Therefore, let the thought of *what life would be without Him* enhance His preciousness.

> *"So all Israel went down to the Philistines*
> *to have their plowshares, mattocks, axes and sickles*
> *sharpened."* — 1 Samuel 13:20

E are engaged in a great war with the Philistines of evil. *Every weapon within our reach must be used.* Preaching, teaching, praying, giving, all must be brought into action, and talents which have been thought too mediocre for service must now be employed. Plowshare, ax, and mattock may all be useful in slaying Philistines; rough tools may deal hard blows, and killing needn't be elegantly done, as long as it is done effectually. Each moment of time, in season or out of season; each fragment of ability, educated or untutored; each opportunity, favorable or unfavorable, must be used because we have many foes and our power to overcome evil is slim.

Most of our tools require sharpening; we need quickness of perception, tact, energy, promptness, in a word, complete adaptation for the Lord's work. Practical common sense is a very scarce thing among the conductors of Christian enterprises. We might learn from our enemies if we would, and so *make the Philistines sharpen our weapons.* This morning let's notice enough to sharpen our zeal during this day by the aid of the Holy Spirit. Look at the energy of the Papists and how they encompass sea and land to make one proselyte. Do they have a monopoly on all the earnestness? Notice the heathen devotees and what tortures they endure in the service of their idols! Are they the only ones to exhibit patience and self-sacrifice? Observe the prince of darkness, how persevering he is in his efforts, how unabashed in his attempts, how daring in his plans, how thoughtful in his plots, how energetic in all! The devils are united together as one person in their infamous rebellion, while we believers in Jesus are divided in our service of God, and scarcely ever work with unanimity. O that from Satan's infernal industry we may learn to go about like good Samaritans, seeking whom we may bless!

*"Although I am less than the least of all God's
people, this grace was given me: to preach to
the Gentiles the unsearchable riches of Christ."*
— *Ephesians 3:8*

HE apostle Paul felt it a great privilege to be allowed to preach the gospel. He didn't look upon his calling as drudgery. On the contrary, he began it with intense delight. However, even though Paul was thus thankful for his assignment, his success in it greatly humbled him. The fuller a vessel becomes, the deeper it sinks in the water. Lazy people may have inflated views of their abilities because they are untried; but the earnest worker soon learns his own weakness. If you seek humility, *try hard work;* if you would know your nothingness, attempt some great thing for Jesus. If you would feel how utterly powerless you are apart from the living God, attempt especially the great work of proclaiming the unsearchable riches of Christ, and you will know, as you never knew before, what a weak unworthy thing you are. Although the apostle both knew and confessed his weakness, he was never perplexed as to the *subject* of his ministry. From his first sermon to his last, Paul preached Christ, and nothing but Christ. He lifted up the cross and praised the Son of God who bled thereon. Follow his example in all your personal efforts to spread the good news of salvation, and let "Christ and Him crucified" be your ever recurring theme. The Christian should be like those lovely spring flowers which, when the sun is shining, open their golden cups, as if to say, "Fill us with your beams!" but when the sun is hidden behind a cloud, close their cups and droop their heads. So should the Christian feel the sweet influence of Jesus; Jesus must be your sun, and you must be the flower which yields itself to the Sun of Righteousness. Oh! to speak of Christ alone, this is the subject which is both "seed for the sower and bread for the eater." This is the live coal for the lip of the speaker, and the master key to the heart of the hearer.

"I have tested you in the furnace of affliction."
— *Isaiah 48:10*

OMFORT yourself, tested believer, with this thought: God says, "I have tested you in the furnace of affliction." Doesn't the word come like a soft shower, assuaging the fury of the flame? Yes, is it not an insulating armor against which the heat has no power? Let affliction come — God has tested me. Poverty, you may stride in at my door, but God is in the house already, and He has tested me. Sickness, you may intrude, but I have a balsam ready — God has tested me. Whatever happens to me in this vale of tears, I know that He has "tested" me. If, believer, you require still greater comfort, remember *that you have Jesus with you in the furnace.* In that silent chamber of yours, One sits by your side whom you have not seen, but whom you love; and even when you aren't aware of it, in your affliction He prepares a bed and smoothes a pillow for you. You are in poverty; but in that lovely house of yours the Lord of life and glory is a frequent visitor. He loves to come into these desolate places, that He may visit you. Your friend sticks closely to you. You can't see Him, but you may feel the pressure of His hands. Can you hear His voice? Even in the valley of the shadow of death He says, "Don't be afraid, I am with you; don't be dismayed, for I am your God." Remember that noble speech of Caesar: "Don't be afraid. You carry Caesar and all his fortune." Christian, don't be afraid; Jesus is with you. In all your fiery trials, His presence is both your comfort and safety. He will never leave one whom He has tested for His own. "Don't be afraid, for I am with you," is His sure word of promise to His chosen ones in the "furnace of affliction." Won't you, then, secure a firm hold on Christ, and say —

> "Through floods and flames, if Jesus lead,
> I'll follow where He goes."

"He saw the Spirit of God descending like a dove."
— *Matthew 3:16*

 s the Spirit of God descended upon the Lord Jesus, the head, so He also, in measure, descends upon the members of the mystical body. His descent is to us after the same fashion as that in which it fell upon our Lord. There is often a singular *rapidity* about it. Even before we are aware of it, we are driven onward and heavenward beyond all expectation. Yet there is none of the hurry of earthly haste, for the wings of the dove are as soft as they are swift. *Quietness* seems essential to many spiritual operations; the Lord is in the still small voice and, like the dew, His grace is distilled in silence. The dove has always been the chosen symbol of *purity,* and the Holy Spirit is holiness itself. Where He comes, everything that is pure and lovely, and of good report, is made to abound, and sin and uncleanness depart. *Peace* also reigns where the Holy Dove comes with power; He bears the olive branch which shows that the waters of divine wrath are assuaged. *Gentleness* is a sure result of the Sacred Dove's transforming power: hearts touched by His benign influence are meek and lowly henceforth and forever. *Harmlessness* follows, as a matter of course; eagles and ravens may hunt their prey — the turtledove can endure harm, but cannot inflict it. We must be harmless as doves. The dove is an apt picture of *love,* the cooing of doves is full of affection; and so the soul, visited by the blessed Spirit, abounds in love to God, in love to believers, in love to sinners and, above all, in love to Jesus. The brooding of the Spirit of God upon the surface of the deep first produced *order and life,* and in our hearts He causes and fosters new life and light. Blessed Spirit, as You descended upon our dear Redeemer, even so descend upon us from this time forward and forever.

"My grace is sufficient for you." — 2 Corinthians 12:9

F none of God's saints were poor and tested, we should not know half so well the consolations of divine grace. When we find the wanderer who has nowhere to lay his head, who yet can say, "Still will I trust in the Lord;" when we see the pauper starving on bread and water who still glories in Jesus; when we see the bereaved widow overwhelmed in affliction yet having faith in Christ, oh! what honor it reflects on the gospel. God's grace is illustrated and magnified in the poverty and trials of believers. Saints bear up under every discouragement, believing that all things work together for their good, and that out of apparent evils a real blessing shall ultimately spring — that their God will either work a deliverance for them speedily, or most assuredly support them in the trouble, as long as He is pleased to keep them in it. This patience of the saints proves the power of divine grace. There is a lighthouse out at sea: it is a calm night — I can't tell whether the structure is firm; the tempest must rage about it, and then I shall know whether it will stand. So with the Spirit's work: if it were not on many occasions surrounded with tempestuous waters, we should not know that it was true and strong; if the winds did not blow upon it, we should not know how firm and secure it was. The masterworks of God are those people who stand in the midst of difficulties, steadfast, unmoveable, —

"Calm mid the bewildering cry,
Confident of victory."

Those who would glorify their God must expect to encounter many trials. No one can be esteemed before the Lord without many conflicts. If, then, your path is marked with many trials, rejoice in it because your life will provide greater evidence of the all-sufficient grace of God. As for His failing you, don't even dream of it — hate the very thought of it. The God who has been sufficient until now, should be trusted to the end.

"They feast on the abundance of your house."
— *Psalm 36:8*

 HEBA'S queen was amazed at the sumptuousness of Solomon's table. She lost all heart when she saw the provision of a single day; and she marvelled equally at the company of servants who were feasted at the royal board. But what is this to the hospitalities of the God of grace? Ten thousand thousand of his people are fed daily; hungry and thirsty, they bring large appetites with them to the banquet, but not one of them returns unsatisfied; there is enough for each, enough for all, enough forevermore. Though the number of people who feed at Jehovah's table is as countless as the stars of heaven, yet each person has a portion of meat. Think how much grace one saint requires, so much that nothing but the Infinite could supply this grace even for one day; and yet the Lord spreads His table, not for one, but many saints, not for one day, but for many years; not for many years only, but for generation after generation. Observe the full feasting spoken of in the text, the guests at mercy's banquet are satisfied, no, more, "abundantly satisfied;" and that not with ordinary fare, but with abundance, the peculiar abundance of God's own house; and such feasting is guaranteed by a faithful promise to all who put their trust under the shadow of Jehovah's wings. I once thought if I could just get the leftovers of the meat at God's backdoor of grace I should be satisfied; like the woman who said, "The dogs eat the crumbs that fall from their master's table;" but no child of God is ever served with scraps and leavings; like Mephibosheth, they all eat from the king's own table. In matters of grace, we all have Benjamin's mess — we all have ten times more than we could have expected, and though our necessities are great, yet are we often amazed at the marvelous plenty of grace which God gives us experimentally to enjoy.

"Let us not be like others, who are asleep."
— 1 Thessalonians 5:6

HERE are many ways of promoting Christian wakefulness. Among others, let me strongly advise Christians to converse together concerning the ways of the Lord. Christian and Hopeful, as they journeyed towards the Celestial City, said to themselves, "To prevent drowsiness in this place, let's fall into good discourse." Christian inquired, "Brother, where shall we begin?" And Hopeful answered, "Where God began with us." Then Christian sang this song —

> "When saints do sleepy grow, let them come hither,
> And hear how these two pilgrims talk together;
> Yea, let them learn of them, in any wise,
> Thus to keep open their drowsy slumb'ring eyes.
> Saints' fellowship, if it be managed well,
> Keeps them awake, and that in spite of hell."

Christians who isolate themselves and walk alone are very liable to grow drowsy. In keeping company with other Christians you will be kept alert, refreshed and encouraged to make quicker progress along the road to heaven. But as you enjoy "sweet fellowship" with others in the ways of God, take care that the theme of your conversation is the Lord Jesus. Let the eye of faith be constantly looking to Him; let your heart be full of Him; let your lips speak of His worth. Friend, live near to the cross, and you will not sleep. *Work to impress yourself with a deep sense of the value of the place to which you are going.* If you remember that you are going to heaven, you will not sleep on the road. If you think that hell is behind you, and the devil pursuing you, you will not loiter. Would the person accused of murder sleep with the avenger of blood behind him, and the city of refuge before him? Christian, will you sleep while the pearly gates are open — the songs of angels waiting for you to join them — a crown of gold ready for your brow? Ah, no! In holy fellowship continue to watch and pray so that you don't enter into temptation.

"Say to my soul, I am your salvation." — *Psalm 35:3*

HAT does this sweet prayer teach me? It shall be my evening's petition; but first it provides me with an instructive meditation. The text informs me, first of all, that *David had his doubts;* for why should he pray, "Say to my soul, 'I am your salvation,' " if he were not sometimes exercised with doubts and fears? Let me be of good cheer, then, for I am not the only saint who has to complain of weakness of faith. If David doubted, I needn't conclude that *I* am not a Christian because I have doubts. The text reminds me that *David was not content while he had doubts and fears,* but he took himself at once to the mercy seat to pray for assurance; for he valued it as much fine gold. I, too, must pursue an abiding sense of my acceptance in the Beloved, and must have no joy when His love is not shed abroad in my soul. When my Bridegroom is gone from me, my soul must and will fast. I learn also that *David knew where to obtain full assurance.* He went to his God in prayer, crying, "Say to my soul, 'I am your salvation.' " I must be frequently alone with God if I expect to have a clear sense of Jesus' love. When I let my prayers cease, my eye of faith grows dim. To be frequently in prayer is to be frequently in heaven; to be slow in prayer is to be slow in progress. I notice that *David would not be satisfied unless his assurance had a divine source.* "*Say* to my soul." Lord, *You* say it! Nothing short of a divine testimony in the soul will ever content the true Christian. Moreover, David couldn't rest unless his assurance had *a vivid personality* about it. "Say to *my* soul, 'I am *your* salvation.' " Lord, if You should say this to all the saints, it means nothing, unless You should say it to me. Lord, I have sinned; I don't deserve your smile; I scarcely dare to ask it; but oh! say to *my* soul, even to *my* soul, "I am *your* salvation." Let me have a present, personal, infallible, indisputable sense that I am Yours, and that You are mine.

"You must be born again." — *John 3:7*

REGENERATION is a subject which lies at the very basis of salvation, and we should make a special effort to determine whether or not we really are "born again," for there are many who fancy they are, who are not. Be assured that the name of a Christian is not the nature of a Christian; and that being born in a Christian land, and being recognized as professing the Christian religion is of no use whatever, unless there is something more added to it — the being "born again," is a matter so *mysterious,* that human words can't describe it. "The wind blows wherever it pleases. You hear its sound, but you cannot tell where it comes from or where it is going. So it is with everyone born of the Spirit." Nevertheless, it is a change which is *known and felt:* known by works of holiness, and felt by a gracious experience. This great work is *supernatural.* It is not an operation which one performs for oneself: a new principle is infused, which works in the heart, renews the soul, and affects the entire person. It is not a change of my name, but a renewal of my nature, so that I'm not the person I used to be, but a new person in Christ Jesus. To wash and dress a corpse is a far different thing from making it alive: man can do the one, God alone can do the other. If, then, you have been "born again," your acknowledgment will be, "O Lord Jesus, the everlasting Father, You are my spiritual Parent; unless Your Spirit had breathed into me the breath of a new, holy, and spiritual life, I had been to this day 'dead in transgressions and sins.' My heavenly life is wholly derived from You, to You I ascribe it. 'My life is now hidden with Christ in God.' It is no longer I who live, but Christ who lives in me." May the Lord enable us to be well assured on this vital point, for to be unregenerate is to be unsaved, unpardoned, without God, and without hope.

"Before his downfall a man's heart is proud."
— Proverbs 18:12

T is an old and common saying, that "coming events cast their shadows before them;" the wise man teaches us that a proud heart is the prophetic prelude of evil. Pride is as surely the sign of destruction as the change of mercury in the barometer is the sign of rain; and far more infallible, too. Whenever people have ridden a high horse, destruction *has* always overtaken them. Let David's aching heart show that there is an eclipse of a man's glory when he dotes upon his own greatness. 2 Sam. 24:10. Immediately what had been said about Nebuchadnezzar was fulfilled. He was driven away from people and ate grass like cattle. His body was drenched with the dew of heaven until his hair grew like the feathers of an eagle and his nails like the claws of a bird. Dan. 4:33. Pride made the boaster a beast, as once before it made an angel a devil. God hates high looks, and never fails to bring them down. All the arrows of God are aimed at proud hearts. O Christian, is your heart prideful this evening? For pride can get into the Christian heart as well as into the sinner's; it can delude us into dreaming that we are "rich and have acquired wealth, and do not need a thing." Are you glorying in your graces or your talents? Are you proud of yourself, that you have had holy postures and sweet experiences? Take note, reader, there is a destruction coming to you also. Your flaunting poppies of self-conceit will be pulled up by the roots, your mushroom graces will wither in the burning heat, and your self-sufficiency shall become as straw for the manure pile. If we forget to live at the foot of the cross in deepest lowliness of spirit, God won't forget to make us feel the pain of His rod. A destruction will come to you, O unduly exalted believer, the destruction of your joys and of your comforts, though there can be no destruction of your soul. Wherefore, "Let him who boasts boast *in the Lord.*"

"Have faith in God." — *Mark 11:12*

FAITH is the foot of the soul by which it can march along the road of the commandments. Love can make the feet move more swiftly; but faith is the foot which carries the soul. Faith is the oil enabling the wheels of holy devotion and of earnest piety to move well; and without faith the wheels are taken from the chariot, and we drag heavily. With faith I can do all things; without faith I shall neither have the inclination nor the power to do anything in the service of God. If you want to find those who serve God the best, you must look for people who have the most faith. Little faith will save a person, but little faith can't do great things for God. Poor Little-faith could not have fought "Apollyon;" it needed "Christian" to do that. Poor Little-faith could not have slain "Giant Despair;" it required "Great-heart's" arm to knock that monster down. Little faith will go to heaven most certainly, but it often has to hide itself in a nutshell, and it frequently loses all but its jewels. Little-faith says, "It is a rough road, beset with sharp thorns, and full of dangers; I am afraid to go;" but Great-faith remembers the promise, "your shoes shall be iron and brass; as your days, so shall your strength be:" and so she boldly ventures. Little-faith stands hopeless, mingling her tears with the flood; but Great-faith sings, "When you pass through the waters, I will be with you; and when you pass through the rivers, they will not sweep over you:" and she fords the stream at once. Would you be comfortable and happy? Would you enjoy religion? Would you have the religion of cheerfulness and not that of gloom? Then "have faith in God." If you love darkness, and are satisfied to dwell in gloom and misery, then be content with little faith; but if you love the sunshine, and would sing songs of rejoicing, covet earnestly this best gift, "great faith."

"It is better to take refuge in the LORD than to trust in man." — Psalm 118:8

OUBTLESS the reader has been tested with the temptation to rely upon the things which are seen, instead of resting alone upon the invisible God. Christians often look to people for help and counsel, and mar the noble simplicity of their reliance upon their God. Does this evening's portion meet the eye of a child of God anxious about material needs? Then let's reason together awhile. You trust in Jesus, and only in Jesus, for your salvation, so why are you troubled? *"Because of my great care."* Isn't it written, "Cast your cares on the Lord"? "Do not be anxious about anything, but in everything, by prayer and petition, with thanksgiving, present your requests to God." Can't you trust God for material needs? *"Ah! I wish I could."* If you can't trust God for material needs, how do you dare trust Him for spiritual needs? Can you trust Him for your soul's redemption, and not rely upon Him for a few lesser mercies? Isn't God enough for your all your needs, or is His all-sufficiency too narrow for your wants? Do you want another eye beside that of Him who sees every secret thing? Is His heart faint? Is His arm weary? If so, seek another God; but if He be infinite, omnipotent, faithful, true, and all-wise, why do you gad about so much seeking another's confidence? Why do you rake the earth to find another foundation, when this is strong enough to bear all the weight which you can ever build on it? Christian, not only mustn't you mix your wine with water, but also don't alloy your gold of faith with the dross of human confidence. Wait only upon God, and let your expectation be from Him. Don't covet Jonah's vine, but rest in Jonah's God. Let the sandy foundations of terrestrial trust be the choice of fools, while you, like one who foresees the storm, build for yourself an abiding place upon the Rock of Ages.

*"We must go through many hardships to enter
the kingdom of God." — Acts 14:22*

 OD'S people have their trials. It was never
designed by God, when He chose His people,
that they should be an untested people. They
were chosen in the furnace of affliction; they
were never chosen to worldly peace and
earthly joy. Freedom from sickness and the
pains of mortality was never promised them; but when
their Lord drew up the charter of privileges, He included
chastisements amongst the things to which they should
inevitably be heirs. Trials are a part of our lot; they were
predestined for us in Christ's last legacy. So surely as the
stars are fashioned by His hands, and their orbits fixed by
Him, so surely are our trials allotted to us: He has ordained their season and their place, their intensity and the
effect they shall have upon us. Good people must never
expect to escape troubles; if they do, they will be disappointed, for none of their predecessors have been without
them. Note the patience of Job; remember Abraham, for
he had his trials, and by his faith under them, he became
the "Father of the faithful." Note well the biographies of
all the patriarchs, prophets, apostles, and martyrs, and you
shall discover none of those whom God made vessels of
mercy who were not made to pass through the fire of
affliction. It is ordained of old that the cross of trouble
should be engraved on every vessel of mercy, as the royal
mark whereby the King's vessels of honor are distinguished. But although hardship is thus the path of God's
children, they have the comfort of knowing that their
Master has traversed it before them; they have His presence and sympathy to cheer them, His grace to support
them, and His example to teach them how to endure; and
when they reach "the kingdom," it will more than make
amends for the "many hardships" through which they
passed to enter it.

"She named her son Ben-Oni (son of sorrow).
But his father named him Benjamin (son of
my right hand)." — Genesis 35:18

O every matter there is a bright as well as a dark side. Rachel was overwhelmed with the sorrow of her own travail and death; Jacob, though weeping the mother's loss, could see the mercy of the child's birth. It is well for us if, while the flesh mourns over trials, our faith triumphs in divine faithfulness. Samson's lion yielded honey, and so will our adversities, if rightly considered. The stormy sea feeds multitudes with its fishes; the wild wood blooms with beauteous flowerets; the stormy wind sweeps away the pestilence, and the biting frost loosens the soil. Dark clouds distill bright drops, and black earth grows gay flowers. A vein of good is to be found in every mine of evil. Sad hearts have peculiar skill in discovering the most disadvantageous point of view from which to gaze upon a trial; if there were only one swamp in the world, they would soon be up to their necks in it, and if there were only one lion in the desert they would hear it roar. About us all there is a tinge of this wretched folly, and we are apt, at times, like Jacob, to cry, "Everything is against me!" Faith's way of walking is to cast all care upon the Lord, and then to anticipate good results from the worst calamities. Like Gideon's men, she does not fret over the broken pitcher, but rejoices that the lamp blazes forth the more. Out of the rough oyster shell of difficulty she extracts the rare pearl of honor, and from the deep ocean caves of distress she uplifts the priceless coral of experience. When her flood of prosperity ebbs, she finds treasures hid in the sands; and when her sun of delight goes down, she turns her telescope of hope to the starry promises of heaven. When death itself appears, faith points to the light of resurrection beyond the grave, thus making our dying Ben-Oni to be our living Benjamin.

"He is altogether lovely." — *Song of Songs 5:16*

 HE superlative beauty of Jesus is all-attracting; it is not so much to be admired as to be loved. He is more than pleasant and fair, He is lovely. Surely the people of God can fully justify the use of this golden word, for He is the object of their warmest love, a love founded on the intrinsic excellence of His person, the complete perfection of His charms. Look, O disciples of Jesus, to your Master's lips, and say, "Aren't they most sweet?" Don't His words cause your hearts to burn within you as He talks with you by the way? You worshippers of Immanuel, look up to His head of much fine gold, and tell me, are not His thoughts precious to you? Is not your adoration sweetened with affection as you humbly bow before that countenance which is as Lebanon, excellent as the cedars? Is there not a charm in His every feature, and is not His whole person fragrant with such a savor of His good ointments, that therefore the virgins love Him? Is there one member of His glorious body which is not attractive? — one portion of His person which is not a fresh lodestone to our souls? — one office which is not a strong cord to bind your heart? Our love is not as a seal set upon His heart of love alone; it is fastened upon His arm of power also; nor is there a single part of Him upon which it does not fix itself. We anoint His whole person with the sweet spikenard of our fervent love. His whole life we would imitate; His whole character we would transcribe. In all other beings we see some lack, in Him there is all perfection. The best even of His favored saints have had blots upon their garments and wrinkles upon their brows; He is nothing but loveliness. All earthly suns have their spots: the fair world itself has its wilderness; we can't love the whole of the most lovely thing; but Christ Jesus is gold without impurities — light without darkness — glory without cloud — "Yes, He is *altogether* lovely."

"Remain in me." — John 15:4

OMMUNION with Christ is a certain cure for every ill. Whether it be the wormwood of woe, or the cloying excess of earthly delight, close fellowship with the Lord Jesus will take bitterness from the one, and satiety from the other. Live near to Jesus, Christian, and it is a matter of secondary importance whether you live on the mountain of honor or in the valley of humiliation. Living near to Jesus, you are covered with the wings of God, and underneath you are the everlasting arms. Let nothing keep you from that hallowed communication, which is the choice privilege of a soul wedded to THE WELL-BELOVED.Don't be content with an interview now and then, but always seek to retain His company, for only in His presence have you either comfort or safety. Jesus should not be to us a friend who calls upon us now and then, but one with whom we walk forever. You have a difficult road before you: see, O traveler to heaven, that you don't go without your guide. You have to pass through the fiery furnace; don't enter it unless, like Shadrach, Meshach, and Abednego, you have the Son of God as your companion. You have to storm the Jericho of your own corruptions: don't attempt the warfare until, like Joshua, you have seen the Captain of the Lord's host, with His sword drawn in His hand. You are to meet the Esau of your many temptations: meet him not until at Jabbok's brook you have laid hold upon the angel, and prevailed. In every case, in every condition, you will need Jesus; but most of all, when the iron gates of death shall open to you. Keep close to your soul's Husband, lean your head upon His bosom, ask to be refreshed with the spiced wine of His pomegranate, and you shall be found of Him at the last, without spot, or wrinkle, or any such thing. Seeing you have lived with Him, and lived in Him here, you shall remain with Him forever.

"When I felt secure, I said, I will never be shaken."
— *Psalm 30:6*

OAB has "been at rest from youth, like wine left on its dregs, not poured from one jar to another." Give a man wealth; let his ships bring home continually rich freights; let the winds and waves appear to be his servants to bear his vessels across the bosom of the mighty deep; let his lands yield abundantly: let the weather be propitious to his crops; let uninterrupted success attend him; let him stand among men as a successful merchant; let him enjoy continued health; allow him with braced nerve and brilliant eye to march through the world, and live happily; give him the buoyant spirit; let him have the song perpetually on his lips; let his eye be ever sparkling with joy — and the natural consequence of such an easy state to any man, let him be the best Christian who ever breathed, will be *presumption;* even David said, "I will never be shaken;" and we are not better than David, nor half so good. Brothers and sisters, beware of the smooth places of the way; if you are treading them, or if the way be rough, thank God for it. If God should always rock us in the cradle of prosperity; if we were always dandled on the knees of fortune; if we didn't have some stain on the alabaster pillar; if there weren't a few clouds in the sky; if we didn't have some bitter drops in the wine of this life, we should become intoxicated with pleasure, we should dream "we stand;" and stand we should, but it would be upon a pinnacle. Every moment of our lives is in just as much danger as a person asleep upon the mast.

We bless God, then, for our afflictions; we thank Him for our changes; we extol His name for losses of property; for we feel that if He had not chastened us in this manner, we might have become too secure. Continued worldly prosperity is a fiery trial.

"Afflictions, though they seem severe,
In mercy oft are sent."

"Man . . . is of few days and full of trouble."
— Job 14:1

T may be of great service to us, before we fall asleep, to remember this mournful fact, for it may lead us to loosen our grip on earthly things. There is nothing very pleasant in the recollection that we are not above the shafts of adversity, but it may humble us and prevent our boasting like the Psalmist in our morning's portion. "My mountain stands firm: I will never be shaken." It may keep us from taking too deep a root in this soil from which we are so soon to be transplanted into the heavenly garden. Let's recollect the frail tenure upon which we hold our *temporal mercies.* If we would remember that all the trees of earth are marked for the woodsman's ax, we should not be so ready to build our nests in them. We should love, but we should love with the love which expects death, and which expects separations. Our dear relations are but loaned to us, and the hour when we must return them to the lender's hand may be even at the door. The same is certainly true for our *worldly goods.* Doesn't wealth grow wings and fly away? Our *health* is equally precarious. Frail flowers of the field, we must not count on blooming forever. There is a time appointed for weakness and sickness, when we shall have to glorify God by suffering, and not by earnest activity. There is no single point in which we can hope to escape from the sharp arrows of affliction; out of our few days no one is safe from sorrow. Man's life is a cask full of bitter wine. Those who look for joy in it had better seek for honey in an ocean of brine. Beloved reader, don't set your affections upon things of earth: but seek those things which are above, for *here* the moth devours, and the thief breaks through, but *there* all joys are perpetual and eternal. The path of trouble is the way home. Lord, make this thought a pillow for many a weary head!

"Sin . . . utterly sinful." — Romans 7:13

EWARE of thinking lightly of sin. At the time of conversion, the conscience is so tender, that we are afraid of the slightest sin. Young converts have a holy timidity, a godly fear lest they should offend against God. But alas! very soon the fine bloom upon these first ripe fruits is removed by the rough handling of the surrounding world: the sensitive plant of young piety turns into a willow in the life which follows, too pliant, too easily yielding. It is sadly true, that even a Christian may grow by degrees so callous that the sin which once startled him does not alarm him in the least. By degrees we get familiar with sin. The ear in which the cannon has been booming will not notice slight sounds. At first a little sin startles us; but soon we say, "Isn't it just a little one?" Then there comes another, larger, and then another, until by degrees we begin to regard sin as only a little ill; and then follows an unholy presumption: "We haven't fallen into open sin. True, we tripped a little, but we stood upright for the most part. We may have uttered one unholy word, but mainly our conversation has been consistent." This is how we palliate sin; we throw a cloak over it; we call it by dainty names. Christian, beware how you think lightly of sin. Take heed lest you fall little by little. Sin, a *little* thing? Isn't it poison? Who knows its deadliness? Sin, a little thing? Don't little foxes spoil the grapes? Doesn't the tiny coral insect build a rock which wrecks a navy? Don't little strokes fell lofty oaks? Won't continual droppings wear away stones? Sin, a little thing? It girded the Redeemer's head with thorns, and pierced His heart! It made Him suffer anguish, bitterness, and woe. If you could but weigh the least sin in the scales of eternity, you would fly from it as from a serpent, and abhor the least appearance of evil. Look upon all sin as that which crucified the Savior, and you will see it to be "utterly sinful."

"You will be called Sought After." — *Isaiah 62:12*

HE surpassing grace of God is seen very clearly in that we were not only sought, but sought *after*. We *seek* for a thing which is lost on the floor of the house, but in such a case there is only seeking, not seeking *out*. The loss is more perplexing and the search more persevering when a thing is sought *out*. We were mingled with the mire: we were like precious pieces of gold that had fallen into the sewer and could only be accumulated again by carefully inspecting a mass of abominable filth and continuing to stir, rake, and search among the heap until all of the treasure is found. Or, to put it another way, we were lost in a labyrinth where we then wandered here and there. When mercy came after us with the gospel, it did not find us at first. It had to search for us and seek us out because, as lost sheep, we were so desperately lost, having wandered into such a strange country, that it did not seem possible that even the Good Shepherd should track our devious roaming. Glory be to unconquerable grace, we were sought *after!* No gloom could hide us, no filthiness could conceal us, we were found and brought home. Glory be to infinite love, God the Holy Spirit restored us!

If they could be written, the lives of some of God's people would fill us with holy astonishment. In many cases, God used strange and marvelous ways to find His own. Blessed be His name. He never relinquishes the search until the chosen are sought after effectually. They are not a people sought today and cast away tomorrow. Omnipotence and wisdom combined will make no mistakes; they shall be called, *"Sought after!"* That *any* should be sought after is matchless grace, but that *we* should be sought after is grace beyond degree! We can find no reason for it but God's own sovereign love, and can only lift up our heart in wonder, and praise the Lord that this night *we* wear the name of *"Sought after."*

"Love your neighbor." — Matthew 5:43

 OVE your neighbor." Perhaps he is rolling in riches, and you are poor and living in your little cottage adjacent to his lordly mansion. Every day you see his estates, his fine linen, and his sumptuous banquets. God has given him these gifts; do not covet his wealth or think resentful thoughts concerning him. Be content with your own lot if you can't better it, but don't look upon your neighbor and wish that he were as yourself. Love him, and then you will not envy him.

Perhaps, on the other hand, you are rich, and the poor live near you. Don't despise them because they are your neighbors. Realize that you are bound to love them. The world calls them your inferiors. In what way are they inferior? They are far more your equals than your inferiors. "God has made of one blood all people that dwell upon the face of the earth." It is your coat which is better than theirs, but you are by no means better than they. They are human beings, and what more than that are you? Take heed that you love your neighbors even though they are in rags, or sunken in the depths of poverty.

Your response might be, "I can't love my neighbors because, for all that I do, they show only ingratitude and contempt in return." So much the more room for the heroism of love. Will you be a featherbed warrior, instead of bearing the rough fight of love? He who dares the most, shall win the most; and if your path of love is rough, tread it boldly, still loving your neighbors through thick and thin. Heap coals of fire on their heads, and if they are difficult to please, don't seek to please *them*, but to please *your Master;* and remember, if *they* spurn your love, your Master has not spurned it, and your deed is as acceptable to Him as if it had been acceptable to them. Love your neighbor, for in so doing you are following the footsteps of Christ.

"To whom do you belong?" — *1 Samuel 30:13*

N O neutralities can exist in religion. We are either ranked under the banner of Prince Immanuel, to serve and fight His battles, or we are vassals of the black prince, Satan. "To whom do you belong?"

Reader, let me assist you in your response. *Have you been "born again"?* If you have, you belong to Christ, but without the new birth you can't be His. *In whom do you trust?* For those who believe in Jesus are the children of God. *Whose work are you doing?* You are sure to serve your master, for he whom you serve is thereby acknowledged to be your lord. *What company do you keep?* If you belong to Jesus, you will fraternize with those who wear the livery of the cross. "Birds of a feather flock together." *What is your conversation?* Is it heavenly or is it earthly? *What have you learned of your Master?* — for servants learn much from their masters to whom they are apprenticed. If you have served your time with Jesus, it will be said of you, as it was of Peter and John, "They took note that these men had been with Jesus."

We press the question, "To whom do you belong?" Answer honestly before you fall asleep. If you are not Christ's, you are in a difficult service — *Run away from your cruel master!* Enter into the service of the Lord of Love, and you shall enjoy a life of blessedness. If you *are* Christ's, let me advise you to do four things. You belong to Jesus — *obey him;* let His word be your law; let His wish be your will. You belong to the Beloved, then *love Him;* let your heart embrace Him; let your whole soul be filled with Him. You belong to the Son of God, then *trust Him;* rest nowhere else but on Him. You belong to the King of kings, then *be decided for Him.* Thus, without needing to be branded on the forehead, all will know to whom you belong.

"Why stay here until we die?" — *2 Kings 7:3*

EAR reader, this little book was mainly intended for the edification of believers, but, if you are yet unsaved, our heart yearns over you: and we would like to speak a word which could prove to be a blessing to you. Open your Bible, and read the story of the lepers, and notice how similar their situation is to yours. If you stay where you are, you will surely perish; if you go to Jesus you can only die. "Nothing ventured, nothing gained," is the old proverb, and in your case the venture is no great one. If you sit still in sullen despair, no one can pity you when your ruin comes; however, if you die after having sought mercy, you would be the object of universal sympathy, should such a thing be possible. No one who refuses to look to Jesus escapes; but you know that some, at any rate, are saved who believe in Him because certain of your own acquaintances have received mercy: then why not you? The Ninevites said, "Who can tell?" Act upon the same hope, and try the Lord's mercy. To perish is so awful that, if there were only a straw to grab at, the instinct of self-preservation should lead you to stretch out your hand. Up to now we have been talking to you on your own unbelieving ground. We would now assure you, as from the Lord, that if you seek Him He will be found by you. Jesus casts out no one who comes to Him. You shall not perish if you trust Him; on the contrary, you shall find treasure far richer than the poor lepers gathered in Syria's deserted camp. May the Holy Spirit encourage you to go at once, and you shall not believe in vain. When you are saved yourself, publish the good news to others. Don't be quiet; tell the King's household first, and unite with them in fellowship; let the gatekeeper of the city, the minister, be informed of your discovery, and then proclaim the good news in every place. The Lord save you before the sun goes down this day.

"He reached out his hand and took the dove and brought it back to himself in the ark." — *Genesis 8:9*

 ORN out by her wanderings, the dove returns at length to the ark as her only resting place. How heavily she flies — she will drop — she will never reach the ark! But she struggles on. Noah has been looking out for his dove all day long, and is ready to receive her. She has just enough strength to reach the edge of the ark, she can hardly alight upon it, and is ready to drop, when Noah reaches out his hand and brings her back to him. Notice that: *"brought the dove back to himself."* She did not fly right in herself, but was too fearful, or too weary to do so. She flew as far as she could, and then he reached out his hand and brought her back to him. This act of mercy was shown to the wandering dove, and she was not reprimanded for her wanderings. She was brought into the ark just as she was. So you, seeking sinner, with all your sin, will be received. "Only return" — those are God's two gracious words — "only return." What! nothing else? No, "only return." She had no olive branch in her mouth this time, nothing at all but just herself and her wanderings; but it is "only return," and she does return, and Noah brings her back. Fly, you wanderer; fly you fainting one, dove as you are, though you think yourself to be as dark as the raven with the mire of sin, back, back to the Savior. Every moment you wait only increases your misery; your attempts to plume yourself and make yourself fit for Jesus are all vanity. Come to Him just as you are. "Return, backsliding Israel." He doesn't say, "Return, *repenting* Israel" (there is no doubt about an invitation of this kind), but "you *backsliding* one," as a backslider with all your backslidings about you, Return, return, return! Jesus is waiting for you! He will reach out His hand and "bring you back" — back to Himself, your heart's true home.

---

*"If you think you are standing firm, be careful
that you don't fall!"* — *1 Corinthians 10:12*

T is a curious fact that there is such a thing as
being proud of grace. A person says, "I have
great faith, I shall not fall; poor little faith
may, but I never shall." "I have fervent love,"
says another, "I can stand, there is no danger
of my going astray." They who boast of grace
have little grace to boast of. Some who do this imagine that
their graces can keep them, not realizing that the stream
must flow constantly from the fountainhead, or else the
brook will soon be dry. If a continuous stream of oil does
not reach the lamp, even though it burns brightly today, it
will smoke tomorrow, and send out a noxious odor. Take
heed that you do not glory in your graces, but let all your
glorying and confidence be in Christ and His strength, for
this is the only way you can be kept from falling. Pray
more often. Spend longer periods of time in holy adoration. Read the Scriptures more earnestly and constantly.
Watch your lives more carefully. Live nearer to God. Take
the best examples for your pattern. Let your conversation
emit the fragrance of heaven. Let your hearts be perfumed
with affection for the souls of others. So live that others
may recognize that you have been with Jesus, and have
learned of Him; and when that happy day shall come,
when He whom you love shall say, "Come up higher," may
it be your happiness to hear Him say, "You have fought the
good fight, you have finished the race, you have kept the
faith. Now there is in store for you the crown of righteousness." On, Christian, with care and caution! On, with holy
fear and trembling! On, with faith and confidence in Jesus
alone, and let your constant petition be, "Sustain me
according to your promise." He, and He alone, is able "to
keep you from falling and to present you before His
glorious presence without fault and with great joy."

"I will watch my ways." — *Psalm 39:1*

ELLOW traveler, do not say in your heart, "I will go here and there, and I shall not sin;" for you are in the most danger of sinning when you are boasting of security. The road is very miry, it will be hard to pick your path so as not to soil your garments. In this world you will often come in contact with sticky resins; always be careful to keep your hands clean of it. There is a robber at every turn of the road to rob you of your jewels; there is a temptation in every mercy; there is a snare in every joy; and, if you ever reach heaven, it will be a miracle of divine grace to be ascribed entirely to your Father's power. Be on your guard. In handling highly-combustible material, we must be careful to avoid any flame that could ignite it and set off an explosion; and you, too, must take care that you enter not into temptation. Even your common actions are edged tools; you must pay attention as to how you handle them. There is nothing in this world to foster a Christian's piety, but everything to destroy it. You should be very anxious, indeed, to look up to God, that *He* may keep you! Your prayer should be, "You hold me up, and I shall be safe." Having prayed, you must also watch, guarding every thought, word, and action, with holy jealousy. Don't expose yourselves unnecessarily; but if called to exposure, if you are summoned to go where the darts are flying, never venture forth without your shield; for if once the devil finds you without your buckler, he will rejoice that his hour of triumph has come, and will soon make you fall down wounded by his arrows. Though you cannot be killed, you may be wounded. "Be sober; be vigilant, danger may be in an hour when everything seems the most secure to you." Therefore, be alert and self-controlled so that you can pray. No one ever fell into error through being too careful. May the Holy Spirit guide us in all our ways, so that they shall always please the Lord.

"Be strong in the grace that is in Christ Jesus."
— *2 Timothy 2:1*

C HRIST has grace without measure in Himself, but He has not retained it for Himself. As the reservoir empties itself into the pipes, so has Christ emptied out His grace for His people. "From the fullness of His grace we have all received one blessing after another." He seems only to have in order to dispense to us. He stands like the fountain, always flowing, but only running in order to supply the empty pitchers and the thirsty lips which draw close to it. Like a tree, He bears sweet fruit, not to hang on boughs, but to be gathered by those who need. Grace, whether its work be to pardon, to purify, to preserve, to strengthen, to enlighten, to quicken, or to restore, is always to be had from Him freely and without price; nor is there one form of the work of grace which He has not given upon His people. As the blood of the body, though flowing from the heart, belongs equally to every member, so the influences of grace are the inheritance of every saint united to the Lamb; and herein there is a sweet communion between Christ and His church, inasmuch as they both receive the same grace. Christ is the head upon which the oil is first poured; but the same oil runs to the very skirts of the garments, so that the meanest saint has an unction of the same costly moisture as that which fell upon the head. This is true communion when the sap of grace flows from the stem to the branch, and when it is perceived that the stem itself is sustained by the very nourishment which feeds the branch. As we daily receive grace from Jesus, and more constantly recognize it as coming from Him, we shall behold Him in communion with us, and enjoy the felicity of communion with Him. Let's make daily use of our riches, and always have recourse to Him as to our own Lord in covenant, taking from Him the supply of all we need with as much boldness as taking money out of our wallets.

"He worked wholeheartedly. And so he prospered."
— *2 Chronicles 31:21*

 HIS is not an unusual occurrence; it is the general rule of the moral universe that those individuals prosper who do their work with all their hearts, while those who go about their work halfheartedly are almost certain to fail. God gives only harvests of thistles to the idle, and is not pleased to send wealth to those who will not dig in the field to find its hidden treasure. It is a universal fact that, if one is to prosper, one must work diligently. The same fact applies to religion. If you want to prosper in your work for Jesus, let it be *heart* work, and let it be done with *all* your heart. Put as much force, energy, heartiness, and earnestness into religion as ever you do into your job, for it deserves far more. The Holy Spirit helps our infirmities, but He does not encourage our idleness; He loves active believers. Who are the most useful people in the Christian church? Those who do what they undertake for God *wholeheartedly.* Who are the most successful Sunday School teachers? The most talented? No; the most zealous; those whose hearts are on fire, the ones who see their Lord riding forth prosperously in the majesty of His salvation. Wholeheartedness shows itself in *perseverance;* there may be failure at first, but the earnest worker will say, "It is the Lord's work, and it must be done; my Lord has summoned me to do it, and in His strength I will accomplish it." Christian, are you serving your Master this way, "wholeheartedly"? Remember the earnestness of Jesus! Think what heart work was His! He could say, *"Zeal for your house consumes me."* When He sweat great drops of blood, it was no light burden He had to carry upon those blessed shoulders; and when He poured out His heart, it was no weak effort He was making for the salvation of His people. Was Jesus in earnest, and are we lukewarm?

"I dwell with you as . . . a stranger." — *Psalm 39:12*

ES, O Lord, *with* You, but I am not a stranger *to* You. All my natural alienation from You, Your grace has effectually removed; and now, in fellowship with Yourself, I walk through this sinful world as a pilgrim in a foreign country. *You* are a stranger in Your own world. Humankind forgets You, dishonors You, sets up new laws and alien customs, and doesn't know You. Your dear Son was in the world, and though the world was made through Him, the world did not recognize Him. He came to that which was His own, but His own did not receive Him. Never was a foreigner so speckled a bird among the denizens of any land as Your beloved Son among His mother's kin. It is no marvel, then, if I who live the life of Jesus, should be unknown and a stranger here below. Lord, I would not be a citizen where Jesus was an alien. His pierced hand has loosened the cords which once bound my soul to earth, and now I find myself a stranger in the land. My speech seems an outlandish tongue to these Babylonians among whom I dwell, my manners are singular, and my actions strange. A Tartar would be more at home in Cheapside than I could ever be in the haunts of sinners. But here is the sweetness of my lot: I am a stranger *with You.* You are my co-sufferer, my fellow traveler. Oh, what joy to wander in such blessed society! My heart burns within me when You speak with me along the way and, though I am a sojourner, I am far more blessed than those who sit on thrones, and far more at home than those who dwell under the ceilings of their houses.

> "To me remains nor place, nor time:
> My country is in every clime;
> I can be calm and free from care
> On any shore, since God is there.
>
> While place we seek, or place we shun,
> The soul finds happiness in none:
> But with a God to guide our way,
> 'Tis equal joy to go or stay."

"Keep your servant also from willful sins."
— *Psalm 19:13*

UCH was the prayer of the *"person after God's own heart."* Did holy David need to pray like this? How necessary such a prayer must be, then, for us babes in grace! It is as if he said, "Keep me from rushing headlong over the precipice of sin." Our evil nature, like an ill-tempered horse, is apt to run away. May the grace of God put the bridle upon it, and hold it in, so that it will be kept from running into mischief. What would the best of us do if it were not for the checks which the Lord sets upon us both in providence and in grace! The psalmist's prayer is directed against the worst form of sin — that which is done with deliberation and willfulness. Even the holiest of persons needs to be "kept from" the vilest transgressions. It is a solemn thing to find the apostle Paul warning saints against the most loathsome sins. "Put to death, therefore, whatever belongs to your earthly nature: sexual immorality, impurity, lust, evil desires and greed, which is idolatry." What! do saints want warning against such sins as these? Yes, they do. The purest robes, unless their purity be preserved by divine grace, will be defiled by the most sinful stains. Experienced Christian, do not boast in your experience; you will trip in spite of this if you look away from Him who is able to keep you from falling. You whose love is fervent, whose faith is constant, whose hopes are bright, do not say, "We shall never sin," but rather cry, "Lead us not into temptation." There is enough tinder in the heart of the best of us to light a fire that shall burn to the lowest hell, unless God quenches the sparks as they fall. Who would have dreamed that righteous Lot could be found drunken, and committing uncleanness? Hazael said, "How could Your servant, a mere dog, accomplish such a feat?" and we are very apt to use the same self-righteous question. May infinite wisdom cure us of the madness of self-confidence.

"Remember the poor." — *Galatians 2:10*

HY does God allow so many of His children to be poor? He could make them all rich if He pleased; He could lay bags of gold at their doors; He could send them a large annual income; or He could scatter round their houses an abundance of provisions, like when he once made the quails lie in heaps round the camp of Israel, and rained bread out of heaven to feed them. There is no need for them to be poor, except that He sees that it is best. "The cattle on a thousand hills are His" — He could supply them; He could make the richest, the greatest, and the mightiest bring all their power and riches to the feet of His children, for the hearts of all people are in His control. But He does not choose to do so; He allows them to be in want, He allows them to pine in penury and obscurity. Why is this? There are many reasons: one is, *to give us, who are favored with enough, an opportunity of showing our love to Jesus.* We show our love to Christ when we sing of Him and when we pray to Him; but if there were no sons or daughters in need in the world we would lose the sweet privilege of evidencing our love, by ministering in giving money or goods to His poorer kin; He has ordained that thus we should prove that our love does not exist in word only, but in deed and in truth. If we truly love Christ, we shall care for those who are loved by Him. Those who are dear to Him will be dear to us. Let's then look upon it not as a duty but as a privilege to relieve the poor of the Lord's flock — remembering the words of the Lord Jesus, "Whatever you did for one of the least of these brothers of Mine, you did for Me." Surely this assurance is sweet enough, and this motive strong enough to lead us to help others with a willing hand and a loving heart — recollecting that all we do for His people is graciously accepted by Christ as done to Himself.

"Blessed are the peacemakers, for they will be called sons of God." — *Matthew 5:9*

HIS is the seventh of the beatitudes: and seven was the number of perfection among the Hebrews. It may be that the Savior placed the peacemaker seventh upon the list because he most nearly approaches the perfect human being in Christ Jesus. He who would have perfect blessedness, so far as it can be enjoyed on earth, must attain to this seventh benediction, and become a peacemaker. There is a significance also in the position of the text. The verse which precedes it speaks of the blessedness of "the pure in heart: for they will see God." It is well to understand that we are to be "first pure, then peaceable." Our peaceableness is never to be a compact with sin, or toleration of evil. We must set our faces like flints against everything which is contrary to God and His holiness: purity being a settled matter in our souls, we can go on to peaceableness. Not less does the verse that follows seem to have been put there on purpose. However peaceable we may be in this world, yet we shall be misrepresented and misunderstood: and no wonder, for even the Prince of Peace, by His very peacefulness, brought fire upon the earth. He Himself, though He loved humankind, and did no wrong, was "was despised and rejected by men, a Man of sorrows, and familiar with suffering." Lest, therefore, the peaceable in heart should be surprised when they meet with enemies, it is added in the following verse, "Blessed are those who are persecuted because of righteousness, for theirs is the kingdom of heaven." Thus, the peacemakers are not only pronounced to be blessed, but they are surrounded with blessings. Lord, give us grace to climb to this seventh beatitude! Purify our minds that we may be "first pure, then peaceable," and fortify our souls, that our peaceableness may not lead us into cowardice and despair when, for Your sake, we are persecuted.

"You are all sons of God through faith in Christ Jesus."
— *Galatians 3:26*

HE *fatherhood of God is common to all His children.* Ah! Little-faith, you have often said, "Oh that I had the courage of Great-heart, that I could wield his sword and be as valiant as he! But, alas, I stumble at every straw, and a shadow makes me afraid." Listen, Little-faith. Great-heart is God's child, and you are God's child too; and Great-heart is not one whit more God's child than you are. Peter and Paul, the highly-favored apostles, were of the family of the Most High; and so are you also; the weak Christian is as much a child of God as the strong one.

> "This cov'nant stands secure,
> Though earth's old pillars bow;
> The strong, the feeble, and the weak,
> Are one in Jesus now."

All the names are in the same family register. One may have more grace than another, but God our heavenly Father has the same tender heart towards all. One may do more mighty works, and may bring more glory to his Father, but he whose name is the least in the kingdom of heaven is as much the child of God as he who stands among the King's mighty men. Let this cheer and comfort us, when we draw near to God and say, "Our Father."

Yet, while we are comforted by knowing this, let's not rest contented with weak faith, but ask, like the Apostles, to have it increased. However feeble our faith may be, if it is real faith in Christ, we shall reach heaven at last, but we shall not honor our Master much on our pilgrimage, neither shall we abound in joy and peace. If then you would live to Christ's glory, and be happy in His service, seek to be filled with the spirit of adoption more and more completely, until perfect love shall cast out fear.

*"As the Father has loved me, so have I loved you.
Now remain in my love." — John 15:9*

 S the Father loves the Son, in the same manner Jesus loves His people. What is that divine method? He loved Him *without beginning,* and thus Jesus loves His members. *"I have loved you with an everlasting love."* You can trace the beginning of human affection; you can easily find the beginning of your love to Christ, but His love to us is a stream whose source is hidden in eternity. God the Father loves Jesus *without any change.* Christian, take comfort in this, that there is no change in Jesus Christ's love to those who rest in Him. Yesterday you were on Tabor's top, and you said, "He loves me:" today you are in the valley of humiliation, but He loves you still the same. On the hill Mizar, and among the Hermons, you heard His voice, which answered so sweetly with the dove cooing of love; and now on the sea, or even *in* the sea, when all His waves and billows go over you, His heart is faithful to His ancient choice. The Father loves the Son *without any end,* and thus does the Son love His people. Saint, you needn't fear the loosening of the silver cord, for His love for you will never cease. Rest confident that even down to the grave Christ will go with you, and that up again from it He will be your guide to the celestial hills. Moreover, the Father loves the Son *without any measure,* and the Son gives the same immeasurable love to His chosen ones. The whole heart of Christ is dedicated to His people. He "loved us and gave Himself for us." His is a love which passes knowledge. Ah! we have indeed an immutable Savior, a precious Savior, one who loves without measure, without change, without beginning, and without end, even as the Father loves Him! There is an abundance of food here for those who know how to digest it. May the Holy Spirit lead us into its marrow and fatness!

"Strengthened in . . . faith." — Romans 4:20

CHRISTIAN, take good care of your faith; for recollect *faith is the only way whereby you can obtain blessings.* If we want blessings from God, nothing can fetch them down but faith. Prayer cannot draw down answers from God's throne except it be the earnest prayer of one who believes. Faith is the angelic messenger between the soul and the Lord Jesus in glory. Let that angel be withdrawn, we can neither send up prayer, nor receive the answers. Faith is the telegraphic wire which links earth and heaven — on which God's messages of love fly so fast that, before we call, He answers and while we are yet speaking, He hears us. But if that telegraphic wire of faith is snapped, how can we receive the promise? Am I in trouble? — I can obtain help for trouble by faith. Am I beaten about by the enemy? — my soul on her dear Refuge leans by faith. But take faith away — in vain I call to God. There is no road between my soul and heaven. In the deepest wintertime faith is a road on which the horses of prayer may travel — yes, and all the better for the biting frost; but blockade the road, and how can we communicate with the Great King? Faith links me with divinity. Faith clothes me with the power of God. Faith engages on my side the omnipotence of Jehovah. Faith insures every attribute of God in my defense. It helps me to defy the hosts of hell. It makes me march triumphant over the necks of my enemies. But without faith how can I receive anything of the Lord? Those who waver — who are like waves in the Sea — cannot expect to receive anything from God! O, then, Christian, watch your faith well; for with it you can win all things, however poor you are, but without it, you can obtain nothing. "Everything is possible for him who believes."

"She ate all she wanted and had some left over."
— Ruth 2:14

HENEVER we are privileged to eat of the bread which Jesus gives, we are, like Ruth, satisfied with the full and sweet repast. When Jesus is the host, no guest goes empty from the table. Our *head* is satisfied with the precious truth which Christ reveals; our *heart* is content with Jesus, as the altogether lovely object of affection; our *hope* is satisfied, for whom have we in heaven but Jesus? and our desire is satiated, for what more can we wish for than "to know Christ and to be found in Him"? Jesus fills our *conscience* until it is at perfect peace; our *judgment* with persuasion of the certainty of His teachings; our *memory* with recollections of what He has done, and our *imagination* with the prospects of what He is yet to do. As Ruth "ate all she wanted and *had some left over*," so is it with us. We have drawn deeply from the cask; we have thought that we could take in all of Christ; but when we have done our best we have had to leave a vast remainder. We've sat at the table of the Lord's love, and said, "Nothing but the infinite can ever satisfy me; I am such a great sinner that I must have infinite merit to wash my sin away;" but we've had our sin removed, and found that there was merit to spare; we've had our hunger relieved at the feast of sacred love, and found that there was an excessive amount of spiritual food remaining. There are certain sweet things in the Word of God which we have not enjoyed yet, and which we are obliged to leave for awhile; for we are like the disciples to whom Jesus said, "I have much more to say to you, more than you can now bear." Yes, there are graces to which we have not attained; places of fellowship nearer to Christ which we have not reached; and heights of communion which our feet have not climbed. At every banquet of love many baskets of leftovers remain. Let's magnify the liberality of our glorious Boaz.

"My lover!" — *Song of Songs 2:8*

HIS was a golden name which the ancient church in her most joyous moments was accustomed to giving to the Anointed of the Lord. When the time of the singing of birds was come, and the cooing of the dove was heard in her land, *her* love note was sweeter than either, as she sang, "*My lover* is mine and I am his: he browses among the lilies." Ever in her song of songs does she call Him by that delightful name, "My lover!" Even in the long winter, when idolatry had withered the garden of the Lord, her prophets found space to lay aside the burden of the Lord for a little season, and to say, as Isaiah did, "I will sing for the one I love a song about His vineyard." Though the saints had never seen His face, though as yet He was not made flesh, nor had dwelt among us, nor had man beheld His glory, yet He was the consolation of Israel, the hope and joy of all the chosen, the "lover" of all those who were upright before the Most High. We, in the summer days of the church, are also accustomed to speaking of Christ as the best beloved of our soul, and to feel that He is very precious, the "outstanding among ten thousand, and altogether lovely." So true is it that the church loves Jesus, and claims Him as her lover, that the apostle dares to defy the whole universe to separate her from the love of Christ, and declares that neither persecutions, distress, affliction, peril, or the sword have been able to do it; no, he joyously boasts, "In all these things we are more than conquerors through Him who loved us."

O that we knew more of You, ever precious one!

> My sole possession is Thy love;
> In earth beneath, or heaven above,
> I have no other store;
> And though with fervent suit I pray,
> And importune Thee day by day,
> I ask Thee nothing more.

"Husbands, love your wives, just as Christ loved the church." — Ephesians 5:25

HAT a golden example Christ gives to His disciples! Few masters could venture to say, "If you would practice my teaching, imitate my life;" but as the life of Jesus is the exact transcript of perfect virtue, He can point to Himself as the paragon of holiness, as well as the teacher of it. The Christian should take nothing short of Christ for his model. Under no circumstances ought we to be content unless we reflect the grace which was in Him. As a husband, the Christian is to look upon the portrait of Christ Jesus, and he is to paint according to that copy. The true Christian is to be such a husband as Christ was to His church. The love of a husband is *special*. The Lord Jesus cherishes for the church a peculiar affection, which is set upon her above the rest of mankind: "I pray for them. I am not praying for the world." The elect church is the favorite of heaven, the treasure of Christ, the crown of His head, the bracelet of His arm, the breastplate of His heart, the very center and core of His love. A husband should love his wife with a *constant* love, for thus Jesus loves His church. He does not vary in His affection. He may change in His display of affection, but the affection itself is still the same. A husband should love his wife with an *enduring* love, for nothing "will be able to separate us from the love of God that is in Christ Jesus our Lord." A true husband loves his wife with a *hearty* love, fervent and intense. It is not mere lip service. Ah! beloved, what more could Christ have done in proof of His love than He has done? Jesus has a *delighted love* towards His spouse: He prizes her affection, and delights in her with sweet complacency. Believer, you wonder at Jesus' love; you admire it — *are you imitating it?* In your domestic relationships is the rule and measure of your love — *"just as Christ loved the church"?*

"You will be scattered, each to his own home.
You will leave me all alone." — John 16:32

EW had fellowship with the sorrows of Gethsemane. The majority of the disciples were
not sufficiently advanced in grace to be admitted to behold the mysteries of "the agony."
Occupied with the passover feast at their own
houses, they represent the many who live
upon the letter, but are mere babes as to the spirit of the
gospel. To twelve, no, to eleven only was the privilege given
to enter Gethsemane and see "this great sight." Out of the
eleven, eight were left at a distance; they had fellowship, but
not of that intimate sort to which the greatly beloved are
admitted. Only three highly-favored ones could approach
the veil of our Lord's mysterious sorrow: within that veil
even these must not intrude; a distance of a stone's throw
must be left between. He must tread the winepress *alone,* and
of the people there must be none with Him. Peter and the
two sons of Zebedee represent the few eminent, experienced
saints, who may be written down as "Fathers;" these having
done business on great waters, can in some degree measure
the huge Atlantic waves of their Redeemer's passion. To
some selected spirits it is given, for the good of others, and
to strengthen them for future, special, and tremendous
conflict, to enter the inner circle and hear the pleadings of
the suffering High Priest; they have fellowship with Him in
His sufferings, and are made conformable to His death. Yet
even these can't penetrate the secret places of the Savior's
woe. "Your unknown sufferings" is the remarkable expression of the Greek liturgy: there was an inner chamber in our
Master's grief, shut out from human knowledge and fellowship. There Jesus is left *"all alone."* Here Jesus was more
than ever an "Unspeakable gift!" Isn't Watts right when
he sings —

> "And all the unknown joys he gives,
> Were bought with agonies unknown."

"Can you bind the beautiful Pleiades? Can you loose the cords of Orion?" — *Job 38:31*

I F inclined to boast of our abilities, the grandeur of nature may soon show us how puny we are. We can't move the least of all the twinkling stars, or quench so much as one of the beams of the morning. We speak of power, but the heavens laugh us to scorn. When the Pleiades shine forth in spring with vernal joy we can't restrain their influences, and when Orion reigns in a higher place, and the year is bound in winter's fetters, we can't relax the icy bands. The seasons revolve according to the divine appointment, neither can the whole human race effect a change therein. Lord, what is mankind?

In the spiritual, as in the natural world, humanity's power is limited on all hands. When the Holy Spirit sheds abroad His delights in the soul, none can disturb; all the cunning and malice of humankind are ineffectual to suppress the genial life-giving power of the Comforter. When He deigns to visit a church and revive it, the most inveterate enemies can't resist the good work; they may ridicule it, but they can no more restrain it than they can push back the spring when the Pleiades rule the hour. God wills it, and so it must be. On the other hand, if the Lord in sovereignty, or in justice, binds us up so that our soul is in soul bondage, who can give us liberty? He alone can remove the winter of spiritual death from an individual or a people. He looses the bands of Orion, and none but He. What a blessing it is that He can do it. O that He would perform the wonder tonight. Lord, end my winter, and let my spring begin. I cannot with all my longings raise my soul out of her death and dullness, but all things are possible with You. I need celestial influences, the clear shinings of Your love, the beams of Your grace, the light of Your countenance, these are the Pleiades to me. I suffer a great deal from sin and temptation, these are my wintry signs, my terrible Orion. Lord, work wonders in me, and for me. Amen.

"Going a little farther, he fell with his face to the ground and prayed." — Matthew 26:39

THERE are several instructive features in our Savior's prayer in His hour of trial. It was *lonely prayer.* He even withdrew from His three favored disciples. Believer, pray often in solitude, especially in times of trial. Family prayer, social prayer, prayer in the church, will not suffice; these are very precious, but the best beaten spice will smoke in your censer in your private devotions, where no ear hears but God's.

It was *humble prayer.* Luke says He knelt, but another evangelist says He "fell with His face to the ground." Where, then, must be YOUR place, humble servant of the great Master? What dust and ashes should cover *your* head! Humility gives us a good foothold in prayer. There is no hope of succeeding with God unless we abase ourselves that He may exalt us in due time.

It was *filial prayer.* "Abba, Father." You will find it a stronghold in the day of trial to plead your adoption. You have no rights as a subject, you have forfeited them by your treason; but nothing can forfeit a child's right to a father's protection. Don't be afraid to say, "My Father, hear my cry."

Observe that it was *persevering prayer.* He prayed three times. Don't cease until you prevail. Be as the importunate widow, whose continual coming earned what her first supplication could not win. Continue in prayer, and watch in the same with thanksgiving.

Lastly, *it was the prayer of resignation.* "Yet not as I will, but as You will." Yield, and God yields. Let it be as God wills, and God will determine for the best. Be content to leave your prayer in His hands, who knows when to give, and how to give, and what to give, and what to withhold. So pleading, earnestly, importunately, yet with humility and resignation, you shall surely succeed.

*"Father, I want those you have given me to be with
me where I am." — John 17:24*

death! why do you touch the tree beneath whose spreading branches weariness has rest? Why do you snatch away the excellent of the earth, in whom is all our delight? If you must use your ax, use it upon the trees which yield no fruit; you might be thanked then. But why will you fell the goodly cedars of Lebanon? O withdraw your ax, and spare the righteous. But no, it must not be; death strikes the comeliest of our friends; the most generous, the most prayerful, the most holy, the most devoted must die. And why? It is through Jesus' prevailing prayer — "Father, I want those You have given to Me to be with Me where I am." It is *that* which bears them on eagle's wings to heaven. Every time a believer mounts from this earth to paradise, it is an answer to Christ's prayer. A good old divine remarks, "Many times Jesus and His people pull against one another in prayer. You bend your knee in prayer and say 'Father, I want Your saints to be with Me where *I* am.' Christ says, 'Father, I want those You have given to Me to be with Me where I am.' " Thus the disciple is at cross-purposes with His Lord. The soul can't be in both places: the loved one can't be with Christ and with you, too. Now, which pleader shall win the day? If you had your choice; if the King should step from His throne, and say, "Here are two supplicants praying in opposition to one another, which shall be answered?" Oh! I am sure, even though it were agonizing for you, you would jump to your feet, and say, "Jesus, not my will, but Yours be done." You would give up your prayer for your loved one's life, if you could realize the thoughts that Christ is praying in the opposite direction — "Father, I want those You have given to Me to be with Me where I am." Lord, You shall have them. By faith we let them go.

*"His sweat was like drops of blood falling
to the ground." — Luke 22:44*

HE mental pressure arising from our Lord's struggle with temptation forced his human body to such an unnatural excitement that his pores sent forth great drops of blood which fell down to the ground. This proves *how tremendous the weight of sin must have been* when it was able to crush the Savior so that He distilled great drops of blood! This demonstrates *the mighty power of His love.* It is a very pretty observation of old Isaac Ambrose that the gum which exudes from the tree without cutting is always the best. This precious camphor tree yielded most sweet spices when it was wounded under the knotty whips, and when it was pierced by the nails on the cross; but see, it gives forth its best spice when there is no whip, no nail, no wound. This sets forth *the voluntariness of Christ's sufferings,* since without a lance the blood flowed freely. No need to put on the leech, or apply the knife; it flows spontaneously. No need for the rulers to cry, "Spring up, O well;" it flows by itself in crimson torrents. If we experience a great pain of mind apparently the blood rushes *to* the heart. The cheeks are pale; a fainting fit comes on; the blood has gone inward as if to nourish the inner person while passing through its trial. But see our Savior in His agony; He is so utterly oblivious of self, that instead of His agony driving His blood to the heart to nourish Himself, it drives it outward to wet the earth with dew. The agony of Christ, inasmuch as it pours Him out upon the ground, pictures the fullness of the offering which He made for humankind.

Do we not perceive how intense must have been the wrestling through which He passed, and will we not hear its voice *to us*? "In your struggle against sin, you have not yet resisted to the point of shedding your blood." Behold the great Apostle and High Priest of our profession, and sweat even to blood rather than yield to the great tempter of your souls.

*"I tell you . . . if they keep quiet, the stones
will cry out."* — Luke 19:40

UT could the stones cry out? Certainly they could if He who opens the mouth of the dumb should bid them lift up their voice. Certainly if they were to speak, they would have much to testify in praise of Him who created them by the word of His power; they could extol the wisdom and power of their *Maker* who called them into being. Shall not *we* speak well of Him who made us anew, and out of stones raised up children to Abraham? The old rocks could tell of chaos and order, and the handiwork of God in successive stages of creation's drama; and can't *we* talk of God's decrees, of God's great work in ancient times, in all that He did for His church in the days of old? If the stones were to speak, they could tell of their *breaker,* how he took them from the quarry, and made them fit for the temple, and can't we tell of our glorious Breaker, who broke our hearts with the hammer of His word, that He might build us into His temple? If the stones should cry out they would magnify their *builder,* who polished them and fashioned them after the similitude of a palace; and shall we not talk of our Architect and Builder, who has put us in our place in the temple of the living God? If the stones could cry out, they might have a long, long story to tell by way of memorial, for many a time has a great stone been rolled as a memorial before the Lord; and we too can testify of Ebenezers, stones of help, pillars of remembrance. The broken stones of the law cry out against us, but Christ Himself, who has rolled away the stone from the door of the sepulcher, speaks for us. Stones might well cry out, but we will not let them: we will silence their noise with ours; we will break into sacred song, and bless the majesty of the Most High, all our days glorifying Him who is called by Jacob the Shepherd and Stone of Israel.

"He was heard because of his reverent submission."
— *Hebrews 5:7*

ID this fear arise from the infernal suggestion *that He was utterly forsaken?* There may be sterner trials than this, but surely it is *one* of the worst to be utterly forsaken? "See," said Satan, "you don't have a friend anywhere! your Father has closed off the heart of His compassion from you. Not an angel in His courts will stretch out his hand to help you. All heaven is alienated from You; You are left alone. See the companions with whom You have taken sweet counsel, what are they worth? Son of Mary, see there Your brother James there, see Your loved disciple John there, and Your bold apostle Peter, how the cowards sleep when You are in Your sufferings! Lo! You have no friend left in heaven or earth. All hell is against You. I have stirred up my infernal den. I have sent my missives throughout all regions summoning every prince of darkness to set upon You this night, and we will spare no arrows, we will use all our infernal might to overwhelm You: and what will You do, You solitary one?" It may be, this was the temptation; we think it was, because the appearance of an angel to Him strengthening Him removed that fear. He was heard in that He feared; He was not alone anymore, but heaven was with Him. It may be that this is the reason of His coming three times to His disciples — as Hart puts it —

> "Backwards and forwards thrice He ran,
> As if He sought some help from man."

He would see for Himself whether it were really true that all men had forsaken Him; He found them all asleep; but perhaps He gained some faint comfort from the thought that they were sleeping, not from treachery, but from sorrow, the spirit indeed was willing, but the flesh was weak. At any rate, He was heard in that He feared. Jesus was heard in His deepest woe; my soul, you shall be heard also.

*"At that time Jesus [was] full of joy through the
Holy Spirit." — Luke 10:21*

HE Savior was "a Man of sorrows," but every thoughtful mind has discovered the fact that down deep in His innermost soul He carried an inexhaustible treasury of refined and heavenly joy. Of all the human race, there was never a man who had a deeper, purer, or more abiding peace than our Lord Jesus Christ. "God has set you above your companions by anointing you with the oil of joy." His vast benevolence must, from the very nature of things, have afforded Him the deepest possible delight, for benevolence is joy. There were a few remarkable seasons when this joy manifested itself. "At that time Jesus, full of joy through the Holy Spirit, said, 'I praise You, Father, Lord of heaven and earth.'" Christ had His songs, though it was night with Him; though His face was marred, and His countenance had lost the luster of earthly happiness, yet sometimes it was lit up with a matchless splendor of unparalleled satisfaction, as He thought upon the compensation of the reward, and in the midst of the congregation sang His praise to God. In this, the Lord Jesus is a blessed picture of His church on earth. At this hour the church expects to walk in sympathy with her Lord along a thorny road; through much tribulation she is forcing her way to the crown. To bear the cross is her office, and to be scorned and counted an alien by her mother's children is her lot; and yet the church has a deep well of joy, of which none can drink but her own children. There are stores of wine, and oil, and corn, hidden in the midst of our Jerusalem, upon which the saints of God are forever sustained and nurtured; and sometimes, as in our Savior's case, we have our seasons of intense delight, for "There is a river whose streams make glad the city of God." Exiles though we are, we rejoice in our King; yes, in Him we exceedingly rejoice, while in His name we set up our banners.

"Are you betraying the Son of Man with a kiss?"
— Luke 22:48

HE "kisses of an enemy are deceitful." Let me be on my guard when the world puts on a loving face, for it will, if possible, betray me as it did my Master, with a kiss. Whenever a man is about to stab religion, he usually professes very great reverence for it. Let me beware of the sleek-faced hypocrisy which is armor bearer to heresy and infidelity. Knowing the deceitfulness of unrighteousness, let me be wise as a serpent to detect and avoid the designs of the enemy. The young man, void of understanding, was led astray by the kiss of the strange woman: may my soul be so graciously instructed all this day, that "the persuasive words" of the world may have no effect upon me. Holy Spirit, don't allow me, a poor frail human being, to be betrayed with a kiss!

But what if I should be guilty of the same accursed sin as Judas, that son of eternal damnation? I have been baptized into the name of the Lord Jesus; I am a member of His visible church; I sit at the communion table: all these are so many kisses of my lips. Am I sincere in them? If not, I am a base traitor. Do I live in the world as carelessly as others do, and yet make a profession of being a follower of Jesus? Then I must expose religion to ridicule, and lead men to speak evil of the holy name by which I am called. Surely, if I act thus inconsistently, I am a Judas, and it were better for me that I had never been born. Dare I hope that I am clear in this matter? Then, O Lord, keep me so. O Lord, make me sincere and true. Preserve me from every false way. Never let me betray my Savior. I do love You, Jesus, and though I often grieve You, yet I would desire to abide faithful even to death. O God, forbid that I should rise to great heights in professing, and then fall at last into the lake of fire, because I betrayed my Master with a kiss.

"The Son of Man." — John 3:13

OW constantly our Master used the title, the "Son of Man!" If He had chosen, He might always have spoken of Himself as the Son of God, the Everlasting Father, the Wonderful, the Advisor, the Prince of Peace; but behold the lowliness of Jesus! He prefers to call Himself the Son of Man. Let's learn a lesson of humility from our Savior; let's never court great titles nor proud degrees. There is here, however, a far sweeter thought. Jesus loved humankind so much, that He delighted to honor it; and since it is a high honor, and indeed, the greatest dignity of being human, that Jesus is the Son of Man, He is accustomed to display this name, that He may as it were hang royal stars upon the breast of humanity, and show forth the love of God to Abraham's seed. *Son of Man* — whenever He said that word, He shed a halo round the head of Adam's children. Yet there is perhaps a more precious thought still. Jesus Christ called Himself the Son of Man to express His oneness and sympathy with His people. He thus reminds us that He is the one whom we may approach without fear. As humans, we may take to Him all our griefs and troubles, for He knows them by experience; in that He Himself has suffered as the "Son of Man," He is able to succor and comfort us. All hail, You blessed Jesus! inasmuch as You are forever using the sweet name which acknowledges that You are a brother and close kin, it is to us a dear token of Your grace, Your humility, Your love.

> "Oh see how Jesus trusts Himself
> Unto our childish love,
> As though by His free ways with us
> Our earnestness to prove!
>
> His sacred name a common word
> On earth He loves to hear;
> There is no majesty in Him
> Which love may not come near."

*"Jesus answered, If you are looking for me,
then let these men go." — John 18:8*

OTICE, my soul, the care which Jesus manifested even in His hour of trial, towards the sheep of His hand! The ruling passion is strong in death. He resigns Himself to the enemy, but He interposes a word of power to set His disciples free. As to Himself, like a sheep before her shearers, He is mute and does not open His mouth, but for His disciples' sake He speaks with Almighty energy. Herein is love, constant, self-forgetting, faithful love. But isn't there far more here than is to be found upon the surface? Haven't we the very soul and spirit of the atonement in these words? The Good Shepherd lays down His life for the sheep, and pleads that they must therefore go free. The Surety is bound, and justice demands that those for whom He stands a substitute should go their way. In the midst of Egypt's bondage, that voice rings as a word of power, *"Let these men go."* Out of the slavery of sin and Satan the redeemed must come. In every cell of the dungeons of Despair, the sound is echoed, *"Let these men go,"* and Despondency and Much-afraid come forth. Satan hears the well-known voice, and lifts his foot from the neck of the fallen; and Death hears it, and the grave opens her gates to let the dead arise. *Go* to progress in holiness, triumph, glory, and none shall dare to keep you from it. No lion shall be in your way, neither shall any ravenous beast prowl upon it. "The hind of the morning" has drawn the cruel hunters to himself, and now the most timid roes and hinds of the field may graze at perfect peace among the lilies of his loves. The thundercloud has burst over the Cross of Calvary, and the pilgrims of Zion shall never be struck by the bolts of vengeance. Come, my heart, rejoice in the immunity which your Redeemer has secured you, and bless His name all the day, and every day.

"When he comes in his Father's glory with the holy angels." — Mark 8:38

F we have been partakers with Jesus in His shame, we shall be sharers with Him in the luster which shall surround Him when He appears again in glory. Are you, loved one, with Christ Jesus? Does a vital union knit you to Him? Then you are today with Him in His shame; you have taken up His cross, and gone with Him without the camp bearing His reproach; you shall doubtless be with Him when the cross is exchanged for the crown. But judge yourself this evening; for if you aren't with Him in the regeneration, neither shall you be with Him when He shall come in His glory. If you start back from the dark side of communion, you shall not understand its bright, its happy period, when the King shall come, and *all His holy angels with Him.* What! are *angels with Him?* And yet He didn't take angels up — He took up the seed of Abraham. Are the holy angels *with Him?* Come, my soul, if you are indeed His own beloved, you cannot be far from Him. If His friends and His neighbors are called together to see His glory, what do you think if you are married to Him? Shall you be distant? Though it is a day of judgment, yet you cannot be far from that heart which, having admitted angels into intimacy, has admitted you into union. Hasn't He said to you, O my soul, "I will betroth you to Me forever; I will betroth you in righteousness and justice, in love and compassion"? Haven't His own lips said it, "I am married to you, and My delight is in you"? If the angels, who are but friends and neighbors, shall be with Him, it is abundantly certain that His own beloved Hephzibah, in whom is all His delight, shall be near to Him, and sit at His right hand. Here is a morning star of hope for you, of such exceeding brilliance, that it may well light up the darkest and most desolate experience.

"Then all the disciples deserted him and fled."
— Matthew 26:56

 E never deserted them, but they in cowardly fear of their lives, fled from Him in the very beginning of His sufferings. This is just one instructive instance of the frailty of all believers if left to themselves; they are but sheep at best, and they flee when the wolf comes. They had all been warned of the danger, and had promised to die rather than leave their Master; and yet they were seized with sudden panic, and took to their heels. It may be, that I, at the opening of this day, have braced up my mind to bear a trial for the Lord's sake, and I imagine myself to be certain to exhibit perfect fidelity; but let me be very jealous of myself, lest having the same evil heart of unbelief, I should depart from my Lord as the apostles did. It is one thing to promise, and quite another to perform. It would have been to their eternal honor to have stood at Jesus' side right manfully; they fled from honor; may I be kept from imitating them! Where else could they have been so safe as near their Master, who could presently call for twelve legions of angels? They fled from their true safety. O God, let me not play the fool also. Divine grace can make the coward brave. The smoking flax can flame forth like fire on the altar when the Lord wills it. These very apostles who were timid as hares, grew to be bold as lions after the Spirit had descended upon them, and even so the Holy Spirit can make my cowardly spirit brave to confess my Lord and witness for His truth.

What anguish must have filled the Savior as He saw His friends so faithless! This was one bitter ingredient in His cup; but that cup is drained dry; let me not put another drop in it. If I forsake my Lord, I shall crucify Him afresh, and put Him to an open shame. Keep me, O blessed Spirit, from an end so shameful.

"Yes, Lord, she said, but even the dogs eat the
crumbs that fall from their masters' table."
— *Matthew 15:27*

HIS woman gained comfort in her misery by thinking GREAT THOUGHTS OF CHRIST. The Master had talked about the children's bread: "Now," she argued, "since You are the Master of the table of grace, I know that You are a generous housekeeper, and there is sure to be abundance of bread on Your table; there will be such an abundance for the children that there will be crumbs to throw on the floor for the dogs, and the children will fare none the worse because the dogs are fed." She thought Him one who kept so good a table that all that she needed would only be a crumb in comparison; yet remember, what she wanted was to have the devil cast out of her daughter. It was a very great thing to her, but she had such a high esteem of Christ, that she said, "It is nothing to Him, it is but a crumb for Christ to give." This is the royal road to comfort. Great thoughts of your sin alone will drive you to despair; but great thoughts of Christ will pilot you into the haven of peace. "My sins are many, but oh! it is nothing to Jesus to take them all away. The weight of my guilt presses me down as a giant's foot would crush a worm, but it is no more than a grain of dust to Him, because He has already borne its curse in His own body on the tree. It will be but a small thing for Him to give me full remission, although it will be an infinite blessing for me to receive it." The woman opens her soul's mouth very wide, expecting great things of Jesus, and He fills it with His love. Dear reader, do the same. She confessed what Christ laid at her door, but she stayed closely by Him, and drew arguments even out of His hard words; she believed great things of Him, and she thus overcame Him. SHE WON THE VICTORY BY BELIEVING IN HIM. Her situation is an example of prevailing faith; and if we would conquer like her, we must imitate her tactics.

"The love of Christ . . . that surpasses knowledge."
— Ephesians 3:19

HE love of Christ in its sweetness, its fullness, its greatness, its faithfulness, passes all human comprehension. Where shall language be found which shall describe His matchless, His unparalleled love towards all human beings? It is so vast and boundless that, as the swallow just skims the water, and does not dive into its depths, so all descriptive words only touch the surface, while depths immeasurable lie beneath. Well might the poet say,

"O love, thou fathomless abyss!"

for this love of Christ is indeed measureless and fathomless; none can attain to it. Before we can have any accurate idea of the love of Jesus, we must understand His previous glory in its height of majesty, and His incarnation upon the earth in all its depths of shame. But who can tell us of the majesty of Christ? When He was enthroned in the highest heavens He was very God of very God; by Him were the heavens made, and all the hosts thereof. His own almighty arm upheld the spheres; the praises of cherubim and seraphim perpetually surrounded Him; the full chorus of the hallelujahs of the universe unceasingly flowed to the foot of His throne: He reigned supreme above all His creatures, God over all, blessed forever. Who can tell His height of glory then? And who, on the other hand, can tell how low He descended? To be a man was something, to be a Man of sorrows was far more; to bleed, and die, and concede, these were much for Him who was the Son of God; but to allow such unparalleled agony — to endure a death of shame and desertion by His Father, this is a depth of condescending love which the most inspired mind must utterly fail to fathom. Herein is love! and truly it is love that "surpasses knowledge." O let this love fill our hearts with adoring gratitude, and lead us to practical manifestations of its power.

"I will accept you as fragrant incense."
— *Ezekiel 20:41*

 HE merits of our great Redeemer are as sweet savor to the Most High. Whether we speak of the active or passive righteousness of Christ, there is an equal fragrance. There was a sweet savor in His active life by which He honored the law of God, and made every precept glitter like a precious jewel in the pure setting of His own person. Such, too, was His passive obedience when He endured with unmurmuring submission, hunger and thirst, cold and nakedness, and at length sweat great drops of blood in Gethsemane, gave His back to the smiters, and His cheeks to them that plucked out the hair, and was fastened to the cruel wood so that He might permit the wrath of God on our behalf. These two things are sweet before the Most High; and for the sake of His doing and His dying, His substitutionary sufferings and His vicarious obedience, the Lord our God accepts us. What a preciousness there must be in Him to overcome our lack of preciousness! What a sweet savor to put away our ill savor! What a purifying power in His blood to take away sin such as ours! and what glory in His righteousness to make such unacceptable creatures to be accepted in the Beloved! Note, believer, how sure and unchanging our acceptance must be, since it is *in Him!* Take care that you never doubt your acceptance in Jesus. You can't be accepted without Christ; but, when you have received His merit, you can't be unaccepted. Notwithstanding all your doubts, and fears, and sins, Jehovah's gracious eye never looks upon you in anger; though He sees sin in you, in yourself, yet when He looks at you through Christ, He sees no sin. You are always accepted in Christ, are always blessed and dear to the Father's heart. Therefore lift up a song, and as you see the smoking incense of the merit of the Savior coming up, this evening, before the sapphire throne, let the incense of your praise go up also.

*"Although he was a son, he learned obedience
from what he suffered."* — *Hebrews 5:8*

E are told that the Captain of our salvation
was made perfect through suffering, therefore we who are sinful, and who are far from
being perfect, must not wonder if we are
called to pass through suffering, too. Shall
the head be crowned with thorns, and shall
the other members of the body be rocked upon the dainty
lap of ease? Must Christ pass through seas of His own
blood to win the crown, and are we to walk to heaven with
dry feet, in silver slippers? No, our Master's experience
teaches us that suffering is necessary, and the trueborn
child of God must not, would not, escape it if he might.
But there is one very comforting thought in the fact of
Christ's "being made perfect through suffering" — it is,
that He can have complete sympathy with us. "For we do
not have a high priest who is unable to sympathize with
our weaknesses." In this sympathy of Christ we find a
sustaining power. One of the early martyrs said, "I can bear
it all, for Jesus suffered, and He suffers in me now; He
sympathizes with me, and this makes me strong." Believer,
lay hold of this thought in all times of agony. Let the
thought of Jesus strengthen you as you follow in His steps.
Find a sweet support in His sympathy; and remember that,
to concede is an honorable thing — to concede for Christ is
glory. The apostles rejoiced that they were counted worthy
to do this. Just as far as the Lord shall give us grace to
concede *for* Christ, to concede *with* Christ, just as far does
He honor us. The jewels of a Christian are his afflictions.
The regalia of the kings whom God has anointed are their
troubles, their sorrows, and their griefs. Let's not, therefore, shun being honored. Let's not turn aside from being
exalted. Griefs exalt us, and troubles lift us up. "If we
endure, we will also reign with Him."

"I called him but he did not answer."
— *Song of Songs 5:6*

RAYER sometimes lingers, like a petitioner at the gate, until the King comes forth to fill her bosom with the blessings which she seeks. The Lord, when He has given great faith, has been known to test it by lengthy delays. He has allowed His servants' voices to echo in their ears as from a brazen sky. They have knocked at the golden gate, but it has remained immovable, as though it were rusted upon its hinges. Like Jeremiah, they have cried, "You have covered Yourself with a cloud, so that no prayer can get through." Thus have true saints continued to wait patiently at length without reply, not because their prayers were not vehement, nor because they were unaccepted, but because it so pleased Him who is a Sovereign, and who gives according to His own pleasure. If it pleases Him to bid our patience exercise itself, shall He not do as He wills with His own! Beggars must not be choosers either as to time, place, or form. But we must be careful not to take delays in prayer for denials: God's past-due bills will be punctually honored; we must not allow Satan to shake our confidence in the God of truth by pointing to our unanswered prayers. Unanswered petitions are not unheard. God keeps a file for our prayers — they are not blown away by the wind, they are treasured in the King's archives. This is a registry in the court of heaven wherein every prayer is recorded. Tested believer, your Lord has a tear bottle in which the costly drops of sacred grief are put away, and a book in which your holy groanings are numbered. Before long, your suit shall prevail. Can't you be content to wait a little while? Won't your Lord's time be better than yours? Before long He will comfortably appear, to your soul's joy, and make you put away the sackcloth and ashes of lengthy waiting, and put on the scarlet and fine linen of full fruition.

"He . . . was numbered with the transgressors."
— *Isaiah 53:12*

HY did Jesus allow Himself to be enrolled among sinners? This wonderful condescension was justified by many powerful reasons. *In such a character He could the better become their advocate.* In some trials there is an identification of the advisor with the client, nor can they be looked upon in the eye of the law as apart from one another. Now, when the sinner is brought to the bar, Jesus appears there Himself. *He* stands to answer the accusation. He points to His side, His hands, His feet, and challenges Justice to bring anything against the sinners whom He represents; He pleads His blood, and pleads so triumphantly, being numbered with them and having a part with them, that the Judge proclaims, "Let them go their way; spare him from going down to the pit, for I have found a ransom for him." Our Lord Jesus was numbered with the transgressors in order that they might *feel their hearts drawn towards Him.* Who can be afraid of one who is written in the same list with us? Surely we may come boldly to Him, and confess our guilt. He who is numbered with us can't condemn us. Wasn't He put down in the transgressor's list *that we might be written in the red roll of the saints?* He was holy, and written among the holy; we were guilty, and numbered among the guilty; He transfers His name from yonder list to this dark indictment, and our names are taken from the indictment and written in the roll of acceptance, for there is a complete transfer made between Jesus and His people. Jesus has taken away our entire estate of misery and sin; and all that Jesus has, comes to us. His righteousness, His blood, and everything that He has He gives us as our dowry. Rejoice, believer, in your union to Him who was numbered among the transgressors; and prove that you are truly saved by being manifestly numbered with those who are new creatures in Him.

"Let us examine our ways and test them, and let us return to the LORD." — *Lamentations 3:40*

HE spouse who fondly loves her absent husband longs for his return; a long protracted separation from her lord is a semi-death to her spirit: and so with souls who love the Savior much, they *must* see His face, they can't bear that He should be away upon the mountains of Bether, and no more hold communion with them. A reproaching glance, an uplifted finger will be grievous to loving children, who fear to offend their tender father, and are only happy in his smile. Beloved, it was so once with you. A text of Scripture, a threatening, a touch of the rod of affliction, and you went to your Father's feet, crying, "Tell me the reason You contend with me?" Is it so now? Are you content to follow Jesus from a distance? Can you contemplate suspended communion with Christ without fear? Can you bear to have your Beloved walking contrary to you because you walk contrary to Him? Have your sins come between you and your God, and is your heart at rest? O let me affectionately warn you, for it is a grievous thing when we can live contentedly without the present enjoyment of the Savior's face. *Let us work to feel what an evil thing this is* — little love to our own dying Savior, little joy in our precious Jesus, little fellowship with the Beloved! Hold a true Lent in your souls, while you sorrow over your hardness of heart. Don't stop at sorrow! Remember where you first received salvation. *Go at once to the cross.* There, and there only, can you get your spirit aroused. No matter how hard, how insensible, how dead we may have become, let's go again in all the rags and poverty, and defilement of our natural condition. Let's clasp that cross, let's look into those languid eyes, let's bathe in that fountain filled with blood — this will bring us back to our first love; this will restore the simplicity of our faith, and the tenderness of our heart.

"By his wounds we are healed." — *Isaiah 53:5*

ILATE delivered our Lord to the Roman officials to be scourged. The Roman scourge was a most dreadful instrument of torture. It was made of the sinews of oxen, and sharp bones were intertwined every here and there among the sinews; so that every time the lash came down these pieces of bone inflicted fearful laceration, and tore off the flesh from the bone. The Savior was, no doubt, bound to the column, and beaten in the manner He had been beaten before; but this beating by the Roman lictors was probably the most severe of His flagellations. My soul, stand here and weep over His poor stricken body.

Believer in Jesus, can you gaze upon Him without tears, as He stands before you the mirror of agonizing love? He is at once fair as the lily for innocence, and red as the rose with the crimson of His own blood. As we feel the sure and blessed healing which His wounds have accomplished in us, doesn't our heart melt at once with love and grief? If ever we have loved our Lord Jesus, surely we must feel that affection glowing now within our hearts.

> "See how the patient Jesus stands,
> Insulted in His lowest case!
> Sinners have bound the Almighty's hands,
> And spit in their Creator's face.
>
> With thorns His temples gor'd and gash'd
> Send streams of blood from every part;
> His back's with knotted scourges lash'd.
> But sharper scourges tear His heart."

We would prefer to go to our rooms and weep; but since our business calls us away, we will first ask our Beloved to print the image of His bleeding self upon the tablets of our hearts all day long, and at nightfall we will return to commune with Him, and grieve that our sin should have cost Him so dearly.

"Rizpah daughter of Aiah took sackcloth and spread it out for herself on a rock. From the beginning of the harvest till the rain poured down from the heavens on the bodies, she did not let the birds of the air touch them by day or the wild animals by night." — 2 Samuel 21:10

IF the love of a woman toward her murdered sons could make her prolong her mournful vigil for so long a period, shall we tire of considering the sufferings of our blessed Lord? She drove away the birds of prey. Shouldn't we chase from our meditations those worldly and sinful thoughts which defile both our minds and the sacred themes upon which we are occupied? Away, you birds of evil wing! Leave the sacrifice alone! Unsheltered and alone, she bore the summer heat, the night dews, and the rains. Sleep was chased from her weeping eyes: her heart was too full for slumber. Notice how she loved her children! Shall Rizpah endure in this manner while we be startled by the first little inconvenience or trial? Are we such cowards that we can't bear to concede with our Lord? With unusual courage, she even chased wild beasts away. Will we be ready to encounter every foe for Jesus' sake? These her children were slain by other hands than hers, and yet she wept and watched: what should we who have by our sins crucified our Lord do? Our obligations are boundless, our love should be fervent and our repentance thorough. To watch with Jesus should be our business, to protect His honor our occupation, to stay by His cross our consolation. Those ghastly corpses might well have frightened Rizpah, especially at night, but in our Lord, whom we view as we sit at the foot of His cross, there is nothing revolting, but everything attractive. Never was living beauty so enchanting as a dying Savior. Jesus, we will watch with You yet awhile. Do graciously unveil Yourself to us; then we shall not sit beneath sackcloth, but in a royal pavilion.

"Let him kiss me with the kisses of his mouth."
— *Song of Songs 1:2*

 OR several days we have been focusing on the Savior's passion, and for a short time to come we shall continue to do so. In beginning a new month, let's seek the same desires for our Lord as those which glowed in the heart of the elect spouse. See how she leaps at once to *Him;* there are no prefatory words; she doesn't even mention His name; she is in the heart of her theme at once, for she speaks of *Him* who was the only Him in the world to her. How bold her love is! it was much condescension which allowed the weeping penitent to anoint His feet with spikenard — it was rich love which allowed the gentle Mary to sit at His feet and learn of Him — but here, love, strong, fervent love, aspires to higher tokens of regard and closer signs of fellowship. Esther trembled in the presence of Xerxes, but the spouse knows no fear in the joyful freedom of perfect love. If we have received the same free spirit, we also may ask the same. By kisses we suppose to be intended those varied manifestations of affection by which the believer is made to enjoy the love of Jesus. The kiss of *reconciliation* we enjoyed at our conversion, and it was sweet as honey dropping from the comb. The kiss of *acceptance* is still warm on our brow, as we know that He has accepted our persons and our works through rich grace. The kiss of daily, present *communion* is that which we long to have repeated day after day until it is changed into the kiss of *reception,* which removes the soul from earth, and the kiss of *consummation* which fills it with the joy of heaven. Faith is our walk, but fellowship sensibly felt is our rest. Faith is the road, but communion with Jesus is the well from which the pilgrim drinks. O lover of our souls, don't be a stranger to us; let the lips of your blessing meet the lips of our asking; let the lips of Your fullness touch the lips of our need, and straightway the kiss will be effected.

"It is time to seek the LORD." — *Hosea 10:12*

HIS month of April is said to derive its name from the Latin verb *aperio*, which signifies *to open* because all the buds and blossoms are now opening, and we have arrived at the gates of the flowery year. Reader, if you are yet unsaved, may your heart, in accord with the universal awakening of nature, be opened to receive the Lord. Every blossoming flower warns you that *it is time to seek the LORD;* don't be out of tune with nature, but let your heart bud and bloom with holy desires. Do you tell me that the warm blood of youth leaps in your veins? then, I entreat you, give your vigor to the Lord. It was my unspeakable happiness to be called in early youth, and I could praise the Lord every day for it. Salvation is priceless whenever it comes, but there is double value in an early salvation. Young men and women, since you may perish before you reach your prime, *"It is time to seek the LORD."* You who feel the first signs of decay, quicken your pace: that hollow cough and hectic flush are warnings which you must not ignore. Indeed, with you it is time to seek the Lord. Did I observe a little gray mingled with your once luxurious tresses? Years are stealing on in haste; death draws nearer with rapid marches. Let each return of spring rouse you to set your house in order. Dear reader, if you are now advanced in years, let me entreat and implore you to delay no longer. There is a day of grace for you now — be thankful for that, but it is a limited season and grows shorter with every passing second on the clock. Here in this silent chamber, on this first night of another month, I address you as best I can with these words; and from my inmost soul, as God's servant, I lay before you this warning, *"It is time to seek the LORD."* Do not neglect this work as it may be your last call from destruction, the final syllable from the lip of grace.

"Jesus made no reply, not even to a single charge."
— *Matthew 27:14*

 E had never been slow of speech when He could bless others, but He would not say a single word for Himself. "No one ever spoke the way this Man does," and no one was ever silent like Him. Was this singular silence *the index of His perfect self-sacrifice?* Did it show that He would not utter a word to stop the slaughter of His sacred person, which He had dedicated as an offering for us? Had He so entirely surrendered Himself that He would not interfere, even to the slightest degree, on His own behalf, but was bound and slain an unstruggling, uncomplaining victim? Was this silence *a type of the defenselessness against sin?* Nothing can be said to whitewash or excuse human guilt; therefore, He who bore its whole weight stood speechless before His judge. Isn't patient silence *the best reply to a contradictory world?* Calm endurance answers some questions infinitely more conclusively than the loftiest eloquence. The best apologists for Christianity in the early days were its martyrs. The anvil breaks a host of hammers by quietly bearing their blows. Didn't the silence of the Lamb of God furnish us with *a grand example of wisdom?* Where every word is an occasion for a new blasphemy, it was the line of duty to add fuel to the fire of sin. The ambiguous and the false, the unworthy and the mean, will before long over-throw and refute themselves; therefore the true can afford to be quiet, and finds silence to be its wisdom. Evidently our Lord, by His silence, furnished *a remarkable fulfillment of prophecy.* A long defense of Himself would have been con-trary to Isaiah's prediction. "He was led like a lamb to the slaughter, and as a sheep before her shearers is silent, so He did not open His mouth." By His quiet He conclusively proved Himself to be the true Lamb of God. As such we salute Him this morning. Be with us, Jesus, and in the silence of our heart, let us hear the voice of Your love.

> *"He will see his offspring and prolong his days, and
> the will of the LORD will prosper in his hand."*
> — *Isaiah 53:10*

PLEAD for the speedy fulfillment of this promise, all of you who love the Lord. It is easy work to pray concerning our needs when we are grounded and established upon God's own promise. How can He that gave the word refuse to keep it? Immutable truth cannot demean itself by a lie, and eternal faithfulness cannot degrade itself by neglect. God must bless His Son; His covenant binds Him to it. That which the Spirit prompts us to ask of Jesus is that which God decrees to give Him. Whenever you are praying for the kingdom of Christ, let your eyes behold the dawning of the blessed day, which draws near, when the Crucified shall receive His coronation in the place where men rejected Him. Courage, you that prayerfully work and toil for Christ with smallest of success. It shall not always be this way. Better times are before you. Your eyes can't see the blissful future: borrow the telescope of faith; wipe the misty breath of your doubts from the glass; look through it and behold the coming glory. Reader, let's ask, *do you* make this your constant prayer? Remember that the same Christ who tells us to say, "Give us each day our daily bread," had first given us this petition, "Hallowed be Your name, Your kingdom come, Your will be done on earth as it is in heaven." Don't let your prayers be just about your own sins, your own wants, your own imperfections, or your own trials. Rather, let them climb the starry ladder, and get up to Christ Himself; and then, as you approach the blood-sprinkled mercy seat, offer this prayer continually, "Lord, extend the kingdom of Your dear Son." Such a petition, fervently presented, will elevate the spirit of all your devotions. Take care to prove the sincerity of your prayer by laboring to promote the Lord's glory.

"The soldiers took charge of Jesus." — John 19:16

 E had been in agony all night; He had spent the early morning at the hall of Caiaphas; He had been hurried from Caiaphas to Pilate, from Pilate to Herod, and from Herod back again to Pilate. Therefore, He had little strength left, yet neither refreshment nor rest were permitted Him. They were eager for His blood, and therefore led Him out to die, burdened with the cross. O sorrowful procession! Well may Salem's daughters weep. My soul, weep also.

What do we learn here as we see our blessed Lord led forth? Don't we perceive that truth which was set forth in shadow by *the scapegoat?* Didn't the high priest bring the scapegoat, and put both his hands upon its head, confessing the sins of the people that, in so doing, those sins might be laid upon the goat, and cease from the people? Then the goat was led away by a fit man into the wilderness, and it carried away the sins of the people, so that if they were sought for they could not be found. Now we see Jesus brought before the priests and rulers, who pronounce Him guilty. God Himself imputes our sins *to Him,* "the LORD has laid on Him the iniquity of us all." "God made Him who had no sin to be sin for us;" and, as the substitute for our guilt, bearing our sin upon His shoulders, represented by the cross; we see the great Scapegoat led away by the appointed officers of justice. Beloved, can you feel assured that He carried *your* sin? As you look at the cross upon His shoulders, does it represent *your* sin? There is one way by which you can tell whether He carried your sin or not. Have you laid your hand upon His head, confessed your sin, and trusted in Him? Then your sin doesn't lie on you; it has all been transferred by blessed imputation to Christ, and He bears it on His shoulder as a load heavier than the cross.

Don't let the picture vanish until you have rejoiced in your own deliverance and adored the loving Redeemer upon whom your iniquities were laid.

"We all, like sheep, have gone astray, each of us has turned to his own way; and the LORD has laid on him the iniquity of us all." — Isaiah 53:6

ERE is a confession of sin *common* to all the elect people of God. They have all fallen, and thereforc, in common chorus, they all say, from the first who entered heaven to the last who shall enter there, "We all, like sheep, have gone astray." The confession, while thus unanimous, is also *special* and particular: "Each of us has turned to his own way." There is a peculiar sinfulness about each of us; all of us are sinful, but each of us has some special annoyance not found in the others. It is the mark of genuine repentance that while it naturally associates itself with other penitents, it also takes up a position of loneliness. "Each of us has turned to his own way" is a confession that each person had sinned against light peculiar to himself, or sinned with a vexation which he could not perceive in others. This confession is *unreserved;* there is not a word to detract from its force, nor a syllable by way of excuse. The confession is *a giving up of all pleas of self-righteousness.* It is the declaration of all human beings who are consciously guilty — guilty with vexations, guilty without excuse: they stand with their weapons of rebellion broken in pieces, and cry, "We all, like sheep, have gone astray, each of us has turned to his own way." Yet we hear no sorrowful wailings attending this confession of sin being that the next sentence makes it almost a song. "The LORD has laid on Him the iniquity of us all." It is the most grievous sentence of the three, but it overflows with comfort. It is strange that, where misery was concentrated, mercy reigned; where sorrow reached her climax, weary souls find rest. The Savior bruised is the healing of bruised hearts. See how the lowliest penitence gives place to assured confidence through simply gazing at Christ on the cross!

*"God made him who had no sin to be sin for us,
so that in him we might become the righteousness
of God." — 2 Corinthians 5:21*

 OURNING Christian! why do you weep? Are you mourning over your own corruptions? Look to your perfect Lord, and remember, you are complete in Him; you are in God's sight as perfect as if you had never sinned; no, more than that, the Lord our Righteousness has put a divine garment upon you, so that you have more than the righteousness of man — you have the righteousness of God. O you who are mourning by reason of inbred sin and depravity, remember, none of your sins can condemn you. You have learned to hate sin; but you have learned also to know that sin is not yours — it was laid upon Christ's head. Your standing is not in yourself — it is in Christ; your acceptance is not in yourself but in your Lord; you are as much accepted of God today, with all your sinfulness, as you will be when you stand before His throne, free from all corruption. O, I beg you, lay hold on this precious thought, *perfection in Christ!* For you are "complete in Him." With your Savior's garment on, you are holy as the Holy one. "Who is he that condemns? Christ Jesus, who died — more than that, who was raised to life — is at the right hand of God and is also interceding for us." Christian, let your heart rejoice, for you are "in the One He loved" — what do you have to fear? Let your face always wear a smile; live near your Master; live in the suburbs of the Celestial City; for soon, when your time has come, you shall rise up where your Jesus sits, and reign at His right hand; and all this because "God made Him who had no sin to be sin for us, so that in Him we might become the righteousness of God."

"Come, let us go up to the mountain of the LORD."
— *Isaiah 2:3*

T is exceedingly beneficial to our souls to rise above this present evil world to something nobler and better. The cares of this world and the deceitfulness of riches are apt to choke everything good within us, and we grow fretful, hopeless, perhaps proud and carnal. It is well for us to cut down these thorns and briers, for heavenly seed sown among them is not likely to yield a harvest; and where shall we find a better sickle with which to cut them down than communion with God and the things of the kingdom? In the valleys of Switzerland many of the inhabitants are deformed, and all wear a sickly appearance, for the atmosphere is charged with miasma, and is close and stagnant; but higher up, on the mountain, you find a hardy race, who breathe the clear fresh air as it blows from the virgin snows of the Alpine summits. It would be well if the dwellers in the valley could frequently leave their homes among the marshes and the fever mists, and inhale the bracing element upon the hills. It is to such an exploit of climbing that I invite you this evening. May the Spirit of God assist us to leave the mists of fear and the fevers of anxiety, and all the ills which gather in this valley of earth, and to ascend the mountains of anticipated joy and blessedness. May God the Holy Spirit cut the cords that keep us here below, and assist us to rise! Too often we sit like chained eagles fastened to the rock; only that, unlike the eagle, we begin to love our chain, and would, perhaps, if it came really to the test, be loath to have it snapped. May God now grant us grace, if we cannot escape from the chain of our flesh, yet to do so with our spirits; and, leaving the body, like a servant, at the foot of the hill, may our soul, like Abraham, arrive at the top of the mountain, there to indulge in communion with the Most High.

"They . . . put the cross on him and made him carry it behind Jesus." — Luke 23:26

E see in Simon's carrying the cross a picture of the work of the church throughout all generations; she is the cross bearer after Jesus. Note then, Christian, Jesus doesn't allow this to occur to the exclusion of your suffering. He bears a cross, not that you may escape it, but that you may endure it. Christ exempts you from sin, but not from sorrow. Remember that, and expect to acknowledge it.

But let's comfort ourselves with this thought, that in our case, as in Simon's, *it is not our cross, but Christ's cross which we carry.* When you are troubled for being pious; when you are cruelly mocked for your religion, then remember it is not *your* cross, it is *Christ's* cross; and how delightful is it to carry the cross of our Lord Jesus!

You carry the cross after Him. You have blessed company; your path is marked with the footprints of your Lord. The mark of His blood-red shoulder is upon that heavy burden. 'Tis *His* cross, and He goes before you as a shepherd goes before his sheep. Take up your cross daily, and follow Him.

Don't forget, also, *that you bear this cross in partnership.* It is the opinion of some that Simon only carried one end of the cross, and not the whole of it. That is very possible; Christ may have carried the heavier part, against the transverse beam, and Simon may have borne the lighter end. Certainly it is so with you; you only have to carry the light end of the cross, Christ bore the heavier end.

And remember, *though Simon had to bear the cross for just a little while, it gave him lasting honor.* Even so, the cross we carry is only for a little while at most, and then we shall receive the crown, the glory. Surely we should love the cross, and, instead of shrinking from it, *count it very dear,* when it works out for us "an eternal glory that far outweighs them all."

"Humility comes before honor." — *Proverbs 15:33*

UMILIATION of soul always *brings a positive blessing with it.* If we empty our hearts of self God will fill them with His love. He who desires close communion with Christ should remember the word of the Lord, "This is the one I esteem: he who is humble and contrite in spirit, and trembles at my word." Stoop if you would climb to heaven. Do we not say of Jesus, "He who descended is the very one who ascended"? So must you. You must grow downwards, that you may grow upwards; for the sweetest fellowship with heaven is to be had by humble souls, and by them alone. God will deny no blessing to a thoroughly humbled spirit. "Blessed are the poor in spirit, for theirs is the kingdom of heaven," with all its riches and treasures. All of God's resources shall be given over by deed of gift to the soul which is humble enough to be able to receive them without growing proud because of it. God blesses us all up to the full measure and extremity of what it is safe for Him to do. If you do not get a blessing, it is because it is not safe for you to have one. If our heavenly Father were to let your unhumbled spirit win a victory in His holy war, you would pilfer the crown for yourself, and meeting with a fresh enemy you would fall a victim; it is for your own safety that you are kept low. When a man is sincerely humble, and never ventures to touch so much as a grain of the praise, there is scarcely any limit to what God will do for him. Humility makes us ready to be blessed by the God of all grace, and fits us to deal efficiently with one another. True humility is a flower which will adorn any garden. This is a sauce with which you may season every dish of life, and you will find an improvement in every case. Whether it be prayer or praise, whether it be work or suffering, the genuine salt of humility cannot be used in excess.

"Let us, then, go to him outside the camp."
— *Hebrews 13:13*

ESUS, bearing His cross, went forth to suffer outside the gate. The Christian's reason for leaving the camp of the world's sin and religion is not because he loves to be distinct, but because *Jesus did so;* and the disciple must follow his Master. Christ was "not of the world:" His life and His testimony were a constant protest against conformity with the world. Never was such overflowing affection for humankind as you find in Him; but still He was separate from sinners. In like manner Christ's people must "go to Him." They must take their positions "outside the camp," as witness bearers for the truth. They must be prepared to tread the straight and narrow path. They must have bold, unflinching, lion-like hearts, loving Christ first, and His truth next, and Christ and His truth beyond all the world. Jesus would have His people "go outside the camp" *for their own sanctification.* You cannot grow in grace to any high degree while you are conformed to the world. The life of separation may be a path of sorrow, but it is the highway of safety; and though the separated life may cost you many pangs, and make every day a battle, yet it is a happy life after all. No joy can excel that of the soldier of Christ: Jesus reveals Himself so graciously, and gives such sweet refreshment, that the warrior feels more calm and peace in his daily strife than others in their hours of rest. The highway of holiness is the highway of communion. It this way we shall hope *to win the crown,* if we are enabled by divine grace faithfully to follow Christ "outside the camp." The crown of glory will follow the cross of separation. A moment's shame will be well recompensed by eternal honor; a little while of bearing witness will seem nothing when we are "forever with the Lord."

"In the name of the LORD I cut them off."
— Psalm 118:12

UR Lord Jesus, by His death, didn't purchase a right to only a *part* of us, but to the *entire* person. In His passion, He contemplated our sanctification in its entirety, spirit, soul, and body, so that, in this triple kingdom, He Himself might reign supreme without a rival. It is the business of the newborn nature which God has given to the regenerate to assert the rights of the Lord Jesus Christ. My soul, inasmuch as you are a child of God, you must conquer all the rest of yourself which yet remains unblessed; you must subdue all your powers and passions to the silver scepter of Jesus' gracious reign, and you must never be satisfied until He who is King by purchase becomes also King by gracious coronation, and reigns in you supreme. Seeing, then, that sin has no right to any part of us, we go about a good and lawful warfare when we seek, in the name of God, to drive it out. O my body, you are a member of Christ: shall I tolerate your subjection to the prince of darkness? O my soul, Christ has suffered for your sins, and redeemed you with His most precious blood: shall I allow your memory to become a storehouse of evil, or your passions to be firebrands of iniquity? Shall I surrender my judgment to be perverted by error, or my will to be led in fetters of iniquity? No, my soul, you are Christ's, and sin has no right to you.

Be courageous concerning this, O Christian! don't be dispirited, as though your spiritual enemies could never be destroyed. You are able to overcome them — not in your own strength — the weakest of them would be too much for you in that; but you can and shall overcome them through the blood of the Lamb. Don't ask, "How shall I dispossess them, for they are greater and mightier than I?" but go to the strong for strength, wait humbly upon God, and the mighty God of Jacob will surely come to the rescue, and you shall sing of victory through His grace.

"How long, O men, will you turn my glory into shame?"
— *Psalm 4:2*

N instructive writer has made a mournful list of the honors which the blinded people of Israel awarded to their long-expected King. (1.) They gave Him *a procession of honor,* in which Roman legionaries, Jewish priests, men and women took part, He Himself bearing His cross. This is the triumph which the world awards to Him who comes to overthrow our direst foes. Derisive shouts are His only acclamations, and cruel taunts His only hymns of praise. (2.) They presented Him with *the wine of honor.* Instead of a golden cup of generous wine they offered Him the criminal's stupefying death draught, which He refused because He would preserve an uninjured taste with which to taste of death; and afterwards when He cried, "I am thirsty," they gave Him vinegar mixed with gall, thrust to His mouth upon a sponge. Oh! wretched, detestable inhospitality to the King's Son. (3.) He was provided with *a guard of honor,* who showed their esteem of Him by gambling over His garments, which they had seized as their booty. Such was the bodyguard of the adored of heaven; a quaternion of brutal gamblers. (4.) *A throne of honor* was found for Him upon the bloody tree; no easier place of rest would rebel men yield to their liege Lord. The cross was, in fact, the full expression of the world's feeling towards Him; "There," they seemed to say, "Son of God, this is the manner in which God Himself should be treated, if we could reach Him." (5.) *The title of honor* was nominally "King of the Jews," but that the blinded nation distinctly repudiated, and really called Him "King of thieves," by preferring Barabbas, and by placing Jesus in the place of highest shame between two thieves. His glory was thus in all things turned into shame by humanity, but it shall yet gladden the eyes of saints and angels, world without end.

*"Save me from bloodguilt, O God, the God who
saves me, and my tongue will sing of your
righteousness." — Psalm 51:14*

 N this SOLEMN CONFESSION, it is pleasing to observe that David plainly names his sin. He doesn't call it manslaughter, nor speak of it as an imprudence by which an unfortunate accident occurred to a worthy man, but he calls it by its true name, blood-guiltiness. He didn't actually kill the husband of Bathsheba; but still it was planned in David's heart that Uriah should be slain, and he was before the Lord his murderer. Learn in confession to be honest with God. Do not give fair names to foul sins; call them what you will, they will smell no sweeter. What God sees them to be is what you must work at feeling them to be; and with all openness of heart acknowledge their real character. Observe, that David was evidently oppressed with the heinousness of his sin. It is easy to use words, but it is difficult to feel their meaning. The fifty-first Psalm is the photograph of a contrite spirit. Let's seek after the same brokenness of heart; for, however excellent our words may be, if our heart is not conscious of the hell-deservingness of sin, we cannot expect to find forgiveness.

Our text has in it AN EARNEST PRAYER— it is addressed to the God of *salvation*. It is His prerogative to forgive; it is His very name and office to save those who seek His face. Better still, the text calls Him the God who saves *me*. Yes, blessed be His name, while I am yet going to Him through Jesus' blood, I can rejoice in the God who saves *me*.

The psalmist ends with A COMMENDABLE VOW: if God will deliver him he will *sing* — no, more, he will "sing *aloud*." Who can sing of such a mercy as this in any other way! But note the subject of the song — "YOUR RIGHTEOUSNESS." We must sing of the finished work of a precious Savior; and he who knows most of forgiving love will sing the loudest.

"For if men do these things when the tree is green,
what will happen when it is dry?" — Luke 23:31

MONG other interpretations of this suggestive question, the following is full of teaching: "If I, the innocent substitute for sinners, allow thus, what will be done when the
sinner himself — the dry tree — shall fall
into the hands of an angry God?" When God
saw Jesus in the sinner's place, He didn't spare Him; and
when He finds the unregenerate without Christ, He will
not spare them. O sinner, Jesus was led away by His
enemies: so shall you be dragged away by fiends to the
place appointed for you. Jesus was deserted of God; and if
He, who was only imputedly a sinner, was deserted, how
much more shall you be? *"Eloi, Eloi, lama sabachthani?"*
what an awful shriek! But what shall be your cry when you
shall say, "My God! my God! why have You forsaken me?"
and the answer shall come back, "Since you ignored all My
advice and would not accept My rebuke, I in turn will
laugh at your disaster; I will mock when calamity overtakes you." If God spared not His own Son, how much less
will He spare you! What whips of burning wire will be
yours when conscience shall strike you with all its terrors.
You richest, you merriest, you most self-righteous sinners
— who would stand in your place when God shall say,
"Awake, O sword, against the man that rejected Me; strike
him, and let him feel the smart forever"? Jesus was spit
upon: sinner, what shame will be yours! We cannot sum up
in one word all the mass of sorrows which met upon the
head of Jesus who died for us, therefore it is impossible for
us to tell you what streams, what oceans of grief must roll
over *your* spirit if you die as you now are. You may die so,
you may die now. By the agonies of Christ, by His wounds
and by His blood, do not bring upon yourselves the wrath
to come! Trust in the Son of God, and you shall never die.

"I will fear no evil, for you are with me."
— Psalm 23:4

 EHOLD, how independent of outward circumstances the Holy Spirit can make the Christian! What a bright light may shine within us when it is all dark without! How firm, how happy, how calm, how peaceful we may be, when the world shakes to and fro, and the pillars of the earth are removed! Even death itself, with all its terrible influences, has no power to suspend the music of a Christian's heart, but rather makes that music become more sweet, more clear, more heavenly, until the last kind act which death can do is to let the earthly strain melt into the heavenly chorus, the temporal joy into the eternal bliss! Let's have confidence, then, in the blessed Spirit's power to comfort us. Dear reader, are you looking forward to poverty? Don't be afraid; in your want, the divine Spirit can give you a greater plenty than the rich have in their abundance. You don't know what joys may be stored up for you in the cottage around which grace will plant the roses of content. Are you conscious of a growing failure of your bodily powers? Do you expect to suffer long nights of languishing and days of pain? O don't be sad! That bed may become a throne to you. Little do you know how every pang that shoots through your body may be a refining fire to consume your dross — a beam of glory to light up the secret parts of your soul. Are the eyes growing dim? Jesus will be your light. Do the ears fail you? Jesus' name will be your soul's best music, and His person your dear delight. Socrates used to say, "Philosophers can be happy without music;" and Christians can be happier than philosophers when all outward causes of rejoicing are withdrawn. In You, my God, my heart shall triumph, come what may of ills without! By your power, O blessed Spirit, my heart shall be exceedingly happy, although all things should fail me here below.

"A large number of people followed him, including women who mourned and wailed for him." — Luke 23:27

MID the rabble rousers who hounded the Redeemer to His doom, there were some gracious souls whose bitter anguish sought vent in mourning and wailing — fit music to accompany that march of woe. When my soul can, in imagination, see the Savior bearing His cross to Calvary, she joins the godly women and weeps with them; for, indeed, there is true cause for grief — cause lying deeper than those mourning women thought. They bewailed innocence maltreated, goodness persecuted, love bleeding, meekness about to die; but my heart has a deeper and more bitter cause to mourn. My sins were the scourges which lacerated those blessed shoulders, and crowned with thorn those bleeding brows: my sins cried "Crucify Him! crucify Him!" and laid the cross upon His gracious shoulders. His being led forth to die is sorrow enough for one eternity: but my having been His murderer, is more, infinitely more, grief than one poor fountain of tears can express.

It wasn't hard to guess why those women loved and wept, but they couldn't have had greater reasons for love and grief than my heart has. Nain's widow saw her son restored — but I myself have been raised to newness of life. Peter's mother-in-law was cured of the fever — but I of the greater plague of sin. Out of Magdalene seven devils were cast — but a whole legion out of me. Mary and Martha were favored with visits — but He dwells with me. His mother bore His body — but He is formed in me the hope of glory. As I am no less behind these holy women in debt, neither shall I wish to be behind them in gratitude or sorrow.

> "Love and grief my heart dividing,
> With my tears His feet I'll lave —
> Constant still in heart abiding,
> Weep for Him who died to save."

"You stoop down to make me great." — *Psalm 18:35*

HE words are capable of being translated, "Your *goodness* has made me great." David gratefully ascribed all his greatness not to his own goodness, but to the goodness of God. "Your *providence*" is another reading; and providence is nothing more than goodness in action. Goodness is the bud of which providence is the flower, or goodness is the seed of which providence is the harvest. Some render it, "Your *help*," which is just another word for providence; providence being the firm ally of the saints, aiding them in the service of their Lord. Or again, "Your *humility* has made me great." "Your *condescension*" may, perhaps, serve as a comprehensive reading, combining the ideas mentioned, including that of *humility*. It is God's making Himself little which is the cause of our being made great. We are so little, that if God should manifest His greatness without condescension, we should be trampled under His feet; but God, who must stoop to view the skies, and bow to see what angels do, turns His eye yet lower, and looks to the lowly and contrite, and makes them great. There are still other readings, such as the Septuagint, which reads, "Your *discipline*" — Your fatherly correction — "has made me great;" while the Chaldee paraphrase reads, "Your *word* has increased me." The idea remains the same. David ascribes all his own greatness to the condescending goodness of his Father in heaven. May this sentiment be echoed in our hearts this evening while we cast our crowns at Jesus' feet, and cry, "You stoop down to make me great." How marvelous our experience of God's gentleness has been! How gentle His corrections have been! How gentle His forbearance! How gentle His teachings! How gentle His drawings! Meditate upon this theme, O believer. Let gratitude be awakened; let humility be deepened; let love be awakened before you fall asleep tonight.

"The place called the Skull." — Luke 23:33

HE hill of comfort is the hill of Calvary; the house of consolation is built with the wood of the cross; the temple of heavenly blessing is founded upon the riven rock — riven by the spear which pierced His side. No scene in sacred history ever gladdens the soul like Calvary's tragedy.

> "Is it not strange, the darkest hour
> That ever dawned on sinful earth,
> Should touch the heart with softer power,
> For comfort, than an angel's mirth?
> That to the Cross the mourner's eye should turn,
> Sooner than where the stars of Bethlehem burn?"

Light springs from the midday-midnight of Golgotha, the place called the Skull, and every herb of the field blooms sweetly beneath the shadow of the once-accursed tree. In that place of thirst, grace has dug a fountain which ever gushes with waters pure as crystal, each drop capable of alleviating the woes of humankind. You who have had your seasons of conflict will confess that it was not at Olivet that you ever found comfort, not on the hill of Sinai, nor on Tabor; but Gethsemane, Gabbatha, and Golgotha have been a means of comfort to you. The bitter herbs of Gethsemane have often taken away the bitters of your life; the scourge of Gabbatha, which is Aramaic for Stone Pavement, has often scourged away your cares, and the groans of Calvary yield us comfort rare and rich. We never should have known Christ's love in all its heights and depths if He had not died; nor could we guess the Father's deep affection if He had not given His Son to die. The common mercies we enjoy all sing of love, just as the seashell, when we put it to our ears, whispers of the deep sea whence it came; but if we desire to hear the ocean itself, we must not look at everyday blessings, but at the transactions of the crucifixion. Those who would know love, go to Calvary and see the Man of sorrows die.

"Last night an angel of the God whose I am and whom I serve stood beside me." — Acts 27:23

 EMPEST and long darkness, coupled with imminent risk of shipwreck, had brought the crew of the vessel into a sad situation; only one man among them remained perfectly calm, and by his word the rest were reassured. Paul was the only man who had heart enough to say, "Keep up your courage, men." There were veteran Roman legionaries on board, and brave old mariners, and yet their poor Jewish prisoner had more spirit than they had. He had a secret Friend who kept his courage up. The Lord Jesus dispatched a heavenly messenger to whisper words of consolation in the ear of His faithful servant, therefore he wore a shining countenance and spoke like a man at ease.

If we fear the Lord, we may look for timely interventions when our case is at its worst. Angels are not kept from us by storms, or hindered by darkness. Seraphs think it no humiliation to visit the poorest of the heavenly family. If angel's visits are few and far between at ordinary times, they shall be frequent in our nights of tempest and tossing. Friends may drop away from us when we are under pressure, but our communication with the inhabitants of the angelic world shall be more abundant; and in the strength of words of love, brought to us from the throne by the way of Jacob's ladder, we shall be strong to do heroic deeds. Dear reader, is this an hour of distress with you? then ask for peculiar help. Jesus is the angel of the covenant, and if His presence is earnestly sought now, it will not be denied. What that presence brings in heart-cheer those remember who, like Paul, have had the angel of God standing by them in a night of storm, when anchors would no longer hold, and rocks were nigh.

"O angel of my God, be near,
Amid the darkness hush my fear;
Loud roars the wild tempestuous sea,
Thy presence, Lord, shall comfort me."

*"I am poured out like water, and all my bones
are out of joint."* — Psalm 22:14

ID earth or heaven ever behold a sadder spectacle of woe! In soul and body, our Lord felt Himself to be weak as water poured upon the ground. The placing of the cross in its socket had shaken Him with great violence, had strained all the ligaments, pained every nerve, and more or less dislocated all His bones. Burdened with His own weight, the august sufferer felt the strain increasing every moment of those six long hours. His sense of faintness and His general weakness were overpowering; while to His own consciousness He became nothing but a mass of misery and swooning sickness. When Daniel saw the great vision, he thus describes his sensations, "I had no strength left, my face turned deathly pale and I was helpless;" how much more faint must have been our greater Prophet when He saw the dread vision of the wrath of God, and felt it in His own soul! To us, sensations such as our Lord endured would have been insupportable, and kind unconsciousness would have come to our rescue; but in His case, He was wounded, and *felt* the sword; He drained the cup and *tasted* every drop.

> "O King of Grief! (a title strange, yet true
> To Thee of all kings only due)
> O King of Wounds! how shall I grieve for Thee,
> Who in all grief preventest me!"

As we kneel before our now ascended Savior's throne, let's remember well the way by which He prepared it as a throne of grace for us; let's in spirit drink of His cup, that we may be strengthened for our hour of heaviness whenever it may come. In His natural body every member suffered, and so it must be in the spiritual; but as out of all His griefs and woes His body came forth uninjured to glory and power, even so shall His mystical body come through the furnace with not so much as the smell of fire upon it.

*"Look upon my affliction and my distress and take
away all my sins."* — *Psalm 25:18*

T is well for us when prayers about our
sorrows are linked with pleas concerning our
sins — when, being under God's hand, we
are not wholly taken up with our pain, but
remember our offenses against God. It is
well, also, to take both sorrow and sin to the
same place. It was to God that David carried his sorrow: it
was to God that David confessed his sin. Observe, then, *we
must take our sorrows to God.* Even your little sorrows you
may roll upon God, for He counts the hairs of your head;
and your great sorrows you may commit to Him, for He
holds the ocean in the hollow of His hand. Go to Him,
whatever your present trouble may be, and you shall find
Him able and willing to relieve you. *But we must take our
sins to God, too.* We must carry them to the cross, that the
blood may fall upon them, to purge away their guilt, and to
destroy their defiling power.

The special lesson of the text is this: — that *we are to go
to the Lord with sorrows and with sins in the right spirit.* Note
that all David asks concerning his sorrow is, *"Look upon
my affliction and my distress;"* but the next petition is
vastly more express, definite, decided, plain — *"Take away
all my sins."* Many sufferers would have put it, "Remove
my affliction and my pain, and look at my sins." But David
doesn't say it this way; he cries, "Lord, as for my affliction
and my distress, I will not dictate to Your wisdom. Lord,
look at them, I will leave them to You, I should delight to
have my pain removed, but do as You will; but as for my
sins, Lord, I know what I want with them; I must have
them forgiven; I cannot endure to lie under their curse for
a moment." A Christian counts sorrow lighter in the scale
than sin; he can bear that his troubles should continue, but
he cannot support the burden of his transgressions.

"My heart has turned to wax; it has melted away
within me." — Psalm 22:14

UR blessed Lord experienced a terrible sinking and melting of soul. "A man's spirit sustains him in sickness, but a crushed spirit who can bear?" Deep depression of spirit is the most grievous of all trials; nothing compares with it. Well might the suffering Savior cry to His God, "Do not be far from me," for above all other seasons a man needs his God when his heart is melted within him because of heaviness. Believer, come near the cross this morning, and humbly adore the King of glory as having once been brought far lower, in mental distress and inward anguish, than any one among us; and note His fitness to become a faithful High Priest, who can be touched with a feeling of our infirmities. Especially let those of us whose sadness springs directly from the withdrawal of a present sense of our Father's love, enter into near and intimate communion with Jesus. Let's not give way to despair, since through this dark room the Master has passed before us. Our souls may sometimes long and faint, and thirst even to anguish, to behold the light of the Lord's countenance: at such times let's stay ourselves with the sweet fact of the sympathy of our great High Priest. Our drops of sorrow may well be forgotten in the ocean of His griefs; but how high ought our love to rise! Come in, O strong and deep love of Jesus, like the sea at the flood in spring tides, cover all my powers, drown all my sins, wash out all my cares, lift up my earthbound soul, and float it right up to my Lord's feet, and there let me lie, a poor broken shell, washed up by His love, having no virtue or value; and only venturing to whisper to Him that if He will put His ear to me, He will hear within my heart faint echoes of the vast waves of His own love which have brought me where it is my delight to lie, even at His feet forever.

"The King's Garden." — Nehemiah 3:15

ENTION of the King's Garden by Nehemiah brings to mind the *paradise* which the King of kings prepared for Adam. Sin has utterly ruined that fair abode of all delights, and driven forth humankind to till the ground, which yields thorns and briers to them. My soul, remember the fall, for it was *your* fall. Weep often because the Lord of love was so shamefully ill-treated by the head of the human race, of which you are a member, as undeserving as any. Behold how dragons and demons dwell on this fair earth, which once was a garden of delights.

See yonder another King's garden, which the King waters with His bloody sweat — *Gethsemane*, whose bitter herbs are sweeter far to renewed souls than even Eden's luscious fruits. There the mischief of the serpent in the first garden was undone: there the curse was lifted from earth, and borne by the woman's promised seed. My soul, frequently reflect on the agony and the passion; resort to the garden of the olive press, and view your great Redeemer rescuing you from your lost estate. This is the garden of gardens indeed, wherein the soul may see the guilt of sin and the power of love, two sights which surpass all others.

Is there no other King's garden? Yes, *my heart*, you are, or should be such. How do the flowers flourish? Do any choice fruits appear? Does the King walk within, and rest in the bowers of my spirit? Let me see that the plants are trimmed and watered, and the mischievous foxes hunted out. Come, Lord, and let the heavenly wind blow at your coming, that the spices of your garden may flow abroad. Nor must I forget the King's garden of *the church*. O Lord, send prosperity to it. Rebuild her walls, nourish her plants, ripen her fruits, and from the huge wilderness, reclaim the barren waste, and make thereof "a King's Garden."

"My lover is to me a sachet of myrrh."
— *Song of Songs 1:13*

YRRH may well be chosen as the type of Jesus on account of its *preciousness*, its *perfume*, its *pleasantness*, its *healing, preserving, disinfecting qualities, and its connection with sacrifice*. But why is He compared to "a *sachet of myrrh*"? First, for *plenty*. He is not a drop of it, He is a casket full. He is not a sprig or flower of it, but a whole sachet. There is enough in Christ for all my necessities; let me not be slow to avail myself of Him. Our well-beloved is compared to a "sachet" again, for *variety:* for there is in Christ not only the one thing needful, but in "Christ all the fullness of the Deity lives in bodily form," everything needful is in Him. Take Jesus in His different characters, and you will see a marvelous variety — Prophet, Priest, King, Husband, Friend, Shepherd. Consider Him in His life, death, resurrection, ascension, second advent; view Him in His virtue, gentleness, courage, self-denial, love, faithfulness, truth, righteousness — everywhere He is a sachet of preciousness. He is a "sachet of myrrh" for *preservation* — not loose myrrh tied up, myrrh to be stored in a casket. We must value Him as our best treasure; we must prize His words and His ordinances; and we must keep our thoughts of Him and knowledge of Him as under lock and key, lest the devil should steal anything from us. Moreover, Jesus is a "sachet of myrrh" *for speciality.* The emblem suggests the idea of distinguishing, discriminating grace. From before the foundation of the world, He was set apart for His people; and He gives forth His perfume only to those who understand how to enter into communion with Him, to have close dealings with Him. Oh! blessed people whom the Lord has admitted into His secrets, and for whom He sets Himself apart. Oh! choice and happy who are thus made to say, "My lover is to me a sachet of myrrh."

---

*"He is to lay his hand on the head of the burnt
offering, and it will be accepted on his behalf to
make atonement for him." — Leviticus 1:4*

 UR Lord's being made "sin for us" is set forth here by the very significant transfer of sin to the bull, which was made by the elders of the people. The laying of the hand wasn't a mere touch of contact, for in some other places of Scripture the original word has the meaning of leaning heavily, as in the expression, "Your wrath lies heavily upon me" (Psalm 88:7). Surely this is the very essence and nature of faith, which doesn't only bring us into contact with the great Substitute, but teaches us to lean upon Him with all the burden of our guilt. Jehovah made to meet upon the head of the Substitute all the offenses of His covenant people, but each one of the chosen is brought personally to ratify this solemn covenant act, when by grace he is enabled by faith to lay his hand upon the head of the "Lamb that was slain from the creation of the world." Believer, do you remember that rapturous day when you first realized pardon through Jesus the sin-bearer? Can't you confess gladly, and join with the writer in saying, "My soul recalls her day of deliverance with delight. Laden with guilt and full of fears, I saw my Savior as my Substitute, and I laid my hand upon Him; oh! how timidly at first, but courage grew and confidence was confirmed until I leaned my soul entirely upon Him; and now it is my unceasing joy to know that my sins are no longer imputed to me, but laid on Him, and like the debts of the wounded traveler, Jesus, like the good Samaritan, has said of all my future sinfulness, 'Put that on My account.' " Blessed discovery! Eternal solace of a grateful heart!

> "My numerous sins transferr'd to Him,
> Shall never more be found,
> Lost in His blood's atoning stream,
> Where every crime is drown'd!"

"All who see me mock me; they hurl insults,
shaking their heads." — Psalm 22:7

 OCKERY was a great ingredient in our Lord's woe. Judas mocked Him in the garden; the chief priests and scribes laughed Him to scorn; Herod considered Him to be of no value; the servants and the soldiers jeered at Him, and brutally insulted Him; Pilate and his guards ridiculed His royalty; and on the tree all sorts of horrid jests and hideous taunts were hurled at Him. Ridicule is always hard to bear, but when we are in intense pain it is so heartless, so cruel, that it cuts us to the quick. Imagine the Savior crucified, racked with anguish far beyond all mortal guess, and then picture that motley crowd, all wagging their heads or thrusting out the lip in bitterest contempt of one poor suffering victim! Surely there must have been something more in the crucified One than they could see, or else such a great and mingled crowd would not unanimously have honored Him with such contempt. Was it not evil confessing, in the very moment of its greatest apparent triumph, that after all it could do no more than mock at that victorious goodness which was then reigning on the cross? O Jesus, "despised and rejected by men," how could You die for men who treated You so badly? Herein is love amazing, love divine, yes, love beyond degree. We, too, have despised You in the days of our unregeneracy, and even since our new birth we have set the world on high in our hearts, and yet You bleed to heal our wounds, and die to give us life. O that we could set You on a glorious high throne in all men's hearts! We would ring out Your praises over land and sea until humankind should as universally adore as once they did unanimously reject.

> Thy creatures wrong Thee, O Thou sovereign Good!
> *Thou art not loved, because not understood:*
> This grieves me most, that vain pursuits beguile
> Ungrateful men, regardless of Thy smile.

"Tell the righteous it will be well with them."
— *Isaiah 3:10*

 T *is* ALWAYS *well with the righteous*. If it had said, "Tell the righteous it is well with them in their prosperity," we would be thankful for such a great boon, for prosperity is an hour of peril, and it is a gift from heaven to be secured from its snares; or if it had been written, "It will be well with them when under persecution," we would be thankful for so sustaining an assurance, for persecution is hard to bear; but when no time is mentioned, all time is included. God's "shalls" must be understood always in their largest sense. From the beginning of the year to the end of the year, from the first gathering of evening shadows until the daystar shines, in all conditions and under all circumstances, it will be well with the righteous. It is so well with him that we could not imagine it to be better, for he is *well fed*, he feeds upon the flesh and blood of Jesus; he is *well clothed*, he wears the imputed righteousness of Christ; he is *well housed*, he dwells in God; he is *well married*, his soul is knit in bonds of marriage union to Christ; he is *well provided for*, for the Lord is his Shepherd; he is well endowed, for heaven is his inheritance. It is well with the righteous — *well upon divine authority;* the mouth of God speaks the comforting assurance. O beloved, if God declares that all is well, ten thousand devils may declare it to be ill, but we laugh them all to scorn. Blessed be God for a faith which enables us to believe God when the creatures contradict Him. "Tell the righteous," says the Word, "it will be well with them"; then, beloved, if you can't see it, let God's word stand in place of your sight; yes, believe it on divine authority more confidently than if your eyes and your feelings told it to you. Whom God blesses is blessed indeed, and what His lip declares is truth most sure and steadfast.

"My God, my God, why have you forsaken me?"
— Psalm 22:1

ERE we behold the Savior in the depth of His sorrows. No other place illustrates so well the griefs of Christ as Calvary, and no other moment at Calvary is so full of agony as that in which His cry rends the air — "My God, my God, why have You forsaken me?" At this moment physical weakness was united with acute mental torture from the shame and ignominy through which He had to pass; and to make His grief culminate with emphasis, He suffered spiritual agony surpassing all expression, resulting from the departure of His Father's presence. This was the black midnight of His horror; then it was that He descended the abyss of suffering. No one can enter into the full meaning of these words. Some of us think at times that *we* could cry, "My God, my God, why have You forsaken me?" There are seasons when the brightness of our Father's smile is eclipsed by clouds and darkness; but let's remember that God never does really forsake us. It is only a seeming forsaking with us, but in Christ's case it was a real forsaking. We grieve at a little withdrawal of our Father's love; but the real turning away of God's face from His Son, who shall calculate how deep the agony which it caused Him?

In our case, our cry is often dictated by unbelief: in His case, it was the utterance of a dreadful fact, for God had really turned away from Him for a season. O you poor, distressed soul, who once lived in the sunshine of God's face, but are now in darkness, remember that He has not really forsaken you. God in the clouds is as much our God as when He shines forth in all the luster of His grace; but since even the *thought* that He has forsaken us gives us agony, what must the woe of the Savior have been when He exclaimed, "My God, my God, why have You forsaken me?"

"Carry them forever." — *Psalm 28:9*

OD'S *people need* to be carried forever. They are very heavy by nature. They have no wings, or if they do, they are like the dove of old which lay among the pots; and they need divine grace to make them mount on wings covered with silver, and with feathers of yellow gold. By nature, sparks fly upward, but the sinful souls of humankind fall downward. O Lord, "carry them forever!" David himself said, "To You, O God, I lift up my soul," and he here feels the necessity that other souls should be lifted up as well as his own. When you ask this blessing for yourself, don't forget to seek it for others also. There are three ways in which God's people require to be carried. *They need to be carried in character.* Lift them up, O Lord; do not allow your people to be like the world's people! The world lies in the wicked one; carry them out of it! The world's people are looking after silver and gold, seeking their own pleasures, and the gratification of their lusts; but, Lord, carry your people above all this; keep them from being "muck-rakers," as John Bunyan calls the man who was always scraping after gold! Set their hearts upon their risen Lord and the heavenly heritage! Moreover, *believers need to be carried in conflict.* In the battle, if they seem to fall, O Lord, be pleased to give them the victory. If the foot of the foe be upon their necks for a moment, help them to grasp the sword of the Spirit, and eventually to win the battle. Lord, carry Your children's spirits in the day of conflict; don't let them sit in the dust, mourning forever. Don't allow the adversary to terrify them, and make them fret; but if, like Hannah, they have been persecuted, let them sing of the mercy of a delivering God.

We may also ask our Lord to *carry them at the last!* Carry them by taking them home, carry their bodies from the tomb, and raise their souls to Your eternal kingdom in glory.

"The precious blood of Christ." — *1 Peter 1:19*

TANDING at the foot of the cross, we see hands, and feet, and side, all distilling crimson streams of precious blood. It is "precious" because of its *redeeming* and *atoning efficacy.* By it, the sins of Christ's people are atoned for; they are redeemed from under the law; they are reconciled to God, made one with Him. Christ's blood is also "precious" in its *purifying power;* it "purifies from all sin." "Though your sins are like scarlet, they shall be as white as snow." Through Jesus' blood there is not a spot left upon any believer, no wrinkle nor any such thing remains. O precious blood, which makes us clean, removing the stains of abundant iniquity, and permitting us to stand accepted in the Beloved, notwithstanding the many ways in which we have rebelled against our God. The blood of Christ is likewise "precious" in its *preserving power.* We are safe from the destroying angel under the sprinkled blood. Remember it is *God's seeing* the blood which is the true reason for our being spared. Here is comfort for us when the eye of faith is dim, for God's eye is still the same. The blood of Christ is "precious" also in its *sanctifying influence.* The same blood which justifies by taking away sin, subsequently quickens the new nature and leads it onward to subdue sin and to follow out the commands of God. There is no motive for holiness as great as that which streams from the veins of Jesus. And "precious," unspeakably precious, is this blood because it has *an overcoming power.* It is written, "They overcame him by the blood of the Lamb." How could they do otherwise? Those who fight with the precious blood of Jesus, fight with a weapon which cannot know defeat. The blood of Jesus! sin dies at its presence, death ceases to be death: heaven's gates are opened. The blood of Jesus! we shall march on, conquering and to conquer, as long as we can trust its power!

"So that his hands remained steady till sunset."
— *Exodus 17:12*

 O mighty was the prayer of Moses, that everything depended upon it. The petitions of Moses thwarted the plans of the enemy more than the fighting of Joshua. Yet both were necessary. No, in the soul's conflict, force and fervor, decision and devotion, valor and vehemence, must join their forces, and all will be well. You must wrestle with your sin, but the major part of the wrestling must be done alone in private with God. Prayer, like that of Moses, holds up the token of the covenant before the Lord. The rod was the emblem of God's working with Moses, the symbol of God's government in Israel. Learn, O pleading saint, to hold up the promise and the oath of God before Him. The Lord cannot deny His own declarations. Hold up the rod of promise, and you have what you will ask for.

Moses grew weary, and then his friends assisted him. When at any time your prayer flags, let faith support one hand, and let holy hope uplift the other, and prayer seating itself upon the stone of Israel, the rock of our salvation, will persevere and prevail. Beware of faintness in devotion; if Moses felt it, how can we escape from it? It is much easier to fight with sin in public than to pray against it in private. It is remarked that Joshua never grew weary in the fighting, but Moses did grow weary in the praying; the more spiritual an exercise, the more difficult it is for flesh and blood to maintain it. Let's cry, then, for special strength, and may the Spirit of God, who helps us in our weakness, as He allowed help to Moses, enable us, like him, to continue with our hands remaining steady *"till sunset;"* until the evening of life is over; until we shall come to the rising of a better sun in the land where prayer is swallowed up in praise.

"You have come . . . to the sprinkled blood that speaks
a better word than the blood of Abel."
— *Hebrews 12:23, 24*

EADER, have *you* come to the sprinkled blood? The question is not whether you have come to a knowledge of doctrine, or an observance of ceremonies, or to a certain form of experience, but *have you come to the blood of Jesus?* The blood of Jesus is the life of all vital godliness. If you have truly come to Jesus, we know how you came — the Holy Spirit sweetly brought you there. You came to the blood of sprinkling with no merits of your own. Guilty, lost, and helpless, you came to take that blood, and that blood alone, as your everlasting hope. You came to the cross of Christ, with a trembling and an aching heart; and oh! what a precious sound it was to you to hear the voice of the blood of Jesus! The dropping of His blood is as the music of heaven to the penitent people of the earth. We are full of sin, but the Savior invites us to lift our eyes to Him, and as we gaze upon His streaming wounds, each drop of blood, as it falls, cries, "It is finished; I have made an end of sin; I have brought in everlasting righteousness." Oh! sweet language of the precious blood of Jesus! If you have come to that blood once, you will come to it constantly. Your life will be "Looking to Jesus." Your whole conduct will be epitomized in this — "To whom coming." Not to whom I *have* come, but to whom I am *always coming.* If you have ever come to the blood of sprinkling, you will feel your need of coming to it every day. He who doesn't desire to wash in it *every day,* has never washed in it at all. The believer always feels it as a joy and privilege that there is still a fountain opened. Past experiences are doubtful food for Christians; only a current coming to Christ can give us joy and comfort. This morning let's sprinkle our doorpost with fresh blood, and then feast upon the Lamb, assured that the destroying angel has to pass us by.

"We would like to see Jesus." — John 12:21

HE motto of worldlings will always be, "Who wants to show us a good time?" They seek satisfaction in earthly comforts, enjoyments, and riches. But regenerated sinners know of only one good. "If only I knew where to find HIM!" When we are truly awakened to feel our guilt, you could pour the gold of India at our feet, but we would say, "Take it away: we want to find HIM" It is a blessed thing when you can bring all your desires into focus so that they all center on one object. When one has fifty different desires, one's heart resembles a small pool of stagnant water, spread out into a marsh, breeding miasma and pestilence; but when all of one's desires are brought into one channel, one's heart becomes like a river of pure water, running swiftly to fertilize the fields. Happy is the person who has one desire, if that one desire is set on Christ, though it may not yet have been realized. If Jesus is a soul's desire, it is a blessed sign of divine work within. Such a person will never be content with mere ordinances. He or she will say, "I want Christ; I *must* have Him — mere ordinances are of no use to me; I want *Himself;* do not offer me these; you offer me the empty pitcher, while I am dying of thirst; give me water, or I die. Jesus is my soul's desire. I would see Jesus!"

Is this your condition, my reader, at this moment? Have you but one desire, and is that after Christ? Then you are not far from the kingdom of heaven. Have you but one wish in your heart, and that one wish that you may be washed from all your sins in Jesus' blood? Can you really say, "I would give all I have to be a Christian; I would give up everything I have and hope for, if I might but feel that I have an interest in Christ"? Then, despite all your fears, be of good cheer, the Lord loves you, and you shall come out into daylight soon, and rejoice in the liberty with which Christ makes us free.

"She tied the scarlet cord in the window." — Joshua 2:21

AHAB depended upon the promise of the spies for her preservation. She saw them as the representatives of the God of Israel. Her faith was simple and firm, but it was very obedient. To tie the scarlet cord in the window was a very trivial act in itself, but she dared not run the risk of omitting it. Come, my soul, isn't there a lesson here for you? Have you been attentive to all your Lord's will, even though some of His commands should seem non-essential? Have you observed in His own way the two ordinances of believers' baptism and the Lord's Supper? Neglecting these indicates that there is an enormous amount of unloving disobedience in your heart. From now on be blameless in all things, even tying a cord, if that is the command.

This act of Rahab sets forth a yet more solemn lesson. Have I implicitly trusted in the precious blood of Jesus? Have I tied the scarlet cord, as with a Gordian knot in my window, so that my trust can never be removed? Or can I look out towards the Dead Sea of my sins, or the Jerusalem of my hopes, without seeing the blood, and seeing all things in connection with its blessed power? The passerby can see a cord of so conspicuous a color, if it hangs from the window: it will be well for me if my life makes the efficacy of the atonement conspicuous to all onlookers. What is there to be ashamed of? Let human beings or devils stare if they want to; the blood is my boast and my song. My soul, there is One who will see that scarlet cord, even when, from weakness of faith, you cannot see it yourself; Jehovah, the Avenger, will see it and pass over you. Jericho's walls fell flat: Rahab's house was on the wall, and yet it stood unmoved; my nature is built into the wall of humanity, and yet when destruction smites the race, I shall be secure. My soul, tie the scarlet cord in the window afresh, and rest in peace.

"You have said, I will surely make you prosper."
— *Genesis 32:12*

HEN Jacob was on the other side of the brook Jabbok, and Esau was coming with armed men, he earnestly sought God's protection, and as a master reason he pleaded, "You have said, 'I will surely make you prosper.' " Oh, the force of that plea! He was holding God to His word — "You have said." The attribute of God's faithfulness is a splendid horn of the altar to lay hold upon; but the promise, which has in it the attribute and something more, is an even mightier holdfast — "I will surely make you prosper." And has *He* said, and shall He not do it? "Let God be true, and every man a liar." Shall *He* not be true? Shall *He* not keep His word? Shall not every word that comes out of His lips stand fast and be fulfilled? Solomon, at the opening of the temple, used this same mighty plea. He pleaded with God to remember the word which He had spoken to his father David, and to bless that place. When a man gives a promissory note, his honor is engaged; he affixes his signature to it, and he must discharge it when the due time comes, or else he loses credit. It shall never be said that God dishonors His bills. The credit of the Most High never was impeached, and never shall be. He is punctual to the moment: He never is before His time, but He never is behind it. Search God's word through, and compare it with the experience of God's people, and you shall find the two tally from the first to the last. Many an old patriarch has said with Joshua, "Not one of all the good promises the LORD your God gave you has failed. Every promise has been fulfilled." If you have a divine promise, you needn't plead it with an "if," you may urge it with certainty. The Lord meant to fulfill the promise, or He would not have given it. God doesn't give His words merely to quiet us, and to keep us hopeful for awhile with the intention of putting us off at last; but when He speaks, it is because He means to do as He has said.

> *"At that moment the curtain of the temple was torn in two from top to bottom."* — Matthew 27:51

O small miracle was wrought in the tearing of so strong and thick a veil; but it wasn't intended merely as a display of power — many lessons were taught us in this. *The old law of ordinances* was put away, and like a worn-out vesture, torn and laid aside. When Jesus died, the sacrifices were all finished, because all fulfilled in Him, and therefore the place of their presentation was marked with an evident token of decay. That tear also *revealed all the hidden things of the old dispensation:* the mercy seat could now be seen, and the glory of God gleamed forth above it. By the death of our Lord Jesus we have a clear revelation of God, for He was "not as Moses, who put a veil over his face." Life and immortality are now brought to light, and things which have been hidden since the foundation of the world are manifest in Him. *The annual ceremony of atonement was thus abolished. The atoning blood* which was once every year sprinkled within the veil, *was now offered once* for all by the great High Priest, and therefore the place of the symbolical rite was broken up. No blood of bulls or of lambs is needed now, for Jesus has entered within the veil with his own blood. Hence *access to God is now permitted,* and is the privilege of every believer in Christ Jesus. There is no small space laid open through which we may peer at the mercy seat, but the tear reaches from the top to the bottom. We may come with boldness to the throne of the heavenly grace. Shall we err if we say that the opening of the Holy of Holies in this marvelous manner by our Lord's expiring cry was *the type of the opening of the gates of paradise* to all the saints by virtue of the Passion? Our bleeding Lord has the key of heaven; He opens and no human closes; let's enter with Him into the heavenly places, and sit with Him there until our common enemies shall be made His footstool.

"The Amen." — *Revelation 3:14*

HE word AMEN solemnly confirms that which
went before; and Jesus is the great Con-
firmer; immutable, forever is "the Amen"
in all *His promises. Sinner,* I would comfort
you with this reflection. Jesus Christ said,
"Come to me, all you who are weary and
burdened, and I will give you rest." If you come to Him,
He will say "Amen" in your soul; His promise shall be true
to you. He said in the days of His flesh, "The bruised reed
I will not break." O you poor, broken, bruised heart, if you
come to Him, He will say "Amen" to you, and that shall be
true in *your* soul as in hundreds of cases in bygone years.
Christian, isn't it also comforting for you to know that
there isn't one word which has gone out of the Savior's lips
which He has ever retracted? The words of Jesus shall
stand when heaven and earth shall pass away. If you grasp
only half of a promise, you shall still find it true. Beware of
one who is called "Clip-promise," who will destroy much
of the comfort of God's word.

Jesus is Yea and Amen in all *His offices.* He was a Priest
to pardon and purify once, He is Amen as Priest still. He
was a King to rule and reign for His people, and to defend
them with His mighty arm, He is an Amen King, the same
still. He was a Prophet of old, to foretell good things to
come, His lips are most sweet, and drop with honey still —
He is an Amen Prophet. He is Amen as to the merit of His
blood; He is Amen as to His righteousness. That sacred
robe shall remain most fair and glorious when nature shall
decay. He is Amen in every single title which He bears;
your Husband, never seeking a divorce; your Friend, stick-
ing closer than a brother; your Shepherd, with you in
death's dark vale; your Help and your Deliverer; your
Castle and your High Tower; the Horn of your strength,
your confidence, your joy, your all in all, and your Yes and
Amen in all.

"So that by his death he might destroy him who holds the power of death." — Hebrews 2:14

child of God, death has lost its sting, because the devil's power over it is destroyed. Then stop being afraid of dying. Ask grace from God the Holy Spirit, that by an intimate knowledge and a firm belief of your Redeemer's death, you may be strengthened for that dread hour. Living near the cross of Calvary you may think of death with pleasure, and welcome it when it comes with intense delight. It is sweet to die in the Lord: it is a covenant blessing to sleep in Jesus. Death is no longer banishment, it is a return from exile, a going home to the many mansions where the loved ones already dwell. The distance between glorified spirits in heaven and militant saints on earth seems great; but it isn't. We are not far from home — a moment will bring us there. The sail is spread; the soul is launched upon the deep. How long will its voyage be? How many wearying winds must beat upon the sail before it shall be reefed in the port of peace? How long shall that soul be tossed upon the waves before it comes to that sea which knows no storm? Listen to the answer, "Absent from the body, present with the Lord." Yon ship has just departed, but it is already at its haven. It just spread its sail and it was there. Like that ship of old, upon the Lake of Galilee, a storm had tossed it, but Jesus said, "Quiet! Be still!" and *immediately* it came to land. Do not think that a long period intervenes between the instant of death and the eternity of glory. When the eyes close on earth they open in heaven. The horses of fire are not an instant on the road. Then, O child of God, what is there for you to fear in death, seeing that through the death of your Lord its curse and sting are destroyed? and now it is but a Jacob's ladder whose foot is in the dark grave, but its top reaches to glory everlasting.

"Fight the battles of the LORD." — *1 Samuel 18:17*

HE sacramental host of God's elect is still warring on earth, Jesus Christ being the Captain of their salvation. He has said, "And surely I am with you always, to the very end of the age." Hark to the shouts of war! Now let the people of God stand fast in their ranks, and let not our hearts fail us. It is true that just now in England the battle is turned against us, and unless the Lord Jesus shall lift His sword, we know not what may become of the church of God in this land; but let's be of good courage, and play the man. There never was a day when Protestantism seemed to tremble more in the scales than now that a fierce effort is making to restore the Romish antichrist to his ancient seat. We greatly want a bold voice and a strong hand to preach and publish the old gospel for which martyrs bled and confessors died. The Savior is, by His Spirit, still on earth; let this cheer us. He is ever in the midst of the fight, and therefore the battle is not doubtful. And as the conflict rages, what a sweet satisfaction it is to know that the Lord Jesus, in His office as our great Intercessor, is prevalently pleading for His people! O anxious gazer, don't look so much at the battle below, for there you shall be enshrouded in smoke, and amazed with garments rolled in blood; but lift your eyes yonder where the Savior lives and pleads, for while He intercedes, the cause of God is safe. Let's fight as if it all depended upon us, but let's look up and know that all depends upon Him.

Now, by the lilies of Christian purity, and by the roses of the Savior's atonement, by the roes and by the hinds of the field, we charge you who are lovers of Jesus, to do valiantly in the Holy War, for truth and righteousness, for the kingdom and crown jewels of your Master. Onward! "for the battle is not yours but God's."

"I know that my Redeemer lives." — *Job 19:25*

 HE marrow of Job's comfort lies in that little word "My" — "My Redeemer," and in the fact that the Redeemer lives. Oh! to get hold of a living Christ. We must get a property in Him before we can enjoy Him. What is gold in the mine to me? It is gold in my purse which will satisfy my necessities, by purchasing the bread I need. So a Redeemer who doesn't redeem *me*, an avenger who will never stand up for *my* blood, of what avail were such? Do not be content until, by faith, you can say "Yes, I cast myself upon my living Lord; and He is mine." It may be you hold Him with a feeble hand; you half think it presumption to say, "He lives as *my* Redeemer;" yet, remember if you only have faith as small as a grain of mustard seed, that little faith *entitles* you to say it. But there is also another word here, expressive of Job's strong confidence, *"I know."* To say, "I hope so, I trust so" is comfortable; and there are thousands in the fold of Jesus who hardly ever get much further. But to reach the essence of consolation you *must* say, "I know." Ifs, buts, and maybes are sure murderers of peace and comfort. Doubts are dreary things in times of sorrow. Like wasps they sting the soul! If I have any suspicion that Christ is not mine, then there is vinegar mingled with the gall of death; but if I know that Jesus lives for me, then darkness is not dark: even the night is light about me. Surely if Job, in those ages before the coming and advent of Christ, could say, "I know," *we* should not speak less positively. God forbid that our positiveness should be presumption. Let's see that our evidences are right, lest we build upon an ungrounded hope; and then let's not be satisfied with the mere foundation, for it is from the upper rooms that we get the widest perspective. A living Redeemer, truly mine, is joy unspeakable.

"Who . . . is at the right hand of God."
— *Romans 8:34*

H E who was once despised and rejected by humankind, now occupies the honorable position of a beloved and honored Son. The right hand of God is the *place of majesty and favor.* Our Lord Jesus is His people's representative. When He died for them, they had rest; when He rose again for them, they had liberty; when He sat down at His Father's right hand, they had favor, and honor, and dignity. The raising and elevation of Christ is the elevation, the acceptance, and enshrinement, the glorifying of all His people, for He is their head and representative. This sitting at the right hand of God, then, is to be viewed as the acceptance of the person of the Surety, the reception of the Representative, and therefore, the acceptance of *our* souls. O saint, see your sure freedom from condemnation in this. "Who is he that condemns?" Who shall condemn those who are in Jesus at the right hand of God?

The right hand is *the place of power.* Christ at the right hand of God has all power in heaven and in earth. Who shall fight against the people who have such power vested in their Captain? O my soul, what can destroy you if Omnipotence is your helper? If the protection of the Almighty covers you, what sword can strike you? Rest secure. If Jesus is your all-prevailing King, and has trampled your enemies beneath His feet; if sin, death, and hell are all vanquished by Him, and you are represented in Him, by no possibility can you be destroyed.

"Jesu's tremendous name
Puts all our foes to flight:
Jesus, the meek, the angry Lamb,
A Lion is in fight.

By all hell's host withstood;
We all hell's host o'erthrow;
And conquering them, through Jesu's blood
We still to conquer go."

"God exalted him." — *Acts 5:31*

JESUS, our Lord, once crucified, dead and buried, now sits upon the throne of glory. The highest place that heaven affords is His by undisputed right. It is sweet to remember that the exaltation of Christ in heaven is a *representative exaltation.* He is exalted at the Father's right hand, and though, like Jehovah, He has eminent glories, in which finite creatures cannot share, yet as the Mediator, the honors which Jesus wears in heaven are the heritage of all the saints. It is delightful to reflect how close Christ's union is with His people. We are actually one with Him; we are members of His body; and His exaltation is *our* exaltation. He will give us to sit upon His throne, even as He has overcome, and is set down with His Father on His throne; He has a crown, and He gives us crowns too; He has a throne, but He is not content with having a throne to Himself, on His right hand there must be His queen, arrayed in "gold of Ophir." He cannot be glorified without His bride. Look up, believer, to Jesus now; let the eye of your faith behold Him with many crowns upon His head; and remember that you will be like Him one day, when you shall see Him as He is; you shall not be as great as He is, you shall not be as divine, but still you shall, in a measure, share the same honors, and enjoy the same happiness and the same dignity which He possesses. Be content to live for a little while without knowing, and to walk your weary way through the fields of poverty, or up the hills of affliction; for before long you shall reign with Christ, for He has "made us kings and priests to God, and we shall reign forever and ever." Oh! wonderful thought for the children of God! We have Christ for our glorious representative in heaven's courts *now,* and soon He will come and receive us to Himself, to be with Him there, to behold His glory, and to share His joy.

"You will not fear the terror of night." — *Psalm 91:5*

HAT is this terror? It may be the cry of fire, or the noise of thieves, or fancied appearances, or the shriek of sudden sickness or death. We live in the world of death and sorrow, we may therefore look for ills as well in the night watches as beneath the glare of the broiling sun. Nor should this alarm us, for whatever the terror is, the promise is that the believer shall not be afraid. Why should one be? Let's put it more specifically, why should *we?* God our Father is here, and will be here all through the lonely hours; He is an almighty Watcher, a sleepless Guardian, a faithful Friend. Nothing can happen without His direction, for even hell itself is under His control. Darkness is not dark to Him. He has promised to be a wall of fire around His people — and who can break through such a barrier? Worldlings may well be afraid, for they have an angry God above them, a guilty conscience within them, and a yawning hell beneath them; but we who rest in Jesus are saved from all these through rich mercy. If we succumb to foolish fear we shall dishonor our profession, and lead others to doubt the reality of godliness. We ought to be afraid of being afraid, lest we should vex the Holy Spirit by foolish distrust. Down, then, you dismal forebodings and groundless apprehensions, God has not forgotten to be gracious, nor shut up His tender mercies. It may be night in the soul, but there is no need to be terrified, for the God of love never changes. Children of light may walk in darkness, but they are not therefore cast away; no, they are now enabled to prove their adoption by trusting in their heavenly Father as hypocrites cannot do.

"Though the night be dark and dreary,
Darkness cannot hide from Thee;
Thou are He, who, never weary,
Watchest where Thy people be."

"No, in all these things we are more than conquerors through him who loved us." — *Romans 8:37*

 E go to Christ for forgiveness, and then too often look to the law for power to fight our sins. Paul thus rebukes us, "You foolish Galatians! Who has bewitched you? Before your very eyes Jesus Christ was clearly portrayed as crucified. I would like to learn just one thing from you: Did you receive the Spirit by observing the law, or by believing what you heard? Are you so foolish? After beginning with the Spirit, are you now trying to attain your goal by human effort?" Take your sins to Christ's cross, for the old self can only be crucified there: we are crucified *with Him*. The only weapon to fight sin with is the spear which pierced the side of Jesus. To give an illustration — you want to overcome an angry temper, how do you do it? It is very possible you have never tried the right way of going to Jesus with it. How did I get salvation? I came to Jesus just as I was, and I trusted Him to save me. Must I kill my angry temper in the same way? It is the only way in which I can ever kill it. I must go to the cross with it, and say to Jesus, "Lord, I trust You to deliver me from it." This is the only way to give it a death blow. Are you covetous? Do you feel the world entangling you? You may struggle against this evil as long as you please, but if this is the sin which persistently troubles you, you will never be delivered from it in any way but by the blood of Jesus. Take it to Christ. Tell Him, "Lord, I have trusted You, and Your name is Jesus, for You do save your people from their sins; Lord, this is one of my sins; save me from it!" Ordinances are nothing without Christ as a means of mortification. Your prayers, and your repentances, and your tears — the whole of them put together — are worth nothing apart from Him. "None but Jesus can do helpless sinners good;" or helpless saints either. You must be conquerors through Him who has loved you, if conquerors at all. Our laurels must grow among His olives in Gethsemane.

"I saw a Lamb, looking as if it had been slain,
standing in the center of the throne."
— *Revelation 5:6*

HY should our exalted Lord appear in glory with His wounds? The wounds of Jesus are His glories, His jewels, His sacred ornaments. To the eye of the believer, Jesus is surpassingly fair because He is "white and ruddy" — white with innocence, and ruddy with His own blood. We see Him as the lily of matchless purity, and as the rose crimsoned with His own gore. Christ is lovely upon Olivet and Tabor, and by the sea, but oh! there never was such a matchless Christ as He that did hang upon the cross. There we beheld all His beauties in perfection, all His attributes developed, all His love drawn out, all His character expressed. Beloved, the wounds of Jesus are far fairer in our eyes than all the splendor and pomp of kings. The thorny crown is more than an imperial diadem. It is true that now He doesn't bear the scepter of reed, but there was a glory in it that never flashed from scepter of gold. Jesus wears the appearance of a slain Lamb as His court dress in which He wooed our souls, and redeemed them by His complete atonement. Nor are these only the ornaments of Christ: they are the *trophies* of His love and of His victory. He has divided the spoil with the strong. He has redeemed for Himself a great multitude whom no one can count, and these scars are the memorials of the fight. Ah! if Christ thus loves to retain the thought of His sufferings for His people, *how precious should his wounds be to us!*

> "Behold how every wound of His
> A precious balm distills,
> Which heals the scars that sin had made,
> And cures all mortal ills.
>
> "Those wounds are mouths that preach His grace;
> The ensigns of His love;
> The seals of our expected bliss
> In paradise above."

"In view of all this, we are making a binding agreement."
— *Nehemiah 9:38*

HERE are many occasions in our experience when we may very rightly, and with benefit, renew our covenant with God. After *recovery from sickness* when, like Hezekiah, we have had a new term of years added to our life, we may fitly do it. After any *deliverance from trouble,* when our joys bud forth anew, let's again visit the foot of the cross, and renew our consecration. Especially, let's do this after any *sin which has grieved the Holy Spirit,* or brought dishonor upon the cause of God; let's then look to that blood which can make us whiter than snow, and again offer ourselves to the Lord. We should not only let our troubles confirm our dedication to God, but *our prosperity* should do the same. If we ever meet with occasions which deserve to be called "crowning mercies" then, surely, if He has crowned *us,* we ought also to crown our God; let's bring forth anew all the jewels of the divine regalia which have been stored in the jewel closet of our heart, and let our God sit upon the throne of our love, arrayed in royal apparel. If we would learn to profit by our prosperity, we should not need so much adversity. If we would gather from a kiss all the good it might confer upon us, we should not so often smart under the rod. Have we lately received some blessing which we hardly expected? Has the Lord put our feet in a large room? Can we sing of mercies multiplied? Then this is the day to put our hand upon the horns of the altar, and say, "Bind me here, my God; bind me here with cords, even forever." Inasmuch as we need the fulfillment of new promises from God, let's offer renewed prayers that our old vows may not be dishonored. Let's this morning make a binding agreement with Him because of the pains of Jesus which for the last month, we have been considering with gratitude.

> *"Flowers appear on the earth; the season of singing has come, the cooing of doves is heard in our land."*
> — *Song of Songs 2:12*

WEET is the season of spring: the long and dreary winter helps us to appreciate its genial warmth, and its promise of summer enhances its present delights. After periods of depression of spirit, it is delightful to behold again the light of the Sun of Righteousness; then our slumbering graces rise from their lethargy, like the crocus and the daffodil from their beds of earth; then is our heart made merry with delicious notes of gratitude, far more melodious than the warbling of birds — and the comforting assurance of peace, infinitely more delightful than the turtledove's note, is heard within the soul. Now is the time for the soul to seek communion with her Beloved; now must she rise from her native sordidness, and come away from her old associations. If we do not hoist the sail when the breeze is favorable, we shall be blameworthy: times of refreshing ought not to pass over us unimproved. When Jesus Himself visits us in tenderness, and entreats us to arise, can we be so base as to refuse His request? He has Himself risen that He may draw us after Him: He now by His Holy Spirit has revived us, that we may, in newness of life, ascend into the heavenlies, and hold communion with Himself. Let our wintry state suffice us for coldness and indifference; when the Lord creates a spring within, let our sap flow with vigor, and our branch blossom with high resolve. O Lord, if it isn't spring time in my chilly heart, I pray that You will make it so, for I am completely weary of living at a distance from You. Oh! the long and dreary winter, when will You bring it to an end? Come, Holy Spirit, and renew my soul! quicken me! restore me, and have mercy on me! This very night I would earnestly implore the Lord to take pity upon His servant, and send me a happy revival of spiritual life!

"Arise, my darling, my beautiful one, and come with me."
— *Song of Songs 2:10*

 O, I hear the voice of my Beloved! He speaks to *me!* Fair weather is smiling upon the face of the earth, and He would not have me spiritually asleep while nature is all around me awaking from her winter's rest. He bids me "Arise," and well He may, for I have been lying among the pots of worldliness long enough. He is risen, I am risen in Him, why then should I cleave to the dust? From lower loves, desires, pursuits, and aspirations, I would rise towards Him. He calls me by the sweet title of "My darling," and counts me beautiful; this is a good argument for my rising. If He has exalted me in this manner, and thinks me thus comely, how can I linger in the tents of Kedar and find congenial associates among humanity? He bids me "Come with me." Further and further from everything selfish, groveling, worldly, sinful, He calls me; yes, from the outwardly religious world which doesn't know Him, and has no sympathy with the mystery of the higher life, He calls me. "Come with me" has no harsh sound in it to my ear, for what is there to hold me in this wilderness of vanity and sin? O my Lord, would that I could come away, but I am taken among the thorns, and cannot escape from them as I would. I would, if it were possible, have neither eyes, nor ears, nor heart for sin. You call me to Yourself by saying "Come with me," and this is a melodious call indeed. To come to You is to come home from exile, to come to land out of the raging storm, to come to rest after long work, to come to the goal of my desires and the summit of my wishes. But Lord, how can a stone rise, how can a lump of clay come away from the horrible pit? O raise me, draw me. Your grace can do it. Send forth your Holy Spirit to kindle sacred flames of love in my heart, and I will continue to rise until I leave life and time behind me, and indeed come with You.

*"If anyone hears my voice and opens the door,
I will come in." — Revelation 3:20*

HAT is your desire this evening? Is it set upon heavenly things? Do you long to enjoy the high doctrine of eternal love? Do you desire liberty in very close communion with God? Do you aspire to know the heights, and depths, and lengths, and breadths? Then you must draw near to Jesus; you must get a clear sight of Him in His preciousness and completeness: you must view Him in His work, in His offices, in His person. Those who understand Christ, receive an anointing from the Holy One, by which He knows all things. Christ is the great master key of all the chambers of God: there is no treasury of God which will not open and yield up all its wealth to the soul that lives near to Jesus. Are you saying, "O that He would dwell in my heart"? "Would that He would make my heart His dwelling place forever"? Open the door, beloved, and He will come into your souls. He has long been knocking, and all with this object, that He may sup with you, and you with Him. *He sups with you* because you find the house or the heart, and *you with Him* because He brings the provision. He couldn't sup with you if it were not in your heart, you finding the house; nor could you sup with Him, for you have a bare cupboard, if He didn't bring provision with Him. Fling wide, then, the portals of your soul. He will come with that love which you long to feel; He will come with that joy into which you cannot work your poor depressed spirit; He will bring the peace which you don't have now; He will come with His flagons of wine and sweet apples of love, and cheer you until you have no other sickness but that of "love o'erpowering, love divine." Only open the door to Him, drive out His enemies, give Him the keys of your heart, and He will dwell there forever. Oh, wondrous love, that brings such a guest to dwell in such a heart!

"Do this in remembrance of me." — *1 Corinthians 11:24*

T seems then, that Christians may forget Christ! There could be no need for this loving exhortation, if there were not a fearful supposition that our memories might prove treacherous. Nor is this a bare supposition: it is, alas! too well confirmed in our experience, not as a possibility, but as a lamentable fact. It appears almost impossible that those who have been redeemed by the blood of the dying Lamb, and loved with an everlasting love by the eternal Son of God, should forget that gracious Savior; but, if startling to the ear, it is, alas! too apparent to the eye to allow us to deny the crime. Forget Him who never forgot us! Forget Him who poured His blood forth for our sins! Forget Him who loved us even to the death! Can it be possible? Yes, it is not only possible, but conscience confesses that it is too sadly a fault with all of us, that we allow Him to be as a traveler, staying only for the night. He whom we should make the abiding tenant of our memories is but a visitor therein. The cross where one would think that memory would linger, and unmindfulness would be an unknown intruder, is desecrated by the feet of forgetfulness. Doesn't your conscience say that this is true? Don't you find yourselves forgetful of Jesus? Some creature steals away your heart, and you are unmindful of Him upon whom your affection ought to be set. Some earthly business engrosses your attention when you should fix your eye steadily upon the cross. It is the incessant turmoil of the world, the constant attraction of earthly things which takes away the soul from Christ. While memory preserves a poisonous weed too well, it permits the rose of Sharon to wither. Let's charge ourselves to bind a heavenly forget-me-not about our hearts for Jesus our Beloved, and, whatever else we let slip, let's hold fast to Him.

"Blessed is he who stays awake." — Revelation 16:15

E die daily," said the apostle. This was the life of the early Christians; they went everywhere with their lives in their hands. We are not in this day called to pass through the same fearful persecutions: if we were, the Lord would give us grace to bear the test; but the tests of Christian life, at the present moment, though outwardly not so terrible, are yet more likely to overcome us than even those of the fiery age. We have to bear the sneer of the world — that isn't so bad; its blandishments, its soft words, its oily speeches, its fawning, its hypocrisy are far worse. Our danger is lest we grow rich and become proud, lest we give ourselves up to the fashions of this present evil world, and lose our faith. Or if wealth isn't the trial, worldly care is quite as mischievous. If we cannot be torn in pieces by the roaring lion, if we may be hugged to death by the bear, the devil doesn't really care which it is, as long as he destroys our love to Christ, and our confidence in Him. I am afraid that the Christian church is far more likely to lose her integrity in these soft and silken days than in those rougher times. We must be awake now, for we traverse the enchanted ground, and are most likely to fall asleep to our own undoing, unless our faith in Jesus is a reality, and our love for Jesus a vehement flame. Many in these days of easy profession are likely to prove tares, and not wheat; hypocrites with fair masks on their faces, but not the trueborn children of the living God. Christian, do not think that these are times in which you can dispense with watchfulness or with holy ardor; you need these things more than ever, and may God the eternal Spirit display His omnipotence in you, that you may be able to say, in all these softer things, as well as in the rougher, "We are more than conquerors through Him who loved us."

"God, our God." — Psalm 67:6

 T is strange how little use we make of the spiritual blessings which God gives us, but it is stranger still how little use we make of God Himself. Though He is "God, our God," we devote ourselves very little to Him, and ask so little of Him. How seldom do we ask counsel at the hands of the Lord! How often do we go about our business, without seeking His guidance! In our troubles how constantly do we strive to bear our burdens ourselves, instead of casting them upon the Lord, that He may sustain us! This is not because we may not, for the Lord seems to say, "I am yours, soul, come and make use of Me as you will; you may freely come to My store, and the more often the better." It is our own fault if we do not freely access the riches of our God. Then, since you have such a friend, and He invites you, draw from Him daily. Never want while you have a God to go to; never fear or faint while you have God to help you; go to your treasure and take whatever you need — there is all that you can want. Learn the divine skill of making God all things to you. He can supply you with all, or, better still, He can be to you instead of all. Let me urge you, then, to make use of your God. Make use of Him *in prayer.* Go to Him often, because He is *your* God. O, will you fail to use so great a privilege? Fly to Him, tell Him all your wants. Use Him constantly *by faith* at all times. If some dark providence has beclouded you, use your God as a "sun;" if some strong enemy has surrounded you, find in Jehovah a "shield," for He is a sun and shield to His people. If you have lost your way in the mazes of life, use Him as a "guide," for He will direct you. Whatever you are, and wherever you are, remember God is just *what* you want, and just *where* you want, and that He can do *all* you want.

"The LORD is King forever and ever." — Psalm 10:16

ESUS Christ is not a despot claiming *divine right,* but He is really and truly the Lord's anointed! "For God was pleased to have all his fullness dwell in Him." God has given to Him all power and all authority. As the Son of Man, He is now head over all things to His church, and He reigns over heaven, and earth, and hell, with the keys of life and death at His belt. Certain princes have delighted to call themselves kings by *the popular will,* and certainly our Lord Jesus Christ is such in His church. If it could be put to the vote whether He should be King in the church, every believing heart would crown Him. O that we could crown Him more gloriously than we do! We would count no expense to be wasted that could glorify Christ. Suffering would be pleasure, and loss would be gain, if thereby we could surround His brow with brighter crowns, and make Him more glorious in the eyes of men and angels. Yes, He shall reign. Long live the King! All hail to You, King Jesus! Go forth, you virgin souls who love your Lord, bow at His feet, strew His way with the lilies of your love, and the roses of your gratitude: "Bring forth the royal diadem, and crown Him Lord of all." Moreover, our Lord Jesus is King in Zion by *right of conquest:* He has taken and carried by storm the hearts of His people, and has slain their enemies who held them in cruel bondage. In the Red Sea of His own blood, our Redeemer has drowned the Pharaoh of our sins: shall He not be King in Jeshurun? He has delivered us from the iron yoke and heavy curse of the law: shall not the Liberator be crowned? We are His portion, whom He has taken out of the hand of the Amorite with His sword and with His bow: who shall snatch His conquest from His hand? All hail, King Jesus! we gladly acknowledge Your gentle sway! Rule in our hearts forever, You lovely Prince of Peace.

*"Remember your word to your servant, for you have
given me hope."* — Psalm 119:49

HATEVER your special need may be, you may readily find some promise in the Bible suited to it. Are you faint and feeble because your way is rough and you are weary? Here is the promise — "He gives strength to the weary." When you read such a promise, take it back to the great Promiser, and ask Him to fulfill His own word. Are you seeking after Christ, and thirsting for closer communion with Him? This promise shines like a star upon you — "Blessed are those who hunger and thirst for righteousness, for they will be filled." Take that promise to the throne continually; don't plead anything else, but go to God over and over again with this — "Lord, You have said it, do as You have said." Are you distressed because of sin, and burdened with the heavy load of your iniquities? Listen to these words — "I, even I, am He who blots out your transgressions, for My own sake, and remembers your sins no more." You have no merit of your own to plead why He should pardon you, but plead His written engagements and He will perform them. Are you afraid lest you shouldn't be able to hold on to the end, lest, after having thought yourself a child of God, you should prove a castaway? If that is your state, take this word of grace to the throne and plead it: "Though the mountains be shaken and the hills be removed, yet My unfailing love for you will not be shaken nor My covenant of peace be removed." If you have lost the sweet sense of the Savior's presence, and are seeking Him with a sorrowful heart, remember the promises: "Return to Me, and I will return to you;" "For a brief moment I abandoned you, but with deep compassion I will bring you back." Feast your faith upon God's own word, and whatever your fears or wants, repair to the Bank of Faith with your Father's note of hand, saying, "Remember Your word to Your servant, for You have given me hope."

"The whole house of Israel is hardened and
obstinate." — *Ezekiel 3:7*

RE there no exceptions? No, not one. Even the favored race are thus described. Are the best so bad? — then what must the worst be? Come, my heart, consider how far you have a share in this universal accusation, and while considering, be ready to be ashamed of yourself of that wherein you may have been guilty. The first charge is *hardness* of forehead, a lack of holy shame, an unhallowed boldness in evil. Before my conversion, I could sin and feel no compunction, hear of my guilt and yet remain unhumbled, and even confess my iniquity and manifest no inward humiliation on account of it. For a sinner to go to God's house and pretend to pray to Him and praise Him argues a brazen-facedness of the worst kind! Alas! since the day of my new birth I have doubted my Lord to His face, murmured unblushingly in His presence, worshipped before Him in a slovenly manner, and sinned without bewailing myself concerning it. If my forehead were not as an adamant, harder than flint, I should have far more holy fear, and a far deeper contrition of spirit. Woe is me, I am one of the hardened house of Israel. The second charge is *obstinacy,* and I must not venture to plead innocent here. Once I had nothing but a heart of stone, and although through grace I now have a new and fleshy heart, much of my former obduracy remains. I am not affected by the death of Jesus as I ought to be; neither am I moved by the ruin of others, the wickedness of the times, the chastisement of my heavenly Father, and my own failures, as I should be. O that my heart would melt at the recital of my Savior's sufferings and death. Would to God I were rid of this nether millstone within me, this hateful body of death. Blessed be the name of the Lord, the disease is not incurable, the Savior's precious blood is the universal solvent, and me, even me, it will effectually soften, until my heart melts as wax before the fire.

"You are my refuge in the day of disaster."
— *Jeremiah 17:17*

 HE path of the Christian is not always bright with sunshine; we have our seasons of darkness and of storm. True, it is written in God's Word, "Her ways are pleasant ways, and all her paths are peace;" and it is a great truth that religion is designed to give us happiness below as well as bliss above; but experience tells us that, if the course of the righteous is "like the first gleam of dawn, shining ever brighter until the full light of day," yet sometimes *that* light is eclipsed. At certain periods clouds cover the believer's sun, and he walks in darkness and sees no light. There are many who have rejoiced in the presence of God for a season; they have basked in the sunshine in the earlier stages of their Christian career; they have walked along the "green pastures" by the side of the "quiet waters," but suddenly they find the glorious sky is clouded; instead of the Land of Goshen they have to tread the sandy desert; in the place of sweet waters, they find troubled streams, bitter to their taste, and they say, "Surely, if I were a child of God, this would not happen." Oh! don't say that, you who are walking in darkness. The best of God's saints must drink the wormwood; the dearest of His children must bear the cross. No Christian has enjoyed perpetual prosperity; no believer can always hang his harp on the poplars (Psalm 137:2). Perhaps the Lord allotted you at first a smooth and unclouded path, because you were weak and timid. He tempered the wind to the shorn lamb, but now that you are stronger in the spiritual life, you must enter upon the riper and rougher experience of God's full-grown children. We need winds and tempests to exercise our faith, to tear off the rotten bough of self-dependence, and to root us more firmly in Christ. The day of evil reveals to us the value of our glorious hope.

"The LORD takes delight in his people."
— Psalm 149:4

OW comprehensive the love of Jesus is! There is no part of His people's interests which He doesn't consider, and there is nothing which concerns their welfare which is not important to Him. Not merely does He think of you, believer, as an immortal being, but as a mortal being, too. Do not deny it or doubt it: "The very hairs of your head are all numbered." "If the LORD delights in a man's way, he makes his steps firm." It would be a sad thing for us if this mantle of love didn't cover all our concerns, for what mischief might be wrought to us in that part of our business which didn't come under our gracious Lord's inspection! Believer, rest assured that the heart of Jesus cares about your lesser affairs. The breadth of His tender love is such that you may resort to Him in all matters; for in all your afflictions He is afflicted, and as a father pities his children, so He pities you. The humblest interests of all His saints are all borne upon the broad bosom of the Son of God. Oh, what a heart is His that not only comprehends each one of His people, but also comprehends the diverse and innumerable concerns of each of those individuals! Do you think, O Christian, that you can measure the love of Christ? Think of what His love has brought you — justification, adoption, sanctification, eternal life! The riches of His goodness are unsearchable; you shall never be able to tell them out or even conceive them. Oh, the breadth of the love of Christ! Shall such a love as this have half our hearts? Shall it have a cold love in return? Shall Jesus' marvelous loving-kindness and tender care meet with but faint response and tardy acknowledgment? O my soul, tune your harp to a glad song of thanksgiving! Go to your rest rejoicing, for you are no desolate wanderer, but a beloved child, watched over, cared for, supplied, and defended by your Lord.

"All the Israelites grumbled." — Numbers 14:2

 HERE are grumblers amongst Christians now, as there were in the camp of Israel of old. There are those who, when the rod falls, cry out against the afflictive dispensation. They ask, "Why am I afflicted like this? What have I done to be chastened in this manner?" A word to you, O grumbler! Why should you grumble against the dispensations of your heavenly Father? Can He treat you in a greater manner than you deserve? Consider what a rebel you were once, but He has pardoned you! Surely, if He in His wisdom sees fit now to chasten you, you shouldn't complain. After all, are you chastened more harshly than your sins deserve? Consider the corruption which is in your breast, and then will you wonder that there needs so much of the rod to fetch it out? Weigh yourself, and discern how much dross is mingled with your gold; and do you think the fire too hot to purge away so much dross as you have? Doesn't that proud rebellious spirit of yours prove that your heart is not thoroughly sanctified? Aren't those grumbling words contrary to the holy submissive nature of God's children? Is not the correction needed? But if you *will* grumble against the chastening, take heed, for it will go hard with grumblers. God always punishes His children twice, if they do not bear the first stroke patiently. But know one thing — "He does not willingly bring affliction or grief to the children of men." All His corrections are sent in love, to purify you, and to draw you nearer to Himself. Surely it must help you to bear the chastening with resignation if you are able to recognize your *Father's* hand. For "the Lord disciplines those He loves, and He punishes everyone He accepts as a son. Endure hardship as discipline; God is treating you as sons." "And do not grumble, as some of them did — and were killed by the destroying angel."

"How precious to me are your thoughts, O God!"
— *Psalm 139:17*

IVINE omniscience affords no comfort to the ungodly mind, but to the child of God it overflows with consolation. God is always thinking of us, never turns aside His mind from us, has us always before His eyes; and this is precisely as we would have it, for it would be dreadful to exist for a moment beyond the observation of our heavenly Father. His thoughts are always tender, loving, wise, prudent, far-reaching, and they bring to us countless benefits: hence it is a special joy to remember them. The Lord always did think of His people: hence their election and the covenant of grace by which their salvation is secured; He always will think of them: hence their final perseverance by which they shall be brought safely to their final rest. In all our wanderings the watchful glance of the Eternal Watcher is forever fixed upon us — we never roam beyond the Shepherd's eye. In our sorrows He observes us incessantly, and not a pang escapes Him; in our toils He sees all our weariness, and writes in His book all the struggles of His faithful ones. These thoughts of the Lord encompass us in all our paths, and penetrate the innermost region of our being. Not a nerve or tissue, valve or vessel, of our bodily organization is uncared for; all the littles of our little world are thought of by the great God.

Dear reader, is this precious to you? then hold to it. Never be led astray by those philosophic fools who preach up an impersonal God, and talk of self-existent, self-governing matter. The Lord lives and thinks of us, this is a truth far too precious for us to be lightly robbed of it. The recognition of a nobleman is valued so highly that he who has it counts his fortune made; but what is it to be thought of by the King of kings! If the Lord thinks of us, all is well, and we may rejoice forever.

"His cheeks are like beds of spice yielding perfume."
— *Song of Songs 5:13*

O, the flowery month has come! March winds and April showers have done their work, and all the earth is adorned with beauty. Come my soul, put on your holiday attire and go forth to gather garlands of heavenly thoughts. You know where to go because, to you, "the beds of spice" are well known, and you have so often smelled the "perfume," that you will go at once to your well-beloved and find all loveliness, all joy in Him. That cheek once so rudely smitten with a rod, often drenched with tears of sympathy and then defiled with spittle — that cheek as it smiles with mercy is like a fragrant aromatic to my heart. You didn't hide your face from shame and spitting, O Lord Jesus, and therefore I will find my dearest delight in praising You. Those cheeks were furrowed by the plow of grief, and crimsoned with red lines of blood from Your thorn-crowned temples; such marks of unbounded love cannot but charm my soul far more than "pillars of perfume." If I may not see the whole of His face I would behold His cheeks, for the least glimpse of Him is exceedingly refreshing to my spiritual sense and yields a variety of delights. In Jesus I find not only fragrance, but a bed of spice; not one flower, but all manner of sweet flowers. He is to me my rose and my lily, my heartsease and my cluster of camphor. When He is with me it is May all the year round, and my soul goes forth to wash her happy face in the morning dew of His grace, and to solace herself with the singing of the birds of His promises. Precious Lord Jesus, let me in very deed know the blessedness which dwells in abiding, unbroken fellowship with You. I am a poor worthless one, whose cheek You have deigned to kiss! O let me kiss You in return with the kisses of my lips.

"I am a rose of Sharon." — *Song of Songs 2:1*

WHATEVER there may be of beauty in the material world, Jesus Christ possesses all that in the spiritual world in a tenfold degree. Among all flowers, the rose is deemed the sweetest, but Jesus is infinitely more beautiful in the garden of the soul than the rose can be in the gardens of earth. He takes the first place as the fairest among ten thousand. He is the sun, and all others are the stars; the heavens and the day are dark in comparison with Him, *for the King in His beauty transcends all.* "I am a rose of *Sharon.*" This was the best and rarest of roses. Jesus is not "a rose" alone, He is "a rose of Sharon," just as He calls His righteousness "gold," and then adds, "the gold of Ophir" — the best of the best. He is positively lovely, and superlatively the loveliest. *There is variety in His charms.* The rose is delightful to the eye, and its scent is pleasant and refreshing; so each of the senses of the soul, whether it be the taste or feeling, the hearing, the sight, or the spiritual smell, finds appropriate gratification in Jesus. *Even the recollection of His love is sweet.* Take the rose of Sharon, and pull it leaf from leaf, and preserve the leaves in the jar of memory, and you shall find each leaf fragrant long afterwards, filling the house with perfume. Christ *satisfies the highest taste* of the most educated spirit to the very full. The greatest amateur in perfumes is quite satisfied with the rose: and when the soul has arrived at her highest pitch of true taste, she shall still be content with Christ, no, she shall be the better able to appreciate Him. Heaven itself possesses nothing which excels the rose of Sharon. What emblem can fully set forth His beauty? Human speech and earthborn things fail to tell of Him. Earth's choicest charms commingled, feebly picture His abounding preciousness. Blessed rose, bloom in my heart forever!

"My prayer is not that you take them out of the world."
— *John 17:15*

 T is a sweet and blessed event which will occur to all believers in God's own time — the going home to be with Jesus. In a few more years, the Lord's soldiers who are now fighting "the good fight of the faith" will be done with conflict, and will have entered into the joy of their Lord. But although Christ prays that His people may eventually be with Him where He is, He does not ask that they may be taken at once away from this world to heaven. He wishes them to stay here. Yet how frequently does the wearied pilgrim put up the prayer, "Oh, that I had the wings of a dove! I would fly away and be at rest;" but Christ does not pray like that, He leaves us in His Father's hands, until, like fully-ripened shocks of corn, we shall each be gathered into our Master's garner. Jesus does not plead for our instant removal by death, for to live in the flesh is necessary for others if not profitable for ourselves. He asks that we may be kept from evil, but He never asks for us to be admitted to the inheritance in glory until we are of full age. Christians often want to die when they have any trouble. Ask them why, and they tell you, "Because we want to be with the Lord." We fear it isn't so much because they are longing to be with the Lord, as because they desire to get rid of their troubles; or else they would feel the same wish to die at other times when not under the pressure of trial. They want to go home, not so much for the Savior's company, but to be at rest. Now it is quite right to desire to depart if we can do it in the same spirit that Paul did, because to be with Christ is far better, but the wish to escape from trouble is a selfish one. Rather let your care and wish be to glorify God by your life here as long as He pleases, even though it be in the midst of toil, and conflict, and suffering, and leave Him to say when "it is enough."

*"All these people were still living by faith
when they died."* — Hebrews 11:13

BEHOLD the epitaph of all those blessed saints who fell asleep before the coming of our Lord! It matters nothing how else they died, whether of old age, or by violent means; this one point, in which they all agree, is the most worthy of record that they "were still living by faith when they died." By faith they lived — it was their comfort, their guide, their motive and their support; and in the same spiritual grace they died, ending their life-song in the sweet strain in which they had so long continued. They didn't die resting in the flesh or upon their own attainments; they made no advance from their first way of acceptance with God, but held to the way of faith to the end. Faith is as precious to die by as to live by.

Dying in faith has distinct reference to *the past*. They believed the promises which had gone before, and were assured that their sins were blotted out through the mercy of God. Dying in faith has to do with *the present*. These saints were confident of their acceptance with God, they enjoyed the beams of His love, and rested in His faithfulness. Dying in faith looks into *the future*. They fell asleep, affirming that the Messiah would surely come, and that when He would in the last days appear upon the earth, they would rise from their graves to behold Him. To them the pains of death were but the birth pangs of a better state. Take courage, my soul, as you read this epitaph. Your course, through grace, is one of faith, and sight seldom cheers you; this has also been the pathway of the brightest and the best. Faith was the orbit in which these stars of the first magnitude moved all the time of their shining here; and happy are you that it is yours. Look anew tonight to Jesus, the author and finisher of your faith, and thank Him for giving you the same precious faith as with those souls now in glory.

"In this world you will have trouble." — *John 16:33*

RE you asking the reason for this, believer? Look *upward* to your heavenly Father, and behold Him pure and holy. Do you know that you are one day to be like Him? Will you easily be conformed to His image? Will you not require much refining in the furnace of affliction to purify you? Will it be an easy thing to get rid of your corruptions, and make you perfect even as your heavenly Father is perfect? Next, Christian, turn your eye *downward.* Do you know what foes you have beneath your feet? You were once a servant of Satan, and no king will willingly lose his subjects. Do you think that Satan will let you alone? No, he will be always at you, for he "prowls around like a roaring lion looking for someone to devour." Expect trouble, therefore, Christian, when you look beneath you. Then look *around you.* Where are you? You are in an enemy's country, a stranger and a sojourner. The world is not your friend. If it is, then you aren't God's friend, for he who is the friend of the world is the enemy of God. Be assured that you shall find enemies everywhere. When you sleep, think that you are resting on the battlefield; when you walk, suspect an ambush in every hedge. As mosquitoes are said to bite strangers more than natives, so will the trials of earth be sharpest to you. Lastly, look *within you,* into your own heart, and observe what is there. *Sin* and *self* are still within. Ah! if you had no devil to tempt you, no enemies to fight you, and no world to ensnare you, you will still find in yourself evil enough to shake you greatly, for "the heart is deceitful above all things and beyond cure." Expect trouble then, but don't be despondent on account of it, for God is with you to help and to strengthen you. He has said, "I will be with you in trouble; I will deliver you and honor you."

"An ever-present help." — Psalm 46:1

 OVENANT blessings are not meant only to be looked at, but to be appropriated. Even our Lord Jesus is given to us for our present use. Believer, you don't make use of Christ as you ought to do. When you are in trouble, why don't you tell Him all your grief? Hasn't He got a sympathizing heart, and can't He comfort and relieve you? No, you are going about to all your friends, except your best Friend, and telling your tale everywhere except into the heart of your Lord. Are you burdened with this day's sins? Here is a fountain filled with blood: use it, saint, use it. Has a sense of guilt returned to you? The pardoning grace of Jesus may be proved again and again. Come to Him at once for purifying. Do you deplore your weakness? He is your strength: why not lean upon Him? Do you feel naked? Come here, soul; put on the robe of Jesus' righteousness. Don't just stand there looking at it; wear it. Strip off your own righteousness, and your own fears, too: put on the fair white linen, for it was meant to be *worn*. Do you feel sick? Pull the nightbell of prayer, and call on the Beloved Physician! He will give you the stimulant that will revive you. You are poor, but then you have "a relative, a man of standing." What! you still won't go to Him and ask Him to give you of His abundance, even after He has given you this promise, that you shall be joint heir with Him, and has transferred ownership of all that He is and all that He has to be yours? There is nothing Christ dislikes more than for His people to make a spectacle of Him, and not to use Him. He loves to be employed by us. The more burdens we put on His shoulders, the more precious He will be to us.

> "Let us be simple with Him, then,
> Not backward, stiff, or cold,
> As though our Bethlehem could be
> What Sinai was of old."

"Do men make their own gods? Yes, but they are not gods!"
— *Jeremiah 16:20*

NE great besetting sin of ancient Israel was idolatry, and the spiritual Israel is vexed with a tendency toward the same folly. Remphan's star shines no longer, and the women weep no more for Tammuz, but Mammon still intrudes his golden calf, and the shrines of pride are not forsaken. Self in various forms struggles to subdue the chosen ones under its dominion, and the flesh sets up its altars wherever it can find space for them. Favorite children are often the cause of excessive sin in believers; the Lord is grieved when He sees us doting upon them above measure; they will live to be as great a curse to us as Absalom was to David, or they will be taken from us to leave our homes desolate. If Christians desire to grow thorns to stuff into their sleepless pillows, let them dote on their dear ones.

It is truly said that "they are not gods," for the objects of our foolish love are very doubtful blessings, the solace which they yield us now is dangerous, and the help which they can give us in the hour of trouble is little indeed. Why, then, are we so bewitched with vanities? We pity the poor heathen who adore a god of stone, and yet worship a god of gold. Where is the vast superiority between a god of flesh and one of wood? The principle, the sin, the folly is the same in either case, only that in ours the crime is more aggravated because we have more light, and sin in the face of it. The heathen bows to a false deity, but the true God he has never known; we commit two evils, inasmuch as we forsake the living God and turn to idols. May the Lord purge us all from this grievous iniquity!

> "The dearest idol I have known,
> Whate'er that idol be;
> Help me to tear it from thy throne,
> And worship only thee."

"You have been born again, not of perishable seed,
but of imperishable." — *1 Peter 1:23*

ETER most earnestly exhorted the scattered saints to love each other "deeply, from the heart" and he wisely fetched his argument, not from the law, from nature, or from philosophy, but from that high and divine nature which God has implanted in His people. Just as some judicious tutor of princes might work to beget and foster in them a kingly spirit and dignified behavior, finding arguments in their position and descent, so, looking upon God's people as heirs of glory, princes of the blood royal, descendants of the King of kings, earth's truest and oldest aristocracy, Peter said to them, "Love one another deeply, from the heart. For you have been born again, not of perishable seed, but of imperishable, through the living and enduring word of God. For, 'All men are like grass, and all their glory is like the flowers of the field; the grass withers and the flowers fall, but the word of the Lord stands forever.'" It would be well if, in the spirit of humility, we recognized the true dignity of our regenerated nature, and lived up to it. What is a Christian? If you compare him with a king, he adds priestly sanctity to royal dignity. The king's royalty often lies only in his crown, but with a Christian it is infused into his inmost nature. He is as much above his fellows through his new birth, as a man is above the beast that perishes. Surely he ought to carry himself, in all his dealings, as one who is not of the multitude, but chosen out of the world, distinguished by sovereign grace, written among "a people belonging to God," and who, therefore, cannot grovel in the dust as others, nor live after the manner of the world's citizens. Let the dignity of your nature, and the brightness of your prospects, O believers in Christ, constrain you to cleave to holiness, and to avoid the very appearance of evil.

"I will be their God, and they will be my people."
— *2 Corinthians 6:16*

 HAT a sweet title: "My people!" What a cheering revelation: "Their God!" How much meaning is couched in those two words, "My people!" Here is *speciality*. The whole world is God's; the heaven, even the heaven of heavens is the Lord's, and He reigns among the children of men; but of those whom He has chosen, whom He has purchased to Himself, He says what He doesn't say of others — "My people." In this word there is the idea of *proprietorship*. In a special manner the "Lord's portion is His people, Jacob His allotted inheritance." All the nations upon earth are His; the whole world is in His power; yet are His people, His chosen, more especially His possession; for He has done more for them than others; He has bought them with His blood; He has brought them nigh to Himself; He has set His great heart upon them; He has loved them with an everlasting love, a love which many waters cannot quench, and which the revolutions of time shall never suffice in the least degree to diminish. Dear friends, can you, by faith, see yourselves in that number? Can you look up to heaven and say, "My Lord and my God: mine by that sweet *relationship* which entitles me to call You Father; mine by that hallowed *fellowship* which I delight to hold with You when You are pleased to manifest Yourself to me as You do not to the world?" Can you read the Book of Inspiration, and find there the indentures of your salvation? Can you read your title written in precious blood? Can you, by humble faith, lay hold of Jesus' garments, and say, "My Christ"? If you can, then God says of you and of others like you, "My people;" for, if God is your God, and Christ your Christ, the Lord has done you a special, peculiar favor; you are the object of His choice, accepted in His beloved Son.

*"Whoever gives heed to instruction prospers, and
blessed is he who trusts in the LORD."*
— *Proverbs 16:20*

ISDOM is man's true strength; and, under its guidance, he best accomplishes the ends of his being. Wisely handling the matter of life gives to humankind the richest enjoyment, and presents the noblest occupation for his powers; hence, by it he finds good in the fullest sense. Without wisdom, man is as the wild ass's colt, running here and there, wasting strength which might be profitably employed. Wisdom is the compass by which we are to steer across the trackless waste of life; without it we are derelict vessels, the sport of winds and waves. We must be prudent in such a world as this, or we will find no good, but be betrayed into unnumbered ills. The pilgrim will sorely wound his feet among the briers of the wood of life if he doesn't choose his steps with the utmost caution. He who is in a wilderness infested with robber bands must handle matters wisely if he would journey safely. If, trained by the Great Teacher, we follow where He leads, we shall find good, even while in this dark abode; there are celestial fruits to be gathered this side of Eden's bowers, and songs of paradise to be sung amid the groves of earth. But where shall this wisdom be found? Many have dreamed of it, but have not possessed it. Where shall we learn it? Let's listen to the voice of the Lord, for He has declared the secret; He has revealed to the sons of men wherein true wisdom lies, and we have it in the text, "Blessed is he who trusts in the LORD." *The true way to handle a matter wisely is to trust in the Lord.* This is the sure clue to the most intricate labyrinths of life, follow it and find eternal bliss. He who trusts in the Lord has a diploma for wisdom granted by inspiration: he is happy now, and shall be happier above. Lord, in this sweet evening, walk with me in the garden and teach me the wisdom of faith.

"We live in him." — 1 John 4:13

O you want a house for your soul? Do you ask, "What does it cost?" It costs something less than proud human nature would like to give. It is without money and without price. Ah! you would like to pay a respectable rent! You would love to do something to win Christ? Then you can't have the house, for it is "without price." Will you take my Master's house on a lease for all eternity, with nothing to pay for it, nothing but the ground rent of loving and serving Him forever? Will you take Jesus and "live in Him?" See, this house is furnished with all you want, it is filled with riches more than you will spend as long as you live. Here you can have intimate communion with Christ and feast on His love; here are tables well-stored with food for you to live on forever; in it, when weary, you can find rest with Jesus; and from it you can look out and see heaven itself. Will you have the house? Ah! if you are homeless, you will say, "I should like to have the house; but may I have it?" Yes; there is the key — the key is, "Come to Jesus." "But," you say, "I am too shabby for such a house." Never mind; there are garments inside. If you feel guilty and condemned, come; and though the house is too good for you, Christ will make you good enough for the house before long. He will wash you and purify you, and you will yet be able to sing, "We live in Him." Believer: three times happy are you to have such a dwelling place! You are greatly privileged, for you have a "strong habitation" in which you are safe forever. And "living in Him," you haven't only a perfect and secure house, but an *everlasting* one. When this world shall have melted like a dream, our house shall live, and stand more imperishable than marble, more solid than granite, self-existent as God, for it is God Himself — "We live in Him."

"All the days of my hard service I will wait."
— *Job 14:14*

 *little stay on earth will make heaven more heav-
enly.* Nothing makes rest so sweet as toil;
nothing renders security so pleasant as exposure to alarms. The bitter quassia cups of
earth will give a relish to the new wine
which sparkles in the golden bowls of glory.
Our battered armor and scarred countenances will render
our victory more illustrious above, when we are welcomed
to the seats of those who have overcome the world. We
should not have full *fellowship with Christ* if we didn't for
awhile sojourn below, for He was baptized with a baptism
of suffering among humankind, and we must be baptized
with the same if we would share His kingdom. Fellowship
with Christ is so honorable that the sorest sorrow is a light
price by which to procure it. Another reason for our
lingering here is *for the good of others.* We would not wish to
enter heaven until our work is done, and it may be that we
are yet ordained to dispense light to souls overtaken by
darkness in the wilderness of sin. Our prolonged stay here
is no doubt *for God's glory.* A tested saint, like a well-cut
diamond, glitters greatly in the King's crown. Nothing
reflects so much honor on a workman as a protracted and
severe trial of his work, and its triumphant endurance of
the ordeal without giving way in any part. We are God's
workmanship, in whom He will be glorified by our afflictions. It is for the honor of Jesus that we endure the trial of
our faith with sacred joy. Let each person surrender one's
own longings to the glory of Jesus, and feel, "If my lying in
the dust would elevate my Lord by so much as an inch, let
me still lie among the pots of earth. If to live on earth
forever would make my Lord more glorious, it should be
my heaven to be shut out of heaven." Our time is fixed and
settled by eternal decree. Don't be anxious about it, but
wait with patience until the pearly gates open.

"Many followed him, and he healed all their sick."
— *Matthew 12:15*

HAT a mass of hideous sickness must have thrust itself under the eye of Jesus! Yet we don't read that He was disgusted, but patiently waited on every case. What a singular variety of evils must have met at His feet! What sickening ulcers and putrefying sores! Yet He was ready for every new shape of the monster evil, and was victor over it in every form. Let the arrow fly from what quarter it might, He quenched its fiery power. The heat of fever, or the cold of dropsy; the lethargy of palsy, or the rage of madness; the filth of leprosy, or the darkness of ophthalmia — all knew the power of His word, and fled at His command. In every corner of the field He was triumphant over evil, and received the homage of delivered captives. He came, He saw, He conquered everywhere. It is even so this morning. Whatever my own case may be, the beloved Physician can heal me; and whatever may be the state of others whom I may remember at this moment in prayer, I may have hope in Jesus that He will be able to heal them of their sins. My child, my friend, my dearest one, I can have hope for each, for all, when I remember the healing power of my Lord; and on my own account, however severe my struggle with sins and infirmities, I may yet be of good cheer. He who on earth walked the hospitals, still dispenses His grace, and works wonders among humanity: let me go to Him at once in right earnest.

Let me praise Him, this morning, as I remember *how* He wrought His spiritual cures, which bring Him most renown. It was by taking upon Himself our sicknesses. "By His wounds we are healed." The church on earth is full of souls healed by our beloved Physician; and the inhabitants of heaven itself confess that "He healed them all." Come, then, my soul, publish abroad the virtue of His grace, and let it be "for the LORD's renown, for an everlasting sign, which will not be destroyed."

"Jesus said to him, Get up! Pick up your mat
and walk." — John 5:8

IKE many others, the invalid had been waiting for a wonder to be wrought, and a sign to be given. Wearily, he watched the pool, but no angel came, or not for him; yet, thinking it to be his only chance, he still waited, and didn't know that there was One near him whose word could heal him in a moment. Many are in the same plight: they are waiting for some singular emotion, remarkable impression, or celestial vision; they wait in vain and watch for nought. Even supposing that, in a few cases, remarkable signs are seen, yet these are rare, and no man has a right to look for them in his own situation; no man especially who feels his infirmity to avail himself of the moving of the water even if it came. It is a very sad reflection that tens of thousands are now waiting in the use of means, and ordinances, and vows, and resolutions, and have so waited time out of mind, in vain, utterly in vain. Meanwhile these poor souls forget the present Savior, who bids them look to Him and be saved. He could heal them at once, but they prefer to wait for an angel and a wonder. To trust Him is the sure way to every blessing, and He is worthy of the most implicit confidence; but unbelief makes them prefer the cold porches of Bethesda to the warm bosom of His love. O that the Lord may turn His eye upon the multitudes who are in this situation tonight; may He forgive the slights which they put upon His divine power, and call them by that sweet constraining voice, to rise from the bed of despair, and in the energy of faith take up their mat and walk. O Lord, hear our prayer for all such at this calm hour of sunset, and before the day breaks may they look and live.

Courteous reader, is there anything in this portion for you?

"The man who was healed had no idea who it was."
— *John 5:13*

EARS are short to the happy and healthy; but thirty-eight years of disease must have dragged a very weary length along the life of the poor invalid man. Therefore, when Jesus healed him by a word, while he lay at the pool of Bethesda, he was delightfully *sensible of a change.* Even so the sinner who has for weeks and months been paralyzed with despair, and has wearily sighed for salvation, is very conscious of the change when the Lord Jesus speaks the word of power, and gives joy and peace in believing. The evil removed is too great to be removed without our discerning it; the life imparted is too remarkable to be possessed and remain inoperative; and the change wrought is too marvelous not to be perceived. Yet the poor man was *ignorant of the author* of his cure; he didn't know the sacredness of His person, the offices which He sustained, or the errand which brought Him among men. Great ignorance of Jesus may remain in hearts which yet feel the power of His blood. We mustn't hastily condemn others for lack of knowledge; but where we can see the faith which saves the soul, we must believe that salvation has been given. The Holy Spirit makes us penitent long before He makes us divine; and those who believe what they know, shall soon know more clearly what they believe. Ignorance is, however, an evil; for this poor man was much *tantalized by the Pharisees,* and was quite unable to cope with them. It is good to be able to answer gainsayers; but we can't do so if we don't know the Lord Jesus clearly and with understanding. The cure of his ignorance, however, soon followed the cure of his infirmity, for he was *visited by the Lord in the temple;* and after that gracious manifestation, he was *found testifying* that "it was Jesus who had made him well." Lord, if You have saved me, show me Yourself, that I may declare You to others.

"Submit to God." — Job 22:21

F we honestly want to "submit to God and be at peace with Him," we must know Him as He has revealed Himself, not only in *the unity of His essence and subsistence,* but also in *the plurality of His persons.* God said, "Let *us* make man in *our* image" — don't be content until you know something of the "us" from whom his being was derived. Make an effort to know the Father; bury your head in His bosom in deep repentance, and confess that you are not worthy to be called His child; receive the kiss of His love; let the ring which is the token of His eternal faithfulness be on your finger; sit at His table and let your heart delight in His grace. Then press forward and seek to know much of *the Son of God* who is the brightness of His Father's glory, and yet in unspeakable condescension of grace became human for our sakes; know Him in the singular complexity of His nature: eternal God, and yet suffering, finite man; follow Him as He walks the waters with the tread of deity, and as He sits upon the well in the weariness of humanity. Don't be satisfied unless you know much of Jesus Christ as your Friend, your Brother, your Husband, your all. Do not forget *the Holy Spirit;* endeavor to obtain a clear view of His nature and character, His attributes, and His works. Behold that Spirit of the Lord, who first of all moved upon chaos, and brought forth order; who now visits the chaos of your soul, and creates the order of holiness. Behold Him as the Lord and giver of spiritual life, the Illuminator, the Instructor, the Comforter, and the Sanctifier. Behold Him as, like holy unction, He descends upon the head of Jesus, and then afterwards rests upon *you* who are like the skirts of His garments. Such an intelligent, scriptural, and experimental belief in the Trinity in Unity is yours if you truly know God; and such knowledge *brings peace indeed.*

"Who has blessed us . . . with every spiritual blessing."
— *Ephesians 1:3*

LL the goodness of the past, the present, and the future, Christ gives to His people. In the mysterious ages of the past the Lord Jesus was His Father's first elect, and in His *election* He gave us an interest, for we were chosen in Him from before the foundation of the world. He had from all eternity the prerogatives of *Sonship*, as His Father's only-begotten and well-beloved Son, and He has, in the riches of His grace, by adoption and regeneration, elevated us to sonship also, so that to us He has given "power to become the people of God." The *eternal covenant*, based upon suretyship and confirmed by oath, is ours, for our strong consolation and security. In the *everlasting settlements of predestining wisdom* and omnipotent decree, the eye of the Lord Jesus was ever fixed on us; and we may rest assured that in the whole roll of destiny there is not a line which militates against the interests of His redeemed. The *great betrothal* of the Prince of Glory is ours, for it is to us that He is betrothed, as the sacred nuptials shall before long declare to an assembled universe. The *marvelous incarnation* of the God of heaven, with all the amazing condescension and humiliation which attended it, is ours. The bloody sweat, the scourge, the cross, are ours forever. Whatever blissful consequences flow from *perfect obedience, finished atonement, resurrection, ascension, or intercession,* all are ours by His own gift. Upon His breastplate He is now bearing our names; and in His authoritative pleadings at the throne He remembers our persons and pleads our cause. His *dominion* over principalities and powers, and His absolute majesty in heaven, He employs for the benefit of them who trust in Him. His high estate is as much at our service as was His condition of abasement. He who gave Himself for us in the depths of woe and death, does not withdraw the grant now that He is enthroned in the highest heavens.

"Come, my lover, let us go to the countryside . . .
to see if the vines have budded."
— *Song of Songs 7:11, 12*

THE church was about to engage in earnest work, and desired her Lord's company in it. She doesn't say, "I will go," but "let us go." It is blessed working when Jesus is at our side! It is the business of God's people to be trimmers of God's vines. Like our first parents, we are put into the garden of the Lord for usefulness; let's therefore go forth into the field. Observe that the church, when she is in her right mind, in all her many labors desires to enjoy communion with Christ. Some imagine that they cannot serve Christ actively, and yet have fellowship with Him: they are mistaken. Doubtless it is very easy to fritter away our inward life in outward exercises, and come to complain with the spouse, "[They] made me take care of the vineyards; my own vineyard I have neglected:" but there is no reason why this should be the case except our own folly and neglect. It is certain that one who professes may do nothing, and yet grow quite as lifeless in spiritual things as those who are most busy. Mary was not praised for sitting still; but for her *sitting at Jesus' feet.* Even so, Christians are not to be praised for neglecting duties under the pretense of having secret fellowship with Jesus: it is not sitting, but sitting at Jesus' feet which is commendable. Do not think that activity is in itself an evil: it is a great blessing, and a means of grace to us. Paul called it a grace given to him to be allowed to preach; and every form of Christian service may become a personal blessing to those engaged in it. Those who have most fellowship with Christ are not recluses or hermits, who have much time to spare, but indefatigable laborers who are toiling for Jesus, and who, in their toil, have Him side by side with them, so that they are workers together with God. Let's remember then, in anything we have to do for Jesus, that we can do it, and should do it in close communion with Him.

"But Christ has indeed been raised from the dead."
— *1 Corinthians 15:20*

 HE whole system of Christianity rests upon the fact that "Christ has indeed been raised from the dead;" for, "If Christ has not been raised, our preaching is useless and so is your faith; you are still in your sins." The *divinity* of Christ finds its surest proof in His resurrection, since He was "through the Spirit of holiness declared with power to be the Son of God by His resurrection from the dead." It would not be unreasonable to doubt His Deity if He had not risen. Moreover, Christ's *sovereignty* depends upon His resurrection, "For this very reason, Christ died and returned to life so that He might be the Lord of both the dead and the living." Again, our *justification,* that choice blessing of the covenant, is linked with Christ's triumphant victory over death and the grave; for "He was delivered over to death for our sins and was raised to life for our justification." No, more, our very *regeneration* is connected with His resurrection, for we are "given new birth into a living hope through the resurrection of Jesus Christ from the dead." And most certainly our *ultimate resurrection* rests here, for "And if the Spirit of Him who raised Jesus from the dead is living in you, He who raised Christ from the dead will also give life to your mortal bodies through His Spirit, who lives in you." If Christ isn't risen, then we shall not rise; but if He is risen then they who are asleep in Christ have not perished, but in their flesh shall surely behold their God. Thus, the silver thread of resurrection runs through all blessings of believers, from our regeneration onwards to our eternal glory, and binds us together. How important then will this glorious fact be in his estimation, and how he will rejoice that beyond a doubt it is established, that "Christ has indeed been raised from the dead."

"The promise is fulfill'd,
Redemption's work is done,
Justice with mercy's reconciled,
For God has raised His Son."

"The One and Only, who came from the Father, full of grace and truth." — *John 1:14*

ELIEVER, you can bear your testimony that Christ *is the One and Only, who came from the Father,* as well as the first begotten from the dead. You can say, "He is divine to me, if He is human to all the world beside. He has done that for me which none but a God could do. He has subdued my stubborn will, melted a heart of adamant, opened gates of brass, and snapped bars of iron. He has turned for me my mourning into laughter, and my desolation into joy; He has led my captives in my train, and made my heart rejoice with unspeakable joy and full of glory. Let others think as they will of Him, to me He must be the One and Only, who came from the Father: blessed be His name. And He is *full of grace.* Ah! had He not been, I should never have been saved. He drew me when I struggled to escape from His grace; and when at last I came all trembling like a condemned culprit to His mercy seat He said, 'your sins which are many are all forgiven you: be of good cheer.' And He is *full of truth.* His promises have been true; not one has failed. I bear witness that no servant has had such a master as I have; no brother such a kinsman as He has been to me; no spouse such a husband as Christ has been to my soul; no sinner a better Savior; no mourner a better comforter than Christ has been to my spirit. I want none beside Him. In life He is my life, and in death He shall be the death of death; in poverty Christ is my riches; in sickness He makes my bed; in darkness He is my star, and in brightness He is my sun; He is the manna of the camp in the wilderness, and He shall be the new corn of the host when they come to Canaan. Jesus is to me all grace and no wrath, all truth and no falsehood: and of truth and grace He is *full,* infinitely full. My soul, this night, bless with all your might 'the One and Only.' "

"Surely I am with you always." — *Matthew 28:20*

IT is well there is One who is always the same, and who is always with us. It is well there is one stable rock amid the billows of the sea of life. O my soul, set not your affections upon rusting, moth-eaten, decaying treasures, but set your heart upon Him who remains faithful to you forever. Do not build your house upon the moving quicksands of a deceitful world, but found your hopes upon this rock, which, amid descending rain and roaring floods, shall stand immovably secure. My soul, I charge you, lay up your treasure in the only secure cabinet; store your jewels where you can never lose them. Put your all in Christ; set all your affections on His person, all your hope in His merit, all your trust in His efficacious blood, all your joy in His presence, and so you may laugh at loss, and defy destruction. Remember that all the flowers in the world's garden fade by turns, and the day comes when nothing will be left but the dark, cold earth. Death's dark extinguisher must soon put out your candle. Oh! how sweet to have sunlight when the candle is gone! The dark flood must soon roll between you and all you have; then wed your heart to Him who will never leave you; trust yourself with Him who will go with you through the dark and surging current of death's stream, and who will land you safely on the celestial shore, and make you sit with Him in heavenly places forever. Go, sorrowing son of affliction, tell your secrets to the Friend who sticks closer than a brother. Trust Him with all your concerns, Him who never can be taken from you, who will never leave you, and who will never let you leave Him, even "Jesus Christ, the same yesterday and today and forever." "Surely I am with you always," is enough for my soul to live on, no matter who else forsakes me.

"Be strong and very courageous." — *Joshua 1:7*

UR God's tender love for His servants makes Him concerned for the state of their inward feelings. He desires them to be of good courage. Some regard it as a small thing for a believer to be vexed with doubts and fears, but God doesn't think so. From this text it is plain that our Master doesn't want us to be entangled with fears. He wants us to be without anxiety, without doubt, without cowardice. Our Master doesn't think so lightly of our unbelief as we do. When we are hopeless we are subject to a grievous malady, not to be trifled with, but to be carried at once to the beloved Physician. Our Lord doesn't love to see our countenance sad. It was a law of Xerxes that no one should come into the king's court dressed in mourning: this is not the law of the King of kings, for we may come mourning as we are; but still He wants us to put off the spirit of heaviness and put on the garment of praise, for there is so much reason to rejoice. The Christian ought to be of a courageous spirit in order to glorify the Lord by enduring trials in an heroic manner. If you are fearful and fainthearted, *you will dishonor your God.* Besides, *what a bad example it is.* This disease of doubtfulness and discouragement is an epidemic which soon spreads among the Lord's flock. One downcast believer makes twenty souls sad. Moreover, unless your courage is kept up, *Satan will be too much for you.* Let your spirit be joyful in God your Savior, the joy of the Lord shall be your strength, and no fiend of hell shall make headway against you: but cowardice throws down the banner. Moreover, *work is light* to a man of cheerful spirit; and *success waits upon cheerfulness.* Those who toil, rejoicing in their God, believing with all their hearts, has success guaranteed. Those who sow in hope shall reap in joy; therefore, dear reader, "be strong and very courageous."

"And show myself to him." — *John 14:21*

HE Lord Jesus gives special revelations of Himself to His people. Even if Scripture didn't declare this, there are many of the children of God who could testify the truth of it from their own experience. They have had manifestations of their Lord and Savior Jesus Christ in a peculiar manner, such as no mere reading or hearing could afford. In the biographies of eminent saints you will find many instances recorded in which Jesus has been pleased, in a very special manner, to speak to their souls and to unfold the wonders of His person; yes, their souls have been steeped in such happiness that they thought they were in heaven, whereas they weren't there, though well nigh on its threshold — for when Jesus manifests Himself to His people, it is heaven on earth; it is paradise in embryo; it is bliss begun. Special manifestations of Christ exercise a holy influence on the believer's heart. One effect will be *humility.* If a man says, "I have had such-and-such spiritual communications, I am a great man," he has never had any communion with Jesus at all; for "The LORD . . . looks upon the lowly, but the proud He knows from afar." He does not need to come near them to know them, and will never give them any visits of love. Another effect will be *happiness;* for in God's presence there are pleasures forevermore. *Holiness* will be sure to follow. A person who has no holiness has never had this manifestation. Some people profess a great deal; but we must not believe them unless we see that their deeds answer to what they say. "Do not be deceived: God cannot be mocked." He will not give His favors to the wicked: for while He will not cast away a perfect person, neither will He respect an evil doer. Thus there will be three effects of nearness to Jesus — humility, happiness, and holiness. May God give them to you, Christian!

"Do not be afraid to go down to Egypt, for I will make you into a great nation there. I will go down to Egypt with you, and I will surely bring you back again." — Genesis 46:3, 4

ACOB must have shuddered at the thought of leaving the land of his father's sojourning, and dwelling among heathen strangers. It was *a new scene, and likely to be a trying one:* who would venture among couriers of a foreign monarch without anxiety? Yet the way was *evidently appointed* for him, and therefore he resolved to go. This is frequently the position of believers now — they are called to perils and temptations altogether untried: at such seasons *let them imitate Jacob's example* by offering sacrifices of prayer to God, and seeking His direction; let them not take a step until they have waited upon the Lord for His blessing: then they *will have Jacob's companion* as their friend and helper. How blessed to feel assured that the Lord is with us in all our ways, and condescends to go down into our humiliations and banishments with us! Even beyond the ocean our Father's love beams like the sun in its strength. We cannot hesitate to go where Jehovah promises His presence; even the valley of deathshade grows bright with the radiance of this assurance. Marching onwards with faith in their God, believers *shall have Jacob's promise.* They shall be brought up again, whether it is from the troubles of life or the chambers of death. Jacob's seed came out of Egypt in due time, and so shall all the faithful pass unscathed through the tribulation of life, and the terror of death. Let's *exercise Jacob's confidence. "Do not be afraid,"* is the Lord's command and His divine encouragement to those who at His bidding are launching upon new seas; the divine presence and preservation forbid so much as one unbelieving fear. Without our God we are afraid to move; but when He tells us to, it is dangerous to linger. Reader, go forward, and don't be afraid.

"Weeping may remain for a night, but rejoicing comes in the morning." — Psalm 30:5

HRISTIAN! If you are in a night of trial, think of tomorrow; cheer up your heart with the thought of the coming of your Lord. Be patient, for

"Lo! He comes with clouds descending."

Be patient! The Farmer waits until He reaps His harvest. Be patient; for you know who has said, "Behold, I am coming soon! My reward is with Me, and I will give to everyone according to what he has done." If you have never been as miserable as you are now, remember

"A few more rolling suns, at most,
Will land thee on fair Canaan's coast."

Your head may be crowned with thorny troubles now, but it shall wear a starry crown before long; your hand may be filled with cares — it shall sweep the strings of the harp of heaven soon. Your garments may be soiled with dust now; they shall be white before long. Wait a little longer. Ah! how despicable our troubles and trials will seem when we look back upon them! Looking at them here in the prospect, they seem immense; but when we get to heaven we shall then

"With transporting joys recount,
The labors of our feet."

Our trials will then seem light and momentary afflictions. Let's go on boldly; even if the night has never been so dark, the morning comes, which is more than they can say who are shut up in the darkness of hell. Do you know what it is thus to live on the future — to live on expectation — to antedate heaven? Happy believer, to have so sure, so comforting a hope. It may be all dark now, but it will soon be light; it may be all trial now, but it will soon be all happiness. What does it matter though "weeping may remain for a night" when "rejoicing comes in the morning?"

"You are my portion, O LORD." — *Psalm 119:57*

OOK at your possessions, O believer, and compare your portion with the lot of your neighbors. Some of them have their portion in the field; they are rich, and their harvests yield them a golden increase; but what are harvests compared with your God, who is the God of harvests? What are bursting granaries compared with Him, who is the Farmer, and feeds you with the bread of heaven? Some have their portion in the city; their wealth is abundant, and flows to them in constant streams, until they become a very reservoir of gold; but what is gold compared with your God? You could not live on it; your spiritual life could not be sustained by it. Put it on a troubled conscience, and could it allay its pangs? Apply it to a hopeless heart, and see if it could stop a solitary groan, or give one grief the less? But you have God, and in Him you have more than gold or riches ever could buy. Some have their portion in that which most men love — applause and fame; but ask yourself, isn't your God more to you than that? What if a myriad of trumpets should sound your praise, would this prepare you to pass the Jordan, or cheer you in prospect of judgment? No, there are griefs in life which wealth cannot alleviate; and there is the deep need of a dying hour, for which no riches can provide. But when you have *God* for your portion, you have more than all else put together. In Him every want is met, whether in life or in death. With God for your portion you are rich indeed, for He will supply your need, comfort your heart, assuage your grief, guide your steps, be with you in the dark valley, and then take you home, to enjoy Him as your portion forever. "I already have plenty," said Esau; this is the best thing a human being can say, but Jacob replies, "I have all I need," which is a note too high for carnal minds.

"Co-heirs with Christ." — Romans 8:17

THE boundless realms of His Father's universe are Christ's by prescriptive right. As "heir of all things," He is the sole proprietor of the vast creation of God, and He has admitted us to claim the whole as ours, by virtue of that deed of co-heir-ship which the Lord has ratified with His chosen people. The golden streets of paradise, the pearly gates, the river of life, the transcendent bliss, and the unutterable glory, are, by our blessed Lord, made over to us for our everlasting possession. All that He has He shares with His people. He has placed the royal crown upon the head of His church, appointing her a kingdom, and calling her sons a royal priesthood, a generation of priests and kings. He uncrowned Himself that we might have a coronation of glory; He would not sit upon His own throne until He had procured a place upon it for all who overcome by His blood. Crown the head and the whole body shares the honor. Behold here the reward of every Christian conqueror! Christ's throne, crown, scepter, palace, treasure, robes, and heritage are yours. Far superior to the jealousy, selfishness, and greed, which admit of no participation of their advantages, Christ deems His happiness completed by His people sharing it. "I have given them the glory that You gave Me." "I have told you this so that My joy may be in you and that your joy may be complete." The smiles of His Father are all the sweeter to Him, because His people share them. The honors of His kingdom are more pleasing, because His people appear with Him in glory. More valuable to Him are His conquests, since they have taught His people to overcome. He delights in His throne because on it there is a place for them. He rejoices in His royal robes since His skirts are spread over them. He delights all the more in His joy because He calls them to enter into it.

> *"He gathers the lambs in his arms and carries them close to his heart."* — *Isaiah 40:11*

 HO is He of whom such gracious words are spoken? He is THE GOOD SHEPHERD. Why does He carry the lambs close to His heart? Because *He has a tender heart, and any weakness at once melts His heart.* The sighs, the ignorance, the feebleness of the little ones of His flock draw forth His compassion. *It is His office,* as a faithful High Priest, to consider the weak. Besides, *He purchased them with blood, they are His property:* He must and will care for *that* which cost Him so dear. Then He is *responsible for each lamb,* bound by covenant engagements not to lose one. Moreover, *they are all a part of His glory and reward.*

But how may we understand the expression, "He *carries* them"? Sometimes He carries them by *not permitting them to endure much trial.* Providence deals tenderly with them. Often they are "carried" by being filled with *an unusual degree of love,* so that they bear up and stand fast. Though their knowledge may not be deep, they have great sweetness in what they do know. Frequently He "carries" them by giving them *a very simple faith,* which takes the promise just as it stands, and believingly runs with every trouble straight to Jesus. The simplicity of their faith gives them an unusual degree of confidence, which carries them above the world.

"He carries the lambs *close to His heart.*" Here is *boundless affection.* Would He put them close to His heart if He didn't love them very much? Here is *tender nearness:* so near are they, that they could not possibly be nearer. Here is *hallowed familiarity:* there are precious love passages between Christ and His weak ones. Here is *perfect safety:* in His bosom who can hurt them? They must hurt the Shepherd first. Here is *perfect rest and sweetest comfort.* Surely we are not sufficiently sensitive to the infinite tenderness of Jesus!

"Everyone who believes is justified." — *Acts 13:39*

HE believer in Christ receives a *present* justification. Faith does not produce this fruit
before long, but *now*. So far as justification is
the result of faith, it is given to the soul in
the moment when it closes with Christ, and
accepts Him as its all in all. Are they who
stand before the throne of God justified now? — so are we,
as truly and as clearly justified as they who walk in white
and sing melodious praises to celestial harps. The thief
upon the cross was justified the moment that he turned the
eye of faith to Jesus; and Paul, the aged, after years of
service, was not more justified than was the thief with no
service at all. We are *today* accepted in the Beloved, *today*
absolved from sin, *today* acquitted at the bar of God. Oh!
soul-transporting thought! There are some clusters of Eshcol's vine which we shall not be able to gather until we
enter heaven; but this is a bough which runs over the wall.
This is not as the corn of the land, which we can never eat
until we cross the Jordan; but this is part of the manna in
the wilderness, a portion of our daily nutriment with
which God supplies us in our journeying to and fro. We are
now — even *now* pardoned; even *now* are our sins put
away; even *now* we stand in the sight of God accepted, as
though we had never been guilty. "Therefore, there is *now*
no condemnation for those who are in Christ Jesus." There
is not a sin in the Book of God, even *now*, against one of
His people. Who dares to lay anything to their charge?
There is neither speck, nor spot, nor wrinkle, nor any such
thing remaining upon any one believer in the matter of
justification in the sight of the Judge of all the earth. Let
present privilege awaken us to present duty, and now,
while life lasts, let's spend and be spent for our sweet Lord
Jesus.

"Made perfect." — *Hebrews 12:23*

ECOLLECT that there are two kinds of perfection which the Christian needs — the perfection of justification in the person of Jesus, and the perfection of sanctification wrought in him by the Holy Spirit. At present, corruption still remains even in the breasts of the regenerate — experience soon teaches us this. Within us are still lusts and evil imaginations. But I rejoice to know that the day is coming when God shall finish the work which He has begun; and He shall present my soul, not only perfect in Christ, but perfect through the Spirit, without spot or blemish, or any such thing. Can it be true that this poor sinful heart of mine is to become holy even as God is holy? Can it be that this spirit, which often cries, "O wretched man that I am! who shall deliver me from the body of this sin and death?" shall get rid of sin and death — that I shall have no evil things to vex my ears, and no unholy thoughts to disturb my peace? Oh, happy hour! may it be hastened! When I cross the Jordan, the work of sanctification will be finished; but not until that moment shall I even claim perfection in myself. Then my spirit shall have its last baptism in the Holy Spirit's fire. It seems to me I long to die to receive that last and final purification which shall usher me into heaven. Not an angel more pure than I shall be, for I shall be able to say, in a double sense, "I am clean," through Jesus' blood, and through the Spirit's work. Oh, how we should extol the power of the Holy Spirit in thus making us fit to stand before our Father in heaven! Yet let not the hope of perfection hereafter make us content with imperfection now. If it does this, our hope cannot be genuine; for a good hope is a purifying thing, even now. The work of grace must be *abiding in us now* or it cannot be *perfected then*. Let's pray to "be filled with the Spirit," that we may *increasingly* bring forth the fruits of righteousness.

*"Who richly provides us with everything
for our enjoyment." — 1 Timothy 6:17*

UR Lord Jesus is always giving, and not for a
single instant does He withdraw His hand.
As long as there is a vessel of grace not yet
full to the brim, the oil shall not be stayed.
He is a sun ever-shining; He is manna always falling round the camp; He is a rock in
the desert, ever sending out streams of life from His
smitten side; the rain of His grace is always dropping; the
river of His bounty is ever-flowing, and the well-spring of
His love is constantly overflowing. As the King can never
die, so His grace can never fail. Daily we pluck His fruit,
and daily His branches bend down to our hand with a fresh
store of mercy. There are seven feast days in His weeks,
and as many as are the days, so many are the banquets in
His years. Who has ever returned from His door unblessed? Who has ever risen from His table unsatisfied, or
from His bosom un-emparadised? His mercies are new
every morning and fresh every evening. Who can know the
number of His benefits, or recount the list of His bounties?
Every sand which drops from the glass of time is but the
tardy follower of a myriad of mercies. The wings of our
hours are covered with the silver of His kindness, and with
the yellow gold of His affection. The river of time bears
from the mountains of eternity the golden sands of His
favor. The countless stars are but as the standard bearers of
a more innumerable host of blessings. Who can count the
dust of the benefits which He gives to Jacob, or tell the
number of the fourth part of His mercies towards Israel?
How shall my soul extol Him who daily loads us with
benefits, and who crowns us with loving-kindness? O that
my praise could be as ceaseless as His bounty! O miserable
tongue, how can you be silent? Wake up, I pray you, lest I
no longer call you my glory, but my shame. "Awake, harp
and lyre! I will awaken the dawn."

*"And he said, This is what the LORD says: Make
this valley full of ditches. For this is what the LORD
says: You will see neither wind nor rain, yet this
valley will be filled with water, and you, your
cattle and your other animals will drink."*
— *2 Kings 3:16, 17*

HE armies of the three kings were famishing
for want of water: God was about to send it,
and in these words the prophet announced
the coming blessing. Here was *a case of human helplessness:* not a drop of water could all
the valiant men procure from the skies or
find in the wells of earth. The people of the Lord are often
at their wits' end in this manner; they see the vanity of the
creature, and learn experimentally where their help is to be
found. Still the people were to make *a believing preparation
for the divine blessing;* they were to dig the trenches in which
the precious liquid would be held. The church must by her
varied agencies, efforts, and prayers, make herself ready to
be blessed; she must make the pools, and the Lord will fill
them. This must be done in faith, in the full assurance that
the blessing is about to descend. Before long there was *a
singular bestowal of the needed boon.* Not as in Elijah's case
did the shower pour from the clouds, but in a silent and
mysterious manner the pools were filled. The Lord has His
own sovereign modes of action: He is not tied to manner
and time as we are, but does as He pleases among humankind. It is ours thankfully to receive from Him, and not to
dictate to Him. We must also notice *the remarkable abundance of the supply* — there was enough for the need of all.
And so it is in the gospel blessing; all the wants of the
congregation and of the entire church shall be met by the
divine power in answer to prayer; and above all this,
victory shall be speedily given to the armies of the Lord.

What am I doing for Jesus? What trenches am I digging? O Lord, make me ready to receive the blessing
which You are so willing to give.

"Walk as Jesus did." — *1 John 2:6*

 HY should Christians imitate Christ? They should do it for *their own sakes.* If they desire to be in a healthy state of soul — if they would escape the sickness of sin, and enjoy the vigor of growing grace, let Jesus be their model. For the sake of their own happiness, if they want to drink wine on the lees, well refined; if they want to enjoy holy and happy communion with Jesus; if they would be lifted up above the cares and troubles of this world, let them walk as Jesus did. There is nothing which can so assist you to walk towards heaven with good speed, as wearing the image of Jesus on your heart to rule all its motions. It is when, by the power of the Holy Spirit, you are enabled to walk with Jesus in His very footsteps, that you are most happy, and most known to be the children of God. Peter, from a distance, is both unsafe and uneasy. Next, for *religion's sake,* strive to be like Jesus. Ah! poor religion, you have been sorely shot at by cruel foes, but you have not been wounded half so dangerously by your foes as by your friends. Who made those wounds in the fair hand of Godliness? Those who profess who used the dagger of hypocrisy. The person who enters the fold with pretenses, being no one but a wolf in sheep's clothing, worries the flock more than the lion outside. There is no weapon half so deadly as a Judas kiss. Those who profess with inconsistency injure the gospel more than the sneering critic or the infidel. But, especially for *Christ's own sake,* imitate His example. Christian, do you love your Savior? Is His name precious to you? Is His cause dear to you? Will you see the kingdoms of the world become His? Is it your desire that He should be glorified? Are you longing that souls should be won to Him? If so, *imitate* Jesus; be a "letter from Christ, known and read by all people."

"You are my servant; I have chosen you."
— *Isaiah 41:9*

 F we have received the grace of God in our hearts, its practical effect has been to make us God's *servants*. We may be unfaithful servants, we certainly are unprofitable ones, but yet, blessed be His name, we *are* His servants, wearing His livery, feeding at His table, and obeying His commands. We were once the servants of sin, but He who made us free has now taken us into His family and taught us obedience to His will. We do not serve our Master perfectly, but we would if we could. As we hear God's voice saying to us, "You are My servant," we can answer with David, "I am Your servant; You have freed me from my chains." But the Lord calls us not only His *servants,* but His *chosen* ones — "I have chosen you." We haven't chosen Him first, but He has chosen us. If we are God's servants, we were not always so; the change must be ascribed to sovereign grace. The eye of sovereignty singled us out, and the voice of unchanging grace declared, "I have loved you with an everlasting love." Long before time began or space was created God had written upon His heart the names of His elect people, had predestined them to be conformed to the image of His Son, and ordained them heirs of all the fullness of His love, His grace, and His glory. What comfort is here! Has the Lord loved us so long, and will He yet cast us away? He knew how stiffnecked we should be, He understood that our hearts were evil, and yet He made the choice. Ah! our Savior is no fickle lover. He does not feel enchanted for awhile with some gleams of beauty from His church's eye, and then afterwards casts her off because of her unfaithfulness. No, He married her in old eternity; and it is written of Jehovah, "He hates divorce." The eternal choice is a bond upon *our* gratitude and upon *His* faithfulness which neither can disown.

> *"In Christ all the fullness of the Deity lives in bodily form,*
> *and you have been given fullness in Christ."*
> — *Colossians 2:9, 10*

LL the attributes of Christ, as God and man, are at our disposal. All the fullness of the Godhead, whatever that marvelous term may comprehend, is ours to make us complete. He cannot endow us with the attributes of Deity; but He has done all that can be done, for He has made even His divine power and Godhead subservient to our salvation. His omnipotence, omniscience, omnipresence, immutability, and infallibility are all combined for our defense. Arise, believer, and behold the Lord Jesus yoking the whole of His divine Godhead to the chariot of salvation! How vast His grace, how firm His faithfulness, how unswerving His immutability, how infinite His power, how limitless His knowledge! All these are by the Lord Jesus made the pillars of the temple of salvation; and all, without decreasing their infinity, are covenanted to us as our perpetual inheritance. The fathomless love of the Savior's heart is every drop of it ours; every sinew in the arm of might, every jewel in the crown of majesty, the immensity of divine knowledge, and the sternness of divine justice, all are ours, and shall be employed for us. The whole of Christ, in His adorable character as the Son of God, is by Himself made over to us most richly to enjoy. His wisdom is our direction, His knowledge our instruction, His power our protection, His justice our surety, His love our comfort, His mercy our solace, and His immutability our trust. He makes no reserve, but opens the recesses of the mountain of God and bids us dig in its mines for the hidden treasures. "All, all, all are yours," He says, "be satisfied with favor and full of the goodness of the Lord." Oh! how sweet thus to behold Jesus, and to call upon Him with the certain confidence that in seeking the intervention of His love or power, we are but asking for that which He has already faithfully promised.

"Later on." — *Hebrews 12:11*

OW happy are tested Christians, *later on.* No calm more deep than that which succeeds a storm. Who hasn't rejoiced in clear shinings after rain? Victorious banquets are for well-exercised soldiers. After killing the lion, we eat the honey; after climbing the Hill Difficulty, we sit down in the arbor to rest; after traversing the Valley of Humiliation, after fighting with Apollyon, the shining one appears, with the healing branch from the tree of life. Our sorrows, like the passing keels of the vessels upon the sea, leave a silver line of holy light behind them "later on." It is peace, sweet, deep peace, which follows the horrible turmoil which once reigned in our tormented, guilty souls. See, then, the happy estate of a Christian! He has the best things last and, therefore, in this world receives the worst things first. But even the worst things are "later on" good things, harsh ploughings yielding joyful harvests. Even now he grows rich by his losses, he rises by his falls, he lives by dying, and becomes full by being emptied; if, then, his grievous afflictions yield him so much peaceable fruit in this life, what shall be the full vintage of joy "later on" in heaven? If dark nights are as bright as the world's days, what shall the days be? If even the starlight is more splendid than the sun, what must the sunlight be? If we can sing in a dungeon, how sweetly will we sing in heaven! If we can praise the Lord in the fires, how will we extol Him before the eternal throne! If evil is good to us *now*, what will the overflowing goodness of God be to us *then*? Oh, blessed "later on!" Who wouldn't be a Christian? Who wouldn't bear the present cross for the crown which comes later on? But herein is work for patience, for the rest is not for today, nor the triumph for the present, but "later on." Wait, O soul, and let patience have her perfect work.

---

*"I have seen slaves on horseback, while princes
go on foot like slaves."* — *Ecclesiastes 10:7*

PSTARTS frequently usurp the highest places, while the truly great pine in obscurity. This is a riddle in providence whose solution will one day gladden the hearts of the upright; but it is so common a fact, that none of us should murmur if it should fall to our own lot. When our Lord was upon the earth, although He is the Prince of the kings of the earth, yet He walked the footpath of weariness and service as the Servant of servants: what wonder is it if His followers, who are princes of the blood, should also be looked down upon as inferior and contemptible persons? The world is upside down, and therefore, the first are last and the last first. See how the servile sons of Satan lord it in the earth! What a high horse they ride! How they lift up their horn on high! Haman is in the court, while Mordecai sits in the gate; David wanders on the mountains, while Saul reigns in state; Elijah is complaining in the cave while Jezebel is boasting in the palace; yet who would wish to take the places of the proud rebels? and who, on the other hand, might not envy the despised saints? When the wheel turns, those who are lowest rise, and the highest sink. Patience, then, believer — eternity will right the wrongs of time.

Let's not fall into the error of letting our passions and carnal appetites ride in triumph, while our nobler powers walk in the dust. Grace must reign as a prince, and make the members of the body instruments of righteousness. The Holy Spirit loves order, and He therefore sets our powers and faculties in due rank and place, giving the highest room to those spiritual faculties which link us with the great King; let's not disturb the divine arrangement, but ask for grace that we may keep under our body and bring it into subjection. We were not newly created to allow our passions to rule over us, but that we, as kings, may reign in Christ Jesus over the triple kingdom of spirit, soul, and body, to the glory of God the Father.

"And prayed that he might die." — *1 Kings 19:4*

T was a remarkable thing that the man who was never to die, for whom God had ordained an infinitely better lot, the man who should be carried to heaven in a chariot of fire, and be translated, that he should not see death — should thus pray, "Take my life, I am no better than my ancestors." We have here a memorable proof that God does not always answer prayer in kind, though He always does in effect. He gave Elijah something better than that which he asked for, and thus really heard and answered him. It was strange that the lion-hearted Elijah should be so depressed by Jezebel's threat as to ask to die, and it was blessedly kind on the part of our heavenly Father that He didn't take His hopeless servant at his word. There is a limit to the doctrine of the prayer of faith. We are not to expect that God will give us everything we choose to ask for. We know that we sometimes ask, and don't receive, because we ask amiss. If we ask for that which is not promised — if we run counter to the spirit which the Lord would have us cultivate — if we ask contrary to His will, or to the decrees of His providence — if we ask merely for the gratification of our own ease, and without an eye to His glory, we mustn't expect that we shall receive. Yet, when we ask in faith, nothing doubting, if we don't receive the precise thing we asked for, we shall receive an equivalent, and more than an equivalent, for it. As one remarks, "If the Lord does not pay in silver, He will in gold; and if He does not pay in gold, He will in diamonds." If He doesn't give you precisely what you ask for, He will give you that which is tantamount to it, and that which you will greatly rejoice to receive instead. Dear reader, pray often, and make this evening a season of earnest intercession, but take heed what you ask.

"The wonder of your great love." — *Psalm 17:7*

WHEN we give our hearts with our alms, we give well, but we must often plead to a failure in this respect. Not so our Master and our Lord. His favors are always performed with the love of His heart. He doesn't send us the cold meat and the broken pieces from the table of His luxury, but He dips our morsel in His own dish, and seasons our provisions with the spices of His fragrant affections. When He puts the golden tokens of His grace into our palms, He accompanies the gift with such a warm pressure of our hand, that the manner of His giving is as precious as the boon itself. He will come into our houses upon His errands of kindness, and He will not act as some austere visitors do in the poor man's cottage, but He sits by our side, not despising our poverty, nor blaming our weakness. Beloved, with what smiles He speaks! What golden sentences drop from His gracious lips! What embraces of affection He gives us! If He had only given us pennies, the way He gave would have gilded them; but as it is, the costly alms are set in a golden basket by His pleasant carriage. It is impossible to doubt the sincerity of His charity, for there is a bleeding heart stamped upon the face of all His benefactions. He gives freely and does not find fault. Not one hint that we are burdensome to Him; not one cold look for His poor pensioners; but He rejoices in His mercy, and presses us close to His heart while He is pouring out His life for us. There is a fragrance in His spikenard which nothing but His heart could produce; there is a sweetness in His honeycomb which couldn't be in it unless the very essence of His soul's affection had been mingled with it. Oh! the rare communion which such singular heartiness effects! May we continually taste and know the blessedness of it!

*"I led them with cords of human kindness,
with ties of love."* — *Hosea 11:4*

UR heavenly Father often draws us with the cords of love; but ah! how reluctant we are to run towards Him! How slowly we respond to His gentle impulses! *He draws us to exercise a more simple faith in Him;* but we have not yet attained to Abraham's confidence; we don't leave our worldly cares with God, but, like Martha, we burden ourselves with much serving. Our meager faith brings leanness into our souls; we don't open our mouths wide, though God has promised to fill them. Doesn't He this evening draw us to trust Him? Can't we hear Him say, "Come, My child, and trust Me. The veil is rent; enter into My presence, and approach boldly to the throne of My grace. I am worthy of your fullest confidence, cast your cares on Me. Shake yourself from the dust of your cares, and put on your beautiful garments of joy." But, alas! though called with tones of love to the blessed exercise of this comforting grace, we will not come. At another time *He draws us to closer communion with Himself.* We have been sitting on the doorstep of God's house, and He bids us advance into the banqueting hall and sup with Him, but we decline the honor. There are secret rooms not yet opened to us; Jesus invites us to enter them, but we hold back. Shame on our cold hearts! We are but poor lovers of our sweet Lord Jesus, not fit to be His servants, much less to be His brides, and yet He has exalted us to be bone of His bone and flesh of His flesh, married to Him by a glorious marriage covenant. Herein is love! But it is love which *takes no denial.* If we do not obey the gentle drawings of His love, He will send affliction to drive us into closer intimacy with Himself. He will have us nearer. What foolish children we are to refuse those bands of love, and so bring upon our backs that whip of cords, which Jesus knows how to use!

"[If] . . . you have tasted that the Lord is good."
— *1 Peter 2:3*

F: — then, this is not a matter to be taken for granted concerning every one of the human race. "If:" — then there is a possibility and a probability that some may not have tasted that the Lord is gracious. "If:" — then this is not a general but a special mercy; and it is necessary to inquire whether we know the grace of God by inward experience. There is no spiritual favor which may not be a matter for heart-searching.

But while this should be a matter of earnest and prayerful inquiry, no one ought to be content while there is any doubt about his having tasted that the Lord is good. A jealous and holy distrust of self may give rise to the question even in the believer's heart, but the *continuance* of such a doubt would be an evil indeed. We mustn't rest without a desperate struggle to clasp the Savior in the arms of faith, and say, "I know whom I have believed, and am convinced that He is able to guard what I have entrusted to Him for that day." Do not rest, O believer, until you have a full assurance of your interest in Jesus. Let nothing satisfy you until, by the infallible witness of the Holy Spirit bearing witness with your spirit, you are certified that you are a child of God. Oh, do not trifle here; don't let "perhaps" and "peradventure" and "if" and "maybe" satisfy your soul. Build on eternal verities, and verily build upon them. Get the sure mercies of David, and surely get them. Let your anchor be cast into that which is within the veil, and see to it that your soul is linked to the anchor by a cable that will not break. Advance beyond these dreary "ifs;" do not live any longer in the wilderness of doubts and fears; cross the Jordan of distrust, and enter the Canaan of peace, where the Canaanite still lingers, but where the land flows unceasingly with milk and honey.

"There is grain in Egypt." — Genesis 42:2

AMINE pinched all the nations, and it seemed inevitable that Jacob and his family should suffer great want; but the God of providence, who never forgets the objects of electing love, had stored a granary for His people by giving the Egyptians warning of the scarcity, and leading them to treasure up the grain of the years of plenty. Little did Jacob expect deliverance from Egypt, but there was the grain in store for him. Believer, though all things are apparently against you, rest assured that God has made a reservation on your behalf; in the catalogue of your griefs there is a saving clause. Somehow He will deliver you, and somewhere He will provide for you. The quarter from which your rescue shall arise may be a very unexpected one, but help will assuredly come in your extremity, and you shall magnify the name of the Lord. If people do not feed you, ravens shall; and if earth yields no wheat, heaven shall drop with manna. Therefore, be of good courage, and rest quietly in the Lord. God can make the sun rise in the west if He pleases, and make the source of distress the channel of delight. The grain in Egypt was all in the hands of the beloved Joseph; he opened or closed the granaries at will. And so the riches of providence are all in the absolute power of our Lord Jesus, who will dispense them freely to His people. Joseph was abundantly ready to help his own family; and Jesus is unceasing in His faithful care for His brothers and sisters. Our business is to go after the help which is provided for us: we must not sit still in despondency, but move quickly, waken ourselves. Prayer will bear us soon into the presence of our royal Brother: once before His throne we have only to ask and have: His stores are not exhausted; there is grain still: His heart is not hard, He will give the grain to us. Lord, forgive our unbelief, and this evening constrain us to draw largely from your fullness and receive grace for grace.

"He led them by a straight way." — Psalm 107:7

HANGEABLE experiences often lead an anxious believer to ask, "Why is this happening to me?" I looked for light, but lo, darkness came; for peace, but behold, trouble. I said in my heart, my mountain stands firm, I shall never be moved. Lord, You do hide your face, and I am troubled. It was only yesterday that I could read my name clearly; today my evidences are made dim, and my hopes are clouded. Yesterday I could climb to Pisgah's top, and look over the landscape, and rejoice with confidence in my future inheritance; today, my spirit has no hopes, but many fears; no joys, but much distress. Is this part of God's plan with me? Can this be the way in which God would bring me to heaven? Yes, it is even so. The eclipse of your faith, the darkness of your mind, the fainting of your hope, all these things are but parts of God's method of making you ripe for the great inheritance upon which you shall soon enter. These trials are for the testing and strengthening of your faith — they are waves that wash you further upon the rock — they are winds which waft your ship the more swiftly towards the desired haven. According to David's words, so it might be said of you, "He guided them to their desired haven." By honor and dishonor, by evil report and by good report, by plenty and by poverty, by joy and by distress, by persecution and by peace, by all these things is the life of your souls maintained, and by each of these are you helped on your way. Oh, do not think, believer, that your sorrows are out of God's plan; they are necessary parts of it. "We must go through many hardships to enter the kingdom." Learn, then, even to "consider it pure joy . . . whenever you face trials of many kinds."

> "O let my trembling soul be still,
> And wait Thy wise, Thy holy will!
> I cannot, Lord, Thy purpose see,
> Yet all is well since ruled by Thee."

"How handsome you are, my lover!"
— *Song of Songs 1:16*

 ROM every point our Well-beloved is most handsome. Our various experiences are meant by our heavenly Father to furnish fresh standpoints from which we may view the loveliness of Jesus; how amiable are our trials when they carry us aloft where we may gain clearer views of Jesus than ordinary life could afford us! We have seen Him from the top of Amana, from the top of Shenir and Hermon, and He has shone upon us as the sun in His strength; but we have seen Him also "from the lions' dens and the mountain haunts of the leopards," and He has lost none of His loveliness. From the languishing of a sick bed, from the borders of the grave, have we turned our eyes to our soul's spouse, and He has never been otherwise than "all handsome." Many of His saints have looked upon Him from the gloom of dungeons, and from the red flames of the stake, yet have they never uttered an ill word of Him, but have died extolling His surpassing charms. Oh, noble and pleasant employment to be forever gazing at our sweet Lord Jesus! Is it not unspeakably delightful to view the Savior in all His offices, and to perceive Him matchless in each? — to shift the kaleidoscope, as it were, and to find fresh combinations of peerless graces? In the manger and in eternity, on the cross and on His throne, in the garden and in His kingdom, among thieves or in the midst of cherubim, He is everywhere "altogether lovely." Examine carefully every little act of His life, and every trait of His character, and He is as lovely in the minute as in the majestic. Judge Him as you will, you cannot censure; weigh Him as you please, and He will not be found wanting. Eternity shall not discover the shadow of a spot in our Beloved, but rather, as ages revolve, His hidden glories shall shine forth with yet more inconceivable splendor, and His unutterable loveliness shall more and more beautify all celestial minds.

"The LORD will fulfill his purpose for me." — *Psalm 138:8*

OST manifestly the confidence which the Psalmist here expressed was a *divine confidence.* He didn't say, *"I* have grace enough to perfect that which concerns me — my faith is so steady that it will not stagger — my love is so warm that it will never grow cold — my resolution is so firm that nothing can move it;" no, his dependence was on the Lord alone. If we indulge in any confidence which is not grounded on the Rock of ages, our confidence is worse than a dream, it will fall upon us, and cover us with its ruins, to our sorrow and confusion. All that Nature spins time will unravel, to the eternal confusion of all who are clothed therein. The Psalmist was wise, he rested upon nothing short of the *Lord's* work. It is the Lord who has begun the good work within us; it is He who has carried it on; and if He does not finish it, it never will be complete. If there is one stitch in the celestial garment of our righteousness which we are to insert ourselves, then we are lost; but this is our confidence, the Lord who began will fulfill. He *has* done it all, *must* do it all, and *will* do it all. Our confidence must not be in what we have done, nor in what we have resolved to do, but entirely in what *the Lord* will do. Unbelief insinuates — "You will never be able to stand. Look at the evil of your heart, you can never conquer sin; remember the sinful pleasures and temptations of the world that surround you, you will be certainly allured by them and led astray." Ah! yes, we should indeed perish if left to our own strength. If we had to navigate our frail vessels over so rough a sea all by ourselves, we might well give up the voyage in despair; but, thanks be to God, He will fulfill His purpose for us, and bring us to the desired haven. We can never be too confident when we confide in Him alone, and never too much concerned to *have such* a trust.

"You have not bought any fragrant calamus for me."
— Isaiah 43:24

 ORSHIPPERS at the temple were accustomed to bringing presents of sweet perfumes to be burned upon the altar of God: but Israel, in the time of her backsliding, became ungenerous, and made only a few votive offerings to her Lord: this was an evidence of coldness of heart towards God and His house. Reader, does this ever occur with you? Might not the complaint of the text be occasionally, if not frequently, brought against you? Those who are poor in pocket, if rich in faith, will be accepted none the less because their gifts are small; but, poor reader, do you give in fair proportion to the Lord, or is the widow's small coin kept back from the sacred treasury? The rich believer should be thankful for the talent entrusted to him, but should not forget his large responsibility, for where much is given much will be required; but, rich reader, are you mindful of your obligations, and rendering to the Lord according to the benefit received? Jesus gave His blood for us, what shall we give to Him? We are His, and all that we have, for He has purchased us to Himself — can we act as if we were our own? O for more consecration! and to this end, O for more love! Blessed Jesus, how good it is of You to accept our fragrant calamus! nothing is too costly as a tribute to your unrivaled love, and yet You do receive with favor the smallest sincere token of affection! You do receive our poor forget-me-nots and love tokens as though they were intrinsically precious, though indeed they are but as the bunch of wild flowers which the child brings to its mother. May we never grow niggardly towards You, and from this hour never may we hear You complain of us again for withholding the gifts of our love. We will give You the first fruits of our increase, and pay You tithes of all, and then we will confess "we have given You only what comes from Your hand."

"Praise be to God, who has not rejected my prayer."
— *Psalm 66:20*

 N looking back upon the character of our prayers, if we do it honestly, we shall be filled with wonder that God has ever answered them. There may be some who think their prayers worthy of acceptance — as the Pharisee did; but the true Christian, in a more enlightened retrospect, weeps over his prayers, and if he could retrace his steps he would desire to pray more earnestly. Remember, Christian, how *cold* your prayers have been. When in your prayer room you should have wrestled as Jacob did; but instead thereof, your petitions have been faint and few — far removed from that humble, believing, persevering faith, which cries, "I will not let You go unless You bless me." Yet, wonderful to say, God has heard these cold prayers of yours, and not only heard, but answered them. Reflect also, how *infrequent* your prayers have been, unless you have been in trouble, and *then* you have gone often to the mercy seat: but when deliverance has come, where has your constant supplication been? Yet in spite of the fact that you have stopped praying as you once did, God has not ceased to bless. When you have neglected the mercy seat, God has not deserted it, but the bright light of the Shekinah has always been visible between the wings of the cherubim. Oh! it is marvelous that the Lord should regard those intermittent spasms of insistent requests which come and go with our necessities. What a God is He thus to hear the prayers of those who come to Him when they have pressing wants, but neglect Him when they have received a mercy; who approach Him when they are forced to come, but who almost forget to address Him when mercies are plentiful and sorrows are few. Let His gracious kindness in hearing such prayers touch our hearts, so that we may henceforth be found to "pray in the Spirit on all occasions with all kinds of prayers and requests."

"Whatever happens, conduct yourselves in a manner worthy of the gospel of Christ." — *Philippians 1:27*

 HE word "conduct" does not merely mean our talk and converse with one another, but the whole course of our life and behavior in the world. The Greek word signifies the actions and the privileges of citizenship: and thus we are commanded to let our actions, as citizens of the New Jerusalem, be worthy of the gospel of Christ. What sort of conduct is this? In the first place, *the gospel is very simple.* So Christians should be simple and plain in their habits. There should be about our manner, our speech, our dress, our whole behavior, that simplicity which is the very soul of beauty. The gospel is *pre-eminently true,* it is gold without dross; and the Christian's life will be lusterless and valueless without the jewel of truth. The gospel is a very *fearless gospel,* it boldly proclaims the truth, whether men like it or not: we must be equally faithful and unflinching. But the gospel is also *very gentle.* Notice this spirit in its Founder: "a bruised reed He will not break." Some of those who profess are sharper than a thorny hedge; such persons are not like Jesus. Let's seek to win others by the gentleness of our words and acts. The gospel is *very loving.* It is the message of the God of love to a lost and fallen race. Christ's last command to His disciples was, "Love each other." O for more real, hearty union and love to all the saints; for more tender compassion towards the souls of the worst and vilest of men! We must not forget that the gospel of Christ is *holy.* It never excuses sin: it pardons it, but only through an atonement. If our life is to resemble the gospel, we must shun, not merely the grosser vices, but everything that would hinder our perfect conformity to Christ. For His sake, for our own sakes, and for the sakes of others, we must strive day by day to let our conduct be more in accordance with His gospel.

"O Lord, do not forsake me." — Psalm 38:21

REQUENTLY we pray that God would not forsake us in the hour of trial and temptation, but we too often forget that we need to use this prayer *at all times.* There is no moment of our life, however holy, in which we can do without His constant upholding. Whether in light or in darkness, in communion or in temptation, we alike need the prayer, "O Lord, do not forsake me." "Uphold me, and I will be delivered." A little child, while learning to walk, always needs a parent's help. The ship without its captain immediately drifts off course. We can't do without continued aid from above; let it then be your prayer today, "Do not forsake me. Father, do not forsake Your child, lest he fall by the hand of the enemy. Shepherd, forsake not Your lamb, lest he wander from the safety of the fold. Great Farmer, forsake not Your plant, lest it wither and die. 'O Lord, do not forsake me,' now; and do not forsake me at any moment of my life. Do not forsake me in my joys, lest they absorb my heart. Do not forsake me in my sorrows, lest I murmur against You. Do not forsake me in the day of my repentance, lest I lose the hope of pardon, and fall into despair; and do not forsake me in the day of my strongest faith, lest faith degenerate into presumption. Do not forsake me for without You I am weak, but with You I am strong. Do not forsake me, for my path is dangerous, and full of snares, and I cannot do without Your guidance. The hen doesn't abandon her brood, so then cover me forever with Your feathers, and let me find refuge under Your wings. 'Do not be far from me, for trouble is near, and there is no one to help.' 'Do not reject me or forsake me, O God my Savior!' "

> "O ever in our cleansed breast,
> Bid Thine Eternal Spirit rest;
> And make our secret soul to be
> A temple pure and worthy Thee."

"They got up and returned at once to Jerusalem. . . .
Then the two told what had happened on the way,
and how Jesus was recognized by them."
— *Luke 24:33, 35*

 HEN the two disciples had reached Emmaus, and were refreshing themselves at the evening meal, the mysterious stranger who had so enchanted them upon the road, took bread and broke it, made Himself known to them, and then vanished out of their sight. They had urged Him to stay with them, because the day was far spent; but now, although it was much later, their love was a lamp to their feet, yes, wings also; they forgot the darkness, their weariness was all gone, and immediately they journeyed back the threescore furlongs to tell the good news of a risen Lord, who had appeared to them by the way. They reached the Christians in Jerusalem, and were received by a burst of joyful news before they could tell their own tale. These early Christians were all on fire to speak of Christ's resurrection, and to proclaim what they knew of the Lord; they made common property of their experiences. This evening let their example impress us deeply. We, too, must bear our witness concerning Jesus. John's account of the sepulcher needed to be supplemented by Peter; and Mary could speak of something further still; combined, we have a full testimony from which nothing can be spared. We have each of us peculiar gifts and special manifestations; but the one object God has in view is the perfecting of the whole body of Christ. We must, therefore, bring our spiritual possessions and lay them at the apostle's feet, and make distribution to all of what God has given to us. Do not keep any part of the precious truth, but speak what you know, and testify what you have seen. Do not let the toil or darkness, or possible unbelief of your friends, weigh one moment in the scale. Up, and be marching to the place of duty, and there tell what great things God has shown to your soul.

"Cast your cares on the LORD and he will sustain you."
— *Psalm 55:22*

 ARE, even though exercised upon legitimate objects, if carried to excess, has in it the nature of sin. The precept to avoid anxious care is earnestly inculcated by our Savior, again and again; it is reiterated by the apostles; and it is one which cannot be neglected without involving transgression: for the very essence of anxious care is the imagining that we are wiser than God, and the thrusting ourselves into His place to do for Him that which He has undertaken to do for us. We attempt to think that which we fancy He will forget; we work to take upon ourselves our weary burden, as if He were unable or unwilling to take it for us. Now this disobedience to His plain precept, this unbelief in His Word, this presumption in intruding upon His province, is all sinful. Yet more than this, anxious care often leads to acts of sin. He who cannot calmly leave his affairs in God's hand, but will carry his own burden, is very likely to be tempted to use wrong means to help himself. This sin leads to a forsaking of God as our advisor, and resorting instead to human wisdom. This is going to the "broken cistern" instead of to the "fountain;" a sin which was laid against Israel of old. Anxiety makes us doubt God's loving-kindness, and thus our love to Him grows cold; we feel mistrust, and thus grieve the Spirit of God, so that our prayers become hindered, our consistent example marred, and our life one of self-seeking. Thus want of confidence in God leads us to wander far from Him; but if through simple faith in His promise, we cast each care as it comes upon Him, and are "not anxious about anything" because He undertakes to care for us, it will keep us close to Him, and strengthen us against much temptation. "You will keep in perfect peace him whose mind is steadfast, because he trusts in You."

"Remain true to the faith." — *Acts 14:22*

ERSEVERANCE is the badge of true saints. The Christian life is not a *beginning* only in the ways of God, but also a *continuance* in the same as long as life lasts. It is with a Christian as it was with the great Napoleon: he said, "Conquest has made me what I am, and conquest must maintain me." So, under God, dear brother in the Lord, conquest has made you what you are, and conquest must sustain you. Your motto must be, "Excelsior." He only is a true conqueror, and shall be crowned at the last, who continues until war's trumpet is blown no more. Perseverance is, therefore, the target of all our spiritual enemies. The *world* does not object to your being a Christian for a time, if she can but tempt you to cease your pilgrimage, and settle down to buy and sell with her in Vanity Fair. The *flesh* will seek to ensnare you, and to prevent your pressing on to glory. "It is weary work being a pilgrim; come, give it up. Am I always to be mortified? Am I never to be indulged? Give me at least a furlough from this constant warfare." *Satan* will make many a fierce attack on your perseverance; it will be the mark for all his arrows. He will strive to hinder you *in service:* he will insinuate that you are doing no good; and that you want rest. He will try to make you weary of *suffering,* he will whisper, "Curse God, and die." Or he will attack your *steadfastness:* "What is the good of being so zealous? Be quiet like the rest; sleep as others do, and let your lamp go out as the other virgins do." Or he will assail your *doctrinal sentiments:* "Why do you hold to these denominational creeds? Sensible people are getting more liberal; they are removing the old landmarks: get with the times." Wear your shield, Christian, therefore, close upon your armor, and cry mightily to God, that by His Spirit you may endure to the end.

"And Mephibosheth lived in Jerusalem, because he always ate at the king's table, and he was crippled in both feet." — 2 Samuel 9:13

EPHIBOSHETH was no great ornament to a royal table, yet he had a continual place at David's board, because the king could see in his face the features of the beloved Jonathan. Like Mephibosheth, we may cry to the King of Glory, "What is your servant, that you should notice a dead dog like me?" but still the Lord indulges us with most familiar communication with Himself, because He sees in our countenances the remembrance of His dearly-beloved Jesus. The Lord's people are *dear for another's sake.* Such is the love which the Father bears to His only begotten, that for His sake He raises His lowly brethren from poverty and banishment, to courtly companionship, noble rank, and royal provision. Their *deformity shall not rob them of their privileges.* Lameness is no bar to sonship; the cripple is as much the heir as if he could run like Asahel. Our right does not limp, though our might may. A king's table is a noble hiding place for lame legs, and at the gospel feast we learn to glory in infirmities, because the power of Christ rests upon us. Yet grievous *disability may mar the persons of the best-loved saints.* Here is one feasted by David, and yet so lame in both his feet that he could not go up with the king when he fled from the city, and was therefore maligned and injured by his servant Ziba. Saints whose faith is weak, and whose knowledge is slender, are great losers; they are exposed to many enemies, and cannot follow the king wherever he goes. This *disease frequently arises from falls.* Bad nursing in their spiritual infancy often causes converts to fall into a despondency from which they never recover, and sin in other cases brings broken bones. Lord, help the lame to leap like a deer, and satisfy all Your people with the bread of Your table!

*"What is your servant, that you should notice a
dead dog like me?"* — 2 Samuel 9:8

 F Mephibosheth was thus humbled by David's kindness, what shall *we* be in the presence of our gracious Lord? The more grace we have, the less we shall think of ourselves, for grace, like light, reveals our impurity. Eminent saints have scarcely known to what to compare themselves, their sense of unworthiness has been so clear and keen. "I am," says holy Rutherford, "a dry and withered branch, a piece of dead carcass, dry bones, and not able to step over a straw." In another place he writes, "Except as to open outbreakings, I want nothing of what Judas and Cain had." The meanest objects in nature appear to the humbled mind to have a preference above itself, because they have never contracted sin: a dog may be greedy, fierce, or filthy, but it has no conscience to violate, no Holy Spirit to resist. A dog may be a worthless animal, and yet by a little kindness it is soon won to love its master, and is faithful to death; but we forget the goodness of the Lord, and do not follow at His call. The term "dead dog" is the most expressive of all terms of contempt, but it is not strong enough to express the self-abhorrence of instructed believers. They do not affect mock modesty, they mean what they say, they have weighed themselves in the balances of the sanctuary, and found out the vanity of their nature. At best, we are but clay, animated dust, mere walking hillocks; but viewed as sinners, we are monsters indeed. Let it be published in heaven as a wonder, that the Lord Jesus should set His heart's love upon such as we are. Dust and ashes though we be, we must and will "magnify the exceeding greatness of His grace." Couldn't His heart find rest in heaven? Must He come to these tents of Kedar for a spouse, and choose a bride upon whom the sun had looked? O heavens and earth, break forth into a song, and give all glory to our sweet Lord Jesus.

"Those he justified, he also glorified." — *Romans 8:30*

 ERE is a precious truth for you, believer. You may be poor, or in suffering, or unknown, but, for your encouragement, review your "calling" and the consequences that flow from it, and especially that blessed result spoken of here. As surely as you are God's child today, so surely shall all your trials soon be at an end, and you shall be rich to all the intents of bliss. Wait awhile, and that weary head shall wear the crown of glory, and that hand of work shall grasp the palm branch of victory. Do not lament your troubles, but rather rejoice that before long you will be where "there will be no more . . . mourning or crying or pain." The chariots of fire are at your door, and a moment will suffice to bear you to the glorified. The everlasting song is almost on your lip. The portals of heaven stand open for you. Don't think that you can fail entering into rest. If He has called you, nothing can divide you from His love. Distress cannot sever the bond; the fire of persecution cannot burn the link; the hammer of hell cannot break the chain. You are secure; that voice which called you at first, shall call you yet again from earth to heaven, from death's dark gloom to immortality's unuttered splendors. Rest assured, the heart of Him who has justified you beats with infinite love towards you. You shall soon be with the glorified, where your portion is; you are only waiting here to make preparation for the inheritance, and that done, the wings of angels shall waft you far away, to the mountain of peace, and joy, and blessedness, where,

"Far from a world of grief and sin,
With God eternally shut in,"

you shall rest forever and ever.

"This I call to mind and therefore I have hope."
— Lamentations 3:21

EMORY is frequently the bondservant of despondency. Despairing minds call to remembrance every dark foreboding in the past, and dilate upon every gloomy feature in the present; thus memory, clothed in sackcloth, presents to the mind a cup of mingled gall and wormwood. There is, however, no necessity for this. Wisdom can readily transform memory into an angel of comfort. That same recollection which in its left hand brings so many gloomy omens, may be trained to bear in its right a wealth of hopeful signs. She needn't wear a crown of iron, she may encircle her brow with a golden band, all spangled with stars. Thus it was in Jeremiah's experience: in the previous verse memory had brought him to deep humiliation of soul: "I well remember them, and my soul is downcast within me;" and now this same memory restored him to life and comfort. "This I call to mind and therefore I have hope." Like a two-edged sword, his memory first killed his pride with one edge, and then slew his despair with the other. As a general principle, if we would exercise our memories more wisely, we might, in our very darkest distress, strike a match which would instantaneously kindle the lamp of comfort. There is no need for God to create a new thing upon the earth in order to restore believers to joy; if they would prayerfully rake the ashes of the past, they would find light for the present; and if they would turn to the book of truth and the throne of grace, their candle would soon shine as in the past. Be it ours to remember the loving-kindness of the Lord, and to rehearse His deeds of grace. Let's open the volume of recollection which is so richly illuminated with memorials of mercy, and we shall soon be happy. Thus memory may be, as Coleridge calls it, "the bosom-spring of joy," and when the Divine Comforter bends it to His service, it may be chief among earthly comforters.

"You . . . hate wickedness." — Psalm 45:7

 N your anger do not sin." There can hardly be goodness in a person who is not angry at sin; those who love truth must hate every false way. How our Lord Jesus hated it when the temptation came! Three times it assailed Him in different forms, but He always met it with, "Get behind me, Satan." He hated it in others; none the less fervently because He showed His hate oftener in tears of pity than in words of rebuke; yet what language could be more stern, more Elijah-like, than the words, "Woe to you, teachers of the law and Pharisees, you hypocrites! You devour widows' houses and for a show make lengthy prayers." He hated wickedness, so much that He bled to wound it to the heart; He died that it might die; He was buried that He might bury it in His tomb; and He rose that He might forever trample it beneath His feet. Christ is in the Gospel, and that Gospel is opposed to wickedness in every shape. Wickedness dresses itself in attractive garments, and imitates the language of holiness; but the precepts of Jesus, like His famous whip of cords, chase it out of the temple, and will not tolerate it in the church. So, too, in the heart where Jesus reigns, what war there is between Christ and Belial! And when our Redeemer shall come to be our Judge, those thundering words, "Depart, you who are cursed" which are, indeed, but a prolongation of His life-teaching concerning sin, shall manifest His abhorrence of iniquity. As warm as is His love to sinners, so hot is His hatred of sin; as perfect as is His righteousness, so complete shall be the destruction of every form of wickedness. O you glorious champion of right, and destroyer of wrong, for this cause has God, even your God, anointed you with the oil of gladness above your fellows.

"Cursed before the LORD is the man who undertakes to rebuild this city, Jericho." — *Joshua 6:26*

INCE he who rebuilt Jericho was cursed, much more the man who labors to restore Popery among us. In our fathers' days the gigantic walls of Popery fell by the power of their faith, the perseverance of their efforts, and the blast of their gospel trumpets; and now there are some who would rebuild that accursed system upon its old foundation. O Lord, be pleased to thwart their unrighteous endeavors, and pull down every stone which they build. It should be a serious business with us to be thoroughly purged of every error which may have a tendency to foster the spirit of Popery, and when we have made a clean sweep at home we should seek in every way to oppose its all too rapid spread abroad in the church and in the world. This last can be done in secret by fervent prayer, and in public by decided testimony. We must warn with judicious boldness those who are inclined towards the errors of Rome; we must instruct the young in gospel truth, and tell them of the black doings of Popery in the times long past. We must aid in spreading the light more thoroughly through the land, for priests, like owls, hate daylight. Are we doing all we can for Jesus and the gospel? If not, our negligence plays into the hands of the priest-craft. What are we doing to spread the Bible, which is the Pope's bane and poison? Are we casting abroad good, sound gospel writings? Luther once said, "The devil hates goose quills" and, doubtless, he has good reason, for ready writers, by the Holy Spirit's blessing, have done his kingdom much damage. If the thousands who will read this short word this night will do all they can to hinder the rebuilding of this accursed Jericho, the Lord's glory shall speed among the sons of men. Reader, what can you do? What will you do?

*"Catch for us the foxes, the little foxes that ruin
the vineyards."* — *Song of Songs 2:15*

 little thorn may cause much suffering. A little cloud may hide the sun. Little foxes spoil the vines; and little sins do mischief to the tender heart. These little sins burrow in the soul, and make it so full of that which is hateful to Christ, that He will not have comfortable fellowship and communion with us. A great sin cannot destroy a Christian, but a little sin can make him miserable. Jesus will not walk with His people unless they drive out every known sin. He says, "If you obey My commands, you will remain in My love, just as I have obeyed My Father's commands and remain in His love." Some Christians very seldom enjoy their Savior's presence. How is this? Surely it must be an affliction for a tender child to be separated from his father. Are you a child of God, and yet satisfied to go on without seeing your Father's face? What! You are the spouse of Christ, and yet content without His company! Surely, you have fallen into a sad state, for the chaste spouse of Christ mourns like a dove without her mate when he has left her. What has driven Christ from you? He hides His face behind the wall of your sins. That wall may be built up of *little* pebbles as easily as of great stones. The sea is made of drops; the rocks are made of grains: and the sea which divides you from Christ may be filled with the drops of your little sins; and the rock which has well nigh wrecked your ship, may have been made by the daily working of the coral insects of your little sins. If you will live with Christ, and walk with Christ, and see Christ, and have fellowship with Christ, watch out for "the little foxes that ruin the vineyards, our vineyards that are in bloom." Jesus invites you to go *with Him* and catch them. He will surely, like Samson, catch the foxes at once and easily. Go with Him on the hunt.

"That we should no longer be slaves to sin."
— Romans 6:6

HRISTIAN, what have you to do with sin? *Has it not cost you enough already?* Burnt child, will you play with the fire? What! After having already been caught in the jaws of the lion, you still want to walk into his den again? Haven't you had enough of the old serpent? Didn't he poison all your veins once, and will you play upon the hole of the asp, and put your hand upon the serpent's den a second time? Oh, don't be so foolish! so unconscious! Did sin ever provide you with real pleasure? Did you find solid satisfaction in it? If so, go back to your old drudgery, and wear the chain again, if that is what pleases you. But inasmuch as sin never gave you what it promised to give you, but deluded you with lies, don't be snared a second time by the old fowler — be free, and let the remembrance of your ancient bondage forbid you to enter the net again! *It is contrary to the designs of eternal love,* which all have an eye to your purity and holiness; therefore don't run opposite to the purposes of your Lord. Another thought should restrain you from sin. *Christians can never sin cheaply;* they pay a heavy price for iniquity. Transgression destroys peace of mind, obscures fellowship with Jesus, hinders prayer, brings darkness over the soul; therefore don't be the serf and bondservant of sin. There is yet a higher argument: each time you become "a slave to sin" you are *"crucifying the Son of God all over again and subjecting him to public disgrace."* Can you bear *that* thought? Oh! if you have fallen into any special sin during this day, it may be my Master has sent this admonition this evening, to bring you back before you backslide very far. Turn to Jesus anew; He has not forgotten His love to you; His grace is still the same. With weeping and repentance, come to His footstool, and you shall be once more received into His heart; you shall be set upon a rock again, and your goings shall be established.

"The king also crossed the Kidron Valley."
— *2 Samuel 15:23*

AVID passed that gloomy valley when fleeing with his company of mourners from his traitor son. The man after God's own heart was not exempt from trouble. On the contrary, his life was full of it. He was both the Lord's Anointed, and the Lord's Afflicted. Why then should we expect to escape? The noblest of our race have waited at sorrow's gates with ashes on their heads. Why, then, should we complain as though some strange thing had happened to us?

The KING of kings himself was not favored with a more cheerful or royal road. He passed over the filthy ditch of Kidron, through which the filth of Jerusalem flowed. God had one Son without sin, but not a single child without the rod. It is a great joy to believe that Jesus has been tempted in all points like as we are. What is our Kidron this morning? Is it a faithless friend, a sad bereavement, a slanderous reproach, a dark foreboding? The King has passed over all these. Is it bodily pain, poverty, persecution, or contempt? Over each of these Kidrons the King has gone before us. "In all our distress He too was distressed." The idea of strangeness in our trials must be banished once and forever, for He who is the Head of all saints, knows by experience the grief which we think so distinctive. All the citizens of Zion must be free of the Honorable Company of Mourners, of which the Prince Immanuel is Head and Captain.

Regardless of David's humiliation, he still returned in triumph to his city, and David's Lord arose victorious from the grave; let's then be of good courage, for we also shall win the day. We shall yet with joy draw water out of the wells of salvation, though now for a season we have to pass by the noxious streams of sin and sorrow. Courage, soldiers of the Cross, the King himself triumphed after going over Kidron, and so shall you.

"Who . . . heals all your diseases." — *Psalm 103:3*

UMBLING as the statement is, yet the fact remains: we are all more or less suffering under the disease of sin. What a comfort to know that we have a great Physician who is both able and willing to heal us! Let's think of Him for a while tonight. His cures are very *speedy* — there is life in a look at Him; His cures are *radical* — He strikes at the center of the disease; and hence, His cures are *sure* and certain. He never fails, and *the disease never returns*. There is no relapse where Christ heals; no fear that His patients should be merely patched up for a season, He makes them new men and women by putting a new heart and right spirit within them. He is well-skilled in *all* diseases. Physicians generally have some *specialty*. Although they may know a little about almost all of our pains and illnesses, there is usually one disease which they have studied more specifically than all others; but Jesus Christ is thoroughly acquainted with the whole of human nature. He is as much at home with one sinner as with another, and He has never yet met with an out-of-the-way case that was difficult for Him. He has had to deal with extraordinarily complicated and strange diseases but, with one glance of His eye, He has known exactly how to treat the patient. He is the only universal doctor; and the medicine He gives is the only true panacea, healing in every instance. Whatever our spiritual malady may be, we should appeal at once to this Divine Physician. There is no heartbreak which Jesus cannot bandage. "His blood purifies from all sin." We only have to remind ourselves of the myriads who have been delivered from all sorts of diseases through the power and virtue of His touch, and we shall joyfully put ourselves in His hands. We trust Him, and sin dies; we love Him, and grace lives; we wait for Him and grace is strengthened; we see Him as He is, and grace is perfected forever.

"And there was evening, and there was morning —
the first day." — Genesis 1:5

AS it so even in the beginning? Did light and darkness divide the realm of time in the first day? Then it is little wonder that I also have changes in my circumstances from the sunshine of prosperity to the midnight of adversity. It will not always be the blaze of noon even in the concerns of my soul. At times, I must expect to mourn the absence of my former joys, and seek my Beloved in the night. Nor am I alone in this, for all the Lord's loved ones have had to sing the mingled song of judgment and of mercy, of trial and deliverance, of mourning and of delight. It is one of the arrangements of Divine providence that day and night shall not cease either in the spiritual or natural creation until we reach the land of which it is written, "There will be no more night." What our heavenly Father ordains is wise and good.

What, then, my soul, is best for you to do? First learn *to be content* with this divine order, and be willing, with Job, to receive evil from the hand of the Lord as well as good. Then study to make the *morning dawns and evening fades call forth songs of joy.* Praise the Lord for the sun of joy when it rises, and for the gloom of evening as it falls. There is beauty both in sunrise and sunset. Sing of it and glorify the Lord. Like the nightingale, pour forth your notes at all hours. *Believe that the night is as useful as the day.* The dews of grace fall heavily in the night of sorrow. The stars of promise shine forth gloriously amid the darkness of grief. *Continue your service* under all changes. If, in the day, your rallying cry is *work*, exchange it at night for *watch*. Every hour has its duty; continue in your calling as the Lord's servant until He shall suddenly appear in His glory. My soul, your evening of old age and death is drawing near. Do not dread it, for it is part of the day; and the Lord has said, "The LORD shields him all day long."

"He will make her deserts like Eden." — *Isaiah 51:3*

T seems to me I see a vision of a howling wilderness, a great and terrible desert resembling the Sahara. I perceive nothing in it to relieve the eye. I am surrounded and exhausted by a vision of hot and arid sand strewn with ten thousand bleaching skeletons of miserable men who have expired in anguish, having lost their way in the merciless wasteland. What an appalling sight! How horrible! a sea of sand without a shore and without an oasis, a gloomy graveyard for a race forlorn! But behold and wonder! All of a sudden, I see a familiar plant springing up from the scorching sand; and as it grows it buds, the bud expands — it is a rose, and at its side a lily bows its modest head; and, miracle of miracles, as the fragrance of those flowers is diffused, the wilderness is transformed into a fruitful field, and all around it bursts into bloom; it rejoices greatly and shouts for joy. The glory of Lebanon will be given to it, the splendor of Carmel and Sharon. Don't call it Sahara; call it Paradise. Don't speak of it any longer as the valley of death shade, for where the skeletons lay bleaching in the sun, behold a resurrection is proclaimed, and up spring the dead, a mighty army, full of life immortal. Jesus is that familiar plant, and His presence makes all things new. Nor is there less amazement in each individual's salvation. Yonder I behold you, dear reader, cast out, an infant, unswathed, unwashed, defiled with your own blood, left to be food for beasts of prey. But, lo, a jewel has been thrown into your heart by a divine hand, and for its sake you have been pitied and tended by divine providence, you are washed and cleansed from your defilement, you are adopted into heaven's family, the fair seal of love is upon your forehead, and the ring of faithfulness is on your hand — you are now a royal member of God's family, though once an orphan, cast away. Of extremely great value is the matchless power and grace which changes deserts into gardens, and makes the barren heart sing for joy.

"For the sinful nature desires what is contrary to the Spirit, and the Spirit what is contrary to the sinful nature." — Galatians 5:17

 N every believer's heart there is a constant struggle between the old nature and the new. The old nature is very active, and loses no opportunity to wield all the weapons of its deadly armory against newborn grace; while, on the other hand, the new nature is constantly watching to resist and destroy its enemy. Grace within us will employ prayer, faith, hope, and love to cast out the evil; it takes to it the "full armor of God" and wrestles earnestly. These two opposing natures will never cease to struggle so long as we are in this world. The battle of "Christian" with "Apollyon" lasted three hours, but the battle of Christian with himself lasted all the way from the Wicket Gate in the river Jordan. The enemy is so securely entrenched within us that he can never be driven out while we are in this body: but although we are besieged on all sides, and often in painful conflict, we have an Almighty helper, even Jesus, the Captain of our salvation, who is always with us, and who assures us that we shall eventually come away from the conflict more than conquerors through Him. With such assistance, the newborn nature is more than a match for its foes. Are you fighting with the adversary today? Are Satan, the world, and the flesh all against you? Don't be discouraged or dismayed. Fight on! For God Himself is with you; *Jehovah Nissi* is your banner, and *Jehovah Rophi* is the healer of your wounds. Don't be afraid; you shall overcome, for who can defeat Omnipotence? Fight on, "looking to Jesus." Although the conflict is lengthy and severe, the victory will be sweet, and the promised reward glorious.

> "From strength to strength go on;
> Wrestle, and fight, and pray,
> Tread all the powers of darkness down,
> And win the well-fought day."

"Teacher." — *Matthew 19:16*

 F the young man in the gospel used this title in speaking to our Lord, how much more fitting it is for me to address Him this way! Indeed, He is my Teacher in two respects: a ruling Teacher and an educating Master. I take great pleasure in running His errands and sitting at His feet. I am both His servant and His disciple, and count it my highest honor to own this double identity. If He should ask me why I call Him *"good,"* I should have a ready answer. It is true that "no one is good — except God alone," but then He is God, and all the goodness of Deity shines forth in Him. In my experience, I have found Him good, so good, in fact, that all the good I have has come to me through Him. He was good to me when I was dead in sin, for He raised me by His Spirit's power; He has been good to me in all my needs, trials, struggles, and sorrows. There could never be a better Teacher, for His service is freedom, His rule is love: I wish I were one thousandth part as good a servant. When He teaches me as my Rabbi, He is unspeakably good; His doctrine is divine, His manner is condescending, His spirit is gentleness itself. No error mingles with His instruction — the golden truth which He brings forth is pure, and all His teachings lead to goodness, sanctifying as well as edifying the disciple. Angels find Him a good Teacher and take great pleasure in paying Him homage at His footstool. The ancient saints proved Him to be a good Teacher, and each of them rejoiced to sing, "I am your servant, O Lord!" My own humble testimony must certainly be to the same effect. I will bear this witness before my friends and neighbors, for possibly they may be led by my testimony to seek my Lord Jesus as their Teacher. O that they would do so! They would never regret such a wise act. If they would only take His easy yoke, they would find themselves in such a royal service that they would enlist in it forever.

"They were the potters who lived at Netaim and Gederah;
they stayed there and worked for the king."
— 1 Chronicles 4:23

OTTERS were not the very highest category of workers, but "the king" needed potters and, therefore, they were engaged in royal service, although the material of their profession was nothing but clay. We, too, may be engaged in the most menial part of the Lord's work, but it is a great privilege to do anything for "the king." Therefore, we will stay with our calling, hoping that, "even while you sleep among the campfires, the wings of *my* dove are sheathed with silver, its feathers with shining gold." There also lived at Netaim and Gederah those having rough, rustic hedging and ditching work to do. They may have desired to live in the city, amid its life, society, and refinement, but they kept their appointed places, for they also were doing the king's work. The place of our habitation is fixed, and we are not to leave it on a whim or just to suit our fancy, but seek to serve the Lord in it, by being a blessing to those among whom we reside. These potters and gardeners had *royal company,* for they lived with the king and, although among hedges and plants, they lived with the king *there.* No lawful place or gracious occupation, however menial, can debar us from communion with our divine Lord. In visiting hovels, swarming tenements, workhouses, or jails, we may go *with the king.* In all works of faith we may count upon Jesus' fellowship. It is when we are in His work that we may count on His smile. You unknown workers who are occupied for your Lord amid the dirt and wretchedness of the lowest of the low, be of good cheer, for jewels have been found upon dunghills before now, earthen pots have been filled with heavenly treasure, and unhealthy weeds have been transformed into precious flowers. Live with the King for His work, and when He writes His chronicles, your name shall be recorded.

"He humbled himself." — *Philippians 2:8*

ESUS is the great teacher of lowliness of heart. Every day we need to learn about Him. See the Master taking a towel and washing His disciples' feet! Follower of Christ, won't you humble yourself? See Him as the Servant of servants, and surely you can't be proud! Isn't this sentence, "He humbled Himself" the compendium of His biography? While on earth, wasn't He always stripping off first one robe of honor and then another until, naked, He was fastened to the cross, and didn't He empty out His inmost self there, pouring out His lifeblood, giving up for all of us, until they laid Him penniless in a borrowed grave? How low our dear Redeemer was brought! Therefore, how can we be proud? Stand at the foot of the cross, and count the purple drops by which you have been cleansed; see the crown of thorns; mark His scourged shoulders, still gushing with encrimsoned rills; see hands and feet given up to the rough iron, and His whole self to mockery and scorn; see the bitterness, and the pangs, and the throes of inward grief, showing themselves in His outward frame; hear the thrilling shriek, "My God, my God, why have You forsaken me?" And if you don't lie prostrate on the ground before that cross, you have never seen it: if you are not humbled in the presence of Jesus, you don't know Him. You were so lost that nothing could save you but the sacrifice of God's only begotten. Think of that, and as Jesus lowered Himself for you, bow yourself in lowliness at His feet. A sense of Christ's amazing love to us has a greater tendency to humble us than even the conscious awareness of our own guilt. May the Lord bring us in contemplation to Calvary, then our position will no longer be that of a person filled with pompous pride. Rather, we shall take the humble place of one who loves greatly because much has been forgiven him. Pride cannot live beneath the cross. Let's sit there and learn our lesson, and then rise and put it into practice.

OW sweet it is to behold the Savior communing with His own beloved people! There can be nothing more delightful than to be led by the Divine Spirit into this fertile field of delight. Let the mind for an instant consider the history of the Redeemer's love, and a thousand enchanting acts of affection will suggest themselves, all of which have had for their design the weaving of the heart into Christ, and the intertwining of the thoughts and emotions of the renewed soul with the mind of Jesus. When we meditate upon this amazing love, and behold the all-glorious Kinsman of the church endowing her with all His ancient wealth, our souls may well faint for joy. Who is he that can endure such a weight of love? That partial sense of it, which the Holy Spirit is sometimes pleased to make readily available to us, is more than the soul can contain; how transporting a complete view of it must be! When the soul shall have understanding to discern all the Savior's gifts, wisdom with which to estimate them, and time in which to meditate upon them, such as the world to come will make readily available to us, we shall then commune with Jesus in a closer manner than at present. But who can imagine the sweetness of such fellowship? It must be one of the things which has not entered into the heart of man, but which God has prepared for them that love Him. Oh, to burst open the door of our Joseph's granaries, and see the plenty which He has stored up for us! This will overwhelm us with love. By faith we see, imperfectly as in a mirror, the reflected image of His unbounded treasures, but when we shall actually see the heavenly things themselves, with our own eyes, how deep the stream of fellowship, in which our soul shall bathe itself, will be! Until then, our loudest sonnets shall be reserved for our loving benefactor, Jesus Christ our Lord, whose love to us is wonderful, surpassing human love.

"Taken up in glory." — 1 Timothy 3:16

E have seen our well-beloved Lord in the days of His flesh, humiliated and in anguish; for He was "despised and rejected by men, a Man of sorrows, and familiar with suffering." He whose brightness is as the morning, wore the sackcloth of sorrow as His daily dress: shame was His mantle, and reproach was His vesture. Yet now, inasmuch as He has triumphed over all the powers of darkness upon the bloody tree, our faith beholds our King returning with dyed garments from Edom, robed in the splendor of victory. How glorious He must have been in the eyes of seraphs, when a cloud received Him out of mortal sight, and He ascended up to heaven! Now He wears the glory which He had with God before the earth was, and yet another glory above all — that which He has well earned in the fight against sin, death, and hell. As victor He wears the illustrious crown. Hark how the song swells high! It is a new and sweeter song: "Worthy is the Lamb, who was slain, for with His blood He has purchased us for God!" He wears the glory of an Intercessor who can never fail, of a Prince who can never be defeated, of a Conqueror who has vanquished every foe, of a Lord who has the heart's allegiance of every subject. Jesus wears all the glory which the pomp of heaven can bestow upon Him, which ten thousand times ten thousand angels can minister to Him. You cannot with the utmost stretch of your imagination conceive of His exceeding greatness; yet there will be a further revelation of it when He shall descend from heaven in great power, with all the holy angels — "Then He will sit on His throne in heavenly glory." Oh, the splendor of that glory! It will move His people's hearts to delight. Nor is this the end, for eternity shall sound His praise, "Your throne, O God, will last for ever and ever!" Reader, if you want to enjoy Christ's glory hereafter, He must be glorious in your sight now. *Is He?*

"Then the LORD shut him in." — *Genesis 7:16*

OAH was shut in *away from all the world* by the hand of divine love. The door of electing purpose comes between us and the world which lies in the wicked one. We are not of the world even as our Lord Jesus was not of the world. We cannot enter into the sin, the gaiety, the pursuits of the multitude; we cannot play in the streets of Vanity Fair with the children of darkness, for our heavenly Father has shut us in. Noah was shut in *with his God.* *"Go* into the ark," was the Lord's invitation, by which He clearly showed that He Himself intended to dwell in the ark with His servant and his family. Thus all the chosen dwell in God and God in them. Happy people to be enclosed in the same circle which contains God in the Trinity of His persons, Father, Son, and Spirit. Let's never be inattentive to that gracious call, "Go, my people, enter your rooms and shut the doors behind you; hide yourselves for a little while until his wrath has passed by." Noah was shut in so that *no evil could reach him.* Floods only lifted him heavenward, and winds only wafted him on his way. Outside of the ark all was ruin, but inside all was rest and peace. Without Christ we perish, but in Christ Jesus there is perfect safety. Noah was so shut in that *he could not even desire to come out,* and those who are in Christ Jesus are in Him forever. They shall not leave ever again, for eternal faithfulness has shut them in, and infernal malice cannot drag them out. The Prince of the house of David closes and no person opens; and when once, in the last days as Master of the house, He shall rise up and shut the door, those who barely profess will knock in vain, and cry Lord, Lord open to us, for that same door which shuts in the wise virgins will shut out the foolish forever. Lord, shut me in by your grace.

"Whoever does not love does not know God."
— 1 John 4:8

 HE distinguishing mark of a Christian is a confidence in the love of Christ, and a yielding of affections to Christ in return. Faith first sets her seal upon a person by enabling that soul to say with the apostle, "Christ, the Son of God, loved me and gave Himself for me." Then love gives the password, and stamps upon a heart gratitude and love for Jesus in return. "We love because He first loved us." In those grand old ages, which are the heroic period of the Christian religion, this double mark was clearly to be seen in all believers in Jesus; they were people who knew the love of Christ, and rested upon it the way a person leans upon a staff whose trustiness has been tried. The love which those early believers felt towards the Lord was not a quiet emotion which they hid within themselves in the secret chamber of their souls, and which they only spoke of in their private assemblies when they met on the first day of the week, and sang hymns in honor of Christ Jesus the crucified. Rather, it was a passion with them of such a vehement and all-consuming energy, that it was visible in all their actions, heard in their common talk, and seen in their eyes even in their commonest glances. Love for Jesus was a flame which fed upon the core and heart of their being; and, therefore, from its own force burned its way into the outer person, and shone there. Zeal for the glory of King Jesus was the seal and mark of all genuine Christians. Because of their dependence upon Christ's love they *dared* much, and because of their love to Christ they *did* much, and it is the same now. The children of God are ruled in their inmost powers by love — the love of Christ constrains them; they rejoice that divine love is set upon them, in their hearts they feel it being poured out by the Holy Spirit, who is given to them, and then by force of gratitude they love the Savior with a pure heart, fervently. My reader, do *you* love Him? Before you sleep give an honest answer to a weighty question!

"I am unworthy." — *Job 40:4*

NE cheering word, poor lost sinner, for you! You think you mustn't come to God because you are unworthy. Now, there isn't a saint alive on this earth who hasn't been made to feel that he is unworthy. If Job, and Isaiah, and Paul were all obliged to say "I am unworthy," oh, poor sinner, will you be ashamed to join in the same confession? If divine grace doesn't eradicate all sin from the believer, how do you hope to do it yourself? and if God loves His people while they are yet unworthy, do you think your loathsomeness will prevent His loving you? Believe on Jesus, you outcast of the world's society! Jesus calls *you*, just as you are.

> "Not the righteous, not the righteous;
> Sinners, Jesus came to call."

Even now say, "You have died for sinners; I am a sinner, Lord Jesus, sprinkle your blood on me;" if you will confess your sin you shall find pardon. If, now, with all your heart, you will say, "I am unworthy, wash me," you shall be washed *now*. If the Holy Spirit shall enable you from your heart to cry

> "Just as I am, without one plea
> But that Thy blood was shed for me,
> And that thou bidd'st me come to Thee,
> O Lamb of God, I come!"

you shall rise from reading this morning's portion with all your sins pardoned; and, although you woke this morning with every sin that humankind has ever committed on your head, you shall rest tonight accepted in the Beloved; though once degraded with the rags of sin, you shall be adorned with a robe of righteousness, and appear as pure as the angels are. For "now," take heed, "*Now* is the time of God's favor." If you "trust God who justifies the wicked, your faith is credited as righteousness." Oh! may the Holy Spirit give you saving faith in Him who receives the most unworthy.

"Are they Israelites? So am I." — *2 Corinthians 11:22*

E have here A PERSONAL CLAIM, and one that *needs proof.* The apostle knew that *His* claim was indisputable, but there are many persons who have no right to the title who yet claim to belong to the Israel of God. If we are with confidence declaring, "I am also an Israelite," let's only say it after having searched our heart as in the presence of God. But if we can give proof that we are following Jesus, if we can from the heart say, "I trust Him wholly, trust Him only, trust Him simply, trust Him now, and trust Him ever," then the position which the saints of God hold belongs to us — all their enjoyments are our possessions; we may be the very least in Israel, "less than the least of all saints," yet since the mercies of God belong to the saints AS SAINTS, and not as advanced saints, or well-taught saints, we may put in our plea, and say, "Are they Israelites? So am I. Therefore the promises are mine, grace is mine, glory will be mine." The claim, rightfully made, is one which will yield untold comfort. When God's people are rejoicing that they are His, what a happiness if they can say, "SO AM I!" When they speak of being pardoned, and justified, and accepted in the Beloved, how joyful to respond, "Through the grace of God, SO AM I." But this claim not only has its enjoyments and privileges, but also its conditions and duties. We must share with God's people in cloud as well as in sunshine. When we hear them spoken of with contempt and ridicule for being Christians, we must come boldly forward and say, "So am I." When we see them working for Christ, giving their time, their talent, their whole heart to Jesus, we must be able to say, "So do I." O let's prove our gratitude by our devotion, and live as those who, having claimed a privilege, are willing to take the responsibility connected with it.

"Let those who love the LORD hate evil." — Psalm 97:10

OU have good reason to "hate evil," for only consider what harm it has already wrought you. Oh, what a world of mischief sin has brought into your heart! Sin blinded you so that you could not see the beauty of the Savior; it made you deaf so that you could not hear the Redeemer's tender invitations. Sin turned your feet into the way of death, and poured poison into the very fountain of your being; it tainted your heart, and made it "deceitful above all things and beyond cure." Oh, what a creature you were when evil had done its utmost with you, before divine grace intervened! You were an heir of wrath even as others; you did "follow the crowd in doing wrong." Such were all of us; but Paul reminds us, "but you were washed, you were sanctified, you were justified in the name of the Lord Jesus Christ and by the Spirit of our God." We have good reason, indeed, for hating evil when we look back and trace its deadly workings. Such mischief did evil do us, that our souls would have been lost had not omnipotent love interfered to redeem us. Even now it is an active enemy, ever watching to do us hurt, and to drag us to eternal damnation. Therefore "hate evil," O Christians, unless you desire trouble. If you would strew your path with thorns, and plant nettles in your death pillow, then neglect to "hate evil;" but if you would live a happy life, and die a peaceful death, then walk in all the ways of holiness, hating evil, even to the end. If you truly love your Savior, and would honor Him, then "hate evil." We know of no cure for the love of evil in a Christian like abundant communication with the Lord Jesus. Dwell much with Him, and it is impossible for you to be at peace with sin.

"Order my footsteps by Thy Word,
And make my heart sincere;
Let sin have no dominion, Lord,
But keep my conscience clear."

"Be earnest." — *Revelation 3:19*

F you would see souls converted, if you would hear the cry that "the kingdom of the world has become the kingdom of our Lord;" if you would place crowns upon the head of the Savior, and see His throne lifted high, then be earnest. For, under God, the way of the world's conversion must be by the zeal of the church. Every grace shall do exploits, but this shall be first; prudence, knowledge, patience, and courage will follow in their places, but zeal must lead the van. It is not the extent of your knowledge, though that is useful; it is not the extent of your talent, though that is not to be despised; it is your zeal that shall do great exploits. This zeal is the fruit of the Holy Spirit: it draws its vital force from *the continued operations of* the Holy Spirit in the soul. If our inner life dwindles, if our heart beats slowly before God, we shall not know zeal; but if all be strong and vigorous within, then we cannot but feel a loving anxiety to see the kingdom of Christ come, and His will done on earth, even as it is in heaven. A deep *sense of gratitude* will nourish Christian zeal. Looking to the hole of the pit whence we were dug, we find abundant reason why we should spend and be spent for God. And zeal is also stimulated by *the thought of the eternal future.* It looks with tearful eyes down to the flames of hell, and it cannot slumber: it looks up with anxious gaze to the glories of heaven, and it cannot but move quickly, wake itself. It feels that time is short compared with the work to be done, and therefore it devotes all that it has to the cause of its Lord. And it is ever strengthened by *the remembrance of Christ's example.* He was clothed with zeal as with a cloak. How swift the chariot wheels of duty went with Him! He knew no loitering by the way. Let's prove that we are His disciples by manifesting the same spirit of zeal.

"Many others fell slain, because the battle was God's."
— *1 Chronicles 5:22*

ARRIOR, fighting under the banner of the Lord Jesus, observe this verse with holy joy, for as it was in the days of old so is it now, if the battle is God's the victory is sure. The sons of Reuben, and the Gadites, and the half tribe of Manasseh could barely muster five and forty thousand fighting men, and yet in their war with the Hagarites, they slew "men, a hundred thousand," "because they cried out to Him during the battle. He answered their prayers, because they trusted in Him." The Lord does not save by many nor by few; it is ours to go forth in Jehovah's name if we are just a handful of people, for the Lord of Hosts is with us for our Captain. They didn't neglect shield, and sword, and bow; neither did they place their trust in these weapons. We must use all fitting means, but our confidence must rest in the Lord alone, for He is the sword and the shield of His people. The great reason for their extraordinary success lay in the fact that "the battle was God's." Beloved, in fighting with sin without and within, with error doctrinal or practical, with spiritual wickedness in high places or low places, with devils and the devil's allies, you are waging Jehovah's war, and unless He Himself can be worsted, you need not fear defeat. Faint not before superior numbers, shrink not from difficulties or impossibilities, flinch not at wounds or death, strike with the two-edged sword of the Spirit, and the slain shall lie in heaps. The battle is the Lord's and He will deliver His enemies into our hands. With steadfast foot, strong hand, dauntless heart, and flaming zeal, rush to the conflict, and the hosts of evil shall fly like chaff before the gale.

Stand up! stand up for Jesus!
The strife will not be long;
This day the noise of battle,
The next the victor's song:

To him that overcometh,
A crown of life shall be;
He with the King of glory
Shall reign eternally.

"You will now see whether or not what I say will
come true for you." — Numbers 11:23

OD had made a positive promise to Moses that for the space of a whole month He would feed the vast host in the wilderness with flesh. Moses, being overtaken by a fit of unbelief, looks to the outward means, and is at a loss to know how the promise can be fulfilled. He looked to the creature instead of the Creator. But does the Creator expect the creature to fulfill His promise for Him? No; He who makes the promise ever fulfills it by His own unaided omnipotence. If He speaks, it is done — done by Himself. His promises don't depend for their fulfillment upon the cooperation of the puny strength of man. We can at once perceive the mistake which Moses made. And yet how commonly we do the same! God has promised to supply our needs, and we look to the creature to do what God has promised to do; and then, because we perceive the creature to be weak and feeble, we indulge in unbelief. Why look we to that quarter at all? Will you look to the north pole to gather fruits ripened in the sun? Verily, you would act no more foolishly if you did this than when you look to the weak for strength, and to the creature to do the Creator's work. Let us, then, put the question on the right footing. The ground of faith is not the sufficiency of the visible means for the performance of the promise, but the all-sufficiency of the invisible God, who will most surely do as He has said. If after clearly seeing that the onus lies with the Lord and not with the creature, we dare to indulge in mistrust, the question of God comes home mightily to us: "Is the LORD's arm too short?" May it happen, too, in His mercy, that with the question there may flash upon our souls that blessed declaration, "You will now see whether or not what I say will come true for you."

"The LORD has done great things for us,
and we are filled with joy." — Psalm 126:3

OME Christians are sadly prone to *look* on the *dark* side of everything, and to dwell more upon what they have gone through than upon what God has done for them. Ask for their impression of the Christian life, and they will describe their continual conflicts, their deep afflictions, their sad adversities, and the sinfulness of their hearts, yet with scarcely any allusion to the mercy and help which God has vouchsafed them. But a Christian whose soul is in a *healthy* state, will come forward joyously, and say, "I will speak, not about myself, but to the honor of my God. He lifted me out of the slimy pit, out of the mud and mire; He set my feet on a rock and gave me a firm place to stand. He put a new song in my mouth, a hymn of praise to our God." Such an abstract of experience as this is the very best that any child of God can present. It is true that we endure trials, but it is just as true that we are delivered out of them. It is true that we have our corruptions, and mournfully do we know this, but it is quite as true that we have an all-sufficient Savior, who overcomes these corruptions, and delivers us from their dominion. In looking back, it would be wrong to deny that we have been in the Slough of Despond, and have crept along the Valley of Humiliation, but it would be equally wicked to forget that we have been *through* them safely and profitably; we have not remained in them, thanks to our Almighty Helper and Leader, who has "brought us to a place of abundance." The deeper our troubles, the louder our thanks to God, who has led us through all, and preserved us until now. Our griefs cannot mar the melody of our praise, we reckon them to be the bass part of our life's song, "The LORD has done great things for us, and we are filled with joy."

"You diligently study the Scriptures." — John 5:39

HE Greek word here rendered *study* signifies a strict, close, diligent, curious search, such as men make when they are seeking gold, or hunters when they are in earnest after game. We must not rest content with having given a superficial reading to a chapter or two, but with the candle of the Spirit we must deliberately seek out the hidden meaning of the word. Holy Scripture *requires study* — much of it can only be learned by careful study. There is milk for babes, but also meat for strong men. The rabbis wisely say that a mountain of matter hangs upon every word, yea, upon every title of Scripture. Tertullian exclaims, "I adore the fullness of the Scriptures." No man who merely skims the book of God can profit thereby; we must dig and mine until we obtain the hid treasure. The door of the word only opens to the key of diligence. The Scriptures *claim searching.* They are the writings of God, bearing the divine stamp and imprimatur — who shall dare to treat them with levity? He who despises them despises the God who wrote them. God forbid that any of us should leave our Bibles to become swift witnesses against us in the great day of account. The word of God *will repay diligent study.* God doesn't bid us sift a mountain of chaff with here and there a grain of wheat in it, but the Bible is winnowed corn — we have but to open the granary door and find it. Scripture grows upon the student. It is full of surprises. Under the teaching of the Holy Spirit, to the searching eye it glows with the splendor of revelation, like a vast temple paved with wrought gold, and roofed with rubies, emeralds, and all manner of gems. No merchandise like the merchandise of Scripture truth. Lastly, *the Scriptures reveal Jesus:* "These are the Scriptures that testify about Me." No more powerful motive can be urged upon Bible readers than this: those who find Jesus find life, heaven, all things. Happy are they who, searching their Bibles, discover their Savior.

"We live to the Lord." — *Romans 14:8*

F God had willed it, each of us might have entered heaven at the moment of conversion. It was not absolutely necessary for our preparation for immortality that we should linger here. It is possible for a man to be taken to heaven, and to be found acceptable to be a participant in the inheritance of the saints in light, though he has but just believed in Jesus. It is true that our sanctification is a long and continued process, and we shall not be perfected until we lay aside our bodies and enter within the veil; but nevertheless, had the Lord so willed it, He might have changed us from imperfection to perfection, and have taken us to heaven at once. Why then are we here? Would God keep His children out of paradise a single moment longer than was necessary? Why is the army of the living God still on the battlefield when one charge might give them the victory? Why are His children still wandering here and there through a maze, when a solitary word from His lips would bring them into the center of their hopes in heaven? The answer is — they are here that they may *"live to the Lord,"* and may bring others to know His love. We remain on earth as sowers to scatter good seed; as ploughmen to break up the fallow ground; as heralds publishing salvation. We are here as the "salt of the earth," to be a blessing to the world. We are here to glorify Christ in our daily life. We are here as workers for Him, and "as God's fellow workers." Let's see that our life answers its end. Let's live earnest, useful, holy lives "to the praise of His glorious grace." Meanwhile we long to be with Him, and daily sing —

> "My heart is with Him on His throne,
> And ill can brook delay;
> Each moment listening for the voice,
> 'Rise up, and come away.' "

"These are the Scriptures that testify about me."
— *John 5:39*

ESUS Christ is the Alpha and Omega of the Bible. He is the constant theme of its sacred pages; from first to last they testify of Him. At the creation we at once discern Him as one of the sacred Trinity; we catch a glimpse of Him in the promise of the woman's seed; we see Him typified in the ark of Noah; we walk with Abraham, as he sees Messiah's day; we dwell in the tents of Isaac and Jacob, feeding upon the gracious promise; we hear the venerable Israel talking of Shiloh; and in the numerous types of the law, we find the Redeemer abundantly foreshadowed. Prophets and kings, priests and preachers, all look one way — they all stand as the cherubs did over the ark, desiring to look within, and to read the mystery of God's great propitiation. Still more manifestly in the New Testament we find our Lord the one pervading subject. It is not an ingot here and there, or dust of gold thinly scattered, but here you stand upon a solid floor of gold; for the whole substance of the New Testament is Jesus crucified, and even its closing sentence is bejeweled with the Redeemer's name. We should always read Scripture in this light; we should consider the word to be as a mirror into which Christ looks down from heaven; and then we, looking into it, see His face reflected as in a mirror — poorly, it is true, but still in such a way as to be a blessed preparation for seeing Him as we shall see Him face to face. This volume contains Jesus Christ's letters to us, perfumed by His love. These pages are the garments of our King, and they all smell of myrrh, and aloes, and cassia. Scripture is the royal chariot in which Jesus rides, and it is paved with love for the daughters of Jerusalem. The Scriptures are the swaddling clothes of the holy child Jesus; unroll them and you find your Savior. The quintessence of the word of God is Christ.

"We love him, because he first loved us."
— 1 John 4:19

HERE is no light in the planet but that which proceeds from the sun; and there is no true love for Jesus in the heart but that which comes from the Lord Jesus Himself. From this overflowing fountain of the infinite love of God, all our love to God must spring. This must ever be a great and certain truth, that we love Him for no other reason than because He first loved us. Our love for Him is *the fair offspring* of His love to us. Cold admiration, when studying the works of God, anyone may have, but the warmth of love can only be kindled in the heart by God's Spirit. How great the wonder that such as we should ever have been brought to love Jesus at all! How marvelous that when we had rebelled against Him, He should, by a display of such amazing love, seek to draw us back. No! never should we have had a grain of love towards God unless it had been sown in us by the sweet seed of His love to us. Love, then, has for its parent the love of God shed abroad in the heart: but after it is thus divinely born, it must be *divinely nourished.* Love is an exotic; it is not a plant which will flourish naturally in human soil, it must be watered from above. Love for Jesus is a flower of a delicate nature, and if it received no nourishment but that which could be drawn from the rock of our hearts it would soon wither. As love comes from heaven, so it must feed on heavenly bread. It cannot exist in the wilderness unless it is fed by manna from on high. Love must feed on love. The very soul and life of our love for God is His love for us.

> "I love thee, Lord, but with no love of mine,
> For I have none to give;
> I love thee, Lord; but all the love is thine,
> For by thy love I live.
> I am as nothing, and rejoice to be
> Emptied, and lost, and swallowed up in thee."

> *"There he broke the flashing arrows, the shields and
> the swords, the weapons of war."* — *Psalm 76:3*

UR Redeemer's glorious cry of "It is finished," was the death knell of all the adversaries of His people, the breaking of "the
flashing arrows, the shields and the swords,
the weapons of war." Behold the hero of
Golgotha using His cross as an anvil, and
His woes as a hammer, dashing to shivers bundle after
bundle of our sins, those poisoned "flashing arrows;"
trampling on every indictment, and destroying every accusation. What glorious blows the mighty Breaker gives with
a hammer far more ponderous than the fabled weapon of
Thor! How the diabolical darts fly to fragments, and the
infernal shields are broken like potters' vessels! Behold,
He draws from its sheath of hellish workmanship the
dread sword of Satanic power! He snaps it across His knee,
as a man breaks the dry wood of a twig, and casts it into the
fire. Beloved, no sin of a believer can now be an arrow to
mortally wound him, no condemnation can now be a
sword to kill him, for the punishment of our sin was borne
by Christ, a full atonement was made for all our iniquities
by our blessed Substitute and Surety. Who now accuses?
Who now condemns? Christ has died, yes rather, has risen
again. Jesus has emptied the quivers of hell, has quenched
every fiery dart, and broken off the head of every arrow of
wrath; the ground is strewn with the splinters and relics of
the weapons of hell's warfare, which are only visible to us
to remind us of our former danger, and of our great
deliverance. Sin has no more dominion over us. Jesus has
made an end of it, and put it away forever. O you enemy,
destructions have come to a perpetual end. Talk of all the
wondrous works of the Lord, you who make mention of
His name, don't keep silence, neither by day, nor when the
sun goes to his rest. Bless the Lord, O my soul.

"You have been weighed on the scales and
found wanting." — Daniel 5:27

 T is well frequently to weigh ourselves on the scale of God's Word. You will find it a holy exercise to read some psalm of David, and, as you meditate upon each verse, to ask yourself, "Can I say this? Have I felt as David felt? Has my heart ever been broken on account of sin, as his was when he penned his penitential psalms? Has my soul been full of true confidence in the hour of difficulty as his was when he sang of God's mercies in the cave of Adullam, or in the holds of Engedi? Do I 'lift up the cup of salvation and call on the name of the LORD'?" Then turn to the life of Christ, and as you read, ask yourselves how far you are conformed to His likeness. Try to discover whether you have the meekness, the humility, the lovely spirit which He constantly inculcated and displayed. Take, then, the epistles, and see whether you can go with the apostle in what he said of his experience. Have you ever cried out as he did — "What a wretched man I am! Who will rescue me from this body of death?" Have you ever felt his self-abasement? Have you seemed to yourself the chief of sinners, and less than the least of all saints? Have you known anything of his devotion? Could you join with him and say, "For to me, to live is Christ and to die is gain"? If we thus read God's Word as a test of our spiritual condition, we shall have good reason to stop many a time and say, "Lord, I feel I have never yet been here, O bring me here! give me true penitence, such as this I read of. Give me real faith; give me warmer zeal; inflame me with more fervent love; grant me the grace of meekness; make me more like Jesus. Let me no longer be 'found wanting,' when weighed in the balances of the sanctuary, lest I be found wanting in the scales of judgment." "But if we judged ourselves, we would not come under judgment."

"Who has saved us and called us to a holy life."
— 2 Timothy 1:9

HE apostle uses the perfect tense and says, "Who *has* saved us." Believers in Christ Jesus *are* saved. They are not looked upon as persons who are in a hopeful state, and may ultimately be saved, but they *are* already saved. Salvation is not a blessing to be enjoyed upon the dying bed, and to be sung of in a future state above, but a matter to be obtained, received, promised, and enjoyed now. The Christian is perfectly saved *in God's purpose;* God has ordained him to salvation, and that purpose is complete. He is saved also as to the *price which has been paid for him:* "It is finished" was the cry of the Savior before He died. The believer is also perfectly saved *in His covenant head,* for as he fell in Adam, so he lives in Christ. This complete salvation is accompanied by *a calling to a holy life.* Those whom the Savior saved upon the cross are in due time effectually called by the power of God the Holy Spirit to holiness: they leave their sins; they try to be like Christ; they choose holiness, not out of any compulsion, but from the stress of a new nature, which leads them to rejoice in holiness just as naturally as in the past they delighted in sin. God neither chose them nor called them because they were holy, but He called them that they might be holy, and holiness is the beauty produced by His workmanship in them. The excellencies which we see in a believer are as much the work of God as the atonement itself. Thus is brought out very sweetly the fullness of the grace of God. Salvation must be of grace, because the Lord is the author of it: and what motive but grace could move Him to save the guilty? Salvation must be of grace, because the Lord works in such a manner that our righteousness is forever excluded. Such is the believer's privilege — *a present salvation;* such is the evidence that he is called to it — *a holy life.*

"Whoever wishes, let him take the free gift of the water of life." — Revelation 22:17

ESUS says, "take the free gift." He wants no payment or preparation. He seeks no recommendation from our virtuous emotions. If you have no good feelings, if you are only willing, you are invited; therefore come! You have no belief and no repentance, — come to Him, and He will give them to you. Come, just as you are, and take "the free gift" without money and without price. He gives Himself to needy ones. The drinking fountains at the street corners are valuable institutions; and we can hardly imagine anyone so foolish as to reach for his purse when he stands before one of them and cry, "I can't drink because I haven't any money in my pocket." No matter how poor a person is, there is the fountain, and you may drink from it just as you are. Thirsty passersby, whether dressed in fustian or in broadcloth, don't look for any warrant for drinking; its being there is the warrant for taking its water freely. The liberality of some good friends has put the refreshing crystal there and we take it, and ask no questions. Perhaps the only persons who go thirsty through the streets where there is a drinking fountain are the fine ladies and gentlemen who are in their carriages. They are very thirsty, but cannot think of being so vulgar as to get out to drink. It would demean them, they think, to drink at a common drinking fountain: so they ride by with parched lips. Oh, how many there are who are rich in their own good works and cannot therefore come to Christ! "I will not be saved," they say, "in the same way as the harlot or the swearer." What! go to heaven in the same way as a chimney sweep! Is there no pathway to glory but the path which led the thief there? I will not be saved that way. Such proud boasters must remain without the living water; but, "WHOSOEVER WISHES, LET HIM *TAKE THE FREE GIFT OF THE WATER OF LIFE.*"

"Keep falsehood and lies far from me."
— *Proverbs 30:8*

E not far from me O my God." Psalm 38:21. Here we have two great lessons — what to express disapproval of and what to ask for earnestly. The happiest state of a Christian is the holiest state. As there is the most heat nearest to the sun, so there is the most happiness nearest to Christ. No Christian enjoys comfort when his eyes are fixed on vanity — he finds no satisfaction unless his soul is quickened in the ways of God. The world may win happiness elsewhere, but he can't. I don't blame ungodly people for rushing to their pleasures. Why should I? Let them have their fill. That is all they have to enjoy. A converted wife who despaired of her husband was always very kind to him, for she said, "I fear that this is the only world in which he will be happy, and therefore I have made up my mind to make him as happy as I can in it." Christians must seek their delights in a higher sphere than the insipid frivolities or sinful enjoyments of the world. Vain pursuits are dangerous to renewed souls. We have heard of a philosopher who, while he looked *up* to the stars, fell into a pit; but how deeply do they fall who look *down*. Their fall is fatal. No Christian is safe when his soul is lazy, and his God is far from him. Every Christian is always safe as to the great matter of his standing in Christ, but he is not safe as regards his experience in holiness, and communion with Jesus in this life. Satan doesn't often attack a Christian who is living near to God. It is when the Christian departs from his God, becomes spiritually starved, and endeavors to feed on vanities, that the devil discovers his advantageous hour. He may sometimes stand foot to foot with the child of God who is active in his Master's service, but the battle is generally short: he who slips as he goes down into the Valley of Humiliation, every time he takes a false step invites Apollyon to assail him. O for grace to walk humbly with our God!

"Delight yourself in the LORD." — *Psalm 37:4*

HE teaching of these words must seem very surprising to those who are strangers to vital godliness, but to the sincere believer it is only the inculcation of a recognized truth. The life of the believer is here described as a *delight* in God, and we are thus certified of the great fact that true religion overflows with happiness and joy. Ungodly persons and those who merely profess faith never look upon religion as a joyful thing; to them it is service, duty, or necessity, but never pleasure or delight. If they attend to religion at all, it is either that they may gain thereby, or else because they dare not do otherwise. The thought of *delight* in religion is so strange to most people, that no two words in their language stand further apart than "holiness" and "delight." But believers who know Christ understand that delight and faith are so blessedly united, that the gates of hell cannot prevail to separate them. They who love God with all their hearts, find that His ways are pleasant ways, and all His paths are peace. Such joys, such brimful delights, such overflowing blessings, do the saints discover in their Lord, that so far from serving Him from custom, they would follow Him though all the world cast out His name as evil. We don't fear God because of any compulsion; our faith is no fetter, our profession is no bondage, we are not dragged to holiness, nor driven to duty. No, our piety is our pleasure, our hope is our happiness, our duty is our delight.

Delight and true religion are as allied as root and flower; as indivisible as truth and certainty; they are, in fact, two precious jewels glittering side by side in a setting of gold.

> "'Tis when we taste Thy love,
> Our joys divinely grow,
> Unspeakable like those above,
> And heaven begins below."

"O LORD, we . . . are covered with shame because
we have sinned against you." — Daniel 9:8

deep sense and clear sight of sin, its heinousness, and the punishment which it deserves,
should make us lie low before the throne. We
have sinned as Christians. Alas! that it
should be so. Favored as we have been, we
have yet been ungrateful: privileged beyond
most, we have not brought forth fruit in proportion. Who
is there, although he may long have been engaged in the
Christian warfare, that will not blush when he looks back
upon the past? As for our days before we were regenerated,
may they be forgiven and forgotten; but since then, though
we have not sinned as before, yet we have sinned against
light and against love — light which has really penetrated
our minds, and love in which we have rejoiced. Oh, the
atrocity of the sin of a pardoned soul! An unpardoned
sinner sins cheaply compared with the sin of one of God's
own elect ones, who has had communion with Christ and
leaned his head upon Jesus' bosom. Look at David! Many
will talk of his sin, but I pray you look at his repentance,
and hear his broken bones, as each one of them moans out
its dolorous confession! Notice his tears, as they fall upon
the ground, and the deep sighs with which he accompanies
the softened music of his harp! We have erred: let's,
therefore, seek the spirit of penitence. Look, again, at
Peter! We speak a great deal about Peter's denying his
Master. Remember, it is written, "He wept bitterly." Have
we no denials of our Lord to be lamented with tears? Alas!
these sins of ours, before and after conversion, would
consign us to the place of inextinguishable fire if it were
not for the sovereign mercy which has made us to differ,
snatching us like brands from the burning. My soul, bow
down under a sense of your natural sinfulness, and worship your God. Admire the grace which saves you — the
mercy which spares you — the love which pardons you!

---

*"Sarah said, God has brought me laughter, and everyone
who hears about this will laugh with me."*
— *Genesis 21:6*

T was far above the power of nature, and even contrary to its laws, that the aged Sarah should be honored with a son; and even so it is beyond all ordinary rules that I, a poor, helpless, undone sinner, should find grace to bear about in my soul the indwelling Spirit of the Lord Jesus. I, who once despaired, as well I might, for my nature was as dry, and withered, and barren, and accursed as a howling wilderness, even I have been made to bring forth fruit to holiness. Well may my mouth be filled with joyous laughter, because of the singular, surprising grace which I have received of the Lord, for I have found Jesus, the promised seed, and He is mine forever. This day I will lift up psalms of triumph to the Lord who has remembered my low estate, for "my heart rejoices in the LORD; in the LORD my horn is lifted high. My mouth boasts over my enemies, for I delight in Your deliverance."

I would have all those that hear of my great deliverance from hell, and my most blessed visitation from on high, laugh for joy with me. I would surprise my family with my abundant peace; I would delight my friends with my ever-increasing happiness; I would edify the church with my grateful confessions; and even impress the world with the cheerfulness of my daily conversation. Bunyan tells us that Mercy laughed in her sleep, and no wonder when she dreamed of Jesus; my joy shall not stop short of hers while my Beloved is the theme of my daily thoughts. The Lord Jesus is a deep sea of joy: my soul shall dive therein, shall be swallowed up in the delights of His society. Sarah looked on her Isaac, and laughed with excess of rapture, and all her friends laughed with her; and you, my soul, look on your Jesus, and bid heaven and earth unite in your unspeakable joy.

"What he opens no one can shut." — *Revelation 3:7*

 ESUS is the keeper of the gates of paradise and before every believing soul He sets an open door, which no person or devil shall be able to close. What joy it will be to find that faith in Him is the golden key to the everlasting doors. My soul, do you carry this key in your heart, or are you trusting to some deceitful lock picker, who will fail you in the end? Hear this parable of the preacher, and remember it. The great King has made a banquet, and He has proclaimed to all the world that none shall enter but those who bring with them the fairest flower that blooms. The spirits of humanity advance to the gate by thousands, bringing with them the flower which each regards as the queen of the garden; but they are driven from the royal presence in droves, and do not enter the festive halls. Some bear in their hand the deadly nightshade of superstition, or the flaunting poppies of Rome, or the hemlock of self-righteousness, but these are not dear to the King. The bearers are shut out of the pearly gates. My soul, have you gathered the rose of Sharon? Do you wear the lily of the valley constantly close to your heart? If so, when you come up to the gates of heaven you will know its value, for you have only to show this choicest of flowers, and the Gatekeeper will open: He will not deny you admission for a moment, for to that rose the Gatekeeper opens forever. You shall find your way with the rose of Sharon in your hand up to the throne of God Himself, for heaven itself possesses nothing that excels its radiant beauty, and of all the flowers that bloom in paradise there is none that can rival the lily of the valley. My soul, get Calvary's blood-red rose into your hand by faith, by love wear it, by communion preserve it, by daily watchfulness make it your all in all, and you shall be blessed beyond all bliss, happy beyond a dream. Jesus, be mine forever, my God, my heaven, my all.

"I give them eternal life, and they shall never perish."
— *John 10:28*

HE Christian should never think or speak lightly of unbelief. For a child of God to mistrust His love, His truth, His faithfulness, must be greatly displeasing to Him. How can we ever grieve Him by doubting His upholding grace? Christian! it is contrary to every promise of God's precious Word that you should ever be forgotten or left to perish. If it could be so, how could He be true who has said, "Can a mother forget the baby at her breast and have no compassion on the child she has borne? Though she may forget, I will not forget you." What about the value of that promise — " 'Though the mountains be shaken and the hills be removed, yet My unfailing love for you will not be shaken nor My covenant of peace be removed,' says the LORD, who has compassion on you." What about the truth of Christ's words — "I give [My sheep] eternal life, and they shall never perish; no one can snatch them out of My hand. My Father, who has given them to Me, is greater than all; no one can snatch them out of My Father's hand." What about the doctrines of grace? They would be all disproved if one child of God should perish. What about the veracity of God, His honor, His power, His grace, His covenant, His oath, if any of those for whom Christ has died, and who have put their trust in Him, should nevertheless be cast away? Banish those unbelieving fears which so dishonor God. Arise, shake yourself from the dust, and put on your beautiful garments. Remember it is sinful to doubt His Word wherein He has promised you that you shall never perish. Let the eternal life within you express itself in confident rejoicing.

"The gospel bears my spirit up:
A faithful and unchanging God
Lays the foundation for my hope,
In oaths, and promises, and blood."

"The LORD is my light and my salvation — whom
shall I fear? The LORD is the stronghold of my life
— of whom shall I be afraid?" — *Psalm 27:1*

HE LORD is my light and my salvation." Here is personal interest, *"my light," "my salvation;"* the soul is assured of it, and therefore declares it boldly. Into the soul at the new birth divine light is poured as the precursor of salvation; where there is not enough light to reveal our own darkness and to make us long for the Lord Jesus, there is no evidence of salvation. After conversion our God is our joy, comfort, guide, teacher and, in every sense, our light: He is light within, light around, light reflected from us, and light to be revealed to us. Note, it is not said merely that the Lord gives light, but that He is light; nor that He gives salvation, but that He is salvation; he, then, who by faith has laid hold upon God, has all covenant blessings in his possession. This being made sure as a fact, the argument drawn from it is put in the form of a question, *"Whom shall I fear?"* A question which is its own answer. The powers of darkness are not to be feared, for the Lord, our light, destroys them; and the damnation of hell is not to be dreaded by us, for the Lord is our salvation. This is a very different challenge from that of boastful Goliath, for it rests, not upon the conceited vigor of an arm of flesh, but upon the real power of the omnipotent I AM. *"The Lord is the stronghold of my life."* Here is a third glowing epithet, to show that the writer's hope was fastened with a threefold cord which could not be broken. We may well accumulate terms of praise where the Lord lavishes deeds of grace. Our life derives all its strength from God; and if He deigns to make us strong, we cannot be weakened by all the machinations of the adversary. *"Whom shall I fear?"* The bold question looks into the future as well as the present. "If God is for us," who can be against us, either now or in time to come?

*"Help, L*ORD*." — Psalm 12:1*

HE *prayer itself is remarkable,* for it is *short,* but *seasonable, sententious,* and *suggestive.* David mourned the shortage of faithful people, and therefore lifted up his heart in supplication; when the creature failed, he flew to the Creator. He evidently felt his own weakness, or he wouldn't have cried for help; but at the same time he intended honestly to exert himself for the cause of truth, for the word "help" is inapplicable where we ourselves do nothing. There is a good deal of *directness, clearness of perception,* and *distinctness of utterance* in this petition of two words; much more, indeed, than in the long rambling outpourings of certain ones who profess the faith. The Psalmist runs directly to his God, with a well-considered prayer; he knows what he is seeking, and where to seek it. Lord, teach us to pray in the same blessed manner.

The occasions for the use of this prayer are frequent. In *providential afflictions* how suitable it is for tested believers who find all helpers failing them. Students, in *doctrinal difficulties,* may often obtain aid by lifting up this cry of "Help, LORD," to the Holy Spirit, the great Teacher. Spiritual warriors in *inward conflicts* may send to the throne for reinforcements, and this will be a model for their request. Workers in *heavenly work* may thus obtain grace in time of need. Seeking sinners, in *doubts and alarms,* may offer up the same weighty supplication; in fact, in all these cases, times, and places, this will serve the turn of needy souls. "Help, LORD," will suit us living and dying, suffering or laboring, rejoicing or sorrowing. In Him our help is found, let's not be slack to cry to Him.

The answer to the prayer is certain, if it is sincerely offered through Jesus. The Lord's character assures us that He will not leave His people; His relationship as Father and Husband guarantee us His aid; His gift of Jesus is a pledge of every good thing; and His sure promise stands, "Do not fear, I WILL HELP YOU."

"Then Israel sang this song: Spring up, O well!
Sing about it." — *Numbers 21:17*

AMOUS was the well of Beer in the wilderness, because it was *the subject of a promise:* That is "the well where the LORD said to Moses, 'Gather the people together and I will give them water.' " The people needed water, and it was promised by their gracious God. We need fresh supplies of heavenly grace, and in the covenant the Lord has pledged Himself to give all we require. The well next became *the cause of a song.* Before the water gushed forth, cheerful faith prompted the people to sing; and as they saw the crystal fount bubbling up, the music grew yet more joyous. In like manner, we who believe the promise of God should rejoice in the prospect of divine revivals in our souls, and as we experience them our holy joy should overflow. Are we thirsting? Let's not murmur, but sing. Spiritual thirst is bitter to bear, but we needn't bear it — the promise indicates a well; let's be of good heart, and look for it. Moreover, the well was *the center of prayer.* "Spring up, O well." What God has engaged to give, we must inquire after, or we reveal that we have neither desire nor faith. This evening let's ask that the Scripture we have read, and our devotional exercises, may not be an empty formality, but a channel of grace to our souls. O that God the Holy Spirit would work in us with all His mighty power, filling us with all the fullness of God. Lastly, the well was *the object of effort.* "The nobles of the people sank — the nobles with scepters and staffs." The Lord would have us active in obtaining grace. Our staffs are ill adapted for digging in the sand, but we must use them to the utmost of our ability. Prayer must not be neglected; the assembling of ourselves together must not be forsaken; sacraments must not be slighted. The Lord will give us His peace most plenteously, but not in a way of idleness. Let's, then, move quickly, awaken ourselves to seek Him in whom are all our fresh springs.

"Your Redeemer." — *Isaiah 54:5*

 ESUS, the Redeemer, is altogether ours and ours forever. All the *offices* of Christ are held on our behalf. He is king for us, priest for us, and prophet for us. Whenever we read a new title of the Redeemer, let's appropriate Him as ours under that name as much as under any other. The shepherd's staff, the father's rod, the captain's sword, the priest's miter, the prince's scepter, the prophet's mantle, all are ours. Jesus has no dignity which He will not employ for our exaltation, and no prerogative which He will not exercise for our defense. His fullness of *Godhead* is our unfailing, inexhaustible treasury.

His *humanity* also, which He took upon Himself for us, is ours in all its perfection. To us our gracious Lord communicates the spotless virtue of a stainless character; to us He gives the meritorious efficacy of a devoted life; to us He gives the reward procured by obedient submission and incessant service. He makes the unsullied garment of His life our covering beauty; the glittering virtues of His character our ornaments and jewels; and the superhuman meekness of His death our boast and glory. He bequeaths us His manger, from which to learn how God came down to humankind; and His Cross to teach us how humankind may go up to God. All His thoughts, emotions, actions, utterances, miracles, and intercessions were for us. He trod the road of sorrow on our behalf, and has given over to us as His heavenly legacy the full results of all the labors of His life. He is now as much ours as heretofore; and He does not blush to acknowledge Himself *"our* Lord Jesus Christ," though He is the blessed and only Potentate, the King of kings, and Lord of lords. Christ everywhere and every way is our Christ, forever and ever most richly to enjoy. O my soul, by the power of the Holy Spirit, call Him "Your Redeemer" this morning.

"I have come into my garden, my sister, my bride."
— *Song of Songs 5:1*

HE heart of the believer is Christ's garden. He bought it with His precious blood, and He enters it and claims it as His own. A garden *implies separation.* It is not the open common; it is not a wilderness; it is walled around, or hedged in. If only we could see the wall of separation between the church and the world made broader and stronger. It makes one sad to hear Christians saying, "Well, there is no harm in this; there is no harm in that," thus getting as near to the world as possible. Grace is at a low ebb in that soul which can even raise the question of how far it may go in worldly conformity. A garden is *a place of beauty,* it far surpasses the wild uncultivated lands. The genuine Christian must seek to be more excellent in his life than the best moralist, because Christ's garden ought to produce the best flowers in all the world. Even the best is poor compared with Christ's deservings; let's not put Him off with withering and dwarf plants. The rarest, richest, choicest lilies and roses ought to bloom in the place which Jesus calls His own. The garden is *a place of growth.* The saints are not to remain undeveloped, always mere buds and blossoms. We should grow in grace, and in the knowledge of our Lord and Savior Jesus Christ. Growth should be rapid where Jesus is the Farmer, and the Holy Spirit the dew from above. A garden is *a place of retirement.* So the Lord Jesus Christ would have us reserve our souls as a place in which He can manifest Himself, as He doesn't to the world. O that Christians were more retired, that they kept their hearts more closely shut up for Christ! We often worry and trouble ourselves, like Martha, with too much serving, so that we haven't the room for Christ that Mary had, and we don't sit at His feet as we should. The Lord grant the sweet showers of His grace to water His garden this day.

"All of them were filled with the Holy Spirit." — *Acts 2:4*

HE blessings of this day would be rich if all of us were filled with the Holy Spirit. It would be impossible to overestimate the consequences of this sacred filling of the soul. Life, comfort, light, purity, power, peace; and many other precious blessings are inseparable from the Spirit's benign presence. As sacred *oil*, He anoints the head of the believer, sets him apart to the priesthood of saints, and gives him grace to execute his office correctly. As the only truly purifying *water* He cleanses us from the power of sin and sanctifies us to holiness, working in us to will and to act according to His good purpose. As the *light*, He manifested to us at first our lost condition, and now He reveals the Lord Jesus to us and in us, and guides us in the way of righteousness. Enlightened by His pure celestial ray, we are no more darkness but light in the Lord. *As fire*, He both purges us from dross, and sets our consecrated nature on fire. He is the sacrificial flame by which we are enabled to offer our whole souls as a living sacrifice to God. As heavenly *dew*, He removes our barrenness and fertilizes our lives. O that He would descend on us from above at this early hour! Such morning dew would be a sweet commencement for the day. As the *dove*, with wings of peaceful love He broods over His church and over the souls of believers, and as a Comforter He dispels the cares and doubts which mar the peace of His beloved. He descends upon the chosen as upon the Lord in the Jordan, and bears witness to their sonship by working in them a filial spirit by which they cry Abba, Father. As the *wind*, He brings the breath of life to humankind; blowing where He chooses, He performs the life-giving operations by which the spiritual creation is animated and sustained. Would to God, that we might feel His presence this day and every day.

"My lover is mine and I am his; he browses among the lilies. Until the day breaks and the shadows flee, turn, my lover, and be like a gazelle or like a young stag on the rugged hills." — Song of Songs 2:16, 17

URELY if there is a happy verse in the Bible it is this — "My lover is mine, and I am His." So peaceful, so full of assurance, so overrunning with happiness and contentment is it, that it might well have been written by the same hand which penned the twenty-third Psalm. Yet though the prospect is exceedingly fair and lovely — earth cannot show its superior — it is not entirely a sunlit landscape. There is a cloud in the sky which casts a shadow over the scene. Listen, "Until the day breaks and the shadows flee."

There is a word, too, about the "rugged hills," or, "the mountains of division," and to our love, anything like division is bitterness. Beloved, this may be your present state of mind; you don't doubt your salvation; you know that Christ is yours, but you are not feasting with Him. You understand your vital interest in Him, so that you have no shadow of a doubt of your being His, and of His being yours, but still His left hand is not under your head, nor does His right hand embrace you. A shade of sadness is cast over your heart, perhaps by affliction, certainly by the temporary absence of your Lord, so even while exclaiming, "I am His," you are forced to take to your knees, and to pray, "Until the day breaks and the shadows flee, turn, my lover."

"Where is He?" asks the soul. And the answer comes, "He browses among the lilies." If we want to find Christ, we must get into communion with His people, we must come to the ordinances with His saints. Oh, for an evening glimpse of Him! Oh, to sup with Him tonight!

> *"For I will give the command, and I will*
> *shake the house of Israel among all the nations*
> *as grain is shaken in a sieve, and not a pebble*
> *will reach the ground."* — *Amos 9:9*

 VERY sifting comes by *divine command and permission.* Satan must ask permission before he can lay a finger upon Job. No, more, in some sense our siftings are *directly the work of heaven,* for the text says, "I will shake the house of Israel." Satan, like a drudge, may hold the sieve, hoping to destroy the grain; but the overruling hand of the Master is accomplishing the purity of the grain by the very process which the enemy intended to be destructive. Precious, but much sifted grain of the Lord's floor, be comforted by the blessed fact that the Lord directs both flail and sieve to His own glory, and to your eternal profit.

The Lord Jesus will surely use the fan which is in His hand, and will *divide the precious from the unworthy.* All are not Israel that are of Israel; the heap on the barn floor is not clean provender, and hence the winnowing process must be performed. In the sieve true weight alone has power. Husks and chaff being devoid of substance must fly before the wind, and only solid grain will remain.

Observe the *complete safety of the Lord's wheat;* even the least grain has a promise of preservation. God Himself sifts, and therefore it is stern and terrible work; He sifts them in all places, "among all the nations;" He sifts them in the most effectual manner, "as grain is shaken in a sieve;" and yet for all this, not the smallest, lightest, or most shriveled grain, is permitted to fall to the ground. Every individual believer is precious in the sight of the Lord, a shepherd would not lose one sheep, nor a jeweler one diamond, nor a mother one child, nor a man one limb of his body, nor will the Lord lose one of His redeemed people. However little we may be, if we are the Lord's, we may rejoice that we are preserved in Christ Jesus.

"At once they left their nets and followed him."
— *Mark 1:18*

HEN they heard the call of Jesus, Simon and Andrew obeyed at once without pause. If we would always, punctually and with resolute zeal, put in practice what we hear upon the spot, or at the first fit occasion, our attendance at the means of grace, and our reading of good books, could not fail to enrich us spiritually. He will not lose his loaf who has taken care at once to eat it, neither can he be deprived of the benefit of the doctrine who has already acted upon it. Most readers and hearers become moved so far as to purpose to amend; but, alas! the proposal is a blossom which has not been knit, and therefore no fruit comes of it; they wait, they waver, and then they forget, until, like the ponds in nights of frost, when the sun shines by day, they are only thawed in time to be frozen again. That fatal *tomorrow* is blood-red with the murder of fair resolutions; it is the slaughterhouse of the innocents. We are very concerned that our little book of "Evening Readings" should not be fruitless, and therefore we pray that readers may not be readers only, but doers, of the word. *The practice of truth is the most profitable reading of it.* Should the reader be impressed with any duty while perusing these pages, let him hasten to fulfill it before the holy glow has departed from his soul, and let him leave his nets, and all that he has, sooner than be found rebellious to the Master's call. Don't give place to the devil by delay! Haste while opportunity and life-giving are in happy conjunction. Don't be caught in your own nets, but break the meshes of worldliness, and go where glory calls you. Happy is the writer who shall meet with readers resolved to carry out his teachings: his harvest shall be a hundredfold, and his Master shall have great honor. Would to God that such might be our reward upon these brief meditations and hurried hints. Grant it, O Lord, to your servant!

"You are the most excellent of men." — Psalm 45:2

HE entire person of Jesus is just like a gem, and His life is all along like a single imprint of a seal. He is altogether complete; not only in His several parts, but as a gracious all-glorious whole. His character is not a mass of fair colors mixed confusedly, nor a heap of precious stones laid carelessly one upon another; He is a picture of beauty and a breastplate of glory. In Him, all the "things of good repute" are in their proper places, and assist in adorning each other. Not one feature in His glorious person attracts attention at the expense of others; but He is perfectly and altogether lovely.

Oh, Jesus! Your power, Your grace, Your justice, Your tenderness, Your truth, Your majesty, and Your immutability make up such a man, or rather such a God-man, as neither heaven nor earth has seen elsewhere. Your infancy, Your eternity, Your sufferings, Your triumphs, Your death, and Your immortality, are all woven in one gorgeous tapestry, without seam or tear. You are music without discord; You are many, and yet not divided; You are all things, and yet not diverse. As all the colors blend into one resplendent rainbow, so all the glories of heaven and earth meet in You, and unite so wondrously, that there is none like You in all things; no, if all the virtues of the most excellent were bound in one bundle, they could not rival You, You mirror all perfection. You have been anointed with the holy oil of myrrh and cassia, which Your God has reserved for You alone; and as for Your fragrance, it is as the holy perfume, the like of which none other can ever mingle, even with the art of the apothecary; each spice is fragrant, but the compound is divine.

> "Oh, sacred symmetry! oh, rare connection
> Of many perfects, to make one perfection!
> Oh, heavenly music, where all parts do meet
> In one sweet strain, to make one perfect sweet!"

"God's solid foundation stands firm."
— *2 Timothy 2:19*

HE foundation upon which our faith rests is this, "that God was reconciling the world to Himself in Christ, not counting men's sins against them." The great fact on which genuine faith relies is, that "The Word became flesh and made His dwelling among us," and that "Christ died for sins once for all, the righteous for the unrighteous, to bring you to God;" "He Himself bore our sins in His body on the tree;" "the punishment that brought us peace was upon Him, and by His wounds we are healed." In one word, the great pillar of the Christian's hope is *substitution.* The vicarious sacrifice of Christ for the guilty, Christ being made sin for us that we might be made the righteousness of God in Him, Christ offering up a true and proper expiatory and substitutionary sacrifice in the room, place, and stead of as many as the Father gave Him, who are known to God by name, and are recognized in their own hearts by their trusting in Jesus — this is the cardinal fact of the gospel. If this foundation were to be removed, what could we do? But it stands firm as the throne of God. We know it; we rest on it; we rejoice in it; and our delight is to hold it, to meditate upon it, and to proclaim it, while we desire to be actuated and moved by gratitude for it in every part of our life and conversation. In these days a direct attack is made upon the doctrine of the atonement. Humanity cannot bear substitution. They gnash their teeth at the thought of the Lamb of God bearing the sin of humankind. But we, who know by experience the preciousness of this truth, will proclaim it in defiance of them confidently and unceasingly. We will neither dilute it nor change it, nor fritter it away in any shape or fashion. It shall still be Christ, a *positive substitute,* bearing human guilt and suffering in the stead of humankind. We cannot, dare not, give it up, for it is our life, and despite every controversy we feel that, nevertheless, "God's solid foundation stands firm."

*"He . . . will build the temple of the LORD, and he will be
clothed with majesty." — Zechariah 6:13*

HRIST Himself is the builder of His spiritual temple, and He has built it on the mountains of His unchangeable affection, His omnipotent grace, and His infallible truthfulness. But as it was in Solomon's temple, so in this; the materials need to be prepared. There are the "Cedars of Lebanon," but they are not framed for the building; they are not cut down, and shaped, and made into those planks of cedar, whose odoriferous beauty shall make glad the courts of the Lord's house in Paradise. There are also the rough stones still in the quarry, they must be hewn thence, and squared. All this is Christ's own work. Each individual believer is being prepared, and polished, and made ready for his place in the temple; but Christ's own hand performs the preparation work. Afflictions cannot sanctify, except as they are used by Him to this end. Our prayers and efforts cannot make us ready for heaven, apart from the hand of Jesus, who fashions our hearts towards what is right.

As in the building of Solomon's temple, "no hammer, chisel or any other iron tool was heard at the temple site," because all was brought perfectly ready for the exact spot it was to occupy — so is it with the temple which Jesus builds; the preparation is all done on earth. When we reach heaven, there will be no sanctifying us there, no squaring us with affliction, no planing us with suffering. No, we must be prepared here — all *that* Christ will do beforehand; and when He has done it, we shall be ferried by a loving hand across the stream of death, and brought to the heavenly Jerusalem, to abide as eternal pillars in the temple of our Lord.

> "Beneath His eye and care,
> The edifice shall rise,
> Majestic, strong, and fair,
> And shine above the skies."

> *"That what cannot be shaken may remain."*
> — *Hebrews 12:27*

E have many things in our possession at the present moment which *can* be shaken, and it does not suit Christians to set much store by them, for there is nothing stable beneath these rolling skies; change is written upon all things. Yet, we have certain things that *"cannot* be shaken," and I invite you this evening to think of them, that if the things which can be shaken should all be taken away, you may derive real comfort from the things that cannot be shaken, which will remain. Whatever your losses have been, or may be, you enjoy present salvation. You are standing at the foot of His cross, trusting alone in the merit of Jesus' precious blood, and no rise or fall of the markets can interfere with your salvation in Him; no breaking of banks, no failures and bankruptcies can touch that. Then you are *a child of God* this evening. God is your Father. No change of circumstances can ever rob you of *that.* Although by losses brought to poverty, and stripped bare, you can say, "He is my Father still. In my Father's house are many rooms; therefore will I not be troubled." You have another permanent blessing, namely, *the love of Jesus Christ.* He who is God and Man loves you with all the strength of His affectionate nature — nothing can affect *that.* The fig tree may not blossom, and the flocks may cease from the field, it doesn't matter to the person who can sing, "My lover is mine, and I am His." Our best portion and richest heritage we cannot lose. Whatever troubles come, let's be mature; let's show that we are not such little children as to be cast down by what may happen in this poor fleeting state of time. Our country is Immanuel's land, our hope is above the sky, and therefore, calm as the summer's ocean; we will see the collapse of everything earthborn, and yet rejoice in the God of our salvation.

"Ephraim is a flat cake not turned over." — *Hosea 7:8*

 pancake which is not flipped over is *uncooked on one side;* and so Ephraim was, in many respects, untouched by divine grace: though there was some partial obedience, there was very much rebellion left. My soul, I charge you, see whether this be your case. Are you thorough in the things of God? Has grace gone through the very center of your being so as to be felt in its divine operations in all your powers, your actions, your words, and your thoughts? To be sanctified, spirit, soul, and body, should be your aim and prayer; and although sanctification may not be perfect in you anywhere in degree, yet it must be universal in its action; there mustn't be the appearance of holiness in one place and reigning sin in another, or else you, too, will be a pancake not turned over.

A cake not turned is *soon burnt on the side nearest the fire,* and although no one can have too much religion, there are some who seem burnt black with bigoted zeal for that part of truth which they have received, or are charred to a cinder with a conceited Pharisaic ostentation of those religious performances which suit their humor. The assumed appearance of superior sanctity frequently accompanies a total absence of all vital godliness. The saint in public is a devil in private. He deals in flour by day and in soot by night. The pancake which is burned on one side, is dough on the other.

If it is so with me, O Lord, turn me over! Turn my unsanctified nature to the fire of your love and let it feel the sacred glow, and let my burnt side cool a little while I learn my own weakness and want of heat when I am removed from your heavenly flame. Do not let me be found to be of a double mind, but one entirely under the powerful influence of reigning grace; for I know very well that, if I am left like a pancake unturned, and am not the subject of your grace on both sides, I must be consumed forever amid everlasting burnings.

"Wait eagerly for our adoption." — *Romans 8:23*

VEN in this world saints are God's children, but men cannot discover them to be so, except by certain moral characteristics. The adoption is not manifested, the children are not yet openly declared. Among the Romans a man might adopt a child, and keep it private for a long time: but there was a second adoption in public; when the child was brought before the constituted authorities its former garments were taken off, and the father who took it to be his child gave it clothing suitable to its new condition of life. "Dear friends, now we are children of God, and what we will be has not yet been made known." We are not yet arrayed in the apparel which befits the royal family of heaven; we are wearing in this flesh and blood just what we wore as the sons of Adam; but we know that "when *He* appears" who is the "firstborn among many brothers," we shall be like Him, we shall see Him as He is. Cannot you imagine that a child taken from the lowest ranks of society, and adopted by a Roman senator, would say to himself, "I long for the day when I shall be publicly adopted. Then I shall leave off these plebeian garments, and be robed as becomes my senatorial rank"? Happy in what he has received, for that very reason he groans to get the fullness of what is promised him. So it is with us today. We are waiting until we shall put on our proper garments, and shall be manifested as the children of God. We are young nobles, and have not yet worn our coronets. We are young brides, and the marriage day is not yet come, and by the love our Spouse bears us, we are led to long and sigh for the bridal morning. Our very happiness makes us groan after more; our joy, like a swollen spring, longs to well up like an Iceland geyser, leaping to the skies, and it heaves and groans within our spirit for want of space and room by which to manifest itself to humankind.

*"A woman in the crowd called out, Blessed is
the mother who gave you birth and nursed you.
He replied, Blessed rather are those who hear the
word of God and obey it."* — Luke 11:27, 28

 T is fondly imagined by some that it must
have involved very special privileges to have
been the mother of our Lord, because they
supposed that she had the benefit of looking
into His very heart in a way in which we
cannot hope to do. There may be an appearance of plausibility in the supposition, but not much. We
don't know that Mary knew more than others; what she
did know she did well to treasure in her heart; but she
doesn't appear from anything we read in the Evangelists to
have been a better-instructed believer than any other of
Christ's disciples. All that she knew we also may discover.
Do you wonder that we should say so? Here is a text to
prove it: "The LORD confides in those who fear Him; He
makes His covenant known to them." Remember the Master's words — "I no longer call you servants, because a
servant does not know his master's business. Instead, I
have called you friends, for everything that I learned from
My Father I have made known to you." So blessedly does
this Divine Revealer of secrets tell us His heart, that He
keeps back nothing which is profitable to us; His own
assurance is, "If it were not so, I would have told you."
Does He not this day manifest Himself to us as He does not
to the world? It is even so; and therefore we will not
ignorantly cry out, "Blessed is the mother who gave You
birth," but we will intelligently bless God that, having
heard the Word and kept it, we have first of all as true a
communion with the Savior as the Virgin had, and in the
second place as true an acquaintance with the secrets of
His heart as she can be supposed to have obtained. Happy
soul to be thus privileged!

"Shadrach, Meshach and Abednego replied . . . we want you to know, O king, that we will not serve your gods." — Daniel 3:16, 18

T HE narrative of the manly courage and marvelous deliverance of the three holy children, or rather champions, is well calculated to excite in the minds of believers firmness and steadfastness in upholding the truth in the teeth of tyranny and in the very jaws of death. Let young Christians especially learn from their example, both in matters of faith in religion, and matters of uprightness in business, never to sacrifice their consciences. Lose all rather than lose your integrity, and when all else is gone, still hold fast a clear conscience as the rarest jewel which can adorn the bosom of a mortal. Be not guided by the will-o'-the-wisp of policy, but by the polestar of divine authority. Follow the right at all hazards. When you see no present advantage, walk by faith and not by sight. Do God the honor to trust Him when it comes to matters of loss for the sake of principle. See whether He will be your debtor! See if He doesn't even in this life prove His word that "Godliness with contentment is great gain," and that they who "seek first His kingdom and His righteousness, and all these things will be given to you as well." Should it happen that, in the providence of God, you are a loser by conscience, you shall find that if the Lord pays you not back in the silver of earthly prosperity, He will discharge His promise in the gold of spiritual joy. Remember that a man's life consists not in the abundance of that which he possesses. To wear a guileless spirit, to have a heart void of offense, to have the favor and smile of God, is greater riches than the mines of Ophir could yield, or the traffic of Tyre could win. "Better a meal of vegetables where there is love than a fattened calf with hatred." An ounce of heart's-ease is worth a ton of gold.

"Go up on a high mountain." — Isaiah 40:9

UR knowledge of Christ is somewhat like climbing one of our Welsh mountains. When you are at the base you see but little: the mountain itself appears to be but half as high as it really is. Confined in a little valley, you discover scarcely anything but the rippling brooks as they descend into the stream at the foot of the mountain. Climb the first rising knoll, and the valley lengthens and widens beneath your feet. Go higher, and you see the country for four or five miles around, and you are delighted with the widening prospect. Mount still, and the scene enlarges; until at last, when you are on the summit, and look east, west, north, and south, you see almost all England lying before you. Yonder is a forest in some distant county, perhaps two hundred miles away, and here the sea, and there a shining river and the smoking chimneys of a manufacturing town, or the masts of the ships in a busy port. All these things please and delight you, and you say, "I could not have imagined that so much could be seen at this elevation." Now, the Christian life is of the same order. When we first believe in Christ we see but little of Him. The higher we climb the more we discover of His beauties. But who has ever gained the summit? Who has known all the heights and depths of the love of Christ which passes knowledge? Paul, when grown old, sitting gray-haired, shivering in a dungeon in Rome, could say with greater emphasis than we can, "I know whom I have believed," for each experience had been like the climbing of a hill, each trial had been like ascending another summit, and his death seemed like gaining the top of the mountain, from which he could see the whole of the faithfulness and the love of Him to whom he had committed his soul. Climb up, dear friend, into the high mountain.

"The dove could find no place to set its feet."
— *Genesis 8:9*

EADER, can you find rest apart from the ark, Christ Jesus? Then be assured that your religion is vain. Are you satisfied with anything short of a conscious knowledge of your union and interest in Christ? Then woe to you. If you profess to be a Christian, yet find full satisfaction in worldly pleasures and pursuits, your profession is false. If your soul can stretch herself at rest, and find the bed long enough, and the coverlet broad enough to cover her in the chambers of sin, then you are a hypocrite, and far enough from any right thoughts of Christ or perception of His preciousness. But if, on the other hand, you feel that if you could indulge in sin without punishment, yet it would be a punishment of itself; and that if you could have the whole world, and abide in it forever, it would be quite enough misery not to be parted from it; for your God — your God — is what your soul craves after; then be of good courage, you are a child of God. With all your sins and imperfections, take this to your comfort: if your soul has no rest in sin, you are not as the sinner is! If you are still crying after and craving after something better, Christ has not forgotten you, for you have not quite forgotten Him. The believer cannot do without his Lord; words are inadequate to express his thoughts of Him. We cannot live on the sands of the wilderness, we want the manna which drops from on high; our skin bottles of creature confidence cannot yield us a drop of moisture, but we drink of the rock which follows us, and that rock is Christ. When you feed on Him your soul can sing, "He has satisfied my mouth with good things, so that my youth is renewed like the eagle's," but if you have Him not, your bursting wine vat and well-filled barn can give you no sort of satisfaction: rather lament over them in the words of wisdom, "Meaningless! Meaningless! . . . Everything is meaningless."

"You have become like us." — Isaiah 14:10

HAT must be the apostate professing Christian's doom when his naked soul appears before God? How will he bear that voice, "Depart, you cursed; you have rejected Me, and I reject you; you have played the harlot, and departed from Me: I also have banished you forever from My presence, and will not have mercy upon you." What will be this wretch's shame at the last great day when, before assembled multitudes, the apostate shall be unmasked? See the profane, and sinners who never professed religion, lifting themselves up from their beds of fire to point at him. "There he is," says one, "will he preach the gospel in hell?" "There he is," says another, "he rebuked me for cursing, and was a hypocrite himself!" "Aha!" says another, "here comes a psalm-singing Methodist — one who was always at his meeting; he is the man who boasted of his being sure of everlasting life; and here he is!" No greater eagerness will ever be seen among Satanic tormentors, than in that day when devils drag the hypocrite's soul down to eternal damnation. Bunyan pictures this with massive but awful grandeur of poetry when he speaks of the back way to hell. Seven devils bound the wretch with nine cords, and dragged him from the road to heaven, in which he had professed to walk, and thrust him through the back-door into hell. Mind that back way to hell, you who profess faith! "Examine yourselves, to see whether you are in the faith." Look well to your state; see whether you are in Christ or not. It is the easiest thing in the world to give a lenient verdict when oneself is to be tried; but O, be just and true here. Be just to all, but be rigorous to yourself. Remember if it is not a rock on which you build, when the house shall fall, great will be the fall of it. O may the Lord give you sincerity, constancy, and firmness; and in no day, however evil, may you be led to turn aside.

*"Escape the corruption in the world caused
by evil desires."* — 2 Peter 1:4

ANISH forever all thought of indulging the flesh if you would live in the power of your risen Lord. It were ill that a man who is alive in Christ should dwell in the corruption of sin. "Why do you look for the living among the dead?" said the angel to Magdalene. Should the living dwell in the sepulcher? Should divine life be immured in the charnel house of fleshly lust? How can we partake of the cup of the Lord and yet drink the cup of Belial? Surely, believer, from open lusts and sins you are delivered: have you also escaped from the more secret and delusive snares of the Satanic fowler? Have you come forth from the lust of pride? Have you escaped from slothfulness? Have you made a clean escape from carnal security? Are you seeking day by day to live above worldliness, the pride of life, and the ensnaring vice of avarice? Remember, it is for this that you have been enriched with the treasures of God. If, indeed, you are the chosen of God, and beloved by Him, don't allow all the lavish treasure of grace to be wasted upon you. Follow after holiness; it is the Christian's crown and glory. An unholy church! it is useless to the world, and of no esteem among men. It is an abomination, hell's laughter, heaven's abhorrence. The worst evils which have ever come upon the world have been brought upon her by an unholy church. O Christian, the vows of God are upon you. You are God's priest: act as such. You are God's king: reign over your lusts. You are God's chosen: don't associate with Belial. Heaven is your portion: live like a heavenly spirit, so shall you prove that you have true faith in Jesus, for there cannot be faith in the heart unless there is holiness in the life.

> "Lord, I desire to live as one
> Who bears a blood-bought name,
> As one who fears but grieving Thee,
> And knows no other shame."

"But you must not go very far." — *Exodus 8:28*

HIS is a crafty word from the lip of the archtyrant Pharaoh. If the poor bondaged Israelites have to go out of Egypt, then he bargains with them that it shall not be very far away; not too far for them to escape the terror of his arms, and the observation of his spies. In the same way, the world loves not the nonconformity of nonconformity, or the dissidence of dissent, it would have us be more charitable and not carry matters with too severe a hand. Death to the world, and burial with Christ, are experiences which carnal minds treat with ridicule, and hence the ordinance which sets them forth is almost universally neglected, and even condemned. Worldly wisdom recommends the path of compromise and talks of "moderation." According to this carnal policy, purity is admitted to be very desirable, but we are warned against being too precise; truth is of course to be followed, but error is not to be severely denounced. "Yes," says the world, "be spiritually minded by all means, but don't deny yourself a little gay society, an occasional ball, and a Christmas visit to a theater. What's the good of crying down a thing when it is so fashionable, and everybody does it?" Multitudes of professing Christians yield to this cunning advice, to their own eternal ruin. If we would follow the Lord wholly, we must go right away into the wilderness of separation, and leave the Egypt of the carnal world behind us. We must leave its maxims, its pleasures, and its religion too, and go far away to the place where the Lord calls His sanctified ones. When the town is on fire, our house cannot be too far from the flames. When the plague is abroad, a man cannot be too far from its haunts. The further from a viper the better, and the further from worldly conformity the better. To all true believers let the trumpet call be sounded, "Come out from them and be separate."

"Each one should remain in the situation which he was in when God called him." — 1 Corinthians 7:20

OME persons have the foolish notion that the only way in which they can live for God is by becoming ministers, missionaries, or Bible women. Alas! how many would be shut out from any opportunity of magnifying the Most High if this were the case. Beloved, it is not office, it is earnestness; it is not position, it is grace which will enable us to glorify God. God is most surely glorified in that cobbler's stall, where the godly worker, as he plies the awl, sings of the Savior's love, ay, glorified far more than in many a church pew where official religiousness performs its scanty duties. The name of Jesus is glorified by the poor unlearned carter as he drives his horse, and blesses his God, or speaks to his fellow laborer by the roadside, as much as by the popular divine who, throughout the country, like Boanerges, is thundering out the gospel. God is glorified by our serving Him in our proper vocations. Take care, dear reader, that you don't forsake the path of duty by leaving your occupation, and take care you don't dishonor your profession while in it. Think little of yourselves, but don't think too little of your callings. Every lawful trade may be sanctified by the gospel to noblest ends. Turn to the Bible, and you will find the most menial forms of work connected either with most daring deeds of faith, or with persons whose lives have been illustrious for holiness. Therefore be not discontented with your calling. Whatever God has made your position, or your work, abide in that, unless you are quite sure that He calls you to something else. Let your first care be to glorify God to the utmost of your power where you are. Fill your present sphere to His praise, and if He needs you in another He will show it to you. This evening lay aside vexatious ambition, and embrace peaceful content.

"Fix our eyes on Jesus." — *Hebrews 12:2*

T is ever the Holy Spirit's work to turn our eyes away from self to Jesus; but Satan's work is just the opposite of this, for he is constantly trying to make us regard ourselves instead of Christ. He insinuates, "Your sins are too great for pardon; you have no faith; you don't repent enough; you will never be able to continue to the end; you don't have the joy of His children; you have such a wavering hold of Jesus." All these are thoughts about self, and we shall never find comfort or assurance by looking within. But the Holy Spirit turns our eyes entirely away from self: He tells us that we are nothing, but that "Christ is all, and is in all." Remember, therefore, it is not *your hold* of Christ that saves you — it is Christ; it is not *your joy* in Christ that saves you — it is Christ; it is not even faith in Christ, although that is the instrument — it is Christ's blood and merits; therefore, don't be fixing your eyes so much on your hand with which you are grasping Christ, as on Christ; don't be looking at your hope, but to Jesus, the source of your hope; don't be looking to your faith, but to Jesus, the author and finisher of your faith. We shall never find happiness by looking at our prayers, our doings, or our feelings; it is what *Jesus* is, not what *we* are, that gives rest to the soul. If we would at once overcome Satan and have peace with God, it must be by "fixing our eyes on Jesus." Simply keep your eye on Him; let His death, His sufferings, His merits, His glories, His intercession, be fresh upon your mind; when you wake in the morning look to Him; when you lie down at night look to Him. Oh! don't let your hopes or fears come between you and Jesus; follow closely after Him, and He will never fail you.

> "My hope is built on nothing less
> Than Jesu's blood and righteousness:
> I dare not trust the sweetest frame,
> But wholly lean on Jesu's name."

"But Aaron's staff swallowed up their staffs."
— *Exodus 7:12*

HIS incident is an instructive emblem of the sure victory of the divine handiwork over all opposition. Whenever a divine principle is cast into the heart, though the devil may fashion a counterfeit, and produce swarms of opponents, as sure as ever God is in the work, it will swallow up all its foes. If God's grace takes possession of a man, the world's magicians may throw down all their rods; and every rod may be as cunning and poisonous as a serpent, but Aaron's rod will swallow up their rods. The sweet attractions of the cross will woo and win the man's heart, and he who lived only for this deceitful earth will now have an eye for the upper spheres, and a wing to mount into celestial heights. When grace has won the day the worldling seeks the world to come. The same fact is to be observed in the life of the believer. What multitudes of foes has our faith had to meet! Our old sins — the devil threw them down before us, and they turned to serpents. What hosts of them! Ah, but the cross of Jesus destroys them all. Faith in Christ makes short work of all our sins. Then the devil has launched forth another host of serpents in the form of worldly trials, temptations, unbelief; but faith in Jesus is more than a match for them, and overcomes them all. The same absorbing principle shines in the faithful service of God! With an enthusiastic love for Jesus difficulties are surmounted, sacrifices become pleasures, sufferings are honors. But if religion is thus a consuming passion in the heart, then it follows that there are many persons who profess religion but have it not; for what they have will not bear this test. Examine yourself, my reader, on this point. Aaron's rod *proved* its heaven-given power. Is your religion doing so? If Christ is anything He must be everything. O rest not until love and faith in Jesus are the master passions of your soul!

"God will bring with Jesus those who have fallen asleep in him." — *1 Thessalonians 4:14*

ET'S not imagine that *the soul* sleeps in insensibility. "Today you will be with me in paradise," is the whisper of Christ to every dying saint. They have "fallen asleep in Jesus," but their souls are before the throne of God, praising Him day and night in His temple, singing hallelujahs to Him who washed them from their sins in His blood. The body sleeps in its lonely bed of earth, beneath the coverlet of grass. But what is this sleep? The idea connected with sleep is *"rest,"* and that is the thought which the Spirit of God would convey to us. Sleep makes each night a Sabbath for the day. Sleep shuts fast the door of the soul, and bids all intruders stand, be left, linger for a while, that the life within may enter its summer garden of ease. The toilworn believer quietly sleeps, as does the weary child when it slumbers on its mother's breast. Oh! happy they who die in the Lord; they rest from their labors, and their works follow them. Their quiet repose shall never be broken until God shall rouse them to give them their full reward. Guarded by angel watchers, curtained by eternal mysteries, they sleep on, the inheritors of glory, until the fullness of time shall bring the fullness of redemption. What an awaking shall be theirs! They were laid in their last resting place, weary and worn, but such they shall not rise. They went to their rest with the furrowed brow, and the wasted features, but they wake up in beauty and glory. The shriveled seed, so destitute of form and comeliness, rises from the dust a beauteous flower. The winter of the grave gives way to the spring of redemption and the summer of glory. Blessed is death, since it, through the divine power, disrobes us of this workday garment, to clothe us with the wedding garment of incorruption. Blessed are those who "have fallen asleep in Him."

"But when envoys were sent by the rulers of
Babylon to ask him about the miraculous sign that
had occurred in the land, God left him to test him
and to know everything that was in his heart."
— *2 Chronicles 32:31*

EZEKIAH was growing so inwardly great and priding himself so much upon the favor of God, that self-righteousness crept in and, through his carnal security, the grace of God was for a time, in its more active operations, withdrawn. Here is quite enough to account for his folly with the Babylonians; for if the grace of God should leave the best Christian, there is enough of sin in his heart to make him the worst of transgressors. If left to yourselves, you who are warmest for Christ would cool down like Laodicea into sickening lukewarmness: you who are sound in the faith would be white with the leprosy of false doctrine; you who now walk before the Lord in excellency and integrity would reel to and fro, and stagger with a drunkenness of evil passion. Like the moon, we borrow our light; bright as we are when grace shines on us, we are darkness itself when the Sun of Righteousness withdraws Himself. *Therefore let's cry to God never to leave us.* "Lord, don't take Your Holy Spirit from us! Don't withdraw Your indwelling grace from us! Haven't You said, 'I the Lord do keep it; I will water it every moment: lest any hurt it, I will keep it night and day'? Lord, keep us everywhere. Keep us when in the valley, so that we don't mumble against your humbling hand; keep us when on the mountain, so that we are not overcome with giddiness through being lifted up; keep us in youth, when our passions are strong; keep us in old age, when becoming conceited of our wisdom, we may therefore prove greater fools than the young and giddy; keep us when we come to die, lest, at the very last, we should deny You! Keep us living, keep us dying, keep us laboring, keep us suffering, keep us fighting, keep us resting, keep us everywhere, for we need You everywhere, O our God!"

"I have given them the glory that you gave me."
— *John 17:22*

EHOLD the superlative liberality of the Lord Jesus, for He has given us His all. Although a tithe of His possessions would have made a universe of angels rich beyond all thought, yet He was not content until He had given us all that He had. It would have been surprising grace if He had allowed us to eat the crumbs of His bounty beneath the table of His mercy; but He will do nothing by halves, He makes us sit with Him and share the feast. Had He given us some small pension from His royal treasury, we should have had cause to love Him eternally; but no, He will have His bride as rich as Himself, and He will not have a glory or a grace in which she shall not share. He has not been content with less than making us co-heirs with Himself, so that we might have equal possessions. He has emptied all His estate into the treasury of the church, and has all things common with His redeemed. There is not one room in His house the key of which He will withhold from His people. He gives them full liberty to take all that He has to be their own; He loves them to make free with His treasure, and appropriate as much as they can possibly carry. The boundless fullness of His all-sufficiency is as free to avail yourself of, believer, as the air you breathe. Christ has put the flagon of His love and grace to the believer's lip, and bids him to drink forever; for could he drain it, he is welcome to do so, and as he cannot exhaust it, he is bidden to drink abundantly, for it is all his own. What truer proof of fellowship can heaven or earth afford?

"When I stand before the throne
Dressed in beauty not my own;
When I see Thee as Thou art,
Love Thee with unsinning heart;
Then, Lord, shall I fully know —
Not till then — how much I owe."

*"Ah, Sovereign LORD, you have made the heavens
and the earth by your great power and outstretched
arm. Nothing is too hard for you." — Jeremiah 32:17*

T the very time when the Chaldeans surrounded Jerusalem, and when the sword,
famine and pestilence had desolated the land,
Jeremiah was commanded by God to purchase a field, and have the deed of transfer
legally sealed and witnessed. This was a
strange purchase for a rational man to make. Prudence
could not justify it, for it was buying with scarcely a
probability that the person purchasing could ever enjoy
the possession. But it was enough for Jeremiah that his
God had bidden him, for well he knew that God will be
justified of all His children. He reasoned thus: "Ah, Lord
God! You can make this plot of ground of use to me; You
can rid this land of these oppressors; You can make me yet
sit under my vine and my fig-tree in the heritage which I
have bought; for 'You have made the heavens and the earth
by Your great power and outstretched arm. Nothing is too
hard for You.' " This gave a majesty to the early saints, that
they dared to do at God's command things which carnal
reason would condemn. Whether it be a Noah who is to
build a ship on dry land, an Abraham who is to offer up his
only son, or a Moses who is to despise the treasures of
Egypt, or a Joshua who is to besiege Jericho seven days,
using no weapons but the blasts of rams' horns, they all act
upon God's command, contrary to the dictates of carnal
reason; and the Lord gives them a rich reward as the result
of their obedient faith. If only we had in the religion of
these modern times a more potent infusion of this heroic
faith in God. If we would venture more upon the naked
promise of God, we should enter a world of wonders to
which as yet we are strangers. Let Jeremiah's place of
confidence be ours — nothing is too hard for the God that
created the heavens and the earth.

"Living water will flow . . . in summer and in winter."
— *Zechariah 14:8*

HE streams of living water which flow from Jerusalem are not dried up by the parching heats of sultry midsummer any more than they were frozen by the cold winds of blustering winter. Rejoice, O my soul, that you are spared to testify to the faithfulness of the Lord. The seasons change and you change, but your Lord stays the same forever, and the streams of His love are as deep, as broad and as full as ever. The heats of business cares and scorching trials make me need the cooling influences of the river of His grace; I may go at once and drink to the full from the inexhaustible fountain, for in summer and in winter it pours forth its flood. The upper springs are never scanty, and blessed be the name of the Lord, the lower springs cannot fail either. Elijah found that the brook Cherith dried up, but Jehovah was still the same God of providence. Job said his brothers were like deceitful brooks, but he found his God an overflowing river of consolation. The Nile is the great confidence of Egypt, but its floods are variable; our Lord is the same forever. By turning the course of the Euphrates, Cyrus took the city of Babylon, but no power, human or infernal, can divert the current of divine grace. All of the tracks of ancient rivers have been found dry and desolate, but the streams which take their rise on the mountains of divine sovereignty and infinite love shall ever be full to the brim. Generations melt away, but the course of grace is unaltered. The river of God may sing with greater truth than the brook in the poem —

"Men may come, and men may go,
But I go on for ever."

How happy my soul is to be led beside such still waters! Never wander to other streams, lest you hear the Lord's rebuke, "Now why go to Egypt to drink water from the Shihor?"

*"The sound of the LORD God as he was walking in
the garden in the cool of the day."* — *Genesis 3:8*

Y soul, now that the cool of the day has come, retire awhile and hearken to the voice of your God. He is always ready to speak with you when you are prepared to hear. If there is any slowness to commune it isn't on His part, but altogether on your own, for He stands at the door and knocks, and if His people would just open, He rejoices to enter. But in what state is my heart, which is my Lord's garden? May I venture to hope that it is well trimmed and watered, and is bringing forth fruit fit for Him? If not, He will have much to reprove, but still I pray Him to come to me, for nothing can so certainly bring my heart into a right condition as the presence of the Sun of Righteousness, who brings healing in His wings. Come, therefore, O Lord, my God, my soul invites You earnestly, and waits for You eagerly. Come to me, O Jesus, my well-beloved, and plant fresh flowers in my garden, such as I see blooming in such perfection in Your matchless character! Come, O my Father, who is the Farmer, and deal with me in Your tenderness and prudence! Come, O Holy Spirit, and wet my whole nature with dew, as the herbs are now moistened with the evening dews. O that God would speak to me. Speak, Lord, for Your servant hears! O that He would walk with me; I am ready to give up my whole heart and mind to Him, and every other thought is hushed. I am only asking what He delights to give. I am sure that He will condescend to have fellowship with me, for He has given me His Holy Spirit to stay with me forever. Sweet is the cool twilight, when every star seems like the eye of heaven, and the cool wind is as the breath of celestial love. My Father, my elder Brother, my sweet Comforter, speak now in loving-kindness, for You have opened my ear and I am not rebellious.

"In him our hearts rejoice." — *Psalm 33:21*

LESSED is the fact that Christians can rejoice even in the deepest distress; although trouble may surround them, they still sing; and, like many birds, they sing best in their cages. The waves may roll over them, but their souls soon rise to the surface and see the light of God's countenance; they have a buoyancy about them which keeps their heads always above the water, and helps them to sing amid the tempest, "God is with me still." To whom shall the glory be given? Oh! to *Jesus* — it is all by Jesus. Trouble doesn't necessarily bring consolation with it to the believer, but the presence of the Son of God in the fiery furnace with him fills his heart with joy. He is sick and suffering, but Jesus visits him and makes his bed for him. He is dying, and the cold chilly waters of the Jordan are gathering about him up to the neck, but Jesus puts His arms around him, and cries, "Don't be afraid, beloved; to die is to be blessed; the waters of death have their fountainhead in heaven; they are not bitter, they are sweet as nectar, for they flow from the throne of God." As the departing saint wades through the stream, and the billows gather around him, and heart and flesh fail him, the same voice sounds in his ears, "So do not fear, for I am with you; do not be dismayed, for I am your God." As he nears the borders of the infinite unknown, and is almost afraid to enter the realm of shades, Jesus says, "Do not be afraid, for your Father has been pleased to give you the kingdom." Thus strengthened and consoled, the believer is not afraid to die; no, he is even willing to depart, for since he has seen Jesus as the morning star, he longs to gaze upon Him as the sun in his strength. Truly, the presence of Jesus is all the heaven we desire. He is at once

> "The glory of our brightest days;
> The comfort of our nights."

"To you I [cry], O LORD my Rock; do not turn
a deaf ear to me. For if you remain silent
I will be like those who have gone down
to the pit." — Psalm 28:1

 cry is the natural expression of sorrow, and a suitable utterance when all other modes of appeal fail us; but the cry must be alone directed to the Lord, for to cry to human-kind is to waste our entreaties into the air. When we consider the readiness of the Lord to hear, and His ability to aid, we shall see good reason for directing all our appeals at once to the God of our salvation. It will be in vain to call to the rocks in the day of judgment, but our Rock attends to our cries.

"Do not turn a deaf ear to me." Mere formalists may be content without answers to their prayers, but genuine suppliants cannot; they are not satisfied with the results of prayer itself in calming the mind and subduing the will — they must go further, and obtain actual replies from heaven, or they cannot rest; and those replies they long to receive at once, they dread even a little of God's silence. God's voice is often so terrible that it shakes the wilderness; but His silence is equally full of awe to an eager suppliant. When God seems to close His ear, we must not therefore close our mouths, but rather cry with more earnestness; for when our note grows shrill with eagerness and grief, He will not deny us a hearing for long. What a dreadful situation we would be in if the Lord should become forever silent to our prayers? *"For if You remain silent, I will be like those who have gone down to the pit."* Deprived of the God who answers prayer, we should be in a more pitiable plight than the dead in the grave, and should soon sink to the same level as the lost in hell. We *must* have answers to prayer: ours is an urgent case of dire necessity; surely the Lord will speak peace to our agitated minds, for He never can find it in His heart to permit His own elect to perish.

"The cows that were ugly and gaunt and ate up the seven sleek, fat cows." — *Genesis 41:4*

 HARAOH'S dream has too often been my waking experience. My days of laziness have ruinously destroyed all that I had achieved in times of zealous industry; my seasons of coldness have frozen all the genial glow of my periods of fervency and enthusiasm; and my fits of worldliness have thrown me back from my advances in the divine life. I need to beware of lean prayers, lean praises, lean duties, and lean experiences, for these will eat up the fat of my comfort and peace. If I neglect prayer for even just a short time, I lose all the spirituality to which I had attained; if I draw no fresh supplies from heaven, the old corn in my granary is soon consumed by the famine which rages in my soul. When the caterpillars of indifference, the cankerworms of worldliness, and the palmerworms of self-indulgence, lay my heart completely desolate, and make my soul to languish, all my former fruitfulness and growth in grace is of no use to me whatsoever. How anxious should I be to have no lean-fleshed days, no ill-favored hours! If every day I journeyed towards the goal of my desires I should soon reach it, but backsliding leaves me still far off from the prize of my high calling, and robs me of the advances which I had so laboriously made. The only way in which all my days can be as the "fat cows" is to feed them in the right meadow, to spend them with the Lord, in His service, in His company, in His fear, and in His way. Why shouldn't every year be richer than the past, in love, and usefulness, and joy? — I am nearer the celestial hills, I have had more experience of my Lord, and should be more like Him. O Lord, keep far from me the curse of leanness of soul; let me not have to cry, "I waste away, I waste away! Woe to me!" but may I be well-fed and nourished in Your house, that I may praise Your name.

"If we [suffer], we will also reign with him."
— *2 Timothy 2:12*

E must not imagine that we are suffering for Christ, and with Christ, if we are not in Christ. Beloved friend, are you trusting in Jesus only? If not, whatever you may have to mourn over on earth, you are not "suffering with Christ," and have no hope of reigning with Him in heaven. Neither are we to conclude that all a Christian's sufferings are sufferings with Christ, for *it is essential that he be called by God to suffer.* If we are rash and imprudent, and run into positions for which neither providence nor grace has fitted us, we ought to question whether or not we are sinning instead of communing with Jesus. If we let passion take the place of judgment, and self-will reign instead of Scriptural authority, we shall fight the Lord's battles with the devil's weapons, and if we cut our own fingers we must not be surprised. Again, *in troubles which come upon us as the result of sin, we must not dream that we are suffering with Christ.* When Miriam spoke evil of Moses, and the leprosy polluted her, she was not suffering for God. Moreover, suffering which God accepts *must have God's glory as its end.* If I suffer that I may earn a name, or win applause, I shall get no other reward than that of the Pharisee. It is requisite also *that love for Jesus, and love for His elect, be ever the mainspring of all our patience. We must manifest the Spirit of Christ* in meekness, gentleness, and forgiveness. Let's search and see if we truly *suffer with Jesus.* And if we do thus suffer, what are our "light and momentary troubles" compared with *reigning with Him?* Oh it is so blessed to be in the furnace with Christ, and such an honor to stand in the pillory with Him, that if there were no future reward, we might count ourselves happy in present honor; but when the compensation is so eternal, so infinitely more than we had any right to expect, shall we not take up the cross with alacrity, and go on our way rejoicing?

"Sanctify them by the truth." — *John 17:17*

ANCTIFICATION begins in regeneration. The Spirit of God infuses into each of us that new living principle by which we become "a new creation" in Christ Jesus. This work, which begins in the new birth, is carried on in two ways — mortification, whereby the lusts of the flesh are subdued and kept under; and vivification, by which the life which God has put within us is made to be a well of water springing up to everlasting life. This is carried on every day in what is called "perseverance," by which the Christian is preserved and continued in a gracious state, and is made to abound in good works to the praise and glory of God; and it culminates or comes to perfection, in "glory," when the soul, being thoroughly purged, is caught up to dwell with holy beings at the right hand of the Majesty on high. But while the Spirit of God is thus the author of sanctification, yet there is a visible agency employed which must not be forgotten. "Sanctify them," said Jesus, "by the *truth:* Your word is truth." The passages of Scripture which prove that the instrument of our sanctification is the Word of God are very many. The Spirit of God brings to our minds the precepts and doctrines of truth, and applies them with power. These are heard in the ear, and being received in the heart, they work in us to will and to do of God's good pleasure. The truth is the sanctifier, and if we do not hear or read the truth, we shall not grow in sanctification. We only progress in sound living as we progress in sound understanding. "Your word is a lamp to my feet and a light for my path." Do not say of any error, "It is a mere matter of opinion." No one indulges in an error of judgment without, sooner or later, tolerating an error in practice. Hold fast to the truth, for by so holding the truth shall you be sanctified by the Spirit of God.

"He who has clean hands and a pure heart,
who does not lift up his soul to an idol or
swear by what is false." — Psalm 24:4

 UTWARD practical holiness is a very precious mark of grace. It is to be feared that many who profess the faith have perverted the doctrine of justification by faith in such a way as to treat good works with contempt; if so, they will receive everlasting contempt at the last great day. If our hands are not clean, let's wash them in Jesus' precious blood, and so let's lift up pure hands to God. But *"clean hands"* will not suffice, unless they are connected with *"a pure heart."* True religion is heart work. We may wash the outside of the cup and the platter as long as we please, but if the inward parts are filthy, we are filthy altogether in the sight of God, for our hearts are more truly ourselves than our hands are; the very life of our being lies in the inner nature, and hence the imperative need of purity within. The pure in heart shall see God, all others are only blind bats.

The man who is born for heaven *"does not lift up his soul to an idol."* All of us have our joys by which our souls are uplifted; the worldling lifts up his soul in human delights, which are mere empty vanities; but the saint loves more substantial things; like Jehoshaphat, he is lifted up in the ways of the Lord. He who is content with husks, will be reckoned with the swine. Does the world satisfy you? Then you have your reward and portion in this life; get as much of it as you can because you will know no other joy.

"Or swear by what is false." The saints are people of honor still. The Christian's word is his only oath; but that is as good as twenty oaths from others. False speaking will shut any man out of heaven, for a liar shall not enter into God's house, whatever his professions or doings may be. Reader, does the text before us condemn you, or do you hope to ascend into the hill of the Lord?

"Called to be saints." — *Romans 1:7*

E are very apt to regard the apostolic saints as if they were "saints" in a more special manner than the other children of God. All are "saints" whom God has called by His grace, and sanctified by His Spirit; but we are apt to look upon the *apostles* as extraordinary beings, scarcely subject to the same weaknesses and temptations as ourselves. Yet in so doing we're forgetting this truth, that the nearer a man lives to God the more intensely he has to mourn over his own evil heart; and the more his Master honors him in His service, the more also does the evil of the flesh vex and tease him day by day. The fact is, if we had seen the apostle Paul, we should have thought him remarkably like the rest of the chosen family: and if we had talked with him, we should have said, "We find that his experience and ours are very similar. He is more faithful, more holy, and more deeply taught than we are, but he has the selfsame trials to endure. No, in some respects he is more sorely tested than ourselves." Do not, then, look upon the ancient saints as being exempt either from infirmities or sins; and do not regard them with that mystic reverence which will almost make us idolaters. Their holiness is attainable even by us. We are "called to be saints" by that same voice which constrained them to their high vocation. It is a Christian's duty to force his way into the inner circle of saintship; and if these saints were superior to us in their attainments, as they certainly were, let's follow them; let's emulate their ardor and holiness. We have the same light that they had, the same grace is accessible to us, and why should we rest satisfied until we have equaled them in heavenly character? They lived *with* Jesus, they lived *for* Jesus, therefore they grew *like* Jesus. Let's live by the same Spirit as they did, "looking to Jesus," and our saintship will soon be apparent.

"Trust in the LORD forever, for the LORD, the LORD,
is the Rock eternal." — Isaiah 26:4

EEING that we have such a God to trust in, let's rest upon Him with all our weight; let's resolutely drive out all unbelief, and endeavor to get rid of doubts and fears, which injure our comfort so much; since there is no excuse for fear where God is the foundation of our trust. A loving parent would be bitterly attacked if his child couldn't trust him; and how ungenerous, how unkind is our conduct when we put so little confidence in our heavenly Father who has never failed us, and who never will. It were well if doubting were banished from the household of God; but it is to be feared that old Unbelief is as nimble nowadays as when the psalmist asked, "Has His unfailing love vanished forever? Has His promise failed for all time?" David hadn't tested the mighty sword of the giant Goliath for very long, and yet he said, "There is none like it." He had tried it once in the hour of his youthful victory, and it had proved itself to be of the right metal, and therefore he praised it ever afterwards; even so should we speak well of our God, there is none like Him in the heaven above or the earth beneath; "'To whom will you compare Me? Or who is My equal?' says the Holy One." There is no rock like the rock of Jacob, our enemies themselves being judges. So far from allowing doubts to live in our hearts, we will take the whole detestable crew, as Elijah did the prophets of Baal, and slay them over the brook; and for a stream to kill them at, we will select the sacred torrent which wells forth from our Savior's wounded side. We have been in many trials, but we have never yet been cast where we could not find in our God all that we needed. Let's then be encouraged to trust in the Lord forever, assured that the Rock eternal will be, as it has been, our help and stay.

"Whoever listens to me will live in safety and be at ease, without fear of harm." — Proverbs 1:33

IVINE love becomes conspicuous when it shines in the midst of judgments. Fair is that lone star which smiles through the rifts of the thunder clouds; bright is the oasis which blooms in the wilderness of sand; so fair and so bright is love in the midst of wrath. When the Israelites provoked the Most High by their continued idolatry, He punished them by withholding both dew and rain, so that their land experienced a great famine; but while He did this, He took care that His own chosen ones should be secure. If all other brooks are dry, yet shall there be one reserved for Elijah; and when that fails, God shall still preserve for him a place of sustenance; no, not only so, the Lord had not simply one "Elijah," but He had a remnant according to the election of grace, who were hidden by fifties in a cave, and though the whole land was subject to famine, yet these fifties in the cave were fed, and fed from Ahab's table too by His faithful, God-fearing steward, Obadiah. Let's draw the inference from this, that come what may, God's people are safe. Let convulsions shake the solid earth, let the skies themselves be rent in two, yet amid the wreck of worlds the believer shall be as secure as in the calmest hour of rest. If God cannot save His people *under* heaven, He will save them *in* heaven. If the world becomes too hot to hold them, then heaven shall be the place of their reception and their safety. Be confident then, when you hear of wars, and rumors of wars. Let no agitation distress you, but be quiet from fear of evil. Whatever comes upon the earth, you, beneath the broad wings of Jehovah, shall be secure. Secure yourself upon His promise; rest in His faithfulness, and bid defiance to the darkest future, for there is nothing direful in it for you. Your sole concern should be to show forth to the world the blessedness of hearkening to the voice of wisdom.

"How many wrongs and sins have I committed?"
— *Job 13:23*

AVE you ever really weighed and considered how great the sin of God's people is? Think how heinous your own transgression is, and you will find that not only does a sin here and there tower up like a high mountain, but that your iniquities are heaped upon each other, as in the old fable of the giants who piled Pelian upon Ossa, mountain upon mountain. What an aggregate of sin there is in the life of one of the most sanctified of God's children! Attempt to multiply this, the sin of one only, by the multitude of the redeemed, "a great multitude that no one could count," and you will have some conception of the great mass of the guilt of the people for whom Jesus shed His blood. But we arrive at a more adequate idea of the magnitude of sin by the greatness of the remedy provided. It is the blood of Jesus Christ, God's only and well-beloved Son. God's Son! Angels cast their crowns before Him! All the choral symphonies of heaven surround His glorious throne. "God over all, forever praised! Amen." And yet He takes upon Himself the form of a servant, and is scourged and pierced, bruised and torn, and at last slain; since nothing but the blood of the incarnate Son of God could make atonement for our offenses. No human mind can adequately estimate the infinite value of the divine sacrifice, for as great as the sin of God's people is, the atonement which takes it away is immeasurably greater. Therefore, the believer, even when sin rolls like a dark flood and the remembrance of the past is bitter, can yet stand before the blazing throne of the great and holy God, and cry, "Who is he that condemns? Christ Jesus, who died — more than that, who was raised to life." While the recollection of his sin fills him with shame and sorrow, he at the same time makes it a foil to show the brightness of mercy — guilt is the dark night in which the fair star of divine love shines with serene splendor.

"Brothers, pray for us." — *1 Thessalonians 5:25*

T HIS one morning in the year we reserved to refresh the reader's memory upon the subject of prayer for ministers, and we do most earnestly implore every Christian household to grant the fervent request of the text first uttered by an apostle and now repeated by us. Brothers and sisters, our work is Solemnly momentous, involving weal or woe to thousands; we deal with souls for God on eternal business, and our word is either a savor of life to life, or of death to death. A very heavy responsibility rests upon us, and it will be no small mercy if at the last we are found clear of the blood of all humankind. As officers in Christ's army, we are the special mark of the enmity of humanity and devils; they watch for our halting, and work to take us by the heels. Our sacred calling involves us in temptations from which you are exempt, above all it too often draws us away from our personal enjoyment of truth into a ministerial and official consideration of it. We meet with many knotty situations, and our wits are baffled; we observe very sad backslidings, and our hearts are wounded; we see millions perishing, and our spirits sink. We want you to profit from our preaching; we desire to be a blessing to your children; we long to be useful both to saints and sinners; therefore, dear friends, intercede for us with our God. We are miserable without the aid of your prayers, but happy if we live in your supplications. You do not look to us but to our Master for spiritual blessings, and yet how many times has He given those blessings through His ministers; ask then, again and again, that we may be the earthen vessels into which the Lord may put the treasure of the gospel. We, the whole company of missionaries, ministers, city missionaries, and students, do in the name of Jesus beg you

"BROTHERS, PRAY FOR US."

"Then I passed by and . . . said to you, Live!"
— *Ezekiel 16:6*

ITH one exception, consider gratefully this mandate of mercy. Note that this fiat of God is *majestic*. In our text, we perceive a sinner with nothing in him but sin, expecting nothing but wrath; but the eternal Lord passes by in His glory; He looks. He pauses, and He pronounces the solitary but royal word, "Live!" There speaks a God. Who but He could venture thus to deal with life and dispense it with a single syllable? Again, this fiat is *manifold*. When He says "Live," it includes many things. Here is judicial life. The sinner is ready to be condemned, but the mighty One says, "Live," and he rises pardoned and absolved. It is spiritual life. We didn't know Jesus — our eyes couldn't see Christ, our ears couldn't hear His voice — Jehovah said "Live," and we who were dead in trespasses and sins were made alive. Moreover, it includes glory life, which is the perfection of spiritual life. "Then I passed by and said to you, 'Live!' " That word rolls on through all the years of time until death comes, and in the midst of the shadows of death, the Lord's voice is still heard, "Live!" In the morning of the resurrection it is that selfsame voice which is echoed by the archangel, "Live," and as holy spirits rise to heaven to be blessed forever in the glory of their God, it is in the power of this same word, "Live!" Note again, that it is an *irresistible* mandate. Saul of Tarsus is on the road to Damascus to arrest the saints of the living God. A voice is heard from heaven and a light is seen above the brightness of the sun, and Saul is crying out, "What shall I do, Lord?" This mandate is a mandate of *free grace*. When sinners are saved, it is only and solely because God *will* do it to magnify His free, unpurchased, unsought grace. Christians, see your position, debtors to grace; show your gratitude by earnest, Christ-like lives, and as God has requested, see to it that you live in earnest.

"Tell me the secret of your great strength." — Judges 16:6

HERE lies the secret strength of faith? It lies in the food it feeds on; for faith studies *what the promise is* — an emanation of divine grace, an overflowing of the great heart of God; and faith says, "My God could not have given this promise, except from love and grace; therefore it is quite certain His Word will be fulfilled." Then faith thinks, *"Who gave* this promise?" It considers not so much its greatness, as, "Who is the author of it?" She remembers that it is God who cannot lie — God omnipotent, God immutable; and therefore concludes that the promise must be fulfilled; and she advances forward in this firm conviction. She remembers, *why the promise was given,* — namely, for God's glory, and she feels perfectly sure that God's glory is safe, that He will never stain His own escutcheon, nor mar the luster of His own crown; and therefore the promise must and will stand. Then faith also considers the amazing *work of Christ* as being a clear proof of the Father's intention to fulfill His word. "He who did not spare His own Son, but gave Him up for us all — how will He not also, along with Him, graciously give us all things?" Moreover faith looks back upon *the past,* for her battles have strengthened her, and her victories have given her courage. She remembers that God has never failed her; no, that He never did once fail any of His children. She recollects times of great peril, when deliverance came; hours of awful need, when as her day her strength was found, and she cries, "No, I never will be led to think that He can change and leave His servant now. Up to now the Lord has helped me, and He will help me still." Thus faith views each promise in its connection with the giver of the promise, and, because she does so, can say with assurance, "Surely goodness and love will follow me all the days of my life!"

*"Guide me in your truth and teach me, for you
are God my Savior, and my hope is in you
all day long."* — *Psalm 25:5*

HEN the believer has begun with trembling feet to walk in the way of the Lord, he asks to be still led onward like a little child upheld by its parent's helping hand, and he craves to be further instructed in the alphabet of truth. Experimental teaching is the burden of this prayer. David knew a great deal, but he felt ignorant, and still desired to be in the Lord's school: four times over in two verses he applies for a scholarship in the college of grace. It would be beneficial for many who profess the faith if, instead of following their own devices and cutting out new paths of thought for themselves, they would inquire for the good old ways of God's own truth, and beg the Holy Spirit to give them sanctified understandings and teachable spirits. *"You are God my Savior."* The Three-One Jehovah is the Author and Perfecter of salvation to His people. Reader, is He God *your* Savior? Do you find in the Father's election, in the Son's atonement, and in the Spirit's life-giving, all the grounds of your eternal hopes? If so, you may use this as an argument for obtaining further blessings; if the Lord has ordained to save you, surely He will not refuse to instruct you in His ways. It is a happy thing when we can address the Lord with the confidence which David here manifests, it gives us great power in prayer, and comfort in trial. *"My hope is in You all day long."* Patience is the fair handmaid and daughter of faith; we cheerfully wait when we are certain that we shall not wait in vain. It is our duty and our privilege to wait upon the Lord in service, in worship, in expectancy, in trust all the days of our life. Our faith will be tested faith, and if it be of the true kind, it will bear continued trial without yielding. We shall not grow weary of waiting upon God if we remember how long and how graciously He once waited for us.

"Forget not all his benefits." — *Psalm 103:2*

 T is a delightful and profitable occupation to see the hand of God in the lives of ancient saints, and to observe His goodness in delivering them, His mercy in pardoning them, and His faithfulness in keeping His covenant with them. But wouldn't it be even more interesting and profitable for us to remark the hand of God in our own lives? Oughtn't we to look upon our own history as being at least as full of God, as full of His goodness and of His truth, as much a proof of His faithfulness and veracity, as the lives of any of the saints who have gone before? We do our Lord an injustice when we suppose that He wrought all His mighty acts, and showed Himself strong for those in the early time, but doesn't perform wonders or lay bare His arm for the saints who are now upon the earth. Let's review our own lives. Surely in these we may discover some happy incidents, refreshing to ourselves and glorifying to our God. Have you had no *deliverances?* Have you passed through no rivers, supported by the divine presence? Have you walked through no fires unharmed? Have you had no *manifestations?* Have you had no choice *favors?* The God who gave Solomon the desire of his heart, has He never listened to you and answered your requests? That God of lavish bounty of whom David sang, "Who satisfies your desires with good things," has He never satiated *you* with fatness? Have you never been made to lie down in green pastures? Have you never been led by the quiet waters? Surely the goodness of God has been the same to us as to the saints of old. Let's, then, weave His mercies into a song. Let's take the pure gold of thankfulness, and the jewels of praise and make them into another crown for the head of Jesus. Let our souls give forth music as sweet and as exhilarating as came from David's harp, while we praise the Lord whose mercy endures forever.

"And he separated the light from the darkness."
— *Genesis 1:4*

 believer has two principles at work within him. In his natural estate he was subject to one principle only, which was darkness; now light has entered, and the two principles disagree. Note the apostle Paul's words in the seventh chapter of Romans: "So I find this law at work: When I want to do good, evil is right there with me. For in my inner being I delight in God's law; but I see another law at work in the members of my body, waging war against the law of my mind and making me a prisoner of the law of sin at work within my members." How is this state of things occasioned? The Lord "separated the light from the darkness." Darkness, by itself, is quiet and undisturbed, but when the Lord sends in light, there is a conflict, for the one is in opposition to the other: a conflict which will never cease until the believer is altogether light in the Lord. If there is a division *within* the individual Christian, there is certain to be *a division without*. As soon as the Lord gives light to us, we proceed to separate ourselves from the darkness around; we secede from a merely worldly religion of outward ceremonial, for nothing short of the gospel of Christ will now satisfy us, and we withdraw ourselves from worldly society and frivolous amusements, and seek the company of the saints, for "We know that we have passed from death to life, because we love our brothers." The light gathers to itself, and the darkness to itself. What God has separated, let's never try to unite, but as Christ went outside the camp, bearing His reproach, so let's come out from the ungodly, and be a peculiar people. He was holy, harmless, undefiled, separate from sinners; and, as He was, so we are to be nonconformists to the world, dissenting from all sin, and distinguished from the rest of mankind by our likeness to our Master.

"Fellow citizens with God's people." — *Ephesians 2:19*

HAT is meant by our being citizens in heaven? It means that *we are under heaven's government*. Christ the king of heaven reigns in our hearts; our daily prayer is, "Your will be done on earth as it is in heaven." The proclamations issued from the throne of glory are freely received by us: we cheerfully obey the decrees of the Great King. Then as citizens of the New Jerusalem, *we share heaven's honors*. The glory which belongs to beatified saints belongs to us, for we are already sons and daughters of God, already princes and princesses of the imperial blood; already we wear the spotless robe of Jesus' righteousness; already we have angels for our servitors, saints for our companions, Christ for our Brother, God for our Father, and a crown of immortality for our reward. We share the honors of citizenship, for we have come to the general assembly and church of the firstborn whose names are written in heaven. As citizens, we have *common rights to all the property of heaven*. Ours are its gates of pearl and walls of chrysolite; ours the azure light of the city that needs no candle nor light of the sun; ours the river of the water of life, and the twelve crops of fruits which grow on the trees planted on the banks thereof; there is nothing in heaven that doesn't belong to us. "The present or the future," all are ours. Also as citizens of heaven we *enjoy its delights*. Do they there rejoice over sinners that repent — prodigals that have returned? So do we. Do they chant the glories of triumphant grace? We do the same. Do they cast their crowns at Jesus' feet? Such honors as we have we cast there too. Are they charmed with His smile? It is not less sweet to us who dwell below. Do they look forward, waiting for His second advent? We also look and long for His appearing. If, then, we are thus *citizens of heaven*, let our walk and actions be consistent with our high dignity.

> *"And there was evening, and there was morning —*
> *the first day."* — Genesis 1:5

HE evening was "darkness" and the morning was "light," and yet *the two together are called by the name that is given to the light alone!* This is somewhat remarkable, but it has an exact analogy in spiritual experience. In every believer there is darkness and light, and yet we are not to be called sinners because there is sin in us, but we are to be named saints because we possess some degree of holiness. This will be a most comforting thought to those who are mourning their infirmities, and who ask, "Can I be a child of God while there is so much darkness in me?" Yes; for you, like the day, don't take your name from the evening, but from the morning; and you are spoken of in the word of God as if you were even now perfectly holy as you will be soon. You are called the child of light, though there is darkness in you still. You are named after what is the predominating quality in the sight of God, which will one day be the only principle remaining. Observe that *the evening comes first.* Naturally we are darkness first in order of time, and the gloom is often first in our mournful apprehension, driving us to cry out in deep humiliation, "God have mercy on me, a sinner." The place of the morning is second, it dawns when grace overcomes nature. It is a blessed aphorism of John Bunyan, "That which is last, lasts forever." That which is first, yields in due season to the last; but nothing comes after the last. So that though you are naturally darkness, when once you become light in the Lord, there is no evening to follow; "Your sun will never set again." The first day in this life is an evening and a morning; but the second day, when we shall be with God, forever, shall be a day with no evening, but one, sacred, high, eternal noon.

*"After you have suffered a little while, will himself
restore you and make you strong, firm and
steadfast." — 1 Peter 5:10*

OU have seen the arch of heaven as it spans the plain: its colors are glorious, and its hues rare. It is beautiful, but, alas, it passes away, and lo, it is no more. The fair colors give way to the fleecy clouds, and the sky is no longer brilliant with the tints of heaven. It is not *established.* How can it be? A glorious show made up of transitory sunbeams and passing raindrops, how can it abide? The graces of the Christian character must not resemble the rainbow in its transitory beauty, but, on the contrary, must be strong, firm, steadfast. Seek, O believer, that every good thing you have may be an abiding thing. May your character not be a writing upon the sand, but an inscription upon the rock! May your faith be no "baseless fabric of a vision," but may it be built of material able to endure that awful fire which shall consume the wood, hay, and stubble of the hypocrite. May you be rooted and grounded in love. May your convictions be deep, your love real, your desires earnest. May your whole life be so firm and strong, that all the blasts of hell, and all the storms of earth shall never be able to remove you. But notice how this blessing of being "strong in the faith" is gained. The apostle's words point us to *suffering* as the means employed — *"After you have suffered a little while."* It is of no use to hope that we shall be well rooted if no rough winds pass over us. Those old knots on the root of the oak tree, and those strange twistings of the branches, all tell of the many storms that have swept over it, and they are also indicators of the depth into which the roots have forced their way. So the Christian is made strong, and firmly rooted by all the trials and storms of life. Therefore, don't shrink from the tempestuous winds of trial, but take comfort, believing that by their rough discipline God is fulfilling this benediction to you.

*"Tell it to your children, and let your children tell
it to their children, and their children to
the next generation." — Joel 1:3*

N this simple way, by God's grace, a living testimony for truth is always to be kept alive in the land — the beloved of the Lord are to hand down their witness for the gospel, and the covenant to their heirs, and these again to their next descendants. This is our *first* duty, we are to begin at the family hearth: he is a bad preacher who does not begin his ministry at home. The heathen are to be sought by all means, and the highways and hedges are to be searched, but home has a prior claim, and woe to those who reverse the order of the Lord's arrangements. To teach our children is a *personal* duty; we cannot delegate it to Sunday School teachers, or other friendly aids. These can assist us, but cannot deliver us from the sacred obligation; proxies and sponsors are wicked devices in this case: mothers and fathers must, like Abraham, command their households in the fear of God, and talk with their offspring concerning the wondrous works of the Most High. Parental teaching is a *natural* duty — who so fit to look to the child's well-being as those who are the authors of his actual being? To neglect the instruction of our offspring is worse than brutish. Family religion is *necessary* for the nation, for the family itself, and for the church of God. By a thousand plots Popery is covertly advancing in our land, and one of the most effectual means for resisting its inroads is left almost neglected, namely, the instruction of children in the faith. Would that parents would awaken to a sense of the importance of this matter. It is a *pleasant* duty to talk of Jesus to our sons and daughters, and the more so because it has often proved to be an *accepted* work, for God has saved the children through the parents' prayers and admonitions. May every house into which this volume shall come honor the Lord and receive His smile.

"To those who have been called, who are loved
by God the Father." — Jude 1
"Sanctified in Christ Jesus." — 1 Corinthians 1:2
"Through the sanctifying work of the Spirit." — 1 Peter 1:2

OTICE the union of the Three Divine Persons in all their gracious acts. How unwisely do those believers talk who make preferences in the Persons of the Trinity; who think of Jesus as if He were the embodiment of everything lovely and gracious, while the Father they regard as severely just, but destitute of kindness. Equally wrong are those who magnify the decree of the Father, and the atonement of the Son, so as to depreciate the work of the Spirit. In deeds of grace none of the Persons of the Trinity act apart from the rest. They are as united in their deeds as in their essence. In their love towards the chosen they are one, and in the actions which flow from that great central source they are still undivided. Specially notice this in the matter of sanctification. While we may without mistake speak of sanctification as the work of the Spirit, yet we must take heed that we do not view it as if the Father and the Son had no part therein. It is correct to speak of sanctification as the work of the Father, of the Son, and of the Spirit. Still does Jehovah say, "Let *us* make man in our image, in our likeness," and thus we are "*God's* workmanship, created in Christ Jesus to do good works, which God prepared in advance for us to do." See the value which God sets upon real holiness, since the Three Persons in the Trinity are represented as working together to produce a church without "stain or wrinkle or any other blemish." And you, believer, as the follower of Christ, must also set a high value on holiness — upon purity of life and godliness of conversation. Value the blood of Christ as the foundation of your hope, but never speak disparagingly of the work of the Spirit which makes you suitable for the inheritance of the saints in light. This day let's so live as to manifest the work of the Triune God in us.

"His heavenly kingdom." — *2 Timothy 4:18*

ONDER city of the great King is a place of *active service*. Ransomed spirits serve Him day and night in His temple. They never cease to fulfill the good pleasure of their King. They always "rest," as far as ease and freedom from care is concerned; and never "rest," in the sense of indolence or inactivity. Jerusalem the golden is the place of *communion* with all the people of God. We shall sit with Abraham, Isaac, and Jacob, in eternal fellowship. We shall hold high communication with the noble host of the elect, all reigning with Him who by His love and His potent arm has brought them safely home. We shall not sing solos, but in chorus shall we praise our King. Heaven is a place of *victory realized*. Whenever, Christians, you have achieved a victory over your lusts — whenever after hard struggling, you have laid a temptation dead at your feet — you have in that hour experienced in a limited way the joy that awaits you when the Lord shall shortly tread Satan under your feet, and you shall find yourself more than conquerors through Him who has loved you. Paradise is a place of *security*. When you enjoy the full assurance of faith, you have the pledge of that glorious security which shall be yours when you are perfect citizens of the heavenly Jerusalem. O my sweet home, Jerusalem, you happy harbor of my soul! Thanks, even now, to Him whose love has taught me to long for You; but louder thanks in eternity, when I shall possess You.

> "My soul has tasted of the grapes,
> And now it longs to go
> Where my dear Lord His vineyard keeps
> And all the clusters grow.
>
> "Upon the true and living vine,
> My famish'd soul would feast,
> And banquet on the fruit divine,
> An everlasting guest."

"God said to Jonah, Do you have a right to be angry?"
— *Jonah 4:9*

NGER is not always or necessarily sinful, but it has such a tendency to run wild that whenever it displays itself, we should be quick to question its character, with this inquiry, "Do you have a right to be angry?" It may be that we can answer, "YES." Very frequently anger is the madman's firebrand, but sometimes it is Elijah's fire from heaven. We do well when we are angry with sin, because of the wrong which it commits against our good and gracious God; or with ourselves because we remain so foolish after so much divine instruction; or with others when the sole cause of anger is the evil which they do. Those who are not angry at transgressions become partakers in them. Sin is a loathsome and hateful thing, and no renewed heart can patiently endure it. God Himself is angry with the wicked every day, and it is written in His Word, "Let those who love the Lord hate evil."

Far more frequently it is to be feared that our anger is not commendable or even justifiable, and then we must answer, "NO." Why should we be irritable with children, hot-blooded with servants, and wrathful with companions? Is such anger honorable to our Christian profession, or glorifying to God? Isn't it the old evil heart seeking to gain dominion, and shouldn't we resist it with all the might of our newborn nature? Many who are professing Christians give way to temper as though it were useless to attempt resistance; but let the believer remember that he must be a conqueror in every point, or else he cannot be crowned. If we cannot control our tempers, what has grace done for us? Someone told Mr. Jay that grace was often grafted on a crabstump. "Yes," said he, "but the fruit will not be crabs." We must not make natural infirmity an excuse for sin, but we must fly to the cross and pray the Lord to crucify our tempers, and renew us in gentleness and meekness after His own image.

"Then my enemies will turn back when I call
for help. By this I will know that God is
for me." — Psalm 56:9

 T is impossible for any human speech to
express the full meaning of this delightful
phrase, *"God is for me."* He was "for me" before
the worlds were made; He was "for me," or
He would not have given His well-beloved
son; He was "for me" when He struck the
Only-begotten, and laid the full weight of His wrath upon
Him — He was "for *me*," though He was against *Him;* He
was "for me," when we were ruined in the fall — He loved
me notwithstanding all; He was "for me," when I was a
rebel against Him, and with a high hand was bidding Him
defiance; He was "for me," or He wouldn't have brought
me humbly to seek His face. He has been "for me" in many
struggles; I have been summoned to encounter hosts of
dangers; I have been assailed by temptations from without
and within — how could I have remained unharmed to
this hour if He had not been "for me"? He is "for me," with
all the infinity of His being; with all the omnipotence of
His love; with all the infallibility of His wisdom; arrayed
in all His divine attributes, He is "for me," — eternally
and immutably "for me;" "for me" when those blue skies
in the distance shall be rolled up like a worn out vesture;
"for me" throughout eternity. And because He is "for me,"
the voice of prayer will always ensure His help. *"Then my*
enemies will turn back when I call for help." This is no
uncertain hope, but a well-grounded assurance — by *"this*
I will know." I will direct my prayer to You, and will look
up for the answer, assured that it will come, and that my
enemies shall be defeated for, "God is for me." O believer,
how happy are you with the King of kings on your side!
How safe with such a Protector! How sure your cause
pleaded by such an Advocate! If God is for you, who can be
against you?

"You will defile it if you use a tool on it." — *Exodus 20:25*

OD'S altar was to be built of unhewn stones, so that no trace of human skill or work might be seen upon it. Human wisdom delights to trim and arrange the doctrines of the cross into a system more artificial and more congenial with the depraved tastes of fallen nature; however, instead of improving the gospel, carnal wisdom pollutes it, until it becomes another gospel, and not the truth of God at all. All alterations and amendments of the Lord's own Word are defilements and pollutions. The proud heart of man is very anxious to have a hand in the justification of the soul before God; preparations for Christ are dreamed of, humblings and repentings are trusted in, good works are cried up, natural ability is much vaunted, and by all means the attempt is made to lift up human tools upon the divine altar. It were well if sinners would remember that as far from perfecting the Savior's work is concerned, their carnal confidences only pollute and dishonor it. The Lord alone must be exalted in the work of atonement, and not a single mark of man's chisel or hammer will be endured. There is an inherent blasphemy in seeking to add to what Christ Jesus in His dying moments declared to be finished, or to improve that in which the Lord Jehovah finds perfect satisfaction. Trembling sinner, away with your tools, and fall upon your knees in humble supplication; and accept the Lord Jesus to be the altar of your atonement, and rest in Him alone.

Many professing Christians may take warning from this morning's text as to the doctrines which they believe. There is among Christians far too much inclination to square and reconcile the truths of revelation; this is a form of irreverence and unbelief, let's strive against it, and receive truth as we find it; rejoicing that the doctrines of the Word are unhewn stones, and so are all the more fit to build an altar for the Lord.

*"At dawn . . . Mary Magdalene . . . went to look
at the tomb."* — Matthew 28:1

 ET'S learn from Mary Magdalene how to obtain fellowship with the Lord Jesus. Notice how she sought. She sought the Savior *very early* in the morning. If you can wait for Christ, and be patient in the hope of having fellowship with Him at some distant season, you will never have fellowship at all; for the heart that is fitted for communion is a hungering and a thirsting heart. She sought Him also with *very great boldness*. Other disciples fled from the tomb, for they trembled and were amazed; but Mary, it is said, "stood" at the tomb. If you would have Christ with you, seek Him boldly. Let nothing hold you back. Defy the world. Press on where others flee. She sought Christ *faithfully* — she stood *at the tomb*. Some find it hard to stand by a living Savior, but she stood by a dead one. Let's seek Christ after this mode, cleaving to the very least thing that has to do with Him, remaining faithful though all others should forsake Him. Note further, she sought Jesus *earnestly* — she stood *"crying."* Those teardroppings were as spells that led the Savior captive, and made Him come forth and show Himself to her. If you desire Jesus' presence, cry after it! If you cannot be happy unless He comes and says to you, "You are My beloved," you will soon hear His voice. Lastly, she sought the Savior *only*. What did she care for angels, she turned her back on them; her search was only for her Lord. If Christ is your one and only love, if your heart has cast out all rivals, you will not long lack the comfort of His presence. Mary Magdalene sought thus *because she loved so much*. Let's arouse ourselves to the same intensity of affection; let our hearts, like Mary's, be full of Christ, and our love, like hers, will be satisfied with nothing short of Himself. O Lord, reveal Yourself to us this evening!

"The fire must be kept burning on the altar continuously;
it must not go out." — *Leviticus 6:13*

EEP the altar of *private prayer* burning. This is the very life of all piety. The sanctuary and family altars borrow their fires here, therefore let this burn well. Secret devotion is the very essence, evidence, and barometer, of vital and experimental religion.

Burn the fat of your sacrifices here. If possible, let your seasons of prayer be regular, frequent, and undisturbed. The prayer of a righteous person is powerful and effective. Do you have nothing to pray for? Let's suggest the church, the ministry, your own soul, your children, your relations, your neighbors, your country, and the cause of God and truth throughout the world. Let's examine ourselves on this important matter. Do we engage with lukewarmness in private devotion? Is the fire of devotion burning dimly in our hearts? Do the chariot wheels drag heavily? If so, let's be alarmed at this sign of decay. Let's go with weeping, and ask for the Spirit of grace and of supplications. Let's set apart special seasons for extraordinary prayer. For if this fire should be smothered beneath the ashes of a worldly conformity, it will dim the fire on the family altar, and lessen our influence both in the church and in the world.

The text will also apply to *the altar of the heart.* This is a golden altar indeed. God loves to see the hearts of His people glowing towards Himself. Let's give to God our hearts, all blazing with love, and seek His grace, that the fire may never be quenched; for it will not burn if the Lord does not keep it burning. Many foes will attempt to extinguish it; but if the unseen hand behind the wall pours the sacred oil on the fire, it will blaze higher and higher. Let's use texts of Scripture as fuel for our hearts' fires, they are live coals; let's listen to sermons, but above all, let's be frequently alone with Jesus.

"He appeared first to Mary Magdalene."
— *Mark 16:9*

 ESUS "appeared first to Mary Magdalene," probably not only on account of her great love and persevering seeking, but because, as the context intimates, *she had been a special trophy of Christ's delivering power.* Learn from this, that the greatness of our sin before conversion should not make us imagine that we may not be specially favored with the very highest grade of fellowship. She was one who had left all to become *a constant attendant on the Savior.* He was her first, her chief object. Many who were on Christ's side didn't take up Christ's cross; *she* did. *She spent her substance in relieving His wants.* If we would see a great deal of Christ, let's *serve* Him. Tell me who they are that sit most often under the banner of His love, and drink deepest draughts from the cup of communion, and I am sure they will be those who give most, who serve best, and who abide closest to the bleeding heart of their dear Lord. But notice *how* Christ revealed Himself to this sorrowing one — by a *word,* "Mary." It only took one word *in His voice,* and at once she knew Him, and *her heart owned allegiance by another word,* her heart was too full to say more. That one word would naturally be the most fitting for the occasion. It implies obedience. She said, *"Teacher."* There is no state of mind in which this confession of allegiance will be too cold. No, when your spirit glows most with the heavenly fire, then you will say, "I am your servant, You have loosed my bonds." If you can say, "Teacher," if you feel that His will is your will, then you stand in a happy, holy place. He must have said, "Mary," or else you could not have said, "Rabboni." See, then, from all this, how Christ honors those who honor Him, how love draws our Beloved, how it only takes one word of His to turn our weeping to rejoicing, how His presence makes the heart's sunshine.

"Each morning everyone gathered as much as he needed."
— *Exodus 16:21*

 ORK to maintain a sense of your entire dependence upon the Lord's good will and pleasure for the continuance of your richest enjoyments. Never try to live on the old manna, nor seek to find help in Egypt. All must come from Jesus, or you are undone forever. Old anointings will not suffice to impart unction to your spirit; your head must have fresh oil poured upon it from the golden horn of the sanctuary, or it will cease from its glory. Today you may be upon the summit of the mountain of God, but He who has put you there must keep you there, or you will sink far more speedily than you dream. Your mountain only stands firm when He settles it in its place; if He were to hide His face, you would soon be troubled. If the Savior should see fit, there is not a window through which you see the light of heaven which He could not darken in an instant. Joshua commanded the sun to stand still, but Jesus can shroud it in total darkness. He can withdraw the joy of your heart, the light of your eyes, and the strength of your life; in His hand your comforts lie, and at His will they can depart from you. Our Lord is determined that we shall feel and recognize this hourly dependence, for He alone permits us to pray for "daily bread," and alone promises that "your strength will equal your days." Isn't it best for us that it should be so, that we may often go to His throne, and constantly be reminded of His love? Oh! how rich the grace which supplies us so continually, and does not refrain itself because of our ingratitude! The golden shower never ceases, the cloud of blessing tarries forever above our habitation. O Lord Jesus, we would bow at Your feet, conscious of our utter inability to do anything without You, and in every favor which we are privileged to receive, we would adore Your blessed name and acknowledge Your unexhausted love.

"You will arise and have compassion on Zion, for it is time to show favor to her; the appointed time has come. For her stones are dear to your servants; her very dust moves them to pity." — Psalm 102:13, 14

 selfish man in trouble is exceedingly hard to comfort, because the springs of his comfort lie entirely within himself, and when he is sad all his springs are dry. But a generous man, full of Christian philanthropy, has other springs from which to supply himself with comfort beside those which lie within. He can go to his God first of all, and there find abundant help; and he can discover arguments for consolation in things relating to the world at large, to his country, and, above all, to the church. David in this Psalm was exceedingly sorrowful; he wrote, "I am like a desert owl, like an owl among the ruins. I lie awake; I have become like a bird alone on a roof." The only way in which he could comfort himself, was in the reflection that God would arise, and have mercy upon Zion: though *he* was sad, yet Zion should prosper; however low his own estate, yet Zion should arise. Christian! learn to comfort yourself in God's gracious dealing towards the church. That which is so dear to your Master, shouldn't it be dear above everything else to you? Even if your way is dark, can't you gladden your heart with the triumphs of His cross and the spread of His truth? Our own personal troubles are forgotten while we look, not only upon what God *has* done, and *is* doing for Zion, but on the glorious things He *will yet do* for His church. Try this prescription, O believer, whenever you are sad of heart and in heaviness of spirit: forget yourself and your little concerns, and seek the welfare and prosperity of Zion. When you bend your knee in prayer to God, do not limit your petition to the narrow circle of your own life, difficult though it is, but send out your longing prayers for the church's prosperity, "Pray for the peace of Jerusalem," and your own soul shall be refreshed.

---

*"For we know, brothers loved by God, that he
has chosen you."* — *1 Thessalonians 1:4*

ANY persons want to know of their election before they look to Christ, but they cannot learn it this way; it is only to be discovered by "looking to Jesus." If you desire to ascertain your own election — after the following manner, you shall assure your heart before God. Do you feel yourself to be a lost, guilty sinner? go straightway to the cross of Christ, and tell Jesus so, and tell Him that you have read in the Bible, "Whoever comes to Me I will never drive away." Tell Him that He has said, "Here is a trustworthy saying that deserves full acceptance: Christ Jesus came into the world to save sinners." Look to Jesus and believe in Him, and you shall make proof of your election directly, for as surely as you believe, you are elect. If you will give yourself wholly up to Christ and trust Him, then you are one of God's chosen ones; but if you stop and say, "I want to know first whether I am elect," you do not know what you are asking. Go to Jesus, as guilty as you are, just as you are. Leave all curious inquiry about election alone. Go straight to Christ and hide in His wounds, and you shall know your election. The assurance of the Holy Spirit shall be given to you, so that you shall be able to say, "I know whom I have believed, and am convinced that He is able to guard what I have entrusted to Him." Christ was at the everlasting council: He can tell you whether you were chosen or not; but you cannot find it out in any other way. Go and put your trust in Him, and His answer will be — "I have loved you with an everlasting love; I have drawn you with loving-kindness." There will be no doubt about His having chosen *you*, when you have chosen *Him*.

"Sons we are through God's election,
Who in Jesus Christ believe."

"Don't let anyone get away!" — *1 Kings 18:40*

HEN the prophet Elijah had received the answer to his prayer, and the fire from heaven had consumed the sacrifice in the presence of all the people, he called upon the assembled Israelites to take the priests of Baal, and sternly cried, "Don't let anyone get away!" He took them all down to the brook Kishon, and slew them there. So it must be with our sins — they are all doomed, not one must be preserved. Our darling sin must die. Do not spare it because of its incessant tears. Strike, though it be as dear as an Isaac. Strike, for God struck at sin when it was laid upon His own Son. With stern unflinching purpose must you condemn to death that sin which was once the idol of your heart. Do you ask how you are to accomplish this? Jesus will be your power. You have grace to overcome sin given you in the covenant of grace; you have strength to win the victory in the crusade against inward lusts, because Christ Jesus has promised to be with you even to the end. If you want to triumph over darkness, set yourself in the presence of the Sun of Righteousness. There is no place so well adapted for the discovery of sin, and recovery from its power and guilt, as the immediate presence of God. Job never knew how to get rid of sin half as well as he did when his eye of faith rested upon God, and then he abhorred himself, and repented in dust and ashes. The fine gold of the Christian is often dimmed. We need the sacred fire to consume the dross. Let's fly to our God, He is a consuming fire; He will not consume our spirit, but our sins. Let the goodness of God excite us to a sacred jealousy, and to a holy revenge against those iniquities which are hateful in His sight. Go forth to battle with Amalek in His strength, and utterly destroy the accursed crew: don't let anyone get away!

"They will set out last, under their standards."
— *Numbers 2:31*

HE camp of Dan brought up the rear when the armies of Israel were on the march. The Danites occupied *the last place,* but what does their position matter since they were as truly part of the host as were the foremost tribes; they followed the same fiery cloudy pillar, they ate of the same manna, drank of the same spiritual rock, and journeyed to the same inheritance. Come, my heart, cheer up, though last and least; it is your privilege to be in the army, and to fare as they fare who lead the caravan. Someone must be last in honor and esteem, someone must do menial work for Jesus, and why shouldn't I? In a poor village, among an ignorant peasantry; or in a back street, among degraded sinners, I will work on, and "set out last" with my standard.

The Danites occupied *a very useful place.* Stragglers have to be picked up along the march, and lost property has to be gathered from the field. Fiery spirits may dash forward over untrodden paths to learn fresh truth, and win more souls to Jesus; but some of a more conservative spirit may be well engaged in reminding the church of her ancient faith, and restoring her fainting sons and daughters. Every position has its duties, and the slowly moving children of God will find their peculiar state one in which they may be eminently a blessing to the whole host.

The rear guard is *a place of danger.* There are foes behind us as well as before us. Attacks may come from any quarter. We read that Amalek fell upon Israel, and slew some of the last of them. The experienced Christian will find frequent work for his weapons in aiding those poor doubting, hopeless, wavering souls who are last in faith, knowledge, and joy. These must not be left unaided; therefore, it is the business of well-taught saints to bear their standards among the last. My soul, tenderly watch to help the last this day.

*"They do not jostle each other; each marches
straight ahead." — Joel 2:8*

OCUSTS always keep their rank, and although their number is legion, they do not crowd upon each other, so as to throw their columns into confusion. This remarkable fact in natural history shows how thoroughly the Lord has infused the spirit of order into His universe, since the smallest animate creatures are as much controlled by it as are the rolling spheres or the seraphic messengers. It would be wise for believers to be ruled by the same influence in all their spiritual life. *In their Christian graces* no one virtue should usurp the sphere of another, or eat out the vitals of the rest for its own support. Affection must not smother honesty, courage must not elbow weakness out of the field, modesty must not jostle energy, and patience must not slaughter resolution. So also with *our duties,* one must not interfere with another; public usefulness must not injure private piety; church work must not push family worship into a corner. It is not good to offer God one duty stained with the blood of another. Each thing is beautiful in its season, but not otherwise. It was to the Pharisee that Jesus said, "You should have practiced the latter, without neglecting the former." The same rule applies to *our personal position,* we must take care to know our place, take it, and keep to it. We must minister as the Spirit has given us ability, and not intrude upon our fellow servant's domain. Our Lord Jesus taught us not to covet the high places, but to be willing to be the least among the brothers and sisters. An envious, ambitious spirit is to be kept far from us; let's feel the force of the Master's command, and do as He bids us, keeping rank with the rest of the host. Tonight let's see whether we are keeping the unity of the Spirit in the bonds of peace, and let our prayer be that, in all the churches of the Lord Jesus, peace and order may prevail.

"The LORD our God has shown us his glory."
— *Deuteronomy 5:24*

OD'S great design in all His works is the manifestation of His own glory. Any aim less than this is unworthy of Himself. But how shall the glory of God be manifested to such fallen creatures as we are? Humankind's eye is not single. We always glance sideways towards our own honor, have too high an estimation of our own powers, and aren't qualified therefore to behold the glory of the Lord. It is clear, then, that self must stand out of the way, that there may be room for God to be exalted; and this is the reason why He frequently brings His people into straits and difficulties, that, being made conscious of their own folly and weakness, they may be fitted to behold the majesty of God when He comes forward to work their deliverance. He whose life is one even and smooth path, will see just a little of the glory of the Lord, for he has few occasions of self-emptying, and hence, is only slightly fitted for being filled with the revelation of God. They who navigate little streams and shallow creeks know a little about the God of tempests; but they who "do business in great waters," these see His "wonders in the deep." Among the huge Atlantic waves of bereavement, poverty, temptation, and reproach we learn the power of Jehovah because we feel the littleness of humankind. Thank God, then, if you have been led by a rough road: it is this which has given you your experience of God's greatness and loving-kindness. Your troubles have enriched you with a wealth of knowledge to be gained by no other means: your trials have been the cleft of the rock in which Jehovah has set you, as He did His servant Moses, that you might behold His glory as it passed by. Praise God that you have not been left in the darkness and ignorance which continued prosperity might have involved, but that in the great fight of affliction, you have been capacitated for the outshinings of His glory in His wonderful dealings with you.

"A bruised reed he will not break, and a smoldering wick he will not snuff out." — Matthew 12:20

HAT is weaker than the bruised reed or the smoldering wick? *A reed* that grows in the fen or marsh snaps as soon as the wild duck lights upon it; just let a foot brush against it, and it bruises and breaks; every wind that flits across the river moves it to and fro. One cannot conceive of anything more frail or brittle, or whose existence is more in jeopardy, than a bruised reed. Then look at the smoldering wick — what is it? It has a spark within it, it is true, but it is almost smothered; an infant's breath could blow it out; nothing has a more precarious existence than its flame. *Weak things* are described here, yet Jesus says of them, "A bruised reed He will not break, and a smoldering wick He will not snuff out." Some of God's children are made strong to do mighty works for Him; God has His Samsons here and there who can pull up Gaza's gates, and carry them to the top of the hill; He has a few mighty men who are lion-like men, but the majority of His people are a timid, trembling race. They are like starlings, frightened at every passerby; a little fearful flock. If temptation comes, they are taken like birds in a snare; if trial threatens, they are ready to faint; their frail skiff is tossed up and down by every wave, they are drifted along like a sea bird on the crest of the billows — weak things, without strength, without wisdom, without foresight. Yet, weak as they are, and *because* they are so weak, they have this promise made specially to them. Herein is grace and graciousness! Herein is love and loving-kindness! How it opens to us the compassion of Jesus — so gentle, tender, considerate! We need never shrink back from *His* touch. We need never fear a harsh word from *Him;* though He might well chide us for our weakness, He does not rebuke. Bruised reeds shall not have any harsh blows from Him, nor the smoldering wick any damping frowns.

"A deposit guaranteeing our inheritance." — *Ephesians 1:14*

H! what enlightenment, what joys, what consolation, what delight of heart is experienced by that person who has learned to feed on Jesus, and on Jesus alone. Yet the realization which we have of Christ's preciousness is, in this life, imperfect at best. As an old writer says, "'Tis but a taste!" We have tasted "that the Lord is gracious," but we do not yet know *how* good and gracious He is, although what we know of His sweetness makes us long for more. We have enjoyed the firstfruits of the Spirit, and they have set us hungering and thirsting for the fullness of the heavenly vintage. We groan within ourselves, waiting for the adoption. *Here* we are like Israel in the wilderness, who had only one cluster from Eshcol, *there* we shall be in the vineyard. Here we see the manna falling small, like coriander seed, but there shall we eat the bread of heaven and the old corn of the kingdom. We are but beginners now in spiritual education; for although we have learned the first letters of the alphabet, we cannot read words yet, much less can we put sentences together; but as one says, "He that has been in heaven but five minutes, knows more than the general assembly of divines on earth." We have many ungratified desires at present, but soon every wish shall be satisfied; and all our powers shall find the sweetest employment in that eternal world of joy. O Christian, antedate heaven for a few years. Within a very little time you shall be rid of all your trials and your troubles. Your eyes now suffused with tears shall weep no longer. You shall gaze in ineffable rapture upon the splendor of Him who sits upon the throne. No, more, you shall sit upon His throne. The triumph of His glory shall be shared by you; His crown, His joy, His paradise, these shall be yours, and you shall be co-heir with Him who is the heir of all things.

"Now why go to Egypt to drink water from the Shihor?" — *Jeremiah 2:18*

Y various miracles, by several mercies, by strange deliverances Jehovah had proved Himself to be worthy of Israel's trust. Yet they broke down the hedges with which God had enclosed them as a sacred garden; they forsook their own true and living God, and followed after false gods. The Lord reproved them constantly for this infatuation, and our text contains one instance of God's expostulating with them, "Now why go to Egypt to drink the water of the muddy river Shihor?" — for so it may be translated. "Why do you wander afar and leave your own cool stream from Lebanon? Why do you forsake Jerusalem to turn aside to Noph and to Tahapanes? Why are you so strangely set on mischief that you can't be content with the good and healthful, but will follow after that which is evil and deceitful?" Isn't there a word of expostulation and warning here to the Christian? O true believer, called by grace and washed in the precious blood of Jesus, you have tasted of better drink than the muddy river of this world's pleasure can give you; you have had fellowship with Christ; you have obtained the joy of seeing Jesus, and leaning your head upon His heart. Do the trifles, the songs, the honors, the merriment of this earth satisfy you after that? Have you eaten the bread of angels, and can you live on husks? Good Rutherford once said, "I have tasted of Christ's own manna, and it has put my mouth out of taste for the brown bread of this world's joys." It seems to me it should be so with you. If you are wandering after the waters of Egypt, O return quickly to the one living fountain: the waters of Shihor may be sweet to the Egyptians, but they will prove only bitterness to you. What have *you* to do with them? *Jesus asks you this question* this evening — what will you answer Him?

"The Daughter of Jerusalem tosses her head as you flee."
— *Isaiah 37:22*

EASSURED by the Word of the Lord, the poor trembling citizens of Zion grew bold, and shook their heads at Sennacherib's boastful threats. Strong faith enables the servants of God to look with calm contempt upon their most haughty foes. *We know that our enemies are attempting impossibilities.* They seek to destroy the eternal life, which cannot die while Jesus lives; to overthrow the citadel, against which the gates of hell shall not prevail. They kick against thorns and wound themselves, and rush upon the raised ornamentation of Jehovah's shield and hurt themselves.

We know their weakness. What are they but men? And what is man but a worm? They roar and swell like waves of the sea, foaming out their own shame. When the Lord arises, they shall fly as chaff before the wind, and be consumed as crackling thorns. Their utter powerlessness to do damage to the cause of God and His truth may make the weakest soldiers in Zion's ranks laugh them to scorn.

Above all, *we know that the Most High is with us*, and when He dresses Himself in arms, where are His enemies? If He comes forth from His place, the potsherds of the earth will not long contend with their Maker. His rod of iron shall dash them in pieces like a potter's vessel, and their very remembrance shall perish from the earth. Away, then, all fears, the kingdom is safe in the King's hands. Let's shout for joy, for the Lord reigns, and His foes shall be as straw for the manure pile.

> "As true as God's own word is true;
> Nor earth, nor hell, with all their crew,
> Against us shall prevail.
> A jest, and by-word, are they grown;
> God *is* with us, we *are* his own,
> Our victory cannot fail."

"Why must I go about mourning?" — Psalm 42:9

AN you answer this, believer? Can you find any reason why you are so often mourning instead of rejoicing? Why yield to gloomy anticipations? Who told you that the night would never end in day? Who told you that the sea of circumstances would ebb out until there should be nothing left but long leagues of the mud of horrible poverty? Who told you that the winter of your discontent would proceed from frost to frost, from snow, and ice, and hail, to deeper snow, and yet more heavy tempest of despair? Don't you know that day follows night, that flood comes after ebb, that spring and summer succeed winter? Hope then! Hope always! For God does not fail you. Don't you know that your God loves you in the midst of all this? Mountains, when in darkness hidden, are as real as in day, and God's love is as true to you now as it was in your brightest moments. No father chastens always: your Lord hates the rod as much as you do; He only cares to use it for that reason which should make you willing to receive it, namely, that it brings about your lasting good. You shall yet climb Jacob's ladder with the angels, and behold Him who sits at the top of it — your covenant God. You shall yet, amidst the splendors of eternity, forget the trials of time, or only remember them to bless the God who led you through them, and wrought your lasting good by them. Come, sing in the midst of tribulation. Rejoice even while passing through the furnace. Make the wilderness blossom like the rose! Cause the desert to ring with your exulting joys, for these light afflictions will soon be over, and then "forever with the Lord," your bliss shall never wane.

> "Faint not nor fear, His arms are near,
> He changeth not, and thou art dear;
> Only believe and thou shalt see,
> That Christ is all in all to thee."

"I am your husband." — *Jeremiah 3:14*

HRIST Jesus is joined to His people in the bond of marriage. In love He espoused His church as a chaste virgin, long before she fell under the yoke of bondage. Full of burning affection He toiled, like Jacob for Rachel, until the whole of her purchase money had been paid, and now, having sought her by His Spirit, and brought her to know and love Him, He awaits the glorious hour when their mutual bliss shall be consummated at the marriage supper of the Lamb. The glorious Bridegroom has not yet presented His betrothed, perfected and complete, before the Majesty of heaven; not yet has she actually entered upon the enjoyment of her dignities as His wife and queen: she is as yet a wanderer in a world of woe, a dweller in the tents of Kedar; but she is even now the bride, the spouse of Jesus, dear to His heart, precious in His sight, written on His hands, and united with His person. On earth He exercises towards her all the affectionate offices of Husband. He makes rich provision for her wants, pays all her debts, allows her to assume His name, and to share in all His wealth. Nor will He ever act otherwise to her. The word divorce He will never mention, for "He hates divorce." Death must sever the conjugal tie between the most loving mortals, but it cannot divide the links of this immortal marriage. In heaven they do not marry, but are as the angels of God; yet there is this one marvelous exception to the rule, for in Heaven Christ and His church shall celebrate their joyous nuptials. Just as this affinity is more lasting, so is it more near than earthly wedlock. Let the love of a husband be never so pure and fervent, it is but a faint picture of the flame which burns in the heart of Jesus. Passing all human union is that mystical cleaving to the church, for which Christ left His Father, and became one flesh with her.

"Here is the man!" — *John 19:5*

I F there is one place where our Lord Jesus most fully becomes the joy and comfort of His people, it is where He plunged deepest into the depths of woe. Come here, gracious souls, and behold the Man in the garden of Gethsemane; behold His heart so brimming with love that He cannot hold it in — so full of sorrow that it must find a vent. Behold the bloody sweat as it distills from every pore of His body, and falls upon the ground. Behold the Man as they drive the nails into His hands and feet. Look up, repenting sinners, and see the sorrowful image of your suffering Lord. See Him, as the ruby drops stand on the thorny crown, and adorn with priceless gems the diadem of the King of Misery. Behold the Man when all His bones are out of joint, and He is poured out like water and brought into the dust of death; God has forsaken Him, and hell compasses Him about. Behold and see, was there ever sorrow like His sorrow that is done to Him? All you that pass by draw near and look upon this spectacle of grief, unique, unparalleled, a wonder to mortals and angels, a prodigy unmatched. Behold the Emperor of Woe who had no equal or rival in His agonies! Gaze upon Him, you mourners, for if there is no consolation in a crucified Christ there is no joy in earth or heaven. If in the ransom price of His blood there is no hope, you harps of heaven, there is no joy in you, and the right hand of God shall know no pleasures forevermore. We have only to sit more continually at the foot of the cross to be less troubled with our doubts and woes. We have but to see *His* sorrows, and *our* sorrows we shall be ashamed to mention; we have but to gaze into His wounds and heal our own. If we would live properly, it must be by the contemplation of His death; if we would rise to dignity, it must be by considering His humiliation and His sorrow.

"You were like one of them." — Obadiah 1:11

ROTHERLY kindness was due from Edom to Israel in the time of need; instead, the men of Esau made common cause with Israel's foes. Special stress in the sentence before us is laid upon the word *you;* as when Caesar cried to Brutus, "and *you* Brutus;" a bad action may be all the worse because of the person who has committed it. When *we* sin, who are the chosen favorites of heaven, we sin with an emphasis; ours is a crying offense, because we are so peculiarly indulged. If an angel should lay his hand upon us when we are doing evil, he needn't use any other rebuke than the question, "What *you?* What are *you* doing here?" Much forgiven, much delivered, much instructed, much enriched, much blessed, shall we dare to put forth our hand to evil? God forbid!

A few minutes of confession may be beneficial to you, gentle reader, this morning. Have you never behaved like the wicked? At an evening party certain men laughed at uncleanness, and the joke was not altogether offensive to your ear, *even you were like one of them.* When hard things were spoken concerning the ways of God, you were bashfully silent; and so, to onlookers, *you were like one of them.* When worldlings were bartering in the market, and driving hard bargains, were you not like one of them? When they were pursuing vanity with a hunter's foot, were you not as greedy for gain as they were? Could any difference be discerned between you and them? *Is there any difference?* Here we come to close quarters. Be honest with your own soul, and make sure that you are a new creation in Christ Jesus; but when this is sure, walk jealously, lest any should again be able to say, "You were like one of them." You will not desire to share their eternal doom, why then behave like them here? Do not come into their secret, lest you come into their ruin. Side with the afflicted people of God, and not with the world.

*"The blood of Jesus, his Son,
purifies us from all sin." — 1 John 1:7*

URIFIES," says the text — not "*shall* purify."
There are multitudes who think that as a
dying hope they may look forward to pardon.
Oh! how infinitely better to have purifying
now than to depend on the bare possibility
of forgiveness when I come to die. Some
imagine that a sense of pardon is an attainment only
obtainable after many years of Christian experience. But
forgiveness of sin is a *present* thing — a privilege for this
day, a joy for this very hour. The moment a sinner trusts
Jesus he is fully forgiven. The text, being written in the
present tense, also indicates *continuance;* it was "purifies"
yesterday, it is "purifies" today, it will be "purifies" tomorrow: it will be always so with you, Christian, until you
cross the river; every hour you may come to this fountain,
for it purifies still. Notice, likewise, the *completeness* of the
purifying, "The blood of Jesus, His Son, purifies us from
all sin" — not only from sin, but "from *all* sin." Reader,
I cannot tell you the exceeding sweetness of this word, but I
pray that God the Holy Spirit would give you a taste of it.
Our sins are manifold against God. Whether the bill be
little or great, the same prescription can apply to the one as
to the other. The blood of Jesus Christ is as blessed and
divine a payment for the transgressions of blaspheming
Peter as for the shortcomings of loving John; our iniquity
is gone, all gone at once, and all gone forever. Blessed
completeness! What a sweet theme to dwell upon as one
gives oneself to sleep.

> "Sins against a holy God;
> Sins against His righteous laws;
> Sins against His love, His blood;
> Sins against His name and cause;
> Sins immense as is the sea —
> From them all He cleanseth me."

*"Stand firm and you will see the deliverance the LORD
will bring you today."* — *Exodus 14:13*

HESE words contain God's command to the
believer when he is reduced to great straits
and brought into extraordinary difficulties.
You cannot retreat; you cannot go forward;
you are shut up on the right hand and on the
left; what are you going to do now ? The
Master's words to you are, "Stand firm." It would be wise for
you if, at such times, you would just listen to your Master's
words, for other and evil advisors come with their suggestions. *Despair* whispers, "Lie down and die; give it all up."
But God would have us put on a cheerful courage, and even
in our worst times, rejoice in His love and faithfulness.
Cowardice says, "Retreat; go back to the worldling's way of
action; you cannot play the Christian's part, it is too difficult. Relinquish your principles." But, however much Satan
may urge this course upon you, you cannot follow it if you
are a child of God. His divine fiat has bid you go from
strength to strength, and so you shall, and neither death nor
hell shall turn you from your course. What, if for a while you
are called to stand still, yet this is only to renew your
strength for some greater advance in due time. *Precipitancy*
cries, "do something. Stir yourself; to stand still and wait is
sheer idleness." We *must* be doing something at once — *we*
must do it so we think — instead of looking to the Lord,
who will not only do something but will do everything.
Presumption boasts, "If the sea is before you, march into it
and expect a miracle." But Faith listens neither to Presumption, nor to Despair, nor to Cowardice, nor to Precipitancy,
but it hears God say, "Stand firm," and immovable as a rock
it stands. "*Stand* firm;" — keep the posture of an upright
person, ready for action, expecting further orders, cheerfully
and patiently awaiting the directing voice; and it will not be
long before God shall say to you, as distinctly as Moses said
it to the people of Israel, "Go forward."

"His forces are beyond number." — *Joel 2:11*

ONSIDER, my soul, the mightiness of the Lord who is your glory and defense. He is a man of war, Jehovah is His name. All *the forces of heaven* are at His beck and call, legions wait at His door, cherubim and seraphim, watchers and holy ones, principalities and powers, are all attentive to His will. If our eyes were not blinded by the ophthalmia of the flesh, we should see horses of fire and chariots of fire round about the Lord's beloved. *The powers of nature* are all subject to the absolute control of the Creator: stormy wind and tempest, lightning and rain, and snow, and hail, and the soft dews and cheering sunshine, come and go at His decree. He releases the bands of Orion and binds the sweet influences of the Pleiades. Earth, sea, and air, and the places under the earth, are the barracks for Jehovah's great armies; space is His camping ground, light is His banner, and flame is His sword. When He goes forth to war, famine ravages the land, pestilence smites the nations, hurricane sweeps the sea, tornado shakes the mountains, and earthquake makes the solid world tremble. As for *animate creatures,* they all own His dominion, and from the great fish which swallowed the prophet, down to "all sorts of flies," which plagued the field of Zoan, all are His servants, and like the palmerworm, the caterpillar, and the cankerworm, are squadrons of His great army, for His forces are beyond number. My soul, see to it that you are at peace with this mighty King, yes, more, be sure to enlist under His banner, for to war against Him is madness, and to serve Him is glory. Jesus, Immanuel, God with us, is ready to receive recruits for the army of the Lord: if I am not already enlisted let me go to Him before I sleep, and beg to be accepted through His merits; and if I already am, as I hope I am, a soldier of the cross, let me be of good courage; for the enemy is powerless compared with my Lord, whose forces are beyond number.

"He left his cloak in her hand and ran out of the house."
— *Genesis 39:12*

N contending with certain sins there remains no mode of victory but by flight. The ancient naturalists wrote a great deal about lizards, whose eyes fascinated their victims and rendered them easy victims; so the mere gaze of wickedness puts us in solemn danger. They who would be safe from acts of evil must hasten away from occasions of it. A covenant must be made with our eyes not even to look upon the cause of temptation, for such sins only need a spark to begin with and a blaze follows in an instant. Who would wantonly enter the leper's prison and sleep amid its horrible corruption? Only he who desires to be leprous himself would thus court contagion. If the mariner knew how to avoid a storm, he would do anything rather than run the risk of weathering it. Cautious pilots have no desire to see how close they can get to a sandbar before getting stuck, or how often they may touch a rock without springing a leak; their aim is to keep, as nearly as possible, in the middle of a safe channel.

This day I may be exposed to great peril, let me have the serpent's wisdom to keep out of it and avoid it. The wings of a dove may be of more use to me today than the jaws of a lion. It is true I may be an apparent loser by declining evil company, but I had better leave my cloak than lose my character; it is not absolutely necessary for me to be rich, but it is imperative for me to be pure. No ties of friendship, no chains of beauty, no flashings of talent, no shafts of ridicule must turn me from the wise resolve to flee from sin. I only need to resist the devil and *he* will flee from me; but the lusts of the flesh, *I* must flee, or they will surely overcome me. O God of holiness preserve your Josephs, that Potiphar's wife would not bewitch them with her vile suggestions. May the horrible trinity of the world, the flesh, and the devil, never overcome us!

"In their misery they will earnestly seek me."
— *Hosea 5:15*

LOSSES and adversities are frequently the means which the great Shepherd uses to fetch home His wandering sheep; like fierce dogs they worry the wanderers back to the fold. There is no making lions tame if they are too well fed; they must be brought down from their great strength, and their stomachs must be lowered, and then they will submit to the tamer's hand; and often have we seen the Christian rendered obedient to the Lord's will by the difficulty of hard work. When rich and increased in goods many professing Christians carry their heads much too loftily, and speak exceedingly boastfully. Like David, they flatter themselves, "My mountain stands fast; I shall never be moved." When the Christian grows wealthy, is in good repute, has good health, and a happy family, he too often invites Mr. Carnal Security to feast at his table, and then, if he is a true child of God, there is a rod preparing for him. Wait awhile, and it may be you will see his substance melt away as a dream. There goes a portion of his estate — how soon the acres change hands. That debt, that dishonored bill — how fast his losses roll in, where will they end? It is a blessed sign of divine life if when these embarrassments occur one after another he begins to be distressed about his backslidings, and takes himself to his God. Blessed are the waves that wash the mariner upon the rock of salvation! Losses in business are often sanctified to our soul's enriching. If the chosen soul will not come to the Lord full-handed, it shall come empty. If God, in His grace, finds no other means of making us honor Him among humankind, He will cast us into the deep; if we fail to honor Him on the pinnacle of riches, He will bring us into the valley of poverty. Yet do not faint, heir of sorrow, when you are rebuked this way, rather recognize the loving hand which chastens, and say, "I will set out and go back to My Father."

> *"Make every effort to add to your faith goodness; and to goodness, knowledge; and to knowledge, self-control; and to self-control, perseverance; and to perseverance, godliness; and to godliness, brotherly kindness; and to brotherly kindness, love."* — 2 Peter 1:5, 6

 F you will enjoy the eminent grace of the full assurance of faith, under the blessed Spirit's influence, and assistance, do what the Scripture tells you, *"Make every effort."* Take care that your *faith* is of the right kind — that it is not a mere belief of doctrine, but a simple faith, depending on Christ, and on Christ alone. Give diligent heed to your *courage.* Plead with God that He would give you the face of a lion, that you may, with a consciousness of right, go on boldly. Study the Scriptures well, and get *knowledge;* for a knowledge of doctrine will tend very much to confirm faith. Try to understand God's Word; let it dwell in your heart richly.

When you have done this, "Add to your knowledge *self-control."* Take heed to your body: exhibit self-control without. Take heed to your soul: exhibit self-control within. Get control of lip, life, heart, and thought. Add to this, by God's Holy Spirit, *perseverance;* ask Him to give you that patience which endures affliction, which, when it is tested, shall come forth as gold. Clothe yourself in perseverance, that you may not murmur nor be depressed in your afflictions. When that grace is won look to *godliness.* Godliness is something more than religion. Make God's glory your object in life; live in His sight; dwell close to Him; seek fellowship with Him; and you have "godliness;" and to that add *brotherly love.* Have a brotherly love for all the saints: and add to that a *love* which opens its arms to all people, and loves their souls. When you are adorned with these jewels, and just in proportion as you practice these heavenly virtues, will you come to know by the clearest evidence "your calling and election." "Make every effort," if you want assurance, for lukewarmness and doubting very naturally go hand in hand.

"He seats them with princes." — *Psalm 113:8*

OUR spiritual privileges are of the highest order. "With princes" *is the place of select society.* Truly, "our fellowship is with the Father and with His Son, Jesus Christ." Speaking of a select society, there is none like this! We "are a chosen people, a royal priesthood, a holy nation." We "have come to thousands upon thousands of angels in joyful assembly, to the church of the firstborn, whose names are written in heaven." The saints *have courtly audience:* princes have admittance to royalty when common people must stand afar off. The child of God has free access to the inner courts of heaven. "For through Him we both have access to the Father by one Spirit." "Let us then approach *the throne* of grace with confidence," says the apostle. Among princes there is *abundant wealth,* but what is the abundance of princes compared with the riches of believers? for "all things are yours, and you are Christ's, and Christ is God's." "He who did not spare His own Son, but gave Him up for us all — how will He not also, along with Him, graciously give us all things?" Princes have *peculiar power.* A prince of heaven's empire has great influence: he wields a scepter in his own domain; he sits upon Jesus' throne, for He has "made them to be a kingdom and priests to serve our God, and they will reign on the earth." We reign over the united kingdom of time and eternity. Princes, again, have *special honor.* We may look down upon all earthborn dignity from the eminence upon which grace has placed us. For what is human grandeur to this, "God raised us up with Christ and seated us with Him in the heavenly realms in Christ Jesus"? We share the honor of Christ, and compared with this, earthly splendors are not worth a thought. Communion with Jesus is a richer gem than ever glittered in imperial diadem. Union with the Lord is a coronet of beauty outshining all the blaze of imperial pomp.

"Very great and precious promises." — 2 Peter 1:4

F you would know experimentally the preciousness of the promises, and enjoy them in your own heart, *meditate much upon them.* There are promises which are like grapes in the winepress; if you will tread them the juice will flow. Thinking over the hallowed words will often be the prelude to their fulfillment. While you are musing upon them, the boon which you are seeking will insensibly come to you. Many a Christian who has thirsted for the promise has found the favor which it ensured gently distilling into his soul even while he has been considering the divine record; and he has rejoiced that he was ever led to lay the promise near his heart.

But besides *meditating* upon the promises, *seek in your soul to receive them as being the very words of God.* Speak to your soul like this, "If I were dealing with a man's promise, I would carefully consider the ability and the character of the man who had covenanted with me. So with the promise of God; my eye must not be so much fixed upon the greatness of the mercy — that may stagger me; as upon the greatness of the promiser — that will cheer me. My soul, it is God, even your God, God that cannot lie, who speaks to you. This word of His which you are now considering is as true as His own existence. He is an unchangeable God. He has not altered one thing which has gone out of His mouth, nor called back one single consolatory sentence. Nor does He lack any power; it is the God that made the heavens and the earth who has spoken in this manner. Nor can He fail in wisdom as to the time when He will give the favors, for He knows when it is best to give and when better to withhold. Therefore, seeing that it is the word of a God so true, so immutable, so powerful, so wise, I will and must believe the promise." If we thus meditate upon the promises, and consider the Promiser, we shall experience their sweetness, and obtain their fulfillment.

> *"Who will bring any charge against those whom*
> *God has chosen?"* — *Romans 8:33*

OST blessed challenge! How unanswerable it is! Every sin of the elect was laid upon the great Champion of our salvation, and by the atonement carried away. There is no sin in God's book against His people: He sees no sin in Jacob, neither iniquity in Israel; they are justified in Christ forever. When the guilt of sin was taken away, the punishment of sin was removed. For the Christian there is no stroke from God's angry hand — no, not so much as a single frown of punitive justice. The believer may be chastised by his Father, but God the Judge has nothing to say to the Christian, except "I have absolved you: you are acquitted." For the Christian there is no legally punishable death in this world, much less any second death. He is completely freed from all the punishment as well as the guilt of sin, and the power of sin is removed, too. It may stand in our way, and agitate us with perpetual warfare; but sin is a conquered foe to every soul in union with Jesus. There is no sin which a Christian cannot overcome if he will only rely upon his God to do it. They who wear the white robe in heaven overcame through the blood of the Lamb, and we may do the same. No lust is too mighty, no besetting sin too strongly entrenched; we can overcome through the power of Christ. Do believe it, Christian, that your sin is a condemned thing. It may kick and struggle, but it is doomed to die. God has written condemnation across its brow. Christ has crucified it, "nailing it to His cross." Go now and mortify it, and the Lord help you to live to His praise, for sin with all its guilt, shame, and fear, is gone.

> "Here's pardon for transgressions past,
> It matters not how black their cast;
> And, O my soul, with wonder view,
> For sins to come here's pardon too."

*"I was senseless and ignorant; I was a brute beast
before you."* — Psalm 73:22

 EMEMBER this is the confession of the man after God's own heart; and in telling us his inner life, he writes, "I was senseless and ignorant." The word *"senseless,"* here, means more than it signifies in ordinary language. David, in an earlier verse of the Psalm, writes, "I envied the arrogant when I saw the prosperity of the wicked," which shows that the folly he intended had *sin* in it. He puts himself down as being thus "senseless." *How foolish* he couldn't tell. It was a sinful folly, a folly which was not to be excused by frailty, but to be condemned because of its perverseness and willful ignorance, for he had been envious of the present prosperity of the ungodly, forgetful of the dreadful end awaiting all such. And are we better than David that *we* should call ourselves wise! Do we profess that we have attained perfection, or to have been so chastened that the rod has taken all our willfulness out of us? Ah, this is pride indeed! If *David* was foolish, how foolish *we* would look, in our own estimation, if we could but see ourselves! Look back, believer: think of how you doubted God when He has been so faithful to you — think of your foolish outcry of "Not so, my Father," when He crossed His hands in affliction to give you the larger blessing; think of the many times when you have read His providences in the dark, misinterpreted His dispensations, and groaned out, "Everything is against me," when they are all working together for your good! Think how often you have chosen sin because of its pleasure, when indeed, that pleasure was a root of bitterness to you! Surely, if we know our own hearts, we must plead guilty to the indictment of a sinful folly; and conscious of this "senselessness," we must make David's consequent resolve our own — *"You guide me with Your counsel."*

"He went around doing good." — *Acts 10:38*

EW words, but yet an exquisite miniature of the Lord Jesus Christ. There are not many touches, but they are the strokes of a master's pencil. Of the Savior, and only of the Savior, is it true in the fullest, broadest, and most unqualified sense. "He went around doing good." From this description it is evident that He did good *personally.* The evangelists constantly tell us that He touched the leper with His own finger, that He anointed the eyes of the blind, and that in situations where He was asked to speak the word only at a distance, He didn't usually comply, but went Himself to the sick bed, and there personally wrought the cure. A lesson to us, if we want to do good, to do it ourselves. Give alms with your own hand; a kind look, or word, will enhance the value of the gift. Speak to a friend about his soul; your loving appeal will have more influence than a whole library of tracts. Our Lord's mode of doing good sets forth His *incessant activity!* He didn't just do the good which was close at hand, but He "went around" on His errands of mercy. Throughout the whole land of Judea there was scarcely a village or a hamlet which was not gladdened by the sight of Him. How this reproves the creeping, loitering manner, in which many professing Christians serve the Lord. Let's prepare our minds for action, and let's not become weary in doing good. Doesn't the text imply that Jesus Christ *went out of His way to do good?* "He went *about* doing good." He was never deterred by danger or difficulty. He sought out the objects of His gracious intentions. So must we. If old plans don't work, we must try new ones, for fresh experiments sometimes achieve more than regular methods. Christ's *perseverance,* and the *unity* of His purpose, are also hinted at, and the practical application of the subject may be summed up in the words, "leaving us an example, that we should follow in His steps."

"Yet I am always with you." — Psalm 73:23

ET," — As if, notwithstanding all the foolishness and ignorance which David had just been confessing to God, it was not one atom less true and certain that David was saved and accepted, and that the blessing of being constantly in God's presence was undoubtedly his. Fully conscious of his own lost estate, and of the deceitfulness and vileness of his nature, yet, by a glorious outburst of faith, he sings "Yet I am always with You." Believer, you are forced to enter into Asaph's confession and acknowledgment, endeavor, in like spirit, to say "yet, since I belong to Christ I am continually with God!" By this is meant continually upon His *mind*, He is always thinking of me for my good. Continually before His *eye;* — the eye of the Lord never closes in sleep, but is perpetually watching over my welfare. Continually in His *hand*, so that no one shall be able to pluck me out of it. Continually on His *heart*, worn there as a memorial, even as the high priest bore the names of the twelve tribes upon his heart forever. You always think of me, O God. The depths of Your love continually yearn towards me. You are always making providence work for my good. You have set me as a signet ring upon Your arm; Your love is as strong as death, many waters cannot quench it; neither can the floods drown it. Surprising grace! You see me in Christ, and though in myself abhorred, You behold me as wearing Christ's garments, and washed in His blood, and thus I stand accepted in Your presence. I am thus always in Your favor — "always with You." Here is comfort for the tested and afflicted soul; vexed with the tempest within — look at the calm without. *"Yet"* — O say it in your heart, and take the peace it gives. "Yet I am always with You."

"All that the Father gives me will come to me."
— *John 6:37*

HIS declaration involves *the doctrine of election:* there are some whom the Father gave to Christ. It involves *the doctrine of effectual calling:* these who are given must and shall come; however stoutly they may set themselves against it, yet they shall be brought out of darkness into God's marvelous light. It teaches us *the indispensable necessity of faith;* for even those who are given to Christ are not saved unless they come to Jesus. Even *they* must come, for there is no other way to heaven but by the door, Christ Jesus. All that the Father gives to our Redeemer *must come to Him,* therefore none can come to heaven except they come to Christ.

Oh! the power and majesty which rest in the words *"will come."* He doesn't say they have power to come, nor that they may come if they want to, but they *"will come."* The Lord Jesus does by His messengers, His word, and His Spirit, sweetly and graciously compel men to come in that they may eat of His marriage supper; and this He does, not by any violation of the free agency of man, but by the power of His grace. I may exercise power over another man's will, and yet that other man's will may be perfectly free, because the constraint is exercised in a manner accordant with the laws of the human mind. Jehovah Jesus knows how, by irresistible arguments addressed to the understanding, by mighty reasons appealing to the affections, and by the mysterious influence of His Holy Spirit operating on all the powers and passions of the soul, so to subdue the entire person, that whereas one was once rebellious, one yields cheerfully to His government, subdued by sovereign love. But how shall those be known whom God has chosen? By this result: that they willingly and joyfully accept Christ, and come to Him with simple and unfeigned faith, resting upon Him as their complete salvation and their complete desire. Reader, have you come to Jesus in this manner?

"And he broke down and wept." — *Mark 14:72*

T has been thought by some that as long as Peter lived, the fountain of his tears began to flow whenever he remembered his denying his Lord. It is not unlikely that it was so, for his sin was very great, and grace in him had afterwards a perfect work. This same experience is common to all the redeemed family according to the degree in which the Spirit of God has removed the natural heart of stone. We, like Peter, remember *our boastful promise:* "Even if all fall away on account of You, I never will." We eat our own words with the bitter herbs of repentance. When we think of what we vowed we would be, and of what we have been, we may weep whole showers of grief. He thought about *his denying his Lord.* The place in which he did it, the little cause which led him into such heinous sin, the oaths and blasphemies with which he sought to confirm his falsehood, and the dreadful hardness of heart which drove him to do so again and yet again. Can we, when we are reminded of our sins, and their exceeding sinfulness, remain apathetic and stubborn? Won't we make our house a Bochim, and cry to the Lord for renewed assurances of pardoning love? May we never take a dry-eyed look at sin, lest before long we have a tongue parched in the flames of hell. Peter also thought upon *his Master's look of love.* The Lord followed up the cock's warning voice with an admonitory look of sorrow, pity, and love. That glance was never out of Peter's mind as long as he lived. It was far more effectual than ten thousand sermons would have been without the Spirit. The penitent apostle would be sure to weep when he recollected the *Savior's full forgiveness,* which restored him to his former place. To think that we have offended so kind and good a Lord is more than sufficient reason for being constant weepers. Lord, strike our rocky hearts, and make the waters flow.

"Whoever comes to me I will never drive away."
— *John 6:37*

 O limit is set to *the duration* of this promise. It doesn't merely say, "I will never drive away a sinner at his first coming," but, "I will never drive away." The original reads, "I will *never, never* drive away." The text means that Christ will not *at first* reject a believer; and that as He will not do it at first, so He will not *to the last.*

But suppose the believer sins after coming? "If anybody does sin, we have one who speaks to the Father in our defense — Jesus Christ, the Righteous One." But suppose that believers backslide? "I will heal their waywardness and love them freely, for My anger has turned away from them." But believers may fall under temptation! "God is faithful; He will not let you be tempted beyond what you can bear. But when you are tempted, He will also provide a way out so that you can stand up under it." But the believer may fall into sin as David did! Yes, but He will "Cleanse me with hyssop, and I will be clean; wash me, and I will be whiter than snow." "I will cleanse them from all the sin they have committed."

> "Once in Christ, in Christ for ever,
> Nothing from His love can sever."

"I give them," says He, "eternal life, and they shall never perish; no one can snatch them out of my hand." What do you say to this, O trembling feeble mind? Is this not a precious mercy, that coming to Christ, you do not come to One who will treat you well for a little while, and then send you about your business, but He will receive you and make you His bride, and you shall be His forever? Receive no longer the spirit of bondage again to fear, but the spirit of adoption whereby you shall cry, *Abba,* Father! Oh! the grace of these words: "I will never drive away."

"I in them." — John 17:23

F this is the union which subsists between our souls and the person of our Lord, how deep and broad is the channel of our communion! This is no narrow pipe through which a thread-like stream may wind its way. It is a channel of amazing depth and breadth, along whose glorious length a ponderous volume of living water may roll its floods. Behold He has set before us an open door, let's not be slow to enter. This city of communion has many pearly gates, every single gate is of one pearl, and each gate is thrown open to the uttermost that we may enter, assured of welcome. If there were but one small loophole through which to talk with Jesus, it would be a high privilege to thrust a word of fellowship through the narrow door; how much we are blessed in having so large an entrance! Had the Lord Jesus been far away from us, with many a stormy sea between, we should have longed to send a messenger to Him to carry Him our love, and bring us tidings from His Father's house; but see His kindness, He has built His house next door to ours, no, more, He lodges with us, and tabernacles in poor humble hearts, so that He may have perpetual communication with us. O how foolish must we be, if we do not live in habitual communion with Him. When the road is long, and dangerous, and difficult, we needn't wonder that friends seldom meet each other, but when they live together, shall Jonathan forget his David? A wife may, when her husband is upon a journey, abide many days without holding conversation with him, but she could never endure to be separated from him if she knew him to be in one of the rooms of her own house. Why, believer, don't you sit at His banquet of wine? Seek your Lord, for He is near; embrace Him, for He is your Brother. Hold Him fast, for He is your Husband; and press Him to your heart, for He is of your own flesh.

*"Those who were musicians . . . were responsible for
the work day and night."* — 1 Chronicles 9:33

T was so well organized in the temple that
the sacred chant never ceased: the singers
constantly praised the Lord, whose mercy
endures forever. Just as mercy didn't cease
to rule either by day or by night, neither did
music hush its holy ministry. My heart,
there is a lesson sweetly taught to you in the ceaseless song
of Zion's temple, you too are a constant debtor, and see to
it that your gratitude, like charity, never fails. God's praise
is constant in heaven, which is to be your final dwelling
place, learn to practice the eternal hallelujah. As the sun
scatters its light around the earth, its beams awaken grateful believers to tune their morning hymn, so that by the
priesthood of the saints perpetual praise is kept up at all
hours, they swathe our globe in a mantle of thanksgiving,
and belt it with a golden belt of song.

The Lord always deserves to be praised for what He is in
Himself, for His works of creation and providence, for His
goodness towards His creatures, and especially for the
transcendent act of redemption, and all the marvelous
blessing flowing therefrom. It is always beneficial to praise
the Lord; it cheers the day and brightens the night; it
lightens toil and softens sorrow; and over earthly gladness
it sheds a sanctifying radiance which makes it less liable to
blind us with its glare. Have we not something to sing
about at this moment? Can't we weave a song out of our
present joys, or our past deliverances, or our future hopes?
Earth yields her summer fruits: the hay is housed, the
golden grain invites the sickle, and the sun, lingering at
length to shine upon a fruitful earth, shortens the interval
of shade that we may lengthen the hours of devout worship. By the love of Jesus, let's be stirred up to close the day
with a psalm of sanctified gladness.

"Let me go to the fields and pick up the leftover grain."
— *Ruth 2:2*

OWNCAST and troubled Christian, come and glean today in the broad field of promise. Here is an abundance of precious promises which exactly meet your needs. Take this one: "A bruised reed He will not break, and a smoldering wick He will not snuff out." Doesn't that suit your situation? A reed, helpless, insignificant, and weak, a bruised reed, out of which no music can come; weaker than weakness itself; a reed, and that reed bruised, yet, He will not break you; on the contrary, He will restore and strengthen you. You are like the smoldering wick: no light or warmth can come from you; but He will not quench you; He will blow with His sweet breath of mercy until He fans you to a flame. Won't you pick up some more grain? "Come to Me, all you who are weary and burdened, and I will give you rest." What soft words! your heart is tender, and the Master knows it, and therefore He speaks so gently to you. Won't you obey Him, and come to Him even now? Take more grain: "'Do not be afraid, O worm Jacob, O little Israel, for I myself will help you,' declares the LORD, your Redeemer, the Holy One of Israel." How can you fear with such a wonderful assurance as this? You may pick up a ton of golden grain like this! "I have swept away your offenses like a cloud, your sins like the morning mist." Or this, "Though your sins are like scarlet, they shall be as white as snow; though they are red as crimson, they shall be like wool." Or this, "The Spirit and the bride say, 'Come!' And let him who hears say, 'Come!' Whoever is thirsty, let him come; and whoever wishes, let him take the free gift of the water of life." Our Master's field is very rich; behold the handfuls. See, there they lie before you, poor timid believer! Pick them up, make them your own, for Jesus bids you to take them. Don't be afraid, only believe! Grasp these sweet promises, thresh them out by meditation and feed on them with joy.

"You crown the year with your bounty."
— *Psalm 65:11*

LL the year round, every hour of every day, God is richly blessing us; both when we sleep and when we wake His mercy waits upon us. The sun may leave us a legacy of darkness, but our God never ceases to shine upon His children with beams of love. Like a river, His loving-kindness is always flowing, with a fullness as inexhaustible as His own nature. Like the atmosphere which constantly surrounds the earth and is always ready to support human life, the benevolence of God surrounds all His creatures; in it, as in their element, they live, and move, and have their being. Yet as the sun on summer days gladdens us with beams more warm and bright than at other times, and as rivers are at certain seasons swollen by the rain, and as the atmosphere itself is sometimes fraught with more fresh, more bracing, or more balmy influences than formerly, so is it with the mercy of God; it has its golden hours; its days of overflow, when the Lord magnifies His grace before us. Among the blessings of the springs below, *the joyous days of harvest* are a special season of excessive favor. It is in the glory of autumn that the ripe gifts of providence are then abundantly given; it is the mellow season of realization, whereas all before was but hope and expectation. Great is the joy of harvest. Happy are the reapers who fill their arms with the liberality of heaven. The Psalmist tells us that the harvest is the crowning of the year. Surely these crowning mercies call for crowning thanksgiving! Let's render it by the *inward emotions of gratitude.* Let our hearts be warmed; let our spirits remember, meditate, and think upon this goodness of the Lord. Then let's *praise Him with our lips,* and laud and magnify His name from whose bounty all this goodness flows. Let's glorify God by yielding *our gifts* to His cause. A practical proof of our gratitude is a special thank offering to the Lord of the harvest.

"Who works out everything in conformity with the purpose of his will." — *Ephesians 1:11*

UR belief in God's wisdom supposes and necessitates that He has a settled purpose and plan in the work of salvation. What would *creation* have been without His design? Is there a fish in the sea or a fowl in the air which was left to chance for its formation? No, in every bone, joint, and muscle, sinew, gland, and blood vessel, you mark the presence of a God working everything according to the design of infinite wisdom. And shall God be present in creation, ruling over all, and not in *grace?* Shall the new creation have the fickle genius of free will to preside over it when divine counsel rules the old creation? Look at *Providence!* Who doesn't know that not one sparrow falls to the ground without your Father? Even the hairs of your head are all numbered. God weighs the mountains of our grief in scales and the hills of our tribulation in balances. And will there be a God in providence and not in grace? Shall the shell be ordained by wisdom and the kernel be left to blind chance? No! He knows the end from the beginning. He sees in its appointed place not merely the cornerstone which He has laid in fair colors, in the blood of His dear Son, but He beholds in their ordained position each of the chosen stones taken out of the quarry of nature, and polished by His grace; He sees the whole from corner to cornice, from base to roof, from foundation to pinnacle. He has in His mind a clear knowledge of every stone which shall be laid in its prepared space, and how vast the edifice shall be, and when the capstone shall be brought forth with shoutings of "God bless it! God bless it!" At the last it shall be clearly seen that in every chosen vessel of mercy, Jehovah did as He willed with His own; and that in every part of the work of grace He accomplished His purpose, and glorified His own name.

"So Ruth gleaned in the field until evening."
— Ruth 2:17

ET me learn from Ruth, the gleaner. Just as she went out to gather the ears of corn, so must I go forth into the fields of prayer, meditation, the ordinances, and hearing the word to gather spiritual food. *The gleaner gathers her portion ear by ear;* her gains are little by little: so must I be content to search for single truths, if there is no larger quantity of them. Every ear helps to make a bundle, and every gospel lesson assists in making us wise to salvation. *The gleaner keeps her eyes open:* if she stumbled among the stubble in a dream, she would have no load to carry home rejoicingly at evening. I must be watchful in religious exercises lest they become unprofitable to me; I fear I have lost much already — O that I may rightly estimate my opportunities and glean with greater diligence. *The gleaner stoops for all she finds,* and so must I. High spirits criticize and object, but lowly minds glean and receive benefit. A humble heart is a great help towards profitably hearing the gospel. The engrafted soul-saving word is not received except with meekness. A stiff back makes a bad gleaner; down, master pride, you are a vile robber, not to be endured for a moment. *What the gleaner gathers she holds:* if she dropped one ear to find another, the result of her day's work would be but scant; she is as careful to retain as to obtain, and so at last her gains are great. How often I forget all that I hear; the second truth pushes the first out of my head, and so my reading and hearing end in much ado about nothing! Do I feel duly the importance of storing up the truth? A hungry belly makes the gleaner wise; if there is no corn in her hand, there will be no bread on her table; she labors under the sense of necessity, and hence her tread is nimble and her grasp is firm; I have even a greater necessity, Lord, help me to feel it, that it may urge me onward to glean in fields which yield so generous a reward to diligence.

"The Lamb is its lamp." — *Revelation 21:23*

UIETLY contemplate the Lamb as the light of heaven. Light in Scripture is the emblem of *joy*. The joy of the saints in heaven is comprised of this: *Jesus* chose us, loved us, bought us, cleansed us, robed us, kept us, glorified us: we are here entirely through the Lord Jesus. Each one of these thoughts shall be to them like a cluster of the grapes of Eshcol. Light is also the cause of *beauty*. Nothing of beauty is left when light is gone. Without light no radiance flashes from the sapphire, no peaceful ray proceeds from the pearl; and thus all the beauty of the saints above comes from Jesus. As planets, they reflect the light of the Sun of Righteousness; they live as beams proceeding from the central orb. If He withdrew, they must die; if His glory were veiled, their glory must expire. Light is also the emblem of *knowledge*. In heaven our knowledge will be perfect, but the Lord Jesus Himself will be the fountain of it. Dark providences, never understood before, will then be clearly seen, and all that puzzles us now will become plain to us in the light of the Lamb. Oh! what unfoldings there will be and what glorifying of the God of love! Light also means *manifestation*. Light manifests. In this world it does not yet appear what we shall be. God's people are a hidden people, but when Christ receives His people into heaven, He will touch them with the wand of His own love, and change them into the image of His manifested glory. They were poor and wretched, but what a transformation! They were stained with sin, but one touch of His finger, and they are bright as the sun, and clear as crystal. Oh! what a manifestation! All this proceeds from the exalted Lamb. Whatever there may be of bright splendor, Jesus shall be the center and soul of it all. Oh! to be present and to see Him in His own light, the King of kings, and Lord of lords!

"As Jesus was on his way." — Luke 8:42

ESUS is passing through the throng to the house of Jairus, to raise the ruler's dead daughter; but He is so full of goodness that He works another miracle while on the road. While yet this rod of Aaron bears the blossom of an unaccomplished wonder, it yields the ripe almonds of a perfect work of mercy. It is all we can do if we have just one purpose, then straightway go to accomplish; it would be imprudent to expend our energies along the way. Hastening to the rescue of a drowning friend, we cannot afford to exhaust our strength upon another in similar danger. It is enough for a tree to yield one sort of fruit, and for a man to fulfill his own peculiar calling. But our Master knows no limit of power or boundary of mission. He is so prolific in grace that, like the sun which shines as it rolls onward in its orbit, His path is radiant with loving-kindness. He is a swift arrow of love, which not only reaches its ordained target, but perfumes the air through which it flies. Virtue is forever going out of Jesus, as sweet odors exhale from flowers; and it always will be emanating from Him, as water from a sparkling fountain. What delightful encouragement this truth provides us! If our Lord is so ready to heal the sick and bless the needy, then, my soul, don't be slow to put yourself in His way, that He may smile on you. Don't be slack in asking if He is so abundant in bestowing. Give earnest heed to His word now, and at all times, that Jesus may speak through it to your heart. Where He is to be found there make your resort, that you may obtain His blessing. When He is present to heal, may He not heal you? But surely He is present even now, for He always comes to hearts which need Him. And don't you need Him? Ah, *He* knows how much! You Son of David, turn Your eyes and look upon the distress which is now before You, and make Your suppliant whole.

"The people who know their God will firmly resist him."
— *Daniel 11:32*

 VERY believer understands that to know God is the highest and best form of knowledge; and this spiritual knowledge is a source of strength to the Christian. It strengthens his *faith.* Believers are constantly spoken of in the Scriptures as being persons who are enlightened and taught by the Lord; they are said to "have an anointing from the Holy One," and it is the Spirit's peculiar office to lead them into all truth, and all this for the increase and the fostering of their faith. Knowledge strengthens *love,* as well as faith. Knowledge opens the door, and then through that door we see our Savior. Or, to use another similitude, knowledge paints the portrait of Jesus, and when we see that portrait then we love Him, we cannot love a Christ whom we don't know, at least, to some degree. If we know just a little of the excellences of Jesus, what He has done for us, and what He is doing now, we cannot love Him much; but the more we know Him, the more we shall love Him. Knowledge also strengthens *hope.* How can we hope for a thing if we don't know of its existence? Hope may be the telescope, but until we receive instruction, our ignorance stands in the front of the glass, and we can see nothing whatever; knowledge removes the interposing object, and when we look through the bright optic glass we discern the glory to be revealed, and anticipate it with joyous confidence. Knowledge gives us reasons for *patience.* How shall we have patience unless we know something of the sympathy of Christ and understand the good which is to come out of the correction which our heavenly Father sends us? Nor is there one single grace of the Christian which, under God, will not be fostered and brought to perfection by holy knowledge. How important, then, it is that we should grow, not only in grace, but in the "knowledge" of our Lord and Savior Jesus Christ.

*"I struck all the work of your hands with blight,
mildew and hail."* — *Haggai 2:17*

OW destructive hail is to the standing crops, beating out the precious grain upon the ground! How grateful we ought to be when the corn is spared so terrible a ruin! Let's offer to the Lord thanksgiving. Even more to be dreaded are those mysterious destroyers — parasites, fungi, rust, and mildew. These turn the ear into a mass of soot, or render it putrid, or dry up the grain, and all in a manner so beyond all human control that the farmer is compelled to cry, "This is the finger of God." Innumerable minute fungi cause the mischief, and if it were not for the goodness of God, the rider on the black horse would soon scatter famine over the land. Infinite mercy spares the food of humanity, but in view of the active agents which are ready to destroy the harvest, very wisely we are taught to pray, "Give us each day our daily bread." The curse is abroad; we have constant need of the blessing. When blight and mildew come they are chastisements from heaven, and we must learn to hear the rod, and Him that has appointed it.

Spiritually, mildew is no uncommon evil. When our work is most promising this blight appears. We hoped for many conversions, and lo! a general apathy, an abounding worldliness, or a cruel hardness of heart! There may be no open sin in those for whom we are laboring, but there is a deficiency of sincerity and decision sadly disappointing our desires. We learn our dependence upon the Lord from this, and the need of prayer that no blight may fall upon our work. Spiritual pride or laziness will soon bring upon us the dreadful evil, and only the Lord of the harvest can remove it. Mildew may even attack our own hearts and shrivel our prayers and religious exercises. May it please the great Farmer to avert so serious a calamity. Shine, blessed Sun of Righteousness, and drive the blights away.

"We know that in all things God works for the good of those who love him." — *Romans 8:28*

PON some points a believer is absolutely sure. He knows, for instance, that God sits in the stern sheets of the vessel when it rocks most. He believes that an invisible hand is always on the world's tiller, and that wherever providence may drift, Jehovah steers it. That reassuring knowledge prepares him for everything. He looks over the raging waters and sees the spirit of Jesus treading the billows, and he hears a voice saying, "It is I, be not afraid." He knows too that God is always wise, and, knowing this, he is confident that there can be no accidents, no mistakes; that nothing can occur which oughtn't to arise. He can say, "If I should lose all I have, it is better that I should lose than have, if God so wills: the worst calamity is the wisest and the kindest thing that could befall me if God ordains it." "We know that in all things God works for the good of those who love Him." The Christian doesn't merely hold this as a theory, but *he knows it* as a matter of fact. Everything *has* worked for good as yet; the poisonous drugs mixed in fit proportions have worked the cure; the sharp cuts of the lancet have cleansed out the proud flesh and facilitated the healing. Every event as yet has worked out the most divinely blessed results; and so, believing that God rules all, that He governs wisely, that He brings good out of evil, the believer's heart is assured, and he is enabled calmly to meet each trial as it comes. The believer can in the spirit of true resignation pray, "Send me what you will, my God, so long as it comes from You; there never came an ill portion from Your table to any of Your children."

"Say not my soul, 'From whence can God relieve my care?'
Remember that Omnipotence has servants everywhere.
His method is sublime, His heart profoundly kind,
God never is before His time, and never is behind."

*"Shall your countrymen go to war while you
sit here?"* — *Numbers 32:6*

INDRED has its obligations. The Reubenites and Gadites would have been unbrotherly if they had claimed the land which had been conquered, and had left the rest of the people to fight for their portions by themselves. We have received a great deal through the efforts and sufferings of the saints in years gone by, and if we don't make some return to the church of Christ by giving her our best energies, we are unworthy to be enrolled in her ranks. Others are combating the errors of the age manfully, or excavating perishing ones from amid the ruins of the fall, and if we fold our hands in idleness we'd better be warned, lest the curse of Meroz fall upon us. The Master of the vineyard says, "Why have you been standing here all day long doing nothing?" What is the idler's excuse? Personal service of Jesus becomes all the more the duty of all because it is cheerfully and abundantly rendered by some. The toils of devoted missionaries and fervent ministers shame us if we sit still in indolence. Shrinking from trial is the temptation of those who are at ease in Zion: they would preferably escape the cross and yet wear the crown; to them the question for this evening's meditation is very applicable. If the most precious are tested in the fire, are we to escape the crucible? If the diamond must be vexed upon the wheel, are we to be made perfect without suffering? Who has commanded the wind to cease from blowing because our vessel is on the deep? Why and wherefore should we be treated better than our Lord? The firstborn felt the rod, and why not the younger brethren? It is a cowardly pride which would choose a downy pillow and a silken couch for a soldier of the cross. Wiser far is he who, being first resigned to the divine will, grows by the energy of grace to be pleased with it, and so learns to gather lilies at the foot of the cross, and, like Samson, to find honey in the lion.

"Watchman, what is left of the night?" — *Isaiah 21:11*

HAT enemies are abroad? Errors are a numerous horde, and new ones appear every hour: against what heresy am I to be on my guard? Sins creep from their lurking places when the darkness reigns; I must myself mount the watchtower, and watch to prayer. Our heavenly Protector foresees all the attacks which are about to be made upon us, and when as yet the evil designed for us is but in the desire of Satan, He prays for us that our faith will not fail, when we are sifted as wheat. Continue O gracious Watchman, to forewarn us of our foes, and for Zion's sake do not hold Your peace.

"Watchman, what is left of the night?" *What weather is coming* for the church? Are the clouds lowering, or is it all clear and fair overhead? We must care for the church of God with anxious love; and now that heresy and infidelity are both threatening, let's observe the signs of the times and prepare for conflict.

"Watchman, what is left of the night?" *What stars are visible?* What precious promises suit our present situation? You sound the alarm, give us the consolation also. Christ, the polestar, is ever fixed in His place, and all the stars are secure in the right hand of their Lord.

But watchman, *when does the morning come?* The Bridegroom tarries. Are there no signs of His coming forth as the Sun of Righteousness? Hasn't the morning star arisen as the pledge of day? When will the day dawn, and the shadows flee away? O Jesus, if You do not come in person to Your waiting church this day, yet come in Spirit to my sighing heart, and make it sing for joy.

> "Now all the earth is bright and glad
> With the fresh morn;
> But all my heart is cold, and dark and sad:
> Sun of the soul, let me behold Thy dawn!
> Come, Jesus, Lord,
> O quickly come, according to Thy word."

"May the whole earth be filled with his glory.
Amen and Amen." — Psalm 72:19

THIS is a large petition. To intercede for a whole city needs a stretch of faith, and there are times when a prayer for one person is enough to stagger us. But how far-reaching was the psalmist's dying intercession! How comprehensive! How sublime! "May the whole earth be filled with His glory. Amen and Amen." It doesn't exempt a single country however crushed by the foot of superstition; it doesn't exclude a single nation however barbarous. For the cannibal as well as for the civilized, for all climes and races this prayer is uttered: it encompasses the whole circle of the earth, and omits no one. We must be up and doing for our Master, or we cannot honestly offer such a prayer. The petition is not asked with a sincere heart unless we endeavor as God shall help us, to extend the kingdom of our Master. Aren't there some who *neglect* both to plead and to work? Reader, is it *your* prayer? Turn your eyes to Calvary. Behold the Lord of Life nailed to a cross, with the crown of thorns about His brow, with bleeding head, and hands, and feet. What! Can you look upon this miracle of miracles, the death of the Son of God, without feeling within your heart a marvelous adoration that language never can express? And when you feel the blood applied to your conscience, and know that He has blotted out your sins, *you are not human* unless you start from your knees and cry, "May the whole earth be filled with His glory. Amen and Amen." Can you bow before the Crucified in loving homage, and not wish to see your Monarch master of the world? Shame on you if you can pretend to love your Prince, and not desire to see Him the universal ruler. Your piety is worthless unless it leads you to wish that the same mercy which has been extended to you may bless the whole world. Lord, it is harvest time, put in Your sickle and reap.

"How right they are to adore you!" — *Song of Songs 1:4*

ELIEVERS love Jesus with a deeper affection than they dare to give to any other being. They would sooner lose father and mother than part with Christ. They hold all earthly comforts with a loose hand, but they carry Him closely locked in their hearts. They voluntarily deny themselves for His sake, but they are not to be driven to deny *Him.* It is scant love which the fire of persecution can dry up; the true believer's love is a deeper stream than this. Many have labored to divide the faithful from their Master, but their attempts have been fruitless in every age. Neither crowns of honor, now frowns of anger, have untied this more than Gordian knot. This is no everyday attachment which the world's power may at length dissolve. Neither human being nor devil have found a key which opens this lock. Never has the craft of Satan been more at fault than when he has exercised it in seeking to rend asunder this union of two divinely welded hearts. It is written, and nothing can blot out the sentence, *"How right they are to adore You."* The intensity of the love of the upright, however, is not so much to be judged by what it appears as by what the upright long for. It is our daily lament that we cannot love enough. Would that our hearts were capable of holding more, and reaching further. Like Samuel Rutherford, we sigh and cry, "Oh, for as much love as would go round about the earth, and over heaven — yes, the heaven of heavens, and ten thousand worlds — that I might let all out upon fair, fair, only fair Christ." Alas! our longest reach is but a span of love, and our affection is but as a drop in a bucket compared with His deserts. Measure our love by our intentions, and it is high indeed; it is in this manner, we trust, that our Lord judges it. Oh, that we could give all the love in all hearts in one great mass, a gathering together of all loves to Him who is altogether lovely!

"Satan stopped us." — *1 Thessalonians 2:18*

INCE the first hour in which goodness came into conflict with evil, it has never ceased to be true in spiritual experience, that Satan hinders us. From all points of the compass, all along the line of battle, in the vanguard and in thc rcar, at the dawn of day and in the midnight hour, Satan hinders us. If we toil in the field, he seeks to break the ploughshare; if we build the wall, he labors to cast down the stones; if we would serve God in suffering or in conflict — everywhere Satan hinders us. He hinders us when we are first coming to Jesus Christ. Fierce conflicts we had with Satan when we first looked to the cross and lived. Now that we are saved, he tries to hinder the completeness of our personal character. You may be congratulating yourself, "I have up to now walked consistently; no man can challenge my integrity." Beware of boasting, for your virtue will yet be tried; Satan will direct his engines against that very virtue for which you are the most famous. If you have been up to now a firm believer, your faith will before long be attacked; if you have been meek like Moses, expect to be tempted to speak unadvisedly with your lips. The birds will peck at your ripest fruit, and the wild boar will dash his tusks at your choicest vines. Satan is sure to hinder us when we are earnest in prayer. He checks our insistent requests and weakens our faith in order that, if possible, we may miss the blessing. Nor is Satan less vigilant in obstructing Christian effort. There was never a revival of religion without a revival of his opposition. As soon as Ezra and Nehemiah begin to work, Sanballat and Tobiah are stirred up to hinder them. What then? We are not alarmed because Satan hinders us, for it is proof that we are on the Lord's side, and are doing the Lord's work, and in His strength we shall win the victory, and triumph over our adversary.

"They . . . spin a spider's web." — Isaiah 59:5

EE the spider's web, and behold in it a most suggestive picture of the hypocrite's religion. *It is meant to catch his prey:* the spider fattens himself on flies, and the Pharisee has his reward. Foolish persons are easily entrapped by the loud professions of pretenders, and even the more judicious cannot always escape. Philip baptized Simon Magus, whose guileful declaration of faith was so soon exploded by the stern rebuke of Peter. Custom, reputation, praise, advancement, and other flies, are the small game which hypocrites take in their nets. A spider's web is *a marvel of skill:* look at it and admire the cunning hunter's wiles. Is not a deceiver's religion equally wonderful? How does he make so barefaced a lie appear to be a truth? How can he make his tinsel look so much like gold? The entire spider's web *comes from the creature's own abdomen.* The bee gathers her wax from flowers, the spider sucks no flowers, and yet she spins out her material to any length. Even so hypocrites find their trust and hope within themselves; their anchor was forged on their own anvil, and their cable twisted by their own hands. They lay their own foundation, and hew out the pillars of their own house, disdaining to be debtors to the sovereign grace of God. But a spider's web is *very frail.* It is curiously wrought, but not enduringly manufactured. It is no match for the servant's broom, or the traveler's staff. The hypocrite needs no battery of Armstrongs to blow his hope to pieces, a mere puff of wind will do it. Hypocritical cobwebs will soon come down when the broom of destruction begins its purifying work. Which reminds us of one more thought, namely, that such cobwebs *are not to be endured in the Lord's house:* He will see to it that they and those who spin them shall be destroyed forever. O my soul, rest on something better than a spider's web. Let the Lord Jesus be your eternal hiding place.

"Everything is possible for him who believes."
— Mark 9:23

ANY professing Christians are always doubting and fearing, and they forlornly think that this is the necessary state of believers. This is a mistake, for "everything is possible for him who believes;" and it is possible for us to mount into a state in which a doubt or a fear shall be but as a bird of passage flitting across the soul, but never lingering there. When you read of the high and sweet communions enjoyed by favored saints, you sigh and murmur in the chamber of your heart, "Alas! these are not for me." O climber, if you just have faith, you shall yet stand upon the sunny pinnacle of the temple, for "everything is possible for him who believes." You hear of exploits which holy men have done for Jesus; what they have enjoyed of Him; how much like Him they have been; how they have been able to endure great persecutions for His sake; and you say, "Ah! as for me, I am but a worm; I can never attain to this." But there is nothing which one saint was, that you may not be. There is no elevation of grace, no attainment of spirituality, no clearness of assurance, no post of duty, which is not open to you if you just have the power to believe. Lay aside your sackcloth and ashes, and rise to the dignity of your true position; you are little in Israel because you will be so, not because there is any necessity for it. It is not right that you should grovel in the dust, O child of a King. Ascend! The golden throne of assurance is waiting for you! The crown of communion with Jesus is ready to bedeck your brow. Wrap yourself in scarlet and fine linen, and fare sumptuously every day; for if you believe, you may eat the fat of kidneys of wheat; your land shall flow with milk and honey, and your soul shall be satisfied as with marrow and fatness. Gather golden sheaves of grace, for they wait for you in the fields of faith. "Everything is possible for him who believes."

*"The city does not need the sun or the moon
to shine on it."* — *Revelation 21:23*

VER there in the better world, the inhabitants are independent of all creature comforts. They have no need of clothing; their white robes never wear out, neither shall they ever be defiled. They need no medicine to heal diseases, for "no one living in Zion will say, 'I am ill.' " They need no sleep to rejuvenate their bodies — they rest not day nor night, but unweariedly praise Him in His temple. They need no social relationship to minister comfort, and whatever happiness they may derive from association with their friends is not essential to their bliss, for their Lord's society is enough for their largest desires. They need no teachers there; they doubtless commune with one another concerning the things of God, but they don't require this by way of instruction; they shall all be taught of the Lord. Ours are the alms at the king's gate, but they feast at the table itself. Here we lean upon the friendly arm, but there they lean upon their Beloved and upon Him alone. Here we must have the help of our companions, but there they find all they want in Christ Jesus. Here we look to the meat which perishes, and to the clothing which decays before the moth, but there they find everything in God. We use the bucket to fetch us water from the well, but there they drink from the fountainhead, and put their lips down to the living water. Here the angels bring us blessings, but we shall not be needing messengers from heaven then. They shall need no Gabriels there to bring their love notes from God, for there they shall see *Him* face to face. Oh! what a blessed time shall that be when we shall have mounted above every second cause and shall rest upon the bare arm of God! What a glorious hour when God and not His creatures, the Lord and not His works, shall be our daily joy! Our souls shall then have attained the perfection of bliss.

"He appeared first to Mary Magdalene,
out of whom he had driven seven demons."
— *Mark 16:9*

ARY Magdalene was *the victim of a fearful evil.* She was possessed by not just one devil, but seven. These dreadful inmates caused much pain and pollution to the poor frame in which they had found a lodging. Hers was a hopeless, horrible situation. She couldn't help herself, neither could any human help avail. But Jesus passed that way, and unsought, and probably even resisted by the poor demoniac, He uttered the word of power, and Mary Magdalene became *a trophy of the healing power of Jesus.* All the seven demons left her, left her never to return, forcibly ejected by the Lord of all. What a blessed deliverance! What a happy change! From delirium to delight, from despair to peace, from hell to heaven! At once she became *a constant follower of Jesus,* catching His every word, following in His wandering paths, sharing His toilsome life; and in all things she became *His generous helper,* first among that band of healed and grateful women who ministered to Him of their substance. When Jesus was lifted up in crucifixion, Mary remained *the sharer of His shame:* we find her first beholding from afar, and then drawing near to the foot of the cross. She could not die on the cross with Jesus, but she stood as near to it as she could, and when His blessed body was taken down, she watched to see how and where it was laid. She was *the faithful and watchful believer,* last at the sepulcher where Jesus slept, first at the grave whence He arose. Her holy fidelity made her *a favored beholder of her beloved Rabboni,* who deigned to call her by her name, and to make her *His messenger of good news* to the trembling disciples and Peter. Thus grace found her a maniac and made her a minister, cast out devils and gave her to behold angels, delivered her from Satan, and united her forever to the Lord Jesus. May I also be such a miracle of grace!

"Christ, who is your life." — *Colossians 3:4*

PAUL'S marvelously rich expression indicates that Christ is the *source* of our life. "He has enlivened you who were dead in trespasses and sins." That same voice which brought Lazarus out of the tomb raised us to newness of life. He is now the *substance* of our spiritual life. It is by His life that we live; He is in us, the hope of glory, the spring of our actions, the central thought which moves every other thought. *Christ is the sustenance of our life.* What can the Christian feed upon but Jesus' flesh and blood? "Here is the bread that comes down from heaven, which a man may eat and not die." O weary pilgrims in this wilderness of sin, you will never get a morsel to satisfy the hunger of your spirits, unless you find it in Him! *Christ is the solace of our life.* All our true joys come from Him; and in times of trouble, His presence is our consolation. There is nothing worth living for but Him; and His loving-kindness is better than life! *Christ is the object of our life.* As the ship speeds towards the port, so the believer hastens towards the haven of his Savior's bosom. As the arrow flies to its goal, so the Christian flies towards the perfecting of his fellowship with Christ Jesus. As the soldier fights for his captain, and is crowned in his captain's victory, so the believer contends for Christ, and gets his triumph out of the triumphs of his Master. "For to him to live is Christ." *Christ is the exemplar of our life.* Where there is the same life within, there will, there must be, to a great extent, the same developments without; and if we live in near fellowship with the Lord Jesus we shall grow like Him. We shall set Him before us as our Divine copy, and we shall seek to walk in His footsteps, until He shall become *the crown of our life in glory.* Oh! how safe, how honored, how happy you are when "Christ is your life!"

"The Son of Man has authority on earth
to forgive sins." — *Matthew 9:6*

EHOLD one of the great Physician's mightiest arts: He has power to forgive sin! While He lived here below, before the ransom had been paid, before the blood had been literally sprinkled on the mercy seat, He had power to forgive sin. Doesn't He have the power to do it now that He has died? What power must dwell in Him who to the utmost penny has faithfully paid the debts of His people! He has boundless power now that He has finished transgression and put an end of sin. If you doubt it, see Him rising from the dead! behold Him in ascending splendor raised to the right hand of God! Hear Him pleading before the eternal Father, pointing to His wounds, urging the merit of His sacred passion! What power to forgive is here! "When You ascended on high, You received gifts from men." "He is exalted on high to give repentance and remission of sins." The most crimson sins are removed by the crimson of His blood. At this moment, dear reader, whatever your sinfulness, Christ has power to pardon, power to pardon *you*, and millions like you. A word will speak it. He has nothing more to do to win your pardon; all the atoning work is done. He can, in answer to your tears, forgive your sins today, and make you know it. He can breathe into your soul at this very moment a peace with God which passes all understanding, which shall spring from perfect remission of your manifold iniquities. Do you believe that? I hope you so. May you experience now the power of Jesus to forgive sin! Don't waste any time in applying to the Physician of souls, but hasten to Him with words like these: —

> "Jesus! Master! hear my cry;
> Save me, heal me with a word;
> Fainting at Thy feet I lie,
> Thou my whisper'd plaint hast heard."

"How I long for the months gone by." — *Job 29:2*

UMBERS of Christians can view the past with pleasure, but regard the present with dissatisfaction; they look back upon the days which they have passed in communing with the Lord as being the sweetest and the best they have ever known, but as to the present, it is clad in a black garb of gloom and dreariness. Once they lived near to Jesus, but now they feel that they have wandered from Him, and they say, "O that I were as in months past!" They complain that they have lost their evidences, or that they have no present peace of mind, or that they have no enjoyment in the means of grace, or that their conscience is not so tender, or that they don't have as much zeal for God's glory. The causes of this mournful state of things are manifold. It may arise through a comparative *neglect of prayer,* for a neglected prayer time is the beginning of all spiritual decline. Or it may be the result of *idolatry.* The heart has been occupied with something else, more than with God; the affections have been set on the things of earth, instead of the things of heaven. A jealous God will not be content with a divided heart; He must be loved first and best. He will withdraw the sunshine of His presence from a cold, wandering heart. Or the cause may be found in *self-confidence* and *self-righteousness.* Pride is busy in the heart, and self is exalted instead of lying low at the foot of the cross. Christian, if you are not now as you "were in months past," don't just be satisfied with *wishing* for a return of former happiness, but go at once to seek your Master, and tell Him your sad state. Ask His grace and strength to help you to walk more closely with Him; humble yourself before Him, and He will lift you up, and once more give you joy in the light of His countenance. Don't sit down to sigh and lament; while the beloved Physician lives there is hope, no, there is a certainty of recovery for the worst cases.

"Eternal encouragement." — *2 Thessalonians 2:16*

NCOURAGEMENT." There is music in the word: like David's harp, it charms away the evil spirit of melancholy. It was a distinguished honor to Barnabas to be called "the son of encouragement;" no, it is one of the illustrious names of one greater than Barnabas, for the Lord Jesus is "the encouragement of Israel." *"Eternal encouragement"* — here is the cream of it all, for the eternity of comfort is the crown and glory of it. What is this "eternal encouragement"? It includes a sense of pardoned sin. Christians have received in their heart the witness of the Spirit that their iniquities are put away like a cloud, and their transgressions like a thick cloud. If sin is pardoned, isn't that eternal encouragement? Next, the Lord gives His people an abiding sense of acceptance in Christ. Christians know that God looks upon them as standing in union with Jesus. Union with the risen Lord is an encouragement of the most abiding order; it is, in fact, eternal. Let sickness prostrate us, haven't we seen hundreds of believers as happy in the weakness of disease as they would have been in the strength of hale and blooming health? Let death's arrows pierce us to the heart, our comfort does not die, for haven't our ears very often heard the songs of saints as they have rejoiced because the living love of God was poured out into their hearts in dying moments? Yes, a sense of acceptance in the Beloved is an eternal encouragement. Moreover, Christians have a conviction of their security. God has promised to save those who trust in Christ: Christians do trust in Christ, and they believe that God will be as good as His word, and will save them. They feel that they are safe by virtue of their being bound up with the person and work of Jesus.

"The Lord reigns, let the earth be glad." — *Psalm 97:1*

HERE is no cause for anxiety as long as this blessed sentence is true. *On earth* the Lord's power as easily controls the rage of the wicked as the rage of the sea; His love as easily refreshes the poor with mercy as the earth with showers. Majesty gleams in flashes of fire amid the tempest's horrors, and the glory of the Lord is seen in its grandeur in the fall of empires, and the crash of thrones. In all our conflicts and tribulations, we may behold the hand of the divine King.

> "God is God; He sees and hears
> All our troubles, all our tears.
> Soul, forget not, 'mid thy pains,
> God o'er all for ever reigns."

In hell, evil spirits admit, with misery, His undoubted supremacy. When permitted to roam abroad, it is with a chain at their heel; the bit is in the mouth of behemoth, and the hook in the jaws of leviathan. Death's darts are under the Lord's lock, and the grave's prisons have divine power as their watchman. The terrible vengeance of the Judge of all the earth makes fiends cower and tremble, even as dogs in the kennel fear the hunter's whip.

> "Fear not death, nor Satan's thrusts,
> God defends who in Him trusts;
> Soul, remember, in thy pains,
> God o'er all for ever reigns."

In heaven none doubt the sovereignty of the King Eternal, but all fall on their faces to do Him homage. Angels are His courtiers, the redeemed His favorites, and all delight to serve Him day and night. May we soon reach the city of the great King!

> "For this life's long night of sadness
> He will give us peace and gladness.
> Soul, remember, in thy pains,
> God o'er all for ever reigns."

"The rainbow appears in the clouds." — *Genesis 9:14*

HE rainbow, the symbol of the covenant with Noah, is typical of our Lord Jesus, who is the Lord's witness to the people. When may we *expect to see the token of the covenant?* The rainbow is only to be seen painted in the *clouds.* When the sinner's conscience is dark with clouds, when he remembers his past sin, and mourns and laments before God, Jesus Christ is revealed to him as the covenant Rainbow, displaying all the glorious hues of the divine character and betokening peace. To the believer, when his trials and temptations surround him, it is sweet to behold the person of our Lord Jesus Christ — to see Him bleeding, living, rising, and pleading for us. God's rainbow is hung over the cloud of our sins, our sorrows, and our woes, to prophesy deliverance. Nor does a *cloud* alone give a rainbow, there must be *the crystal drops* to reflect the light of the sun. So, our sorrows must not only threaten, but they must really fall upon us. There would have been no Christ for us if the vengeance of God had been merely a threatening cloud: punishment must fall in terrible drops upon the Surety. Until there is a *real* anguish in the sinner's conscience, there is no Christ for him; until the chastisement which he feels becomes grievous, he cannot see Jesus. But there must also be *a sun;* for clouds and drops of rain don't make rainbows unless the sun shines. Beloved, our God, who is as the sun to us, always shines, but we don't always see Him — clouds hide His face; but it does not matter what drops may be falling or what clouds may be threatening. If *He* only shines, there will be a rainbow at once. It is said that when we see the rainbow, the shower is over. It is certain that, when Christ comes, our troubles withdraw; when we behold Jesus, our sins vanish, and our doubts and fears subside. When Jesus walks on the waters of the sea, how profound the calm!

"The cedars of Lebanon that he planted." — Psalm 104:16

EBANON'S cedars are emblematic of Christians in that *they owe their planting entirely to the Lord.* This is quite true of every child of God. We are not planted by other mortals, nor by ourselves, but by God. The mysterious hand of the divine Spirit dropped the living seed into a heart which He had Himself prepared for its reception. Every true heir of heaven recognizes the great Farmer as his planter. Moreover, the cedars of Lebanon *are not dependent upon human beings for their watering;* they stand on the lofty rock, unmoistened by human irrigation; and yet our heavenly Father supplies them. Thus it is with Christians who have learned to live by faith. They are independent of humanity, even in temporal things; for their continued maintenance they look to the Lord their God, and to Him alone. The dew of heaven is their portion, and the God of heaven is their fountain. Again, the cedars of Lebanon *are not protected by any mortal power.* They owe nothing to humankind for their preservation from stormy wind and tempest. They are God's trees, kept and preserved by Him, and by Him alone. It is precisely the same with Christians. We are not hothouse plants, sheltered from temptation; we stand in the most exposed position; we have no shelter, no protection, except this, that the broad wings of the eternal God always cover the cedars which He Himself has planted. Like cedars, believers are *full of sap,* having vitality enough to be ever green, even amidst winter's snows. Lastly, the flourishing and majestic condition of the cedar *is to the praise of God only.* The Lord, even the Lord alone has been everything to the cedars, and, therefore David very sweetly puts it in one of the psalms, "Praise the LORD from the earth . . . fruit trees and all cedars." In the believer there is nothing that can magnify humankind; we are planted, nourished, and protected by the Lord's own hand, and to Him let all the glory be ascribed.

"I will remember my covenant." — Genesis 9:15

OTICE the form of the promise. God doesn't say, "And when *you* shall look upon the rainbow, and *you* shall remember My covenant, *then* I will not destroy the earth," but it is gloriously put, not upon *our* memory, which is fickle and frail, but upon *God's* memory, which is infinite and immutable. "Whenever I bring clouds over the earth and the rainbow appears in the clouds, I will remember my covenant between me and you and all living creatures of every kind." Oh! it is not *my* remembering God, it is God's remembering *me* which is the ground of my safety; it is not *my* laying hold of His covenant, but His covenant's laying hold on me. Glory be to God! All of the ramparts and citadels of salvation are secured by divine power, and even the minor towers, which we may imagine might have been left to mortals, are guarded by almighty strength. Even the *remembrance* of the covenant is not left to our memories, for *we* might forget, but our Lord cannot forget the saints whom He has engraved on the palms of His hands. It is with us as with Israel in Egypt; the blood was upon the top and both sides of the doorframe, but the Lord didn't say, "When *you* see the blood I will pass over you," but "When *I* see the blood I will pass over you." My looking to Jesus brings me joy and peace, but it is God's looking to Jesus which secures my salvation and that of all His elect, since it is impossible for our God to look at Christ, our bleeding Surety, and then to be angry with us for sins already punished in Him. No, it is not left up to *us* even to be saved by remembering the covenant. There is no impure blend here — not a single thread of the creature mars the fabric. It is not *of* humankind, neither *by* humankind, but of the Lord alone. We *should* remember the covenant, and we *shall* do it, through divine grace; but the hinge of our safety doesn't hang there — it is God's remembering *us,* not our remembering *Him;* and hence the covenant is *an everlasting covenant.*

"You make me glad by your deeds." — *Psalm 92:4*

O you believe that your sins are forgiven, and that Christ has made a full atonement for them? Then what a joyful Christian *you ought to be!* You should live above the common trials and troubles of the world! Since sin is forgiven, can it matter what happens to you now? Luther said, "Strike, Lord, strike, for my sin is forgiven; if You have but forgiven me, strike as hard as You will;" and in a similar spirit you may say, "Send sickness, poverty, losses, crosses, persecution, what You will, *You have forgiven me,* and my soul is glad." Christian, if you are thus saved, while you are glad, *be grateful and loving.* Cling to that cross which took your sin away; serve Him who served you. "Therefore, I urge you, in view of God's mercy, to offer your bodies as living sacrifices, holy and pleasing to God — this is your spiritual act of worship." Don't let your zeal evaporate in some little outburst of song. Show your love in expressive tokens. Love the brothers and sisters of Him who loved you. If there is a Mephibosheth anywhere who is lame or crippled, help him for Jonathan's sake. If there is a poor tested believer, weep with him, and bear his cross for the sake of Him who wept for you and carried your sins. Since you are thus forgiven freely for Christ's sake, go and tell others the joyful news of pardoning mercy. Don't be content with this unspeakable blessing for yourself alone, but publish abroad the story of the cross. Holy gladness and holy boldness will make you a good preacher, and all the world will be a pulpit for you to preach in. Cheerful holiness is the most forcible of sermons, but the Lord must give it you. Seek it this morning before you go into the world. When it is the Lord's work in which we rejoice, we needn't be afraid of being too happy.

"I am concerned about their suffering."
— *Exodus 3:7*

HE child is cheered as he sings, "My father knows this;" and shouldn't we be comforted as we discern that our dear Friend and tender soul-husband knows all about us?

1. *He is the Physician,* and if He knows all, there is no need for the patient to know. Hush, you silly, fluttering heart, prying, peeping, and suspecting! What you don't know now, you shall know hereafter, and meanwhile Jesus, the beloved Physician, knows your soul in adversities. Why does the patient need to analyze all the medicine, or estimate all the symptoms? This is the Physician's work, not mine; it is my business to trust, and His to prescribe. If He shall write His prescription in coarse characters which I cannot decipher, I won't be uncomfortable because of it; rather, I rely upon His unfailing skill to make all plain in the end, however mysterious the workings.

2. *He is the Master,* and His knowledge is to serve us instead of our own; we are to obey, not to judge: "A servant does not know his master's business." Shall the architect explain his plans to every construction worker on the job? If he knows his own intent, isn't that enough? The vessel on the potter's wheel cannot guess to what pattern it shall be conformed, but if the potter understands his art, what does the ignorance of the clay matter? My Lord must not be cross-examined any more by one so ignorant as I.

3. *He is the Head.* All understanding centers there. What judgment can an arm make? What kind of comprehension does a foot have? All the power to know lies in the head. Why should an arm or a foot have a brain of its own when the head fulfills every intellectual office for it? Here, then, must the believer rest his comfort in sickness, not that he himself can see the end, but that Jesus knows all. Sweet Lord, forever be eye, soul, and head for us, and let's be content to know only what You choose to reveal.

"He went out to the field one evening to meditate."
— *Genesis 24:63*

 IS activity is very admirable. If those who spend so many hours in idle company, light reading, and useless pastimes, could learn wisdom, they would find more profitable society and more interesting engagements in meditation than in the vanities which now have such charms for them. We would all know more, live nearer to God, and grow in grace if we spent more time alone. Meditation chews the cud and extracts the real nutriment from the mental food gathered elsewhere. When Jesus is the theme, meditation is sweet indeed. Isaac found Rebecca while engaged in private musings; many others have found their best beloved there.

His choice of place is likewise very admirable. In the field we have a study surrounded with texts for thought. From the cedar to the hyssop, from the soaring eagle down to the chirping grasshopper, from the blue expanse of heaven to a drop of dew, all things are full of teaching, and when the eye is divinely opened, that teaching flashes upon the mind far more vividly than from written books. Our little rooms are neither as healthy, or suggestive, or agreeable, or so inspiring as the fields. Let's count nothing common or unclean, but feel that all created things point to their Maker, and the field will at once be hallowed.

The season is also very admirable. The season of sunset, as it draws a veil over the day, suits that resting of the soul when earthborn cares yield to the joys of heavenly communion. The glory of the setting sun excites our wonder, and the solemnity of approaching night awakens our awe. If the business of this day will permit it, it would be a good thing, dear reader, if you can spare an hour to walk in the field at evening; but, if not, the Lord is in the town also and will meet with you in your room or in the crowded street. Let your heart go forth to meet Him.

"I will . . . give you a heart of flesh."
— *Ezekiel 36:26*

 heart of flesh is known by its *tenderness concerning sin.* To have indulged a foul imagination, or to have allowed a wild desire to linger even for a moment, is quite enough to make a heart of flesh grieve before the Lord. The heart of stone calls a great iniquity nothing, but this is not true for the heart of flesh.

> "If to the right or left I stray,
> That moment, Lord, reprove;
> And let me weep my life away,
> For having grieved thy love."

The heart of flesh is *tender to God's will.* My will is a great blusterer, and it is hard to subject it to God's will; but when the heart of flesh is given, the will quivers like an aspen leaf in every breath of heaven, and bows like a willow in every breeze of God's Spirit. The natural will is cold, hard iron, which is not to be hammered into form, but the renewed will, like molten metal, is soon molded by the hand of grace. In the fleshy heart there is a *tenderness of affections.* The hard heart doesn't love the Redeemer, but the renewed heart burns with affection towards Him. The hard heart is selfish and coldly demands, "Why should I weep for sin? Why should I love the Lord?" But the heart of flesh says; "Lord, You know that I love You; help me to love You more!" The renewed heart has many privileges; "'Tis here the Spirit dwells, 'tis here that Jesus rests." It is fitted to receive every spiritual blessing, and every blessing comes to it. It is prepared to yield every heavenly fruit to the honor and praise of God, and therefore the Lord delights in it. A tender heart is the best defense against sin, and the best preparation for heaven. A renewed heart stands on its watchtower looking for the coming of the Lord Jesus. Do you have this heart of flesh?

"Ascribe to the LORD the glory due his name."
— *Psalm 29:2*

OD'S glory is the result of His nature and acts. He is glorious in His character, for there is such a store of everything that is holy, and good, and lovely in God, that He must be glorious. The actions which flow from His character are also glorious; but while He intends that they should manifest to His creatures His goodness, and mercy, and justice, He is equally concerned that the glory associated with them should be given only to Himself. Nor is there anything whatever in ourselves in which we may glory; for who makes us different from one another? And what do we have that we didn't receive from the God of all grace? Then how careful should we be *to walk humbly before the Lord!* The moment we glorify ourselves, since there is only room for one glory in the universe, we set ourselves up as rivals to the Most High. Shall the insect of an hour glorify itself against the sun which warmed it into life? Shall a piece of broken pottery exalt itself above the one who shaped it on the wheel? Shall the dust of the desert fight against the whirlwind, or the drops of the ocean struggle with the tempest? "Ascribe to the LORD, O families of nations, ascribe to the LORD glory and strength, ascribe to the LORD the glory due His name." Yet it is, perhaps, one of the hardest struggles of the Christian life to learn this sentence — "Not to us, O LORD, not to us but to Your name be the glory." It is a lesson which God is always teaching us, and teaching us sometimes by the most painful discipline. Let a Christian begin to boast, "I can do everything," without adding "through Him who gives me strength," and before long he will have to groan, "I can do nothing," and lament over himself in the dust. When we do anything for the Lord, and He is pleased to accept what we have done, let's lay our crown at His feet, and exclaim, "Not I, but the grace of God which was with me!"

> *"We ourselves, who have the firstfruits*
> *of the Spirit."* — Romans 8:23

RESENT possession is declared. At this present moment we have the firstfruits of the Spirit. We have repentance, that gem of the first water; faith, that priceless pearl; hope, the heavenly emerald; and love, the glorious ruby. We are already made "new creations in Christ Jesus," by the effectual working of God the Holy Spirit. This is called the firstfruits because *it comes first.* As the wave-sheaf was the first of the harvest, so the spiritual life, and all the graces which adorn that life, are the first operations of the Spirit of God in our souls. *The firstfruits were the pledge of the harvest.* As soon as the Israelite had plucked the first handful of ripe ears, he looked forward with glad anticipation to the time when the wagon should creak beneath the sheaves. So, believer, when God gives us things which are pure, lovely, and of good report, as the work of the Holy Spirit, these are to us the prognostics of the coming glory. *The firstfruits were always holy to the Lord,* and our new nature, with all its powers, is a consecrated thing. The new life is not ours that we should ascribe its excellence to our own merit; it is Christ's image and creation, and is ordained for His glory. But *the firstfruits were not the harvest,* and the works of the Spirit in us at this moment are not the consummation — the perfection is yet to come. We must not boast that we have attained, and so reckon the wave-sheaf to be all the produce of the year: we must hunger and thirst after righteousness, and pant for the day of full redemption. Dear reader, this evening open your mouth wide, and God will fill it. Let the boon in present possession excite in you a sacred greed for more grace. Groan within yourself for higher degrees of consecration, and your Lord will grant them to you, for He is able to do immeasurably more than all we ask or imagine.

"God's unfailing love." — Psalm 52:8

 EDITATE for a while on God's unfailing love. It is *tender love*. With a gentle touch, He heals the brokenhearted, and binds up their wounds. He is as gracious in the manner of His unfailing love as in the matter of it. It *is great unfailing love*. There is nothing little in God; His unfailing love is like Himself — it is infinite. You cannot measure it. His unfailing love is so great that it forgives great sins to great sinners, after great lengths of time, and then gives great favors and great privileges, and raises us up to great enjoyments in the great heaven of the great God. It is *undeserved unfailing love,* as indeed all true unfailing love must be, for deserved unfailing love is only a misnomer for justice. There was no right on the sinner's part to the kind consideration of the Most High; had the rebel been doomed at once to eternal fire he would have richly deserved the doom, and if delivered from wrath, sovereign love alone has found a cause, for there was none in the sinner himself. It *is rich unfailing love*. Some things are great, but have little efficacy in them, but this love is a cordial to your drooping spirits; a golden ointment to your bleeding wounds; a heavenly bandage to your broken bones; a royal chariot for your weary feet; a bosom of love for your trembling heart. It *is manifold mercy and love*. As Bunyan says, "All the flowers in God's garden are double." There is no single mercy. You may think you have but one mercy, but you shall find it to be a whole cluster of mercies. It *is abounding love*. Millions have received it, yet far from its being exhausted, it is as fresh, as full, and as free as ever. It *is unfailing love*. It will never leave you. If this love is within you, God's love will be with you in temptation to keep you from yielding; with you in trouble to prevent you from sinking; with you living to be the light and life of your countenance; and with you dying to be the joy of your soul when earthly comfort is ebbing fast.

"This sickness will not end in death." — *John 11:4*

ROM our Lord's words we learn that there is a limit to sickness. Here is an "in" which means that its ultimate end is restrained, and a there is a limit beyond which it cannot go. Lazarus might pass through death, but death was not to be the end of his sickness. In all sickness, the Lord says to the waves of pain, "Up to now shall you go, but no further." His fixed purpose is not the destruction, but the instruction of His people. Wisdom hangs up the thermometer at the furnace mouth, and regulates the heat.

1. *The limit is encouragingly comprehensive.* The God of providence has limited the time, manner, intensity, repetition, and effects of all our sicknesses; each throb is decreed, each sleepless hour predestined, each relapse ordained, each depression of spirit foreknown, and each sanctifying result eternally purposed. Nothing great or small escapes the ordaining hand of Him who numbers the hairs of our head.

2. *This limit is wisely adjusted* to our strength, to the end designed, and to the grace apportioned. Affliction is not a haphazard event — the weight of every stroke of the rod is accurately measured. He who made no mistakes in balancing the clouds and measuring out the heavens, commits no errors in measuring out the ingredients which constitute the medicine of souls. We cannot allow too much nor be relieved too late.

3. *The limit is tenderly appointed.* The knife of the heavenly Surgeon never cuts deeper than is absolutely necessary. "He does not willingly bring affliction or grief to the children of men." A mother's heart cries, "Spare my child;" but no mother is more compassionate than our gracious God. When we consider how hard-mouthed we are, it is a wonder that we are not driven with a sharper bit. The thought is full of consolation, that He who has fixed the bounds of our habitation, has also fixed the bounds of our tribulation.

"Foreigners have entered the holy places of the Lord's house." — Jeremiah 51:51

 N this account the faces of the Lord's people were covered with shame, for it was a terrible thing that lay persons should intrude into the Holy Place reserved for the priests alone. Everywhere about us we see the same reason for sorrow. How many ungodly people are now being educated with the view of entering into the ministry! What a crying sin is that solemn lie by which our whole population is nominally comprehended in a National Church! How fearful it is that the sacraments should be pressed upon the unconverted, and that among the more enlightened churches of our land there should be such laxity of discipline. If the thousands who will read this portion shall all take this matter before the Lord Jesus this day, He will interfere and avert the evil which will otherwise come upon His church. To adulterate the church is to pollute a well, to pour water upon fire, to sow a fertile field with stones. May we all have grace to maintain in our own proper way the purity of the church, as being an assembly of believers, and not a nation, an unsaved community of unconverted men.

Our zeal must, however, begin at home. Let's examine *ourselves* as to our right to eat at the Lord's table. Let's see to it that we have on our wedding garment, lest we ourselves be intruders in the Lord's sanctuaries. Many are called, but few are chosen; the way is narrow, and the gate is strait. O for grace to come to Jesus properly, with the faith of God's elect. He who struck Uzzah for touching the ark is very jealous of His two sacraments; as a true believer I may approach them freely, as an alien I must not touch them lest I die. Heart searching is the duty of all who are baptized or come to the Lord's table. "Search me, O God, and know my heart; test me and know my anxious thoughts."

*"Then they offered him wine mixed with myrrh, but
he did not take it."* — Mark 15:23

golden truth is couched in the fact that the
Savior put the cup of wine mixed with myrrh
from His lips. On the heights of heaven the
Son of God stood of old, and as He looked
down upon our globe He measured the long
descent to the utmost depths of human misery; He cast up the sum total of all the agonies which
expiation would require, and abated not a jot. He solemnly
determined that to offer a sufficient atoning sacrifice He
must go the whole way, from the highest to the lowest,
from the throne of highest glory to the cross of deepest
woe. This myrrhed cup, with its sleep-inducing influence,
would have kept Him from all but a little of the utmost
limit of misery, therefore He refused it. He would not stop
short of all He had undertaken to allow for His people. Ah,
how many of us have pined after reliefs to our grief which
would have been injurious to us! Reader, did you never
pray for a discharge from hard service or suffering with a
petulant and willful eagerness? Providence has taken from
you the desire of your eyes with a stroke. Say, Christian, if
it had been said, "If you so desire it, that loved one of yours
shall live, but God will be dishonored," could you have put
away the temptation, and said, "your will be done"? Oh, it
is sweet to be able to say, "My Lord, if for other reasons I
need not suffer, yet if I can honor You more by suffering,
and if the loss of my earthly all will bring You glory, then
so let it be. I refuse the comfort, if it comes in the way of
Your honor." O that we thus walked more in the footsteps
of our Lord, cheerfully enduring trial for His sake,
promptly and willingly putting away the thought of self
and comfort when it would interfere with our finishing the
work which He has given us to do. Great grace is needed,
but great grace is provided.

> *"He will stand and shepherd his flock in the strength of the LORD."* — Micah 5:4

HRIST'S reign in His church is that of a *shepherd-king.* He has supremacy, but it is the superiority of a wise and tender shepherd over his needy and loving flock; He commands and receives obedience, but it is the willing obedience of the well-cared-for sheep, rendered joyfully to their beloved Shepherd, whose voice they know so well. He rules by the force of love and the energy of goodness.

His reign is *practical in its character.* It is said, "He will *stand and shepherd.*" The great Head of the church is actively engaged in providing for His people. He doesn't sit down upon the throne in empty state, or hold a scepter without wielding it in government. No, He stands and shepherds. The expression "shepherd," in the Greek, means to do everything expected of a shepherd: to guide, to watch, to preserve, to restore, to tend, as well as to feed.

His reign is *continual in its duration.* It is said, *"He will stand* and shepherd;" not "He will feed now and then, and leave His position;" not, "He will for one day grant a revival, and then on next day leave His church to barrenness." His eyes never slumber, and His hands never rest; His heart never ceases to beat with love, and His shoulders are never weary of carrying His people's burdens.

His reign is *effectually powerful in its action;* "He shall shepherd His flock in the strength of the LORD." Wherever Christ is, there is God; and whatever Christ does is the act of the Most High. Oh! it is a joyful truth to consider that He who stands today representing the interests of His people is very God of very God, to whom every knee shall bow. Happy are we who belong to such a shepherd, whose humanity communes with us, and whose divinity protects us. Let's worship and bow down before Him as the people of His pasture.

"Free me from the trap that is set for me, for you are
my refuge." — Psalm 31:4

UR spiritual foes are the serpent's brood, and seek to trap us using subtlety as a trap. The prayer before us supposes the possibility of the believer being caught like a bird. So deftly does the fowler do his work, that simple ones are soon surrounded by the trap. The text asks that even out of Satan's meshes the captive one may be delivered; this is a proper petition, and one which can be granted: eternal love can rescue the saint from between the jaws of the lion, and out of the belly of hell. It may take a sharp *pull* to save a soul from the trap of temptations, and a mighty pull to extricate a person from the snares of malicious cunning, but the Lord is equal to every emergency, and the most skillfully placed traps of the hunter shall never be able to hold His chosen ones. Woe to those who are so clever at laying traps; they who tempt others shall be destroyed themselves.

"For You are my refuge." What an inexpressible sweetness is to be found in these few words! How joyfully may we encounter toils, and how cheerfully may we endure sufferings, when we can lay hold upon celestial strength. Divine power will tear apart all the toils of our enemies, confound their politics, and frustrate their knavish tricks; he is a happy man who has such matchless might engaged upon his side. Our own strength would be of little service when embarrassed in the traps of base cunning, but the Lord's strength is always available; we only have to invoke it, and we shall find it near at hand. If by faith we are depending alone upon the strength of the mighty God of Israel, we may use our holy reliance as a plea in supplication.

"Lord, evermore Thy face we seek:
Tempted we are, and poor, and weak;
Keep us with lowly hearts, and meek.
Let us not fall. Let us not fall."

"Israel's singer of songs." — 2 Samuel 23:1

MONG all the saints whose lives are recorded in Holy Scripture, David possesses an experience of the most striking, varied, and instructive character. In his history we meet with trials and temptations not to be discovered, as a whole, in other saints of ancient times, and hence he is all the more suggestive a type of our Lord. David knew the trials of people of all ranks and conditions. Kings have their troubles, and David wore a crown: the peasant has his cares, and David handled a shepherd's crook: the wanderer has many hardships, and David lived in the caves of Engedi: the captain has his difficulties, and David found the sons of Zeruiah too hard for him. The psalmist was also tested in his friends, his adviser Ahithophel forsook him, "He who shares my bread has lifted up his heel against me." His worst foes were of his own household: his children were his greatest affliction. The temptations of poverty and wealth, of honor and reproach, of health and weakness, all tried their power upon him. He had temptations from without to disturb his peace, and from within to mar his joy. David no sooner escaped from one trial than he fell into another; no sooner emerged from one season of despondency and alarm, than he was again brought into the lowest depths, and all God's waves and billows rolled over him. It is probably because of this that David's psalms are so universally the delight of experienced Christians. Whatever our frame of mind, whether ecstasy or depression, David has exactly described our emotions. He was an able master of the human heart, because he had been tutored in the best of all schools — the school of heart-felt, personal experience. As we are instructed in the same school, as we mature in grace and in years, we increasingly appreciate David's psalms, and find them to be "green pastures." My soul, let David's experience cheer and counsel you this day.

"They restored Jerusalem as far as the Broad Wall."
— Nehemiah 3:8

 ITIES well fortified have broad walls, and so had Jerusalem in her glory. The New Jerusalem must, in like manner, be surrounded and preserved by a broad wall of nonconformity to the world, and *separation* from its customs and spirit. The tendency of these days is to break down the holy barrier, and make the distinction between the church and the world merely nominal. Professing Christians are no longer strict and Puritanical, questionable literature is read on all hands, frivolous pastimes are currently indulged, and a general laxity threatens to deprive the Lord's peculiar people of those sacred singularities which separate them from sinners. It will be an ill day for the church and the world when the proposed amalgamation shall be complete, and the sons of God and the daughters of men shall be as one: then shall another deluge of wrath be ushered in. Beloved reader, let it be your aim in heart, in word, in dress, in action to maintain the broad wall, remembering that the friendship of this world is enmity against God.

The broad wall afforded a pleasant place of *resort* for the inhabitants of Jerusalem. From they wall they had a commanding view of the surrounding country. This reminds us of the Lord's exceedingly broad commandments, in which we walk at liberty in communion with Jesus, overlooking the scenes of earth, and looking out towards the glories of heaven. Separated from the world, and denying ourselves all ungodliness and fleshly lusts, we are nevertheless not in prison, nor restricted within narrow bounds; no, we walk at liberty, because we keep His precepts. Come, reader, this evening walk with God in His statutes. As friend met friend upon the city wall, so meet your God in the way of holy prayer and meditation. You have a right to travel the ramparts and citadels of salvation, for you are a freeman of the royal town, a citizen of the metropolis of the universe.

"He who refreshes others will himself be refreshed."
— *Proverbs 11:25*

ERE we are taught the great lesson, that to get, we must give; that to accumulate, we must scatter; that to make ourselves happy, we must make others happy; and that in order to become spiritually vigorous, we must seek the spiritual good of others. In watering others, we are ourselves watered. How? Our efforts to be useful *bring out our powers for usefulness.* We have latent talents and dormant faculties, which are brought to light by exercise. Our strength for work is hidden even from ourselves, until we venture forth to fight the Lord's battles, or to climb the mountains of difficulty. We don't know what tender sympathies we possess until we try to dry the widow's tears, and soothe the orphan's grief. We often find, in attempting to teach others, that we *gain instruction for ourselves.* Oh, what gracious lessons some of us have learned at sick beds! We went to teach the Scriptures, we came away blushing that we knew so little of them. In our conversation with poor saints, we are taught the way of God more perfectly for ourselves and get a deeper insight into divine truth. So that watering others *makes us humble.* We discover how much grace there is where we had not looked for it; and how much the poor saint may outstrip us in knowledge. Our own *comfort is also increased* by our working for others. We try to cheer them up, and the consolation gladdens our own heart. Like the two men in the snow; one chafed the other's limbs to keep him from dying, and in so doing kept his own blood in circulation, and saved his own life. The poor widow of Sarepta gave from her scanty store a supply for the prophet's wants, and from that day she never again knew what want was. "Give, and it will be given to you. A good measure, pressed down, shaken together and running over, will be poured into your lap."

*"I have not said to Jacob's descendants,
Seek me in vain."* — *Isaiah 45:19*

E can gain great comfort by considering what God has *not* said. What He *has* said is inexpressibly full of comfort and delight; what He has *not* said is scarcely less rich in consolation. It was one of these *"has not saids"* which preserved the kingdom of Israel in the days of Jeroboam the son of Joash, for "the LORD had not said that He would blot out the name of Israel from under heaven." 2 Kings 14:27. In our text we have an assurance that God *will* answer prayer, because He has "not said to Jacob's descendants, 'Seek Me in vain.' " You who write bitter things against yourselves should remember that, let your doubts and fears say what they will, if *God* has not cut you off from mercy, there is no room for despair: even the voice of conscience is of little weight if it is not seconded by the voice of God. What God *has* said, tremble at! But do not allow your vain imaginings to overwhelm you with despondency and sinful despair. Many timid persons have been vexed by the suspicion that there may be something in God's decree which shuts *them* out from hope, but here is a complete refutation to that troublesome fear, for no true seeker can be decreed to wrath. "I have not spoken in secret, from somewhere in a land of darkness; I have not said," even in the secret of my unsearchable decree, "Seek Me in vain." God has clearly revealed that He *will* hear the prayer of those who call upon Him, and that declaration cannot be contravened. He has so firmly, so truthfully, so righteously spoken, that there can be no room for doubt. He doesn't reveal His mind in unintelligible words, but He speaks plainly and positively, "Ask, and you shall receive." Believe, O trembler, this sure truth — that prayer must and shall be heard, and that never, even in the secrets of eternity, has the Lord said to any living soul, "Seek Me in vain."

"O daughters of Jerusalem, I charge you — if you find my lover, what will you tell him? Tell him I am faint with love." — Song of Songs 5:8

UCH is the language of the believer panting after present fellowship with Jesus, *he is faint with love for his Lord.* Gracious souls are never perfectly at ease unless they are in a state of nearness to Christ; for when they are away from Him they lose their peace. The nearer to Him, the nearer to the perfect calm of heaven; the nearer to Him, the fuller the heart is, not only of peace, but of life, and vigor, and joy, for these all depend on constant communication with Jesus. What the sun is to the day, what the moon is to the night, what the dew is to the flower, such is Jesus Christ to us. What bread is to the hungry, clothing to the naked, the shadow of a great rock to the traveler in a weary land, such is Jesus Christ to us; and, therefore, if we are not consciously one with Him, little marvel if our spirit cries in the words of the Song, "O daughters of Jerusalem, I charge you — if you find my lover, what will you tell him? Tell him I am faint with love." *This earnest longing after Jesus has a blessing attending it:* "Blessed are those who hunger and thirst for righteousness;" and therefore, supremely blessed are they who thirst after the Righteous One. Blessed is that hunger, since it comes from God: if I may not have the full-blown blessedness of being filled, I would seek the same blessedness in its sweet bud-pining in emptiness and eagerness until I am filled with Christ. If I may not feed on Jesus, it shall be next door to heaven to hunger and thirst after Him. There is a hallowedness about that hunger, since it sparkles among the beatitudes of our Lord. But the blessing *involves a promise.* Such hungry ones *"shall be filled"* with what they are desiring. If Christ thus causes us to long after Himself, He will certainly satisfy those longings; and when He does come to us, as come He will, *oh, how sweet it will be!*

"The unsearchable riches of Christ." — *Ephesians 3:8*

Y Master has riches beyond the count of arithmetic, the measurement of reason, the dream of imagination, or the eloquence of words. They are *unsearchable!* You may look, and study, and weigh, but Jesus is a greater Savior than you think Him to be when your thoughts are at the greatest. My Lord is more ready to pardon than you to sin, more able to forgive than you to transgress. My Master is more willing to supply your wants than you are to confess them. Never tolerate low thoughts of my Lord Jesus. When you put the crown on His head, you will only crown Him with silver when He deserves gold. *My Master has riches of happiness to give to you now.* He can make you to lie down in green pastures, and lead you beside quiet waters. There is no music like the music of His pipe, when He is the Shepherd and you are the sheep, and you lie down at His feet. There is no love like His, neither earth nor heaven can match it. To know Christ and to be found in Him — oh! this is life, this is joy, this is marrow and fatness, wine on the sediment well refined. My Master doesn't treat His servants churlishly; He gives to them as a king gives to a king; He gives them two heavens — a heaven below in serving Him here, and a heaven above in delighting in Him forever. *His unsearchable riches will be best known in eternity.* He will give you all you need on the way to heaven; your place of defense shall be the munitions of rocks, your bread shall be given to you, and your waters shall be sure; but it is there, THERE, where you shall hear the song of them that triumph, the shout of them that feast, and shall have a face-to-face view of the glorious and loved one. The unsearchable riches of Christ! This is the tune for the minstrels of earth, and the song for the harpers of heaven. Lord, teach us more and more of Jesus, and we will speak of the good news to others.

*"The sound of weeping and of crying will be heard . . .
no more."* — Isaiah 65:19

HE glorified weep no more, for *all outward causes of grief are gone.* There are no broken friendships, nor blighted prospects in heaven. Poverty, famine, peril, persecution, and slander, are unknown there. No pain distresses, no thought of death or bereavement saddens. They weep no more, for *they are perfectly sanctified.* No "sinful, unbelieving heart" prompts them to depart from the living God; they are without fault before His throne, and are fully conformed to His image. Well may they cease to mourn who have ceased to sin. They weep no more, because *all fear of change is past.* They know that they are eternally secure. Sin is shut out, and they are shut in. They dwell within a city which shall never be stormed; they bask in a sun which shall never set; they drink of a river which shall never dry; they pluck fruit from a tree which shall never wither. Countless cycles may revolve, but eternity shall not be exhausted, and while eternity endures, their immortality and blessedness shall co-exist with it. They are forever with the Lord. They weep no more, because *every desire is fulfilled.* They cannot wish for anything which they don't already have in their possession. Eye and ear, heart and hand, judgment, imagination, hope, desire, will, all the faculties, are completely satisfied; and imperfect as our present ideas are of the things which God has prepared for them that love Him, yet we know enough, by the revelation of the Spirit, that the saints above are supremely blessed. The joy of Christ, which is an infinite fullness of delight, is in them. They bathe themselves in the bottomless, shoreless sea of infinite beatitude. That same joyful rest remains for us. It may not be far distant. Before long the weeping willow shall be exchanged for the palm branch of victory, and sorrow's dewdrops will be transformed into the pearls of everlasting bliss. "Therefore encourage each other with these words."

"That Christ may dwell in your hearts
through faith." — *Ephesians 3:17*

EYOND measure it is desirable that we, as believers, should have the person of Jesus constantly before us, to inflame our love towards Him, and to increase our knowledge of Him. I would to God that my readers were all entered as diligent scholars in Jesus' college, students of Corpus Christi, or the body of Christ, resolved to attain to a good degree in the learning of the cross. But to have Jesus always near, the heart must be full of Him, welling up with His love, even to overrunning; hence the apostle prays "that Christ may *dwell in your hearts.*" See how near he would have Jesus be! You cannot get a subject closer to you than to have it in the heart itself. *"That Christ may dwell;"* not that Christ may call upon you sometimes, as a casual visitor enters into a house and stays overnight, but that Christ may *dwell;* that He may become the Lord and Tenant of your inmost being, never to leave.

Observe the words — that Christ may dwell *in your hearts,* that best room of the house of mortals; not in your thoughts alone, but in your affections; not merely in the mind's meditations, but in the heart's emotions. We should pant after love for Christ of a most abiding character, not a love that flames up and then dies out into the darkness of a few embers, but a constant flame, fed by sacred fuel, like the fire upon the altar which never went out. This cannot be accomplished except by faith. Faith must be strong, or love will not be fervent; the root of the flower must be healthy, or we cannot expect the bloom to be sweet. Faith is the lily's root, and love is the lily's bloom. Now, reader, Jesus cannot be in your heart's love unless you have a firm hold on Him by your heart's faith. Therefore, pray that you may always trust Christ in order that you may always love Him. If love is cold, you can be confident that faith is drooping.

"One who breaks open the way will go up before them."
— *Micah 2:13*

 NASMUCH as Jesus has gone before us, things are not the same as they would have been had He never passed that way. He has *conquered every foe* that obstructed the way. Cheer up now, you faint-hearted warrior. Not only has Christ traveled the road, but He has slain your enemies. Do you dread sin? He has nailed it to His cross. Do you fear death? He has been the death of Death. Are you afraid of hell? He has barred it against the advent of any of His children; they shall never see the gulf of eternal damnation. Whatever foes may be before the Christian, they are all overcome. There are lions, but their teeth are broken; there are serpents, but their fangs are extracted; there are rivers, but they are bridged or fordable; there are flames, but we wear that matchless garment which renders us invulnerable to fire. The sword that has been forged against us is already blunted; the instruments of war which the enemy is preparing have already lost their point. God has taken away in the person of Christ all the power that anything can have to hurt us. Well then, the army may safely march on, and you may go joyously along your journey, for all your enemies are conquered beforehand. What shall you do but march on to take the prey? They are beaten, they are vanquished; all you have to do is to divide the spoil. You shall, it is true, often engage in combat; but your fight shall be with a vanquished foe. His head is broken; he may attempt to injure you, but his strength shall not be sufficient for his malicious design. Your victory shall be easy, and your treasure shall be beyond all count.

> "Proclaim aloud the Savior's fame,
> Who bears *the Breaker's* wond'rous name;
> Sweet name; and it becomes him well,
> Who breaks down earth, sin, death, and hell."

*"If a fire breaks out and spreads into thornbushes so
that it burns shocks of grain or standing grain or
the whole field, the one who started the fire must
make restitution."* — Exodus 22:6

UT what restitution can he make who casts abroad the firebrands of error, or the coals of lasciviousness, and sets men's souls on a blaze with the fire of hell? The guilt is inestimable, and the result is irretrievable. If such an offender be forgiven, what grief it will cause him in retrospect, since he can't undo the mischief which he has done! An ill example may kindle a flame which years of amended character cannot quench. To burn the food of man is bad enough, but how much worse to destroy the soul! It may be useful for us to reflect how far we may have been guilty in the past, and to inquire whether, even in the present, there might yet be evil in us which has a tendency to bring damage to the souls of our relatives, friends, or neighbors.

The fire of strife is a terrible evil when it breaks out in a Christian church. Where converts were multiplied, and God was glorified, jealousy and envy do the devil's work most effectually. Where the golden grain was being housed, to reward the toil of the great Boaz, the fire of enmity comes in and leaves little else but smoke and a heap of blackness. Woe to those by whom offenses come. May they never come through us, for although we cannot make restitution, we shall certainly be the chief sufferers if we are the chief offenders. Those who feed the fire deserve just censure, but he who first kindles it is most to blame. Discord usually takes first hold upon the thorns; it is nurtured among the hypocrites and base professing Christians in the church, and away it spreads among the righteous, blown by the winds of hell, and no one knows where it may end. O Lord and giver of peace, make us peacemakers, and never let us aid and abet the men of strife, or even unintentionally cause the least division among Your people.

"His fruit is sweet to my taste." — *Song of Songs 2:3*

AITH, in Scripture, is spoken of under the emblem of all the senses. It is *sight:* "Turn to Me and be saved." It is *hearing:* "Hear Me, that your soul may live." Faith is *smelling:* "All Your robes are fragrant with myrrh and aloes and cassia;" "Your name is like perfume poured out." Faith is spiritual *touch.* By this faith the woman came behind and touched the hem of Christ's garment, and by this we handle the things of the good word of life. Faith is equally the spirit's *taste.* "How sweet are Your words to my taste, sweeter than honey to my mouth!" "Unless you eat the flesh of the Son of Man and drink His blood, you have no life in you."

This *"taste"* is faith *in one of its highest operations.* One of the first performances of faith is *hearing.* We hear the voice of God, not with the outward ear alone, but with the inward ear; we hear it as God's Word, and we believe it to be so; that is the "hearing" of faith. Then our minds *look* upon the truth as it is presented to us; that is to say, we understand it, we perceive its meaning; that is the "seeing" of faith. Next we discover its preciousness; we begin to admire it, and find how fragrant it is; that is faith in its *"smell."* Then we appropriate the mercies which are prepared for us in Christ; that is faith in its *"touch."* Hence follow the enjoyments, peace, delight, communion, which are faith in its "taste." Any one of these acts of faith is saving. To hear Christ's voice as the sure voice of God in the soul will save us; but that which gives true enjoyment is the aspect of faith wherein Christ, by holy taste, is received into us, and made, by inward and spiritual understanding of His sweetness and preciousness, to be the food of our souls. It is then we "delight to sit in His shade," and find His fruit is sweet to our taste.

"If you believe with all your heart, you may."
— *Acts 8:37*

HESE words may answer your scruples, devout reader, concerning *the sacraments*. Perhaps you say, "I am afraid to be baptized; it is such a solemn thing to confess myself to be dead with Christ, and buried with Him. I don't feel free to come to the Master's table; I am afraid of eating and drinking damnation to myself, not discerning the Lord's body." Ah! poor trembler, Jesus has given you freedom; don't be afraid. If a stranger came to your house, he would stand at the door, or wait in the hall; he wouldn't dream of intruding uninvited into your living room — he is not at home: but your child moves very freely about the house; and so is it with the child of God. A stranger may not intrude where a child may venture. When the Holy Spirit has allowed you to feel the spirit of adoption, you may come to Christian sacraments without fear. The same rule holds true for the *Christian's inward privileges*. You think, poor seeker, that you are not allowed to rejoice with unspeakable joy and full of glory; if you are permitted to get inside Christ's door, or sit at the base of His table, you would be very content. Ah! but you shall not have fewer privileges than the very greatest. God makes no differentiation in His love for His children. A child is a child to Him; He will not make him a hired servant; but he shall feast upon the fatted calf, and shall have the music and the dancing as much as if he had never gone astray. When Jesus comes into the heart, He issues a general license to delight in the Lord. No chains are worn in the court of King Jesus. Our admission into full privileges may be gradual, but it is sure. Perhaps our reader is saying, "I wish I could enjoy the promises, and walk freely in my Lord's commands." "If you believe with all your heart, you may." Loose the chains around your neck, O captive daughter, for Jesus makes you free.

"He ordained his covenant forever." — *Psalm 111:9*

HE Lord's people delight in the covenant itself. It is an unfailing source of consolation to them as often as the Holy Spirit leads them into its banqueting house and waves its banner of love. They delight to contemplate *the antiquity* of that covenant, remembering that before the daystar knew its place, or planets ran their rotations, the interests of the saints were made secure in Christ Jesus. It is peculiarly pleasing to them to remember *the sureness* of the covenant, while meditating upon the "faithful love promised to David." They delight to celebrate it as "signed, and sealed, and ratified, in all things ordered well." It often makes their hearts expand with joy to think of its *immutability*, as a covenant which neither time nor eternity, life nor death, shall ever be able to violate — a covenant as old as eternity and as everlasting as the Rock of ages. They rejoice also to feast upon *the fullness* of this covenant, for they see in it all things provided for them. God is their portion, Christ their companion, the Spirit their Comforter, earth their shelter, and heaven their home. They see in it an inheritance reserved and entailed to every soul possessing an interest in its ancient and eternal deed of gift. Their eyes sparkled when they saw it as a treasure-trove in the Bible; but oh! how their souls were gladdened when they saw in the last will and testament of their divine kinsman, that it was bequeathed to them! More especially it is the pleasure of God's people to contemplate *the graciousness* of this covenant. They see that the law was made void because it was a covenant of works and depended upon merit, but this they perceive to be enduring because grace is the basis, grace the condition, grace the strain, grace the bulwark, grace the foundation, grace the capstone. The covenant is a treasury of wealth, a granary of food, a fountain of life, a storehouse of salvation, a charter of peace, and a haven of joy.

"As soon as all the people saw Jesus, they were
overwhelmed with wonder and ran to greet him."
— *Mark 9:15*

OW great the difference between Moses and Jesus! When the prophet of Horeb had been on the mountain forty days, he underwent a kind of transfiguration, so that his countenance shone with exceeding brightness, and he put a veil over his face, for the people could not endure to look upon his glory. Not so our Savior. He had been transfigured with a greater glory than that of Moses, and yet, it is not written that the people were blinded by the blaze of His countenance, but rather they were amazed, and running to Him they saluted Him. The glory of the law repels, but the greater glory of Jesus attracts. Although Jesus is holy and just, also blended with His purity is so much truth and grace that sinners run to Him amazed at His goodness, fascinated by His love; they salute Him, become His disciples, and take Him to be their Lord and Master. Reader, it may be that just now you are blinded by the dazzling brightness of the law of God. You feel its claims on your conscience, but you can't keep it in your life. Not that you find fault with the law; on the contrary, it commands your profoundest esteem. Even so, the law doesn't draw you to God; you are rather hardened in heart, and are verging towards desperation. Ah, poor heart! turn your eye from Moses, with all his repelling splendor, and look to Jesus, resplendent with milder glories. Behold His flowing wounds and thorn-crowned head! He is the Son of God, and therein He is greater than Moses. More importantly, He is the Lord of love, and therein more tender than the lawgiver. He bore the wrath of God, and in His death revealed more of God's justice than Sinai on fire, but that justice is now vindicated, and henceforth it is the guardian of believers in Jesus. Look, sinner, to the bleeding Savior, and as you feel the attraction of His love, fly to His arms, and you shall be saved.

"How long will they refuse to believe in me?"
— Numbers 14:11

TRIVE *with all diligence to keep out that monster unbelief.* It so dishonors Christ, that He will withdraw His visible presence if we insult Him by indulging it. It is true it is a weed, the seeds of which we can never entirely extract from the soil, but we must aim at its root with zeal and perseverance. Among hateful things it is the most to be abhorred. Its injurious nature is so venomous that he that exercises it and he upon whom it is exercised are both hurt thereby. In your situation, O believer! it is most wicked, for the mercies of your Lord in the past increase your guilt in doubting Him now. When you do distrust the Lord Jesus, He may well cry out, "Now then, I will crush you as a cart crushes when loaded with grain." This is crowning His head with thorns of the sharpest kind. It is very cruel for a well-beloved wife to mistrust a kind and faithful husband. The sin is needless, foolish, and unwarranted. Jesus has never given the slightest ground for suspicion, and it is hard to be doubted by those to whom our conduct is uniformly affectionate and true. Jesus is the Son of the Highest, and has unbounded wealth; it is shameful to doubt Omnipotence and distrust all-sufficiency. The cattle on a thousand hills will suffice for our most hungry feeding, and the granaries of heaven are not likely to be emptied by our eating. If Christ were only a cistern, we might soon exhaust His fullness, but who can drain a fountain? Myriads of spirits have drawn their supplies from Him, and not one of them has murmured at the scantiness of His resources. Away, then, with this lying traitor unbelief, for his only errand is to cut the bonds of communion and make us mourn an absent Savior. Bunyan tells us that unbelief has "as many lives as a cat:" if so, let's kill one life now, and continue the work until the whole nine are gone. Down with you, you traitor, my heart despises you.

"Into your hands I commit my spirit; redeem me,
O LORD, the God of truth." — *Psalm 31:5*

 HESE words have been frequently used by holy men in their hour of departure. We may profitably consider them this evening. The object of the faithful person's concern for another in life and death is not his body or his estate, but his spirit; this is his choice treasure — if this is safe, all is well. What is this mortal state compared with the soul? The believer commits his soul to the hand of his God; it came from Him, it is His own, He has in the past sustained it, He is able to keep it, and it is most fit that He should receive it. All things are safe in Jehovah's hands; what we entrust to the Lord will be secure, both now and in that day of days towards which we are hastening. It is peaceful living, and glorious dying, to repose in the care of heaven. At all times we should commit our all to Jesus' faithful hand; then, though life may hang on a thread, and adversities may multiply as the sands of the sea, our soul shall dwell at ease, and delight itself in quiet resting places.

"Redeem me, O LORD, the God of truth." Redemption is a solid basis for confidence. David had not known Calvary as we have, but temporal redemption cheered him; and won't eternal redemption yet more sweetly console us? Past deliverances are strong pleas for present assistance. What the Lord has done He will do again, for He does not change. He is faithful to His promises and gracious to His saints; He will not turn away from His people.

> "Though Thou slay me I will trust,
> Praise Thee even from the dust,
> Prove, and tell it as I prove,
> Thine unutterable love.
>
> Thou mayst chasten and correct,
> But Thou never canst neglect;
> Since the ransom price is paid,
> On Thy love my hope is stay'd."

"Olive oil for the light." — *Exodus 25:6*

Y soul, how much you need this, for your lamp will not burn for very long without it. Your snuff will smoke and become an offense if light is gone, and gone it will be if oil is absent. You have no oil well springing up in your human nature, and therefore you must go to them that sell and buy for yourself, or like the foolish virgins, you will have to cry, "My lamp is going out." Even the consecrated lamps could not give light without oil; though they shone in the tabernacle they needed to be fed, though no rough winds blew upon them they required to be trimmed, and your need is equally as great. Under the most happy circumstances you cannot give light for another hour unless the fresh oil of grace is given to you.

It was not every oil that might be used in the Lord's service; neither the petroleum which exudes so plentifully from the earth, nor the produce of fishes, nor that extracted from nuts would be accepted; one oil only was selected, and that the best olive oil. Pretended grace from natural goodness, fancied grace from priestly hands, or imaginary grace from outward ceremonies will never serve the true saint of God; he knows that the Lord would not be pleased with rivers of such oil. He goes to the olive press of Gethsemane, and draws his supplies from Him who was crushed therein. The oil of gospel grace is pure and free of sediment, and hence the light which feeds on it is clear and bright. Our churches are the Savior's golden candelabra, and if they are to be lights in this dark world, they must have a great supply of holy oil. Let's pray for ourselves, our ministers, and our churches, that they may never lack oil for the light. Truth, holiness, joy, knowledge, love, these are all beams of the sacred light, but we cannot emit them unless, in private, we receive oil from God the Holy Spirit.

"Sing, O barren woman." — *Isaiah 54:1*

HOUGH we have brought forth some fruit to Christ, and have a joyful hope that we are "plants of His own right hand planting," yet there are times when we feel very barren. Prayer is lifeless, love is cold, faith is weak, each grace in the garden of our heart languishes and droops. We are like flowers in the hot sun, requiring the refreshing shower. In such a condition what are we to do? The text is addressed to us in just such a state. *"Sing, O barren woman . . . burst into song, shout for joy."* But what can I sing about? I cannot talk about the present, and even the past looks full of barrenness. Ah! I *can* sing of *Jesus Christ*. I can talk of visits which the Redeemer has paid to me in the past; or if not of these, I can magnify the great love with which He loved His people when He came from the heights of heaven for their redemption. I will go to the cross again. Come, my soul, you were once burdened, and you rid yourself of your burden there. Go to Calvary again. Perhaps that very cross which gave you life may give you fruitfulness. What is my barrenness? It is the platform for His fruit-creating power. What is my desolation? It is the dark setting for the sapphire of His everlasting love. I will go in poverty, I will go in helplessness, I will go in all my shame and backsliding, I will tell Him that I am still His child, and in confidence in His faithful heart, even I, the barren one, will sing and cry aloud.

Sing, believer, for it will cheer your own heart, and the hearts of other desolate ones. Sing on, for now that you are really ashamed of being barren, you will be fruitful soon; now that God makes you *loath* to be without fruit, He will soon cover you with clusters. The experience of our barrenness is painful, but the Lord's visitations are delightful. A sense of our own poverty drives us to Christ, and that is where we need to be, for in Him is our fruit found.

"Have mercy on me, O God." — *Psalm 51:1*

HEN Dr. Carey was suffering from a dangerous illness, the inquiry was made, "If this sickness should prove fatal, what passage would you select as the text for your funeral sermon?" He replied, "Oh, I feel that such a poor sinful creature as myself is unworthy of having anything said about him; but if a funeral sermon must be preached, let it be from the words: 'Have mercy on me, O God, according to Your unfailing love; according to your great compassion blot out my transgressions.' " In the same spirit of humility he directed in his will that the following inscription and nothing more should be engraved on his gravestone: —

WILLIAM CAREY, BORN AUGUST 17th, 1761:

DIED —

"A wretched, poor, and helpless worm
On Thy kind arms I fall."

Only on the footing of free grace can the most experienced and most honored of the saints approach their God. The best of us are conscious above all others that we are mere mortals at best. Empty boats float high, but heavily laden vessels are low in the water; merely professing Christians can boast, but true children of God cry for mercy upon their unprofitableness. We need the Lord to have mercy upon our good works, our prayers, our preachings, our alms-givings, and our holiest things. The blood was not only sprinkled upon the doorposts of Israel's dwelling houses, but upon the sanctuary, the mercy seat, and the altar, because as sin intrudes into our holiest things, the blood of Jesus is needed to purify them from defilement. If mercy needs to be exercised towards our duties, what shall be said of our sins? How sweet the remembrance that inexhaustible mercy is waiting to be gracious to us, to restore our backslidings, and make our broken bones rejoice!

*"As long as he is a Nazirite, he must not eat
anything that comes from the grapevine, not even
the seeds or skins."* — Numbers 6:4

 AZIRITES had taken, among other vows, one which excluded them from the use of wine. In order that they might not violate the obligation, they were forbidden to drink the vinegar of wine or strong liquors, and to make the rule still more clear, they were not to touch the unfermented juice of grapes, nor even to eat the fruit either fresh or dried. In order, altogether, to secure the integrity of the vow, they were not even allowed anything that had to do with the vine; they were, in fact, to avoid the appearance of evil. Surely this is a lesson to the Lord's separated ones, teaching them to come away from sin in every form, to avoid not merely its grosser shapes, but even its spirit and similitude. An uncompromising walk is quite despised these days, but rest assured, dear reader, it is both the safest and the happiest. He who yields a point or two to the world is in fearful peril; he who eats the grapes of Sodom will soon drink the wine of Gomorrah. A little crevice in the dike in Holland lets in the sea, and the gap speedily swells until a province is drowned. Worldly conformity, in any degree, is a snare to the soul, and makes it more and more liable to presumptuous sins. Moreover, as the Nazirite who drank grape juice could not be quite sure whether it might not have endured a degree of fermentation, and consequently could not be clear in heart that his vow was intact, so the yielding, temporizing Christian cannot wear a conscience void of offense, without feeling that the inward monitor is in doubt of him. We do not need to doubt about doubtful things; they are wrong to us. We must not flirt with things that tempt us, but flee from them with speed. Better be sneered at as a Puritan than be despised as a hypocrite. Walking carefully may involve quite a bit of self-denial, but it has compensatory pleasures of its own which more than suffice.

"Wait for the LORD." — *Psalm 27:14*

 T may seem an easy thing to *wait*, but it is one of the postures which a Christian doesn't learn without years of teaching. Marching and quick-marching are much easier for God's soldiers than standing still. There are hours of perplexity when the most willing spirit, anxiously desirous to serve the Lord, doesn't know what part to take. Then what shall it do? Vex itself by despair? Fly back in cowardice, turn to the right hand in fear, or rush forward in presumption? No, but simply wait. *Wait in prayer,* however. Call upon God, and spread the situation before Him; tell Him your difficulty, and plead His promise of aid. In dilemmas between one duty and another, it is sweet to be humble as a child, and *wait with simplicity of soul* upon the Lord. It is sure to be well with us when we feel and know our own folly, and are heartily willing to be guided by the will of God. But *wait in faith.* Express your unstaggering confidence in Him; for unfaithful, untrusting waiting, is but an insult to the Lord. Believe that if He keeps you tarrying even until midnight, yet He will come at the right time; the vision shall come and shall not linger. *Wait in quiet patience,* not rebelling because you are under the affliction, but blessing your God for it. Never murmur against the second cause, as the children of Israel did against Moses; never wish you could go back to the world again, but accept the situation as it is, and put it as it stands, simply and with your whole heart, without any self-will, into the hand of your covenant God, saying, "Now, Lord, not my will, but Yours be done. I don't know what to do; I am brought to extremities, but I will wait until You shall halt the floods, or drive back my foes. I will wait, if You keep me many a day, for my heart is fixed upon You alone, O God, and my spirit waits for You in the full conviction that You will yet be my joy and my salvation, my refuge and my strong tower."

"Heal me, O LORD, and I will be healed."
— Jeremiah 17:14
"I have seen his ways, but I will heal him."
— Isaiah 57:18

T is the sole prerogative of God to remove spiritual disease. Natural disease may be instrumentally healed by mortals, but even then the honor is to be given to God who gives virtue to medicine, and bestows power to the human frame to cast off disease. As for spiritual sicknesses, these remain with the great Physician alone; He claims it as His prerogative, "I put to death and I bring to life, I have wounded and I will heal;" and one of the Lord's choice titles is Jehovah Rophi, the Lord that heals you. "I will heal your wounds," is a promise which could not come from the lips of a mortal, but only from the mouth of the eternal God. On this account the psalmist cried to the Lord, "O Lord, heal me, for my bones are in agony," and again, "Heal me, for I have sinned against You." For this, also, the godly praise the name of the Lord, saying, "He heals all our diseases." He who made us can restore us; He who was at first the creator of our nature can create it anew. What a transcendent comfort it is that in the person of Jesus "all the fullness of the Deity lives in bodily form!" My soul, whatever your disease may be, this great Physician can heal you. If He is God, there can be no limit to His power. Come then with the blind eye of darkened understanding, come with the limping foot of wasted energy, come with the maimed hand of weak faith, the fever of an angry temper, or the ague of shivering despondency, come just as you are, for He who is God can certainly restore you to health. None shall restrain the healing virtue which proceeds from Jesus our Lord. Legions of devils have been made to own the power of the beloved Physician, and never once has He been baffled. All His patients have been cured in the past and shall be in the future, and you shall be one among them, my friend, if you would just rest in Him this night.

"Wait in hope for my arm." — *Isaiah 51:5*

 N seasons of severe trial, Christians have nothing on earth in which to trust, and we are therefore compelled to cast ourselves on our God alone. When our vessel is tilting so far over it is in danger of capsizing, and no human deliverance can avail, we must simply and entirely trust ourselves to the providence and care of God. Happy storm that wrecks us on such a rock as this! O blessed hurricane that drives the soul to God and God alone! There is no getting at our God sometimes because of the multitude of our friends; but when we are so poor, so friendless, so helpless that we have nowhere else to turn, we fly into our Father's arms, and are blessedly clasped therein! When we are burdened with troubles so pressing and so peculiar, that we cannot tell them to anyone but our God, we may be thankful for them; for we will learn more of our Lord then than at any other time. Oh, tempest-tossed believer, it is a happy trouble that drives you to your Father! Now that you have only your God in which to trust, see that you put your full confidence in Him. Do not dishonor your Lord and Master by unworthy doubts and fears; but be strong in faith, giving glory to God. Show the world that your God is worth ten thousand worlds to you. Show the wealthy how rich you are in your poverty when the Lord God is your helper. Show the strong how strong you are in your weakness when underneath you are the everlasting arms. Now is the time for feats of faith and valiant exploits. Be strong and very courageous, and the Lord your God shall certainly, as surely as He built the heavens and the earth, glorify Himself in your weakness, and magnify His might in the midst of your distress. The grandeur of the arch of heaven would be spoiled if the sky were supported by a single visible column, and your faith would lose its glory if it rested on anything discernible by the carnal eye. May the Holy Spirit let you rest in Jesus this closing day of the month.

"If we walk in the light, as he is in the light."
— *1 John 1:7*

 S He is in the light! Can we ever attain to this? Shall we ever be able to walk as clearly in the light as He whom we call "Our Father," of whom it is written, "God is light; in Him there is no darkness at all"? Certainly, this is the model which it sets before us, for the Savior Himself said, "Be perfect, therefore, as your heavenly Father is perfect;" and although we may feel that we can never rival the perfection of God, yet we are to seek after it, and never to be satisfied until we attain to it. The youthful artist, as he grasps his first pencil, can hardly hope to equal Raphael or Michelangelo, but still, if he didn't have a noble *beau ideal* before his mind, he would only attain to something very mean and ordinary. But what is meant by the expression that the Christian is to walk in light as God is in the light? We conceive it to mean *likeness*, but not *degree*. We are as truly in the light, we are as heartily in the light, we are as sincerely in the light, as honestly in the light, though we cannot be there in the same measure. I cannot dwell in the sun. It is too bright a place for my residence, but I can *walk* in the light of the sun; and so, though I cannot attain to that perfection of purity and truth which belongs to the Lord of hosts by nature as the infinitely good, yet I can set the Lord always before me, and strive, by the help of the indwelling Spirit, after conformity to His image. That famous old commentator, John Trapp, says, "We may be in the light as God is in the light for *quality*, but not for *equality*." We are to have the same light, and are as truly to have it and walk in it as God does, though, as for equality with God in His holiness and purity, that must be left until we cross the Jordan and enter into the perfection of the Most High. Notice that the blessings of sacred fellowship and perfect purifying are bound up with walking in the light.

> *"You guide me with your counsel, and afterward you*
> *will take me into glory."* — Psalm 73:24

HE Psalmist felt his need of divine guidance. He had just been discovering the foolishness of his own heart, and lest he should be constantly led astray by it, he resolved that God's counsel should henceforth guide him. A sense of our own folly is a great step towards being wise, when it leads us to rely on the wisdom of the Lord. The blind man leans on a friend's arm and reaches home in safety, and so should we give ourselves up implicitly to divine guidance, doubting nothing; assured that, although we cannot see, it is always safe to trust the God who sees all. *"You will,"* is a blessed expression of confidence. He was sure that the Lord would not decline the condescending task. There is a word for you, O believer; rest in it. Be assured that your God will be your advisor and friend; He shall guide you; He will direct all your ways. In His written Word you have this assurance in part fulfilled, for holy Scripture is His counsel to you. We are happy to have God's Word always to guide us! Where is the mariner without his compass? And where would the Christian be without the Bible? This is the unerring chart, the map in which every shallow is described, and all the channels from the quicksands of destruction to the haven of salvation mapped and marked by One who knows the way. Blessed be You, O God, that we may trust You to guide us now, and guide us even to the end! After this guidance through life, the Psalmist anticipates a divine reception at last — *"and afterward You will take me into glory."* What a thought for you, believer! *God* Himself will take *you* into glory — *you!* Wandering, erring, straying, yet He will take you, safe at last, *into glory!* This is your reward; live on it this day, and if perplexities should surround you, go straight to the throne in the strength of this text.

"Trust in him at all times." — *Psalm 62:8*

 AITH is as much the rule of temporal as of spiritual life. We ought to have faith in God for our earthly affairs as well as for our heavenly business. It is only as we learn to trust in God for the supply of all our daily needs that we shall live above the world. We are not to be idle, *that* would show we did *not* trust in God who works up to now, but in the devil, who is the father of idleness. We are not to be imprudent or rash; that would be trusting chance and not the living God, who is a God of economy and order. Acting in all prudence and uprightness, we are to rely simply and entirely upon the Lord at all times.

Let me commend to you a life of trust in God in temporal things. Trusting in God, you will not be compelled to mourn because you have used sinful means to grow rich. Serve God with integrity, and if you achieve no success, at least no sin will lie upon your conscience. Trusting God, you will not be guilty of self-contradiction. Those who trust in skill sail this way today and that way the next, like a vessel tossed about by the fickle wind; but they who trust in the Lord are like a vessel propelled by steam, which cuts through the waves, defies the wind, and makes one bright, straight, silvery track to her destined haven. Be someone with living principles within; never bow to the varying customs of worldly wisdom. Walk in your path of integrity with firm steps, and show that you are invincibly strong in the strength which confidence in God alone can confer. This is how you will be delivered from anxiety; you will not be troubled by bad news, your heart will be fixed, trusting in the Lord. How pleasant to float along the stream of providence! There is no more blessed a way of living than a life of dependence upon a covenant-keeping God. We have no care, for He cares for us; we have no troubles, because we cast our burdens upon the Lord.

"Simon's mother-in-law was in bed with a fever, and they told Jesus about her." — Mark 1:30

ERY interesting is this little glimpse into the house of the apostolic fisherman, Simon Peter. We see at once that household joys and cares are not a hindrance to the full exercise of ministry since they furnish an opportunity for personally witnessing the Lord's gracious work upon one's own flesh and blood. They may even instruct the teacher better than any other earthly discipline. True Christianity and household life agree well with each other. Simon's house was probably a poor fisherman's hut, but the Lord of glory entered it, lodged in it, and wrought a miracle in it. If this page is being read this morning in some very humble home, let this fact encourage the inhabitants to seek the company of King Jesus. God is more often in little cottages than in rich palaces. Jesus is looking around your room now, and is waiting to be gracious to you. Into Simon's house sickness had entered, fever in a deadly form had prostrated his mother-in-law. As soon as Jesus came, they told Him of the sad affliction, and He hastened to the patient's bed. Do you have any sickness in the house this morning? You will find Jesus by far the best physician. Go to Him at once and tell Him all about the matter. Immediately lay the situation before Him. It concerns one of His people; therefore, it will not be trivial to Him. Observe, that the Savior restored the sick woman *at once;* no one can heal like He does. We cannot make sure that the Lord will instantly remove all disease from those we love, but we can know that believing prayer for the sick is far more likely to be followed by restoration than anything else in the world; and where this does not avail, we must meekly bow to His will by whom life and death are determined. The tender heart of Jesus waits to hear our griefs. Let's pour them into His patient ear.

"Unless you people see miraculous signs and
wonders . . . you will never believe." — *John 4:48*

craving after marvels was symptomatic of the direction in which people's minds were going in our Lord's day. They refused solid nourishment, and pined after mere wonder. They would have nothing to do with the gospel, which they so greatly needed. Yet they eagerly demanded the miracles which Jesus did not always choose to perform. Many in these days insist on seeing signs and wonders or else they refuse to believe. Some have said in their heart, "Unless I feel deep horror in my soul, I will never will believe in Jesus." But what if you never should feel such horror, as probably you never may? Will you go to hell out of spite against God because He will not treat you like another? Someone once said to himself, "If I had a dream, or if I could feel a sudden shock of, I don't know, something, then I would believe." Is this what you undeserving mortals imagine — that my Lord is to be dictated to by you! You are beggars at His gate, asking for mercy, and you really think you ought to determine the rules and regulations for how He shall give that mercy. Do you really believe that He will submit to this? My Master is of a generous spirit, but He has a fittingly royal heart. He spurns all dictation and maintains His sovereignty of action. Why, dear reader, if such is the case with you, do you crave signs and wonders? Isn't the gospel its own sign and wonder? Isn't this a miracle of miracles, that "God so loved the world that He gave His one and only Son, that whoever believes in Him shall not perish but have eternal life"? Surely, that precious word, "Whoever is thirsty, let him come; and whoever wishes, let him take the free gift of the water of life," and that solemn promise, "whoever comes to Me I will never drive away," are better than signs and wonders! A truthful Savior ought to be believed. He is truth itself. Why will you ask proof of the veracity of One who can't lie? The devils themselves declared Him to be the Son of God. Will you mistrust Him?

"You whom I love." — *Song of Songs 1:7*

T is good to be able to say of the Lord Jesus, without any "ifs, ands, or buts," — *"You whom I love."* Many can only say of Jesus that they *hope* they love Him; they *trust* they love Him; but only a poor and shallow experience will be content to stay here. Our spirits ought not to rest until we feel quite sure about a matter of such vital importance. We shouldn't be satisfied with a superficial *hope* that Jesus loves us, and with a bare *trust* that we love Him. The saints of old spoke without qualification; they spoke positively and plainly. "I *know* whom I have believed," said Paul. "I *know* that my Redeemer lives," said Job. Get positive knowledge of your love of Jesus, and don't be satisfied until you can speak of your interest in Him as a reality, which you have made sure by having received the witness of the Holy Spirit, and His seal upon your soul by faith.

True love for Christ is, in every situation, the Holy Spirit's work, and must be wrought in the heart by Him. He is the *efficient cause* of it; but the logical reason why we love Jesus lies in *Himself. Why* do we love Jesus? *Because He first loved us. Why* do we love Jesus? Because He *"gave Himself for us."* We have life through His death; we have peace through His blood. Though He was rich, yet *for our sakes* He became poor. *Why* do we love Jesus? Because of the *excellency of His person.* We are filled with a sense of His beauty! an admiration of His charms! a consciousness of His infinite perfection! His greatness, goodness, and loveliness, in one resplendent ray, combine to enchant the soul until it is so enraptured that it exclaims, "Yes, He is altogether lovely." Blessed love is this — a love which binds the heart with chains softer than silk, and yet firmer than the hardest metal!

"The LORD [tests] the righteous." — *Psalm 11:5*

LL events are under the control of Providence; consequently all the trials of our outward life are traceable at once to the great First Cause. Out of the golden gate of God's ordinance the armies of trial march forth in array, clad in their iron armor, and armed with weapons of war. All providences are doors to trial. Even our mercies, like roses, have their thorns. Men may be drowned in seas of prosperity as well as in rivers of affliction. Our mountains are not too high, and our valleys are not too low for temptations: trials lurk on all roads. Everywhere, above and beneath, we are beset and surrounded with dangers. Yet no shower falls unpermitted from the threatening cloud; every drop has its order before it hastens to the earth. The trials which come from God are sent to prove and strengthen our graces, and so at once to illustrate the power of divine grace, to test the genuineness of our virtues, and to add to their energy. Our Lord in His infinite wisdom and superabundant love sets so high a value upon His people's faith that He will not screen them from those trials by which faith is strengthened. You would never have possessed the precious faith which now supports you if the trial of your faith had not been like fire. You are a tree that never would have rooted so well if the wind had not rocked you to and fro, and made you take firm hold upon the precious truths of the covenant grace. Worldly ease is a great foe to faith; it loosens the joints of holy valor, and snaps the sinews of sacred courage. The balloon never rises until the cords are cut; affliction is the scissors to believing souls. While the wheat sleeps comfortably in the husk it is useless to humanity. It must be threshed out of its resting place before its value can be known. Thus it is good that Jehovah tests the righteous, for it allows them to grow rich towards God.

"I am willing . . . Be clean!" — *Mark 1:41*

RIMEVAL darkness heard the Almighty fiat, "Let there be light," and without delay, there was light. The word of the Lord Jesus is equal in majesty to that ancient word of power. Redemption, like Creation, has its word of might. Jesus speaks and it is done. Leprosy yielded to no human remedies, but it fled at once at the Lord's "I am willing." The disease exhibited no hopeful signs or tokens of recovery, nature contributed nothing to its own healing, but the unaided word effected the entire work on the spot and forever. The sinner is in a plight more miserable than the leper; let him imitate his example and go to Jesus, "begging Him on his knees." Let him exercise what little faith he has, even though it should go no further than "Lord, if You are willing, You can make me clean;" and there needn't be doubt as to the result of the application. Jesus heals all who come, and casts out none. In reading the narrative in which our morning's text occurs, it is worthy of devout notice that Jesus touched the leper. This unclean person had broken through the regulations of the ceremonial law and pressed into the house, yet Jesus, instead of chiding him, broke through the law Himself in order to meet him. He made an interchange with the leper, for while He cleansed him, He contracted by that touch a Levitical defilement. This is how Jesus Christ was made sin for us, although in Himself He knew no sin, that we might be made the righteousness of God in Him. O that poor sinners would go to Jesus, believing in the power of His blessed substitutionary work, and they would soon learn the power of His gracious touch. That hand which multiplied the loaves, which saved sinking Peter, which upholds afflicted saints, which crowns believers, that same hand will touch every seeking sinner, and in a moment make him clean. The love of Jesus is the source of salvation. He loves, He looks, He touches us, WE LIVE.

---

*"Use honest scales and honest weights, an honest
ephah and an honest hin."* — *Leviticus 19:36*

LL weights, scales, and measures were to be according to the standard of justice. Surely Christians will not need to be reminded of this in business, for even if righteousness were to be banished from the entire world, it would find shelter in believing hearts. There are, however, other balances which weigh moral and spiritual things, and these often need examining. We will call in an official tonight.

Are the balances in which we weigh our own and others' characters quite accurate? Don't we turn our own ounces of goodness into pounds, and other peoples' gallons of excellence into quarts? See to weights and measures here, Christian. Are the scales in which we measure our trials and troubles according to standard? Paul, who had endured more than we have, called his afflictions light, and yet we often consider ours to be heavy — surely something must be wrong with the weights! We must see to this matter, lest we get reported to the court above for unjust dealing. Are those weights with which we measure our doctrinal belief quite fair? The doctrines of grace should have the same weight with us as the precepts of the word — no more and no less; but it is to be feared that, with many, one scale or the other is unfairly weighted. It is a grand matter to give just measure in truth. Christian, be careful here. Those measures in which we estimate our obligations and responsibilities look rather small. When a rich man gives no more to the cause of God than the poor contribute, is that an honest ephah and an honest hin? When ministers are half starved, is that honest dealing? When the poor are despised, while the ungodly rich are held in admiration, is that a just balance? The list could go on, but we prefer to let it become your evening's assignment to discover and destroy all unrighteous balances, weights, and measures.

"Woe to me that I dwell in Meshech, that I live among the tents of Kedar!" — Psalm 120:5

S a Christian you have to live in the midst of an ungodly world, and it is of little use for you to cry "Woe to me." Jesus didn't pray that you should be taken out of the world, and what He didn't pray for you need not desire. Better far in the Lord's strength to meet the difficulty, and glorify Him in it. The enemy is always on the watch to detect inconsistency in your conduct; therefore, be very *holy*. Remember that all eyes are upon you, and that more is expected from you than from others. Strive to give no opportunity for blame. Let your goodness be the only fault they can discover in you. Like Daniel, compel them to say of you, "We will never find any basis for charges against this man Daniel unless it has something to do with the law of his God." Seek to be *useful* as well as consistent. Perhaps you think, "If I were in a more favorable position, I might serve the Lord's cause, but I can't do any good where I am;" but the worse the people are among whom you live, the more need they have of your efforts; if they are crooked, the more necessary it is that you should set them straight; and if they are perverse, the more need you have to turn their proud hearts to the truth. Where should the physician be but where many are sick? Where is honor to be won by the soldier but in the hottest fire of the battle? And when you grow weary of the strife and sin that meets you on every hand, consider that all the saints have endured the same trial. They were not carried to heaven on feather beds, and you mustn't expect to travel more easily than they. They had to risk their lives to the death in the high places of the field, and you will not be crowned until you also have endured hardness as a good soldier of Jesus Christ. Therefore, "stand firm in the faith; be men of courage; be strong."

"Have you journeyed to the springs of the sea?"
— *Job 38:16*

 OME things in nature must remain a mystery to the most intelligent and enterprising investigators. Human knowledge has bounds beyond which it cannot go. Universal knowledge is for God alone. If this is true concerning things which are seen and temporal, I may rest assured that it is even more true for matters spiritual and eternal. Why, then, have I been torturing my brain with speculations as to destiny and will, fixed fate, and human responsibility? These deep and dark truths I am no more able to comprehend than to find out the depth which lurks below, from which the old ocean draws her watery stores. Why am I so curious to know the reason of my Lord's providences, the motive of His actions, the design of His visitations? Shall I ever be able to clasp the sun in my fist, and hold the universe in my palm? Yet these are just a drop in the bucket compared with the Lord my God. Let me not strive to understand the infinite, but spend my strength in love. What I can't gain by intellect I can possess by affection, and let that satisfy me. I can't penetrate the heart of the sea, but I can enjoy the healthful breezes which sweep over its bosom, and I can sail over its blue waves with propitious winds. If I could journey to the springs of the sea, the feat would serve no useful purpose either to myself or to others. It would not save the sinking vessel or give back the drowned mariner to his weeping wife and children. Neither would my solving deep mysteries do me one single bit of good, for the least love for God, and the simplest act of obedience to Him, are better than the profoundest knowledge. My Lord, I leave the infinite to You, and pray that You put far from me such a love for the tree of knowledge as might keep me from the tree of life.

"In a crooked and depraved generation, in which you shine like [lights] in the universe." — *Philippians 2:15*

 E use lights to *expose, make apparent.* A Christian's life should so shine that no one could live with him a week without knowing the gospel. His conversation should be such that all who are around him can clearly perceive whose he is and whom he serves, and see reflected in his actions the image of Jesus. Lights are intended for *guidance.* We are to help those around us who are in the dark. We are to hold forth to them the Word of life. We are to point sinners to the Savior, and the weary to a divine resting place. We sometimes read our Bibles, but fail to understand them; we should be ready, like Philip, to instruct the inquirer in the meaning of God's Word, the way of salvation, and the life of godliness. Lights are also used for *warning.* On our rocks and shoals a lighthouse is sure to be erected. Christians should know that there are many false lights shown everywhere in the world, and therefore the right light is needed. The wreckers of Satan are always abroad, tempting the ungodly to sin under the name of pleasure; they hoist the wrong light. Let's shine the true light upon every dangerous rock, point out every sin and tell what it leads to, so that we can be clear of the blood of human beings, and shine as lights in the world. Lights also have a very *cheering* influence, and so have Christians. We ought to be comforters, with kind words on our lips and sympathy in our hearts; we should carry sunshine wherever we go, and spread happiness around.

> Gracious Spirit dwell with me;
> I myself would gracious be,
> And with words that help and heal
> Would thy life in mine reveal,
> And with actions bold and meek
> Would for Christ my Savior speak.

"If you are led by the Spirit, you are not under law." — *Galatians 5:18*

E who look at our own character and position from a legal point of view will not only despair when we come to the *end* of our reckoning, but, if we're smart, will despair at the *beginning;* for, if we are to be judged on the footing of the law, no living human being will ever be justified. How blessed to know that we dwell in the domains of grace and not of law! When thinking of my state before God the question isn't, "Am I perfect in myself before the law?" but, "Am I perfect in Christ Jesus?" That is a very different matter. We needn't inquire, "Am I without sin naturally?" but, "Have I been washed in the fountain opened for sin and for uncleanness?" It isn't "Am I in myself well pleasing to God?" but "Am I accepted in the Beloved?" We look at our proof from the top of Sinai and grow alarmed concerning our salvation. It is much better for us if we read our title by the light of Calvary. "Why," we say, "my faith has unbelief in it, it is not able to save me." Suppose we had considered *the object* of our faith instead of our faith, then we would have said, "There is no failure in *Him,* and therefore I am safe." We sigh over our hope: "Ah! my hope is marred and dimmed by an anxious distress about present things; how can I be accepted?" Had we regarded *the ground* of our hope, we would have seen that the promise of God stands sure, and that whatever our doubts may be, the oath and promise never fail. Ah! believer, it is always safer for you to be led by the Spirit into gospel liberty than to wear legal handcuffs. Judge yourself by what *Christ* is rather than by what *you* are. Satan will try to mar your peace by reminding you of your sinfulness and imperfections: you can only meet his accusations by faithfully adhering to the gospel and refusing to wear the yoke of bondage.

"Since they could not get him to Jesus because of the crowd, they made an opening in the roof above Jesus and, after digging through it, lowered the mat the paralyzed man was lying on." — Mark 2:4

AITH *is full of inventions.* The house was full, a crowd was blocking the doorway, but faith found a way to get to the Lord and place the paralyzed man before Him. If we can't get sinners where Jesus is by ordinary methods we must use extraordinary ones. It seems, according to Luke 5:19, that roof tiles had to be removed, which would make dust and cause a measure of danger to those below, but when the situation is very urgent, we must not mind running some risks and shocking some proprieties. Jesus was there to heal and, therefore, come what may, faith risked all so that her poor paralyzed charge might have his sins forgiven. O that we had more daring faith among us! Can't we, dear reader, seek it this morning for ourselves and for our fellow workers. Won't we today try to perform some gallant act for the love of souls and the glory of the Lord.

The world is constantly inventing; genius serves all the purposes of human desire: can't faith also invent and, by some new means, reach the outcasts who lie perishing around us? It was the presence of Jesus which excited victorious courage in the four bearers of the paralyzed man: isn't the Lord among us now? Have we seen His face for ourselves this morning? Have we felt His healing power in our own souls? If so, then through door, through window, or through roof, let's, breaking through all impediments, work to bring poor souls to Jesus. All means are good and acceptable when faith and love are truly set on winning souls. If hunger for bread can break through stone walls, surely hunger for souls is not to be hindered in its efforts. O Lord, make us quick to suggest methods of reaching your poor sin-sick ones, and bold to carry them out despite the risks.

"They are disheartened, troubled like the restless sea." — Jeremiah 49:23

ITTLE do we know of what sorrow may be upon the restless sea at this moment. We are safe in our quiet room, yet far away, on the salty sea, the hurricane may be cruelly searching for human lives. Hear how the death fiends howl among the ropes in the ship's riggings; how every timber shakes as the waves beat like battering rams upon the vessel! God help you, poor drenched and wearied ones! My prayer goes up to the great Lord of sea and land, that He will make the storm a calm, and bring you to your desired haven! Nor ought I to offer prayer alone, I should try to benefit those hardy sailors who risk their lives so constantly. Have I ever done anything for them? What can I do? How often does the boisterous sea swallow up the mariner! Thousands of corpses lie where pearls lie deep. There is death-sorrow on the sea, which is echoed in the long wail of widows and orphans. The salt of the sea is in the eyes of many mothers and wives. Remorseless billows, you have devoured the love of women, and the provider of households. What a resurrection shall there be from the caverns of the deep when the sea gives up her dead! Until then there will be sorrow on the sea. As if in sympathy with the woes of earth, the sea is forever fretting along a thousand shores, wailing with a sorrowful cry like her own birds, booming with a hollow crash of unrest, raving with uproarious discontent, chafing with hoarse wrath, or jangling with the voices of ten thousand murmuring pebbles. The roar of the sea may be joyous to a rejoicing spirit, but to the sorrowful the wide, wide ocean is even more forlorn than the wide, wide world. This is not our rest, and the restless billows tell us so. There is a land where there is no more sea — our faces are steadfastly set towards it; we are going to the place of which the Lord has spoken. Until then, we cast our sorrows on the Lord who trod the sea of old, and who creates a way for His people through the depths thereof.

"Your fruitfulness comes from me." — *Hosea 14:8*

UR fruitfulness comes from our God as to *union*. The fruit of the branch is directly traceable to the root. Sever the connection, the branch dies, and no fruit is produced. By virtue of our union with Christ we bring forth fruit. Every bunch of grapes has been first in the root, it has passed through the stem, and flowed through the sap vessels, and fashioned itself externally into fruit, but it was first in the stem; so also every good work was first in Christ, and then is brought forth in us. O Christian, prize this precious union to Christ; for it must be the source of all the fruitfulness which you can hope to know. If you were not joined to Jesus Christ, you will be a barren bough indeed.

Our fruitfulness comes from God as to *spiritual providence*. When the dewdrops fall from heaven, when the cloud looks down from on high, and is about to distill its liquid treasure, when the bright sun swells the berries of the cluster, each heavenly boon may whisper to the tree and say, "Your fruitfulness comes from Me." The fruit owes much to the root — that is essential to fruitfulness — but it owes very much also to external influences. How much we owe to God's grace-providence in which He provides us constantly with life-giving, teaching, consolation, strength, or whatever else we want. To this we owe all our usefulness or virtue.

Our fruitfulness comes from God as to *wise farming*. The gardener's sharp-edged knife promotes the fruitfulness of the tree, by thinning the clusters, and by cutting off superfluous shoots. So is it, Christian, with that pruning which the Lord gives to you. "I am the true vine, and My Father is the gardener. He cuts off every branch in Me that bears no fruit, while every branch that does bear fruit He prunes so that it will be even more fruitful." Since our God is the author of our spiritual graces, let's give to Him all the glory of our salvation.

*"His incomparably great power for us who believe.
That power is like the working of his mighty
strength, which he exerted in Christ when he
raised him from the dead." — Ephesians 1:19, 20*

 N the resurrection of Christ, as in our salvation, nothing short of a *divine power* was put forth. What shall we say of those who think that conversion is the work of the free will of individuals, and is due to improving one's own disposition? When we can see the dead rise from the grave by their own power, then we can expect to see ungodly sinners of their own free will turning to Christ. It isn't the word preached, nor the word read in itself; all life-giving power proceeds from the Holy Spirit. This power was *irresistible*. All the soldiers and the high priests could not keep the body of Christ in the tomb; death itself could not hold Jesus in its bonds: this is how irresistible the power put forth in the believer is when one is raised to newness of life. No sin, no corruption, no devils in hell nor sinners upon earth, can stop the hand of God's grace when it intends to convert a person. If God omnipotently says, "You shall," we cannot say, "I won't." Observe that the power which raised Christ from the dead was *glorious*. It reflected honor upon God and shocked the hosts of evil. So there is great glory to God in the conversion of every sinner. It was *everlasting power.* "Since Christ was raised from the dead, He cannot die again; death no longer has mastery over Him." So we, being raised from the dead, do not go back to our dead works nor to our old corruptions, but we live to God. "Because He lives we live also." "For you died, and your life is now hidden with Christ in God." "Just as Christ was raised from the dead through the glory of the Father, we too may live a new life." Lastly, in the text, mark the *union of the new life to Jesus.* The same power which raised the Head works life in the members. What a blessing to be made alive together with Christ!

"I will answer you and tell you great and unsearchable
things you do not know." — Jeremiah 33:3

HERE are different translations of these words. One version renders it, "I will show you great and *fortified* things." Another, "Great and *reserved* things." Now, there are reserved and special things in Christian experience: not all of the developments of spiritual life are attained with the same degree of ease. There are the common frames and feelings of repentance, and faith, and joy, and hope, which are enjoyed by the entire family; but there is an upper realm of rapture, of communion, and conscious union with Christ, which is far from being the common dwelling place of believers. Not all of us have the high privilege of John, to lean upon Jesus' bosom; nor of Paul, to be caught up into the third heaven. There are heights in experimental knowledge of the things of God which the eagle's eye of acumen and philosophic thought has never seen: God alone can bear us there; but the chariot in which He takes us up, and the fiery steeds with which that chariot is dragged, are prevailing prayers. Prevailing prayer is victorious over the God of mercy, "As a man he struggled with God. He struggled with the angel and overcame him; he wept and begged for his favor. He found him at Bethel and talked with him there." Prevailing prayer takes the Christian to Carmel, and enables him to cover heaven with clouds of blessing, and earth with floods of mercy. Prevailing prayer bears the Christian aloft to Pisgah, and shows him the inheritance reserved; it elevates us to Tabor and transfigures us, until in the likeness of our Lord, as He is, so are we also in this world. If you would reach to something higher than ordinary groveling experience, look to the Rock that is higher than you, and gaze with the eye of faith through the window of burning prayer. When you open the window on your side, it will not be bolted on the other.

"Surrounding the throne were twenty-four other thrones, and seated on them were twenty-four elders. They were dressed in white." — Revelation 4:4

 HESE representatives of the saints in heaven are said to be *surrounding the throne.* In the passage in Song of Songs, where Solomon sings of the King sitting at his table, some render it "a round table." From this, some interpreters, I think, without stretching the meaning of the text, have said, "There is an equality among the saints." That idea is conveyed by the equal nearness of the twenty-four elders. The condition of glorified saints in heaven is that of nearness to Christ, clear vision of His glory, constant access to His court, and familiar fellowship with His person: nor is there any difference in this respect between one saint and another, but all the people of God, apostles, martyrs, ministers, or private and obscure Christians, shall all be seated *near the throne,* where they shall forever gaze upon their exalted Lord, and be satisfied with His love. They shall all be near to Christ, all delighted with His love, all eating and drinking at the same table with Him, all equally beloved as His favorites and friends even if not all equally rewarded as servants.

Let believers on earth imitate the saints in heaven in their nearness to Christ. Let's on earth be as the elders are in heaven, sitting around the throne. May Christ be the object of our thoughts, the center of our lives. How can we bear to live at such a distance from our Beloved? Lord Jesus, draw us nearer to Yourself! Say to us, "Abide in Me, and I in you;" and permit us to sing, "His left arm is under my head, and his right arm embraces me."

> O lift me higher, nearer Thee,
> And as I rise more pure and meet,
> O let my soul's humility
> Make me lie lower at Thy feet;
> Less trusting self, the more I prove
> The blessed comfort of Thy love.

*"Jesus went up on a mountainside and called to him
those he wanted, and they came to him."*
— *Mark 3:13*

ERE was sovereignty. Impatient spirits may fret and fume, because they are not called to the highest places in the ministry; but reader, it is your place to rejoice that Jesus calls whom He wills. If He shall leave me to be a doorkeeper in His house, I will cheerfully bless Him for His grace in permitting me to do anything in His service. The call of Christ's servants comes from above. Jesus stands on the mountain, forever above the world in holiness, earnestness, love and power. Those whom He calls must go up the mountain to Him, they must seek to rise to His level by living in constant communion with Him. They may not be able to mount to classic honors, or attain scholastic eminence, but they must, like Moses, go up into the mountain of God and have familiar communication with the unseen God, or they will never be fitted to proclaim the gospel of peace. Jesus went apart to hold high fellowship with the Father, and we must enter into the same divine companionship if we would bless others. No wonder that the apostles were clothed with power when they came down fresh from the mountain where Jesus was. This morning we must try to ascend the mountain of communion, that there we may be ordained to the lifework for which we are set apart. Let's not look upon a human face today until we have seen Jesus. Time spent with Him is laid out at blessed interest. We too shall cast out devils and work wonders if we go down into the world girded with that divine energy which Christ alone can give. It is of no use going to the Lord's battle until we are armed with heavenly weapons. We *must* see Jesus, this is essential. At the mercy seat we will linger until He shall manifest Himself to us as He does not to the world, and until we can truthfully say, "We were with Him in the Holy Mountain."

"Wolves at dusk." — *Habakkuk 1:8*

HILE preparing the present volume, this particular expression kept recurring to me so, in order to put its constant nagging at rest, I determined to give a page to it. The wolf at dusk, infuriated by a day of hunger, was fiercer and more ravenous than he would have been in the morning. Couldn't the furious creature represent our doubts and fears after a day of distraction of mind, losses in business, and perhaps ungenerous tauntings from others? How our thoughts howl in our ears, "Where is your God now?" How voracious and greedy they are, swallowing up all suggestions of comfort, and remaining as hungry as before. Great Shepherd, slay these wolves at dusk, and allow your sheep to lie down in green pastures, undisturbed by insatiable unbelief. How similar the fiends of hell are to wolves at dusk, for when the flock of Christ is in a cloudy and dark day, and their sun seems to be going down, they hasten to tear and to devour. They will seldom attack the Christian in the daylight of faith, but in the gloom of soul conflict, they fall upon him. O You who have laid down Your life for the sheep, preserve them from the fangs of the wolf.

False teachers who craftily and industriously hunt for the precious life, devouring us with their lies, are as dangerous and detestable as wolves at dusk. Darkness is their element, deceit is their character, destruction is their end. We are most in danger from them when they wear sheepskins. Blessed is he who is kept from them, for thousands are made the prey of grievous wolves that enter within the fold of the church.

What a wonder of grace it is when fierce persecutors are converted, for then the wolf dwells with the lamb, and men of cruel ungovernable dispositions become gentle and teachable. O Lord, convert many who are like this: we pray for this tonight.

"Be separate." — *2 Corinthians 6:17*

HE Christian, while in the world, is not to be of the world. He should be distinguished from it in *the great object of his life.* To him, "to live," should be "Christ." Whether he eats, or drinks, or whatever he does, he should do all to God's glory. You may store up treasures; but store them up in heaven, where moth and rust do not destroy, and where thieves do not break in and steal. You may strive to be rich; but let your ambition be to be "rich in faith," and good works. You may have pleasure; but when you are merry, sing psalms and make melody in your hearts to the Lord. In your *spirit,* as well as in your aim, you should differ from the world. Waiting humbly before God, always conscious of His presence, delighting in communion with Him, and seeking to know His will, you will prove that you are of the heavenly race. And you should be separate from the world in your *actions.* If something is right, though you may lose by it, it must be done; if it is wrong, though you would gain by it, you must scorn the sin for your Master's sake. You must have no fellowship with the unfruitful works of darkness, but rather reprove them. Walk worthy of your high calling and dignity. Remember, O Christian, that you are a son of the King of kings. Therefore, keep yourself unspotted from the world. Do not dirty the fingers which are soon to sweep celestial strings; do not let your eyes, which are soon to see the King in His beauty, become the windows of lust — do not let those feet, which are soon to walk the golden streets, be defiled in muddy places — do not let those hearts which are before long to be filled with heaven and to overflow with ecstatic joy, be filled with pride and bitterness.

Then rise my soul! and soar away,
Above the thoughtless crowd;
Above the pleasures of the gay,
And splendors of the proud;

Up where eternal beauties bloom,
And pleasures all divine;
Where wealth, that never can consume,
And endless glories shine.

"Lead me, O LORD, in your righteousness because of my enemies." — Psalm 5:8

HE enmity of the world is very bitter against the people of Christ. Men will forgive a thousand faults in others, but they will magnify the most trivial offense in the followers of Jesus. Instead of regretting the futility of this, let's turn it to account, and since so many are watching for our halting, let this be a special motive for walking very carefully before God. If we live carelessly, the lynx-eyed world will soon see it, and with its hundred tongues, it will spread the story, exaggerated and emblazoned by the zeal of slander. They will shout triumphantly. "Aha! Just like we said it would be! See how these Christians act! They are all hypocrites." Thus will much damage be done to the cause of Christ, and much insult offered to His name. The cross of Christ is in itself an offense to the world; let's take heed that we add no offense of our own. It is "a stumbling block to the Jew": let's be careful not to put any stumbling blocks where there are already enough. "To the Gentiles it is foolishness": let's not add our folly to put a point on the scorn with which the wise of the world poke fun at the gospel. How watchful we should be of ourselves! How rigid with our consciences! In the presence of adversaries who will misrepresent our best deeds, and impugn our motives where they can't censure our actions, how circumspect should we be! Pilgrims travel as suspected persons through Vanity Fair. Not only are we under surveillance, but there are more spies than we are aware of. The espionage is everywhere, at home and abroad. If we fall into the enemies' hands we may sooner expect generosity from a wolf, or mercy from a fiend, than anything like patience with our infirmities from those who spice their infidelity towards God with scandals against His people. O Lord, always lead us, lest our enemies trip us up!

"The Lord is a jealous . . . God." — *Nahum 1:2*

YOUR Lord is very jealous of your love, O believer. Did He choose you? He can't bear that you should choose another. Did He buy you with His own blood? He can't endure that you should think that you are your own, or that you belong to this world. He loved you with such a love that He would not stop in heaven without you; He would sooner die than have you perish, and He can't endure that anything should stand between your heart's love and Himself. *He is very jealous of your trust.* He will not permit you to trust in an arm of flesh. He can't bear that you should hew out broken cisterns, when the overflowing fountain is always freely available to you. When we lean upon Him, He is glad, but when we transfer our dependence to another, when we rely upon our own wisdom, or the wisdom of a friend — worst of all, when we trust in any works of our own, He is displeased, and will chasten us that He may bring us to Himself. *He is also very jealous of our company.* There should be no one with whom we converse so much as with Jesus. To abide in Him only, this is true love; but to commune with the world, to find sufficient solace in our carnal comforts, to prefer even the society of our fellow Christians to secret communication with Him, this is grievous to our jealous Lord. He would preferably have us abide in Him, and enjoy constant fellowship with Himself; and many of the trials which He sends us are for the purpose of weaning our hearts from the creature, and fixing them more closely upon Himself. Let this jealousy which would keep us near to Christ *be also a comfort* to us, for if He loves us so much as to care this much about *our* love, we may be sure that He won't allow anything to harm us, and will protect us from all our enemies. Oh that we may have grace this day to keep our hearts in sacred chastity for our Beloved alone, with sacred jealousy shutting our eyes to all the fascinations of the world!

"I will sing of your love and justice." — Psalm 101:1

AITH triumphs in trial. When reason is thrust into the inner prison, with her feet fastened in the stocks, faith makes the dungeon walls ring with her merry notes as she cries, "I will sing of Your love and justice. To You, O LORD, I will sing praise." Faith pulls the dark mask from the face of trouble, and discovers the angel beneath. Faith looks up at the cloud, and sees that

> "'Tis big with mercy and shall break
> In blessings on her head."

There is reason for singing even in the judgments of God towards us. For, first, the trial is *not so heavy as it might have been;* next, the trouble is *not so severe as we deserved to have borne;* and our affliction is *not so crushing as the burden which others have to carry.* Faith sees that in her worst sorrow there is nothing legally punishable; there is not a drop of God's wrath in it; it is all sent in love. Faith discerns love gleaming like a jewel on the breast of an angry God. Faith says of her grief, "This is a badge of honor, for the child must feel the rod"; and then she sings of the sweet result of her sorrows, because they work her spiritual good. No, more, says Faith, "For our light and momentary troubles are achieving for us an eternal glory that far outweighs them all." So Faith rides forth on the dark horse, conquering and to conquer, trampling down carnal reason and fleshly sense, and chanting notes of victory amid the thickest of the brawl.

> "All I meet I find assists me
> In my path to heavenly joy:
> Where, though trials now attend me,
> Trials never more annoy.
>
> "Blest there with a weight of glory,
> Still the path I'll ne'er forget,
> But, exulting, cry, it led me
> To my blessed Savior's seat."

*"As they pass through the Valley of Baca, they make it
a place of springs; the autumn rains also cover it
with pools."* — Psalm 84:6

 HIS teaches us that the *comfort* obtained by one can often prove serviceable to another; just as wells can be used by the company who came after. We read some book full of consolation, which is like Jonathan's rod, dropping with honey. Ah! we think our brother has been here before us, and dug this well for us as well as for himself. Many a "Night of Weeping," "Midnight Harmonies," an "Eternal Day," "A Crook in the Lot," a "Comfort for Mourners," has been a well dug by a pilgrim for himself, but has proved quite as useful to others. Especially we notice this in the Psalms, such as that beginning, "Why are you downcast, O my soul?" Travelers have been delighted to see the footprint of man on a barren shore, and we love to see the road signs of pilgrims while passing through the vale of tears.

The pilgrims dig the well, but, strange enough, it fills from the top instead of the bottom. We use the means, but the blessing does not spring from the means. We dig a well, but heaven fills it with rain. The horse is prepared against the day of battle, but safety is of the Lord. The means are connected with the end, but they do not of themselves produce it. See here, the rain fills the pools so that the wells become useful as reservoirs for the water; work is not lost, but yet it does not supersede divine help.

Grace may well be compared to rain for its purity, for its refreshing and vivifying influence, for its coming alone from above, and for the sovereignty with which it is given or withheld. May our readers have showers of blessing, and may the wells they have dug be filled with water! Oh, what are means and ordinances without the smile of heaven! They are as clouds without rain, and pools without water. O God of love, open the windows of heaven and pour us out a blessing!

"This man welcomes sinners." — Luke 15:2

BSERVE *the condescension* of this fact. This Man, who towers above all other men, holy, harmless, undefiled, and separate from sinners — *this* Man receives sinners. This Man, who is no other than the eternal God, before whom angels veil their faces — *this* Man receives sinners. It requires an angel's tongue to describe such a mighty stoop of love. That any of *us* should be willing to seek after the lost is nothing wonderful — they are of our own race; but that He, the offended God, against whom the transgression has been committed, should take upon Himself the form of a servant, and bear the sin of many, and should then be willing to receive the vilest of the vile, this is marvelous.

"This Man welcomes sinners"; not, however, that they may remain sinners, but He welcomes them that He may pardon their sins, justify their persons, cleanse their hearts by His purifying word, preserve their souls by the indwelling of the Holy Spirit, and enable them to serve Him, to show forth His praise, and to have communion with Him. Into His heart's love He welcomes sinners, takes them from the manure pile, and wears them as jewels in His crown; plucks them as brands from the burning, and preserves them as costly monuments of His mercy. None are so precious in Jesus' sight as the sinners for whom He died. When Jesus receives sinners, He has not some out-of-doors reception place, no casual ward where He charitably entertains them as men do passing beggars, but He opens the golden gates of His royal heart, and welcomes the sinner right into Himself — yes, He admits the humble penitent into personal union and makes Him a member of His body, of His flesh, and of His bones. There was never such a reception as this! This fact is still most sure this evening, He is still welcoming sinners: if only sinners would welcome Him.

"There were also other boats with him." — Mark 4:36

ESUS was the Lord High Admiral of the sea that night, and His presence preserved the whole convoy. It is well to sail with Jesus, even though it is in a little ship. When we sail in Christ's company, we cannot assume we will always have fair weather, for great storms may toss the vessel which carries the Lord Himself, and we must not expect to find the sea less boisterous around our little boat. If we go with Jesus we must be content to fare as He fares; and when the waves are rough to Him, they will be rough to us. It is by tempest and tossing that we shall come to land, as He did before us.

When the storm swept over Galilee's dark lake all faces gathered darkness, and all hearts dreaded shipwreck. When all human help was useless, the slumbering Savior arose, and with a word, transformed the riot of the tempest into the deep quiet of a calm; then were the little vessels at rest as well as that which carried the Lord. Jesus is the star of the sea; and though there be sorrow upon the sea, when Jesus is on it there is joy, too. May our hearts make Jesus their anchor, their rudder, their lighthouse, their lifeboat, and their harbor. His church is the Admiral's flagship, let's attend her movements, and cheer her officers with our presence. He Himself is the great attraction; let's always follow in His wake, mark His signals, steer by His chart, and never fear while He is within hail. Not one ship in the convoy shall suffer a wreck; the great Commodore will steer every vessel in safety to the desired haven. By faith we will slip our cable for another day's cruise, and sail forth with Jesus into a sea of tribulation. Winds and waves will not spare us, but they all obey Him; and, therefore, whatever squalls may occur without, faith shall feel a blessed calm within. He is always in the center of the weather-beaten company: let's rejoice in Him. His vessel has reached the haven, and so shall ours.

*"I acknowledged my sin to you and did not cover
up my iniquity. I said, I will confess my
transgressions to the LORD — and you forgave
the guilt of my sin." — Psalm 32:5*

AVID'S grief for sin was bitter. Its effects were visible upon his outward frame: "his bones wasted away"; "his strength was sapped as in the heat of the summer." He could find no remedy until he made a full confession before the throne of the heavenly grace. He tells us that for a time he kept silence, and his heart became more and more filled with grief: like a small mountain lake whose outlet is blocked up, his soul was swollen with torrents of sorrow. He fashioned excuses; he endeavored to divert his thoughts, but it was all to no purpose; like a festering sore his anguish gathered, and as he would not use the lancet of confession, his spirit was full of torment, and knew no rest. At last it came to this, that he must return to his God in humble penitence, or die outright; so he hastened to the mercy seat, and there unrolled the volume of his iniquities before the all-seeing One, acknowledging all the evil of his ways in language such as you read in Psalm 51 and other penitential Psalms. Having done this, a work so simple and yet so difficult to pride, he received at once the token of divine forgiveness; the bones which had been wasting away began to rejoice, and he came forth from his time of prayer to sing of the blessedness of a man whose transgression is forgiven. See the value of a grace-wrought confession of sin! It is to be prized above all price, for in every situation where there is a genuine, gracious confession, mercy is freely given, not because the repentance and confession *deserve* mercy, but for *Christ's sake.* Blessed be God, there is always healing for the broken heart; the fountain is ever flowing to purify us from our sins. Truly, O Lord, You are a God "ready to pardon!" Therefore will we acknowledge our iniquities.

"He will have no fear of bad news." — *Psalm 112:7*

HRISTIAN, you ought not to dread the arrival of bad news; because if you are distressed by it, *how do you differ from others?* Others don't have your God to fly to; they have never proved His faithfulness as you have done, and it is no wonder if they are bowed down with alarm and cowed with fear: but you profess to be of another spirit; you have been begotten again to a lively hope, and your heart lives in heaven and not on earthly things; now, if you are seen to be distracted as others, what is the value of that grace which you profess to have received? Where is the dignity of that new nature which you claim to possess?

Again, if you should be filled with alarm, as others are, *you would, doubtless, be led into the sins so common to others under trying circumstances.* The ungodly, when they are overtaken by bad news, rebel against God; they murmur, and think that God deals harshly with them. Will you fall into that same sin? Will you provoke the Lord as they do?

Moreover, unconverted people often run to the wrong means in order to escape from difficulties, and you will surely do the same if your mind yields to the present pressure. Trust in the Lord, and wait patiently for Him. Your wisest course is to do as Moses did at the Red Sea, "Stand still and see the salvation of God." For if you give way to fear when you hear of bad news, you will be unable to meet the trouble with that calm composure which nerves for duty, and sustains under adversity. How can you glorify God if you play the coward? Saints have often sung God's high praises in the fires, but will your doubting and hopelessness, as if you had no one to help you, magnify the Most High? Then take courage, and relying in sure confidence upon the faithfulness of your covenant God, "do not let your heart be troubled, neither let it be afraid."

"The people close to his heart." — *Psalm 148:14*

HE dispensation of the old covenant was that of distance. When God appeared even to His servant Moses, He said, "Do not come any closer. Take off your sandals"; and when He manifested Himself upon Mount Sinai, to His own chosen and separated people, one of the first commands was, "Put limits around the mountain." Both in the sacred worship of the tabernacle and the temple, the thought of distance was always prominent. The mass of the people didn't even enter the outer court. Into the inner court none but the priests might dare to intrude; while into the innermost place, or the holy of holies, the high priest entered but once in the year. It was as if the Lord in those early ages would teach man that sin was so utterly loathsome to Him, that He must treat men as lepers put without the camp; and when He came nearest to them, He yet made them feel the width of the separation between a holy God and an impure sinner. When the gospel came, we were placed on quite another footing. The word "Go" was exchanged for "Come;" distance was made to give place to nearness, and we who in the past were afar off, were drawn close by the blood of Jesus Christ. Incarnate Deity has no wall of fire about it. "Come to Me, all you who are weary and burdened, and I will give you rest," is the joyful proclamation of God as He appears in human flesh. Now He doesn't teach the leper his leprosy by setting him at a distance, but by Himself suffering the penalty of His defilement. What a state of safety and privilege is this nearness to God through Jesus! Do you know it by experience? If you know it, are you living in the power of it? As marvelous as this nearness is, it is yet to be followed by a dispensation of greater nearness still, when it shall be said, "Now the dwelling of God is with men, and He will live with them." Hasten it, O Lord.

"Participate in the divine nature." — 2 Peter 1:4

O be a participant in the divine nature is not, of course, to become God. That can't be. The essence of Deity is not to be participated in by the creature. Between the creature and the Creator there must always be a gulf fixed in respect of essence; but as the first man Adam was made in the image of God, so we, by the renewal of the Holy Spirit, are in a yet diviner sense made in the image of the Most High, and are participants in the divine nature. We are, by grace, made like God. "God is love;" we become love — "Everyone who loves has been born of God." God is truth; we become true, and we love that which is true: God is good, and He makes us good by His grace, so that we become the pure in heart who shall see God. Moreover, we become participants in the divine nature in even a higher sense than this — in fact, in as lofty a sense as can be conceived, short of our being absolutely divine. Do we not become members of the body of the divine person of Christ? Yes, the same blood which flows in the head flows in the hand: and the same life which makes Christ alive makes His people alive, for "You are dead, and your life is now hidden with Christ in God." No, as if this were not enough, we are married to Christ. He has pledged to marry us to Himself in righteousness and in faithfulness, and He who is joined to the Lord is one spirit. Oh! marvelous mystery! we look into it, but who shall understand it? One with Jesus — so one with Him that the branch is no more one with the vine than we are a part of the Lord, our Savior, and our Redeemer! While we rejoice in this, let's remember that those who are made participants in the divine nature will manifest their high and holy relationship in their communication with others, and make it evident by their daily walk and conversation that they have escaped the corruption that is in the world through lust. O for more divine holiness of life!

*"Am I the sea, or the monster of the deep, that you
put me under guard?"* — *Job 7:12*

HIS was a strange question for Job to ask of the Lord. He felt himself to be too insignificant to be so strictly watched and chastened, and he hoped that he was not so unruly as to need to be so restrained. The inquiry was natural from one surrounded with such insupportable miseries, but after all, it is capable of a very humbling answer. It is true that man is not the sea, but he is even more troublesome and unruly. The sea obediently respects its boundary, and though that boundary is only a belt of sand, it does not overleap the limit. Mighty as it is, it hears the divine *up to now,* and when most raging with tempest it respects the word; but obstinate, willful people defy heaven and oppress earth, neither is there any end to this rebellious rage. The sea, obedient to the moon, ebbs and flows with ceaseless regularity, and thus renders an active as well as a passive obedience; but humankind, restless beyond its sphere, sleeps within the lines of duty, lazy where it should be active. We will neither come nor go at the divine command, but sullenly prefer to do what we shouldn't, and to leave undone that which is required of us. Every drop in the ocean, every beaded bubble, every shell and pebble, feels the power of law, and yields or moves at once. O that our nature were but one thousandth part as much conformed to the will of God! We call the sea fickle and false, but how constant it is! Since our fathers' days, and the time long past before them, the sea is where it was, beating on the same cliffs to the same tune; we *know* where to find it, it does not abandon its bed or change its ceaseless boom; but where is humankind — vain, fickle humanity? Can the wise man guess by what folly he will next be seduced from his obedience? We need more watching than the billowy sea, and are far more rebellious. Lord, rule us for Your own glory. Amen.

"Bring the boy to me." — *Mark 9:19*

ESPAIRINGLY the poor disappointed father turned away from the disciples to their Master. His son was in the worst possible condition, and all means had failed, but the miserable child was soon delivered from the evil one when the parent in faith obeyed the Lord Jesus' word, "Bring the boy to Me." Children are a precious gift from God, but a great deal of anxiety accompanies them. They may be a great joy or a great bitterness to their parents; they may be filled with the Spirit of God, or possessed with the spirit of evil. In all cases, the Word of God gives us one prescription for the curing of all their ills, "Bring the boy to Me." O for more agonizing prayer on their behalf while they are yet babes! Sin is there, let our prayers begin to attack it. Our cries for our offspring should precede those cries which betoken their actual advent into a world of sin. In the days of their youth, we shall see sad tokens of that dumb and deaf spirit which will neither pray correctly, nor hear the voice of God in the soul, but Jesus still commands, "Bring them to Me." When they are grown up, they may wallow in sin and seethe with animosity against God; then when our hearts are breaking we should remember the great Physician's words, "Bring them to Me." We must never cease to pray until they cease to breathe. No situation is hopeless while Jesus lives.

The Lord sometimes allows His people to be driven into a corner that they may experimentally know how necessary He is to them. Ungodly children, when they show us our own powerlessness against the depravity of their hearts, drive us to flee to the strong for strength, and this is a great blessing to us. Whatever our morning's need may be, let it bear us, like a strong current, to the ocean of divine love. Jesus can soon remove our sorrow. He delights to comfort us. Let's hurry to Him while He waits to meet us.

"Encourage him." — *Deuteronomy 1:38*

OD employs His people to encourage one another. He didn't say to an angel, "Gabriel, my servant Joshua is about to lead my people into Canaan — go, encourage him." God never works needless miracles; if His purposes can be accomplished by ordinary means, He will not use miraculous agency. Gabriel wouldn't have been half so well fitted for the work as Moses. A brother's sympathy is more precious than an angel's embassy. The angel, swift of wing, had better known the Master's bidding than the people's temper. An angel had never experienced the hardness of the road, nor seen the fiery serpents, nor had he led the stiff-necked multitude in the wilderness as Moses had done. We should delight that God usually works for human beings with other human beings. It forms a bond of friendship, and being mutually dependent on one another, we are fused more completely into one family. Brothers and sisters, take the text as God's message to you. Work to help others, and especially strive to *encourage* them. Talk cheerily to the young and anxious inquirer, lovingly try to remove obstacles out of his way. When you find a spark of grace in the heart, kneel down and blow it into a flame. Leave the young believer to discover the roughness of the road by degrees, but tell him of the strength which dwells in God, of the sureness of the promise, and of the charms of communion with Christ. Aim to comfort the sorrowful, and to animate the hopeless. Speak a word in season to him who is weary, and encourage those who are fearful to go on their way with gladness. God encourages you by His promises; Christ encourages you as He points to the heaven He has won for you, and the spirit encourages *you* as He works in you to will and to do of His own will and pleasure. Imitate divine wisdom, and encourage others, according to the word of this evening.

*"Since we live by the Spirit, let us keep in step
with the Spirit." — Galatians 5:25*

HE two most important things in our holy
religion are the *life of faith* and the *walk of
faith*. He who shall understand these correctly isn't far from being a master in experimental theology, for they are vital points to a
Christian. You will never find true faith un-
attended by true godliness; on the other hand, you will
never discover a truly holy life which has not for its root a
living faith upon the righteousness of Christ. Woe to those
who seek after the one without the other! There are some
who cultivate faith and forget holiness; these may be very
high in orthodoxy, but they shall be very deep in condemnation, for they hold the truth in unrighteousness; and
there are others who have strained after holiness of life,
but have denied the faith, like the Pharisees of old, of
whom the Master said, they were "whitewashed tombs."
We must have faith, for this is the foundation; we must
have holiness of life, for this is the superstructure. Of what
service is the mere foundation of a building to a man in the
day of tempest? Can he hide himself therein? He needs a
house to cover him, as well as a foundation for that house.
Even so, we need the superstructure of spiritual life if we
would have comfort in the day of doubt. But do not seek a
holy life without faith, for that would be to erect a house
which can afford no permanent shelter, because it has no
foundation on a rock. Let faith and life be put together,
and, like the two abutments of an arch, they will make our
piety enduring. Like light and heat streaming from the
same sun, they are alike full of blessing. Like the two
pillars of the temple, they are for glory and for beauty.
They are two streams from the fountain of grace; two
lamps lit with holy fire; two olive trees watered by heavenly care. O Lord, give us this day life within, and it will
reveal itself without to Your glory.

"And they follow me." — John 10:27

E should follow our Lord as unhesitatingly as sheep follow their shepherd, for *He has a right to lead us wherever He pleases.* We are not our own, we are bought with a price — let's recognize the rights of the redeeming blood. The soldier follows his captain, the servant obeys his master, even more so must we follow our Redeemer, to whom we are a purchased possession. We are not true to our profession of being Christians if we question the bidding of our Leader and Commander. Submission is our duty, judging too severely is our folly. Often our Lord might say to us as to Peter, "What *is* that to you? You must follow Me." Wherever Jesus may lead us, *He goes before us.* If we don't know where we are going, we know *with whom* we go. With such a companion, who will dread the perils of the road? The journey may be long, but His everlasting arms will carry us to the end. The presence of Jesus is the assurance of eternal salvation, because He lives, we shall live also. We should follow Christ in simplicity and faith, because *the paths in which He leads us all end in glory and immortality.* It is true they may not be *smooth* paths — they may be covered with sharp flinty trials, but they lead to the "city with foundations, whose architect and builder is God." "All the ways of the Lord are loving and faithful for those who keep the demands of His covenant." Let's put full trust in our Leader, since we know that, come prosperity or adversity, sickness or health, popularity or contempt, His purpose shall be worked out, and that purpose shall be pure, unmingled good to every heir of mercy. We shall find it sweet to go up the bleak side of the hill with Christ; and when rain and snow blow into our faces, His dear love will make us far more blessed than those who sit at home and warm their hands at the world's fire. To the top of Amana, to the dens of lions, or to the hills of leopards, we will follow our Beloved. Precious Jesus, draw us, and we will run after You.

"It is for freedom that Christ has set us free."
— Galatians 5:1

 HIS "freedom" makes us *free to avail ourselves of* heaven's charter — *the Bible.* Here is a choice passage, believer, "When you pass through the waters, I will be with you." You are free to avail yourself of that. Here is another: "Though the mountains be shaken and the hills be removed, yet My unfailing love for you will not be shaken;" you are free to avail yourself of that. You are a welcome guest at the table of the promises. Scripture is a never-failing treasury filled with boundless stores of grace. It is the bank of heaven; you may draw from it as much as you please, without impediment. Come in faith and you are welcome to all *covenant blessings.* There is not a promise in the Word which shall be withheld. In the depths of tribulations let this freedom comfort you; amid waves of distress let it cheer you; when sorrows surround you let it be your solace. This is your Father's token of love; you are free to avail yourself of it at all times. You are also *free to avail yourself of the throne of grace.* It is the believer's privilege to have access at all times to His heavenly Father. Whatever our desires, our difficulties, our wants, we are at liberty to spread all before Him. It doesn't matter how much we may have sinned, we may ask and expect pardon. It signifies nothing how poor we are, we may plead His promise that He will provide all necessary things. We have permission to approach His throne at all times — in midnight's darkest hour, or in noontide's most burning heat. Exercise your right, O believer, and live up to your privilege. You are free to avail yourself of all that is treasured up *in Christ* — wisdom, righteousness, sanctification, and redemption. It doesn't matter what your need is, for there is fullness of supply in Christ, and it is there *for you.* O what a "freedom" is yours! freedom from condemnation, freedom to the promises, freedom to the throne of grace, and at last freedom to enter heaven!

"I prayed for this child." — *1 Samuel 1:27*

EVOUT souls delight to look upon those mercies which they have obtained in answer to supplication, for they can see God's special love in them. When we can name our blessings "Samuel," that is, "asked of God," they will be as dear to us as her child was to Hannah. Peninnah had many children, but they came as common blessings unsought in prayer: Hannah's one heaven-given child was dearer far, because he was the fruit of earnest pleadings. How sweet that water was to Samson which he found at "the well of him that prayed!" Quassia cups turn all waters bitter, but the cup of prayer puts a sweetness into the draughts it brings. Did we pray for the conversion of our children? How doubly sweet, when they are saved, to see in them our own petitions fulfilled! Better to rejoice over them as the fruit of our pleadings than as the fruit of our bodies. Have we sought of the Lord some choice spiritual gift? When it comes to us, it will be wrapped up in the gold cloth of God's faithfulness and truth, and so be doubly precious. Have we petitioned for success in the Lord's work? How joyful is the prosperity which comes flying upon the wings of prayer! It is always best to get blessings into our house in the legitimate way, by the door of prayer; then they are blessings indeed, and not temptations. Even when prayer isn't speedy, the blessings grow all the richer for the delay; the child Jesus was all the more lovely in the eyes of Mary when she found Him after having sought Him sorrowing. That which we win by prayer we should dedicate to God, as Hannah dedicated Samuel. The gift came from heaven, let it go to heaven. Prayer brought it, gratitude sang over it, let devotion consecrate it. Here will be a special occasion for saying, "Of Your own have I given to You." Reader, is prayer your element or your weariness? Which?

"A sword for the LORD and for Gideon!" — *Judges 7:20*

IDEON ordered his men to do two things: covering up a torch in an earthen pitcher, he commanded them, at an appointed signal, to break the pitcher and let the light shine, and then sound with the trumpet, crying, "A sword for the LORD and for Gideon! A sword for the LORD and for Gideon!" This is precisely what all Christians must do. First, *you must shine;* break the pitcher which conceals your light; throw aside the bushel which has been hiding your candle, and shine. "Let your light shine before men, that they may see your good deeds and praise your Father in heaven." Then *there must be the sound,* the blowing of the trumpet. There must be active exertions for the ingathering of sinners by proclaiming Christ crucified. Take the gospel to them; carry it to their door; put it in their way; don't allow them to escape it; blow the trumpet right against their ears. Remember that the true slogan for action of the church is Gideon's watchword, *"A sword for the LORD and for Gideon!"* God must do it, it is His own work. But we are not to be idle; instrumentality is to be used — "A sword for the LORD *and for Gideon!*" If we only cry, "A sword for the LORD!" we shall be guilty of an idle presumption; and if we shout, "and for Gideon!" alone, we shall manifest idolatrous reliance on an arm of flesh: we must blend the two in practical harmony, "A sword for the LORD and for Gideon!" We can do nothing of ourselves, but we can do everything by the help of our God; let's, therefore, in His name determine to go out personally and serve with our flaming torch of holy example, and with our trumpet tones of earnest declaration and testimony, and God shall be with us, and Midian shall be put to confusion, and the Lord of hosts shall reign forever and ever.

"At evening let not your hands be idle."
— *Ecclesiastes 11:6*

N *the evening of the day* opportunities are plentiful: men and women return from their work, and the zealous soul winner finds time to tell abroad the love of Jesus. Have I no evening work for Jesus? If I haven't, let me no longer let my hand be idle from a service which requires abundant work. Sinners are perishing for lack of knowledge; he who loiters may find his skirts crimson with the blood of souls. Jesus gave both His hands to the nails, how can I keep back one of mine from His blessed work? Night and day He toiled and prayed for me, how can I give a single hour to the pampering of my flesh with luxurious ease? Up, idle heart; stretch out your hand to work, or uplift it to pray; heaven and hell are in earnest, let me be so, and this evening sow good seed for the Lord my God.

The evening of life also has its calls. Life is so short that a morning of manhood's vigor, and an evening of decay, make the whole of it. To some it seems long, but a few pennies seem like a great sum of money to a poor man. Life is so brief that no man can afford to lose a day. It has been well said that if a great king should bring us a great heap of gold, and bid us take as much as we could count in a day, we should make a long day of it; we should begin early in the morning, and in the evening we should not withhold our hand; but to win souls is far nobler work, how is it that we so soon withdraw from it? Some are spared to a long evening of green old age; if this is my situation, let me use such talents as I still retain, and to the last hour serve my blessed and faithful Lord. By His grace I will die in harness, and lay down my charge only when I lay down my body. Age may instruct the young, cheer the faint, and encourage the hopeless; if evening has less of vigorous heat, it should have more of calm wisdom, therefore in the evening I will not let my hands be idle.

"I will rejoice in doing them good." — *Jeremiah 32:41*

OD'S delight in His saints cheers the heart of every believer! We can't see any reason in ourselves why the Lord should take pleasure in us; we can't take delight in ourselves, for we often have to groan, being burdened; conscious of our sinfulness, and deploring our unfaithfulness; and we fear that God's people can't take much delight in us, for they must perceive so much of our imperfections and our follies, that they may rather lament our infirmities than admire our graces. But we love to dwell upon this transcendent truth, this glorious mystery: that as the bridegroom rejoices over the bride, so does the Lord rejoice in us. We do not read anywhere that God delights in the cloud-capped mountains, or the sparkling stars, but we do read that He delights in the habitable parts of the earth, and that His delights are with humankind. We do not find it written that even angels give His soul delight; nor does He say, concerning cherubim and seraphim, "You will be called Hephzibah . . . for the LORD will take delight in you;" but He does say all that to poor fallen creatures like ourselves, debased and depraved by sin, but saved, exalted, and glorified by His grace. In what strong language He expresses His delight in His people! Who could have conceived of the eternal One as bursting forth into a song? Yet it is written, "He will take great delight in you, He will quiet you with His love, He will rejoice over you with singing." As He looked upon the world He had made, He said, "It is very good;" but when He beheld those who are the purchase of Jesus' blood, His own chosen ones, it seemed as if the great heart of the Infinite couldn't restrain itself any longer, but overflowed in divine exclamations of joy. Shouldn't we utter our grateful response to such a marvelous declaration of His love, and sing, "I will rejoice in the LORD, I will be joyful in God my Savior"?

"Do not take away my soul along with sinners."
— Psalm 26:9

EAR made David pray this way, for something whispered, "Perhaps, after all, you may be gathered with the wicked." That fear, although marred by unbelief, springs, in the main, from holy anxiety, arising from the recollection of past sin. Even the pardoned man will inquire, "What if at the end my sins should be remembered, and I should be left out of the list of the saved?" He recollects his present unfruitfulness — so little grace, so little love, so little holiness, and looking forward to the future, he considers his weakness and the many temptations which surround him, and he fears that he may fall, and become a prey to the enemy. A sense of sin and present evil, and his prevailing corruptions, compel him to pray, in fear and trembling, "Do not take away my soul along with sinners." Reader, if you have prayed this prayer, and if your character is accurately described in the Psalm from which it is taken, you needn't be afraid that you shall be taken away with sinners. Have you the two virtues which David had — the outward walking in integrity, and the inward trusting in the Lord? Are you resting upon Christ's sacrifice, and can you compass the altar of God with humble hope? If so, rest assured, you shall never be taken away with the wicked, for that calamity is impossible. The gathering at the judgment is like to like. "First collect the weeds and tie them in bundles to be burned; then gather the wheat and bring it into my barn." If, then, you are *like* God's people, you shall be *with* God's people. You can't be gathered with the wicked, for you are too dearly bought. Redeemed by the blood of Christ, you are His forever, and where He is, there must His people be. You are loved too much to be cast away with criminals. Shall one dear to Christ perish? Impossible! Hell can't hold you! Heaven claims you! Trust in your Surety and don't be afraid!

"Let Israel rejoice in their Maker." — *Psalm 149:2*

 ET your heart be glad, O believer, but take care that your gladness has its spring *in the Lord.* You have many reasons for being glad in your God, for you can sing with David, "God, my joy and my delight." Be glad that the Lord reigns, that Jehovah is King! Rejoice that He sits upon the throne, and rules all things! Every attribute of God should become a fresh ray in the sunlight of our gladness. That He is *wise* should make us glad, knowing as we do our own foolishness. That He is *mighty,* should cause us to rejoice who tremble at our weakness. That He is *everlasting,* should always be a theme of joy when we know that *we* wither as the grass. That He is *unchanging,* should perpetually yield us a song, since *we* change every hour. That He is full of grace, that He is overflowing with it, and that this grace in covenant He has given to us; that it is ours to purify us, ours to keep us, ours to sanctify us, ours to perfect us, ours to bring us to glory — all this should tend to make us glad in Him. This gladness in God is as a deep river. So far we have only touched its brink; we know a little of its clear sweet, heavenly streams, but onward the depth is greater, and the current more impetuous in its joy. The Christian feels that he may delight himself not only in what God *is,* but also in all that God *has done* in the past. The Psalms show us that God's people in times long past were accustomed to thinking a great deal about God's actions and having a song concerning each of them. So let God's people now rehearse the deeds of the Lord! Let them tell of His mighty acts, and "sing to the Lord, for He is highly exalted." Nor let them ever stop singing, for as new mercies flow to them day by day, so should their gladness in the Lord's loving acts in providence and in grace show itself in continued thanksgiving. Be glad, children of Zion. Rejoice in the Lord your God.

"I call as my heart grows faint; lead me to the rock
that is higher than I." — Psalm 61:2

OST of us know what it is to be overwhelmed in heart; feeling as empty as a dish which has been wiped and turned upside down; submerged and thrown on our beam ends like a vessel mastered by the storm. Discoveries of inward corruption will do this, if the Lord allows the great depth of our depravity to become troubled and cast up mire and dirt. Disappointments and heartbreaks will do this when billow after billow rolls over us, and we are like a broken shell hurled to and fro by the surf. Blessed be God that, at these times, we are not without an all-sufficient solace. Our God is the harbor of weather-beaten sails, the hospice of forlorn pilgrims. He is higher than we are, His mercy is higher than our sins, His love higher than our thoughts. It is pitiful to see men putting their trust in something lower than themselves; but our confidence is fixed upon an exceedingly high and glorious Lord. He is a Rock because He does not change, and a high Rock because the tempests which overwhelm us roll far beneath His feet; He is not disturbed by them, but rules them at His will. If we get under the shelter of this lofty Rock we may defy the hurricane; all is calm under the protection of that towering cliff. Alas! such is the confusion in which the troubled mind is often cast, that we need piloting to this divine shelter. Hence the prayer of the text. O Lord, our God, by Your Holy Spirit, teach us the way of faith, lead us into Your rest. The wind blows us out to sea, the helm does not respond to our puny hand; You, You alone, can steer us over the bar, between submerged rocks which lie ahead, and safely into the fair haven. How dependent we are upon You — we need You to bring us to You. To be wisely directed and steered into safety and peace is Your gift, and Yours alone. This night be pleased to deal well with Your servants.

"In love he predestined us to be adopted as his sons through Jesus Christ, in accordance with his pleasure and will — to the praise of his glorious grace, which he has freely given us in the One he loves." — Ephesians 1:4–6

HAT a state of privilege! It includes our *justification* before God. It signifies that we are the objects of *divine complacency,* no, even of *divine delight.* How marvelous that we, worms, mortals, sinners, should be the objects of divine love! But it is only *"in the One He loves."* Some Christians seem to be accepted in their own experience, at least, that is their apprehension. When their spirit is lively, and their hopes bright, they think God accepts them, for they feel so high, so heavenly-minded, so drawn above the earth! But when their souls cleave to the dust, they are the victims of the fear that they are no longer accepted. If they could but see that all their high joys do not exalt them, and all their low despondencies do not really depress them in their Father's sight, but that they stand accepted in One who never alters, in One who is always the one God loves, always perfect, always without spot or wrinkle, or any such thing, how much happier they would be, and how much more they would honor the Savior! Rejoice then, believer, in this: you are accepted "in the One He loves." You look within, and you say, "There is nothing acceptable *here!*" But look at Christ, and see if there is not everything acceptable *there.* Your sins trouble you; but God has cast your sins behind His back, and you are accepted in the Righteous One. You have to fight with corruption, and to wrestle with temptation, but you are already accepted in Him who has overcome the powers of evil. The devil tempts you; be of good cheer, he can't destroy you, for you are accepted in Him who has broken Satan's head. Know by full assurance your glorious standing. Even glorified souls are not more accepted than you are. They are only accepted in heaven "in the One He loves," and you are even now accepted in Christ after the same manner.

"If you can, said Jesus." — Mark 9:23

certain man had a demoniac son, who was afflicted with a dumb spirit. The father, having seen the futility of the efforts of the disciples to heal his child, had little or no faith in Christ, and therefore, when he was invited to bring his son to Him, he said to Jesus, "If You can do anything, take pity on us, and help us." Now, to be sure, there needed to be an "if" in the question, but the poor trembling father had put the "if" in the wrong place: Jesus Christ, therefore, without commanding him to retract the "if," kindly puts it in its legitimate position. "No, if the truth be told," He seemed to say, "there should be no 'if' about My power, nor concerning My willingness. The 'if' lies somewhere else." " *'If you can,'* said Jesus. 'Everything is possible for him who believes.' " The man's trust was strengthened, he offered a humble prayer for an increase of faith, and instantly Jesus spoke the word, and the devil was cast out, with an injunction never to return. There is a lesson here which we need to learn. We, like this man, often see that there is an "if" somewhere, but we are perpetually blundering by putting it in the wrong place. *"If"* Jesus can help me — *"if"* He can give me grace to overcome temptation — *"if"* He can give me pardon — *"if"* He can make me successful? No, *"if"* you can believe, He both can and will. You have misplaced your "if." If you can confidently trust, even as all things are possible for Christ, so shall all things be possible for you. Faith stands in God's power, and is robed in God's majesty; it wears the royal apparel, and rides on the King's horse, for it is the grace which the King delights to honor. Girding itself with the glorious might of the all-working Spirit, it becomes, in the omnipotence of God, mighty to do, to dare, and to allow. Everything, without limit, is possible to those who believe. My soul, can you believe your Lord tonight?

*"I was ashamed to ask the king for soldiers and horsemen
to protect us from enemies on the road, because we had
told the king, The gracious hand of our God is on
everyone who looks to him, but his great anger is
against all who forsake him."* — Ezra 8:22

A convoy on many accounts would have been desirable for the pilgrim band, but a holy reluctance would not allow Ezra to seek one. He feared that the heathen king would think his professions of faith in God were mere hypocrisy, or imagine that the God of Israel was not able to preserve His own worshippers. He could not bring his mind to lean on an arm of flesh in a matter so evidently of the Lord, and therefore the caravan set out with no visible protection, guarded by Him who is the sword and shield of His people. It is to be feared that few believers feel this holy jealousy for God. Even those who, to a certain degree, walk by faith, occasionally mar the luster of their life by craving aid from man. It is a most blessed thing to have no props and no buttresses, but to stand upright on the Rock of Ages, upheld by the Lord alone. Would any believers seek state endowments for their church, if they remembered that the Lord is dishonored by their asking Caesar's aid, as if the Lord could not supply the needs of His own cause? Would we be running so hastily to friends and relations for assistance if we remembered that the Lord is magnified by our implicit reliance upon His solitary arm? My soul, wait only upon God. "But," says one, "are not means to be used?" Of course they are, but our fault seldom lies in their neglect: far more frequently it springs out of foolishly believing in them instead of believing in God. Few go the extreme of neglecting the creature's arm, but very many sin greatly in making too much of it. Learn, dear reader, to glorify the Lord by leaving means untried, if by using them you will dishonor the name of the Lord.

"I slept but my heart was awake."
— *Song of Songs 5:2*

ARADOXES abound in Christian experience, and here is one — the spouse was asleep, and yet she was awake. We can only read this believer's riddle if we have plowed with the heifer of this experience. The two points in this evening's text are — a mournful sleepiness and a hopeful wakefulness. *I slept.* Through sin that dwells in us we may become lax in holy duties, lazy in religious exercises, dull in spiritual joys, and altogether lethargic and unconcerned. This is a shameful state for one in whom the life-giving Spirit dwells; and it is dangerous to the highest degree. Even wise virgins sometimes slumber, but it is high time for all to shake off the bands of laziness. It is to be feared that many believers lose their strength as Samson lost his locks, while sleeping in the lap of material security. With a perishing world around us, to sleep is cruel; with eternity so near at hand, it is madness. Yet none of us are as awake as we ought to be; a few thunderclaps would do us all good, and it may be, unless we soon move quickly, wake ourselves up, we shall have them in the form of war, or pestilence, or personal bereavements and losses. O that we may leave forever the couch of physical comfort, and go forth with flaming torches to meet the coming Bridegroom! *My heart was awake.* This is a happy sign. Life is not extinct, though sadly smothered. When our renewed heart struggles against our natural heaviness, we should be grateful to sovereign grace for keeping a little vitality within the body of this death. Jesus will hear our hearts, will help our hearts, will visit our hearts; for the voice of the wakeful heart is really the voice of our Beloved, saying, "Open to Me." Holy zeal will surely unbar the door.

> "Oh lovely attitude! He stands
> With melting heart and laden hands;
> My soul forsakes her every sin;
> And lets the heavenly stranger in."

*"To be just and the one who justifies those who
have faith."* — Romans 3:26

 EING justified by faith, we have peace with God. Conscience accuses no longer. Judgment now decides for the sinner instead of against him. Memory looks back upon past sins, with deep sorrow for the sin, but yet with no dread of any penalty to come; for Christ has paid the debt of His people to the last jot and tittle, and received the divine prescription; and unless God can be so unjust as to demand double payment for one debt, no soul for whom Jesus died as a substitute can ever be cast into hell. It seems to be one of the very principles of our enlightened nature to believe that God is just; we feel that it must be so, and this gives us our terror at first; but isn't it marvelous that this very same belief that God is just, later becomes the pillar of our confidence and peace! If God is just, I, a sinner, alone and without a substitute, must be punished; but Jesus stands in my place and is punished for me; and now, if God is just, I, a sinner, standing in Christ, can never be punished. God must change His nature before one soul, for whom Jesus was a substitute, can ever by any possibility suffer the lash of the law. Therefore, Jesus having taken the place of the believer — having supplied Himself as the full equivalent to divine wrath for all that His people ought to have suffered as the result of sin, the believer can shout with glorious triumph, "Who will bring any charge against those whom God has chosen? It is God who justifies. Who is he that condemns? Christ Jesus, who died — more than that, who was raised to life." My hope lives not because I am not a sinner, but because I am a sinner for whom Christ died; my trust is not that I am holy, but that being unholy, *He* is my righteousness. My faith rests not upon what I am, or shall be, or feel, or know, but in what Christ is, in what He has done, and in what He is now doing for me. On the lion of justice the fair maid of hope rides like a queen.

"Who has become for us wisdom from God."
— *1 Corinthians 1:30*

UMAN intellect seeks after rest, and by nature seeks it apart from the Lord Jesus Christ. Educated individuals are apt, even when converted, to look upon the simplicities of the cross of Christ with an eye too little reverent and loving. They are snared in the old net in which the Greeks were taken, and have a hankering to mix philosophy with revelation. The temptation with a man of refined thought and high education is to depart from the simple truth of Christ crucified, and to invent, as the term is, a more *intellectual* doctrine. This led the early Christian churches into Gnosticism, and bewitched them with all sorts of heresies. This is the root of Neology, and the other fine things which, in days gone, by were so fashionable in Germany, and are now so ensnaring to certain classes of divines. Whoever you are, good reader, and whatever your education may be, if you are the Lord's, be assured you will find no rest in philosophizing divinity. You may receive this dogma of one great thinker, or that dream of another profound reasoner, but what the chaff is to the wheat, that will these be to the pure word of God. All that reason, when best guided, can find out is but the A B C of truth, and even that lacks certainty, while in Christ Jesus there is treasured up all the fullness of wisdom and knowledge. All attempts on the part of Christians to be content with systems such as Unitarian and Broad-Church thinkers would approve of, must fail; true heirs of heaven must come back to the grandly simple reality which makes the plowman's eye flash with joy, and gladdens the pious pauper's heart — "Jesus Christ came into the world to save sinners." Jesus satisfies the most elevated intellect when He is believingly received, but apart from Him the mind of the regenerate discovers no rest. "The fear of the LORD is the beginning of knowledge." "All who follow His precepts have good understanding."

"Among the myrtle trees in a ravine." — *Zechariah 1:8*

HE vision in this chapter describes the condition of Israel in Zechariah's day; but being interpreted in its aspect towards *us*, it describes the church of God as we find it now in the world. The church is compared to a myrtle grove flourishing in a valley. It is *hidden*, unobserved, secret; courting no honor and attracting no observation from the unconcerned gazer. The church, like her head, has a glory, but it is concealed from carnal eyes, for the time of her breaking forth in all her splendor has not yet come. The idea of *tranquil security* is also suggested to us: for the myrtle grove in the valley is still and calm, while the storm sweeps over the mountain summits. Tempests expend their force upon the craggy peaks of the Alps, but down yonder where the stream which brings joy to the city of our God flows, the myrtles flourish by the still waters, all unshaken by the impetuous wind. How great is the inward tranquillity of God's church! Even when opposed and persecuted, she has a peace which the world doesn't give, and which, therefore, it can't take away: the peace of God which passes all understanding keeps the hearts and minds of God's people. Does not the metaphor forcibly picture the peaceful, *perpetual growth* of the saints? The myrtle does not shed her leaves, she is always green; and the church in her worst time still has a blessed vibrant greenness of grace about her; no, she has sometimes exhibited *most* vibrant greenness when her winter has been sharpest. She has prospered most when her adversities have been most severe. Hence the text *hints at victory*. The myrtle is the emblem of peace, and a significant token of *triumph*. The brows of conquerors were bound with myrtle and with laurel; and isn't the church always victorious? Aren't we more than conquerors through Him who loved us? Living in peace, the saints fall asleep in the arms of victory.

"Wail, O pine tree, for the cedar has fallen."
— *Zechariah 11:2*

WHEN the crash of a falling oak is heard in the forest, it is a sign that the woodsman is present, and every tree in the whole company may tremble lest tomorrow the sharp edge of the ax should find it out. We are all like trees marked for the ax, and the fall of one should remind us that for every one, whether great as the cedar, or humble as the fir, the appointed hour is stealing on in haste. I trust we do not, by often hearing of death, become callous to it. May we never be like the birds in the steeple, which build their nests when the bells are tolling, and sleep quietly when the solemn funeral peals are startling the air. May we regard death as the most weighty of all events, and be sobered by its approach. It ill suits us to sport while our eternal destiny hangs on a thread. The sword is out of its scabbard — let's not trifle; it is sharpened and polished, and the edge is sharp — let's not play with it. He who does not prepare for death is more than an ordinary fool, he is a madman. When the voice of God is heard among the trees of the garden, let fig tree and sycamore, and elm and cedar, alike hear the sound thereof.

Be ready, servant of Christ, for your Master comes suddenly, when an ungodly world least expects Him. See to it that you are faithful in His work, for the grave shall soon be dug for you. Be ready, parents. See that your children are brought up in the fear of God, for they will soon be orphans. Business professionals, take care that your affairs are in order, and that you serve God with all your hearts, for the days of your terrestrial service will soon be ended, and you will be called to give account for the deeds done in the body, whether they be good or whether they be evil. May we all prepare for the tribunal of the great King with a care which shall be rewarded with the gracious commendation, "Well done, good and faithful servant!"

"Blessed are you, O Israel! Who is like you, a people saved by the LORD?" — *Deuteronomy 33:29*

E who affirms that Christianity makes people miserable, is himself an utter stranger to it. It would be strange indeed if it made us wretched, since we can see *to what a position it exalts us!* It makes us sons and daughters of God. Do you suppose that God will give all the happiness to His enemies, and reserve all the mourning for His own family? Shall His foes have mirth and joy, and shall His homeborn children inherit sorrow and wretchedness? Shall the sinner, who has no part in Christ, call himself rich in happiness, and shall we go mourning as if we were penniless beggars? No, we will rejoice in the Lord always, and glory in our inheritance, for we "did not receive a spirit that makes [us] a slave again to fear, but [we] received the Spirit of sonship. And by Him we cry, '*Abba*, Father.' " The rod of chastisement must rest upon us in our measure, but it works for us the comfortable fruits of righteousness; and therefore by the aid of the divine Comforter, we, the "people saved by the Lord," will joy in the God of our salvation. We are married to Christ; and shall our great Bridegroom permit His spouse to linger in constant grief? Our hearts are knit to Him: we are His members, and though for awhile we may suffer as our Head once suffered, yet we are even now blessed with heavenly blessings in Him. We have the deposit guaranteeing our inheritance in the comforts of the Spirit, which are neither few nor small. Inheritors of joy forever, we have tastes of our portion. There are streaks of the light of joy to herald our eternal sunrising. Our riches are beyond the sea; our city with firm foundations lies on the other side the river; gleams of glory from the spirit world cheer our hearts, and urge us onward. Truly is it said of us, "Blessed are you, O Israel! Who is like you, a people saved by the LORD?"

*"My lover thrust his hand through the
latch-opening; my heart began to pound
for him."* — *Song of Songs 5:4*

 NOCKING was not enough, for my heart was too full of sleep, too cold and ungrateful to arise and open the door, but the touch of His effectual grace has stirred my soul to wakefulness. Oh, the long-suffering of my Lover, to linger when He found Himself shut out, and me asleep upon the bed of laziness! Oh, the greatness of His patience, to knock and knock again, and to add His voice to His knockings, begging me to open to Him! How could I have refused Him! Base heart, blush and be confused! But what greatest kindness of all is this, that He becomes His own porter and unbars the door Himself! Three times blessed is the hand which condescends to lift the latch and turn the key. Now I see that nothing but my Lord's own power can save such a naughty mass of wickedness as I am; ordinances fail, even the gospel has no effect upon me, until His hand is stretched out. Now, also, I perceive that His hand is good where all else is unsuccessful, He can open when nothing else will. Blessed be His name, I feel His gracious presence even now. Well may my heart lament for Him, when I think of all that He has suffered for me, and of my ungenerous return. I have allowed my affections to wander. I have set up rivals. I have grieved Him. Sweetest and dearest of all beloveds, I have treated You as an unfaithful wife treats her husband. Oh, my cruel sins, my cruel self! What can I do? Tears are a poor show of my repentance, my whole heart boils with indignation at myself. Wretch that I am, to treat my Lord, my All in All, my exceeding great joy, as though He were a stranger. Jesus, you forgive freely, but this is not enough, prevent my unfaithfulness in the future. Kiss away these tears, and then purge my heart and bind it with sevenfold cords to Yourself, never to wander again.

> *"From heaven the* LORD *looks down and sees all mankind."* — *Psalm 33:13*

ERHAPS no figure of speech represents God in a more gracious light than when He is spoken of as stooping from His throne, and coming down from heaven to attend to the wants and to behold the woes of humanity. We love Him, who, when Sodom and Gomorrah were full of iniquity, would not destroy those cities until He had made a personal visitation of them. We can't help pouring out our heart in affection for our Lord who inclines His ear from the highest glory, and puts it to the lip of the dying sinner, whose failing heart longs after reconciliation. How can we but love Him when we know that He numbers the very hairs of our heads, marks our path, and orders our ways? Especially is this great truth brought near to our heart, when we recollect how attentive He is, not merely to the temporal interests of His creatures, but to their spiritual concerns. Though leagues of distance lie between the finite creature and the infinite Creator, yet there are links uniting both. When a tear is wept by you, do not think that God does not see; for, "As a father has compassion on his children, so the Lord has compassion on those who fear Him." Your sigh is able to move the heart of Jehovah; your whisper can incline His ear to you; your prayer can stay His hand; your faith can move His arm. Do not think that God sits on high taking no account of you. Remember that however poor and needy you are, yet the Lord thinks upon you. For the eyes of the Lord run to and fro throughout the whole earth, to show Himself strong in the behalf of them whose heart is perfect towards Him.

> Oh! then repeat the truth that never tires;
> No God is like the God my soul desires;
> He at whose voice heaven trembles, even He,
> *Great as He is, knows how to stoop to me.*

"Seven times . . . go back." — *1 Kings 18:43*

UCCESS is certain when the Lord has promised it. Although you may have pleaded month after month without evidence of an answer, it is not possible for the Lord to be deaf when His people are earnest in a matter which concerns IIis glory. The prophet on the top of Carmel continued to wrestle with God, and never for a moment gave way to a fear that he should be unsuitable in Jehovah's courts. Six times the servant returned, but on each occasion no word was spoken but "Go back." We must not dream of unbelief, but hold to our faith even to seventy times seven. Faith sends expectant hope to look from Carmel's brow, and if nothing is beheld, she sends again and again. So far from being crushed by repeated disappointment, faith is animated to plead more fervently with her God. She is humbled, but not abashed: her groans are deeper, and her sighings more vehement, but she never relaxes her hold or stays her hand. It would be more agreeable to flesh and blood to have a speedy answer, but believing souls have learned to be submissive, and to find it good to wait *for* as well as *upon* the Lord. Delayed answers often set the heart searching itself, and so lead to contrition and spiritual reformation: deadly blows are thus struck at our corruption, and the chambers of imagery are cleansed. The great danger is lest men should faint, and miss the blessing. Reader, do not fall into that sin, but continue in prayer and watching. At last the little cloud was seen, the sure forerunner of torrents of rain, and even so with you, the token for good shall surely be given, and you shall rise as a prevailing prince to enjoy the mercy you have sought. Elijah was a man of passions similar to ours: his power with God didn't lie in his own merits. If his believing prayer availed so much, why not yours? Plead the precious blood with unceasing insistent requests, and it shall be with you according to your desire.

"If the disease has covered his whole body, he shall pronounce that person clean." — Leviticus 13:13

 TRANGE enough this regulation appears, yet there was wisdom in it, for the throwing out of the disease proved that the constitution was sound. This morning it may be well for us to see the typical teaching of so singular a rule. We, too, are lepers, and may read the law of the leper as applicable to ourselves. When a man sees himself to be altogether lost and ruined, covered all over with the defilement of sin, and no part free from pollution; when he disclaims all righteousness of his own, and pleads guilty before the Lord, then is he clean through the blood of Jesus, and the grace of God. Hidden, unfelt, unconfessed iniquity is the true leprosy, but when sin is seen and felt it has received its death blow, and the Lord looks with eyes of mercy upon the soul afflicted with it. Nothing is more deadly than self-righteousness, or more hopeful than contrition. We must confess that we are "nothing else but sin," for no confession short of this will be the whole truth, and if the Holy Spirit is at work within us, convincing us of sin, there will be no difficulty about making such an acknowledgment — it will spring spontaneously from our lips. What comfort does the text afford to those under a deep sense of sin! Sin mourned and confessed, however dark and foul, shall never shut a person out from the Lord Jesus. Whoever comes to Him, He will not at all cast out. Though dishonest as the thief, though unchaste as the woman who was a sinner, though fierce as Saul of Tarsus, though cruel as Manasseh, though rebellious as the prodigal, the great heart of love will look upon those who feels themselves to have no soundness in them, and will pronounce them clean, when they trust in Jesus crucified. Come to Him, then, poor heavy-laden sinner,

> Come needy, come guilty, come loathsome and bare;
> You can't come too filthy — come just as you are.

"I found the one my heart loves. I held him and would not let him go." — *Song of Songs 3:4*

OES Christ receive us when we come to Him, notwithstanding all our past sinfulness? Does He never chide us for having tried all other refuges first? And is there none on earth like Him? Is He the best of all the good, the fairest of all the fair? Oh, then let's praise Him! Daughters of Jerusalem, extol Him with tambourine and harp! Down with your idols, up with the Lord Jesus. Now let the standards of pomp and pride be trampled under foot, but let the cross of Jesus, which the world frowns and scoffs at, be lifted on high. O for a throne of ivory for our King Solomon! Let Him be set on high forever, and let my soul sit at His footstool, and kiss His feet, and wash them with my tears. Oh, how precious is Christ! How can it be that I have thought so little of Him? How is it I can go abroad for joy or comfort when He is so full, so rich, so satisfying? Fellow believer, make a covenant with your heart that you will never depart from Him, and ask your Lord to ratify it. Bid Him set you as a signet ring upon His finger, and as a bracelet upon His arm. Ask Him to bind you about Him, as the bride adorns herself with ornaments, and as the bridegroom puts on his jewels. I would live in Christ's heart; in the clefts of that rock my soul would eternally abide. The sparrow has made a house, and the swallow a nest for herself where she may lay her young, even Your altars, O Lord of hosts, my King and my God; and so too would I make my nest, my home, in You, and never may the soul of Your turtle dove go forth from You again, but may I nestle close to You, O Jesus, my true and only rest.

"When my precious Lord I find,
All my ardent passions glow;
Him with cords of love I bind,
Hold and will not let Him go."

"Sing the glory of his name; make his praise glorious!"
— *Psalm 66:2*

T is not an option for us whether or not we will praise God. Praise is God's most righteous due, and every Christian, as the recipient of His grace, is bound to praise God from day to day. It is true we have no authoritative rubric for daily praise; we have no commandment prescribing certain hours of song and thanksgiving: but the law written upon the heart teaches us that it is right to praise God; and the unwritten mandate comes to us with as much force as if it had been recorded on the tables of stone, or handed to us from the top of thundering Sinai. Yes, it is the Christian's *duty* to praise God. It is not only a pleasurable exercise, but it is the absolute obligation of his life. You who are always mourning, don't think that you are guiltless in this respect, or imagine that you can discharge your duty to your God without songs of praise. You are bound by the bonds of His love to bless His name as long as you live, and His praise should continually be in your mouth, for you are blessed, in order that you may bless Him; "the people I formed for Myself that they may proclaim My praise;" and if you do not praise God, you are not bringing forth the fruit which He, as the Divine Farmer, has a right to expect at your hands. Therefore, do not let your harp hang upon the willows, but take it down, and strive, with a grateful heart, to bring forth its loudest music. Arise and chant His praise. With every morning's dawn, lift up your notes of thanksgiving, and let every setting sun be followed with your song. Belt the earth with your praises; surround it with an atmosphere of melody, and God Himself will hearken from heaven and accept your music.

"E'en so I love Thee, and will love,
And in Thy praise will sing,
Because Thou art my loving God,
And my redeeming King."

"A live dog is better off than a dead lion!"
— *Ecclesiastes 9:4*

IFE is a precious thing, and in its humblest form it is superior to death. This truth is eminently certain in spiritual things. It is better to be the least in the kingdom of heaven than the greatest out of it. The lowest degree of grace is superior to the noblest development of unregenerate nature. Where the Holy Spirit implants divine life in the soul, there is a precious deposit which none of the refinements of education can equal. The thief on the cross excels Caesar on his throne; Lazarus among the dogs is better than Cicero among the senators; and the most unlettered Christian is in the sight of God superior to Plato. Life is the badge of nobility in the realm of spiritual things, and those without it are only coarser or finer specimens of the same lifeless material, needing to be made alive, for they are dead in trespasses and sins.

A living, loving, gospel sermon, however unlearned in matter and uncouth in style, is better than the finest discourse devoid of unction and power. A living dog keeps better watch than a dead lion, and is of more service to his master; and so the poorest spiritual preacher is infinitely to be preferred to the exquisite orator who has no wisdom but that of words, no energy but that of sound. The same holds true for our prayers and other religious exercises; if we are awakened in them by the Holy Spirit, they are acceptable to God through Jesus Christ, though we may think them to be worthless things; while our grand performances in which our hearts were absent, like dead lions, are mere carrion in the sight of the living God. O for living groans, living sighs, living despondencies, rather than lifeless songs and dead calms. Anything's better than death. The snarlings of the dog of hell will at least keep us awake, but dead faith and dead profession, what greater curses can a man have? Wake us, wake us, O Lord!

"Every delicacy, both new and old, that I have stored up for you, my lover." — *Song of Songs 7:13*

HE spouse desires to give to Jesus all that she produces. Our heart has "every delicacy," both "new and old," and they are laid up for our Beloved. At this rich autumnal season of fruit, let's survey our stores. We have *new* fruits. We desire to feel new life, new joy, new gratitude; we wish to make new resolves and carry them out by new labors; our heart blossoms with new prayers, and our soul is pledging herself to new efforts. But we have some *old* fruits too. There is our first love: a choice fruit at that, and Jesus delights in it. There is our first faith: that simple faith by which, having nothing, we became possessors of all things. There is our joy when first we knew the Lord: let's revive it. We have our old remembrances of the promises. How faithful God has been! In sickness, how softly He made our bed! In deep waters, how placidly He buoyed us up! In the flaming furnace, how graciously He delivered us. Old fruits, indeed! We have many of them, for His mercies have been more than the hairs of our head. We must regret old sins, but then we have had repentances which He has given us, by which we have wept our way to the cross and learned the merit of His blood. We have every delicacy, this morning, both new and old; but here is the point — *they are all stored up for Jesus.* Truly, those are the best and most acceptable services in which Jesus is the solitary aim of the soul, and His glory, without any admixture whatever, the end of all our efforts. Let our many delicacies be stored up only for our Beloved; let's display them when He is with us, and not hold them up before the gaze of humanity. Jesus, we will turn the key in our garden door, and none shall enter to rob You of one good fruit from the soil which You have watered with Your bloody sweat. Our all shall be Yours, Yours only, O Jesus, our Beloved!

"The LORD bestows favor and honor."
— *Psalm 84:11*

 T is Jehovah's nature to be generous; to give is His delight. His gifts are precious beyond measure, and are as freely given as the light of the sun. He gives grace to His elect because He wills it, to His redeemed because of His covenant, to the called because of His promise, to believers because they seek it, to sinners because they need it. He gives grace abundantly, seasonably, constantly, readily, sovereignly; doubly enhancing the value of the benefit by the way in which it is bestowed. Grace in all its forms He renders freely to His people: comforting, preserving, sanctifying, directing, instructing, assisting grace He generously pours into their souls without ceasing, and He always will do so, whatever may occur. Sickness may occur, but the Lord will give grace; poverty may happen to us, but grace will surely be affordable; death must come, but grace will light a candle at the darkest hour. Reader, how blessed it is as the years roll around, and the leaves begin to fall again, to enjoy such an unfading promise as this, "The Lord bestows favor."

The little conjunction *"and"* in this verse is a diamond rivet binding the present with the future: favor and honor always go together. God has married them, and no one can divorce them. The Lord would never deny honor to the soul He has freely allowed to live upon His favor; indeed, honor is nothing more than favor in its Sabbath dress, favor in full bloom, favor like autumn fruit, mellow and perfected. We cannot tell how soon this honor will be ours! It may be that before October has run its course we shall see the Holy City; but whether the interval is longer or shorter, we shall be glorified before long. Honor, the honor of heaven, the honor of eternity, the honor of Jesus, the honor of the Father, the Lord will surely give to His chosen. Oh, rare promise of a faithful God!

Two golden links of one celestial chain:
Who owneth grace shall surely glory gain.

"The hope that is stored up for you in heaven."
— *Colossians 1:5*

OUR hope in Christ for the future is the main-spring and the mainstay of our joy here. It will animate our hearts to think often of heaven, for all that we can desire is promised there. Here we are weary and haggard, but yonder is the land of *rest* where the sweat of work shall no more wet the worker's brow with dew, and fatigue shall be banished forever. To those who are weary and spent, the word "rest" is full of heaven. We are always in the field of battle; we are so tempted within and so molested by foes without that we have little or no peace; but in heaven we shall enjoy the *victory,* when the banner shall be waved aloft in triumph, and the sword shall be sheathed, and we shall hear our Captain say, "Well done, good and faithful servant!" We have suffered bereavement after bereavement, but we are going to the land of the *immortal* where graves are unknown things. Here sin is a constant grief to us, but there we shall be perfectly *holy,* for by no means shall anything enter into that kingdom which defiles. Hemlock does not spring up in the furrows of celestial fields. Oh! isn't it wonderful that you aren't going to live in banishment for-ever, that you aren't going to dwell in this wilderness eter-nally, but shall soon inherit Canaan? Nevertheless, don't let it be said of us that we are dreaming about the *future* and forgetting the *present.* Let the future sanctify the present to highest uses. Through the Spirit of God the hope of heaven is the most potent force for the product of virtue; it is a fountain of joyous effort; it is the cornerstone of cheerful holiness. Those who carry this hope within themselves works with vigor, for the joy of the Lord is their strength. They fight against temptation with enthusiasm, for the hope of the next world repels the flaming arrows of the adversary. They can work without present reward, for they look for a reward in the world to come.

"You who are highly esteemed." — *Daniel 10:11*

HILD of God, do you hesitate to assume this title? Ah! Has your unbelief made you forget that *you*, too, are greatly loved? Wouldn't you have to be loved a great deal to have been bought with the precious blood of Christ, as of a lamb without blemish and without spot? When God punished His only begotten Son for you, how could you be anything less than greatly loved? You lived in sin, and reveled in it; wouldn't you have been greatly loved for God to have put up with you so patiently? You were called by grace and led to a Savior, and made a child of God and an heir of heaven. Isn't all of this proof of the existence of a very great and superabounding love? Since that time, whether your path has been rough with troubles, or smooth with mercies, it has been full of proofs that you are a person who is greatly loved. If the Lord has chastened you, yet it was not out of anger; if He has made you poor, yet you have been rich in grace. The more unworthy you feel about yourself, the more evidence you have that nothing but unspeakable love could have led the Lord Jesus to save such a soul as yours. The more inferior you feel, the clearer the display of the abounding love of God becomes in having chosen you, called you, and made you an heir of bliss. Now, if there is such love between God and us let's live under the influence and sweetness of it, and exercise the privilege of our position. Let's not approach our Lord as though we were strangers, or as though He were unwilling to hear us — for we are greatly loved by our loving Father. "He who did not spare His own Son, but gave Him up for us all — how will He not also, along with Him, graciously give us all things?" Come boldly, O believer, for despite the whisperings of Satan and the doubtings of your own heart, you are greatly loved. Meditate on the exceeding greatness and faithfulness of divine love this evening, and in this frame of mind go to your bed in peace.

"Are not all angels ministering spirits sent to serve those who will inherit salvation?" — *Hebrews 1:14*

NGELS are the unseen attendants of the saints of God; they bear us up in their hands, lest we dash our foot against a stone. Loyalty to their Lord leads them to take a deep interest in the children of His love; they rejoice over the return of the prodigal to his father's house below, and they welcome the advent of the believer to the King's palace above. In times long past the sons and daughters of God were favored with their visible appearance, and at this day, although unseen by us, heaven is still opened, and the angels of God ascend and descend upon the Son of man, that they may visit the heirs of salvation. Seraphim still fly with live coals from off the altar to touch the lips of people greatly loved. If our eyes could be opened, we should see horses of fire and chariots of fire around the servants of the Lord; for we have come to an innumerable company of angels, who are all watchers and protectors of the royal seed. Spenser's line is not poetic fiction, where he sings —

> "How often do they with golden pinions cleave
> The flitting skies, like flying pursuivant
> Against foul fiends to aid us militant!"

To what dignity the chosen are elevated when the brilliant courtiers of heaven become their willing attendants! What a communion we are raised into since we communicate with spotless celestials! How well we are defended since all the twenty thousand chariots of God are armed for our deliverance! To whom do we owe all of this? Let the Lord Jesus Christ be forever endeared to us, for through Him we are allowed to sit in heavenly places far above principalities and powers. He it is whose camp is around about them that fear Him; He is the true Michael whose foot is upon the dragon. All hail, Jesus! you Angel of Jehovah's presence, to You this family offers its morning vows.

"He himself suffered when he was tempted."
— *Hebrews 2:18*

 T is a commonplace thought, and yet it tastes like nectar to the weary heart — Jesus was tempted as I am. You have heard that truth many times: have you grasped it? He was tempted to the very same sins into which we fall. Do not dissociate Jesus from our common humanity. It is a dark room which you are going through, but Jesus went through it before. It is a sharp fight which you are waging, but Jesus has stood foot to foot with the same enemy. Let's be of good cheer, Christ has borne the load before us, and the blood-stained footsteps of the King of glory may be seen along the road which we traverse at this hour. There is something sweeter yet — Jesus was tempted, but Jesus never sinned. Then, my soul, it isn't necessary for you to sin, for Jesus was a man, and if one man endured these temptations and didn't sin, then in His power His members may also cease from sin. Some beginners in the divine life think that they cannot be tempted without sinning, but they are mistaken; there is no sin in *being tempted,* but there *is* sin in *yielding to temptation.* Herein is comfort for the sorely tempted ones. There is still more to encourage them if they reflect that the Lord Jesus, though tempted, gloriously triumphed, and as He overcame, so surely shall His followers also, for Jesus is the representative man for His people; the Head has triumphed, and the members share in the victory. Fears are unnecessary, for Christ is with us, armed for our defense. Our place of safety is the heart of the Savior. Perhaps we are tempted just now, in order to drive us nearer to Him. Blessed is any wind that blows us into the port of our Savior's love! Happy wounds, which make us seek the beloved Physician. You tempted ones, come to your tempted Savior, for He can be touched with a feeling of your infirmities, and will help every tested and tempted one.

"When evening comes, there will be light."
— *Zechariah 14:7*

FTENTIMES we look forward with forebodings to *the time of old age*, forgetful that at evening it shall be light. To many saints, old age is the choicest season in their lives. A balmier air fans the mariner's cheek as he nears the shore of immortality, fewer waves ruffle his sea, quiet reigns, deep, still and solemn. From the altar of age the flashes of the fire of youth are gone, but the more real flame of earnest feeling remains. The pilgrims have reached Beulah land, that happy country whose days are as the days of heaven upon earth. Angels visit it, celestial gales blow over it, flowers of paradise grow in it, and the air is filled with seraphic music. Some dwell here for years, and others come to it only a few hours before their departure, but it is an Eden on earth. We may well long for the time when we shall recline in its shady groves and be satisfied with hope until the time of fruition comes. The setting sun seems larger than when aloft in the sky, and a splendor of glory tinges all the clouds which surround his going down. Pain does not break the calm of the sweet twilight of age, for strength made perfect in weakness bears up with patience under it all. Ripe fruits of choice experience are gathered as the rare repast of life's evening, and the soul prepares itself for rest.

The Lord's people shall also enjoy light in *the hour of death*. Unbelief laments; the shadows fall, the night is coming, existence is ending. Ah no, cries faith, the night is far spent, the true day is at hand. Light is come, the light of immortality, the light of a Father's countenance. Gather up your feet in the bed, see the waiting bands of spirits! Angels waft you away. Farewell, loved one, you are gone, you wave your hand. Ah, now it is light. The pearly gates are open, the golden streets shine in the jasper light. We cover our eyes, but you behold the unseen; adieu, believer; you have light at evening the likes of which we do not have yet.

*"But if anybody does sin, we have one who speaks
to the Father in our defense — Jesus Christ, the
Righteous One." — 1 John 2:1*

F anybody does sin, we *have* one who speaks to the Father in our defense." Yes, though we sin, we have Him still. John does not say, "If anybody sins he has forfeited his advocate," but "we *have* one who speaks to the Father in our defense," sinners though we are. All the sin that a believer ever did, or can be allowed to commit, cannot destroy his interest in the Lord Jesus Christ, as his advocate. The name here given to our Lord is suggestive. *"Jesus."* Ah! then He is an advocate such as we need, for Jesus is the name of One whose business and delight it is to save. "They shall call His name Jesus, for *He shall save* His people from their sins." His sweetest name implies His success. Next, it is "Jesus *Christ*" — Christos, the anointed. This shows *His authority* to plead. The Christ has a right to plead, for He is the Father's own appointed advocate and elected priest. If He were of our choosing He might fail, but if God has laid help upon one that is mighty, we may safely lay our trouble where God has laid His help. He is Christ, and therefore authorized; He is Christ, and therefore *qualified*, for the anointing has fully fitted Him for His work. He can plead so as to move the heart of God and prevail. What words of tenderness, what sentences of persuasion will the anointed use when He stands up to plead for me! One more letter of His name remains, "Jesus Christ *the Righteous One*." This is not only His character BUT His plea. It is His character, and if the Righteous One is my advocate, then my cause is good, or He would not have espoused it. It is His plea, for He meets the charge of unrighteousness against me by the plea that *He* is righteous. He declares Himself my substitute and puts His obedience to my account. My soul, you have a friend well fitted to be your advocate, He cannot help but succeed; leave yourself entirely in His hands.

"He got up and ate and drank. Strengthened by that food,
he traveled forty days and forty nights."
— *1 Kings 19:8*

LL the strength supplied to us by our gracious God is meant for service, not for wantonness or boasting. When the prophet Elijah found the cake baked over hot coals, and the jar of water placed by his head, as he lay under the broom tree, he was no gentleman to be gratified with dainty fare that he might stretch himself at his ease; far from it, he was commissioned to go forty days and forty nights strengthened by it, journeying towards Horeb, the mountain of God. When the Master invited the disciples to "Come and dine" with Him, after the feast was concluded He said to Peter, "Feed my sheep;" further adding, "Follow me." Even thus it is with us; we eat the bread of heaven, that we may expend our strength in the Master's service. We come to the Passover, and eat of the paschal lamb ready, staff in hand, so as to start off at once when we have satisfied our hunger. Some Christians are for living *on* Christ, but are not so anxious to live *for* Christ. Earth should be a preparation for heaven; and heaven is the place where saints feast most and work most. They sit down at the table of our Lord, and they serve Him day and night in His temple. They eat of heavenly food and render perfect service. Believer, in the strength you daily gain from Christ, work for Him. Some of us have yet to learn much concerning the design of our Lord in giving us His grace. We are not to retain the precious grains of truth as the Egyptian mummy held the wheat for ages, without giving it an opportunity to grow: we must sow it and water it. Why does the Lord send down the rain upon the thirsty earth, and give the genial sunshine? Isn't it so these may all help the fruits of the earth to yield food for man? Even so the Lord feeds and refreshes our souls that we may afterwards use our renewed strength in the promotion of His glory.

"Whoever believes and is baptized will be saved."
— *Mark 16:16*

R. MacDonald asked the inhabitants of the island of St. Kilda how a man must be saved. An old man replied, "We shall be saved if we repent, and forsake our sins, and turn to God." "Yes," said a middle-aged woman, "and with a true heart too." "Ay," answered a third, "and with prayer;" and, added a fourth, "It must be the prayer of the heart." "And we must be diligent too," said a fifth, "in keeping the commandments." Thus, each having contributed a mite, feeling that a very decent creed had been made up, they all looked and listened for the preacher's approbation, but they had aroused his deepest pity. The carnal mind always maps out for itself a way in which self can work and become great, but the Lord's way is quite the reverse. Believing and being baptized are no matters of merit to be gloried in — they are so simple that boasting is excluded, and free grace bears the palm. It may be that the reader is unsaved — what is the reason? Do you think the way of salvation as laid down in the text to be dubious? How can that be when God has pledged His own word for its certainty? Do you think it too easy? Why, then, don't you attend to it? Its ease leaves those without excuse who neglect it. To believe is simply to trust, to depend, to rely upon Christ Jesus. To be baptized is to submit to the sacrament which our Lord fulfilled at the Jordan, to which the converted ones submitted at Pentecost, to which the jailer yielded obedience the very night of his conversion. The outward sign doesn't save, but it sets forth to us our death, burial, and resurrection with Jesus, and, like the Lord's Supper, is not to be neglected. Reader, do you believe in Jesus? Then, dear friend, dismiss your fears, you shall be saved. Are you still an unbeliever? Then remember there is only one door, and if you will not enter by it, you will perish in your sins.

"Whoever drinks the water I give him will never thirst."
— *John 4:14*

HE who is a believer in Jesus finds enough in his Lord to satisfy him now, and to content him forever. The believer is not the man whose days are weary for want of comfort, and whose nights are long from absence of heart-cheering thought, for he finds in religion such a spring of joy, such a fountain of consolation, that he is content and happy. Put him in a dungeon and he will find good company; place him in a barren wilderness, he will eat the bread of heaven; drive him away from friendship, he will meet the "friend who sticks closer than a brother." Blast all his gourds, and he will find shadow beneath the Rock of Ages; sap the foundation of his earthly hopes, but his heart will still be fixed, trusting in the Lord. The heart is as insatiable as the grave until Jesus enters it, and then it is a cup full to overflowing. There is such a fullness in Christ that He alone is the believer's all. The true saint is so completely satisfied with the all-sufficiency of Jesus that he thirsts no more — except when it is for deeper draughts of the living fountain. In that sweet manner, believer, shall you thirst; it shall not be a thirst of pain, but of loving desire; you will find it a sweet thing to be panting after a fuller enjoyment of Jesus' love. One in days gone by has said, "I have been sinking my bucket down into the well very frequently, but now my thirst after Jesus has become so insatiable, that I long to put the well itself up to my lips, and drink from it." Is this the feeling of your heart now, believer? Do you feel that all your desires are satisfied in Jesus, and that you have no want now, but to know more of Him, and to have closer fellowship with Him? Then come continually to the fountain, and take of the water of life freely. Jesus will never think you take too much, but will always welcome you, saying, "Drink, yes, drink abundantly, O beloved."

"He had married a Cushite." — *Numbers 12:1*

TRANGE choice of Moses, but how much more strange the choice of Him who is a prophet like Moses, and greater than he! Our Lord, who is fair as the lily, has entered into marriage union with one who confesses herself to be dark, because the sun has looked upon her. It is the wonder of angels that the love of Jesus should be set upon poor, lost, guilty human beings. Each believer must, when filled with a sense of Jesus' love, be also overwhelmed with astonishment that such love should be lavished on an object so utterly unworthy of it. Knowing as we do our secret guiltiness, unfaithfulness, and darkness of heart, we are dissolved in grateful admiration of the matchless freedom and sovereignty of grace. Jesus must have found the cause of His love in His own heart, He could not have found it in us, for it is not there. Even since our conversion we have been dark, though grace has made us comely. Holy Rutherford said of himself what we must each subscribe to — "His relation to me is, that I am sick, and He is the Physician of whom I stand in need. Alas! how often I play fast and loose with Christ! He binds, I loose; He builds, I cast down; I quarrel with Christ, and He agrees with me twenty times a day!" Most tender and faithful Husband of our souls, pursue Your gracious work of conforming us to Your image until You shall present even us poor Cushites to Yourself, without spot, or wrinkle, or any such thing. Moses met with opposition because of his marriage, and both himself and his spouse were the subjects of an evil eye. Can we wonder if this vain world opposes Jesus and His spouse, and especially when great sinners are converted? This is constantly the Pharisee's ground of objection, "This man welcomes sinners." Still the old cause of quarrel is revived, because "He had married a Cushite."

"Why have you brought this trouble on your servant?"
— *Numbers 11:11*

UR heavenly Father sends us frequent troubles *to test our faith.* If our faith is worth anything, it will stand the test. Gilt is afraid of fire, but gold is not: the *paste* gem dreads to be touched by the diamond, but the true jewel fears no test. It is a poor faith which can only trust God when friends are true, the body full of health, and the business profitable; but that is true faith which holds by the Lord's faithfulness when friends are gone, when the body is sick, when spirits are depressed, and the light of our Father's countenance is hidden. A faith which can say, in the direst trouble, "Though He slay me, yet will I hope in Him," is heaven-born faith. The Lord afflicts His servants *to glorify Himself,* for He is greatly glorified in the graces of His people, which are His own handiwork. When "tribulation works patience; and patience, experience; and experience, hope," the Lord is honored by these growing virtues. We would never know how the music of the harp sounds if the strings were left untouched, nor enjoy the juice of the grape if it weren't trampled in the winepress; nor discover the sweet perfume of cinnamon if it weren't pressed and beaten; nor feel the warmth of fire if the coals were not utterly consumed. The wisdom and power of the great Workman are discovered by the trials through which His vessels of mercy are permitted to pass. Present afflictions *tend also to heighten future joy.* There must be shades in the picture to bring out the beauty of the lights. Could we be so supremely blessed in heaven, if we hadn't known the curse of sin and the sorrow of earth? Won't peace be sweeter after conflict, and rest more welcome after toil? Won't the recollection of past sufferings enhance the bliss of the glorified? There are many other comfortable answers to the question with which we opened our brief meditation: Why have You brought this trouble on Your servant? Let's muse upon it all day long.

"On whom are you depending?" — *Isaiah 36:5*

 EADER, this is an important question. Listen to the Christian's answer, and see if it is yours. "On whom are you depending?" "I trust," says the Christian, "in a triune God. I trust *the Father,* believing that He has chosen me from before the foundations of the world; I trust Him to provide for me in providence, to teach me, to guide me, to correct me if need be, and to bring me home to His own house where the many mansions are. I trust *the Son.* Very God of very God is He — the man Christ Jesus. I trust in Him to take away all my sins by His own sacrifice, and to adorn me with His perfect righteousness. I trust Him to be my Intercessor, to present my prayers and desires before His Father's throne, and I trust Him to be my Advocate at the last great day, to plead my cause, and to justify me. I trust Him for what He is, for what He has done, and for what He has promised yet to do. And I trust *the Holy Spirit* — He has begun to save me from my inbred sins; I trust Him to drive them all out; I trust Him to curb my temper, to subdue my will, to enlighten my understanding, to check my passions, to comfort my despondency, to help my weakness, to illuminate my darkness; I trust Him to dwell in me as my life, to reign in me as my King, to sanctify me wholly, spirit, soul, and body, and then to take me up to dwell with the saints in light forever."

Oh, blessed trust! To trust Him whose power will never be exhausted, whose love will never wane, whose kindness will never change, whose faithfulness will never fail, whose wisdom will never be nonplused, and whose perfect goodness can never decrease! Happy are you, reader, if this trust is yours! So trusting, you shall enjoy sweet peace now, and glory hereafter, and the foundation of your trust shall never be removed.

"Put out into deep water, and let down the nets for a catch." — Luke 5:4

 E learn from this narrative the *necessity of human agency.* The catch of fishes was miraculous, yet neither the fisherman nor his boat, nor his fishing tackle were ignored; but all were used to take the fish. So in the saving of souls, God works by means; and while the present economy of grace shall stand, God will be pleased by the foolishness of preaching to save them that believe. When God works without instruments, doubtless He is glorified; but He has Himself selected the plan of instrumentality as being that by which He is most magnified in the earth. *Means of themselves are utterly unavailing.* "Master, we've worked hard all night and haven't caught anything." What was the reason for this? Were they not fishermen plying their special calling? Certainly, they were no novices; they understood the work. Had they gone about the toil unskillfully? No. Had they lacked industry? No, they had worked hard. Had they lacked perseverance? No, they had *worked all night.* Was there a deficiency of fish in the sea? Certainly not, for as soon as the Master came, they swam to the net in shoals. What, then, is the reason? Is it because there is no power in the means of themselves apart from the presence of Jesus? "Without Him we can do nothing." But with Christ we can do all things. *Christ's presence confers success.* Jesus sat in Peter's boat, and His will, by a mysterious influence, drew the fish to the net. When Jesus is lifted up in His church, His presence is the church's power — the shout of a king is in the midst of her. "But I, when I am lifted up from the earth, will draw all men to Myself." Let's go out this morning on our work of soul fishing, looking up in faith, and around us in solemn anxiety. Let's toil until night comes, and we shall not work in vain, for He who bids us let down the net, will fill it with fish.

"Pray in the Holy Spirit." — Jude 20

OTICE the grand characteristic of true prayer — *"In the Holy Spirit."* The seed of acceptable devotion must come from heaven's storehouse. Only the prayer which comes from God can go to God. We must shoot the Lord's arrows back to Him. That desire which He writes upon our heart will move His heart and bring down a blessing, but the desires of the flesh have no power with Him.

Praying in the Holy Spirit is praying in *fervency.* Cold prayers ask the Lord not to hear them. Those who do not plead with fervency, do not plead at all. It is as well to speak of lukewarm fire as of lukewarm prayer — it is essential that it be red hot. It is praying *perseveringly.* The true suppliant gathers force as he proceeds, and grows more fervent when God delays the answer. The longer the gate is closed, the more vehemently does he use the knocker, and the longer the angel lingers the more resolved is he that he will never let him go without the blessing. Beautiful in God's sight are tearful, agonizing, unconquerable, insistent requests. It means praying *humbly,* for the Holy Spirit never puffs us up with pride. It is His office to convince of sin, and so to bow us down in contrition and brokenness of spirit. We shall never sing *Gloria in excelsis* unless we pray to God *De profundis:* out of the depths must we cry, or we shall never behold glory in the highest. It is *loving* prayer. Prayer should be perfumed with love, saturated with love — love for our fellow saints, and love for Christ. Moreover, it must be a prayer full of *faith.* A man prevails only as he believes. The Holy Spirit is the author of faith, and strengthens it, so that we pray believing God's promise. O that this blessed combination of excellent graces, priceless and sweet as the spices of the merchant, might be fragrant within us because the Holy Spirit is in our hearts! Most blessed Comforter, exert Your mighty power within us, helping our infirmities in prayer.

"Able to keep you from falling." — *Jude 24*

 N some sense the path to heaven is very safe, but in other respects there is *no road as dangerous*. It is surrounded with difficulties. One false step (and how easy it is to take that if grace is absent), and down we go. What a slippery path is that which some of us have to tread! How many times have we to exclaim with the Psalmist, "My feet had almost slipped; I had nearly lost my foothold." If we were strong, sure-footed mountaineers, this wouldn't matter so much; but in ourselves, *how weak we are!* In the best roads *we soon falter*, in the smoothest paths we quickly stumble. These feeble knees of ours can scarcely support our tottering weight. A straw may throw us, and a pebble can wound us; we are mere children tremblingly taking our first steps in the walk of faith, our heavenly Father holds us by the arms or we should soon be down. Oh, if we are kept from falling, how must we bless the patient power which watches over us day by day! Think, how prone we are to sin, how apt to choose danger, how strong our tendency to cast ourselves down, and these reflections will make us sing more sweetly than we have ever done, "Glory be to Him, who is able to keep us from falling." *We have many foes* who try to push us down. The road is rough and we are weak. In addition to this, enemies lurk in ambush, who rush out when we least expect them, and work to trip us up, or hurl us down the nearest precipice. Only an Almighty arm can preserve us from these unseen foes, who are seeking to destroy us. Such an arm is engaged for our defense. He is faithful that has promised, and He is able to keep us from falling, so that with a deep sense of our utter weakness, we may cherish a firm belief in our perfect safety, and say, with joyful confidence,

> "Against me earth and hell combine,
> But on my side is power divine;
> Jesus is all, and He is mine!"

"Jesus did not answer a word." — *Matthew 15:23*

ENUINE seekers who as yet have not obtained the blessing, may take comfort from the story before us. The Savior didn't at once give the blessing, even though the woman had great faith in Him. He intended to give it, but He waited awhile. "Jesus did not answer a word." Weren't her prayers good? Never better in the world. Wasn't her situation needy? Sorrowfully needy. Didn't she *feel* her need sufficiently? She felt it overwhelmingly. Wasn't she earnest enough? She was intensely so. Didn't she have any faith? She had such a high degree of it that even Jesus wondered, and said, "Woman, you have great faith." See then, although it is true that faith brings peace, yet it does not always bring it instantaneously. There may be certain reasons calling for the trial of faith, rather than the reward of faith. Genuine faith may be in the soul like a hidden seed, but as yet it may not have budded and blossomed into joy and peace. A painful silence from the Savior is the grievous trial of many a seeking soul, but heavier still is the affliction of a harsh cutting reply such as this, "It is not right to take the children's bread and toss it to their dogs." Many, in waiting upon the Lord, find immediate delight, but this isn't the case with everyone. Some, like the jailer, are in a moment turned from darkness to light, but others are plants of slower growth. A deeper sense of sin may be given to you instead of a sense of pardon, and in such a case you will need patience to bear the heavy blow. Ah! poor heart, though Christ beat and bruise you, or even slay you, trust Him; though He should give you an angry word, believe in the love of His heart. I beg you, don't give up seeking or trusting my Master just because you haven't yet obtained the conscious joy which you long for. Cast yourself on Him, and perseveringly depend even in situations where you can't rejoicingly hope.

"Before his glorious presence without fault." — *Jude 24*

URN this wonderful phrase around in your mind, *"without fault!"* We are far off from it now; but as our Lord never stops short of perfection in His work of love, we shall reach it one day. The Savior who will keep His people to the end, will also present them at last to Himself, as "a radiant church, without stain or wrinkle or any other blemish, but holy and blameless." All the jewels in the Savior's crown are of the first water and without a single flaw. All the maids of honor who attend the Lamb's wife are pure virgins without spot or stain. But how will Jesus make us faultless? He will wash us from our sins in His own blood until we are white and fair as God's purest angel; and we shall be clothed in His righteousness, that righteousness which makes the saint who wears it positively faultless; yes, perfect in the sight of God. We shall be blameless and unreproveable even in His eyes. His law will not only have no charge against us, but it will be magnified in us. Moreover, the work of the Holy Spirit within us will be altogether complete. He will make us so perfectly holy, that we shall have no lingering tendency to sin. Judgment, memory, will — every power and passion shall be emancipated from the slavery of evil. We shall be holy even as God is holy, and in His presence we shall dwell forever. Saints will not be out of place in heaven, their beauty will be as great as that of the place prepared for them. Oh the rapture of that hour when the everlasting doors shall be lifted up, and we, being made fit for the inheritance, shall dwell with the saints in light. Sin gone, Satan shut out, temptation past forever, and ourselves "faultless" before God, this will be heaven indeed! Let's be joyful now as we rehearse the song of eternal praise so soon to roll forth in full chorus from all the bloodwashed host; let's copy David's exultings before the ark as a prelude to our ecstasies before the throne.

"I will save you from the hands of the wicked and redeem you from the grasp of the cruel."
— *Jeremiah 15:21*

 OTE the glorious personality of the promise. *I will, I* will. The Lord Jehovah Himself intercedes to deliver and redeem His people. He pledges Himself personally to rescue them. His own arm shall do it, that He may have the glory. Here is not a word said of any effort of our own which may be needed to assist the Lord. Neither our strength nor our weakness is taken into the account, but the lone *I*, like the sun in the heavens, shines out resplendent in all-sufficiency. Why then do we calculate our forces, and consult with flesh and blood to our grievous wounding? Jehovah has power enough without borrowing from our puny arm. Peace, you unbelieving thoughts, be still, and know that the Lord reigns. Nor is there a hint concerning secondary means and causes. The Lord says nothing of friends and helpers: He undertakes the work alone, and feels no need of human arms to aid Him. All of our looking around to companions and relatives is in vain; they are broken reeds if we lean upon them — often unwilling when able, and unable when they are willing. Since the promise comes from God alone, it would be well to wait only upon Him; and when we do so, our expectation never fails us. Who are the wicked that we should fear them? The Lord will utterly consume them; they are to be pitied rather than feared. As for terrible ones, they are only terrors to those who have no God to fly to, for when the Lord is on our side, whom shall we fear? If we run into sin to please the wicked, we have cause to be alarmed, but if we hold fast to our integrity, the rage of tyrants shall be overruled for our good. When the fish swallowed Jonah, he found him a morsel which he could not digest; and when the world devours the church, it is glad to be rid of it again. In all times of fiery trial, in patience let's possess our souls.

> *"Let us lift up our hearts and our hands to God*
> *in heaven."* — *Lamentations 3:41*

HE act of prayer *teaches us our unworthiness,* which is a very salutary lesson for such proud beings as we are. If God gave us favors without constraining us to pray for them we should never know how poor we are, but a true prayer is an inventory of wants, a catalog of necessities, a revelation of hidden poverty. While it is an application to divine wealth, it is a confession of human emptiness. The most healthy state of a Christian is to be always empty in self and constantly depending upon the Lord for supplies; to be always poor in self and rich in Jesus; weak as water personally, but mighty through God to do great exploits; and hence the use of prayer, because, while it adores God, it lays the creature where it should be, in the very dust. Apart from the answer which it brings, prayer is a great benefit in itself to the Christian. As the runner gains strength for the race by daily exercise, so for the great race of life we acquire energy by the hallowed work of prayer. Prayer plumes the wings of God's young eaglets, that they may learn to mount above the clouds. Prayer puts on the loins of God's warriors, and sends them forth to combat with their sinews braced and their muscles firm. An earnest pleader comes out of his prayer time, even as the sun rises from the chambers of the east, rejoicing like a strong man to run his race. Prayer is that uplifted hand of Moses which routs the Amalekites more than the sword of Joshua; it is the arrow shot from the chamber of the prophet foreboding defeat to the Syrians. Prayer puts on human weakness with divine strength, turns human folly into heavenly wisdom, and gives to troubled mortals the peace of God. We don't know what prayer cannot do! We thank you, great God, for the mercy seat, a choice proof of your marvelous loving-kindness. Help us to use it correctly throughout this day!

"Those he predestined, he also called."
— Romans 8:30

 N 2 Timothy 1:9 we read — "Who has saved us and called us to a *holy* life." Now, here is a touchstone by which we may try our calling. It is "a holy life — not because of anything we have done but because of His own purpose and grace." This calling forbids all trust in our own doings, and conducts us to Christ alone for salvation, but it afterwards purges us from dead works to serve the living and true God. As He that has called you is holy, so must you be holy. If you are living in sin, you are not called, but if you are truly Christ's, you can say, "Nothing pains me so much as sin; I desire to be rid of it; Lord, help me to be holy." Is this the panting of your heart? Is this the tenor of your life towards God, and His divine will? Again, in Philippians 3:13, 14, we are told of "the goal to win the prize for which God has called me heavenward in Christ Jesus." Is this then the prize you want to win? Has it ennobled your heart, and set it upon heavenly things? Has it elevated your hopes, your tastes, your desires? Has it raised the constant tenor of your life, so that you spend it with God and for God? Another test we find in Hebrews 3:1 — those "who share in the *heavenly* calling." Heavenly calling means a call *from* heaven. If an individual alone calls you, you are uncalled. Is your calling of God? Is it a call *to* heaven as well as from heaven? Unless you are a stranger here, and heaven your home, you have not been called with a heavenly calling; for those who have been so called, declare that they look for a city with foundations, whose architect and builder is God, and they themselves are strangers and pilgrims upon the earth. Is your calling thus holy, high, heavenly? Then, beloved, you have been called of God, for such is the calling with which God calls His people.

"I meditate on your precepts." — *Psalm 119:15*

HERE are times when solitude is better than society, and silence is wiser than speech. We would be better Christians if we were alone more, waiting upon God, and gathering through meditation on His Word spiritual strength for work in His service. We ought to muse *upon the things of God, because we thus get the real nutriment out of them.* Truth is something like the cluster of the vine: if we would have wine from it, we must bruise it; we must press and squeeze it many times. The bruiser's feet must come down joyfully upon the bunches, or else the juice will not flow; and they must tread the grapes well, or else much of the precious liquid will be wasted. So we must, by meditation, tread the clusters of truth, if we would get the wine of consolation out of them. Our bodies are not supported by merely taking food into the mouth, but the process which really supplies the muscle, and the nerve, and the sinew, and the bone, is the process of digestion. It is by digestion that the outward food becomes assimilated with the inner life. Our souls are not nourished merely by listening awhile to this, that, and the other part of divine truth. Hearing, reading, seeing, and learning, all require inwardly digesting to complete their usefulness, and the inward digesting of the truth lies for the most part in meditating upon it. Why is it that some Christians, although they hear many sermons, make such slow advances in the divine life? Because they neglect their times of prayer, and do not thoughtfully meditate on God's Word. They love the wheat, but they do not grind it; they want have the corn, but they will not go out into the fields to gather it; the fruit hangs upon the tree, but they will not pluck it; the water flows at their feet, but they will not stoop to drink it. From such folly deliver us, O Lord. Our resolve this morning is, "I meditate on Your precepts."

"The [Comforter], the Holy Spirit." — John 14:26

HIS age is peculiarly the dispensation of the Holy Spirit, in which Jesus cheers us, not by His personal presence, as He shall do by-and-by, but by the indwelling and constant abiding of the Holy Spirit, who is forever the Comforter of the church. It is His office to console the hearts of God's people. He convinces of sin; He illuminates and instructs; but still the main part of His work lies in making glad the hearts of the renewed, in confirming the weak, and lifting up all those that are bowed down. He does this by revealing Jesus to them. The Holy Spirit consoles, but Christ *is the consolation.* If we may use the figure, the Holy Spirit is the Physician, but Jesus is the medicine. *He* heals the wound, but it is by applying the holy ointment of Christ's name and grace. He does not take of His own things, but of the things of Christ. So if we give to the Holy Spirit the Greek name of *Paraclete,* as we sometimes do, then our heart confers on our blessed Lord Jesus the title of *Paraclesis.* If the one is the Comforter, the other is the Comfort. Now, with such rich provision for his need, why should the Christian be sad and hopeless? The Holy Spirit has graciously engaged to be your Comforter: do you imagine, O you weak and trembling believer, that He will be negligent of His sacred trust? Can you suppose that He has undertaken what He cannot or will not per-form? If it is His special work to strengthen you, and to comfort you, do you suppose He has forgotten His busi-ness, or that He will fail in the loving office which He sustains towards you? No, don't think so harshly of the tender and blessed Spirit whose name is "the Comforter." He is pleased to provide the oil of joy for mourning, and the garment of praise for the spirit of heaviness. Trust in Him, and He will surely comfort you until the house of mourning is closed forever, and the marriage feast has begun.

"Godly sorrow brings repentance." — *2 Corinthians 7:10*

ENUINE spiritual mourning for sin is *the work of the Spirit of God.* Repentance is too choice a flower to grow in nature's garden. Pearls grow naturally in oysters, but penitence never shows itself in sinners unless divine grace works it in them. If you have one particle of real hatred for sin, God must have given it to you, for human nature's thorns never produced a single fig. "Flesh gives birth to flesh."

True repentance *has a distinct reference to the Savior.* When we repent of sin, we must have one eye upon sin and another upon the cross, or it will be better still if we fix both our eyes upon Christ and see our transgressions only in the light of His love.

True sorrow for sin is *eminently practical.* We cannot say we hate sin, if we live in it. Repentance makes us see the evil of sin, not merely as a theory, but experimentally — as a burnt child dreads fire. We should be as frightened of it as a person, who has recently been stopped and robbed, is afraid of the thief upon the highway; and we shall shun it — shun it in everything — not in great things only, but in little things, as we shun little vipers as well as great snakes. True mourning for sin will make us very careful with our tongues, lest they should say a wrong word; we shall be very watchful over our daily actions, lest in anything we offend. Each night we will close the day with painful confession of our shortcomings, and each morning wake with anxious prayers, that this day God would hold us up that we may not sin against Him.

Sincere repentance is *continual.* Believers repent until their dying day. This dropping well is not intermittent. Every other sorrow yields to time, but this dear sorrow grows with our growth, and it is so sweet a bitter, that we thank God we are permitted to enjoy and to endure it until we enter our eternal rest.

"Love is as strong as death." — *Song of Songs 8:6*

 HOSE love can this be which is as mighty as the conqueror of monarchs, the destroyer of the human race? Wouldn't it sound like satire if it was applied to my poor, weak, and scarcely living love to Jesus my Lord? I do love Him, and perhaps by His grace, I could even die for Him, but as for my love in itself, it can scarcely endure a scoffing jest, much less a cruel death. Surely it is my Beloved's love which is spoken of here — the love of Jesus, the matchless lover of souls. His love was indeed stronger than the most terrible death, for it endured the trial of the cross triumphantly. It was a lingering death, but love survived the torment; a shameful death, but love despised the shame; a legally punishable death, but love bore our iniquities; a forsaken, lonely death, from which the eternal Father hid His face, but love endured the curse, and gloried over all. Never such love, never such death. It was a desperate duel, but love was the victor. What then, my heart? Don't you have any emotions stirred within you at the contemplation of such heavenly affection? Yes, my Lord, I long, I pant to feel Your love flaming like a furnace within me. Come Yourself and excite the ardor of my spirit.

"For every drop of crimson blood
Thus shed to make me live,
O wherefore, wherefore have not I
A thousand lives to give?"

Why should I despair of loving Jesus with a love as strong as death? He deserves it: I desire it. The martyrs felt such love, and they were only flesh and blood, then why not I? They mourned their weakness, and yet out of weakness were made strong. Grace gave them all their unflinching constancy — there is the same grace for me. Jesus, lover of my soul, shed abroad such love, even Your love in my heart, this evening.

"I consider everything a loss compared to the
surpassing greatness of knowing Christ Jesus
my Lord." — *Philippians 3:8*

PIRITUAL knowledge of Christ will be a *personal* knowledge. I cannot know Jesus through another person's acquaintance with Him. No, *I* must know Him *myself;* I must know Him on my own account. It will be an *intelligent* knowledge — I must know *Him,* not as the visionary dreams of Him, but as the Word reveals Him. I must know His natures, divine and human. I must know His offices — His attributes — His works — His shame — His glory. I must meditate upon Him until I "have power, together with all the saints, to grasp how wide and long and high and deep is the love of Christ, and to know this love that surpasses knowledge." It will be an *affectionate* knowledge of Him; indeed, if I know Him at all, I must love Him. An ounce of heart knowledge is worth a ton of head learning. Our knowledge of Him will be a *satisfying* knowledge. When I know my Savior, my mind will be full to the brim — I shall feel that I have that which my spirit panted after. "This is that bread whereof if a man eat he will never go hungry." At the same time it will be an *exciting* knowledge; the more I know of my Beloved, the more I shall want to know. The higher I climb, the loftier will be the summits which invite my eager footsteps. The more I get, the more I want.. Like the miser's treasure, my gold will make me covet more. To conclude; this knowledge of Christ Jesus will be a most *happy* one; in fact, so elevating that, sometimes, it will completely bear me up above all trials, and doubts, and sorrows; and it will, while I enjoy it, make me something more than "Man born of woman is of few days and full of trouble;" for it will fling about me the immortality of the ever-living Savior, and gird me with the golden belt of His eternal joy. Come, my soul, sit at Jesus' feet and learn of Him all this day.

"Do not conform any longer to the pattern of this world." — *Romans 12:2*

 F a Christian can possibly be saved while he conforms to this world, at any rate it must be so as by fire. Such a bare salvation is almost as much to be dreaded as desired. Reader, would you wish to leave this world in the darkness of a hopeless death bed, and enter heaven as a shipwrecked mariner climbs the rocks of his native country? Then be worldly. Be mixed up with Mammonites, and refuse to go outside the camp bearing Christ's reproach. But would you have a heaven below as well as a heaven above? Would you have power, together with all the saints, to grasp how wide and long and high and deep is the love of Christ, and to know this love that surpasses knowledge? Would you receive an abundant entrance into the joy of your Lord? Then come out from among them, and be separate, and don't touch the unclean thing. Would you attain the full assurance of faith? You cannot gain it while you commune with sinners. Would you flame with vehement love? Your love will be dampened by the drenchings of godless society. You cannot become a great Christian — you may be a babe in grace, but you never can be perfect in Christ Jesus while you yield yourself to the worldly maxims and modes of business of this world. It is unhealthy for an heir of heaven to be a great friend with the heirs of hell. It looks bad when a courtier is too intimate with his king's enemies. Even small inconsistencies are dangerous. Little thorns make great blisters, little moths destroy fine garments, and little frivolities and little rogueries will rob religion of a thousand joys. O professing Christian, too little separated from sinners, you don't know what you lose by your conformity to the world. It cuts the tendons of your strength, and makes you creep where you ought to run. Then, for your own comfort's sake, and for the sake of your growth in grace, if you are a Christian, be a Christian, and be a marked and distinct one.

"But who can endure the day of his coming?"
— Malachi 3:2

IS first coming was without external pomp or show of power, and yet in truth there were few who could tolerate its testing might. Herod and all Jerusalem with him were stirred at the news of the wondrous birth. Those who supposed themselves to be waiting for Him, showed the fallacy of their professions by rejecting Him when He came. His life on earth was a winnowing fan, which tested the great heap of religious profession, and few enough could survive the process. But what will His second advent be? What sinner can endure to think of it? "He will strike the earth with the rod of His mouth; with the breath of His lips He will slay the wicked." When in His humiliation He had only said to the soldiers, "I am He," they fell backward; what will be the terror of His enemies when He shall more fully reveal Himself as the *"I am"*? His death shook earth and darkened heaven. What will the dreadful splendor of that day be like in which, as the living Savior, He shall summon the living and dead before Him? O that the terrors of the Lord would persuade us to forsake our sins and kiss the Son lest He be angry! Though a lamb, He is yet the lion of the tribe of Judah, tearing the prey in pieces; and though He does not break the bruised reed, yet He will break His enemies with a rod of iron, and dash them into pieces like a potter's vessel. None of His foes shall bear up before the tempest of His wrath, or hide themselves from the sweeping hail of His indignation; but His beloved blood-washed people look for His appearing with joy, and hope to abide it without fear: to them He sits as a refiner even now, and when He has tested them they shall come forth as gold. Let's search ourselves this morning and make our calling and election sure, so that the coming of the Lord may cause no dark forebodings in our minds. O for grace to cast away all hypocrisy, and to be found by Him sincere and without rebuke in the day of His appearing.

"Redeem the firstborn donkey with a lamb,
but if you do not redeem it, break its neck."
— *Exodus 34:20*

 VERY firstborn creature must be the Lord's, but since the donkey was unclean, it couldn't be presented in sacrifice. What then? Should it be allowed to go free from the universal law? By no means. God makes no exceptions. The donkey is His due, but He will not accept it; He will not abate the claim, but yet He cannot be pleased with the victim. No way of escape remained but redemption — the creature must be saved by the substitution of a lamb in its place; or if not redeemed, it must die. My soul, here is a lesson for you. That unclean animal is yourself; you are justly the property of the Lord who made you and preserves you, but you are so sinful that God will not, cannot, accept you; and it has come to this, the Lamb of God must stand in your stead, or you must die eternally. Let all the world know of your gratitude to that spotless Lamb who has already bled for you, and so redeemed you from the fatal curse of the law. Must it not sometimes have been a question with the Israelite which should die, the donkey or the lamb? Wouldn't the good man pause to estimate and compare? Certainly, there was no comparison between the value of the soul of a mortal and the life of the Lord Jesus, and yet the Lamb dies, and the mortal donkey is spared. My soul, admire the boundless love of God to you and others of the human race. Worms are bought with the blood of the Son of the Highest! Dust and ashes redeemed with a price far above silver and gold! What doom would have been mine had not generous redemption been found! The breaking of the neck of the donkey was but a momentary penalty, but who shall measure the wrath to come to which no limit can be imagined? Inestimably dear is the glorious Lamb who has redeemed us from such a doom.

"Jesus said to them, Come and have breakfast."
— John 21:12

 N these words the believer is invited to a holy *nearness to Jesus.* "Come and have breakfast," implies the same table, the same meat; yes, and sometimes it means to sit side-by-side, and lean our head upon the Savior's bosom. It is being brought into the banqueting house, where the banner of redeeming love waves. "Come and have breakfast," gives us a vision of *union with Jesus,* because the only food that we can feast upon when we dine with Jesus is *Himself.* Oh, what union this is! It is a depth which reason cannot fathom, that we thus feed upon Jesus. "Whoever eats My flesh and drinks My blood remains in Me, and I in him." It is also an invitation to enjoy *fellowship with the saints.* Christians may differ on a variety of points, but they all have one spiritual appetite; and if we cannot all *feel* alike, we can all *feed* alike on the bread of life sent down from heaven. At the table of fellowship with Jesus we are one bread and one cup. As the loving cup goes round we pledge one another heartily therein. Get nearer to Jesus, and you will find yourself linked more and more in spirit to all who are like yourself, supported by the same heavenly manna. If we were nearer to Jesus we would be nearer to one another. We likewise see in these words the *source of strength* for every Christian. To look at Christ is to live, but for strength to serve Him you must "come and have breakfast." We work under much unnecessary weakness on account of neglecting this precept of the Master. None of us needs to put ourselves on a low diet; on the contrary, we should fatten on the marrow and fatness of the gospel that we may accumulate strength therein, and urge every power to its full tension in the Master's service. Thus, then, if you would realize *nearness* to Jesus, *union* with Jesus, *love* to His people and *strength from Jesus,* "come and have breakfast" with Him by faith.

"With you is the fountain of life." — Psalm 36:9

HERE are times in our spiritual experience when human counsel or sympathy, or religious sacraments, fail to comfort or help us. Why does our gracious God permit this? Perhaps it is because we have been living too much without Him, and He therefore takes away everything upon which we have been in the habit of depending, that He may drive us to Himself. It is a blessed thing to live at the fountainhead. While our canteens are full, we are content, like Hagar and Ishmael, to go into the wilderness; but when they are empty, nothing will serve us but "God, You see me." We are like the prodigal, we love the pig sty and forget our Father's house. Remember, we can make pig stys and husks even out of the forms of religion; they are blessed things, but we may put them in God's place, and then they are of no value. Anything becomes an idol when it keeps us away from God: even the brazen serpent is to be despised as "Nehushtan," if we worship it instead of God. The prodigal was never safer than when he was driven to his father's bosom, because he could find sustenance nowhere else. Our Lord favors us with a famine in the land that it may make us seek after Himself the more. The best position for a Christian is living wholly and directly on God's grace — still abiding where he stood at first — "Having nothing, and yet possessing everything." Let's never for a moment think that our standing is in our sanctification, our mortification, our graces, or our feelings, but know that because Christ offered a full atonement, therefore we are saved; for we are complete in Him. Having nothing of our own to trust to, but resting upon the merits of Jesus — His passion and holy life furnish us with the only sure ground of confidence. Beloved, when we are brought to a thirsting condition, we are sure to turn to the fountain of life with eagerness.

"But David thought to himself, One of these days I will be destroyed by the hand of Saul." — 1 Samuel 27:1

 HE thought of David's heart at this time was a *false* thought, because he certainly had no ground for thinking that God's anointing him by Samuel was intended to be left as an empty unmeaning act. On no one occasion had the Lord deserted His servant. He had frequently been placed in perilous positions, but not one instance had occurred in which divine intervention had not delivered him. The trials to which he had been exposed had been varied; they had not assumed only one form, but many — yet in every case He who sent the trial had also graciously ordained a way of escape. David could not put his finger upon any entry in his diary, and say of it, "Here is evidence that the Lord will forsake me," for the entire tenor of his past life proved the very reverse. He should have argued from what God *had* done for him, that God would be his defender still. But is it not just in the same way that *we* doubt God's help? Is it not *mistrust without a cause?* Have we ever had the shadow of a reason to doubt our Father's goodness? Have not His loving-kindnesses been marvelous? Has He *once* failed to justify our trust? Ah, no! our God has not left us at any time. We have had dark nights, but the star of love has shone forth amid the blackness; we have been in stern conflicts, but over our head He has held aloft the shield of our defense. We have gone through many trials, but never to our detriment, always to our advantage; and the conclusion from our past experience is that He who has been with us in six troubles will not forsake us in the seventh. What we have known of our faithful God, proves that He will keep us to the end. Let's not, then, reason contrary to evidence. How can we ever be so ungenerous as to *doubt* our God? Lord, throw down the Jezebel of our unbelief, and let the dogs devour it.

"He gathers the lambs in his arms." — *Isaiah 40:11*

UR good Shepherd has in His flock a variety of experiences, some are strong in the Lord, and others are weak in faith, but He is impartial in His care for all His sheep, and the weakest lamb is as dear to Him as the most advanced of the flock. Lambs are accustomed to lag behind, prone to wander, and apt to grow weary, but from all the danger of these infirmities the Shepherd protects them with His arm of power. He finds newborn souls, like young lambs, ready to perish — He nourishes them until life becomes vigorous; He finds weak minds ready to faint and die — He consoles them and renews their strength. All the little ones He gathers, for it is not the will of our heavenly Father that one of them should perish. What a quick eye He must have to see them all! What a tender heart to care for them all! What a far-reaching and potent arm, to gather them all! In His lifetime on earth He was a great gatherer of the weaker sort, and now that He dwells in heaven, His loving heart yearns towards the meek and contrite, the timid and feeble, the fearful and fainting here below. How gently did He gather me to Himself, to His truth, to His blood, to His love, to His church! With what effectual grace did He compel me to come to Himself! Since my first conversion, how frequently has He restored me from my wanderings, and once again folded me within the circle of His everlasting arm! The best of all is, that He does it all Himself, personally, not delegating the task of love, but condescending Himself to rescue and preserve His most unworthy servant. How shall I love Him enough or serve Him worthily? I would preferably make His name great to the ends of the earth, but what can my feebleness do for Him? Great Shepherd, add to Your mercies this one other, a heart to love You more truly as I ought.

"Your [paths] overflow with abundance." — Psalm 65:11

ANY are "the paths of the Lord" which "overflow with abundance," but a special one is the *path of prayer*. No believer, who is often praying, will have need to cry, "My leanness, my leanness; woe is me." Starving souls live at a distance from the mercy seat, and become like the parched fields in times of drought. Prevalence with God in wrestling prayer is sure to make the believer strong — if not happy. The nearest place to the gate of heaven is the throne of the heavenly grace. Often alone, and you will have much assurance; seldom alone with Jesus, your religion will be shallow, polluted with many doubts and fears, and not sparkling with the joy of the Lord. Since the soul-enriching path of prayer is open to the very weakest saint; since no high attainments are required; since you are not bidden to come because you are an advanced saint, but freely invited if you are a saint at all; see to it, dear reader, that you are often on the path of private devotion. Be on your knees often, for so Elijah drew the rain upon famished Israel's fields.

There is another special path overflowing with abundance to those who walk therein. It is the secret walk of *communion*. Oh! the delights of fellowship with Jesus! Earth has no words which can set forth the holy calm of a soul leaning on Jesus' bosom. Few Christians understand it, they live in the lowlands and seldom climb to the top of Nebo: they live in the outer court, they do not the holy place, they do not take up the privilege of priesthood. At a distance they see the sacrifice, but they don't sit down with the priest to eat it, and to enjoy the fat of the burnt offering. But, reader, always sit under the shadow of Jesus; come up to that palm tree, and take hold of the branches; let your beloved be to you as the apple tree among the trees of the wood, and you shall be satisfied as with marrow and fatness. O Jesus, visit us with Your salvation!

"To obey is better than sacrifice." — *1 Samuel 15:22*

AUL had been commanded to slay utterly all the Amalekites and their cattle. Instead of doing so, he preserved the king, and allowed his people to take the best of the oxen and of the sheep. When called to account for this, he declared that he did it with a view of offering sacrifice to God; but Samuel met him at once with the assurance that sacrifices were no excuse for an act of direct rebellion. The sentence before us is worthy to be printed in letters of gold, and to be hung up before the eyes of the present idolatrous generation, who are very fond of the fineries of will-worship, but utterly neglect the laws of God. Let it be a constant remembrance to you that to keep strictly in the path of your Savior's command is better than any outward form of religion; and to hearken to His precept with an attentive ear is better than to bring the fat of rams, or any other precious thing to lay upon His altar. If you are failing to keep the least of Christ's commands to His disciples, I pray that you will not be disobedient any longer. All the pretensions you make of attachment to your Master, and all the devout actions which you may perform, are no compensation for disobedience. "To obey," even in the slightest and smallest thing, "is better than sacrifice," however pompous. Don't talk about Gregorian chants, sumptuous robes, incense, and banners; the first thing which God requires of His child is obedience; and even if you give your body to be burned, and all your goods to feed the poor, if you do not hearken to the Lord's precepts, all your formalities shall profit you nothing. It is a blessed thing to be teachable as a little child, but it is a much more blessed thing when one has been taught the lesson, to carry it out to the letter. How many adorn their temples and decorate their priests, but refuse to obey the word of the Lord! My soul, do not come into their secret.

"Mere infants in Christ." — 1 Corinthians 3:1

RE you mourning, believer, because you are so weak in the divine life: because your faith is so small and your love so feeble? Cheer up, for you have cause for gratitude. Remember *that in some things you are equal to the greatest and most full-grown Christian.* You are as much bought with blood as he is. You are as much an adopted child of God as any other believer. An infant is as truly a child of its parents as is the full-grown man. You are as completely justified, for your justification is not a thing of degrees: your little faith has made you every bit as clean. You have as much right to the precious things of the covenant as the most advanced believers, for your right to covenant mercies doesn't lie in your growth, but in the covenant itself; and your faith in Jesus is not the measure, but the token of your inheritance in Him. You are as rich as the richest, if not in enjoyment, yet in real possession. The smallest star that gleams is set in heaven; the faintest ray of light has affinity with the great orb of day. In the family register of glory the small and the great are written with the same pen. You are as dear to your Father's heart as the greatest in the family. Jesus is very tender towards you. You are like the smoldering wick; a rougher spirit would say, "put out that smoldering wick; it fills the room with an offensive odor!" but *He* will not quench the smoking flax. You are like a bruised reed; and any less tender hand than that of the Chief Musician would tread upon you or throw you away, but He will never break the bruised reed. Instead of being downcast by reason of what you are, you should triumph in Christ. Am I but little in Israel? Yet in Christ I am made to sit in heavenly places. Am I poor in faith? Still in Jesus I am heir of all things. Though "less than nothing I can boast, and vanity confess," yet, if the root of the matter is in me I will rejoice in the Lord, and glory in the God of my salvation.

"God my Maker, who gives songs in the night."
— Job 35:10

 NYONE can sing in the day. When the cup is full, one draws inspiration from it. When wealth rolls in abundance around one, anyone can praise the God who gives a generous harvest or sends home a loaded ship. It is easy enough for an Aeolian harp to whisper music when the winds blow — the difficulty is for music to swell forth when no wind is stirring. It is easy to sing when we can read the notes by daylight; but the skillful one sings when there is not a ray of light to read by — who sings from the heart. No one can make a song in the night by oneself; one may attempt it, but will find that a song in the night must be divinely inspired. As long as all things are going well, I can weave songs, fashioning them, wherever I go, out of the flowers that grow upon my path; but put me in a desert, where no green thing grows, and on what shall I frame a hymn of praise to God? How shall a mortal make a crown for the Lord where there are no jewels? Just let my voice be clear, and my body full of health, and I can sing God's praise: silence my tongue, lay me upon the bed of languishing, and how shall I then chant God's high praises, unless He Himself gives me the song? No, it is not in our power to sing when all is adverse, unless an altar coal shall touch our lips. It was a divine song which Habakkuk sang when, in the night, he said, "Though the fig tree does not bud and there are no grapes on the vines, though the olive crop fails and the fields produce no food, though there are no sheep in the pen and no cattle in the stalls, yet I will rejoice in the LORD, I will be joyful in God my Savior." Then, since our Maker gives *songs in the night,* let's wait upon Him for the music. O Chief Musician, don't allow us to remain songless just because affliction is upon us; rather, tune our lips to the melody of thanksgiving.

"In all things grow up into him." — *Ephesians 4:15*

 ANY Christians remain stunted and dwarfed in spiritual things, so as to present the same appearance year after year. No up-springing of advanced and refined feeling is manifest in them. They *exist* but do not *"In all things grow up into Him."* But should we rest content with being in the "green blade," when we might advance to "the ear," and eventually ripen into the "full corn in the ear"? Should we be satisfied to believe in Christ, and to say, "I am safe," without wishing to know in our own experience more of the fullness which is to be found in Him? It shouldn't be like this. We should, as good traders in heaven's market, covet being enriched in the knowledge of Jesus. It is all very well to tend to the vineyards of others, but we mustn't neglect our own spiritual growth and ripening. Why should it always be winter time in our hearts? We must have our seed time, it is true, but O for a spring time — yes, a summer season, which shall give promise of an early harvest. If we would ripen in grace, we must live near to Jesus — in His presence — ripened by the sunshine of His smiles. We must hold sweet communion with Him. We must leave the distant view of His face and come near, as John did, and pillow our head on His breast; then we shall find ourselves advancing in holiness, in love, in faith, in hope — yes, in every precious gift. As the sun rises first on mountain tops and gilds them with his light, and presents one of the most charming sights to the eye of the traveler; so is it one of the most delightful contemplations in the world to see the glow of the Spirit's light on the head of some saint, who has risen up in spiritual stature, like Saul, above his fellows, until, like a mighty Alp, snowcapped, he reflects first among the chosen, the beams of the Sun of Righteousness, and bears the alpenglow of His effulgence high aloft for all to see, and seeing it, to glorify His Father who is in heaven.

"Do not hold . . . back." — Isaiah 43:6

LTHOUGH this message was sent to the south, and referred to the seed of Israel, it may profitably be a summons to ourselves. We are naturally backward regarding all good things, and it is a lesson of grace to learn to go forward in the ways of God. Reader, are you unconverted, but desire to trust in the Lord Jesus? Then *do not hold back.* Love invites you, the promises secure you success, the precious blood prepares the way. Don't let sins or fears hinder you, but come to Jesus just as you are. Do you long to pray? Would you pour out your heart before the Lord? *Do not hold back.* The mercy seat is prepared for such as need mercy; a sinner's cries will prevail with God. You are invited, no, you are commanded to pray, come therefore with boldness to the throne of grace.

Dear friend, are you already saved? Then *do not hold back* from union with the Lord's people. Don't neglect the sacraments of baptism and the Lord's Supper. You may be of a timid disposition, but you must strive against it, lest it leads you into disobedience. There is a sweet promise made to those who confess Christ — by no means miss it, lest you come under the condemnation of those who deny Him. If you have talents *do not hold back* from using them. Don't hoard your wealth, don't waste your time; don't let your abilities rust or your influence be unused. Jesus did not hold back; imitate Him by being foremost in self-denials and self-sacrifices. *Do not hold back* from close communion with God, from boldly appropriating covenant blessings, from advancing in the divine life, from prying into the precious mysteries of the love of Christ. Neither, beloved friend, be guilty of holding others back by your coldness, harshness, or suspicions. For Jesus' sake go forward yourself, and encourage others to do the same. Hell and the harassing bands of superstition and infidelity are at the front line of the fight. O soldiers of the cross, do not hold back.

"For Christ's love compels us." — *2 Corinthians 5:14*

OW much do you owe my Lord? Has He ever done anything for you? Has He forgiven your sins? Has He covered you with a robe of righteousness? Has He set your feet upon a rock? Has He established your goings? Has He prepared heaven for you? Has He prepared you for heaven? Has He written your name in His book of life? Has He given you countless blessings? Has He laid up for you a store of mercies, which eye has not seen nor ear heard? Then do something for Jesus worthy of His love. Don't just give a mere verbal offering to a dying Redeemer. How will you feel when your Master comes, if you have to confess that you *did* nothing for Him, but kept your love shut up, like a stagnant pool, neither flowing forth to His poor or to His work. Throw out such love as that! What do mortals think of a love which never shows itself in action? Why, they say, "Open rebuke is better than secret love." Who will accept a love so weak that it does not actuate you to a single deed of self-denial, of generosity, of heroism, or zeal! Think how *He* has loved you, and given Himself for you! Do you know the power of that love? Then let it be like a rushing mighty wind to your soul to sweep out the clouds of your worldliness, and clear away the mists of sin. "For Christ's sake" let this be the tongue of fire that shall sit upon you: "for Christ's sake" let this be the divine rapture, the heavenly inspiration to bear you aloft from earth, the divine spirit that shall make you bold as lions and swift as eagles in your Lord's service. Love should give wings to the feet of service, and strength to the arms of work. Fixed on God with a constancy that is not to be shaken, resolute to honor Him with a determination that is not to be turned aside, and pressing on with an ardor never to be wearied, let's manifest the compelling love of Jesus. May the divine lodestone draw us heavenward towards itself!

> *"Why are you troubled, and why do doubts rise in*
> *your minds?"* — Luke 24:38

 HY do you say, O Jacob, and complain, O Israel, 'My way is hidden from the LORD; my cause is disregarded by my God' "? The Lord cares for all things, and the meanest creatures share in His universal providence, but His particular providence is over His saints. "The angel of the Lord encamps around those who fear Him." "Precious is their blood in His sight." "Precious in the sight of the Lord is the death of His saints." "We know that in all things God works for the good of those who love Him, who have been called according to His purpose." Let the fact that, while He is the Savior of all mortals, He is especially the Savior of them that believe, cheer and comfort you. You are His peculiar care; His regal treasure, which He guards as the apple of His eye; His vineyard over which He watches day and night. "The very hairs of your head are all numbered." Let the thought of His special love *for you* be a spiritual pain killer, a dear quieting to your woe: "Never will I leave *you;* never will I forsake *you.*" God says that as much to you as to any saint of old. "Do not be afraid . . . I am your shield, your very great reward." We lose much consolation by the habit of reading His promises for the whole church, instead of taking them directly home to ourselves. Believer, grasp the divine word with a personal, appropriating faith. Think that you hear Jesus say, "I have prayed for *you* that your faith may not fail." Do you think you see Him walking on the waters of your trouble? He is there, and He is saying, "Don't be afraid, it is I; don't be afraid." Oh, those sweet words of Christ! May the Holy Spirit make you feel them as spoken to *you;* forget others for awhile — accept the voice of Jesus as addressed to you, and say, "Jesus whispers consolation; I cannot refuse it; I will sit under His shadow with great delight."

"I will . . . love them freely." — Hosea 14:4

HIS sentence is a body of divinity in miniature. He who understands its meaning is a theologian, and he who can dive into its fullness is a true master in Israel. It is a condensation of the glorious message of salvation which was delivered to us in Christ Jesus our Redeemer. The sense hinges upon the word "freely." This is the glorious, the suitable, the divine way by which love streams from heaven to earth, a spontaneous love flowing forth to those who neither deserved it, purchased it, nor sought after it. It is, indeed, the only way in which God can love such as we are. The text is a death blow to all sorts of fitness: "I will love them *freely.*" Now, if there was any fitness necessary in us, then He would not love us freely, at least, this would be a mitigation and a drawback to the freeness of it. But it stands, "I will love you *freely.*" We complain, "Lord, my heart is so hard." "I will love you freely." "But I do not feel my need of Christ as I would wish." "I will not love you because you feel your need; I will love you freely." "But I do not feel that softening of spirit which I would desire." Remember, the softening of spirit is not a condition, for there are no conditions; the covenant of grace has no conditionality whatever; so that, without any fitness, we may venture upon the promise of God which was made to us in Christ Jesus, when He said, "Whoever believes in Him is not condemned." It is blessed to know that the grace of God is free to us at all times, without preparation, without fitness, without money, and without price! "I will love them freely." These words *invite backsliders to return:* indeed, the text was specially written for such — "I will heal their waywardness and love them freely." Backslider! surely the generosity of the promise will at once break your heart, and you will return, and seek your injured Father's face.

*"The Spirit will take from what is mine and make it
known to you."* — *John 16:15*

HERE are times when all the promises and
doctrines of the Bible are of no avail unless a
gracious hand shall apply them to us. We are
thirsty, but too faint to crawl to the stream of
water. When a soldier is wounded in battle it
is of little use for him to know that there are
those at the hospital who can bind up his wounds, and
medicines there to ease all the pains which he now suffers:
what he needs is to be carried there, and to have the
remedies applied. It is thus with our souls, and to meet this
need there is one, even the Spirit of truth, who takes the
things of Jesus, and applies them to us. Do not think that
Christ has placed His joys on heavenly shelves that we may
climb up to them for ourselves, but He draws near, and
sheds His peace abroad in our hearts. O Christian, if you
are tonight laboring under deep distresses, your Father
does not give you promises and then leave you to draw
them up from the Word like buckets from a well, but the
promises He has written in the Word He will write anew
on your heart. He will manifest His love to you, and by His
blessed Spirit, dispel your cares and troubles. Let it be
known to you, O mourner, that it is God's prerogative to
wipe every tear from the eye of His people. The good
Samaritan didn't say, "Here is the wine, and here is the oil
for you;" he actually poured in the oil and the wine. So
Jesus not only gives you the sweet wine of the promise, but
holds the golden chalice to your lips, and pours the life
blood into your mouth. The poor, sick, way-worn pilgrim
is not merely strengthened to walk, but he is borne on
eagles' wings. Glorious gospel! which provides everything
for the helpless, which draws near to us when we cannot
reach after it — brings us grace before we seek for grace!
Here is as much glory in the giving as in the gift. Happy
people who have the Holy Spirit to bring Jesus to them.

"You do not want to leave, too, do you?" — *John* 6:67

ANY have forsaken Christ, and have walked no more with Him; but *what reason have* YOU *to make a change?* Has there been any reason for it in the *past?* Hasn't Jesus proved Himself all-sufficient? He appeals to you this morning — "Have I been a desert to you?" When your soul has simply trusted Jesus, have you ever been confused? Up until now, haven't you found your Lord to be a compassionate and generous friend to you, and hasn't simple faith in Him given you all the peace your spirit could desire? Can you so much as dream of a better friend than He has been to you? Then do not change the old and tested for new and false. As for *the present,* can that compel you to leave Christ? When we are beset with the difficulties of this world, or with the severer trials within the church, we find it a most blessed thing to pillow our head upon the heart of our Savior. This is the joy we have today that we are saved in Him; and if this joy is satisfying, why would we think of changing? Who barters gold for dross? We will not abandon the sun until we find a better light, nor leave our Lord until a brighter lover shall appear; and, since this can never be, we will hold Him with an immortal grasp, and bind His name as a seal upon our arm. As for *the future,* can you suggest anything which can arise that shall render it necessary for you to mutiny, or desert the old flag to serve under another captain? We don't think so. If life is long — He doesn't change. If we are poor, what better than to have Christ who can make us rich? When we are sick, what more do we want than Jesus to make our bed in our sickness? When we die, is it not written that "neither death nor life, neither angels nor demons, neither the present nor the future . . . will be able to separate us from the love of God that is in Christ Jesus our Lord!" We say with Peter, "Lord, to whom shall we go?"

*"Why are you sleeping? he asked them. Get up and
pray so that you will not fall into temptation."*
— *Luke 22:46*

 NDER what conditions are you inclined to sleep? Isn't it when *your temporal circumstances are prosperous?* Haven't you found this true? When you had daily troubles to take to the throne of grace, weren't you more wakeful than you are now? Easy roads make sleepy travelers. Another dangerous time is *when all goes pleasantly in spiritual matters.* Christian didn't go to sleep when lions were in the way, or when he was wading through the river, or when fighting with Apollyon; but when he had climbed half way up the Hill Difficulty, and came to a delightful arbor, he sat down, and without delay fell asleep, to his great sorrow and loss. The enchanted ground is a place of balmy breezes, laden with fragrant odors and soft influences, all tending to lull pilgrims to sleep. Remember Bunyan's description: "Then they came to an arbor, warm, and promising much refreshing to the weary pilgrims; for it was finely wrought above head, beautified with greens, and furnished with benches and settles. It had also in it a soft couch, where the weary might lean." "The arbor was called the Lazy's Friend, and was made on purpose to allure, if it might be, some of the pilgrims to take up their rest there when weary." Depend upon it, it is in the easy places that people shut their eyes and wander into the dreamy land of forgetfulness. Old Erskine wisely remarked, "I like a roaring devil better than a sleeping devil." There is no temptation half so dangerous as not being tempted. The distressed soul does not sleep; it is after we enter into peaceful confidence and full assurance that we are in danger of slumbering. The disciples fell asleep after they had seen Jesus transfigured on the mountain top. Take heed, joyous Christian, good frames of mind are near neighbors to temptations: be as happy as you wish, only be watchful.

"The trees of the LORD are well watered." — *Psalm 104:16*

 ITHOUT sap the tree cannot flourish or even exist. *Vitality* is essential to a Christian. There must be *life* — a vital principle infused into us by God the Holy Spirit, or we cannot be trees of the Lord. The mere name of being a Christian is just a dead thing. We must be filled with the spirit of divine life. This life is *mysterious*. We do not understand the circulation of the sap, by what force it rises, and by what power it descends again. So the life within us is a sacred mystery. Regeneration is the work of the Holy Spirit entering into us and becoming our life. Afterwards, this divine life in a believer feeds upon the flesh and blood of Christ and is thus sustained by divine food; but who can explain to us where it comes from and where it goes? What a *secret* thing the sap is! The roots go searching through the soil with their little spongioles, but we cannot see them suck out the various gases, or transmute the mineral into the vegetable; this work is done down in the dark. Our root is Christ Jesus, and our life is hidden in Him; this is the secret of the Lord. The radix of the Christian life is as secret as the life itself. How *permanently active* the sap in the cedar is! In the Christian, the divine life is always full of energy — not always in bearing fruit, but in inward operations. Aren't every one of the believer's *graces* in constant motion? yet his life never ceases to palpitate within. He is not always working for God, but his heart is always living upon Him. As the sap *manifests itself in producing the foliage and fruit of the tree,* so is this true of a truly healthy Christian where grace is externally manifested in his walk and conversation. If you talk with him, he cannot help speaking about Jesus. If you notice his actions you will see that he has been with Jesus. He has so much sap within, that it must fill his conduct and conversation with life.

"He began to wash his disciples' feet." — *John 13:5*

HE Lord Jesus loves His people so much, that every day He is still doing many things for them that are analogous to washing their soiled feet. He accepts their poorest actions; He feels their deepest sorrow; He hears their slenderest wish, and He forgives their every transgression. He is still their servant as well as their Friend and Master. He not only performs majestic deeds for them, as wearing the miter on His brow, and the precious jewels glittering on His breastplate, and standing up to plead for them, but humbly, patiently, He even goes about among His people with the basin and the towel. He does this when, day by day, He takes from us our constant infirmities and sins. Last night, when you bowed your knee, you mournfully confessed that much of your conduct was not worthy of your profession; and even tonight, you must mourn afresh that you have fallen again into the selfsame folly and sin from which special grace delivered you long ago; and yet Jesus will have great patience with you. He will hear your confession of sin; He will say, "I am willing. Be clean!" He will again apply the blood of sprinkling, and speak peace to your conscience, and remove every blemish. It is a great act of eternal love when Christ once for all absolves the sinner, and puts him into the family of God; but what condescending patience there is when the Savior with much long-suffering bears the often recurring follies of His wayward disciple; day by day and hour by hour, washing away the multiplied transgressions of His erring but yet beloved child! To dry up a flood of rebellion is something marvelous, but to endure the constant dripping of repeated offenses — to bear with a perpetual testing of patience, this is divine indeed! While we find comfort and peace in our Lord's daily purifying, its legitimate influence upon us will be to increase our watchfulness, and hasten our desire for holiness. *Isn't this true?*

*"Because of the truth, which lives in us and will be
with us forever." — 2 John 2*

NCE the truth of God enters into the human heart and wins over the entire person to itself, no power human or infernal can dislodge it. We don't entertain it as a guest but as the master of the house — this is a *Christian necessity;* he is no Christian who does not believe in this manner. Those who feel the vital power of the gospel, and know the might of the Holy Spirit as He opens, applies, and seals the Lord's Word, would sooner be torn to pieces than be rent away from the gospel of their salvation. What a thousand mercies are wrapped up in the assurance that the truth will be with us forever; will be our living support, our dying comfort, our rising song, our eternal glory; this is *Christian privilege,* without it our faith is worth very little. Some truths we outgrow and leave behind, for they are only rudiments and lessons for beginners, but we cannot deal with Divine truth in this manner, for though it is sweet food for babies, it is, in the highest sense, strong meat for adults. The truth that we are sinners is painfully with us to humble and make us watchful; the more blessed truth that whoever believes on the Lord Jesus shall be saved, abides with us as our hope and joy. Experience, far from loosening our hold of the doctrines of grace, has knit us to them more and more firmly; our grounds and motives for believing are now much stronger, more numerous than ever, and we have reason to expect that it will be so until in death we clasp the Savior in our arms.

Wherever this abiding love of truth can be discovered, we are bound to exercise our love. No narrow circle can contain our gracious sympathies; our communion of heart must be as wide as the election of grace. Much error may be mingled with truth received, let's war with the error but still love the brother for the measure of truth which we see in Him; above all let's love and spread the truth ourselves.

"She . . . began to glean in the fields behind the harvesters. As it turned out, she found herself working in a field belonging to Boaz, who was from the clan of Elimelech." — Ruth 2:3

S it turned out. Yes, it seemed nothing but an accident, but how divinely was it overruled! Ruth had gone forth with her mother's blessing, under the care of her mother's God, to humble but honorable toil, and the providence of God was guiding her every step. Little did she know that amid the sheaves she would find a husband, that he should make her the joint owner of all those broad acres, and that she, a poor foreigner, should become one of the progenitors of the great Messiah. God is very good to those who trust in Him, and often surprises them with unlooked for blessings. Little do we know what may happen to us tomorrow, but this sweet fact may cheer us, that no good thing shall be withheld. Chance is banished from the faith of Christians, for they see the hand of God in everything. The trivial events of today or tomorrow may involve consequences of the highest importance. O Lord, deal as graciously with Your servants as You did with Ruth.

How blessed it would it if, in wandering in the field of meditation tonight, as it turned out, we should find ourselves in the place where our next Kinsman will reveal Himself to us! O Spirit of God, guide us to Him. We would sooner glean in His field than bear away the whole harvest from any other. O for the footsteps of His flock, which may conduct us to the green pastures where He dwells! This is a weary world when Jesus is away — we could better do without the sun and the moon than without Him — but how divinely fair all things become in the glory of His presence! Our souls know the virtue which dwells in Jesus, and can never be content without Him. We will wait in prayer this night until, as it turns out, we should find ourselves on a part of the field belonging to Jesus wherein He will manifest Himself to us.

"You expected much, but see, it turned out to be little.
What you brought home, I blew away. Why? declares
the LORD *Almighty. Because of my house, which*
remains a ruin, while each of you is busy
with his own house." — *Haggai 1:9*

 HURLISH souls stint their contributions to the ministry and missionary operations, and call such saving good economy; little do they dream that they are thus impoverishing themselves. Their excuse is that they *must* care for their own families, and they forget that to neglect the house of God is the sure way to bring ruin upon their own houses. Our God has a method in providence by which He can accomplish our endeavors beyond our expectation, or can defeat our plans to our confusion and dismay. With the turn of His hand He can steer our vessel in a profitable channel, or run it aground in poverty and bankruptcy. It is the teaching of Scripture that the Lord enriches the generous and leaves the miserly to find out that withholding tends to poverty. In a very wide sphere of observation, I have noticed that the most generous Christians of my acquaintance have always been the most happy, and almost invariably the most prosperous. I have seen the liberal giver rise to wealth of which he never dreamed; and I have as often seen the mean, ungenerous scoundrel descend to poverty by the very parsimony by which he thought to rise. People trust good stewards with larger and larger sums, and so it frequently is with the Lord; He gives by cartloads to those who give by bushels. Where wealth is not given, the Lord makes the little much by the contentment which the sanctified heart feels in a portion of which the tithe has been dedicated to the Lord. Selfishness looks first at home, but godliness seeks first the kingdom of God and His righteousness; yet, in the long run, selfishness is loss and godliness is great gain. It requires faith to act towards our God with an open hand, but surely He deserves it of us; and all that we can give is a very poor acknowledgment of our amazing indebtedness to His goodness.

"All streams flow into the sea, yet the sea is never
full. To the place the streams come from, there
they return again." — *Ecclesiastes 1:7*

 VERYTHING beneath the moon is on the move; time knows nothing of rest. The solid earth is a rolling ball, and the great sun itself a star obediently fulfilling its course around some greater luminary. Tides move the sea, winds stir the airy ocean, friction wears the rock: change and death rule everywhere. The sea is not a miser's storehouse for a wealth of waters, for as by one force the waters flow into it, by another they are lifted from it. Human beings are born only to die: everything is hurry, worry, and vexation of spirit. Friend of the unchanging Jesus, what a joy it is to reflect upon your changeless heritage; your sea of bliss which will be forever full, since God Himself shall pour eternal rivers of pleasure into it. We seek an abiding city beyond the skies, and we shall not be disappointed.

The passage before us may well teach us gratitude. Father Ocean is a great receiver, but he is a generous distributor. What the rivers bring him he returns to the earth in the form of clouds and rain. The person who takes all but makes no return is out of joint with the universe. To give to others is but sowing seed for ourselves. He who is so good a steward as to be willing to use his substance for his Lord, shall be entrusted with more. Friend of Jesus, are you rendering to Him according to the benefit received? Much has been given to you; what is your fruit? Have you done everything you could? Can't you do more? To be selfish is to be wicked. Suppose the ocean gave up none of its watery treasure; it would bring ruin upon our race. God forbid that any of us should follow the ungenerous and destructive policy of living for ourselves. Jesus did not please Himself. All fullness dwells in Him, but of His fullness we have all received. O for Jesus' spirit, that henceforth we may not live for ourselves!

"Here is a trustworthy saying." — 2 Timothy 2:11

AUL has four of these *"trustworthy sayings."* The first occurs in 1 Timothy 1:15, "Here is a trustworthy saying that deserves full acceptance: Christ Jesus came into the world to save sinners." The next is in 1 Timothy 4:8-9, "Godliness has value for all things, holding promise for both the present life and the life to come. This is a trustworthy saying that deserves full acceptance." The third is in 2 Timothy 2:12, "Here is a trustworthy saying . . . if we endure, we will also reign with Him;" and the fourth is in Titus 3:8, "This is a trustworthy saying . . . that those who have trusted in God may be careful to devote themselves to doing what is good." We may trace a connection between these trustworthy sayings. The first one lays the foundation of our eternal salvation in the free grace of God, as shown to us in the mission of the great Redeemer. The next affirms the double blessedness which we obtain through this salvation — the blessings of the upper and lower springs — of time and of eternity. The third shows one of the duties to which the chosen people are called; we are ordained to endure for Christ with the promise that "if we endure, we will also reign with Him." The last sets forth the active form of Christian service, bidding us to diligently maintain good works. Thus we have the root of salvation in free grace; next, the privileges of that salvation in the life which now is, and in that which is to come; and we have also the two great branches of suffering with Christ and serving with Christ, loaded with the fruits of the Spirit. Treasure up these trustworthy sayings. Let them be the guides of our life, our comfort, and our instruction. The apostle of the Gentiles proved them to be trustworthy, they are trustworthy still, not one word shall fall to the ground; they deserve full acceptance, let's accept them now, and prove their trustworthiness. Let these four trustworthy sayings be written on the four corners of my house.

"All of us have become like one who is unclean."
— *Isaiah 64:6*

HE believer is a new creation, he belongs to a holy generation and a peculiar people — the Spirit of God is in him, and in all respects he is far removed from the natural man; but for all that the Christian is still a sinner. He is so from the imperfection of his nature, and will continue so to the end of his earthly life. The black fingers of sin leave smudges upon our fairest robes. Sin mars our repentance, before the great Potter has finished it upon the wheel. Selfishness defiles our tears, and unbelief tampers with our faith. The best thing we ever did apart from the merit of Jesus only swelled the number of our sins; for when we have been most pure in our own sight, yet, like the heavens, we are not pure in God's sight; and as He charged His angels with folly, much more must He charge us with it, even in our most angelic frames of mind. The song which thrills to heaven, and seeks to emulate seraphic strains, has human discords in it. The prayer which moves the arm of God is still a bruised and battered prayer, and only moves God's arm because the sinless One, the great Mediator, has stepped in to take away the sin of our supplication. The most golden faith or the purest degree of sanctification to which a Christian has ever attained on earth still has so much alloy in it as to be only worthy of the flames, considered in itself. Every night we look in the mirror we see a sinner, and we need to confess, "We are all as an unclean thing, and all our righteousnesses are as filthy rags." Oh, how precious is the blood of Christ to such hearts as ours! How priceless a gift is His perfect righteousness! And how bright the hope of perfect holiness hereafter! Even now, though sin dwells in us, *its power is broken*. It has no dominion; it is a broken-backed snake; we are in bitter conflict with it, but it is with a vanquished foe with which we have to deal. Yet a little while and we shall enter victoriously into the city where nothing defiles.

"But I have chosen you out of the world." — John 15:19

ERE is distinguishing grace and discriminating regard; for some are made the special objects of divine affection. Don't be afraid to dwell upon this high doctrine of election. When your mind is heaviest and most depressed, you will find it to be a bottle of the richest cordial. Those who doubt the doctrines of grace, or who cast them into the shade, miss the richest clusters of Eshcol; they lose the wines on the well-refined sediments, the fat things full of marrow. There is no balm in Gilead comparable to it. If the honey in Jonathan's wood when just touched enlightened *the eyes*, this is honey which will enlighten *your heart* to love and learn the mysteries of the kingdom of God. Eat, and don't be afraid of going to excess; live upon this choice dainty, and don't be afraid that it will be too delicate a diet. Meat from the King's table will hurt none of His courtiers. Desire to have your mind enlarged, that you may comprehend more and more the eternal, everlasting, discriminating love of God. When you have mounted as high as election, stand on its sister mount, the covenant of grace. Covenant engagements are the munitions of stupendous rock behind which we lie entrenched; covenant engagements with the surety, Christ Jesus, are the quiet resting places of trembling spirits.

> "His oath, His covenant, His blood,
> Support me in the raging flood;
> When every earthly prop gives way,
> This still is all my strength and stay."

If Jesus undertook to bring me to glory, and if the Father promised that He would give me to the Son to be a part of the infinite reward of the travail of His soul; then, my soul, until God Himself is unfaithful, until Jesus ceases to be the truth, you are safe. When David danced before the ark, he told Michal that election made him do so. Come, my soul, exult before the God of grace and leap for joy of heart.

*"His head is purest gold; his hair is wavy and black
as a raven."* — *Song of Songs 5:11*

OMPARISONS all fail to describe the Lord Jesus, but the spouse uses the best within her reach. By *the head* of Jesus we may understand His deity, "for the head of Christ is God;" and then the ingot of purest gold is the best conceivable metaphor, but all too poor to describe one so precious, so pure, so dear, so glorious. Jesus is not a grain of gold, but a vast globe of it, a priceless mass of treasure such as earth and heaven cannot excel. The creatures are mere iron and clay, they all shall perish like wood, hay, and stubble, but the ever-living Head of the creation of God shall shine on forever and ever. In Him is no mixture, nor smallest taint of alloy. He is forever infinitely holy and altogether divine. *The wavy hair* depicts His manly vigor. There is nothing effeminate in our Beloved. He is the manliest of men. Bold as a lion, laborious as an ox, swift as an eagle. Every conceivable and inconceivable beauty is to be found in Him, though once He was despised and rejected of men.

> "His head the finest gold;
> With secret sweet perfume,
> His curled locks hang all as black
> As any raven's plume."

The glory of His head is not cut off. He is eternally crowned with peerless majesty. *The black hair* indicates youthful freshness, for Jesus has the dew of His youth upon Him. Others grow languid with age, but He is forever a Priest as was Melchisedek; others come and go, but He abides as God upon His throne, world without end. We will behold Him tonight and adore Him. Angels are gazing upon Him — His redeemed must not turn their eyes away from Him. Where else is there such a Beloved? O for an hour's fellowship with Him! Away, you intruding cares! Jesus draws me, and I run after Him.

"This, then, is how you should pray:
Our Father in heaven, . . ." — Matthew 6:9

HIS prayer begins where all true prayer must commence, with the spirit of *adoption,* "Our Father." There is no acceptable prayer until we can say, "I will set out and go back to my Father." This childlike spirit soon perceives the grandeur of the Father "in heaven," and ascends to *devout adoration,* "Hallowed be Your name." The child lisping, *"Abba,* Father," grows into the cherub crying, "Holy, Holy, Holy." It is only a step from rapturous worship to the *glowing missionary spirit,* which is a sure outgrowth of filial love and reverent adoration — "Your kingdom come, Your will be done on earth as it is in heaven." Next follows the heartfelt *expression of dependence* upon God — "Give us today our daily bread." Being further illuminated by the Spirit, he discovers that he is not only dependent, but sinful, hence he *entreats for mercy,* "Forgive us our debts, as we also have forgiven our debtors:" and being pardoned, having the righteousness of Christ imputed, and knowing his acceptance with God, he humbly *supplicates for holy perseverance,* "Lead us not into temptation." The person who is really forgiven, is anxious not to offend again; the possession of justification leads to an anxious desire for sanctification. "Forgive us our debts," that is justification; "Lead us not into temptation, but deliver us from the evil one," that is sanctification in its negative and positive forms. As the result of all this, there follows a *triumphant ascription of praise,* "Yours is the kingdom, the power, and the glory, forever and ever, Amen." We rejoice that *our* King reigns in providence and shall reign in grace, from the river even to the ends of the earth, and of His dominion there shall be no end. Thus from a sense of adoption, up to fellowship with our reigning Lord, this short model of prayer conducts the soul. Lord, teach us thus to pray.

"But they were kept from recognizing him."
— *Luke 24:16*

HE disciples ought to have known Jesus. They had heard His voice so often, and gazed upon that marred face so frequently, that it is amazing they didn't discover Him. Yet isn't this also true with you? You haven't seen Jesus lately. You've been to His table, and you haven't met Him there. You are in deep distress this evening and, even though He plainly says, "It is I, don't be afraid," you can't recognize Him. Alas! our eyes are restricted. We know His voice; we have looked into His face; we have leaned our head upon His bosom, yet, even though Christ is very near us, we are saying "If only I knew where to find Him!" We should know Jesus because we have the Scriptures to reflect His image, and yet, how possible it is for us to open that precious book and not even have a glimpse of the Well-beloved! Dear child of God, are you in that state? Jesus feeds among the lilies of the word, and you walk among those lilies, and yet you don't see Him. He is accustomed to walking through the glades of Scripture, communing with His people, as the Father did with Adam in the cool of the day, and yet you are in the garden of Scripture, but cannot see Him, though He is always there. And why don't we see Him? In our case, as in the disciples' case, it must be attributed to unbelief. They evidently didn't expect to see Jesus; therefore, they didn't know Him. To a great extent, in spiritual things, we get what we expect of the Lord. Faith alone can bring us to see Jesus. Make it your prayer, "O LORD, open my eyes that I may see my Savior present with me." It is a blessed thing to *want* to see Him; but oh! it is a far better thing to gaze upon Him. To those who seek Him He is kind; but to those who find Him, He is dear beyond expression!

"I will praise you, O LORD." — *Psalm 9:1*

RAISE should always follow answered prayer; as the mist of earth's gratitude rises when the sun of heaven's love warms the ground. Has the Lord been gracious to you, and inclined His ear to the voice of your supplication? Then praise Him as long as you live. Let the ripe fruit drop upon the fertile soil from which it drew its life. Don't deny singing to Him who has answered your prayer and given you the desire of your heart. To be silent over God's mercies is to incur the guilt of ingratitude; it is to act as basely as the nine lepers who, after they had been cured of their leprosy, never returned to give thanks to the healing Lord. To forget to praise God is to refuse to benefit ourselves; for praise, like prayer, is one great means of promoting the growth of the spiritual life. It helps to remove our burdens, to excite our hope, to increase our faith. It is a healthful and invigorating exercise which quickens the pulse of the believer, and steels one for fresh enterprises in the Master's service. To bless God for mercies received is also the way to benefit others; "let the afflicted hear and rejoice." Those who have been in similar circumstances will take comfort if we can say, "Glorify the LORD with me; let us exalt His name together; this poor man called, and the LORD heard him." Weak hearts will be strengthened, and drooping saints will be revived as they listen to our "songs of deliverance." Their doubts and fears will be rebuked, as we teach and admonish one another in psalms and hymns and spiritual songs. They too shall "sing of the ways of the LORD," when they hear us magnify His holy name. Praise is the most heavenly of Christian duties. The angels don't pray, but they never cease to praise both day and night; and the redeemed, clothed in white robes, with palm branches in their hands, are never weary of singing the new song, "Worthy is the Lamb."

"You who dwell in the gardens with friends
in attendance, let me hear your voice!"
— *Song of Songs 8:13*

Y sweet Lord Jesus remembers the garden of Gethsemane well; and, although He has left that garden, He now dwells in the garden of His church: there He opens His heart to those who keep His blessed company. That voice of love with which He speaks to His beloved is more musical than the harps of heaven. There is a depth of melodious love within it which leaves all human music far behind. Tens of thousands on earth and millions above take extravagant pleasure in its harmonious accents. Some whom I know well and greatly envy are listening to the beloved voice at this very moment. O I wish I were a participant in their joys! It is true some of these are poor, others bedridden, and some near the gates of death; but, O my Lord, I would cheerfully starve with them, pine with them, or die with them, if I could just hear Your voice. Once I did hear it often, but I have grieved Your Spirit. Return to me in compassion and once again say to me, "I am your salvation." No other voice can content me; I know Your voice, and cannot be deceived by another. Allow me to hear it, I pray. I don't know what You will say, neither do I set any condition, O my Beloved. Just let me hear You speak and, if it should be a rebuke, I will bless You for it. Perhaps, in order to purify my dull ear, I may need an operation very grievous to the flesh, but, no matter what the cost, I am not turning from the one consuming desire: let me hear Your voice. Bore a new opening in my ear; pierce my ear with Your harshest notes, only don't let me continue to be deaf to Your calls. Tonight, Lord, grant Your unworthy one this desire, for I am Yours, and You have bought me with Your blood. You have opened my eye to see You, and the sight has saved me. Lord, open my ear. I have read Your heart, now let me hear Your lips.

"Renew a steadfast spirit within me." — Psalm 51:10

 backslider, if there is a spark of life left in him, will groan after restoration. In this renewal the same exercise of grace is required as at our conversion. We needed repentance then; we certainly need it now. We wanted faith that we might come to Christ at first; only the same grace can bring us to Jesus now. We wanted a word from the Most High, a word from the lip of the loving One, to end our fears then; we shall soon discover, when under a sense of present sin, that we need it now. No one can be renewed without a manifestation of the Holy Spirit's energy that is as real and true as at the first renewal because the work is as great, and flesh and blood are just as present now as they ever were. Let your personal weakness, O Christian, be an argument to make you pray earnestly to your God for help. Remember, David didn't fold his arms or close his lips when he felt himself to be powerless; instead, he hastened to the mercy seat with "renew a steadfast spirit within me." Don't let the doctrine that you can do nothing unaided make you sleep; but let it be a goad in your side to drive you with great earnestness to Israel's strong Helper. O that you may have grace to plead with God, as though you pleaded for your very life — "Lord, renew a steadfast spirit within me." Those who *sincerely* pray to God to do this, will prove their honesty by using the means through which God works. Pray often; live upon the Word of God often; kill the lusts which have driven your Lord from you; be careful to watch over future uprisings of sin. The Lord has His own appointed ways; sit by the wayside and you will be ready when He passes by. Continue in all those blessed ordinances which will foster and nourish your dying graces; and, knowing that all the power must proceed from Him, never stop saying, "Renew a steadfast spirit within me."

*"I cared for you in the desert, in the land of
burning heat."* — *Hosea 13:5*

ES, Lord, You did indeed know me in my *fallen state.* Nevertheless, You choose me for Yourself. When I was loathsome and abhorred myself, You received me as Your child, and You satisfied my craving wants. Blessed be Your name forever for this free, rich, abounding mercy. Since then, *my inward experience* has often been a wilderness but, just the same, You have owned me as Your beloved, and poured streams of love and grace into me to delight me, and make me fruitful. Yes, when my *outward circumstances* have been at the worst, and I have wandered in a land of drought, Your sweet presence has comforted me. Others haven't known me when scorn was in store for me, but You have known my soul in adversities, for no affliction dims the luster of Your love. Most gracious Lord, I magnify You for all Your faithfulness to me in trying circumstances, and I deplore all the times that I have forgotten You or have been happy with myself when I really owed everything to Your gentleness and love. Have mercy upon Your servant in this thing!

My soul, if Jesus in this manner acknowledged you in your low estate, be sure to acknowledge both Himself and His cause now that you are prosperous. Don't be so elevated by your worldly successes that you are ashamed of the truth or of the poor church with which you have been associated. Follow Jesus into the wilderness: bear the cross with Him when the heat of persecution grows hot. He owned you, O my soul, in your poverty and shame — don't ever be so treacherous as to be ashamed of Him. O for more shame at the thought of being ashamed of my best Beloved! Jesus, my soul cleaves to You.

> "I'll turn to Thee in days of light,
> As well as nights of care,
> Thou brightest amid all that's bright!
> Thou fairest of the fair!"

"To the church that meets in your home." — Philemon 2

S there a church in this house? Are parents, children, and friends all members of it or are some still unconverted? Let's pause here and let the question go around — *Am I a member of the church in this house?* How a father's heart would leap for joy and a mother's eyes fill with holy tears if, from the eldest to the youngest child, all were saved! Let's pray for this great mercy until the Lord grants it to us. It is conceivable that Philemon's dearest object of desire was to have all in his household saved; but, to begin with, this desire was not granted to him in its fullness. He had a wicked servant, Onesimus, who, after having wronged him, ran away from his service. His master's prayers followed him and, at last, as God would have it, Onesimus was led to hear Paul preach; his heart was touched, and he returned to Philemon, not only to be a faithful servant, but also a beloved brother, adding another member to the church in Philemon's house. Is there an unconverted servant or child absent this morning? Make special supplication that such may, on their return to their home, gladden all hearts with the good news of what grace has done! Is there one present? Let him partake in the same earnest entreaty.

If there is such a church in our house, let's order it well, and let all act as in the sight of God. Let's move in the common affairs of life with studied holiness, diligence, kindness, and integrity. More is expected of a church than of an ordinary household; in such a case, family worship must be more devout and hearty; internal love must be warmer and unbroken, and external conduct must be more sanctified and Christlike. We needn't fear that the smallness of our number will keep us off of the list of churches, for the Holy Spirit has here enrolled a family church in the inspired book of remembrance. As a church, let's now draw near to the great head of the one church universal, and let's beg Him to give us grace to shine before all people to the glory of His name.

"And they knew nothing about what would happen
until the flood came and took them all away.
That is how it will be at the coming of the
Son of Man." — Matthew 24:39

HE doom was universal; neither rich nor poor escaped: the learned and the illiterate, the admired and the abhorred, the religious and the profane, the old and the young, all sank in one common ruin. No doubt, some had ridiculed the patriarch — where are their merry jests now? Others had threatened him for his zeal which they took to be madness — where are their boastings and speeches now? The critic who judged Noah's work is drowned in the same sea which covers his sneering companions. Those who spoke patronizingly of the good man's faithfulness to his convictions, but didn't share in them, have sunk to rise no more, and the workers who helped to build the wondrous ark for pay, are all lost also. The flood swept them *all* away, and made no single exception. Even so, outside of Christ, final destruction is sure for every man born of woman; no rank, possession, or character, shall be adequate to save a single soul who has not believed in the Lord Jesus. My soul, behold this widespread judgment and tremble at it.

How marvelous the general apathy! they were all eating and drinking, marrying and giving in marriage, until the awful morning dawned. There wasn't a wise man upon earth outside of the ark. Folly duped the whole race, the folly of self-preservation — the most foolish of all follies. Folly in doubting the most true God — the most malignant foolishness. My soul, isn't it strange? Everyone is negligent of their souls until grace gives them reason; then they leave their madness and act like rational beings, but not until then.

All, blessed be God, were safe in the ark; no corruption entered there. From the huge elephant down to the tiny mouse, all were safe. The timid rabbit was as secure as the courageous lion, the helpless cony as safe as the laborious ox. All are safe in Jesus. My soul, are you in Him?

"I the LORD do not change." — *Malachi 3:6*

 T is well for us that, in the middle of all the changes in life, there is One whom change cannot affect, One whose heart can never alter, and on whose brow mutability can make no furrows. Everything else has gone through changes — all things are changing. The sun itself grows dim with age; the world is growing old; the folding up of the worn-out vesture has begun; the heavens and earth must soon pass away; they shall perish, they shall grow old as does a garment; but there is only One who has immortality, of whose years there is no end, and in whose person there is no change. The gratification which the mariner feels, when, after having been tossed about for many a day, he sets foot again upon solid ground is the satisfaction of a Christian when, amid all the changes of this uneasy, troubled life, he rests the foot of his faith upon this truth — *"I the LORD do not change."*

The stability which the anchor gives the ship when it has at last obtained a holdfast is comparable to the hope of the Christian when it fixes itself upon this glorious truth. God "does not change like shifting shadows." Whatever His attributes were in ages past, they are now; His power, His wisdom, His justice, His truth are unchanged as well. He has always been the refuge of His people, their stronghold in the day of trouble, and He is their sure Helper still. He is unchanged in His *love.* He has loved His people with "an everlasting love;" He loves them now as much as ever He did, and when all earthly things shall have melted in the last conflagration, His love will still wear the dew of its youth. How valuable it is to have the assurance that He doesn't change! The wheel of providence revolves, but its axle is eternal love.

> "Death and change are busy ever,
> Man decays, and ages move;
> But His mercy waneth never;
> God is wisdom, God is love."

*"Indignation grips me because of the wicked, who
have forsaken your law." — Psalm 119:53*

Y soul, do you feel a holy shuddering at the sins of others? If not, you are lacking inward holiness. David's cheeks were wet with rivers of waters because of prevailing unholiness, Jeremiah desired eyes like fountains that he might lament the iniquities of Israel, and Lot was vexed with the conversation of the men of Sodom. Those upon whom the mark was set in Ezekiel's vision were those who sighed and cried for the abominations of Jerusalem. It cannot but grieve gracious souls to see what pains individuals take to go to hell. They know the evil of sin experimentally, and they are alarmed to see others flying like moths into its blaze. Sin makes the righteous shudder because it violates a holy law which it is to every man's highest interest to keep. It pulls down the pillars of the commonwealth. Sin in others horrifies us because it reminds us of the baseness of our own hearts: when we see a transgressor, we cry with the saint mentioned by Bernard, "He fell today, and I could fall tomorrow." Sin to believers is horrible because it crucified the Savior; we see in every iniquity the nails and spear. How can a saved soul look on that cursed Christ-killing sin without abhorrence? Say, my heart, do you sensibly go along with all of this? It is an awful thing to insult God to His face. The good God deserves better treatment, the great God claims it, the just God will have it, or repay His adversary to his face. An awakened heart trembles at the audacity of sin, and stands alarmed at the contemplation of its punishment. How monstrous a thing rebellion is! How direful a doom is prepared for the ungodly! My soul, never laugh at sin's follies lest you come to smile at sin itself. It is your enemy, and your Lord's enemy — view it with extreme dislike, for only in this way can you confirm the possession of holiness, without which no one can see the Lord.

"He is praying." — *Acts 9:11*

 RAYERS are instantly noticed in heaven. The moment Saul began to pray the Lord heard him. Here is comfort for the distressed but praying soul. Frequently, a poor broken-hearted person on bended knee can only express regret in the language of sighs and tears; yet that groan has made all the harps of heaven thrill with music; that tear has been caught by God and treasured in the lachrymatory of heaven. "You list my tears on your scroll," implies that they are recorded as they flow. The suppliant, whose fears prevent his words, will be well understood by the Most High. He may only look up with misty eye; but "prayer is the falling of a tear." Tears are the diamonds of heaven; sighs are a part of the music of Jehovah's court, and are numbered with "the sublimest strains that reach the majesty on high." Do not think that your prayer, however weak or trembling, will be unregarded. Jacob's ladder is lofty, but our prayers shall lean upon the Angel of the covenant and so climb its starry rounds. Our God not only *hears* prayer but also *loves* to hear it. "He does not ignore the cry of the afflicted." True, He does take into consideration haughty looks and lofty words; He doesn't care for the pomp and pageantry of kings; He doesn't listen to the swell of martial music; He doesn't regard the triumph and pride of man; but wherever there is a heart big with sorrow, or a lip quivering with agony, or a deep groan, or a penitential sigh, the heart of Jehovah is open; He marks it down in the registry of His memory; He puts our prayers, like rose leaves, between the pages of His book of remembrance, and when the volume is opened at last, a precious fragrance will release itself from it.

> "Faith asks no signal from the skies,
> To show that prayers accepted rise,
> Our Priest is in His holy place,
> And answers from the throne of grace."

"Their prayer reached heaven, his holy dwelling place." — 2 Chronicles 30:27

 RAYER is the unfailing recourse of the Christian in any situation, in every plight. When you can't use your sword you may take to the weapon of all-prayer. Your powder may be damp, your bowstring may be relaxed, but the weapon of all-prayer needn't ever be out of order. Leviathan laughs at the javelin, but he trembles at prayer. Sword and spear need furbishing, but prayer never rusts, and when we think it at its most blunt, it cuts the best. Prayer is an open door which none can shut. Devils may surround you on all sides, but the way upward is always open; as long as that road is unobstructed, you will not fall into the enemy's hand. We can never be taken by blockade, escalade, mine, or storm as long as heavenly relief can come down to us via Jacob's ladder to relieve us during times of constraining circumstances. Prayer is never out of season: in summer and in winter its merchandise is precious. Prayer gains audience with heaven in the dead of night, in the midst of business, in the heat of noonday, in the shades of evening. In every condition, whether of poverty, or sickness, or obscurity, or slander, or doubt, your covenant God will welcome your prayer and answer it from His holy place. Nor is prayer ever *futile*. True prayer is always true power. You may not always get what you ask, but you shall always have your real wants supplied. When God does not answer His children according to the letter, He does so according to the spirit. If you ask for coarse meal, will you get angry because He gives you the finest flour? If you seek bodily health, will you complain if, instead, He makes your sickness turn to the healing of spiritual maladies? Isn't it better to have the cross sanctified than removed? This evening, my soul, don't forget to offer your petition and request, for the Lord is ready to grant you your desires.

"For my power is made perfect in weakness."
— 2 Corinthians 12:9

 primary qualification for serving God with any amount of success, and for doing God's work well and triumphantly, is a sense of our own weakness. When God's warrior marches forth to battle, strong in his own might, when he boasts, "I know that I shall conquer, my own right arm and my conquering sword shall get me the victory," defeat is not far away. God will not go forth with that man who marches in his own strength. He who counts on victory in this manner has thought wrongly, for it is "'not by might nor by power, but by my Spirit,' says the LORD Almighty." They who go forth to fight, boasting of their prowess, shall return with their brightly-colored banners trailing in the dust and their armor stained with disgrace. Those who serve God must serve Him in His own way, and in His strength, or He will never accept their service. That which man does, unaided by divine strength, God can never own. The mere fruits of the earth He casts away; He will only reap that corn, the seed of which was sown from heaven, watered by grace, and ripened by the sun of divine love. God will empty out all that you have before He will put His own into you; He will first clean out your granaries before He will fill them with the finest of the wheat. The river of God is full of water; but not one drop of it flows from earthly springs. God will have no strength used in His battles but the strength which He Himself imparts. Are you mourning over your own weakness? Take courage, for there must be a consciousness of weakness before the Lord will give you victory. Your emptiness is but the preparation for your being filled, and your casting down is but the making ready for your lifting up.

"When I am weak then am I strong,
Grace is my shield and Christ my song."

"In your light we see light." — *Psalm 36:9*

O lips can tell the love of Christ to the heart until Jesus Himself shall speak within. Descriptions all fall flat and tame unless the Holy Spirit fills them with life and power; until our Immanuel reveals Himself within, the soul does not see Him. If you would see the sun, would you gather together the common means of illumination, and seek in that way to behold the orb of day? No, the wise man knows that the sun must reveal itself, and only by its own blaze can that mighty lamp be seen. It is so with Christ. "Blessed are you, Simon son of Jonah," He said to Peter, "for this was not revealed to you by man." Purify flesh and blood by any educational process you may select, elevate mental faculties to the highest degree of intellectual power, yet none of these can reveal Christ. The Spirit of God must come with power, and overshadow the human being with His wings, and then in that mystic holy of holies the Lord Jesus must display Himself to the sanctified eye, as He does not to blind humanity. Christ must be His own mirror. The great mass of this bleary-eyed world can see nothing of the ineffable glories of Immanuel. He stands before them without form or comeliness, a root out of a dry ground, rejected by the vain and despised by the proud. Only where the Spirit has touched the eye with eye salve, awakened the heart with divine life, and educated the soul to a heavenly taste, only there is He understood. "Now to you who believe, this stone is precious;" to you He is the chief cornerstone, the Rock of your salvation, your all in all; but to others He is "a stone that causes men to stumble and a rock that makes them fall." Happy are those to whom our Lord manifests Himself, for His promise to such is that He will *make His abode with them.* O Jesus, our Lord, our heart is open, come in, and stay forever. Show Yourself to us now! Favor us with a glimpse of Your all-conquering charms.

"No weapon forged against you will prevail."
— *Isaiah 54:17*

HIS day is notable in English history for two great deliverances wrought by God. On this day in 1605, the plot of the Papists to destroy the Houses of Parliament was discovered.

"While for our princes they prepare
In caverns deep a burning snare,
He shot from heaven a piercing ray,
And the dark treachery brought to day."

Secondly, this day in 1688 marks the anniversary of the landing of King William III, at Torbay, by which the hope of Popish ascendancy was quashed, and religious liberty was secured.

This day ought to be celebrated, not by the saturnalia of striplings, but by the songs of saints. Our Puritan forefathers most devoutly made it a special time of thanksgiving. There still exists a record of the annual sermons preached by Matthew Henry on this day. Our Protestant feeling and our love of liberty should make us regard its anniversary with holy gratitude. Let our hearts and lips exclaim, "We have heard with our ears, O God; our fathers have told us what You did in their days, in days long ago." You have made this nation the home of the gospel; and when the foe has risen against her, You have shielded her. Help us to offer repeated songs for repeated deliverances. Grant us more and more a hatred of Antichrist, and hasten on the day of her entire extinction. Until then and ever, we believe the promise, "No weapon forged against You will prevail." Should it not be laid upon the heart of every lover of the gospel of Jesus on this day to plead for the overturning of false doctrines and the extension of divine truth? Would it not be well to search our own hearts, and turn out any of the Popish lumber of self-righteousness which may lie concealed therein?

"Give thanks to him and praise his name."
— Psalm 100:4

UR Lord wants all His people to be rich in elevated, joyful thoughts concerning His blessed person. Jesus is not content that His brethren should think ungenerous thoughts of Him; it is His pleasure that His wedded ones should be delighted with His beauty. We are not to regard Him as a bare necessary, like bread and water, but as a luxurious delicacy, a rare and beautiful delight. To this end He has revealed Himself as "a pearl of great value" in its peerless beauty, as "a sachet of myrrh" in its refreshing fragrance, as "a rose of Sharon" in its lasting perfume, and as "a lily of the valley" in its spotless purity.

To help lift your thoughts of who Christ is, remember the esteem in which Christ is held beyond the skies, where things are measured by the right standard. Think how God esteems the Only Begotten, His unspeakable gift to us. Consider what the angels think of Him, as they count it their highest honor to veil their faces at His feet. Consider what those who are washed in His blood think of Him, as day without night they sing His well-deserved praises. Elevated thoughts of Christ will enable us to act consistently with our relations towards Him. The more loftily we see Christ enthroned, and the more lowly we are when bowing before the foot of the throne, the more truly shall we be prepared to act our part towards Him. Our Lord Jesus wants us to think well of Him, so that we may submit cheerfully to His authority. Exalted thoughts of Him increase our love. Love and esteem go together. Therefore, believer, think often about your Master's excellencies. Study Him in His primeval glory, before He took upon Himself your nature! Think of the mighty love which drew Him from His throne to die upon the cross! Admire Him as He conquers all the powers of hell! See Him risen, crowned, glorified! Bow before Him as the Wonderful, the Advisor, the mighty God, for only in this way will your love for Him be what it should.

"I will pour water on the thirsty land." — *Isaiah 44:3*

 HEN a believer feels very sad and lowly, he or she will often try to lift this depression by punishing himself or herself with dark and doleful fears. This is not a way to rise from the dust, but to continue in it. You may as well chain an eagle's wing to make it fly, as to doubt in order to increase our grace. It is not the law, but the gospel which saves the seeking soul at first; and it is not a legal bondage, but gospel liberty which can restore the fainting believer afterwards. Slavish fear doesn't return the backslider to God, but the sweet wooings of love allure him to Jesus' heart. This morning, are you thirsting for the living God, and unhappy because you can't find Him to the delight of your heart? Have you lost the joy of religion, and is "restore to me the joy of Your salvation" your prayer? Are you conscious also that you are barren, like the dry ground; that you are not bringing forth the fruit to God which He has a right to expect of you; that you are not as useful in the church, or in the world, as your heart desires to be? Then this is exactly the promise you need, "I will pour water on the thirsty land." You shall receive the grace you so much require, and you shall have it to the utmost extremity of your needs. Water refreshes the thirsty: you shall be refreshed; your desires shall be gratified. Water awakens sleeping vegetable life: your life shall be quickened by fresh grace. Water swells the buds and makes the fruits ripen; you shall have fructifying grace: you shall be made fruitful in the ways of God. Whatever good quality there is in divine grace, you shall enjoy it to the full. All the riches of divine grace you shall receive in plenty; you shall be, as it were, drenched with it: and as sometimes the meadows become flooded by the bursting rivers, and the fields are turned into pools, so shall you be — the thirsty land shall be springs of water.

"This is the blood of the covenant, which God has commanded you to keep." — *Hebrews 9:20*

HERE is a strange power about the very word "blood" and the sight of it always has an impact on us. A kind heart cannot bear to see a sparrow bleed, and unless familiarized by use, turns away with horror at the slaughter of a beast. As to the blood of human beings, it is a consecrated thing: it is murder to shed it in anger, it is a dreadful crime to squander it in war. Is this solemnity due to the fact that blood is life, and the spilling out of it the sign of death? We think so. When we advance to considering the blood of the Son of God, our awe increases even more, and we shudder as we think of the guilt of sin, and the terrible penalty which the Sinbearer endured. Blood, always precious, is priceless when it streams from Immanuel's side. The blood of Jesus seals the *covenant* of grace, and makes it forever sure. Covenants in ages past were sealed by sacrifice, and the everlasting covenant was ratified in the same manner. Oh, the delight of being saved upon the sure foundation of divine engagements which cannot be dishonored! Salvation by the works of the law is a frail and broken vessel whose shipwreck is sure; but the covenant vessel fears no storms, for the blood ensures the whole. The blood of Jesus made His *testament* valid. Wills are of no power unless the testators die. In this light the soldier's spear is a blessed aid to faith, since it proved our Lord to be really dead. There can be no doubt about it, and we may boldly appropriate the legacies which He has left for His people. Happy are they who see their title to heavenly blessings assured to them by a dying Savior. But doesn't this blood say something to us? Doesn't it invite us to sanctify ourselves to Him by whom we have been redeemed? Does it not call us to newness of life, and incite us to entire consecration to the Lord? O that the power of the blood might be known and felt in us this night!

"See, I have engraved you on the palms of my hands."
— *Isaiah 49:16*

 O doubt a part of the wonder which is concentrated in the word *"See,"* is excited by the unbelieving lamentation of the preceding sentence. Zion said, "The LORD has forsaken me, the Lord has forgotten me." How amazed the divine mind seems to be at this wicked unbelief! What can be more astounding than the unfounded doubts and fears of God's favored people? The Lord's loving word of rebuke should make us blush; He cries, "How can I have forgotten you, when I have engraved you on the palms of My hands? How dare you doubt My constant remembrance, when the memorial is set upon My very flesh?" O unbelief, how strange a marvel you are! We do not know which most to wonder at, the faithfulness of God or the unbelief of His people. He keeps His promise a thousand times, and yet the next trial makes us doubt Him. He never fails; He is never a dry well; He is never as a setting sun, a passing meteor, or a melting vapor; and yet we are as continually vexed with anxieties, molested with suspicions, and disturbed with fears, as if our God were the mirage of the desert. "See," *is a word intended to excite admiration.* Here, indeed, we have a theme for marveling. Heaven and earth may well be astonished that rebels should obtain so great a nearness to the heart of infinite love as to be written upon the palms of His hands. "I have engraved *you.*" It does not say, "your name." The name is there, but that is not all: "I have engraved *you.*" See the fullness of this! I have engraved your person, your image, your situation, your circumstances, your sins, your temptations, your weaknesses, your wants, your works; I have engraved *you,* everything about you, all that concerns you; I have put you altogether there. Will you ever say again that your God has forsaken you when He has engraved *you* upon His own palms?

"You will be my witnesses." — *Acts 1:8*

N order to learn how to discharge your duty as a witness for Christ, look at His example. He is always witnessing: by the well of Samaria, or in the Temple of Jerusalem: by the lake of Gennesaret, or on the mountain's brow. He is witnessing night and day; His mighty prayers are as vocal to God as His daily services. He witnesses under all circumstances; Scribes and Pharisees cannot shut His mouth; even before Pilate He witnesses a good confession. He witnesses so clearly and distinctly that there is no mistake in Him. Christian, make your life a clear testimony. Be as the brook wherein you may see every stone at the bottom — not as the muddy creek, of which you only see the surface — but clear and transparent, so that your heart's love to God and man may be visible to all. You needn't *say,* "I am true:" *be* true. Do not boast of integrity, but *be* upright. This is how others cannot avoid your testimony. Never, for fear of feeble humankind, restrain your witness. Your lips have been warmed with a coal from off the altar; let them speak as heaven-touched lips should do. "Sow your seed in the morning, and at evening do not let your hands be idle." Don't watch the clouds, don't consult the wind — in season and out of season witness for the Savior, and if it shall come to pass that for Christ's sake and the gospel's you shall endure suffering in any shape, don't shrink from it, but rejoice in the honor thus conferred upon you, that you are counted worthy to endure with your Lord; and be joyful also in this — that your sufferings, your losses, and persecutions shall become the platform from which you shall witness for Christ Jesus all the more vigorously and with greater power. Study your great Exemplar, and be filled with His Spirit. Remember that you need much teaching, much upholding, much grace, and much humility, if your witnessing is to be to your Master's glory.

"As you received Christ Jesus as Lord." — *Colossians 2:6*

HE life of faith is represented as *receiving* — *an act which implies the very opposite of anything like merit.* It is simply the acceptance of a gift. As the earth drinks in the rain, as the sea receives the streams, as night accepts light from the stars, so we, giving nothing, partake freely of the grace of God. The saints are not by nature wells or streams; they are only cisterns into which the living water flows; they are empty vessels into which God pours His salvation. The idea of receiving implies *a sense of realization,* making the matter a *reality.* One cannot very well receive a shadow; we receive that which is substantial: so is it in the life of faith, Christ becomes real to us. While we are without faith, Jesus is a mere name to us — a person who lived a long time ago, so long ago that His life is only history to us now! By an act of faith Jesus becomes a real person in the consciousness of our heart. But receiving also means *grasping or getting possession of.* The thing which I receive becomes my own: I appropriate to myself that which is given. When I receive Jesus, He becomes *my* Savior, so much mine that neither life nor death shall be able to rob me of Him. All this is to receive Christ — to take Him as God's free gift; to realize Him in my heart, and to appropriate Him as mine.

Salvation may be described as the blind receiving sight, the deaf receiving hearing, the dead receiving life; but we have not only received these blessings, we have received CHRIST JESUS Himself. It is true that He gave us life from the dead. He gave us pardon of sin; He gave us imputed righteousness. These are all precious things, but we are not content with them; we have received *Christ Himself.* The Son of God has been poured into us, and we have received Him, and appropriated Him. What a heartful Jesus must be, for heaven itself cannot contain Him!

*"The Teacher asks: Where is my guest room, where I
may eat the Passover with my disciples?"*
— *Mark 14:14*

 ERUSALEM at the time of the Passover was one great inn; each householder had invited his own friends, but no one had invited the Savior, and He had no dwelling of His own. It was by His own supernatural power that He found Himself an upper room in which to keep the feast. It is so even to this day — Jesus is not received by people except where, by His supernatural power and grace, He renews the heart. All doors are open enough to the prince of darkness, but Jesus must clear a way for Himself or lodge in the streets. It was through the mysterious power exerted by our Lord that the householder raised no question, but at once cheerfully and joyfully opened his guest room. Who he was, and what he was, we do not know, but he readily accepted the honor which the Redeemer proposed to confer upon him. We still discover who are and who are not the Lord's chosen in this way; for when the gospel comes to some, they fight against it, and will not have it, but where people receive it and welcome it, this is a sure indication that there is a secret work going on in the soul, and that God has chosen them to eternal life. Are you willing, dear reader, to receive Christ? then there is no difficulty in the way; Christ will be your guest; His own power is working with you, making you willing. What an honor to entertain the Son of God! The heaven of heavens cannot contain Him, and yet He condescends to find a house within our hearts! We are not worthy that He should come under our roof, but what an unutterable privilege when He condescends to enter! for then He makes a feast, and causes us to feast with Him upon royal dainties, we sit at a banquet where the food is immortal, and give immortality to those who feed thereon. Blessed among the children of Adam is he who entertains the angels' Lord.

"Continue to [walk] in him." — *Colossians 2:6*

F we have received Christ Himself in our inmost hearts, our new life will manifest its intimate acquaintance with Him by a *walk of faith in Him*. Walking implies *action*. Our religion is not to be confined to our closet; we must carry out into practical effect that which we believe. If we walk in Christ, then we act as Christ would act; for Christ being in us, our hope, our love, our joy, our life, we are the reflex of the image of Jesus; and others say about us, "They are like their Master; they live like Jesus Christ." Walking signifies *progress*. "Continue to live in Him;" proceed from grace to grace, run forward until you reach the uttermost degree of knowledge that a person can attain concerning our Beloved. Walking implies *continuance*. There must be a perpetual abiding in Christ. How many Christians think that in the morning and evening they ought to come into the company of Jesus, and may then give their hearts to the world all the day: but this is poor living; we should always be with Him, treading in His steps and doing His will. Walking also implies *habit*. When we talk about our walk and conversation, we mean our habits, the constant tenor of our life. Now, if we sometimes enjoy Christ, and then forget Him; sometimes call Him ours, and at another time lose our hold, this is not a habit; we do not *walk* in Him. We must keep to Him, cling to Him, never let Him go, but live and have our being in Him. "Just as you received Christ Jesus as Lord, continue to live in Him;" persevere in the same way in which you have begun, and, as at first, when Christ Jesus was the trust of your faith, the source of your life, the principle of your action, and the joy of your spirit, so let Him be the same until life's end; the same when you walk through the valley of the shadow of death, and enter into the joy and the rest which remain for the people of God. O Holy Spirit, enable us to obey this heavenly precept.

*"Whose refuge will be the mountain fortress. His
bread will be supplied, and water will not
fail him." — Isaiah 33:16*

O you doubt, O Christian, do you doubt as to whether God will fulfill His promise? Shall the munitions of rock be carried by storm? Shall the storehouses of heaven fail? Do you think that your heavenly Father, though He knows that you have need of food and clothing, will yet forget you? When not a sparrow falls to the ground without your Father, and the very hairs of your head are all numbered, will you mistrust and doubt Him? Perhaps your affliction will continue upon you until you dare to trust your God, and then it shall end. There are so many who have been tested and in anguish until, at last, they have been driven in sheer desperation to exercise faith in God, and the moment of their faith has been the instant of their deliverance; they have seen whether God would keep His promise or not. Oh, I pray you, doubt Him no longer! Do not please Satan, and don't vex yourself by indulging any more those hard thoughts of God. Don't think it is such a light matter to doubt Jehovah. Remember, it is a *sin;* and not a little sin either, but in the highest degree criminal. The angels never doubted Him, nor the devils either: we alone, out of all the beings that God has fashioned, dishonor Him by unbelief, and tarnish His honor by mistrust. Shame upon us for this! Our God does not deserve to be so basely suspected; in our earlier life we have proved Him to be true and faithful to His word, and with so many instances of His love and of His kindness as we have received and are daily receiving at His hands, it is base and inexcusable that we allow a doubt to sojourn within our heart. May we henceforth wage constant war against doubts of our God — enemies to our peace and to His honor; and with an unstaggering faith believe that what He has promised He will also perform. "Lord, I do believe; help me overcome my unbelief!"

"The eternal God is your refuge." — *Deuteronomy 33:27*

HE word refuge may be translated "mansion," or "abode," which gives the thought that *God is our abode, our home.* There is a fullness and sweetness in the metaphor, for our home is dear to our hearts, whether it be the humblest cottage, or the scantiest garret; and dearer far is our blessed God, in whom we live, and move, and have our being. It is at home that we *feel safe:* we shut the world out and dwell in quiet security. So when we are with our God we "fear no evil." He is our shelter and retreat, our abiding refuge. At home, *we take our rest;* it is there we find repose after the fatigue and toil of the day. And so our hearts find rest in God, when, wearied with life's conflict, we turn to Him, and our soul dwells at ease. At home, also, we *let our hearts loose;* we are not afraid of being misunderstood, nor of our words being misconstrued. So when we are with God we can commune freely with Him, laying open all our hidden desires; for if the "secret of the Lord is with them that fear Him," the secrets of them that fear Him ought to be, and must be, with their Lord. Home, too, is the place of our *truest and purest happiness:* and it is in God that our hearts find their deepest delight. We have joy in Him which far surpasses all other joy. *It is also for home that we work and make every effort.* The thought of it gives strength to bear the daily burden, and quickens the fingers to perform the task; and in this sense we may also say that God is our home. Love for Him strengthens us. We think of Him in the person of His dear Son; and a glimpse of the suffering face of the Redeemer constrains us to work in His cause. We feel that we must work, for there are brothers and sisters yet to be saved, and we have to gladden our Father's heart by bringing home His wandering sons and daughters; we would fill with holy mirth the sacred family among whom we dwell. Happy are those who have thus the God of Jacob for their refuge!

"It is enough for the student to be like his teacher."
— *Matthew 10:25*

 O one will dispute this statement, for it would be unseemly for the servant to be exalted above his Master. When our Lord was on earth, what was the treatment He received? Were His claims acknowledged, His instructions followed, His perfections worshipped by those whom He came to bless? No; "He was despised and rejected by men." His place was outside the camp: cross-bearing was His occupation. Did the world yield Him solace and rest? "Foxes have holes and birds of the air have nests, but the Son of Man has no place to lay His head." This inhospitable country afforded Him no shelter: it cast Him out and crucified Him. Such — if you are a follower of Jesus, and maintain a consistent, Christlike walk and conversation — you must expect to be the lot of that part of your spiritual life which, in its outward development, comes under the observation of humankind. They will treat it as they treated the Savior — they will despise it. Do not dream that worldlings will admire you, or that the more holy and the more Christlike you are, the more peaceably people will act towards you. They did not prize the polished gem, how could they value the jewel in the rough? "If the head of the house has been called Beelzebub, how much more the members of His household"? If we were more like Christ, we should be more hated by His enemies. It is a sad dishonor to a child of God to be the world's favorite. It is a very ill omen to hear a wicked world clap its hands and shout "Well done" to the Christian. He may begin to look to his character, and wonder whether he has not been doing wrong, when the unrighteous give him their approbation. Let's be true to our Master, and have no friendship with a blind and base world which scorns and rejects Him. Far be it from us to seek a crown of honor where our Lord found a coronet of thorn.

"Underneath are the everlasting arms."
— Deuteronomy 33:27

OD — the eternal God — is Himself *our support* at all times, and especially when we are sinking in deep trouble. There are seasons when a Christian *sinks very low in humiliation.* Under a deep sense of his great sinfulness, he is humbled before God until he scarcely knows how to pray, because he appears, in his own sight, so worthless. Well, child of God, remember that when you are at your worst and lowest, yet underneath you "are everlasting arms." Sin may drag you ever so low, but Christ's great atonement is still under all. You may have descended into the deep, but you cannot have fallen as low as "the uttermost;" and to the uttermost He saves. Again, the Christian sometimes sinks very deeply in *sore trial from without.* Every earthly prop is cut away. What then? Still underneath him are "the everlasting arms." He cannot fall so deep in distress and affliction but what the covenant grace of an ever-faithful God will still encircle him. The Christian may be sinking under *trouble from within* through fierce conflict, but even then he cannot be brought so low as to be beyond the reach of the "everlasting arms" — they are underneath him; and, while thus sustained, all Satan's efforts to harm him avail nothing.

This assurance of support is a comfort to any *weary but earnest worker* in the service of God. It implies a promise of strength for each day, grace for each need, and power for each duty. And, further, *when death comes,* the promise shall still hold good. When we stand in the midst of the Jordan, we shall be able to say with David, "I will fear no evil, for You are with me." We shall descend into the grave, but we shall go no lower, for the eternal arms prevent our further fall. All through life, and at its close, we shall be upheld by the "everlasting arms" — arms that neither flag nor lose their strength, for "the everlasting God will not grow tired or weary."

"He chose our inheritance for us." — Psalm 47:4

ELIEVER, if your inheritance is a lowly one, you should be satisfied with your earthly portion; for you may rest assured that it is the fittest *for you.* Unerring wisdom ordained your lot, and selected for you the safest and best condition. A ship of large tonnage is to be brought up the river; now, in one part of the stream there is a sand bank; should someone ask, "Why does the captain steer through the deep part of the channel and deviate so much from a straight line?" His answer would be, "Because I could not get my vessel into harbor at all if I did not keep to the deep channel." So, it may be, you would run aground and endure shipwreck, if your divine Captain did not steer you into the depths of affliction where waves of trouble follow each other in quick succession. Some plants die if they have too much sunshine. It may be that you are planted where you get only a little, you are put there by the loving Farmer, because only in that situation will you bring forth fruit to perfection. Remember this, had any other condition been better for you than the one in which you are, divine love would have put you there. You are placed by God in the most suitable circumstances, and if you had to choose your lot, you would soon cry, "Lord, choose my inheritance for me, for by my self-will I am pierced through with many sorrows." Be content with such things as you have, since the Lord has ordered all things for your good. Take up your own daily cross; it is the burden best suited for your shoulder, and will prove most effective to make you perfect in every good word and work to the glory of God. Down busy self, and proud impatience, it is not for you to choose, but for the Lord of Love!

> "Trials must and will befall —
> But with humble faith to see
> Love inscribed upon them all;
> This is happiness to me."

"[The trial of] your faith." — 1 Peter 1:7

AITH untested may be true faith, but it is sure to be little faith, and it is likely to remain dwarfish as long as it is without trials. Faith never prospers as well as when all things are against her: tempests are her trainers, and lightnings are her illuminators. When a calm reigns on the sea, spread the sails as you will, the ship does not move into its harbor; for on a slumbering ocean the keel sleeps, too. Let the winds rush howling forth, and let the waters lift up themselves, then, though the vessel may rock, and her deck may be washed with waves, and her mast may creak under the pressure of the full and swelling sail, it is then that she makes headway towards her desired haven. No flowers wear so lovely a blue as those which grow at the foot of the frozen glacier; no stars gleam so brightly as those which glisten in the polar sky; no water tastes so sweet as that which springs amid the desert sand; and no faith is so precious as that which lives and triumphs in adversity. Tested faith brings experience. You couldn't have believed your own weakness if you had not been compelled to pass through the rivers; and you would never have known God's strength if you had not been supported amid the floods of water. Faith increases in solidity, assurance, and intensity the more it is exercised with tribulation. Faith is precious, and its trial is precious, too.

However, don't let this discourage those of you who are young in faith. You will have trials enough without seeking them: the full portion will be measured out to you in due season. Meanwhile, if you cannot yet claim the result of long experience, thank God for what grace you have; praise Him for that degree of holy confidence to which you have attained: walk according to that rule, and you shall yet have more and more of the blessing of God, until your faith shall move mountains and conquer impossibilities.

> *"One of those days Jesus went out to a*
> *mountainside to pray, and spent the*
> *night praying to God."* — Luke 6:12

 F ever one of woman born might have lived without prayer, it was our spotless, perfect Lord, and yet no one was ever so much in supplication as He! Such was His love for His Father that He loved to be in frequent communication with Him; such was His love for His people that He desired to be in frequent intercession for them. *The fact* of this eminent prayerfulness of Jesus is a lesson for us — He has given us an example that we may follow in His steps. *The time* He chose was admirable, it was the hour of silence, when the crowd would not disturb Him; the time of inaction, when all but Himself had ceased to work; and the season when slumber made people forget their woes, and cease their pleadings to Him for relief. While others found rest in sleep, He refreshed Himself with prayer. *The place* was also well selected. He was alone where none would intrude, where none could observe: thus was He free from Pharisaic ostentation and vulgar interruption. Those dark and silent hills were well-suited as a private chapel for the Son of God. Heaven and earth in midnight stillness heard the groans and sighs of the mysterious Being in whom both worlds were blended. *The continuance* of His pleadings is remarkable; the long watches were not too long; the cold wind did not chill His devotions; the grim darkness did not darken His faith, or loneliness check His insistent requests. We cannot watch with Him one hour, but He watched for us whole nights. *The occasion* for this prayer is notable; it was after His enemies had been enraged — prayer was His refuge and solace; it was before He sent forth the twelve apostles — prayer was the gate of His enterprise, the herald of His new work. Shouldn't we learn from Jesus to resort to special prayer when we are under peculiar trial, or contemplate fresh endeavors for the Master's glory? Lord Jesus, teach us to pray.

"No branch can bear fruit by itself." — John 15:4

OW did you begin to bear fruit? It was when you came to Jesus and cast yourselves on His great atonement, and rested on His finished righteousness. Ah! what fruit you had then! Do you remember those early days? Then, indeed, the vine flourished, the tender grape appeared, the pomegranates budded forth, and the beds of spices gave forth their smell. Have you declined since then? If you have, we charge you to remember that time of love, and repent, and do your first works. *Dedicate yourself to those engagements which you have experimentally proved draw you nearest to Christ,* because it is from Him that all your fruits proceed. Any holy exercise which will bring you to Him will help you to bear fruit. The sun is, no doubt, a great worker in creating fruit among the trees of the orchard: and Jesus is still more so among the trees of His garden of grace. When have you been the most fruitless? Hasn't it been when you have lived farthest from the Lord Jesus Christ, when you have slackened in prayer, when you have departed from the simplicity of your faith, when your graces have engrossed your attention instead of your Lord, when you have said, "My mountain stands firm; I shall never be shaken;" and have forgotten where your strength dwells — has not it been *then* that your fruit has ceased? Some of us have been taught that we have nothing outside of Christ, by terrible abasements of heart before the Lord; and when we have seen the utter barrenness and death of all creature power, we have cried in anguish, "From Him all my fruit must be found, for no fruit can ever come from me." We are taught, by past experience, that the more simply we depend upon the grace of God in Christ, and wait upon the Holy Spirit, the more we shall bring forth fruit to God. Oh! to trust Jesus for fruit as well as for life.

"They should always pray." — *Luke 18:1*

F men and women should always pray and not faint, much more *Christian men and women.* Jesus has sent His church into the world on the same errand upon which He Himself came, and this mission includes intercession. What if I say that the church is the world's priest? Creation is mute, but the church is to find a mouth for it. It is the church's high privilege to pray with acceptance. The door of grace is always open for her petitions, and they never return empty-handed. The veil was rent *for her,* the blood was sprinkled upon the altar *for her,* God constantly invites *her* to ask what she wills. Will she refuse the privilege which angels might envy her? Isn't she the bride of Christ? Can't she go in to her King at every hour? Will she let the precious privilege go unused? The church always has need for prayer. There are always some in her midst who are declining, or falling into open sin. There are lambs to be prayed for, that they may be carried in Christ's bosom: the strong, lest they grow presumptuous; and the weak, lest they become despairing. If we kept up prayer meetings twenty-four hours in the day, all the days in the year, we might never be without a special subject for supplication. Are we ever without the sick and the poor, the afflicted and the wavering? Are we ever without those who seek the conversion of relatives, the reclaiming of the faithless, or the salvation of the depraved? No, with congregations constantly gathering, with ministers always preaching, with millions of sinners lying dead in trespasses and sins; in a world full of idols, cruelties, deviltries, if the church does not pray, how shall she excuse her base neglect of the commission of her loving Lord? Let the church be in constant supplication, let every private believer cast his mite of prayer into the treasury.

*"I will cut off . . . those who bow down and swear
by the Lord, and who also swear by Molech."*
— *Zephaniah 1:4, 5*

UCH persons thought themselves safe because they were with both parties: they went with the followers of Jehovah, and bowed at the same time to Molech. But duplicity is abominable with God, and His soul hates hypocrisy. The idolater who distinctly gives himself to his false god has one sin less than he who brings his polluted and detestable sacrifice to the temple of the Lord, while his heart is with the world and the its sins. To hold with the hare and run with the hounds is a dastard's policy. In the common matters of daily life, a double-minded man is despised, but in religion he is loathsome to the last degree. The penalty pronounced in the verse before us is terrible, but it is well deserved; for how should divine justice spare the sinner, who knows the right, approves it, and professes to follow it, and all the while loves the evil, and gives it dominion in his heart?

My soul, search yourself this morning, and see whether you are guilty of double-dealing. You profess to be a follower of Jesus — do you truly love Him? Is your heart right with God? Are you of the family of old Father Honest, or are you a relative of Mr. Falsehood? A name to live by is of little value if I am indeed dead in trespasses and sins. To have one foot on the land of truth, and another on the sea of falsehood will involve a terrible fall and a total ruin. Christ will be all or nothing. God fills the whole universe, and hence there is no room for another god; if, then, He reigns in my heart, there will be no space for another reigning power. Do I rest alone on Jesus crucified, and live alone for Him? Is it my desire to do so? Is my heart set upon doing so? If so, blessed be the mighty grace which has led me to salvation; and if not so, O Lord, pardon my sad offense, and unite my heart to fear Your name.

*"Laban replied, It is not our custom here to give the
younger daughter in marriage before the older one."*
— Genesis 29:26

E do not excuse Laban for his dishonesty, but we do not hesitate because of any demands of conscience to learn from the custom which he quoted as his excuse. There are some things which must be taken in order, and if we want to win the second we must secure the first. The second may be the more lovely in our eyes, but the rule of the heavenly country must stand, and the elder must be married first. For instance, many men desire the beautiful and well-favored Rachel of joy and peace in believing, but they must first be wedded to the tender-eyed Leah of repentance. Everyone falls in love with happiness, and many would cheerfully serve twice seven years to enjoy it, but according to the rule of the Lord's kingdom, the Leah of real holiness must be beloved of our soul before the Rachel of true happiness can be attained. Heaven does not stand first but second, and only by persevering to the end can we win a portion in it. The cross must be carried before the crown can be worn. We must follow our Lord in His humiliation, or we shall never rest with Him in glory.

My soul, what do you say? Are you so vain as to hope to break through the heavenly rule? Do you hope for reward without work, or honor without toil? Dismiss the idle expectation, and be content to take the ill-favored things for the sake of the sweet love of Jesus, which will compensate you for all. In such a spirit, laboring and suffering, you will find bitters grow sweet, and hard things easy. Like Jacob, your years of service will seem to you but a few days for the love you have for Jesus; and when the dear hour of the wedding feast shall come, all your toils shall be as though they had never been — an hour with Jesus will make up for ages of pain and work.

Jesus, to win Thyself so fair,
Thy cross I will with gladness bear:
Since so the rules of heaven ordain,
The first I'll wed the next to gain.

"The LORD's portion is his people." — *Deuteronomy 32:9*

 OW are they His? By His own sovereign *choice*. He chose them, and set His love upon them. This He did altogether apart from any goodness in them at the time, or any goodness which He foresaw in them. He had mercy on whom He would have mercy, and ordained a chosen company to eternal life; thus, therefore, they are His by His unconstrained election.

They are not only His by choice, but by *purchase*. He has bought and paid for them to the utmost penny, hence about His title there can be no dispute. Not with corruptible things, as with silver and gold, but with the precious blood of the Lord Jesus Christ, the Lord's portion has been fully redeemed. There is no mortgage on His estate; no suits can be raised by opposing claimants, the price was paid in open court, and the church is the Lord's freehold forever. See the blood mark upon all the chosen, invisible to the human eye, but known to Christ, for "the Lord knows them that are His;" He forgets none of those whom He has redeemed from among humanity; He counts the sheep for whom He laid down His life, and remembers well the church for which He gave Himself.

They are also His by *conquest*. What a battle He had in us before we would be won! How long He laid siege to our hearts! How often He sent us terms of capitulation! but we barred our gates, and fenced our walls against Him. Don't we remember that glorious hour when He carried our hearts by storm? When He placed His cross against the wall, and scaled our ramparts, planting on our strongholds the blood-red flag of His omnipotent mercy? Yes, we are, indeed, the conquered captives of His omnipotent love. Thus chosen, purchased, and subdued, the rights of our divine possessor are inalienable: we rejoice that we never can be our own; and we desire, day by day, to do *His* will, and to show forth *His* glory.

*"Show us your strength, O God,
as you have done before."* — Psalm 68:28

T is our wisdom, as well as our necessity, to beg God continually to strengthen that which He has wrought in us. It is because of their neglect in this, that many Christians may blame themselves for those trials and afflictions of spirit which arise from unbelief. It is true that Satan seeks to flood the fair garden of the heart and make it a scene of desolation, but it is also true that many Christians leave open the sluices themselves, and let in the dreadful deluge through carelessness and lack of prayer to their strong Helper. We often forget that the Author of our faith must be the Preserver of it also. The lamp which was burning in the temple was never allowed to go out, but it had to be replenished daily with fresh oil; in like manner, our faith can only live by being sustained with the oil of grace, and we can only obtain this from God Himself. Foolish virgins we shall prove, if we do not secure the needed sustenance for our lamps. He who built the world upholds it, or it would fall in one tremendous crash; He who made us Christians must maintain us by His Spirit, or our ruin will be speedy and final. Let's, then, evening by evening, go to our Lord for the grace and strength we need. We have a strong argument to plead, for it is *His own work of grace* which we ask Him to strengthen — *"that which You have wrought for us."* Do you think He will fail to protect and sustain *that?* Only let your faith take hold of His strength, and all the powers of darkness, led on by the master fiend of hell, cannot cast a cloud or shadow over your joy and peace. Why faint when you may be strong? Why endure defeat when you may conquer? Oh! take your wavering faith and drooping graces to Him who can revive and replenish them, and earnestly pray, "Show us Your strength, O God, as You have done before."

"I say to myself, The Lord is my portion."
— *Lamentations 3:24*

IT is not "The Lord is *partly* my portion," nor "The Lord is *in* my portion;" but He Himself makes up the sum total of my soul's inheritance. Within the circumference of that circle lies all that we possess or desire. The *Lord* is my portion. Not His grace merely, nor His love, nor His covenant, but Jehovah Himself. He has chosen us for His portion, and we have chosen Him for ours. It is true that the Lord must first choose our inheritance for us, or else we shall never choose it for ourselves; but if we are really called according to the purpose of electing love, we can sing —

> "Lov'd of my God for Him again
> With love intense I burn;
> Chosen of Him ere time began,
> I choose Him in return."

The Lord is our *all-sufficient* portion. God fills Himself; and if God is all-sufficient in Himself, He must be all-sufficient for us. It is not easy to satisfy man's desires. When he dreams that he is satisfied, again he wakes to the perception that there is still something more beyond, and immediately the horse-leech in his heart cries, "Give me, give me." But all that we can wish for is to be found in our divine portion, so that we ask, "Whom have I in heaven but You? And earth has nothing I desire besides You." Well may we "delight ourselves in the Lord" who makes us to drink of the river of His pleasures. Our faith stretches her wings and mounts like an eagle into the heaven of divine love as to her proper dwelling place. "The boundary lines have fallen for me in pleasant places; surely I have a delightful inheritance." Let's rejoice in the Lord always; let's show to the world that we are a happy and a blessed people, and thus induce them to exclaim, "We will go with you, for we have heard that God is with you."

"Your eyes will see the king in his beauty."
— *Isaiah 33:17*

HE more you know about Christ, the less will you be satisfied with superficial views of Him. The more deeply you study His trans-actions in the eternal covenant, His engage-ments on your behalf as the eternal Surety, and the fullness of His grace which shines in all His offices, the more truly will you see the King in His beauty. Have these kinds of outlooks often. Long more and more to see Jesus. *Meditation and contemplation* are often like windows of agate and gates of carbuncle, through which we behold the Redeemer. Meditation puts the tele-scope to the eye, and enables us to see Jesus in a better way than we could have seen Him if we had lived in the days of His flesh. Would that our conversation were more in heaven, and that we were more taken up with the person, the work, the beauty of our incarnate Lord. More medita-tion and the beauty of the King would flash upon us with more resplendence. Beloved, it is very probable that we shall have such a sight of our glorious King as we never had before, *when we come to die.* Many saints in dying have looked up from amidst the stormy waters, and have seen Jesus walking on the waves of the sea, and heard Him say, "It is I. Don't be afraid." Ah, yes! when the tenement begins to shake, and the clay falls away, we see Christ through the rifts, and between the rafters the sunlight of heaven comes streaming in. But if we want to see face to face the "King in His beauty" *we must go to heaven* for the sight, or the King must come here in person. O that He would come on the wings of the wind! He is our Husband, and we are widowed by His absence; He is our Brother dear and fair, and we are lonely without Him. Thick veils and clouds hang between our souls and their true life: when shall the day break and the shadows flee away? Oh, long-expected day, begin!

"To him be the glory forever! Amen." — *Romans 11:36*

O him be the glory forever!" This should be *the single* desire of the Christian. All other wishes must be subservient and tributary to this one. The Christian may wish for prosperity in his business, but only as far as it may help him to promote this — "To Him be the glory forever!" He may desire to attain more gifts and more graces, but it should only be that "To Him be the glory forever!" You are not acting as you ought to do when you are moved by any other motive than a single eye to your Lord's glory. As a Christian, you are "of God, and through God," then live "to God." Let nothing ever set your heart beating so mightily as love for Him. Let this ambition fire your soul; let it be the foundation of every enterprise upon which you enter, and this your sustaining motive whenever your zeal would grow chill; make God your *only* object. Depend upon it, where self begins sorrow begins; but if God is my supreme delight and only object,

> "To me 'tis equal whether love ordain
> My life or death — appoint me ease or pain."

Let your desire for God's glory be a *growing* desire. You blessed Him in your youth; don't be content with such praises as you gave Him then. Has God prospered you in business? Give Him more as He has given you more. Has God given you experience? Praise Him by stronger faith than you exercised at first. Does your knowledge grow? Then sing more sweetly. Do you enjoy happier times than you once had? Have you been restored from sickness, and has your sorrow been turned into peace and joy? Then give Him more music; put more coals and more sweet frankincense into the censer of your praise. In every important aspect of your life give Him honor, putting the "Amen" to this doxology to your great and gracious Lord by your own individual service and increasing holiness.

"Whoever splits logs may be endangered by them."
— *Ecclesiastes 10:9*

PPRESSORS may get their way with poor and needy people as easily as they can split logs of wood, but they had better watch out, for it is a dangerous business, and a splinter from a tree has often killed the woodsman. Jesus is persecuted in every injured saint, and He is mighty to avenge His loved ones. Success in treading down the poor and needy is a thing to be trembled at: if there is no danger to persecutors here there will be great danger hereafter.

To split logs is a common everyday business, and yet it has its dangers. Likewise, reader, there are dangers connected with your calling and daily life which it will be well for you to be aware of. We do not refer to hazards by flood and field, or by disease and sudden death, but to perils of a spiritual sort. Your occupation may be as humble as log splitting, and yet the devil can tempt you in it. You may be a domestic servant, a farm laborer, or a mechanic, and you may be greatly screened from temptations to the grosser vices, and yet some secret sin may do you damage. Those who dwell at home, and do not mingle with the rough world, may yet be endangered by their very seclusion. Nowhere is he safe who thinks himself so. Pride may enter a poor man's heart; avarice may reign in a cottager's bosom; uncleanness may venture into the quietest home; and anger, and envy, and malice may insinuate themselves into the most rural abode. Even in speaking a few words to a servant we may sin; a little purchase at a shop may be the first link in a chain of temptations; the mere looking out of a window may be the beginning of evil. O Lord, how exposed we are! How shall we be secured! To keep ourselves is work too hard for us: only You are able to preserve us in such a world of evils. Spread your wings over us, and we, like little chickens, will cower beneath You, and feel ourselves safe!

"A spring enclosed, a sealed fountain."
— Song of Songs 4:12

N this metaphor, which has reference to the inner life of a believer, we have very plainly the idea of *secrecy.* It is a spring *shut up:* just as there were springs in the East, over which an edifice was built, so that none could reach them except those who knew the secret entrance; so is the heart of a believer when it is renewed by grace: there is a mysterious life within which no human skill can touch. It is a secret which no other person knows; no, which the very possessor of it cannot tell to a neighbor. The text includes not only secrecy, but *separation.* It is not the common spring, of which every passer-by may drink, it is one kept and preserved from all others; it is a fountain bearing a particular mark — a king's royal seal, so that all can perceive that it is not a common fountain, but a fountain owned by a proprietor, and placed specially by itself alone. So is it with the spiritual life. The chosen of God were separated in the eternal decree; they were separated by God in the day of redemption; and they are separated by the possession of a life which others do not have; and it is impossible for them to feel at home with the world, or to delight in its pleasures. There is also the idea of *sacredness.* The spring shut up is preserved for the use of some special person: and such is the Christian's heart. It is a spring kept for Jesus. Every Christian should feel that he has God's seal upon him — and he should be able to say with Paul, "Finally, let no one cause me trouble, for I bear on my body the marks of Jesus." Another idea is prominent — it is that of *security.* Oh! how sure and safe is the inner life of the believer! If all the powers of earth and hell could combine against it, that immortal principle must still exist, for He who gave it pledged His life for its preservation. And who "Who is going to harm you," when God is your protector?

"You are from all eternity." — Psalm 93:2

HRIST is EVERLASTING. Of Him we may sing with David, "Your throne, O God, is forever and ever." Rejoice, believer, in Jesus Christ, the same yesterday, today, and forever. Jesus always *was*. The Babe born in Bethlehem was united to the Word, which was in the beginning, by whom all things were made. The title by which Christ revealed Himself to John in Patmos was, "Him who is, and who was, and who is to come." If He were not God from everlasting, we could not so devoutly love Him; we could not feel that He had any share in the eternal love which is the fountain of all covenant blessings; but since He was from all eternity with the Father, we trace the stream of divine love to Himself equally with His Father and the blessed Spirit. As our Lord always *was*, so also He *is* forevermore. Jesus is not dead; "He always lives to intercede for me." Resort to Him in all your times of need, for He is waiting to bless you still. Moreover, Jesus our Lord *shall be* forever. If God should spare your life to fulfill your full day of threescore years and ten, you will find that His purifying fountain is still opened, and His precious blood has not lost its power; you shall find that the Priest who filled the healing fount with His own blood, lives to purge you from all iniquity. When only your last battle remains to be fought, you shall find that the hand of your conquering Captain has not grown feeble — the living Savior shall cheer the dying saint. When you enter heaven you shall find Him there bearing the dew of His youth; and through eternity the Lord Jesus shall still remain the perennial spring of joy, and life, and glory to His people. Living waters may you draw from this sacred well! Jesus always was, He always is, He always shall be. He is eternal in all His attributes, in all His offices, in all His might, and willingness to bless, comfort, guard, and crown His chosen people.

"Avoid foolish controversies." — *Titus 3:9*

UR days are few, and are far better spent in doing good, than in disputing over matters which are, at best, of minor importance. The old scholars did a world of mischief by their incessant discussion of subjects of no practical importance; and our churches permit such petty wars over profound points and unimportant questions. After everything has been said that can be said, neither party is any the wiser, and therefore the discussion no more promotes knowledge than love, and it is foolish to sow in so barren a field. Questions upon points wherein Scripture is silent; upon mysteries which belong to God alone; upon prophecies of doubtful interpretation; and upon mere modes of observing human ceremonials, are all foolish, and wise men avoid them. Our business is neither to ask nor answer foolish questions, but to avoid them altogether; and if we observe the apostle's precept (Titus 3:8) to be careful to maintain good works, we shall find ourselves far too often occupied with profitable business to take much interest in unworthy, contentious, and needless strivings.

There are, however, some questions which are the reverse of foolish, which we must not avoid, but fairly and honestly meet, such as these: Do I believe in the Lord Jesus Christ? Am I renewed in the spirit of my mind? Am I walking not after the flesh, but after the Spirit? Am I growing in grace? Does my conversation adorn the doctrine of God my Savior? Am I looking for the coming of the Lord, and watching as a servant should do who expects his master? What more can I do for Jesus? Such inquiries as these urgently demand our attention; and if we have been at all given to judging too severely, let's now turn our critical abilities to a service so much more profitable. Let's be peacemakers, and endeavor to lead others, both by our precept and example, to "avoid foolish controversies."

"If only I knew where to find Him." — Job 23:3

 N Job's uttermost extremity he cried after the Lord. The longing desire of an afflicted child of God is once more to see his Father's face. His first prayer is not "O that I might be healed of the disease which now festers in every part of my body!" nor even "O that I might see my children restored from the jaws of the grave, and my property once more brought from the hand of the spoiler!" but the first and uppermost cry is, "O that I knew where I might find HIM, who is my God! that I might come even to His seat!" God's children run home when the storm comes on. It is the heaven-born instinct of a gracious soul to seek shelter from all ills beneath the wings of Jehovah. "He that has made his refuge God," might serve as the title of a true believer. A hypocrite, when afflicted by God, resents the infliction, and, like a slave, would run from the Master who has scourged him; but not so the true heir of heaven, he kisses the hand which struck him, and seeks shelter from the rod in the bosom of the God who frowned upon him. Job's desire to commune with God was intensified by the failure of all other sources of consolation. The patriarch turned away from his sorry friends, and looked up to the celestial throne, just as a traveler turns from his empty canteen, and takes himself with all speed to the well. He bids farewell to earthborn hopes, and cries, "If only I knew where to find Him!" Nothing teaches us so much the preciousness of the Creator, as when we learn the emptiness of all besides. Turning away with bitter scorn from earth's hives, where we find no honey, but many sharp stings, we rejoice in Him whose faithful word is sweeter than honey or the honeycomb. In every trouble we should first seek to realize God's presence with us. Only let's enjoy His smile, and we can bear our daily cross with a willing heart for His dear sake.

"O LORD, you took up my case." — Lamentations 3:58

 BSERVE how *positively* the prophet speaks. He does not say, "I hope, I trust, I sometimes think that God takes up my case;" but he speaks of it as a matter of fact not to be disputed. "You *took* up my case." Let's, by the aid of the gracious Comforter, shake off those doubts and fears which so much mar our peace and comfort. Let this be our prayer, that we may be rid of the harsh croaking voice of surmise and suspicion, and may be able to speak with the clear, melodious voice of full assurance. Notice how *gratefully* the prophet speaks, ascribing all the glory to God alone! You perceive there is not a word concerning himself or his own pleadings. He does not ascribe his deliverance in any measure to any human being, much less to his own merit; but it is "*LORD*" — "O LORD, You took up my case; *You* redeemed my life." A grateful spirit should always be cultivated by the Christian; and especially after deliverances we should prepare a song for our God. Earth should be a temple filled with the songs of grateful saints, and every day should be a censor smoking with the sweet incense of thanksgiving. How *joyful* Jeremiah seems to be while he records the Lord's mercy. How triumphantly he lifts up the strain! He has been in the low dungeon, and is even now no other than the weeping prophet; and yet in the very book which is called "Lamentations," clear as the song of Miriam when she dashed her fingers against the tabor, shrill as the note of Deborah when she met Barak with shouts of victory, we hear the voice of Jeremiah going up to heaven — "You took up my case; You redeemed my life." O children of God, seek after a vital experience of the Lord's loving-kindness, and when you have it, speak positively of it; sing gratefully; shout triumphantly.

*"Coneys are creatures of little power, yet they make
their home in the crags." — Proverbs 30:26*

ONSCIOUS of their own natural defenselessness, the coneys resort to burrows in the
rocks, and are secure from their enemies. My
heart, be willing to gather a lesson from
these feeble folk. You are as weak and as
exposed to peril as the timid coney, be as
wise to seek a shelter. My best security is within the
munitions of an immutable Jehovah, where His unalterable promises stand like giant walls of rock. It will be well
with you, my heart, if you can always hide yourself in the
ramparts and citadels of His glorious attributes, all of
which are guarantees of safety for those who put their trust
in Him. Blessed be the name of the Lord, I have so done,
and have found myself like David in Adullam, safe from
the cruelty of my enemy; I don't have to discover at this
time the blessedness of the man who puts his trust in the
Lord, for long ago, when Satan and my sins pursued me, I
fled to the cleft of the rock Christ Jesus, and in His riven
side I found a delightful resting place. My heart, run to
Him anew tonight, whatever your present grief may be;
Jesus feels for you; Jesus consoles you; Jesus will help you.
No monarch in his impregnable fortress is more secure
than the coney in his rocky burrow. The master of ten
thousand chariots is not one bit better protected than the
little dweller in the mountain's cleft. In Jesus the weak are
strong, and the defenseless safe; they could not be stronger
if they were giants, or safer if they were in heaven. Faith
gives to earthly mortals the protection of the God of
heaven. More they cannot need, and needn't wish. The
coneys cannot build a castle, but they avail themselves of
what is there already: I cannot make myself a refuge, but
Jesus has provided it, His Father has given it, His Spirit
has revealed it, and lo, again tonight I enter it, and am safe
from every foe.

"Do not grieve the Holy Spirit of God."
— *Ephesians 4:30*

LL that the believer has must come from Christ, but it comes solely through the channel of the Spirit of grace. Moreover, as all blessings thus flow to you through the Holy Spirit, so also no good thing can come out of you in holy thought, devout worship, or gracious act, apart from the sanctifying operation of the same Spirit. Even if the good seed is sown in you, it still lies dormant until He works in you to will and to do of His own good pleasure. Do you desire to speak for Jesus — how can you unless the Holy Spirit touches your tongue? Do you desire to pray? Alas! what dull work it is unless the Spirit makes intercession for you! Do you desire to subdue sin? Do you want to be holy? Do you want to imitate your Master? Do you desire to rise to superlative heights of spirituality? Are you wanting to be made like the angels of God, full of zeal and ardor for the Master's cause? You cannot without the Spirit — "Apart from Me you can do nothing." O branch of the vine, you can have no fruit without the sap! O child of God, you have no life within you apart from the life which God gives you through His Spirit! Then let's not grieve Him or provoke Him to anger by our sin. Let's not quench Him in one of His faintest motions in our soul; let's foster every suggestion, and be ready to obey every prompting. If the Holy Spirit is indeed so mighty, let's attempt nothing without Him; let's begin no project, and carry on no enterprise, and conclude no transaction, without imploring His blessing. Let's do Him the due homage of feeling our entire weakness apart from Him, and then depending alone upon Him, having this for our prayer, "Open my heart and my whole being to Your incoming, and uphold me with Your free Spirit when I shall have received that Spirit in my inward parts."

*"Lazarus was among those reclining at the table
with him."* — *John 12:2*

 E *is to be envied.* It was fine to be Martha and
serve, but better to be Lazarus and commune. There are times for each purpose, and
each is comely in its season, but none of the
trees of the garden yield such clusters as the
vine of fellowship. To sit with Jesus, to hear
His words, to see His acts, and receive His smiles, was such
a favor as must have made Lazarus as happy as the angels.
When it has been our happy lot to feast with our Beloved
in His banquet hall, we would not have given half a sigh
for all the kingdoms of the world, if so much breath could
have bought them.

He is to be imitated. It would have been a strange thing if
Lazarus had not been at the table where Jesus was, for he
had been dead, and Jesus had raised him. For the risen one
to be absent when the Lord who gave him life was at his
house, would have been ungrateful indeed. We too were once
dead, yes, and like Lazarus stinking in the grave of sin; Jesus
raised us, and by His life we live — can we be content to live
at a distance from Him? Do we fail to remember Him at His
table, where He deigns to feast with His brothers and
sisters? Oh, this is cruel! It suits us to repent, and do as *He*
has bidden us, for His least wish should be law to us. To have
lived without constant communication with one of whom
the Jews said, "Behold how He loved him," would have been
disgraceful to Lazarus. Isn't it inexcusable in us whom Jesus
has loved with an everlasting love? To have been cold to
Him who wept over his lifeless corpse, would have argued
great brutishness in Lazarus. What does it argue in us over
whom the Savior has not only wept, but bled? Come, believers, who read this portion, let's return to our heavenly
Bridegroom, and ask for His Spirit that we may be on terms
of closer intimacy with Him, and henceforth sit at the table
with Him.

> *"Israel served to get a wife, and to pay for her*
> *he tended sheep."* — Hosea 12:12

ACOB, while expostulating with Laban, describes his own toil like this, ""I have been with you for twenty years now. Your sheep and goats have not miscarried, nor have I eaten rams from your flocks. I did not bring you animals torn by wild beasts; I bore the loss myself. And you demanded payment from me for whatever was stolen by day or night. This was my situation: The heat consumed me in the daytime and the cold at night, and sleep fled from my eyes." Even more toilsome than this was the life of our Savior here below. He watched over all His sheep until He gave in as His last account, "I have not lost one of those You gave Me." His hair was wet with dew, and His locks with the drops of the night. Sleep departed from His eyes, for all night He was in prayer wrestling for His people. One night Peter must be pleaded for; again, another claims His tearful intercession. No shepherd sitting beneath the cold skies, looking up to the stars, could ever utter such complaints because of the hardness of his toil as Jesus Christ might have brought if He had chosen to do so, because of the sternness of His service in order to procure His spouse —

> "Cold mountains and the midnight air,
> Witnessed the fervor of His prayer;
> The desert His temptations knew,
> His conflict and His victory too."

It is sweet to dwell upon the spiritual parallel of Laban having required all the sheep at Jacob's hand. If they were torn by beasts, Jacob must make it good; if any of them died, he must stand as surety for the whole. Wasn't the toil of Jesus for His church the toil of one who was under suretyship obligations to bring every believing one safe to the hand of Him who had committed them to His charge? Look upon toiling Jacob, and you see a representation of Him of whom we read, "He tends His flock like a shepherd."

"The power of his resurrection." — *Philippians 3:10*

HE doctrine of a risen Savior is exceedingly precious. The resurrection is the cornerstone of the entire building of Christianity. It is the keystone of the arch of our salvation. It would take a volume to set forth all the streams of living water which flow from this one sacred source, the resurrection of our dear Lord and Savior Jesus Christ; but to *know* that He has risen, and to have fellowship with Him as such — communing with the risen Savior by possessing a risen life — seeing Him leave the tomb by leaving the tomb of worldliness ourselves, this is even still more precious. The doctrine is the basis of the experience, but as the flower is more lovely than the root, so is the experience of fellowship with the risen Savior more lovely than the doctrine itself. I would have you *believe* that Christ rose from the dead so as to sing of it, and derive all the consolation which it is possible for you to extract from this well-ascertained and well-witnessed fact; but I beg you, do not be content to be only there. Though you cannot, like the disciples, see Him visibly, yet I bid you aspire to see Christ Jesus by the eye of faith; and though, like Mary Magdalene, you may not "touch" Him, yet you are privileged to talk with Him, and to know that He is risen, you yourselves being risen in Him to newness of life. To know a crucified Savior as having crucified all my sins, is a high degree of knowledge; but to know a risen Savior as having justified me, and to realize that He has bestowed upon me new life, having given me to be a new creation through His own newness of life, this is a noble style of experience: no one should be satisfied with less. May you want to know both Christ and the power of His resurrection. Why should souls who are risen with Jesus wear the grave clothes of worldliness and unbelief? Rise, for the Lord is risen.

"Fellowship with him." — *1 John 1:6*

HEN we were united by faith to Christ, we were brought into such complete fellowship with Him, that we were made one with Him, and His interests and ours became mutual and identical. We have fellowship with Christ in His *love*. What He loves we love. He loves the saints — so do we. He loves sinners — so do we. He loves the poor perishing human race, and pants to see earth's deserts transformed into the garden of the Lord — so do we. We have fellowship with Him in His *desires*. He desires the glory of God — we also work for the same. He desires that the saints may be with Him where He is — we desire to be with Him there, too. He desires to drive out sin — behold we fight under His banner. He desires that His Father's name may be loved and adored by all His creatures — we pray daily, "Your kingdom come, Your will be done on earth as it is in heaven." We have fellowship with Christ in His *sufferings*. We are not nailed to the cross, nor do we die a cruel death, but when He is reproached, we are reproached; and a very sweet thing it is to be blamed for His sake, to be despised for following the Master, to have the world against us. The disciple should not be above His Lord. In our measure we commune with Him in His *labors*, ministering to others by the word of truth and by deeds of love. Our meat and our drink, like His, is to do the will of Him who has sent us and to finish His work. We also have fellowship with Christ in His *joys*. We are happy in His happiness, we rejoice in His exaltation. Have you ever tasted that joy, believer? There is no purer or more thrilling delight to be known this side of heaven than that of having Christ's joy fulfilled in us, that our joy may be full. His *glory* awaits us to complete our fellowship, for His church shall sit with Him upon His throne, as His well-beloved bride and queen.

"Go up on a high mountain." — *Isaiah 40:9*

ACH believer should be thirsting for God, for the living God, and longing to climb the hill of the Lord, and see Him face to face. We should not be content in the mists of the valley when the summit of Tabor awaits us. My soul thirsts to drink deep of the cup which is reserved for those who reach the mountain's brow, and bathe their brows in heaven. How pure the dews of the hills are, how fresh the mountain air, how rich the fare of the dwellers aloft, whose windows look into the New Jerusalem! Many saints are content to live like miners in coal mines, who do not see the sun; they eat dust like the serpent when they might taste the ambrosial meat of angels; they are content to wear the miner's garb when they might put on king's robes; tears mar their faces when they might anoint them with celestial oil. I am satisfied that many believers pine in a dungeon when they could be walking on the palace roof, and viewing the goodly land and Lebanon. Rouse, O believer, from your low condition! Cast away your laziness, your lethargy, your coldness, or whatever interferes with your chaste and pure love for Christ, your soul's Husband. Make Him the source, the center, and the circumference of all your soul's range of delight. What enchants you into such folly as to remain in a pit when you may sit on a throne? Don't live in the lowlands of bondage now that mountain liberty is conferred upon you. Don't be satisfied any longer with your dwarfish attainments, but press forward to things more sublime and heavenly. Aspire to a higher, nobler, fuller life. Upward to heaven! Nearer to God!

> "When wilt Thou come unto me, Lord?
> Oh come, my Lord most dear!
> Come near, come nearer, nearer still,
> I'm blest when Thou art near."

*"The LORD will be our Mighty One. It will be like a place
of broad rivers and streams." — Isaiah 33:21*

ROAD rivers and streams produce fertility
and abundance in the land. Places near broad
rivers are remarkable for the variety of
their plants and their plentiful harvests.
God is all this to His church. Having God
she has *abundance*. What can she ask for
that He will not give her? What want can she mention
which He will not supply? "On this mountain the LORD
Almighty will prepare a feast of rich food for all peoples."
Do you want the bread of life? It drops like manna from
the sky. Do you want refreshing streams? The rock follows
you, and that Rock is Christ. If you endure any want it is
your own fault; if you are restricted, you are not restricted
in Him, but in your own heart. Broad rivers and streams
also point to *commerce*. Our glorious Lord is to us a place of
heavenly merchandise. Through our Redeemer we have
commerce with the past; the wealth of Calvary, the treasures of the covenant, the riches of the ancient days of
election, the stores of eternity, all come to us down the
broad stream of our gracious Lord. We have commerce,
too, with the future. What galleys, laden to the water's
edge, come to us from the millennium! What visions we
have of the days of heaven upon earth! Through our
glorious Lord we have commerce with angels; communion
with the bright spirits washed in blood, who sing before
the throne. No! Better than that, we have fellowship with
the Infinite One. Broad rivers and streams are especially
intended to set forth the idea of *security*. Rivers were of old
a defense. Oh! beloved, what a defense is God to His
church! The devil cannot cross this broad river of God.
How he wishes he could turn the current, but don't be
afraid, for God abides immutably the same. Satan may
worry, but he cannot destroy us; no galley with oars shall
invade our river, neither shall gallant ship pass thereby.

"A little sleep, a little slumber, a little folding of the hands to rest — and poverty will come on you like a bandit and scarcity like an armed man." — Proverbs 24:33, 34

 HE laziest of people only ask for a little slumber; they would be indignant if they were accused of total idleness. A little folding of the hands to sleep is all they crave, and they have a multitude of reasons to show that this indulgence is a very proper one. Yet by these littles the day ebbs out, and the time for work is all gone, and the field is grown over with thorns. It is by little procrastinations that men ruin their souls. They have no intention to delay for years — a few months will bring the more convenient season — tomorrow if you will, they will attend to serious things; but the present hour is so occupied and altogether so unsuitable, that they beg to be excused. Like sands from an hourglass, time passes, life is wasted by driblets, and seasons of grace lost by little slumbers. Oh, to be wise, to catch the flying hour, to use the moments on the wing! May the Lord teach us this sacred wisdom, for otherwise a poverty of the worst sort awaits us, eternal poverty which shall want even a drop of water, and beg for it in vain. Like a traveler steadily pursuing his journey, poverty overtakes the lazy, and ruin overthrows the undecided: each hour brings the dreaded pursuer nearer; he does not pause by the way, for he is on his master's business and must not linger. As an armed man enters with authority and power, so shall want come to the idle, and death to the impenitent, and there will be no escape. O that we were wise in time, and would seek the Lord Jesus diligently before the solemn day shall dawn when it will be too late to plow and to sow, too late to repent and believe. In harvest, it is too late to regret that the seed time was neglected. As yet, faith and holy decision are timely. May we obtain them this night.

"To proclaim freedom for the prisoners." — Luke 4:18

O ONE but Jesus can give deliverance to captives. Real freedom comes only from Him. It is a liberty *righteously given;* for the Son, who is Heir of all things, has a right to make us free. The saints honor the justice of God, which now secures their salvation. It is a liberty which has been *dearly purchased.* Christ speaks it by His power, but He bought it by His blood. He makes you free, but it is by His own bonds. You go free because He has borne your burden for you: you are set free because He has suffered in your place. But, though dearly purchased, *He freely gives it.* Jesus asks nothing of us as a preparation for this liberty. He finds us sitting in sackcloth and ashes, and bids us put on the beautiful array of freedom; He saves us just as we are, and all without our help or merit. When Jesus sets free, the liberty is *perpetually entailed;* no chains can bind again. Let the Master say to me, "Captive, I have delivered you," and it is done forever. Satan may plot to enslave us, but if the Lord is on our side, whom shall we fear? The world, with its temptations, may seek to ensnare us, but mightier is He who is for us than all who are against us. The machinations of our own deceitful hearts may harass and annoy us, but He who has begun the good work in us will carry it on and perfect it to the end. The foes of God and the enemies of man may gather their hosts together, and come with concentrated fury against us, but if God acquits, who is he that condemns? The eagle which mounts to his rocky eyrie and, afterward, soars above the clouds is no freer than the soul which Christ has delivered. If we are no more under the law, but free from its curse, let our liberty be *practically exhibited* in our serving God with gratitude and delight. "I am Your servant, the son of Your maidservant; You have freed me from my chains." "Lord, what do You want me to do?"

"For he says to Moses, I will have mercy on whom I have mercy, and I will have compassion on whom I have compassion." — *Romans 9:15*

N these words the Lord in the plainest manner claims the right to give or to withhold His mercy according to His own sovereign will. As the prerogative of life and death is vested in the monarch, so the Judge of all the earth has a right to spare or condemn the guilty, as may seem best in His sight. Men by their sins have forfeited all claim upon God; they deserve to perish for their sins — and if they all do so, they have no ground for complaint. If the Lord steps in to save any, He may do so if the ends of justice are not thwarted; but if He judges it best to leave the condemned to endure the righteous sentence, none may arraign Him at their bar. Foolish and impudent are all those discourses about the rights of men to be all placed on the same footing; ignorant, if not worse, are those contentions against discriminating grace, which are but the rebellions of proud human nature against the crown and scepter of Jehovah. When we are brought to see our own utter ruin and ill desert, and the justice of the divine verdict against sin, we no longer jeer at the truth that the Lord is not bound to save us; we do not murmur if He chooses to save others, as though He were doing us an injury, but feel that if He deigns to look upon us, it will be His own free act of undeserved goodness, for which we shall forever bless His name.

How shall those who are the subjects of divine election sufficiently adore the grace of God? They have no room for boasting, for sovereignty most effectually excludes it. The Lord's will alone is glorified, and the very notion of human merit is cast out to everlasting contempt. There is no more humbling doctrine in Scripture than that of election, none more promoting of gratitude, and, consequently, none more sanctifying. Believers should not be afraid of it, but adoringly rejoice in it.

*"Whatever your hand finds to do, do it with all
your might."* — *Ecclesiastes 9:10*

HATEVER your hands find to do," refers to works that are *possible*. There are many things which our *heart* finds to do which we never should do. It is well it is in our heart; but if we would be eminently useful, we must not be content with forming schemes in our heart, and talking of them; we must practically carry out *"whatever our hand finds to do."* One good deed is worth more than a thousand brilliant theories. Don't wait for large opportunities, or for a different kind of work, but do just the things we "find to do" day by day. We have no other time in which to live. The past is gone; the future has not arrived; we never shall have any time but time *present*. Then do not wait until your experience has ripened into maturity before you attempt to serve God. Endeavor now to bring forth fruit. Serve God now, but be careful as to the way in which you perform what you find to do — *"do it with all your might."* Do it *promptly;* do not fritter away your life in thinking of what you intend to do tomorrow as if that could compensate for the idleness of today. No one ever served God by doing things tomorrow. If we honor Christ and are blessed, it is by the things which we do *today.* Whatever you do for Christ, throw your whole soul into it. Do not give Christ a little slurred work, done as a matter of course now and then; but when you do serve Him, do it with heart, and soul, and strength.

But where is the might of Christians? It is not in ourselves, for we are perfect weakness. Our might lies in the Lord of Hosts. Then let's seek His help; let's proceed with prayer and faith, and when we have done what our "hand finds to do," let's wait upon the Lord for His blessing. What we do in this manner will be well done, and will not fail in its effect.

"Men will rejoice when they see the plumb line in the hand of Zerubbabel." — Zechariah 4:10

MALL things marked the beginning of the work in the hand of Zerubbabel, but no one might despise it, for the Lord had raised up one who would persevere until the headstone should be brought forth with shoutings. *The plumb line was in good hands.* Here is the comfort of every believer in the Lord Jesus; let the work of grace be ever so small in its beginnings, the plumb line is in good hands, a master builder greater than Solomon has undertaken the raising of the heavenly temple, and He will not fail nor be discouraged until the topmost pinnacle shall be raised. If the plumb line were in the hand of a mere human being, we might fear for the building, but the pleasure of the Lord shall prosper in Jesus' hand. The works did not proceed irregularly, and without care, for *the master's hand carried a good instrument.* Had the walls been hurriedly run up without due superintendence, they might have been out of the perpendicular; but the plumb line was used by the chosen overseer. Jesus is forever watching the erection of His spiritual temple, that it may be built securely and well. We are for haste, but Jesus is for judgment. He will use the plumb line, and that which is out of line must come down, every stone of it. Hence the failure of many a flattering work, the overthrow of many a glittering profession. It is not for us to judge the Lord's church, since Jesus has a steady hand, and a true eye, and can use the plumb line well. Don't we rejoice to see judgment left to Him?

The plumb line was in active use — it was in the builder's hand; a sure indication that he meant to push the work on to completion. O Lord Jesus, how would we indeed delight if we could see You at Your great work. O Zion, the beautiful, your walls are still in ruins! Rise, You glorious Builder, and make her desolations to rejoice at Your coming.

*"Joshua the high priest standing before the angel
of the LORD." — Zechariah 3:1*

N Joshua *the high priest* we see a picture of each and every child of God who has been brought near through the blood of Christ, and has been taught to minister in holy things, and enter into that which is within the veil. Jesus has made us priests and kings to God, and even here upon earth we exercise the priesthood of consecrated living and hallowed service. But this high priest is said to be *"standing* before the angel of the LORD," that is, standing to minister. This should be the perpetual position of every true believer. Every place is now God's temple, and His people can as truly serve Him in their daily employments as in His house. They are to be always "ministering," offering the spiritual sacrifice of prayer and praise, and presenting themselves a "living sacrifice." But notice where it is that Joshua stands to minister, it is *before the angel* of Jehovah. It is only through a mediator that we poor defiled ones can ever become priests to God. I present what I have before the messenger, the angel of the covenant, the Lord Jesus; and through Him my prayers find acceptance wrapped up in *His* prayers; my praises become sweet as they are bound up with bundles of myrrh, and aloes, and cassia from Christ's own garden. If I can bring Him nothing but my tears, He will put them with His own tears in His own bottle for He once wept; if I can bring Him nothing but my groans and sighs, He will accept these as an acceptable sacrifice, for He once was broken in heart, and sighed heavily in spirit. I myself, standing in Him, am accepted in the Beloved; and all my polluted works, though in themselves only objects of divine abhorrence, are so received, that God smells a sweet savor. He is content and I am blessed. See, then, the position of the Christian — "a high priest — standing — before the angel of the LORD."

*"The forgiveness of sins, in accordance with the
riches of God's grace."* — *Ephesians 1:7*

OULD there be a sweeter word in any language than that word "forgiveness," when
it sounds in a guilty sinner's ear, like the
silver notes of jubilee to the captive Israelite? Blessed, forever blessed is that dear star
of pardon which shines into the condemned
cell, and gives the perishing a gleam of hope amid the
midnight of despair! Can it be possible that sin, such sin as
mine, can be forgiven, forgiven altogether, and forever?
Hell is my portion as a sinner — there is no possibility of
my escaping from it while sin remains upon me — can the
load of guilt be uplifted, the crimson stain removed? Can
the adamantine stones of my prison ever be loosed from
their mortices, or the doors be lifted from their hinges?
Jesus tells me that I may yet be clear. Forever blessed is the
revelation of atoning love which not only tells me that
pardon is possible, but that it is secured to all who rest in
Jesus. I have believed in the appointed propitiation, even
Jesus crucified, and therefore my sins are at this moment,
and forever, forgiven by virtue of His substitutionary pains
and death. What joy this is! What bliss to be a perfectly
pardoned soul! My soul dedicates all her powers to Him
who of His own unpurchased love became my surety, and
wrought out for me redemption through His blood. What
riches of grace does free forgiveness exhibit! To forgive at
all, to forgive fully, to forgive freely, to forgive forever!
Here is a constellation of wonders; and when I think of
how great my sins were, how dear the precious drops were
which cleansed me from them, and how gracious the
method was by which pardon was sealed home to me, I am
in a maze of wondering worshipping affection. I bow before
the throne which absolves me, I clasp the cross which
delivers me, I serve henceforth all my days the Incarnate
God, through whom I am this night a pardoned soul.

"It gave me great joy to have some brothers come and tell about your faithfulness to the truth and how you continue to walk in the truth." — 3 John 3

HE truth was in Gaius, and Gaius walked in the truth. If the first had not been the case, the second could never have occurred; and if the second could not be said of him the first would have been a mere pretense. Truth must enter into the soul, penetrate and saturate it, or else it is of no value. Doctrines held as a matter of creed are like bread in the hand, which ministers no nourishment to the frame; but doctrine accepted by the heart, is as food digested, which, by assimilation, sustains and builds up the body. In us truth must be a living force, an active energy, an indwelling reality, a part of the woof and warp of our being. If it is *in us*, we cannot henceforth part with it. A man may lose his garments or his limbs, but his inward parts are vital, and cannot be torn away without absolute loss of life. A Christian can die, but he cannot deny the truth. Now it is a rule of nature that the inward affects the outward, as light shines from the center of the lantern through the glass: when, therefore, the truth is kindled within, its brightness soon beams forth in the outward life and conversation. It is said that the food of certain worms colors the cocoons of silk which they spin: and just so the nutriment upon which a man's inward nature lives gives a tinge to every word and deed proceeding from him. To walk in the truth imports a life of integrity, holiness, faithfulness, and simplicity — the natural product of those principles of truth which the gospel teaches, and which the Spirit of God enables us to receive. We may judge the secrets of the soul by their manifestation in the man's conversation. Allow us today, O gracious Spirit, to be ruled and governed by Your divine authority, so that nothing false or sinful may reign in our hearts, lest it extend its malignant influence to our daily walk among others.

"Spoke up for the welfare of all the Jews."
— *Esther 10:3*

ORDECAI was a true patriot, and therefore, being exalted to the highest position under Xerxes, he used his eminence to promote the prosperity of Israel. In this he was a type of Jesus, who, upon His throne of glory, seeks not His own, but spends His power for His people. It would be good if every Christian would be a Mordecai to the church, striving according to his ability for its prosperity. Some are placed in stations of affluence and influence. Let them honor their Lord in the high places of the earth, and testify for Jesus before great men and women. Others have what is far better, namely, close fellowship with the King of kings. Let them be sure to plead daily for the weak of the Lord's people, the doubting, the tempted, and the comfortless. It will have a consequence upon their honor if they make much intercession for those who are in darkness and dare not move near to the mercy seat. Instructed believers may serve their Master greatly if they lay out their talents for the general good, and impart their wealth of heavenly learning to others, by teaching them the things of God. The very least in our Israel may at least *seek* the welfare of his people; and his desire, if he can give no more, shall be acceptable. It is at once the most Christlike and the most happy course for a believer to cease from living for himself. He who blesses others cannot fail to be blessed himself. On the other hand, to seek our own personal greatness is a wicked and unhappy plan of life, its way will be grievous and its end will be fatal.

Here is the place to ask you, my friend, whether you are to the best of your power seeking the wealth of the church in your neighborhood? I trust you are not doing it mischief by bitterness and scandal, nor weakening it by your neglect. Friend, unite with the Lord's poor, bear their cross, do them all the good you can, and you shall not miss your reward.

"Do not go about spreading slander among your people. . . .
Rebuke your neighbor frankly so you will not share
in his guilt." — *Leviticus 19:16, 17*

 PREADING SLANDER emits a threefold poison, for it injures the teller, the hearer, and the person about whom the slander is spread. Whether the report is true or false, we are by this precept of God's Word forbidden to spread it. The reputations of the Lord's people should be very precious in our sight, and we should consider it shameful to help the devil to dishonor the church and the name of the Lord. Some tongues need a bridle rather than a spur. Many feel happy and satisfied in putting down others, as if, in doing so, they raised themselves up. Noah's wise sons cast a mantle over their father, and he who exposed him earned a fearful curse. One of these dark days we, too, may require tolerance and silence from others, so let's give it cheerfully to those who require it now. Let this be our family rule, and our personal agreement — SLANDER NO ONE.

The Holy Spirit, however, permits us to censure sin, and prescribes the way in which we are to do it. It must be done by rebuking our brother to his face, not by railing behind his back. This course is manly, brotherly, Christlike, and under God's blessing will be useful. Does the flesh shrink from it? Then we must lay the greater stress upon our conscience, and keep ourselves to the work, lest by allowing sin in our friend we become ourselves participants in it. Hundreds have been saved from gross sins by the timely, wise, affectionate warnings of faithful ministers and friends. Our Lord Jesus has set us a gracious example of how to deal with erring friends in His warning given to Peter, the prayer with which He preceded it, and the gentle way in which He bore with Peter's boastful denial that he needed such a caution.

"Spices for the anointing oil." — Exodus 35:8

MUCH use was made of this anointing oil under the law, and that which it represents is of primary importance under the gospel. The Holy Spirit, who anoints us for all holy service, is indispensable to us if we would serve the Lord acceptably. Without His aid our religious services are but a vain oblation, and our inward experience is a dead thing. Whenever our ministry is without unction, what miserable stuff it becomes! nor are the prayers, praises, meditations, and efforts of private Christians one jot superior. A holy anointing is the soul and life of piety, its absence the most grievous of all calamities. To go before the Lord without anointing is as though some common Levite had thrust himself into the priest's office — his ministrations would rather have been sins than services. May we never venture upon hallowed exercises without sacred anointings. They drop upon us from our glorious Head; from His anointing we who are as the skirts of His garments take part in a generous unction.

Choice spices were compounded with the rarest art of the apothecary to form the anointing oil, to display to us how rich all the influences of the Holy Spirit are. All good things are found in the divine Comforter. Matchless consolation, infallible instruction, immortal life-giving, spiritual energy, and divine sanctification all lie compounded with other excellencies in that sacred eye salve, the heavenly anointing oil of the Holy Spirit. It imparts a delightful fragrance to the character and person of the man upon whom it is poured. Nothing like it can be found in all the treasuries of the rich, or the secrets of the wise. It is not to be imitated. It comes alone from God, and it is freely given, through Jesus Christ, to every waiting soul. Let's seek it, for we may have it, and may have it this very evening. O Lord, anoint Your servants.

*"Amaziah asked the man of God, But what about the
hundred talents I paid for these Israelite troops?
The man of God replied, The LORD can give you
much more than that." — 2 Chronicles 25:9*

HIS seemed to be a very important question
for the king of Judah, and possibly it is
of even more weight with the tested and
tempted Christian. To lose money is at no
times pleasant, and when principle is involved, the flesh is not always ready to make
the sacrifice. "Why lose that which may be so usefully
employed? May not the truth itself be bought too dear?
What shall we do without it? Remember the children, and
our small income!" All these things and a thousand more
would tempt the Christian to stretch his hand toward
unrighteous gain, or keep himself from carrying out his
conscientious convictions, when they involve serious loss.
Not all people can view these matters in the light of faith;
and even with the followers of Jesus, the doctrine of "we
must live" has quite sufficient weight.

The Lord can give you much more than that is a very
satisfactory answer to the anxious question. Our Father
holds the purse strings, and what we lose for His sake He can
repay a thousandfold. It is our duty to obey His will, and we
may rest assured that He will provide for us. The Lord will
be no one's debtor at the last. Saints know that a grain of
heart's ease is of more value than a ton of gold. The man who
wraps a threadbare coat about a good conscience has gained
a spiritual wealth far more desirable than any he has lost.
God's smile and a dungeon are enough for a true heart; His
frown and a palace would be hell to a gracious spirit. Let
worst come to worst, let all the talents go, we have not lost
our treasure, for that is above, where Christ sits at the right
hand of God. Meanwhile, even now, the Lord makes it
possible for the meek to inherit the earth, He withholds no
good thing from them that walk uprightly.

*"Michael and his angels fought against the dragon,
and the dragon and his angels fought back."*
— *Revelation 12:7*

 AR will always rage between the two great sovereignties until one or other is crushed. Peace between good and evil is an impossibility; in fact, the very pretense of it would be the triumph of the powers of darkness. *Michael will always fight;* his holy soul is vexed with sin, and will not endure it. Jesus will always be the dragon's foe, and that not in a quiet sense, but actively, vigorously, with full determination to exterminate evil. All His servants, whether angels in heaven or messengers on earth, will and must fight; they are born to be warriors — at the cross they enter into covenant never to make truce with evil; they are a warlike company, firm in defense and fierce in attack. The duty of every soldier in the army of the Lord is daily, with all his heart, and soul, and strength, to fight against the dragon.

The dragon and his angels will not decline the melee; they are incessant in their onslaughts, sparing no weapon, fair or foul. We are foolish to expect to serve God without opposition: the more zealous we are, the more sure we are to be assailed by the myrmidons of hell. The church may become lazy, but not so her great antagonist; his restless spirit never allows the war to let up; he hates the woman's seed, and would preferably devour the church if he could. The servants of Satan partake much of the old dragon's energy, and are usually an active race. War rages all around, and to dream of peace is dangerous and futile.

Glory be to God, we know the end of the war. The great dragon shall be cast out and destroyed forever, while Jesus and they who are with Him shall receive the crown. Let's sharpen our swords tonight, and pray that the Holy Spirit would nerve our arms for the conflict. Never was battle so important, never the crown so glorious. Every person to his post, you warriors of the cross, and may the Lord tread Satan under your feet shortly!

"You made both summer and winter." — Psalm 74:17

 Y soul begin this wintry month with your God. The cold snows and the piercing winds all remind you that He keeps His covenant with day and night, and tend to assure you that He will also keep that glorious agreement which He has made with you in the person of Christ Jesus. He who is true to His Word in the revolutions of the seasons of this poor sin-polluted world will not prove unfaithful in His dealings with His own dearly-loved Son.

Winter in the soul is by no means a comfortable season, and if it is upon you just now it will be very painful to you: but there is this comfort, namely, that *the Lord* makes it happen. He sends the sharp blasts of adversity to nip the buds of expectation. He scatters the hoarfrost like ashes over the once verdant meadows of our joy. He releases His ice like morsels freezing the streams of our delight. He does it all; He is the great Winter King, and rules in the realms of frost. Therefore, you cannot murmur. Losses, crosses, heaviness, sickness, poverty, and a thousand other ills, are of the Lord's sending, and come to us with wise design. Frosts kill noxious insects, and limit raging diseases; they break up the clods, and sweeten the soul. O that such good results would always follow our winters of affliction!

How we prize the fire just now! How pleasant its cheerful glow is! Let's in the same manner prize our Lord, who is the constant source of warmth and comfort in every time of trouble. Let's approach Him, and in Him find joy and peace in believing. Let's wrap ourselves in the warm garments of His promises, and accomplish tasks appropriate to the season, for it is unwise to be as the lazy person who won't plow because it is too cold, for he shall beg in summer and have nothing.

"Let them give thanks to the LORD for his unfailing
love and his wonderful deeds for men."
— *Psalm 107:8*

 F we complained less and praised more, we would be happier, and God would be more glorified. Let's praise God daily for *common mercies* — common as we frequently call them, and yet so priceless, that when deprived of them we are ready to perish. Let's bless God for the eyes to watch the sun, for the health and strength to be physically active, for the bread we eat, for the clothes we wear. Let's praise Him that we aren't dismissed to be in the company of the hopeless, or confined among the guilty. Let's thank Him for freedom, for friends, for family associations and comforts. Let's praise Him, in fact, for everything which we receive from His generous hand, for we deserve little, and yet are endowed most abundantly. But, beloved, the sweetest and the loudest note in our songs of praise should be of *redeeming love.* God's redeeming acts towards His chosen are forever the favorite themes of their praise. If we know what redemption means, let's not withhold our sonnets of thanksgiving. We have been redeemed from the power of our corruptions, uplifted from the depth of sin in which we were naturally plunged. We have been led to the cross of Christ — our shackles of guilt have been broken off; we are no longer slaves, but children of the living God, and can antedate the period when we shall be presented before the throne without spot or wrinkle or any such thing. Already, by faith, we wave the palm branch and wrap ourselves in the fair linen which is to be our everlasting garb. Shouldn't we unceasingly give thanks to the Lord our Redeemer? Child of God, can you be silent? Wake up, wake up, you who will possess glory, and take captive your captives as you cry with David, "Praise the LORD, O my soul; all my inmost being, praise His holy name." Let the new month begin with new songs.

"All beautiful you are, my darling." — *Song of Songs 4:7*

T HE Lord's admiration of His church is very wonderful, and His description of her beauty is very glowing. She is not merely *beautiful,* but "*all* beautiful." He views her in Himself, washed in His sin-atoning blood and clothed in His meritorious righteousness, and He considers her to be full of comeliness and beauty. No wonder that such is the case, since it is only His own perfect excellency that He admires; for the holiness, glory, and perfection of His church are His own glorious garments on the back of His own well-beloved spouse. She is not simply pure, or well-proportioned; she is positively lovely and beautiful! She has actual merit! Her deformities of sin are removed; but more, she has through her Lord obtained a meritorious righteousness by which an actual beauty is conferred upon her. Believers have a positive righteousness given to them when they become "accepted in the beloved" (Eph. 1:6, KJV). Nor is the church barely lovely, she is *superlatively so.* Her Lord styles her "You the most beautiful of women." She has a real worth and excellence which cannot be rivaled by all the nobility and royalty of the world. If Jesus could exchange His elect bride for all the queens and empresses of earth, or even for the angels in heaven, He wouldn't because He puts her first and foremost — "most beautiful of women." Like the moon she far outshines the stars. He is not ashamed of this opinion; rather, He invites all men to hear it. He sets an "oh" before it, a special note of exclamation, inviting and arresting attention. "How beautiful you are, my darling! *Oh,* how beautiful! " (Song of Songs 4:1). He publishes His opinion widely even now, and one day from the throne of His glory He will avow the truth of it before the assembled universe. "Come, you who are blessed by My Father" (Matt. 25:34), will be His solemn affirmation of the loveliness of His elect.

*"All of the things that are done under the sun . . .
are meaningless."* — *Ecclesiastes 1:14*

OTHING can satisfy the entire man but the Lord's love and the Lord's own self. Saints have tried to drop anchor in other sheltered areas, but they have been driven out of such fatal refuges. Solomon, the wisest of men, was permitted to make experiments for us all, and to do for us what we must not dare to do for ourselves. Here is his testimony in his own words: "I thought to myself, 'Look, I have grown and increased in wisdom more than anyone who has ruled over Jerusalem before me' . . . I denied myself nothing my eyes desired; I refused my heart no pleasure. My heart took delight in all my work, and this was the reward for all my labor. Yet when I surveyed all that my hands had done and what I had toiled to achieve, everything was meaningless, a chasing after the wind; nothing was gained under the sun." "All of them are meaningless, a chasing after the wind." What! the whole of it meaningless? O favored monarch, is there nothing in all your wealth? Nothing in that wide dominion reaching from the river even to the sea? Nothing in Palmyra's glorious palaces? Nothing in the house of the forest of Lebanon? In all your music and dancing, and wine and luxury, is there nothing? "Nothing," he says, "but weariness of spirit." This was his verdict when he had trampled the whole round of pleasure. To embrace our Lord Jesus, to dwell in His love, and be fully assured of union with Him — this is all in all. Dear reader, you needn't try other forms of life in order to see whether they are better than the Christian's: if you roam the world over, you will see no sights like a sight of the Savior's face; even if you were to have all the comforts of life, you would be wretched if you lost your Savior; but if you win Christ, then even if you were to rot in a prison, you would find it a paradise; if you were to live in obscurity or die with famine, you still would be satisfied with favor and full of the goodness of the Lord.

"There is no flaw in you." — *Song of Songs 4:7*

AVING pronounced His church positively full of beauty, our Lord confirms His praise by a precious negative, "There is no flaw in you." As if the Bridegroom had anticipated that the carping world would insinuate that He had only mentioned her beautiful parts, and had purposely omitted those features which were deformed or defiled, He sums everything up by declaring her universally and entirely beautiful, and utterly devoid of stain. A flaw may soon be removed, and is the very least thing that can disfigure beauty, but even from this little blemish the believer is delivered in his Lord's sight. If He had said there is no hideous scar, no horrible deformity, no deadly ulcer, we might even then have marveled; but when He testifies that she is free from the slightest flaw, all these other forms of defilement are included, and the depth of wonder is increased. If He had only promised to remove all flaws by-and-by, we would only have had an eternal reason for joy; but when He speaks of it as already done, who can restrain the most intense emotions of satisfaction and delight? O my soul, here is marrow and fatness for you; eat your fill, and be satisfied with royal delicacies.

Christ Jesus has no quarrel with His spouse. She often wanders from Him, and grieves His Holy Spirit, but He does not allow her faults to affect His love. He sometimes chides, but it is always in the tenderest manner, with the kindest intentions: it is "my love" even then. There is no remembrance of our follies, He doesn't harbor bad thoughts about us; rather, He pardons and loves as much after the offense as before it. It is fortunate for us that this is so, for if Jesus were as mindful of injuries as we are, how could He commune with us? Many times believers put themselves out of humor with the Lord for some slight turn in providence, but our precious Husband knows our silly hearts too well to take any offense at our bad manners.

"The LORD mighty in battle." — *Psalm 24:8*

ELL may our God be glorious in the eyes of His people, seeing that He has performed such miracles for them, in them, and by them. *For them,* the Lord Jesus defeated every foe on Calvary, breaking all the weapons of the enemy in pieces by His finished work of satisfactory obedience; by His triumphant resurrection and ascension He completely overturned the hopes of hell, taking captive every captive, making a show of our enemies openly, triumphing over them by His cross. Every arrow of guilt which Satan might have shot at us is broken, for who can lay anything to the charge of God's elect? The sharp swords of infernal malice and the perpetual battles of the serpent's seed are of no avail, for in the midst of the church the lame take the prey, and the feeblest warriors are crowned.

The saved may well adore their Lord for His conquests *in them,* since the arrows of their natural hatred are snapped, and the weapons of their rebellion broken. What victories has grace won in our evil hearts! How glorious is Jesus when the will is subdued, and sin dethroned! As for our remaining corruptions, they shall sustain an equally sure defeat, and every temptation, doubt, and fear, shall be utterly destroyed. In the Salem of our peaceful hearts, the name of Jesus is great beyond compare: He has won our love, and He shall wear it. Even thus securely may we look for victories *by us.* We are more than conquerors through Him that loved us. We shall cast down the powers of darkness which are in the world, by our faith, zeal, and holiness; we shall win sinners to Jesus, we shall overturn false systems, we shall convert nations, for God is with us, and none shall stand before us. This evening let the Christian warrior chant the war song, and prepare for tomorrow's fight. Greater is He that is in us than he that is in the world.

"I have many people in this city." — Acts 18:10

HIS should be a great encouragement to try to do good, since God has among the vilest of the vile, the most reprobate, the most debauched and drunken, an elect people who *must* be saved. When you take the Word to them, you do so because God has ordained you to be the messenger of life to their souls, and *they must* receive it, for so the decree of predestination runs. They are as much redeemed by blood as the saints before the eternal throne. They are Christ's property, and yet perhaps they are lovers of the ale-house, and haters of holiness; but if Jesus Christ purchased them He will have them. God is not unfaithful to forget the price which His Son has paid. He will not allow His substitution to be in any case an ineffectual, dead thing. Tens of thousands of redeemed ones are not regenerated yet, but regenerated they must be; and this is our comfort when we go forth to them with the life-giving Word of God.

No! More than this. These ungodly ones are prayed for by Christ before the throne. "My prayer is not for them alone," says the great Intercessor. "I pray also for *those who will believe* in me through their message." Poor, ignorant souls, they know nothing about prayer for themselves, but Jesus prays for them. Their names are on His breastplate, and before long they must bow their stubborn knee, breathing the penitential sigh before the throne of grace. "It was not the season for figs." The predestined moment has not struck; but, when it comes, *they shall obey,* for God will have His own; *they must,* for the Spirit is not to be withstood when He comes forth with fullness of power — *they must* become the willing servants of the living God. "Your troops will be willing on Your day of battle." "He shall justify many." "He will see . . . the suffering of His soul." "I will give Him a portion among the great, and He will divide the spoils with the strong."

*"We ourselves . . . groan inwardly as we wait
eagerly for our adoption as sons, the redemption
of our bodies."* — *Romans 8:23*

 HIS groaning is universal among the saints: to a greater or less extent we all feel it. It is not the groan of murmuring or complaint: it is more the note of desire than of distress. Having received a pledge, we desire the whole of our portion; we are yearning for our entire person, in its trinity of spirit, soul, and body, to be set free from the last vestige of the fall; we long to put off corruption, weakness, and dishonor, and to wrap ourselves in incorruption, in immortality, in glory, in the spiritual body which the Lord Jesus will give to His people. We long for the manifestation of our adoption as the children of God. "We groan," but it is *"within ourselves."* It is not the hypocrite's groan, by which he would make men believe that he is a saint because he is wretched. Our sighs are sacred things, too hallowed for us to tell abroad. We keep our longings to our Lord alone. Then the apostle says we are *"waiting,"* by which we learn that we are not to be petulant, like Jonah or Elijah, when they said, "Let me die;" nor are we to whimper and sigh for the end of life because we are tired of work, nor wish to escape from our present sufferings till the will of the Lord is done. We are to groan for glorification, but we are to wait patiently for it, knowing that what the Lord appoints is best. Waiting implies being ready. We are to stand at the door expecting the Beloved to open it and take us away to Himself. This "groaning" is a *test.* You may judge a man by what he groans after. Some men groan after wealth — they worship Mammon; some groan continually under the troubles of life — they are merely impatient; but the man who sighs after God, who is uneasy until he is made like Christ, that is the blessed man. May God help us to groan for the coming of the Lord, and the resurrection which He will bring to us.

"Ask and it will be given to you." — Matthew 7:7

 E know of a place in England still existing, where a ration of bread is served to every passerby who chooses to ask for it. Whoever the traveler may be, he has but to knock at the door of St. Cross Hospital, and there is the ration of bread for him. Jesus Christ so loves sinners that He has built a St. Cross Hospital, so that whenever a sinner is hungry, he only has to knock and have his wants supplied. No! He has done better. He has attached a bath to this Hospital of the Cross so that whenever a soul is black and filthy, it only has to go there and be washed. The fountain is always full, always efficacious. No sinner ever went into it and found that it could not wash away his stains. Sins which were scarlet and crimson have all disappeared, and the sinner has been made whiter than snow. As if this were not enough, there is attached to this Hospital of the Cross a wardrobe, and a sinner making application simply as a sinner, may be clothed from head to foot; and if he wishes to be a soldier, he may not merely have a garment for ordinary wear, but armor which shall cover him from the sole of his foot to the crown of his head. If he asks for a sword, he shall have that given to him, and a shield too. Nothing that is good for him shall be denied him. He shall have spending money as long as he lives, and he shall have an eternal heritage of glorious treasure when he enters into the joy of his Lord.

If all these things are to be had by merely knocking at mercy's door, O my soul, knock hard this morning, and ask large things of your generous Lord. Leave not the throne of grace until all your wants have been spread before the Lord, and until by faith you have a comfortable prospect that they shall be all supplied. No bashfulness need slow you when Jesus invites. No unbelief should hinder when Jesus promises. No cold-heartedness should restrain when such blessings are to be obtained.

"Then the LORD showed me four craftsmen."
— *Zechariah 1:20*

N the vision described in this chapter, the prophet saw four terrible horns. They were pushing this way and that way, dashing down the strongest and the mightiest; and the prophet asked, "What are these?" The answer was, "These are the horns that scattered Israel." He saw before him a representation of those powers which had oppressed the church of God. There were four horns; for the church is attacked from all quarters. Well might the prophet have felt dismayed; but all of a sudden there appeared before him *four craftsmen.* He asked, "What are these coming to do?" These are the men whom God has found to break those horns in pieces. *God will always find men for His work,* and He will find them at the right time. The prophet did not see the craftsmen *first,* when there was nothing to do, but first the "horns," and then the "craftsmen." Moreover, the Lord finds *enough men.* He did not find *three* craftsmen, but *four;* there were four horns, and there must be four workmen. God finds *the right men;* not four men with pens to write; not four architects to draw plans; but four craftsmen to do rough work. Rest assured, you who tremble for the ark of God, that when the "horns" grow troublesome, the "craftsmen" will be found. You need not fret concerning the weakness of the church of God at any moment; there may be growing up in obscurity the valiant reformer who will shake the nations: Chrysostoms may come forth from our Ragged Schools, and Augustines from the thickest darkness of London's poverty. The Lord knows where to find His servants. He has in ambush a multitude of mighty men, and at His word they shall start up to the battle; "for the battle is the Lord's," and He shall get for Himself the victory. Let's abide faithful to Christ, and He, in the right time, will raise up for us a defense, whether it be in the day of our personal need, or in the season of peril to His church.

"As is the man from heaven, so also are those who are of heaven." — 1 Corinthians 15:48

HE head and members are of one nature, and not like that monstrous image which Nebuchadnezzar saw in his dream. The head was of fine gold, but the belly and thighs were of brass, the legs of iron, and the feet, part of iron and part of clay. Christ's mystical body is no absurd combination of opposites; the members were mortal, and therefore Jesus died; the glorified head is immortal, and therefore the body is immortal too, for thus the record stands, "Because I live, you also will live." As is our loving Head, such is the body, and every member in particular. A chosen Head and chosen members; an accepted Head, and accepted members; a living Head, and living members. If the head is pure gold, all the parts of the body are of pure gold also. Thus is there a double union of nature as a basis for the closest communion. Pause here, devout reader, and see if you can without ecstatic amazement, contemplate the infinite condescension of the Son of God in thus exalting your wretchedness into blessed union with His glory. You are so mean that in remembrance of your mortality, you may say to corruption, "You are my father," and to the worm, "You are my sister;" and yet in Christ you are so honored that you can say to the Almighty, "Abba, Father," and to the Incarnate God, "You are my brother and my husband." Surely if relationships to ancient and noble families make men think highly of themselves, *we* have whereof to glory over the heads of them all. Let the poorest and most despised believer lay hold upon this privilege; let not a senseless indolence make him negligent to trace his pedigree, and let him allow no foolish attachment to present vanities to occupy his thoughts to the exclusion of this glorious, this heavenly honor of union with Christ.

NE like a Son of Man" appeared to John in Patmos, and the beloved disciple noted that He wore a golden sash. *A sash,* for Jesus never was ungirded while upon earth, but stood always ready for service, and now before the eternal throne He ceases not His holy ministry, but as a priest is girt about with "the curious belt of the ephod." Well it is for us that He has not ceased to fulfill His offices of love for us, since this is one of our choicest safeguards that He forever lives to make intercession for us. Jesus is never an idler; His garments are never loose as though His offices were ended; He diligently carries on the cause of His people. *A golden sash,* to manifest the superiority of His service, the royalty of His person, the dignity of His state, the glory of His reward. No longer does He cry out of the dust, but He pleads with authority, a King as well as a Priest. Safe enough is our cause in the hands of our enthroned Melchisedek.

Our Lord presents all His people with an example. We must never unbind our girdles. This is not the time for lying down at ease, it is the season of service and warfare. We need to bind the sash of truth more and more tightly around our loins. It is a golden sash, and so will be our richest ornament, and we greatly need it, for a heart that is not well braced up with the truth as it is in Jesus, and with the fidelity which is wrought of the Spirit, will be easily entangled with the things of this life, and tripped up by the snares of temptation. It is in vain that we possess the Scriptures unless we bind them around us like a sash, surrounding our entire nature, keeping each part of our character in order, and giving compactness to our whole person. If in heaven Jesus doesn't unbind the sash, much less may we upon earth. Stand, therefore, having your waist surrounded about with truth.

"He chose the lowly things of this world."
— 1 Corinthians 1:28

 ALK the streets by moonlight, if you dare, and you will see sinners then. Watch when the night is dark, and the wind is howling, and the picklock is grating in the door, and you will see sinners then. Go to the nearest jail, and walk through the cell blocks, and notice the inmates with heavy overhanging brows, people whom you would not like to meet at night, and there are sinners there. Go to the reform schools, and note those who have betrayed a rampant juvenile depravity, and you will see sinners there. Go across the seas to the place where a person will gnaw a bone upon which is reeking human flesh, and there is a sinner there. Go where you will, you don't need to ransack earth to find sinners, for they are common enough; you may find them in every lane and street of every city, and town, and village, and hamlet. It is for such that Jesus died. If you were to single out for me the grossest specimen of humanity, who, nevertheless, had been born of woman, I still would have hope for him because Jesus Christ has come to seek and to save *sinners.* Love which singles out an individual has picked out some of the worst to be made the best. Pebbles-in-the-brook grace turns into jewels for the royal crown. He transforms worthless dross into pure gold. Redeeming love has set apart many of the worst of human-kind to be the reward of the Savior's passion. Effectual grace calls forth many of the vilest of the vile to sit at the table of mercy. Therefore, let none despair.

Reader, by that love looking out of Jesus' tearful eyes, by that love streaming from those bleeding wounds, by that faithful love, that strong love, that pure, disinterested, and abiding love; by the heart and by the gentle pity of the Savior's compassion, we appeal to you not to turn away as though it were nothing to you; but believe on Him and you shall be saved. Trust your soul with Him and He will bring you to His Father's right hand in glory everlasting.

*"I have become all things to all men so that by all
possible means I might save some."*
— 1 Corinthians 9:22

AUL'S great object was not merely to instruct and to improve, but to save. Anything short of this would have disappointed him; he wanted men to be renewed in heart, forgiven, sanctified, in fact, *saved.* Have our Christian labors been aimed at anything below this great point? Then let's revise our ways for, at the last great day, of what use is it to have taught and moralized humanity if they appear before God unsaved? Our clothes will be blood-red if, throughout life, we have sought inferior objects and forgotten that humankind needed to be saved. Paul knew the ruin of humanity's natural state and did not try to educate them, but to save them; he saw people sinking towards hell and did not talk of refining them, but of saving them from the wrath to come. To understand their salvation, he gave himself up with untiring zeal to speaking the good news at large, warning and begging people to be reconciled to God. His prayers were persistent and his labors incessant. Saving souls was his consuming passion, his ambition, his calling. He became a servant to all people, toiling for his race, feeling distressed if he didn't preach the gospel. He laid aside his preferences to prevent prejudice; he submitted his will in things indifferent, and if humankind would but receive the gospel, he raised no questions about forms or ceremonies: the gospel was the one all-important business with him. If he might save some he would be content. This was the crown for which he strove, the sole and sufficient reward of all his labors and self-denials. Dear reader, have you and I lived to win souls at this noble rate? Are we possessed with the same all-absorbing desire? If not, why not? Jesus died for sinners, can't we live for them? Where is our tenderness, where our love for Christ, if we don't seek His honor in the salvation of all people everywhere? O that the Lord would saturate us through and through with an undying zeal for human souls.

"Yet you have a few people in Sardis who have not soiled their clothes. They will walk with me, dressed in white, for they are worthy." — Revelation 3:4

E may understand this to refer to *justification.* "They will walk with me, dressed in white" means that they will enjoy a constant sense of their own justification by faith; they will understand that the righteousness of Christ is attributed to them, that they have all been washed and made whiter than the newly-fallen snow.

Again, it refers to *joy and gladness:* for white robes were holiday dresses among the Jews. They who have not defiled their garments will have their faces always bright; they will understand what Solomon meant when he said "Go, eat your food with gladness, and drink your wine with a joyful heart, for it is now that God favors what you do. Always be clothed in white." He who is accepted by God will wear white garments of joy and gladness, while he walks in sweet communion with the Lord Jesus. Whence so many doubts, so much misery, and mourning? It is because so many believers defile their garments with sin and error, hence, they lose the joy of their salvation and the comfortable fellowship of the Lord Jesus. They do not walk in white here below.

The promise also refers to *walking in white before the throne of God.* Those who have not defiled their garments here will most certainly walk in white up there, where the white-robed hosts sing perpetual hallelujahs to the Most High. They will possess joys inconceivable, happiness beyond a dream, bliss which imagination has not known, blessedness which even the stretch of desire has not reached. The "undefiled in the way" will have all this — not of merit, nor of works, but of grace. They will walk with Christ in white, for He has made them "worthy." In His sweet company they will drink of the living fountains of waters.

*"From your bounty, O God,
you provided for the poor."* — *Psalm 68:10*

LL God's gifts are prepared gifts laid up in store for wants foreseen. He anticipates our needs and, out of the fullness which He has treasured up in Christ Jesus, He provides for the poor out of His goodness. You may trust Him for all the necessities that can occur, for He has infallibly foreknown every one of them. He can say of us in all conditions, "I knew that you will be this and that." A man takes a journey across the desert, and after he has made a day's progress and pitched his tent, he discovers that he lacks many comforts and provisions which he hasn't brought in his baggage. "Ah!" he says, "I didn't foresee this: if I had this journey to do over, I would bring with me all the things necessary to my comfort." But God has marked with prescient eye all the requirements of His poor wandering children, and when those needs occur, supplies are ready. It is goodness which He has prepared for the poor in heart, goodness and goodness only. "My grace is sufficient for you." "Your strength will equal your days."

Reader, is your heart heavy this evening? God knew it would be. The comfort which your heart lacks lies in the sweet assurance of the text. You are poor and needy, but He has thought about you, and has the exact blessing which you require in store for you. Appeal earnestly for the promise, believe it and obtain its fulfillment. Do you feel that you never were so consciously vile as you are now? Look! The crimson fountain, with all its former efficacy to wash your sin away, is still open to you. You will never be put into any situation where Christ cannot help you. No pinch will ever arrive in your spiritual affairs in which Jesus Christ will not be equal to the emergency, for your history has all been foreknown and provided for in Jesus.

"Yet the LORD longs to be gracious to you."
— *Isaiah 30:18*

OD often DELAYS IN ANSWERING PRAYER. We have several instances of this in sacred Scripture. Jacob did not get the blessing from the angel until nearly dawn of the next day — he had to wrestle all night for it. For a long time the poor woman of Syrian Phoenicia did not receive a word of reply. Paul begged the Lord *three times* that "a thorn in his flesh" might be taken from him, yet he received no guarantee that it would be taken away. Instead, and in place of this assurance, he was given a promise that God's grace would be sufficient for him. If you have been knocking at the gate of mercy and have received no answer, do you want me to tell you why the mighty Maker hasn't opened the door and let you in? Our Father has reasons peculiar to Himself for keeping us waiting in this manner. Sometimes it is to show His power and His sovereignty, that we might know that Jehovah has a right to give or to withhold. More frequently the delay is for our profit. You are perhaps kept waiting in order that your desires may be more fervent. God knows that delay will quicken and increase desire, and that if He keeps you waiting you will see your necessity more clearly, and will seek more earnestly; and that you will prize the mercy all the more for its long delay. There may also be something wrong with you which needs to be removed before the joy of the Lord is given. Perhaps your views of the Gospel plan are confused, or you may be relying on yourself a little too much instead of trusting simply and entirely on the Lord Jesus, or God makes you delay awhile so that He might more fully display the riches of His grace to you at last. Your prayers are all filed in heaven and, if not immediately answered, they are certainly not forgotten. However, in a little while they will be fulfilled to your delight and satisfaction. Don't let despair make you silent, but continue your humble request in good faith.

"My people will live in peaceful dwelling places."
— *Isaiah 32:18*

EACE and rest do not belong to the unregenerate. They are the peculiar possession of the Lord's people, and of them only. The God of Peace gives perfect peace to those whose hearts are fixed upon Him. When humankind was unfallen, God gave them the flowery bowers of Eden as their quiet resting places; alas! how quickly sin blighted this beautiful life of innocence. In the day of universal wrath when the flood swept away a guilty race, the chosen family was quietly secured in the resting place of the ark, which floated them from the old condemned world into the new earth of the rainbow and the covenant, herein typifying Jesus, the ark of our salvation. Israel rested safely beneath the blood-besprinkled habitations of Egypt when the destroying angel struck the firstborn; and in the wilderness the shadow of the pillar of cloud and the flowing rock gave the weary pilgrims sweet rest. At this hour we rest in the promises of our faithful God, knowing that His words are full of truth and power; we rest in the doctrines of His word, which are consolation itself; we rest in the covenant of His grace, which is a haven of delight. More highly-favored are we than David in Adullam, or Jonah beneath his vine, for none can invade or destroy our shelter. The person of Jesus is the quiet resting place of His people, and when we draw near to Him in the breaking of the bread, in the hearing of the word, the searching of the Scriptures, prayer, or praise, we find any form of approach to Him to be the return of peace to our spirits.

"I hear the words of love, I gaze upon the blood,
I see the mighty sacrifice, and I have peace with God.
'Tis everlasting peace, sure as Jehovah's name,
'Tis stable as His steadfast throne, for evermore the same:
The clouds may go and come, and storms may sweep my sky,
This blood-sealed friendship changes not, the cross is ever nigh."

"So we will be with the Lord forever."
— *1 Thessalonians 4:17*

VEN the sweetest visits from Christ, how short they are — and how transitory! One moment our eyes see Him, and we rejoice with joy unspeakable and full of glory, but after a short while we do not see Him because our beloved withdraws Himself from us. Like a wild gazelle or a young deer, He leaps over the mountains of division; He is gone to the land of spices, and feeds no more among the lilies.

> "If today He deigns to bless us
> With a sense of pardoned sin,
> He tomorrow may distress us,
> Make us feel the plague within."

Oh, how sweet the prospect of the time when we will not behold Him at a distance, but see Him face to face: when He will not be as a wayfaring man departing after a night, but will eternally enfold us in the bosom of His glory. We will not see Him for a short time, but

> "Millions of years our wondering eyes,
> Shall o'er our Savior's beauties rove;
> And myriad ages we'll adore,
> The wonders of His love."

In heaven there shall be no interruptions by care or sin; no weeping shall dim our eyes; no earthly business shall distract our happy thoughts; we shall have nothing to hinder us from gazing forever on the Sun of Righteousness with unwearied eyes. Oh, if it is so sweet to see Him now and then, how sweet to gaze on that blessed face forever, never to have a cloud rolling between, never to have to turn one's eyes away to look on a world of weariness and woe! Blessed day, when will you dawn? Rise, O unsetting sun! The joys of sense may leave us as soon as they will, for this shall make glorious amends. If to die is but to enter into uninterrupted communion with Jesus, then death is indeed gain, and the black drop is swallowed up in a sea of victory.

"The Lord opened her heart." — *Acts 16:14*

N Lydia's conversion there are many points of interest. It was brought about by *providential circumstances.* She was a seller of purple cloth, of the city of Thyatira, but just at the right time for hearing Paul we find her at Philippi; providence, which is the handmaid of grace, led her to the right spot. Again, *grace was preparing her soul for the blessing* — grace preparing for grace. She did not know the Savior, but as a Jewess, she knew many truths which were excellent stepping stones to a knowledge of Jesus. Her conversion took place in the use of the means. On the Sabbath she went when prayer was accustomed to be made, and there prayer was heard. Never neglect the means of grace; God *may* bless us when we are not in His house, but we have the greater reason to hope that He *will* when we are in communion with His saints. Observe the words, *"The Lord* opened her heart." She did not open her own heart. Her prayers did not do it; Paul did not do it. The Lord Himself must open the heart, to receive the things which make for our peace. He alone can put the key into the hole of the door and open it, and get admittance for Himself. He is the heart's master just as He is the heart's maker. The first outward evidence of the opened heart was *obedience.* As soon as Lydia had believed in Jesus, she was baptized. It is a sweet sign of a humble and broken heart, when the child of God is willing to obey a command which is not essential to his or her salvation, which is not forced upon him or her by a selfish fear of condemnation, but is a simple act of obedience and of communion with the Master. The next evidence was *love,* manifesting itself in acts of grateful kindness to the apostles. To the saints love has always been a mark of the true convert. Those who do nothing for Christ or His church, show little evidence of an "opened" heart. Lord, constantly give me an opened heart.

"The one who calls you is faithful and he will do it."
— *1 Thessalonians 5:24*

EAVEN is a place where we shall never sin; where we shall cease our constant watch against an indefatigable enemy, because there will be no tempter to ensnare our feet. There the wicked cease from troubling, and the weary are at rest. Heaven is the "undefiled inheritance;" it is the land of perfect holiness, and therefore of complete security. But, even on earth, don't the saints sometimes taste the joys of blissful security? The doctrine of God's word is that all who are in union with the Lamb are safe; that all the righteous shall hold on to their way; that those who have committed their souls to the keeping of Christ shall find Him a faithful and immutable preserver. Sustained by such a doctrine we can enjoy security even on earth; not that high and glorious security which renders us free from every slip, but that holy security which arises from the sure promise of Jesus that none who believe in Him shall ever perish, but shall be with Him where He is. Believer, let's often reflect with joy on the doctrine of the perseverance of the saints, and honor the faithfulness of our God by a holy confidence in Him.

May our God bring home to you a sense of your safety in Christ Jesus! May He assure you that your name is engraved on His hand; and whisper in your ear the promise, "Fear not, I am with you." Look upon Him, the great Surety of the covenant, as faithful and true, and, therefore, bound and engaged to present you, the weakest of the family, with all the chosen race, before the throne of God; and in such a sweet contemplation as this will you drink the juice of the spiced wine of the Lord's pomegranate and taste the dainty fruits of Paradise. You will have a foretaste of the enjoyments which enthrall the souls of the perfect saints above, if you can believe with unstaggering faith that "the One who calls you is faithful and He will do it."

"It is the Lord Christ you are serving."
— *Colossians 3:24*

O what choice order of officials was this word spoken? To kings who proudly boast a divine right? Ah, no! Too often do they serve themselves or Satan, and forget the God whose patient endurance permits them to wear their mimic majesty for their little hour. Does the apostle speak, then, to those so-called "right reverend fathers in God," the bishops, or "the venerable the archdeacons?" No, indeed. Paul knew nothing of these mere inventions of humankind. Not even to pastors and teachers, or to the wealthy and esteemed among believers, was this word spoken, but to servants, yes, and to slaves. Among the toiling multitudes, the journeymen, the day laborers, the domestic servants, the drudges of the kitchen, the apostle found, as we find still, some of the Lord's chosen, and to them he says, "Whatever you do, work at it with all your heart, as working for the Lord, not for people, since you know that you will receive an inheritance from the Lord as a reward. It is the Lord Christ you are serving." This saying exalts the weary routine of earthly employments, and sheds a halo around the most humble occupations. To wash feet may be servile, but to wash *His* feet is royal work. To untie shoelaces is poor employ, but to unloosen the great Master's shoe is a princely privilege. The shop, the barn, the scullery, and the smithy become temples when men and women do all to the glory of God! Then "divine service" is not a thing of a few hours and a few places, but all life becomes holiness to the Lord, and every place and thing, as consecrated as the tabernacle and its golden candlestick.

"Teach me, my God and King, in all things Thee to see;
And what I do in anything to do it as to Thee.
All may of Thee partake, nothing can be so mean,
Which with this tincture, *for Thy sake,* will not grow bright and clean.
A servant with this clause makes drudgery divine;
Who sweeps a room, as for Thy laws, makes that and the action fine."

"His ways are eternal." — *Habakkuk 3:6*

HAT He has done at one time, He will do yet again. Man's ways are variable, but God's ways are eternal. There are many reasons for this most comforting truth: among them are the following — the Lord's ways are *the result of wise deliberation;* He orders all things according to the counsel of His own will. Human action is frequently the hasty result of passion, or fear, and is followed by regret and alteration; but nothing can take the Almighty by surprise, or happen otherwise than He has foreseen. His ways are *the outgrowth of an immutable character,* and in them the fixed and settled attributes of God are clearly to be seen. Unless the Eternal One Himself can undergo change, His ways, which are Himself in action, must remain forever the same. Is He eternally just, gracious, faithful, wise, tender? — then His ways must always be distinguished for the same excellences. Beings act according to their nature: when those natures change, their conduct varies also; but since God cannot know the shadow of a turning, His ways will abide everlastingly the same. Moreover there is no reason from without which could reverse the divine ways, since they are *the embodiment of irresistible might.* The earth is said, by the prophet, to be cleft with rivers, mountains tremble, the deep lifts up its hands, and sun and moon stand still, when Jehovah marches forth for the salvation of His people. Who can stop His hand, or say to Him, "What are You doing?" But it is not might alone which gives stability; God's ways are *the manifestation of the eternal principles of right,* and therefore can never pass away. Evil breeds decay and involves ruin, but the true and the good have about them a vitality which ages cannot diminish.

This morning let's go to our heavenly Father with confidence, remembering that Jesus Christ is the same yesterday, today, and forever, and in Him the Lord is ever gracious to His people.

"They are unfaithful to the LORD." — *Hosea 5:7*

ELIEVER, here is a sorrowful truth! You are the beloved of the Lord, redeemed by blood, called by grace, preserved in Christ Jesus, accepted in the Beloved, on your way to heaven, and yet, "they are unfaithful to the LORD," your best friend; unfaithful to Jesus, whose you are; unfaithful to the Holy Spirit, by whom you have been endowed with life eternal! How unfaithful you have been in the matter of vows and promises. Do you remember the love you had at your wedding, that happy time — the springtide of your spiritual life? Oh, how closely you clung to your Master then, saying, "He shall never charge me with indifference; my feet shall never grow slow in the way of His service; I will not allow my heart to wander after other loves; in Him is every supply of sweetness beyond expression. I give all up for my Lord Jesus' sake." Has it been so? Alas! if conscience were to speak, it would say, "He who promised so much has performed most badly. Prayer has frequently been slurred — it has been short, but not sweet; brief, but not fervent. Communion with Christ has been forgotten. Instead of a heavenly mind, there have been carnal cares, worldly vanities and thoughts of evil. Instead of service, there has been disobedience; instead of fervency, lukewarmness; instead of patience, petulance; instead of faith, confidence in an arm of flesh; and as a soldier of the cross there has been cowardice, disobedience, and desertion, to a very shameful degree." You "are unfaithful." Unfaithful to Jesus! what words shall be used in denouncing it? Words are of little avail: let our penitent thoughts denounce the sin which is so surely in us. Unfaithful to Your wounds, O Jesus! Forgive us, and let's not sin again! How shameful to be unfaithful to Him who never forgets us, but who this day stands with our names etched on His breastplate before the eternal throne.

"Salt without limit." — *Ezra 7:22*

ALT was used in every offering made by fire to the Lord, and from its preserving and purifying properties it was the grateful emblem of divine grace in the soul. It is worthy of our attentive consideration that, when Artaxerxes gave salt to Ezra the priest, he set no limit on the quantity, and we may be quite certain that when the King of kings distributes grace among His royal priesthood, the supply is not cut short by *Him*. Often are we restricted in ourselves, but never in the Lord. Those who choose to gather much manna will find that they may have as much as they desire. There is no such famine in Jerusalem that the citizens should eat their bread by weight and drink their water by measure. Some things in the economy of grace are measured. For instance, our vinegar and gall are given to us with such exactness that we never have a single drop too much, but of the salt of grace no stint is made, "Ask and it will be given to you." Parents need to lock up the fruit cupboard, and the sweet jars, but there is no need to keep the salt-box under lock and key, for few children will eat too greedily from that. A man may have too much money, or too much honor, but he cannot have too much grace. When Jeshurun grew fat in the flesh, he kicked against God, but there is no fear of a man's becoming too full of grace: a *plethora* of grace is impossible. More wealth brings more care, but more grace brings more joy. Increased wisdom is increased sorrow, but abundance of the Spirit is fullness of joy. Believer, go to the throne for a large supply of heavenly salt. It will season your afflictions, which are unsavory without salt; it will preserve your heart which corrupts if salt is absent, and it will kill your sins even as salt kills reptiles. You need much; seek much, and have much.

"I will make your [windows] of rubies."
— Isaiah 54:12

HE church is most instructively symbolized by a building erected by heavenly power, and designed by divine skill. Such a spiritual house must not be dark, for the Israelites had light in their dwellings; therefore, there must be windows to let the light in and to allow the inhabitants to gaze out. These windows are *precious* as rubies: the ways in which the church beholds her Lord and heaven, and spiritual truth in general, are to be held in the highest esteem. Rubies are *not the most transparent* of gems, they are only semi-transparent at best:

"Our knowledge of that life is small,
Our eye of faith is dim."

Faith is one of these precious ruby windows, but alas! it is often so misty and obscured, that we see only darkly, and mistake much that we do see. Yet if we cannot gaze through windows of diamonds and know even as we are known, it is a glorious thing to behold the altogether lovely One, even though the glass be hazy as the ruby. *Experience* is another of these dim but precious windows, yielding to us a subdued religious light in which we see the sufferings of the Man of sorrows through our own afflictions. Our weak eyes could not endure windows of transparent glass to let in the Master's glory, but when they are dimmed with weeping, the beams of the Sun of Righteousness are tempered, and shine through the windows of ruby with a soft radiance inexpressibly soothing to tempted souls. *Sanctification,* as it conforms us to our Lord, is another ruby window. Only as we become heavenly can we comprehend heavenly things. The pure in heart see a pure God. Those who are like Jesus see Him as He is. Because we are so little like Him, the window is only ruby; because we are somewhat like Him, it is ruby. We thank God for what we have, and long for more. When shall we see God and Jesus, and heaven and truth, face to face?

"They go from strength to strength." — *Psalm 84:7*

 HEY go *from strength to strength.* There are various renderings of these words, but all of them contain the idea of progress.

Our own good translation of the authorized version is enough for us this morning. "They go from strength to strength." That is, they grow stronger and stronger. Usually, if we are walking, we go from strength to weakness; we start fresh and in good order for our journey, but before long the road is rough, and the sun is hot, we sit down by the wayside, and then again painfully pursue our weary way. But the Christian pilgrim having obtained fresh supplies of grace, is as vigorous after years of toilsome travel and struggle as when he first set out. He may not be quite so elated and buoyant, nor perhaps quite so hot and hasty in his zeal as he once was, but he is much stronger in all that constitutes real power, and travels, if more slowly, far more surely. Some gray-haired veterans have been as firm in their grasp of truth, and as zealous in diffusing it, as they were in their younger days; but, alas, it must be confessed it is often otherwise, for the love of many waxes cold and iniquity abounds, but this is their own sin and not the fault of the promise which still holds good: "Even youths grow tired and weary, and young men stumble and fall; but those who hope in the LORD will renew their strength. They will soar on wings like eagles; they will run and not grow weary, they will walk and not be faint." Fretful spirits sit down and trouble themselves about the future. "Alas!" they say, "we go from affliction to affliction." Very true, O you of little faith, but then you go from strength to strength also. You shall never find a bundle of affliction which has not bound up in the middle of it sufficient grace. God will give the strength of ripe adulthood with the burden allotted to full-grown shoulders.

"I have been crucified with Christ."
— Galatians 2:20

HE Lord Jesus Christ acted in what He did as a great public representative person, and His dying upon the cross was the virtual dying of all His people. Then all His saints rendered to justice what was due, and made an expiation to divine vengeance for all their sins. The apostle of the Gentiles delighted to think that as one of Christ's chosen people, he died upon the cross in Christ. He did more than believe this doctrinally, he accepted it confidently, resting his hope upon it. He believed that by virtue of Christ's death, he had satisfied divine justice, and found reconciliation with God. Beloved, what a blessed thing it is when the soul can, as it were, stretch itself upon the cross of Christ, and feel, "I am dead; the law has slain me, and I am therefore free from its power, because in my Surety I have borne the curse, and in the person of my Substitute the whole that the law could do, by way of condemnation, has been executed upon me, for I have been crucified with Christ."

But Paul meant even more than this. He not only believed in Christ's death, and trusted in it, but he actually felt its power in himself in causing the crucifixion of his old corrupt nature. When he saw the pleasures of sin, he said, "I cannot enjoy these: I am dead to them." Such is the experience of every true Christian. Having received Christ, he is to this world as one who is utterly dead. Yet, while conscious of death to the world, he can, at the same time, exclaim with the apostle, "Nevertheless I live." He is fully alive to God. The Christian's life is a matchless riddle. No worldling can comprehend it; even the believer himself cannot understand it. Dead, yet alive! crucified with Christ, and yet at the same time risen with Christ in newness of life! Union with the suffering, bleeding Savior, and death to the world and sin, are soul-cheering things. O for more enjoyment of them!

*"Orpah kissed her mother-in-law good-by, but Ruth
clung to her." — Ruth 1:14*

OTH of them had an affection for Naomi, and
therefore set out with her upon her return to
the land of Judah. But the hour of testing
came; Naomi most unselfishly set before each
of them the trials which awaited them, and
commanded them, if they cared for ease and
comfort, to return to their Moabitish friends. At first, both
of them declared that they would cast in their lot with the
Lord's people; but upon still further consideration, Orpah
with much grief and a respectful kiss left her mother-in-law,
and her people, and her God, and went back to her idolatrous friends, while Ruth with all her heart gave herself up
to the God of her mother-in-law. It is one thing to love the
ways of the Lord when everything is beautiful, and quite
another to cleave to them under all discouragements and
difficulties. The kiss of outward profession is very cheap and
easy, but the practical cleaving to the Lord, which must
show itself in holy decision for truth and holiness, is not so
small a matter. How does the case stand with us? Is our heart
fixed upon Jesus? Is the sacrifice bound with cords to the
horns of the altar? Have we counted the cost, and are we
solemnly ready to allow all worldly loss for the Master's
sake? The gain afterwards will be an abundant compensation, for Egypt's treasures are not to be compared with the
glory to be revealed. Orpah is heard of no more; in glorious
ease and idolatrous pleasure her life melts into the gloom of
death; but Ruth lives in history and in heaven, for grace has
placed her in the noble line whence sprung the King of
kings. Blessed among women shall those be who for Christ's
sake can renounce all; but forgotten and worse than forgotten
shall those be who in the hour of temptation do violence to
conscience and turn back to the world. O that this morning
we may not be content with the form of devotion, which may
be no better than Orpah's kiss, but may the Holy Spirit work
in us a cleaving of our whole heart to our Lord Jesus.

"I will build . . . your foundations with sapphires."
— *Isaiah 54:11*

OT only is that which is seen of the church of God beautiful and precious, but also that which is unseen. Foundations are out of sight, and so long as they are firm it is not expected that they should be valuable; but in Jehovah's work everything is of a piece, nothing slurred, nothing mean. The deep foundations of the work of grace are as sapphires for preciousness, no human mind is able to measure their glory. We build upon *the covenant of grace,* which is firmer than the impenetrable stone adamant, and as enduring as jewels upon which age spends itself in vain. Sapphire foundations are eternal, and the covenant abides throughout the lifetime of the Almighty. Another foundation is *the person of the Lord Jesus,* which is clear and spotless, everlasting and beautiful as the sapphire; blending in one the deep blue of earth's ever rolling ocean and the azure of its all-embracing sky. At one time our Lord might have been likened to the ruby as He stood covered with His own blood, but now we see Him radiant with the soft blue of love, love abounding, deep, eternal. Our eternal hopes are built upon *the justice and the faithfulness of God,* which are clear and cloudless as the sapphire. We are not saved by a compromise, by mercy defeating justice, or law suspending its operations; no, we defy the eagle's eye to detect a flaw in the groundwork of our confidence — our foundation is of sapphire, and will endure the fire.

The Lord Himself has laid the foundation of His people's hopes. It is a matter of serious concern to determine whether or not *our* hopes are built upon such a basis. Good works and ceremonies are not a foundation of sapphires, but of wood, hay, and stubble; neither are they laid by God, but by our own conceit. Foundations will all be tested before long: woe to the one whose lofty tower shall come down with a crash because it is built on quicksand. The person who is built on sapphires may await storm or fire with equanimity, and shall endure the trial.

"Come to me." — *Matthew 11:28*

HE cry of the Christian religion is the gentle word, "Come." The Jewish law harshly said, "Go, take heed to your steps as to the path in which you shall walk. Break the commandments, and you shall perish; keep them, and you shall live." The law was a dispensation of terror, which drove men before it as with a scourge; the gospel draws with bands of love. Jesus is the good Shepherd going before His sheep, bidding them follow Him, and ever leading them onwards with the sweet word, "Come." The law repels, the gospel attracts. The law shows the distance which there is between God and man; the gospel bridges that awful chasm, and brings the sinner across it.

From the first moment of your spiritual life until you are ushered into glory, the language of Christ to you will be, *"Come, come* to me." As a mother puts out her finger to her little child and woos it to walk by saying, *"Come,"* even so does Jesus. He will always be ahead of you, bidding you follow Him as the soldier follows his captain. He will always go before you to pave your way, and clear your path, and you shall hear His animating voice calling you after Him all through life; while in the solemn hour of death, His sweet words with which He shall usher you into the heavenly world shall be — "Come, you blessed of My Father."

No! There is more. This is not only Christ's cry to you, but, if you are a believer, this is your cry to Christ — "Come! come!" You will be longing for His second advent; you will be saying, "Come quickly, even so come Lord Jesus." You will be panting for nearer and closer communion with Him. As His voice to you is "Come," your response to Him will be, "Come, Lord, and abide with me. Come, and exclusively inhabit the throne of my heart; reign there without a rival, and consecrate me entirely to Your service."

*"You have neither heard nor understood; from of old
your ear has not been open."* — Isaiah 48:8

T is painful to remember that, to a certain degree, this accusation may be laid at the door of *believers*, who too often are in a measure *spiritually insensible*. We may well mourn for ourselves that *we* do not hear the voice of God as we ought, "You have not heard." There are gentle motions of the Holy Spirit in the soul which are unheeded by us: there are whisperings of divine command and of heavenly love which are alike unobserved by our leaden intellects. Alas! we have been *carelessly ignorant* — "You have not understood." There are matters within which we ought to have seen, corruptions which have made headway unnoticed; sweet affections which are being blighted like flowers in the frost, untended by us; glimpses of the divine face which might be perceived if we did not wall up the windows of our soul. But we "have not understood." As we think about this, we are humbled in the deepest self-abasement. How we must adore the grace of God as we learn, from the context, that all this folly and ignorance on our part *was foreknown by God,* and, notwithstanding that foreknowledge, He yet has been pleased to deal with us in a way of mercy! Admire the marvelous sovereign grace which could have chosen us in the sight of all this! Wonder at the price that was paid for us when Christ knew what we should be! He who hung upon the cross foresaw us as unbelieving, backsliding, cold of heart, indifferent, lax in prayer, and yet He said, "I am the Lord your God, the Holy One of Israel, your Savior . . . Since you are precious and honored in my sight, and because I love you, I will give men in exchange for you, and people in exchange for your life!" O redemption, how you shine with amazing brilliance when we think how black we are! O Holy Spirit, give us henceforth the hearing ear, the understanding heart!

"I remember you." — *Jeremiah 2:2*

ET'S note that Christ delights to think about His church, and to look upon her beauty. As the bird returns often to its nest, and as the traveler hurries to his home, so does the mind continually pursue the object of its choice. We cannot look too often into that face which we love; we always want to have our precious things within sight. This is also true for our Lord Jesus. From all eternity He is "rejoicing in His whole world and delighting in mankind." His thoughts rolled onward to the time when His elect should be born into the world; He viewed them in the mirror of His foreknowledge. "All the days ordained for me were written in your book before one of them came to be." (Ps. 139:16). When the world was set upon its pillars, He was there, and He set the bounds of the people according to the number of the children of Israel. Many a time before His incarnation, He descended to this lower earth in the similitude of a man; on the plains of Mamre (Gen. 18), by the brook of Jabbok (Gen. 32:24–30), beneath the walls of Jericho (Josh. 5:13), and in the fiery furnace of Babylon (Dan. 3:19, 25), the Son of Man visited His people. Because His soul delighted in them, He could not rest away from them, for His heart longed after them. They were never absent from His heart, for He had written their names on His hands, and etched them on His side. As the breastplate containing the names of the tribes of Israel was the most brilliant ornament worn by the high priest, so the names of Christ's elect were His most precious jewels, and glittered on His heart. We may often forget to meditate upon the perfections of our Lord, but He never ceases to remember us. Let's chide ourselves for past forgetfulness, and always pray for grace to keep Him in our fondest memory. Lord, paint upon the eyes of my soul the image of Your Son.

"I am the gate; whoever enters through me will be saved. He will come in and go out, and find pasture." — John 10:9

ESUS, the great I AM, is the entrance into the true church, and the way of access to God Himself. He gives the person who comes to God by Him four choice privileges.

1. *You will be saved.* The fugitive killer passed the gate of the city of refuge, and was safe. Noah entered the door of the ark, and was secure. No one can be lost who takes Jesus as the door of faith to their souls. Entrance through Jesus into peace is the guarantee of entrance by the same door into heaven. Jesus is the only door, an open door, a wide door, a safe door; and blessed is the one who rests all hope of admission to glory upon the crucified Redeemer.

2. *You will go in.* You shall be privileged to go in among the divine family, sharing the children's bread, and participating in all their honors and enjoyments. You shall go into the chambers of communion, to the banquets of love, to the treasures of the covenant, to the storehouses of the promises. You shall go in to the King of kings in the power of the Holy Spirit, and the secret of the Lord shall be with you.

3. *You will go out.* This blessing is frequently forgotten. We go out into the world to work and let come what may, but what a mercy to go in the name and power of Jesus! We are called to bear witness to the truth, to cheer the disconsolate, to warn the unconcerned, to win souls, and to glorify God; and as the angel said to Gideon, "Go in the strength you have," so also the Lord would have us proceed as His messengers in His name and strength.

4. *You will find pasture.* Those who know Jesus shall never want. Going in and out shall be similarly helpful to them: in fellowship with God they shall grow, and in watering others they shall be watered. Having made Jesus their all, they shall find all in Jesus. Their souls shall be like a watered garden, and as a well of water whose waters do not fail.

"Rend your heart and not your garments." — *Joel 2:13*

ARMENT-RENDING and other outward signs of religious emotion are *easily manifested* and are *frequently hypocritical;* but to feel true repentance is far more difficult, and consequently far less common. Humankind will attend to the most multiplied and minute ceremonial regulations — for such things are *pleasing to the flesh* — but true religion is too humbling, too heart-searching, too thorough for the tastes of carnal men; they prefer something more ostentatious, flimsy, and worldly. Outward observances are *temporarily comfortable;* the eye and ear are pleased; self-conceit is fed, and self-righteousness is puffed up: but they are *ultimately delusive,* for in the article of death, and at the day of judgment, the soul needs something more substantial than ceremonies and rituals to lean upon. Apart from vital godliness all religion is *utterly vain;* offered without a sincere heart, every form of worship is a solemn sham and an impudent mockery of the majesty of heaven.

HEART-RENDING is *divinely wrought and solemnly felt.* It is a secret grief which is *personally experienced,* not in mere form, but as a deep, soul-moving work of the Holy Spirit upon the inmost heart of each believer. It is not a matter to be merely talked of and believed in, but keenly and sensitively felt in every living child of the living God. It is *powerfully humiliating,* and *completely sin-purging;* but then it is *sweetly preparative* for those gracious consolations which proud unhumbled spirits are unable to receive; and it is *distinctly discriminating,* for it belongs to the elect of God, and to them alone.

The text commands us to rend our hearts, but they are naturally hard as marble: how, then, can this be done? We must take them to Calvary: a dying Savior's voice ripped open the rocks once, and it is as powerful now. O blessed Spirit, let's hear the death cries of Jesus, and our hearts shall be rent even as men rend their garments in the day of lamentation.

"Be sure you know the condition of your flocks, give careful attention to your herds." — *Proverbs 27:23*

 VERY wise merchant will occasionally take an inventory, when he will calculate the sum of his monetary transactions, examine what he has on hand, and ascertain decisively whether his trade is prosperous or declining. Every person who is wise in the kingdom of heaven will frequently set apart special seasons for self-examination, to discover whether things are right between God and his soul. "Search me, O God, and know my heart; test me and know my anxious thoughts." The God whom we worship is a great searcher of hearts, and since ages past His servants knew Him as the Lord who "searches the heart and examines the mind." Allow me to inspire you, in His name, to diligently inspect and solemnly test your state for fear that you may come short of the promised rest. That which every wise person does and which God Himself does with all of us, I exhort you to do with yourself this evening. Let the oldest saint look well to the fundamentals of his piety, for gray heads may cover black hearts: and don't allow the young professor to despise this word of warning, for the greenness of youth may be joined to the rottenness of hypocrisy. Every now and then a cedar falls into our midst. The enemy still continues to sow tares among the wheat. It is not my aim to introduce doubts and fears into your mind. No; really it isn't. Rather, I would hope that the rough wind of self-examination may help to drive those doubts and fears away. It is not security, but carnal security, which we would kill; not confidence, but fleshly confidence, which we would overthrow; not peace, but false peace, which we would destroy. By the precious blood of Christ, which was not shed to make you a hypocrite but that sincere souls might show forth His praise, I beg you, search and look, lest at the last it be said of you, "MENE, MENE, TEKEL: You have been weighed on the scales and found wanting."

"The lot is cast into the lap, but its every decision is from the LORD." — *Proverbs 16:33*

F the disposal of the lot is the Lord's whose is the arrangement of our whole life? If the simple casting of a lot is guided by Him, how much more the events of our entire life — especially when we are told by our blessed Savior: "Indeed, the very hairs of your head are all numbered. Don't be afraid; you are worth more than many sparrows." It would bring a holy calm over your mind, dear friend, if you were always to remember this continuously. It would relieve your anxious mind to the extent that you would be more capable of being able to walk in patience, quiet, and cheerfulness as a Christian should. An anxious person cannot pray with faith; when troubled about the world, instead of serving your Master, your thoughts are serving you. If you would "seek first the kingdom of God and His righteousness," all things would then be added to you. You are meddling with Christ's business and neglecting your own when you fret about your lot and circumstances. You have been trying "providing" work and forgetting that it is your job is to obey. Be wise and attend to the obeying, and let Christ manage the providing. Come and survey your Father's storehouse, and ask whether He will let you starve while He has laid up so great an abundance in His garner? Look at His heart of mercy; see if that can ever prove unkind! Look at His inscrutable wisdom; see if that will ever be at fault. Above all, look up to Jesus Christ your Intercessor, and ask yourself, while He pleads, can your Father deal ungraciously with you? If He remembers even sparrows, will He forget one of the least of His poor children? "Cast your cares on the LORD and He will sustain you; He will never let the righteous fall."

> My soul, rest happy in thy low estate,
> Nor hope nor wish to be esteem'd or great;
> To take the impress of the Will Divine,
> Be that your glory, and those riches thine.

"And there was no longer any sea."
— *Revelation 21:1*

CARCELY could we rejoice at the thought of losing the glorious old ocean: the new heavens and the new earth are none the fairer to our imagination, if, indeed, literally there is to be no great and wide sea, with its gleaming waves and shelly shores. Is not the text to be read as a metaphor, tinged with the prejudice with which the Oriental mind universally regarded the sea in the times long past? A real physical world without a sea it is mournful to imagine, it would be an iron ring without the sapphire which made it precious. There must be a spiritual meaning here. In the new dispensation there will be no *division* — the sea separates nations and divides peoples from each other. To John in Patmos the deep waters were like prison walls, shutting him off from his brothers and his work: there shall be no such barriers in the world to come. Leagues of rolling billows lie between us and many a kinsman whom tonight we prayerfully remember, but in the bright world to which we go there shall be unbroken fellowship for all the redeemed family. In this sense there shall be no more sea. The sea is the emblem of *change;* with its ebbs and flows, its glassy smoothness and its mountainous billows, its gentle murmurs and its tumultuous roarings, it is never long the same. Slave of the fickle winds and the changeful moon, its instability is proverbial. In this mortal state we have too much of this; earth is constant only in her inconstancy, but in the heavenly state all mournful change shall be unknown, and with it all fear of *storm* to wreck our hopes and drown our joys. The sea of glass glows with a glory unbroken by a wave. No tempest howls along the peaceful shores of paradise. Soon we shall reach that happy land where partings, and changes, and storms shall be ended! Jesus will waft us there. Are we in Him or not? This is the grand question.

"I have loved you with an everlasting love."
— *Jeremiah 31:3*

OMETIMES the Lord Jesus tells His church His love thoughts. "He does not think it appropriate to talk behind her back, so in her very presence He says, 'How beautiful you are, my darling!' It is true, this is not His ordinary method; He is a wise lover, and knows when to keep back the intimation of love and when to let it out; but there are times when He will make no secret of it, times when He will put it beyond all dispute in the souls of His people" (R. Erskine's Sermons). The Holy Spirit is often pleased, in a most gracious manner, to witness with our spirits to the love of Jesus. He takes the things of Christ and reveals them to us. No voice is heard from the clouds, and no vision is seen in the night, but we have a testimony more sure than either of these. If an angel should fly from heaven and inform the saint personally of the Savior's love for him, the evidence would not be one bit more satisfactory than that which is borne in the heart by the Holy Spirit. Ask those of the Lord's people who have lived the nearest to the gates of heaven, and they will tell you that they have had seasons when the love of Christ towards them has been a fact so clear and sure, that they could no more doubt it than they could question their own existence. Yes, beloved believer, you and I have had times of renewal in the presence of the Lord, and, during those times, our faith has climbed to the highest level of assurance. We have had confidence to lean our heads upon the bosom of our Lord, and no more questioned our Master's affection to us than John did when in that blessed posture; no, even the dark question, "Lord, surely not *I*?" has been far removed from us. He has kissed us with the kisses of His mouth, and killed our doubts by the closeness of His embrace. His love has been sweeter than wine to our souls.

"Call the workers and pay them their wages."
— *Matthew 20:8*

OD is a good paymaster; He pays His servants while at work as well as when they have done it; and one of His payments is this: *an easy conscience.* If you have spoken faithfully of Jesus to one person, when you go to bed at night you feel happy in thinking, "Today I have freed my conscience of that person's blood." There is a great *comfort in doing something for Jesus.* Oh, what a happiness to place jewels in His crown, and give Him to see of the travail of His soul! There is also very great reward in *watching the first buddings of conviction in a soul!* To say of that young woman in your class, "She is tender-hearted, I do hope that means that the Lord is working within her." To go home and pray over a young man who said something that afternoon which made you think he must know more about divine truth than you thought he did! Oh, the joy of hope! But as for *the joy of success!* it is unspeakable. This joy, overwhelming as it is, is a hungry thing — you pine for more of it. To be a soul winner is the happiest thing in the world. With every soul you bring to Christ, you get a new heaven upon earth. But who can conceive of the bliss which awaits us above! Oh, how sweet is that sentence, "Come and share your master's happiness!" Do you know what the joy of Christ is over a saved sinner? This is the very joy which we are to possess in heaven. Yes, when He ascends the throne, you shall ascend it with Him. When the heavens ring with "Well done, well done," you shall participate in the reward; you have toiled with Him, you have suffered with Him, you shall now reign with Him; you have sown with Him, you shall reap with Him; your face was covered with sweat like His, and your soul was grieved for the sins of men as His soul was, now your face shall be bright with heaven's splendor as is His countenance; now your soul shall be filled with beatific joys even as His soul is.

"Has he not made with me an everlasting covenant."
— *2 Samuel 23:5*

HIS covenant is *divine in its origin.* "HE has made with me an everlasting covenant." Oh that great word HE! Stop, my soul. God, the everlasting Father, has positively made a covenant with you; yes, that God who spoke the world into existence by a word; He, stooping from His majesty, takes hold of your hand and makes a covenant with you. Is it not a deed, the stupendous condescension of which might ravish our hearts forever if we could really understand it? "HE has made with me a covenant." A king hasn't made a covenant with me — that would be something; but the Prince of the kings of the earth, Shaddai, the Lord All-sufficient, the Jehovah of ages, the everlasting Elohim, "He has made with me an everlasting covenant." But notice, *it is particular in its application.* "He has made with ME an everlasting covenant." Here lies the sweetness of it for each believer. It is not enough for me to know that He made peace for the world; I want to know whether He made peace for *me!* It is of little concern to me that He has made a covenant, I want to know whether He has made a covenant *with me.* Blessed is the assurance that He has made a covenant with me! If God the Holy Spirit gives me assurance of this, then His salvation is mine, His heart is mine, He Himself is mine — *He is my God.*

This covenant is *everlasting in its duration.* An everlasting covenant means a covenant which had no beginning, and which shall never, never end. In the midst of all the uncertainties of life, how sweet it is to know that "the foundation of the Lord stands sure," and to have God's own promise, "I will not violate My covenant or alter what My lips have uttered." Like dying David, I will sing about this even though my house is not as right with God as my heart desires.

*"I clothed you with an embroidered dress and put
leather sandals on you. I dressed you in fine
linen and covered you with costly
garments." — Ezekiel 16:10*

 EE how generously the Lord provides for His people's apparel. They are clothed in such a manner that the divine skill is seen producing an unrivaled *embroidered work*, in which every attribute takes its part and every divine beauty is revealed. No art exists like the art displayed in our salvation, no ingenious workmanship like that seen in the righteousness of the saints. Justification has occupied the attention of learned pens in all ages of the church and will be the theme of admiration in eternity. God has indeed "woven it together." With all this elaboration there is mingled utility and durability, comparable to our wearing *leather sandals*. The animal meant here is unknown, but its skin covered the tabernacle and formed one of the finest and strongest leathers known. The righteousness which is of God by faith endures forever; he who is shod with this divine preparation will tread the desert safely, and may even set his foot upon the lion and the adder. Purity and dignity of our holy vesture are brought out in *the fine linen*. When the Lord sanctifies His people, they are clad as priests in pure white; not even the snow itself excels them; they are in the eyes of human beings and angels beautiful to look at, and even in the Lord's eyes they are unblemished. Meanwhile the royal apparel is delicate and *costly*. No expense is spared, no beauty withheld, no exquisiteness denied.

What, then? Is there no inference from this? Surely there is gratitude to be felt and joy to be expressed. Come, my heart, don't refuse to express your evening hallelujah! Tune your pipes! Touch your chords!

"Strangely, my soul, art thou arrayed
By the Great Sacred Three!
In sweetest harmony of praise
Let all thy powers agree."

"I will strengthen you." — *Isaiah 41:10*

GOD has a strong reserve with which to discharge this engagement; for He is able to do all things. Believer, until you can drain the ocean dry of omnipotence and break the towering mountains of almighty strength into pieces, you never need to be afraid. Don't think that the strength of a human being shall ever be able to overcome the power of God. As long as the earth's huge pillars stand, you have enough reason to remain firm in your faith. The same God who directs the earth in its orbit, feeds the burning furnace of the sun, and trims the lamps of heaven, has promised to supply you with daily strength. While He is able to uphold the universe, don't even dream that He will prove unable to fulfill His own promises. Remember what He did in ages past, in the former generations. Remember how He spoke, and it was done; how He commanded, and it stood fast. Shall He that created the world grow weary? He hangs the world upon nothing; shall He who does this be unable to support His children? Shall He be unfaithful to His word for want of power? Who is it that restrains the tempest? Doesn't He ride upon the wings of the wind, and make the clouds His chariots, and hold the ocean in the hollow of His hand? How can He fail you? When He has put such a faithful promise as this on record, will you for a moment indulge the thought that He has outpromised Himself, and gone beyond His power to fulfill? Ah, no! You cannot doubt any longer.

O you who are my God and my strength, I can believe that this promise shall be fulfilled, for the boundless reservoir of Your grace can never be exhausted, and the overflowing storehouse of Your strength can never be emptied by Your friends or rifled by Your enemies.

> "Now let the feeble all be strong,
> And make Jehovah's arm their song."

"They are no longer his children."
— *Deuteronomy 32:5*

HAT is the secret mark which infallibly iden-
tifies the child of God? It is vain presumption to decide this upon our own judgment;
but God's word reveals it to us, and we may
tread surely where we have revelation to be
our guide. Now, we are told concerning our
Lord, "to all who *received Him*, to those who believed in
His name, He gave the right to become children of God."
Then, if I have received Christ Jesus into my heart, I am a
child of God. That reception is described in the same verse
as *believing on the name of Jesus Christ*. If, then, I believe on
Jesus Christ's name — that is, simply from my heart trust
myself with the crucified, but now exalted, Redeemer, I am
a member of the family of the Most High. Whatever else I
may not have, if I have this, I have the privilege to become
a child of God. Our Lord Jesus puts it another way. "My
sheep listen to My voice; I know them, and they follow
Me." Here is the matter in a nutshell. Christ appears as a
shepherd to His own sheep, not to others. As soon as He
appears, His own sheep perceive Him — they trust Him,
they are prepared to follow Him; He knows them, and they
know Him — there is a mutual knowledge — there is a
constant connection between them. Thus the one mark,
the sure mark, the infallible mark of regeneration and
adoption is a hearty faith in the appointed Redeemer.
Reader, are you in doubt, are you uncertain whether you
bear the secret mark of God's children? Then don't let an
hour go by until you have said, "Search me, O God, and
know my heart." Don't ignore the situation here, I implore
you! If you must procrastinate, let it be about some secondary matter: your health, if you will, or the title deeds of
your estate; but about your soul, your never-dying soul
and its eternal destinies, I beg you to be serious. Settle
eternity once and for all.

"Friend, move up to a better place." — *Luke 14:10*

HEN the life of grace first begins in the soul, we do indeed draw near to God, but it is with great fear and trembling. The soul, conscious of guilt and humbled thereby, is overawed with the solemnity of its position; it is cast to the earth by a sense of the grandeur of Jehovah, in whose presence it stands. With unfeigned bashfulness it takes the lowest room.

But, later in life, as the Christian grows in grace, although never forgetting the solemnity of one's position, and never losing that holy awe which must encompass a gracious person when in the presence of the God who can create or can destroy; yet one's fear has all its terror taken out of it; it becomes a holy reverence, and no more an overshadowing dread. We are called up higher, to greater access to God in Christ Jesus. Then godly Christians, walking amid the splendors of Deity, and veiling our faces like the glorious cherubim with those twin wings, the blood and righteousness of Jesus Christ, will reverently and with bowed spirit approach the throne; and seeing there a God of love, of goodness, and of mercy, will realize the covenant character of God rather than His absolute Deity. We will see in God His goodness rather than His greatness, and more of His love than of His majesty. Then will the soul, bowing still as humbly as in the past, enjoy a more sacred liberty of intercession; for while prostrate before the glory of the Infinite God, it will be sustained by the refreshing consciousness of being in the presence of boundless mercy and infinite love, and by the realization of acceptance "in the Beloved." Thus the believer is bidden to come up higher, and is enabled to exercise the privilege of rejoicing in God, and drawing near to Him in holy confidence, saying, "*Abba,* Father."

> "So may we go from strength to strength,
> And daily grow in grace,
> Till in Thine image raised at length,
> We see Thee face to face."

"Yours [is] also the night." — *Psalm 74:16*

ES, Lord, You do not abdicate your throne when the sun goes down, nor do You leave the world all through these long wintry nights to be the prey of evil; Your eyes watch us as the stars, and Your arms surround us as the zodiac belts the sky. The dews of kindly sleep and all the influences of the moon are in Your hand, and the alarms and solemnities of night are equally with You. This is very sweet to me when watching through the midnight hours, or tossing to and fro in anguish. There are precious fruits put forth by the moon as well as by the sun: may my Lord make me to be a favored partaker in them.

The night of affliction is as much under the arrangement and control of the Lord of Love as the bright summer days when all is bliss. Jesus is in the tempest. His love wraps the night about itself as a mantle, but to the eye of faith the sable robe is scarcely a disguise. From the first watch of the night even to the break of day the eternal Watcher observes His saints, and overrules the shades and dews of midnight for His people's highest good. We believe in no rival deities of good and evil contending for the mastery, but we hear the voice of Jehovah saying, "I form the light and create darkness; I, the LORD, do all these things."

Gloomy seasons of religious indifference and social sin are not exempted from the divine purpose. When the altars of truth are defiled, and the ways of God forsaken, the Lord's servants weep with bitter sorrow, but they may not despair, for the darkest eras are governed by the Lord, and shall come to their end at His bidding. What may seem defeat to us may be victory to Him.

> "Though enwrapt in gloomy night,
> We perceive no ray of light;
> Since the Lord Himself is here,
> 'Tis not meet that we should fear."

"For your sakes he became poor." — *2 Corinthians 8:9*

 HE Lord Jesus Christ was eternally *rich*, glorious, and exalted; but "though *He was rich,* yet for your sakes He became poor." Just as the rich saint cannot be true in his communion with his poor brothers and sisters without ministering to their needs out of this wealth of material possessions, so (the same rule holding with the head as between the members), it is impossible that our Divine Lord could have had fellowship with us unless He had imparted to us of His own abounding wealth, and had become poor to make us rich. Had He remained upon His throne of glory, and had we continued in the ruins of the fall without receiving His salvation, communion would have been impossible on both sides. Our position by the fall, apart from the covenant of grace, made it just as impossible for fallen humanity to communicate with God as it is for Belial to be in concord with Christ. In order, therefore, that communion might be compassed, it was necessary that the rich kinsman should give his estate to his poor relatives, that the righteous Savior should give to His sinning brethren of His own perfection, and that we, the poor and guilty, should receive of His fullness grace for grace; that thus in giving and receiving, the One might descend from the heights, and the other ascend from the depths, and so be able to embrace each other in true and hearty fellowship. Poverty must be enriched by Him in whom are infinite treasures before it can venture to commune; and guilt must lose itself in imputed and imparted righteousness before the soul can walk in fellowship with purity. Jesus must clothe His people in His own garments, or He cannot admit them into His palace of glory; and He must wash them in His own blood, or else they will be too defiled for the embrace of His fellowship.

O believer, here is love! For *your sake* the Lord Jesus "became poor" that He might lift you up into communion with Himself.

> *"The glory of the LORD will be revealed, and all*
> *mankind together will see it. For the mouth of*
> *the LORD has spoken."* — Isaiah 40:5

E anticipate the happy day when the whole world shall be converted to Christ; when the gods of the heathen shall be cast to the moles and the bats; when Romanism shall be exploded, and the crescent of Mohammed shall wane, never again to cast its baleful rays upon the nations; when kings shall bow down before the Prince of Peace, and all nations shall call their Redeemer blessed. Some despair of this. They look upon the world as a vessel breaking up and going to pieces, never to float again. We know that the world and all that is therein is one day to be burned up, and afterwards we look for new heavens and for a new earth; but we cannot read our Bibles without the conviction that —

> "Jesus shall reign where'er the sun
> Does his successive journeys run."

We are not discouraged by the length of His delays; we are not disheartened by the long period which He allots to the church in which to struggle with little success and much defeat. We believe that God will never allow this world, which has once seen Christ's blood shed upon it, to be always the devil's stronghold. Christ came here to deliver this world from the detested sway of the powers of darkness. What a shout shall that be when humankind and angels shall unite to cry "Hallelujah, hallelujah, for the Lord God Omnipotent reigns!" What satisfaction there will be in that day to have had a share in the fight, to have helped to break the arrows of the bow, and to have aided in winning the victory for our Lord! Happy are they who trust themselves with this conquering Lord, and who fight side by side with Him, doing their little in His name and by His strength! How unhappy are those on the side of evil! It is a losing side, and it is a matter wherein to lose is to lose and to be lost forever. Whose side are you on?

*"The virgin will be with child and will give birth
to a son, and will call him Immanuel."*
— *Isaiah 7:14*

ET'S today go down to Bethlehem, and in company with wondering shepherds and adoring Magi, let's see Him who was born King of the Jews, for we by faith can claim an interest in Him, and can sing, *"To us* a child is born, *to us* a son is given."* Jesus is Jehovah incarnate, our Lord and our God, and yet our brother and friend; let's adore and admire. Let's notice at the very first glance *His miraculous conception.* It was a thing unheard of before, and unparalleled since, that a virgin should conceive and bear a Son. The first promise went like this, *"The seed of the woman,"* not the offspring of the man. Since venturous woman led the way in the sin which brought forth Paradise lost, she, and she alone, ushers in the Regainer of Paradise. Our Savior, although truly human, was as to His human nature the Holy One of God. Let's reverently bow before the holy Child whose innocence restores to humanity its ancient glory; and let's pray that He may be formed in us, the hope of glory. Do not fail to note *His humble parentage.* His mother has been described simply as "a virgin," not a princess, or prophetess, nor a matron of large estate. True, the blood of kings ran in her veins; nor was her mind a weak and untaught one, for she could sing most sweetly a song of praise; but yet how humble her position, how poor the man to whom she was betrothed, and how miserable the accommodations available to the newborn King!

Immanuel, God with us in our nature, in our sorrow, in our life work, in our punishment, in our grave, and now with us, or rather we with Him, in resurrection, ascension, triumph, and Second Advent splendor.

*"When a period of feasting had run its course, Job
would send and have them purified. Early in the
morning he would sacrifice a burnt offering for each
of them, thinking, Perhaps my children have sinned
and cursed God in their hearts. This was Job's
regular custom." — Job 1:5*

 HAT the patriarch did early in the morning, after the family festivities, it would be wise for us believers to do for ourselves before resting tonight. Amid the cheerfulness of household gatherings it is easy to slide into sinful levities, and to forget our avowed character as Christians. It ought not to be true, but it is true, that our days of feasting are very seldom days of sanctified enjoyment, but too frequently degenerate into unhallowed mirth. There is a way of joy as pure and sanctifying as though one bathed in the rivers of Eden: holy gratitude should be quite as purifying an element as grief. Alas! for our poor hearts, that facts prove that the house of mourning is better than the house of feasting. Come, believer, in what have you sinned today? Have you been forgetful of your high calling? Have you been even as others in idle words and loose speeches? Then confess the sin, and fly to the sacrifice. The sacrifice sanctifies. The precious blood of the Lamb slain removes the guilt, and purges away the defilement of our sins of ignorance and carelessness. This is the best ending of a Christmas — to wash anew in the purifying fountain. Believer, come to this sacrifice continually; if it is so good tonight, it is good every night. To live at the altar is the privilege of the royal priesthood; to them sin, great as it is, is nevertheless no cause for despair, since they draw near yet again to the sin-atoning victim, and their conscience is purged from dead works.

> Gladly I close this festive day,
> Grasping the altar's hallow'd horn;
> My slips and faults are washed away,
> The Lamb has all my trespass borne.

"The last Adam." — *1 Corinthians 15:45*

ESUS is the federal head of His elect. As in Adam, every heir of flesh and blood has a personal interest, because he is the covenant head and representative of the race as considered under the law of works; so under the law of grace, every redeemed soul is one with the Lord from heaven, since He is the Second Adam, the Sponsor and Substitute of the elect in the new covenant of love. The apostle Paul declares that Levi was in the loins of Abraham when Melchizedek met him: it is a certain truth that the believer was in the loins of Jesus Christ, the Mediator, when in old eternity the covenant settlements of grace were decreed, ratified, and made sure forever. Thus, whatever Christ has done, He has wrought for the whole body of His church. We were crucified in Him and buried with Him (read Col. 2:10–13), and to make it still more wonderful, we are risen with Him and even ascended with Him to the seats on high (Eph. 2:6). It is thus that the church has fulfilled the law, and is "accepted in *the beloved.*" It is thus that she is regarded with complacency by the just Jehovah, for He views her in Jesus, and does not look upon her as separate from her covenant head. As the Anointed Redeemer of Israel, Christ Jesus has nothing distinct from His church, but all that He has He holds for her. Adam's righteousness was ours as long as he maintained it, and his sin was ours the moment that he committed it; and in the same manner, all that the Second Adam is or does, is ours as well as His, seeing that He is our representative. Here is the foundation of the covenant of grace. This gracious system of representation and substitution, which moved Justin Martyr to cry out, "O blessed change, O sweet permutation!" this is the very groundwork of the gospel of our salvation, and is to be received with strong faith and rapturous joy.

"Surely I am with you always." — Matthew 28:20

HE Lord Jesus is in the midst of His church; He walks among the golden candlesticks; His promise is, "Surely I am with you always." He is as surely with us now as He was with the disciples at the lake, when they saw coals of fire, and fish laid thereon and bread. Not in the flesh, but still in real truth, Jesus is with us. And a blessed truth it is, for where Jesus is, *love becomes inflamed.* Of all the things in the world that can set the heart burning, there is nothing like the presence of Jesus! A glimpse of Him so overcomes us, that we are ready to say, "Turn away Your eyes from me, for they have overcome me." Even the smell of the aloes, and the myrrh, and the cassia, which drop from His perfumed garments, causes the sick and the faint to grow strong. Let there be but a moment's leaning of the head upon that gracious bosom, and a reception of His divine love into our poor cold hearts, and we are cold no longer, but glow like seraphs, equal to every work, and capable of every suffering. If we know that Jesus is with us, *every power will be developed,* and every grace will be strengthened, and we shall cast ourselves into the Lord's service with heart, and soul, and strength; therefore is the presence of Christ to be desired above all things. *His presence will be most realized by those who are most like Him.* If you desire to see Christ, you must grow in conformity to Him. Bring yourself, by the power of the Spirit, into union with Christ's desires, and motives, and plans of action, and you are likely to be favored with His company. Remember *His presence may be had.* His promise is as true as ever. He loves being with us. If He doesn't come, it is because we hinder Him by our indifference. He will reveal Himself to our earnest prayers, and graciously allow Himself to be detained by our entreaties, and by our tears, for these are the golden chains which bind Jesus to His people.

"Can papyrus grow tall where there is no marsh?"
— Job 8:11

 HE papyrus is spongy and hollow, and so also is a hypocrite; there is no substance or stability in him. It is shaken to and fro in every wind just as formalists yield to every influence; for this reason the papyrus is not broken by the tempest, neither are hypocrites troubled with persecution. I wouldn't willingly be a deceiver or be deceived; perhaps the text for this day may help me to test myself as to whether or not I am a hypocrite. The papyrus by nature lives in water, and owes its very existence to the mire and moisture wherein it has taken root; let the mire become dry, and the papyrus withers very quickly. Its greenness is absolutely dependent upon circumstances, a present abundance of water makes it flourish, and a drought destroys it at once. Is this my situation? Do I only serve God when I am in good company, or when religion is profitable and respectable? Do I love the Lord only when temporal comforts are received from His hands? If so I am a base hypocrite, and like the withering papyrus, I shall perish when death deprives me of outward joys. But can I honestly assert that when bodily comforts have been few, and my surroundings have been more adverse to grace than at all helpful to it, that I have still held tightly on to my integrity? Then have I hope that there is genuine vital godliness in me. The papyrus cannot grow without mire, but plants of the Lord's right hand planting can and do flourish even in the year of drought. A godly person often grows best when his worldly circumstances decay. He who follows Christ for his purse is a Judas; they who follow for loaves and fishes are children of the devil; but they who attend Him out of love for Himself are His own loved ones. Lord, let me find my life in *You*, and not in the mire of this world's favor or gain.

"The LORD will guide you always." — Isaiah 58:11

HE LORD will guide you always." Not an angel, but JEHOVAH shall guide you. He said He wouldn't go through the wilderness ahead of His people, but that an angel would go before them to lead them in the way; but Moses said, "If *Your* Presence does not go with us, do not send us up from here." Christian, God has not left you in your earthly pilgrimage to an angel's guidance: He Himself leads the caravan. You may not see the cloudy, fiery pillar, but Jehovah will never forsake you. Notice the word *will* — "The LORD will guide you." How certain this makes it! How sure it is that God will not forsake us! His precious "shalls" and "wills" are better than human oaths. "I will never leave you, nor forsake you." Then observe the adverb *always*. We are not merely to be guided once in a while, but we are to have a perpetual monitor; not occasionally to be left to wander only with our own understanding, but we are continually to hear the guiding voice of the Great Shepherd; and if we follow close at His heels, we shall not err, but be led on the right way to a city in which to dwell. If you have to change your position in life; if you have to emigrate to distant shores; if it should happen that you are cast into poverty, or uplifted suddenly into a more responsible position than the one you now occupy; if you are thrown among strangers, or cast among foes, yet do not tremble, for "the LORD will guide you always." There are no dilemmas out of which you shall not be delivered if you live close to God, and your heart is kept warm with holy love. They do not go wrong who go in the company of God. Like Enoch, walk with God, and you cannot mistake your road. You have infallible wisdom to direct you, immutable love to comfort you, and eternal power to defend you. "The LORD" — note the word — "The LORD will guide you always."

"The life I live in the body, I live by faith in the Son of God." — *Galatians 2:20*

HEN the Lord in mercy passed by and saw us in our blood, He first of all said, "Live;" and this He did *first*, because life is one of the absolutely essential things in spiritual matters, and until it is given we are incapable of partaking of the things of the kingdom. Now the life which grace confers upon the saints at the moment of their life-giving is none other than the life of Christ, which, like the sap from the stem, runs into us, the branches, and establishes a living connection between our souls and Jesus. Faith is the grace which perceives this union, having proceeded from it as its firstfruit. It is the neck which joins the body of the church to its all-glorious Head.

"Oh Faith! thou bond of union with the Lord,
Is not this office thine? and thy fit name,
In the economy of gospel types,
And symbols apposite — the Church's *neck;*
Identifying her in will and work
With Him ascended?"

Faith lays hold upon the Lord Jesus with a firm and determined grasp. She knows His excellence and worth, and no temptation can induce her to repose her trust elsewhere; and Christ Jesus is so delighted with this heavenly grace, that He never ceases to strengthen and sustain her by the loving embrace and all-sufficient support of His eternal arms. Here, then, is established a living, sensible, and delightful union which casts forth streams of love, confidence, sympathy, complacency, and joy, whereof both the bride and bridegroom love to drink. When the soul can evidently perceive this oneness between itself and Christ, the pulse may be felt as beating for both, and the one blood as flowing through the veins of each. Then is the heart as near heaven as it can be on earth, and is prepared for the enjoyment of the most sublime and spiritual kind of fellowship.

"I did not come to bring peace, but a sword."
— Matthew 10:34

HE Christian will be sure to make enemies. It will be one of his objectives not to make any; but, if to do what is right and to believe what is true should cause him to lose every earthly friend, he will count it but a small loss, since his great Friend in heaven will be yet more friendly, and reveal Himself to him more graciously than ever. O you who have taken up His cross, don't you know what your Master said? "For I have come to turn 'a man against his father, a daughter against her mother, a daughter-in-law against her mother-in-law — a man's enemies will be the members of his own household.'" Christ is the great Peacemaker; but before peace, He brings war. Where the light comes, the darkness must retire. Where truth is, the lie must flee; or, if it abides, there must be a stern conflict, for the truth cannot and will not lower its standard, and the lie must be trampled under foot. If you follow Christ, you shall have all the dogs of the world yelping at your heels. If you want to live so as to stand the test of the last tribunal, depend upon it, the world will not speak well of you. He who has the friendship of the world is an enemy to God; but if you are true and faithful to the Most High, humankind will resent your unflinching fidelity, since it is a testimony against their iniquities. Fearless of all consequences, you must do what is right. You will need the courage of a lion unhesitatingly to pursue a course which shall turn your best friend into your fiercest foe; but for the love of Jesus you must thus be courageous. For the truth's sake, to risk reputation and affection is such a deed that to do it constantly you will need a degree of moral principle which only the Spirit of God can work in you; yet don't turn your back like a coward, but be strong. Follow courageously in your Master's steps, for He has traversed this rough way before you. Better a brief warfare and eternal rest, than false peace and everlasting torment.

"Thus far has the LORD helped us." — 1 Samuel 7:12

 HE words "thus far" seems like a hand pointing in the direction of the *past.* Twenty years or seventy, and yet, "Thus far has the LORD helped us!" Through poverty, through wealth, through sickness, through health, at home, abroad, on the land, on the sea, in honor, in dishonor, in perplexity, in joy, in trial, in triumph, in prayer, in temptation, "thus far has the LORD helped us!"

We enjoy looking down a long avenue of trees. It is delightful to gaze from one end of the long vista to the other, a sort of verdant temple, with its branching pillars and its arches of leaves; even so look down the long aisles of your years, at the green boughs of mercy overhead, and the strong pillars of loving-kindness and faithfulness which bear up your joys. Are there no birds singing in yonder branches? Surely there must be many, and they all sing of mercy received "thus far."

But the word also points *forward.* For when one arrives a certain mark and writes "thus far," one is not yet at the end, there is still a distance to be traversed. More trials, more joys; more temptations, more triumphs; more prayers, more answers; more toils, more strength; more fights, more victories; and then come sickness, old age, disease, death. Is it over now? No! there is still more — awakening in Jesus' likeness, thrones, harps, songs, psalms, white clothing, the face of Jesus, the society of saints, the glory of God, the fullness of eternity, the infinity of bliss. O be of good courage, believer, and with grateful confidence raise your 'Ebenezer': "Thus far has the LORD helped us," for —

> He who hath helped thee hitherto
> Will help thee all thy journey through.

When read in heaven's light how glorious and marvelous a prospect will your "thus far" unfold to your grateful eye!

"What do you think about the Christ?"
— *Matthew 22:42*

 HE great test of your soul's health is, *What do you think about the Christ?* Is He "the most excellent of men" to you — "the chief among ten thousand" — the "altogether lovely"? Wherever Christ is thus esteemed, all the faculties of the spiritual person exercise themselves with energy. I will judge your piety by this barometer: does Christ stand high or low with you? If you have thought little of Christ, if you have been content to live without His presence, if you have cared little for His honor, if you have been neglectful of His laws, then I know that your soul is sick — God grant that it may not be sick to death! But if the first thought of your spirit has been, "How can I honor Jesus?" If the daily desire of your soul has been, "If only I knew where to find Him!" I tell you that you may have a thousand infirmities, and even scarcely know whether you are a child of God at all, and yet I am persuaded, beyond a doubt, that you are safe, since Jesus is great in your esteem. I don't care about your rags, what do you think about *His* royal apparel? I don't care about your wounds, though they bleed in torrents, what do you think about *His* wounds? are they like glittering rubies in your estimation? I think no less of you, even though you lie like Lazarus on the manure pile, and the dogs lick you — I don't judge you by your poverty: what do you think about the King in His beauty? Has He a glorious high throne in your heart? Would you set Him higher if you could? Would you be willing to die if you could but add another trumpet to the strain which proclaims His praise? Ah! then it is well with you. Whatever you may think of yourself, if Christ is great to you, you shall be with Him before long.

"Though all the world my choice deride,
Yet Jesus shall my portion be;
For I am pleased with none beside,
The fairest of the fair is He."

"The end of a matter is better than its beginning."
— *Ecclesiastes 7:8*

 OOK at David's Lord and Master; see His beginning. He was despised and rejected of humankind; a Man of sorrows and acquainted with grief. Would you take a look at the end? He sits at His Father's right hand, waiting until His enemies are made His footstool. "In this world we are like Him." You must bear the cross, or you shall never wear the crown; you must wade through the mire, or you shall never walk the golden pavement. Cheer up, then, poor Christian. "The end of a matter is better than its beginning." See that creeping worm, how contemptible its appearance! It is the beginning of a thing. Mark that insect with gorgeous wings, playing in the sunbeams, sipping at the flower bells, full of happiness and life; that is the end thereof. That caterpillar is you, until you are wrapped up in the chrysalis of death; but when Christ shall appear you shall be like Him, for you shall see Him as He is. Be content to be like Him, a worm and not human, that like Him you may be satisfied when you wake up in His likeness. That rough-looking diamond is put upon the wheel of the lapidary. He cuts it on all sides. It loses a great deal — much that seemed costly to itself. The king is crowned; the diadem is put upon the monarch's head with trumpet's joyful sound. A glittering ray flashes from that coronet, and it beams from that very diamond which was just now so sorely vexed by the lapidary. You may venture to compare yourself to such a diamond, for you are one of God's people; and this is the time of the cutting process. Let faith and patience have their perfect work, for in the day when the crown shall be set upon the head of the King, Eternal, Immortal, Invisible, one ray of glory shall stream from you. "'They will be mine,' says the LORD Almighty, 'in the day when I make up my treasured possession.'" "The end of a matter is better than its beginning."

"Don't you realize that this will end in bitterness?"
— *2 Samuel 2:26*

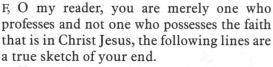

I F, O my reader, you are merely one who professes and not one who possesses the faith that is in Christ Jesus, the following lines are a true sketch of your end.

You are a respectable attendant at a place of worship; you go because others go, not because your heart is right with God. This is your beginning. I will suppose that for the next twenty or thirty years you will be spared to go on as you do now, professing religion by an outward attendance upon the means of grace, but having no heart in the matter. Tread softly, for I must show you the deathbed of such a one as yourself. Let's gaze upon him gently. A clammy sweat is on his brow, and he wakes up crying, "O God, it is hard to die. Did you send for my minister?" "Yes, he is coming." The minister comes. "Sir, I fear that I am dying!" "Have you any hope?" "I cannot say that I have. I fear to stand before my God; oh! pray for me." The prayer is offered for him with sincere earnestness, and the way of salvation is for the ten thousandth time put before him, but before he has grasped the rope, I see him sink. I may put my finger upon those cold eyelids, for they will never see anything here again. But where is the man, and where are the man's true eyes? It is written, "In hell, where he was in torment, he looked up." Ah! why didn't he lift up his eyes before? Because he was so accustomed to hearing the gospel that his soul slept under it. Alas! if you should lift up your eyes there, how bitter your wailings will be. Let the Savior's own words reveal the woe: "Father Abraham, have pity on me and send Lazarus to dip the tip of his finger in water and cool my tongue, because I am in agony in this fire." There is a frightful meaning in those words. May you never have to spell it out by the red light of Jehovah's wrath!

*"On the last and greatest day of the Feast, Jesus stood
and [cried] in a loud voice, If anyone is thirsty, let
him come to me and drink." — John 7:37*

ATIENCE had her perfect work in the Lord Jesus, and until the last day of the Feast He pleaded with the Jews, even as on this last day of the year He pleads with us, and waits to be gracious to us. Admirable indeed is the longsuffering of the Savior in bearing with some of us year after year, notwithstanding our provocations, rebellions, and resistance of His Holy Spirit. Wonder of wonders that we are still in the land of mercy!

Pity expressed herself most plainly, for Jesus *cried,* which implies not only the loudness of His voice, but the tenderness of His tones. He entreats us to be reconciled. "We *pray* you," says the Apostle, "as though God did *beg* you through us." What earnest, pathetic terms these are! How deep the love must be which makes the Lord weep over sinners and, like a mother, woo His children to His heart! Surely at the call of such a cry our willing hearts will come.

Provision is made most plenteously; all is provided that we can need to quench our soul's thirst. To our conscience the atonement brings peace; to our understanding the gospel brings the richest instruction; to our heart the person of Jesus is the noblest object of affection; to the whole person the truth as it is in Jesus supplies the purest nutriment. Thirst is terrible, but Jesus can remove it. Though the soul is utterly famished, Jesus can restore it.

Proclamation is given so freely that everyone who thirsts is welcome. No other distinction is made but that of thirst. Whether it is the thirst of avarice, ambition, pleasure, knowledge, or rest, they who suffer from it are invited. The thirst may be bad in itself, and not be a sign of grace, but rather a mark of inordinate sin longing to be gratified with deeper draughts of lust; but it is not goodness in the creature which brings him the invitation, the Lord Jesus sends it freely, and without respect of persons.

Personality is declared most fully. The sinner must come to *Jesus,* not to works, sacraments, or doctrines, but to a personal Redeemer, who bore our sins Himself in His own body on the tree. The bleeding, dying, rising Savior is the only star of hope to a sinner. Oh for grace to come now and drink, before the sun sets upon the year's last day!

No waiting or preparation is so much as hinted at. Drinking represents a reception for which no fitness is required. A fool, a thief, a harlot can drink; and so sinfulness of character is no bar to the invitation to believe in Jesus. We want no golden cup, no bejeweled chalice, in which to convey the water to the thirsty; the mouth of poverty is welcome to stoop down and quaff the flowing flood. Blistered, leprous, filthy lips may touch the stream of divine love; they cannot pollute it, but shall themselves be purified. Jesus is the fount of hope. Dear reader, hear the dear Redeemer's loving voice as He cries to each of us,

"IF ANYONE IS THIRSTY, LET HIM COME TO ME AND DRINK."

"The harvest is past, the summer has ended, and we
are not saved." — *Jeremiah 8:20*

OT *saved!* Dear reader, is this your mournful plight? Warned of the judgment to come, bidden to escape for your life, and yet at this moment *not saved!* You know the way of salvation, you read it in the Bible, you hear it from the pulpit, it is explained to you by friends, and yet you neglect it, and therefore you are *not saved.* You will be without excuse when the Lord shall judge the living and dead. The Holy Spirit has given more or less of blessing upon the word which has been preached in your hearing, and times of refreshing have come from the divine presence, and yet you are without Christ. All these hopeful seasons have come and gone — your summer and your harvest have past — and yet you are *not saved.* Years have followed one another into eternity, and your last year will soon be here: youth has gone, adulthood is going, and yet you are *not saved.* Let me ask you — *will you ever be saved?* Is there any likelihood of it? Already the most propitious seasons have left you unsaved; will other occasions alter your condition? Means have failed with you — the best of means, used perseveringly and with the utmost affection — what more can be done for you? Affliction and prosperity have alike failed to impress you; tears and prayers and sermons have been wasted on your barren heart. Are not the probabilities of your ever being saved dead against you? Isn't it more than likely that you will live just like you do now until death forever bars the door of hope? Do you recoil from the supposition? Yet it is a most reasonable one: he who is not washed in so many waters will in all probability go filthy to his end. The convenient time never has come, why should it ever come? It is logical to fear that it never will arrive, and that like the governor Felix ("When I find it convenient, I will send for you." Acts 24:25), you will find no convenient season until

you are in hell. O consider what that hell is, and of the
dread probability that you will soon be cast into it!

Reader, suppose you should die unsaved, no words can
describe your doom. Write out your dread estate in tears
and blood, talk of it with groans and gnashing of teeth: you
will be punished with everlasting destruction from the
glory of the Lord, and from the glory of His power. A
brother's voice would preferably startle you into earnestness. O be wise, be wise in time, and before another year
begins, believe in Jesus, who is able to save to the utter
most. Consecrate these last hours to lonely thought, and if
deep repentance be bred in you, it is a good thing; and if it
leads to a humble faith in Jesus, it is the best thing of all. O
see to it that this year does not pass away leaving you
an unforgiven spirit. Don't let the new year's midnight
peals ring upon a joyless spirit! *Now,* NOW, NOW believe,
and live.

"FLEE FOR YOUR LIVES! DON'T LOOK BACK, AND DON'T STOP ANYWHERE IN THE PLAIN! FLEE TO THE MOUNTAINS OR YOU WILL BE SWEPT AWAY!"

Subject Index

(Note: "m" and "e" serve as abbreviations
for "morning" and "evening")

Scripture Index